Ministry through Word and Sacrament

Michael Angelo Angelo

THOMAS C. ODEN

Classical Pastoral Care

VOLUME TWO
MINISTRY THROUGH
WORD & SACRAMENT

Baker Books

A Division of Baker Book House Co
Grand Rapids, Michigan 49516

For John F. Ollom and James M. O'Kane

Originally published 1987 by The Crossroad Publishing Company

Published by Baker Books
a division of Baker Book House Company
P.O. Box 6287, Grand Rapids, MI 49516-6287

Printed in the United States of America

ISBN 0-8010-6764-2

Library of Congress Cataloging-in-Publication data on file in Washington, D.C.

Contents

Preface to the Baker Edition

EVANGELICALS STAND POISED to rediscover the classical pastoral tradition. This series seeks the revitalization of a discipline once familiar to evangelical Protestant scholarship, but now regrettably crippled and enervated.

It has been commonly observed that there is a deep hunger and profound readiness among evangelicals for neglected classical Christian roots as a resource for counsel, teaching, exegesis, and the work of ministry (see the writings of Robert Webber, Mark Noll, Ward Gasque, Donald Bloesch, James I. Packer, Michael Horton, Clark Pinnock, and Os Guinness).

It is well known that classic Protestant and evangelical teachers made frequent and informed references to the ancient Christian pastoral writers. Calvin was exceptionally well grounded in Augustine, but was also thoroughly familiar with the texts of Cyprian, Tertullian, John Chrysostom, Ambrose, Jerome, Leo, and Gregory the Great, and ecumenical council definitions such as those of Nicea, Constantinople I, and Chalcedon. Philipp Melancthon and Martin Chemnitz were especially gifted scholars of classical pastoral care. This tradition was carried forth and deepened by Reformed pastoral theologians (Gerhard, Quenstedt, Bucanus, Ursinus, Wollebius, and Cocceius), and survived healthily well into the eighteenth-century evangelical revival among leading teachers like J.A. Bengel, Philip Doddridge, Jonathan Edwards, John Wesley, and Johann Neander, all of whom read classic Christian writers handily in their original languages. Not until the late nineteenth century did the study of the ancient pastoral writers atrophy among Protestant pastors.

What is notably missing in today's picture is the classic pastoral texts themselves in accessible form, and a vital community of pastors and care-givers in living dialogue with these foundational prototypes.

1

A major long-range objective of this edition is the mentoring of young evangelical pastors and counselors toward greater competence in the classical pastoral tradition. Deliberately included in this collection are the voices of women from the classic Eastern and Western traditions of spiritual formation, exegesis, martyrology, catechesis, and piety. While the documentation of their poignant utterances is regrettably infrequent, they still are exceedingly powerful commentators on care-giving—I am thinking of such voices as Amma Theodora, Julian of Norwich, Hildegaard of Bingen, and Teresa of Avila.

Will benefits accrue to persons in teaching and helping professions who have no evangelical commitments or interests? The study of classical pastoral care is fitting not only for pastors and professionals, but for lay readers interested in their own inward spiritual formation. The arguments contained in this series tend to elicit ripple effects on diverse readers in such widely varied fields as psychology, Western cultural history, liturgies, homiletics, and education. Classical pastoral care is long overdue in contributing something distinctive of its own to the larger dialogue on care-giving, empathy, behavioral change, and therapeutic effectiveness.

By the early eighties it began to be evident that someone needed to pull together a substantial collection of essential sources of classic Christian writers on major themes of pastoral care. The series was first published by Crossroad/Continuum Publishing Company, a general academic publisher of religious books with strong ties to the erudite Herder tradition of Catholic scholarship. In the intervening years, no serious rival or alternative to this collection has appeared. There exists no other anthology of texts of classical pastoral care that presents the variety of textual material offered in this series. I am now deeply pleased to see it come out in an edition more accessible to Protestants. This is the first time the series has been made available in paperback.

The four books can be read either as a single, unified sequence or separately as stand-alone volumes. To this day some readers know of only one or two volumes, but are not aware that each volume is part of a cohesive series. Baker has made this unity clearer by offering the four volumes as a series.

I am deeply grateful for the interest that many working pastors, counselors, and lay persons have shown in this Classical Pastoral Care series. Even though these volumes were chosen as a Religious Book Club selection over several years, the circulation has been disseminated largely through academic audiences. I am pleased that it is now being offered by Baker for the first time to evangelical pastors and evangelically oriented pastoral and lay counselors and lay readers.

These texts are sometimes hard to locate if one is approaching them topically in crumbling, antiquated editions with poor indexes. This edition provides for the first time a well-devised index for the whole series that makes the anthology much more accessible to readers who wish to dip into it thematically.

These four volumes are designed to display the broad range of classical Christian reflections on all major questions of pastoral care. Many practical subjects are included, such as care of the dying, care of the poor, marriage and family counseling, pastoral visitation and care of the sick, counsel on addictive behaviors, vocational counsel, the timing of good counsel, the necessary and sufficient conditions of a helping relationship, body language in pastoral counsel, pastoral care through preaching, pastoral care through prayer, the pastor as educator of the soul, preparing for the Lord's table, clergy homosexuality and sexual ethics, equality of souls beyond sexual difference, the path to ordination, charismatic, healing ministries, and preparation for the care of souls.

The four volumes are:

I. *On Becoming a Minister* (first published 1987)
II. *Ministry through Word and Sacrament* (1989)
III. *Pastoral Counsel* (1989)
IV. *Crisis Ministries* (1986)

This edition for the first time identifies the order of volumes more clearly. Since in the first edition the fourth volume (*Crisis Ministries*, with its bio-bibliographical addendum) appeared first, the sequential order of the series has been confusing to some readers. Many have never seen the four volumes in a collection together, and do not yet realize that the whole sequence is constructed in a well-designed order to cover all major topics of pastoral theology.

There is reason to believe that this series is already being regarded as a standard necessary accession of theological seminary libraries, as well as of the libraries of most colleges and universities in which religious studies are taught, and in many general public libraries.

Meanwhile, out of rootless hunger the prefix "pastoral" has come to mean almost anything. There is no constraint on ascribing any subject matter to the category of pastoral care. In this game pastoral can mean my ultimate concern, transcendental meditation, or worse, my immediate feeling process or group hugging or my racial identity or crystal-gazing—you name it, anything. Then what is called pastoral is no longer related to the work of Christian ministry at all.

The preaching and counseling pastor needs to know that current pastoral care stands in a tradition of two millennia of reflection on the tasks of soul care. If deprived of these sources, the practice of pastoral care may become artificially constricted to modern psychotherapeutic procedures or pragmatic agendas. During the sixties and seventies, these reductionistic models prevailed among many old-line Protestant pastors, and to some degree as the eighties proceeded they also took root among evangelicals. This anthology shows the classic historic roots of contemporary approaches to psychological change, and provides to some degree a critique of those contemporary models.

Pastors today are rediscovering the distinctiveness of pastoral method as distinguished from other methods of inquiry (historical, philosophical, literary, psychological, etc.). Pastoral care is a unique enterprise that has its own distinctive subject-matter (care of souls); its own methodological premise (revelation); its own way of inquiring into its subject-matter (attentiveness to the revealed Word through Scripture and its consensual tradition of exegesis); its own criteria of scholarly authenticity (accountability to canonical text and tradition); its own way of knowing (listening to sacred Scripture with the historic church); its own mode of cultural analysis (with worldly powers bracketed and divine providence appreciated); and its own logic (internal consistency premised upon revealed truth).

The richness of the classic Christian pastoral tradition remains pertinent to ministry today. The laity have a right to competent, historically grounded pastoral care. The pastor has a right to the texts that teach how pastors have understood their work over the centuries. Modern chauvinism has falsely taught us a theory of moral inferiority: that new ideas are intrinsically superior, and old patterns inferior. This attitude has robbed the laity of the pastoral care they deserve, and the ministry of the texts that can best inform the recovery of pastoral identity.

Thomas C. Oden
June, 1994

Introduction

"SOUL" (*psyche, anima*) IS THAT WHICH ENLIVENS, energizes, animates human existence, as distinguished but not separated from the body which is animated. Body minus soul equals corpse. A warm body is one with soul—alive.

The term *soul care* translates the ancient Latin idea of *cura animarum:* the nourishment, guidance, and care of that which animates human existence. Curacy, or soul care, is a vocation set aside to guide souls in their journey through life toward fulfillment of their genuine freedom and possibility.

The previous Volume I, *Becoming a Minister,* set forth classic pastoral writings on the calling and work of the minister. This present Volume II, *Ministry through Word and Sacrament,* asks how that care-giver acts to provide nourishment and guidance for souls in eight crucial arenas of ministry: care of oneself; ministry of the Word; soul care through prayer; ministry of the sacrament of beginnings—baptism; ministry of holy communion; the education of the soul; the nurture of community; and the engendering of support for ministry. The following Volume III, *Pastoral Counsel,* will focus upon individual one-on-one conversations as a major concern of pastoral care. Our present purpose is to show that soul care occurs not only in individual conversations, but also in a community of care, in public settings like preaching and worship, and in sacramental life, in baptizing and celebrating the Eucharist, in the teaching of children and adults, and in the nurturing of community in the parish and the civil order.

The eight questions of this volume are:

- Why do *care-givers themselves need soul care?* And what special nourishment is required to transcend despair over the burdens of care for others?

5

- How does soul care occur through community by means of public witness and the *preaching of good news*?
- In what sense does *the worshipping community and the life of prayer* provide the broader social and necessary spiritual matrix for individual soul care?
- How do sacramental ministries constitute central acts of soul care, beginning with the ministry of *baptism*?
- Why is *confession* intrinsically connected with holy *communion* so as to constitute the quintessential service of soul care?
- How does the pastor *teach* the soul to increase in faith and behavioral excellence?
- How does the pastor nurture *community* in the parish, and *civil justice* beyond the parish?
- How may the care-giver best find and order resources *properly to support ministry* without eliciting abuses?

The Christian pastor struggles for the health of the person and the life of the soul simultaneously in these diverse developmental phases and arenas.

1 On the Pastoral Obligation to Care for Oneself

PASTORAL BURN-OUT is thought to be a distinctively modern dilemma, but the classic pastoral writers repeatedly faced it thoughtfully and resourcefully. They thought that burnout could best be averted by wise preparation and by following the ancient injunction to take care of oneself. This injunction was closely linked with pastoral care in Acts 20:28: "Keep watch over yourselves and over all the flock of which the Holy Spirit has given you charge."

This volume, therefore, begins its search into the diverse arenas of pastoral care by inquiring at closest quarters into the nearest of these: oneself as pastor, one's own needs and dreams. Caring for the flock cannot occur unless one first cares for oneself, watches over one's own welfare, feeds and nurtures one's own body and soul.

The first step toward doing unto others as one would have them do unto oneself is to learn what one's ownself truly needs, proportionally loves, freely fantasizes, and uniquely requires. For if one does not know how one would wish to be treated, one cannot treat others as one would wish to be treated. In pursuit of soul care for the pastor, the pastoral tradition has candidly faced the distinctive challenges of pastoral service, difficulties intrinsic to soul care, reasons for pastoral burnout, and how to avert it.

I ❧ CARE OF THE CARE-GIVER

The principle was firmly established by the classic writers that the care-giver needs regular and special care. Since so much attention in ministry focusses on offering pastoral care to others, the point is easily missed that the pastor often seriously needs to be cared for. Luther stated the principle succinctly:

> Those who take care of souls are worthy of all care. (Luther, *Table Talk*, W-T 5, #6287; WLS 2, p. 939)

Gregory the Great reflected deliberately on ways in which pastors are called to care for themselves. Gregory thought it a specific hazard of ministry that one becomes so focussed upon others' needs that one's own health and well-being may be jeopardized. The sudden death of highly competent ministers may be an oblique witness to their own myopia about their omnicompetencies:

> In restoring others to health by healing their wounds, he must not disregard his own health. . . . Let him not, while helping his neighbours, neglect himself, let him not, while lifting up others, fall himself. In many instances, indeed, the greatness of certain men's virtues has been an occasion of their perdition, in that they have felt inordinately secure in the assurance of their strength, and they died suddenly because of their negligence. (Gregory the Great, *Pastoral Care*, Part IV, ACW 11, p. 234)

John Chrysostom argued that pastors need more help and care than the average person due to the heavy demands and extraordinary expectations associated with the pastoral office:

> The priest's wounds require greater help, indeed as much as those of all the people together. They would not have required greater help if they had not been more serious, and their seriousness is not increased by their own nature but by the extra weight of dignity belonging to the priest who dares to commit them. (Chrysostom, *On the Priesthood*, Ch. VI.10, sec. 16, p. 151)

Keeping guard over oneself is likened to the need of each ship in a crowded harbor to steer carefully to avoid collisions. This is especially so where there is silent anger within, of which one has remained unaware:

> Let us keep guard over ourselves with all care. For when a harbour is full of ships, it is easy for them to get crushed by each other, especially if they are secretly riddled with bad temper as by some worm. (John Climacus, *The Ladder of Divine Ascent*, Step 4, sec. 77, p. 43)

With characteristic balance and good judgment, Gregory the Great grasped the point that effective care of souls is conjointly composed of two aspects—care of others and care of oneself—neither of which should inordinately dominate the other:

> Pastors are called to fulfil their charge over others in such a way as not to fail to accomplish the charge over themselves, and to be ardently solicitous on their own account in such as way as not to grow slack in watching over those entrusted to them. (Gregory the Great, *Pastoral Care*, Part III, Ch. 4, ACW 11, p. 97)*

An appropriate concern for oneself, or proportional self-interest (ordinate self-love), is frequently cited as a pastoral duty. It is not unseemly or selfish for pastors to pray for their own needs. The depth of these needs is seen in this prayer of Aelred:

You know well, O Searcher of my heart, that there is nothing in my soul that I would hide from you, even had I the power to escape your eyes. . . . Further, against the vices and the evil passions which still assault my soul, (whether they come from past bad habit, or from my immeasurable daily negligence, whether their source is in the weakness of my corrupt and vitiated nature, or in the secret tempting of malignant spirits) against these vices, Lord, may your sweet grace afford me strength and courage; that I may not consent thereto, nor let them reign in this my mortal body. (Aelred of Rievaulx, *The Pastoral Prayer*, sec. 5, CFS 2, pp. 110-111)

The notion of ministers sharing in support groups is very old indeed. Anglican Bishop Burnet underscored the need for pastors to care for one another:

The clergy ought to contrive ways to meet often together, to enter into a brotherly correspondence, and into the concerns one of another, both in order to their progress in knowledge, and for consulting together in all their affairs. This would be a means to cement them into one body: hereby they might understand what were amiss in the conduct of any in their division, and try to correct it either by private advices and endeavours, or by laying it before the bishop, by whose private Labours, if his clergy would be assisting to him, and give him free and full informations of things, many disorders might be cured, without rising to a public scandal, or forcing him to extreme censures. It is a false pity in any of the clergy, who see their brethren running into ill courses, to look on and say nothing: it is a cruelty to the church, and may prove a cruelty to the person of whom they are so unseasonably tender: for things may be more easily corrected at first, before they have grown to be public, or are hardened by habit and custom. Upon all these accounts it is of great advantage, and may be matter of great edification to the clergy, to enter into a strict union together, to meet often, and to be helpful to one another. (Gilbert Burnet, *Of the Pastoral Care*, Ch. VIII, pp. 175-176)

If clergy remain passively silent while a fellow pastor is stumbling and falling, it amounts to cruel indifference and "unseasonable tenderness."

II ❦ Difficulties Intrinsic to Care-giving

Suppose one came upon a description of a vocational profile in which hours were long, pay minimal, risks high, accomplishments largely unnoticed, and the level of conflict at times intense. Would it not seem reasonable to avoid it at all costs? Yet if ministry is viewed primarily in terms of hedonic costs/benefits, much of it could be described in this way. Nonetheless the pastoral literature frequently attests to a deep sense of joy in genuine ministry. Amid these struggles there emerges a unique form of happiness and fulfillment from the distinctive pastoral tasks of liturgy, intercession, meditative study, teaching, proclamation, pastoral care, and intimate interpersonal communication.

The classical pastoral writers have tried to make it clear that the office of the pastor is not an easy street, and that there are certain persistent problems and dilemmas that often accompany the task—difficulties intrinsically connected with care-giving.

The household sweat is great; the political sweat is greater; the church sweat is the greatest. (Luther, "Lectures on Genesis Chapters One to Five, 1535–36," WA 42, 159, WLS 2, p. 951; cf. in LW, 1, p. 213)

It is impossible to list in advance all the difficulties one might expect to encounter in ministry:

Making a list of all the difficulties involved is like trying to measure the ocean. (Chrysostom, *On the Priesthood*, Ch. VI, sec. 8, p. 149)

The perplexity is that the deepest joys of ministry are intrinsically related precisely to what makes ministry at times very difficult:

We can engage in no sublimer and greater work on earth than educating people by preaching and teaching. . . . But no work is more difficult than making other people good. Yet this is the best service we can render God. (Luther, WA 36, 216; WLS 2, p. 951)

In the astonishing medieval poetry of Ramon Lull, Christ is the Lover and he the beloved. Lull portrays the joys and trials of ministry as intricately connected. Modern readers may mistake for masochism the subtlety of this intrinsic connection:

The Beloved asked the Lover, "Have you remembered any way in which I have rewarded you for you to love me thus?" "Yes," replied the Lover, "for I make no distinction between the trials which you send and the joys."

The Beloved asked, "Tell me, Lover, if I double your sorrows, will you still be patient?" "Yes," replied the Lover, "so that you will also double my love." (Ramon Lull, *The Book of the Lover and the Beloved*, sec. 8-9, pp. 14-15)

Benedict of Nursia in the sixth century showed the complexity of reasons why care of souls is a demanding task. For it requires at the same time honesty, compassion, accountability, and prudence. It is not meant for one lacking in courage, candor, or imagination:

Let him reflect how difficult and perplexing a business he undertakes, at once to govern many souls and to be subject to as many humours: to suit himself to everyone with regard to their capacity and condition; to win some by fair means, others by reprimands, others by dint of reason: that he may not suffer damage to his flock, but rather rejoice at the increase and improvement of it.

Above all, he is not to dissemble or undervalue the care of souls committed to his charge, for the sake of temporal concerns, which are earthly, transitory, and fleeting; but ever to reflect that the government of souls is his business, and that he is accountable for them. (Benedict of Nursia, Rule, LCC IX, p. 296)

To engage in ministry without succumbing to numerous temptations is like walking a tightrope or balancing on a razor's edge. Without denying the difficulties of the task, Luther commented on how the pastor is to find inner certitude and physical energy to persist in this exacting work:

Thus there are many temptations and hindrances for this ministry on both the right and the left side, the temptation of keeping quiet either to escape harm and persecution or to gain popularity, property, or pleasure. Besides, we are weak, lazy, and listless. Therefore we let ourselves be distracted, and we get tired when we see that things do not progress as we would like, when it all seems useless and the people despise our rebukes and even become the worse on account of them. . . . Our consolation is in the fact that He makes us His salt and will sustain us in our salting. He commands us to do that salting with good cheer, regardless of whether the world refuses to tolerate it and persecutes us. (Luther, "Commentary on the Sermon on the Mount, 1532," LW 21, pp. 57-58)

Among temptations to the church's ministry, Luther described three in particular: persecution, heresy, and antinomianism. First there is the tyrannical persecution of faith's witness by coercive state powers, then false teachings parading as faith, and most subtly, the antinomian spirit of license against the law that imagines the gospel no longer needs the law.

The first trial of the church (from the beginning of the world) always comes from the tyrants, who shed our blood. When the tyrants are almost at an end, the far more harmful trial brought on by heretics follows, reinforcing the violence of the tyrants. After the heretics have been somewhat suppressed, there follows the most harmful trial of all in the time of peace, namely, license and worldly-mindedness in living, life without the Law, without the Word, since we are satiated and surfeited with the Word, which is no longer necessary "because the enemies are defeated." So the worst enemies of a man are those of his own household. These three trials tempt to sin against the Father, the Son, and the Holy Ghost. (Luther, W-Br. 9, pp. 510f.; WLS 1, p. 281)

The tempter is formidable, deceitful, and determined. The temptation of ministers is often treated, but never with more subtlety than by Baxter. That our own highest ideals and principles may cause our downfall anticipates much post-Niebuhrian social criticism:

As wise and learned as you are, take heed to yourselves, lest he outwit you. The devil is a greater scholar than you, and a nimbler disputant: he can transform himself into an angel of light to deceive: he will get within you, and trip up your heels before you are aware: he will play the juggler with you undiscerned, and cheat you of your faith or innocency, and you shall not know that you have lost it; nay he will make you believe it is multiplied or increased, when it is lost. . . . He will be sure to find advantages within you, and make your own principles and inclinations betray you; and whenever he ruineth you, he will make you the instruments of ruin to others. (Baxter, *RP*, pp. 74-75)

Those called to ministry, if faithful to the apostolic tradition, will be given grace to persevere:

We show forth our diligence in preaching the same doctrines that they taught, beside which, according to the admonition of the Apostle, we are forbidden to add anything. For the office of keeping what is committed to our trust is no less dignified than that of handing it down. . . . Shouldn't you expect that God would give you grace to preserve in that which he has given you to preach? So being filled with the Holy Spirit, as it is written, you may set forth that one truth which the Spirit himself has taught you, although with diverse voices. (Ephesus, A.D. 431, The Letter of Pope Celestine to the Synod of Ephesus, The Seven Ecumenical Councils, NPNF 2, XIV, pp. 220-221)*

III ⚡ PASTORAL BURNOUT

Given the difficulties that necessarily accompany the care of souls, it is not surprising that some should experience periods of intense demoralization. This phenomena, which has more recently been called "pastoral burnout," has been recognized, wisely analyzed and creatively faced in previous periods of pastoral care.

Catherine of Siena provides a poignant example. At one point she experienced an overwhelming sense of failure and defeat as a care-giver, as expressed in these dramatic terms in the solitude of prayer:

Oh, unhappy one that I am! Thou hast placed me in charge of souls, assigning to me so many beloved sons, that I should love them with singular love and direct them to Thee by the way of Life, but I have been to them nothing but a mirror of human weakness. I have had no care of them. I have not helped them with continuous and humble prayer in Thy presence, nor have I given them sufficient examples of the good life or the warnings of salutary doctrine. (Catherine of Siena, *Transit of the Saint*, p. 341)*

Similarly Luther wrote of certain periods in which his feelings of frustration, anger, despair, disgust, and weariness caused him to wish to decline the struggle altogether. When despair over the burdens of soul care approached, Luther took comfort in Jesus' specific promise to those who are reviled:

I often become so angry and impatient with our peasants, townsfolk, and nobility that I think I never want to deliver another sermon; for they carry on so shamefully that a person is inclined to be disgusted with life. Besides this, the devil does not stop plaguing me without and within. Therefore I would almost like to say: Let someone else be preacher in my place. I will let matters take their course, for I am getting nothing but the hatred and envy of the world and all sorts of trouble from the devil. Thus flesh and blood rise in revolt, and human nature becomes dejected and disheartened. In such conditions I must find counsel in the Word of God. . . . "How blest are you, when you suffer insults and persecution and every kind of calumny for my sake.

Accept it with gladness and exultation, for you have a rich reward in heaven; in the same way they persecuted the prophets before you" (Matt. 5:11). To these words I cling. (Luther, WA 34 II, pp. 527f.; WLS 3, p. 1120, NEB)*

Some mystical writers have imagined that Christ was the beckoner as one moves into a period of depression. Luther stubbornly asserted the opposite. It is the influence of the adversary that elicits depression. This provided him with a partial clarification of the otherwise complete absurdity of recurrent *Anfechtung* (affliction) accompanying his soul care. During periods of depression about ministry, which he experienced often, he thought that it was not Christ but the demonic that confronted him. The adversary's motive: to drive him out of ministry. Luther's remedy: confront and renounce the demonic, and confess Christ:

We must know this and be guided by it when we must step forth to preach and confess the Word. Then indeed we shall find out, both on the outside among our enemies and on the inside among ourselves, when the devil himself will attack you and show you how hostile he is to you, in order that he may bring you into sorrow, impatience, and heaviness of heart, and inflict every plague on you. Who does all this? Surely not Christ or any good spirit; it is the accursed, desperate enemy. He shoots such darts into your heart, not because you are a sinner as others are, adulterers, thieves, and the like. No, he does so because he is hostile to you for being a Christian. . . . Therefore be prepared, so that when you experience and feel these temptations either in your official capacity or especially in your heart, you can confront the devil and say: "Now I see why the devil assails me this way. He wants to scare and drive me from my office, from my preaching, and confession, and my faith, and to make me despondent. He does not want me to expect anything good from my Lord Christ or to praise, honor, or call upon Him. For the devil is Christ's sworn and declared enemy. But I despise you and your power, you accursed devil. I am determined to defy you and to preach and praise this Man all the more, to comfort my heart with His blood and death, and to put my trust in Him, even if you and all hell should burst asunder." (Luther, "Sermons on the Gospel of St. John Chapter Fifteen, 1537," LW 24, p. 289)

Luther provided the classic description of the crisis of burnout, by speaking in a sermon of his own temptation to depression. He assumed that it could only be the adversary who was saying to him: Cease ministry.

For I know [says Christ] that the devil will harass you severely for My sake, to sadden and weary you, to make you impatient, to induce you to defect, and to make you say: "I wish I had never had anything to do with this!" That is the sentiment of many right now. I myself have been assailed by such aversion and weariness, and the thought has come to me: "If I had not begun to do so, I would never again preach another word; I would let everything take whatever course it may." . . . But Christ declares: "That is not the right attitude. Do not let the devil, the world, or your own flesh overcome you; but think of how I have loved you and still love you." (Luther, "Sermons on the Gospel of St. John Chapter Fifteen, 1537," LW 24, p. 247)

The beleaguered pastor may not always find support among clergy colleagues. Menno Simons is a case in point. In discussing the problem of integrity in ministry, Menno applied the trenchant metaphor of a prostitute talking incessantly about virtue. Having found many hypocrisies among clergy, this persecuted clergyman wrote:

O preachers, preachers, how aptly has the Holy Spirit likened you to wells without water, clouds without rain from which no helpful water can be received, trees without fruit from which nothing edible can be picked. I know not to what you may be better compared than to a woman who lives in all manner of shame and wantonness, but likes to talk about modesty and virtue. (Menno Simons, *Foundations of Christian Doctrine*, 1539, *CWMS*, p. 168)*

In a Sermon of 1531 on Titus 2:13, Luther stated his conviction that the power and goodness of God at times become hidden from view, even while one is actively engaged in Christ's ministry. God allows his power to be perceived as weakness and dying, in order that subsequently it might become known as love and resurrection:

He allows His prophets and apostles to be expelled and murdered: Paul to be beheaded, Peter to be crucified, His holy martyrs to be flung into bonds and prison, to be scourged, stoned, hacked, and stabbed to pieces and miserably done away with. He allows His Christians to suffer want, trouble, and misfortune in the world. He acts as He did in the days of His flesh, when John the Baptist had to lose his head for the sake of a desperate harlot, while He, the Savior and Helper, said nothing about it, departed thence in a ship and withdrew to the solitude of a wilderness (Matt. 14:10ff, Mark 6:27, 32). Is He not a petty, childish God, who does not save Himself and allows His children to suffer as if

He did not see how badly they were faring?

Then, as the writings of the prophets and the psalms state, the godless boast; they mock the Christians and their God, saying: "Where is now their God?" (Ps. 115:2; cf. John 16:20). If He is God, let Him contend for His rights and the rights of His people so that His name may not be rooted out and His people may not suffer. If he does not see what is going on, then He has no eyes to see and no reason to understand. On the other hand, if He does see and know but allows these things to happen, then He is no good, faithful God and has no heart for His people. Likewise, if He sees and knows but cannot help, then He has no hands that are able to do anything, nor does He have power to enable Him to save.

Hence the prophet Isaiah correctly says of God: "Verily Thou art a God that hidest Thyself, O God of Israel, the Savior" (45:15). For He hides His omnipotence, wisdom, power, and might and acts so childishly as though He could do nothing, knew nothing, understood nothing or did not want to do anything. Now He lets our adversaries treat His Word, Sacraments, and Christians as they please. He lets us call and cry and says nothing, as though He were deep in thought or were busy or were out in the field or asleep and heard nothing, as Elijah says of Baal (1 Kings 18:27). (Luther, WA 34 II, pp. 128f.; WLS 1, p. 282)

John Chrysostom thought that the strength of a ministry could only be known through testing. The life of monk and priest are contrasted just at this point—the priestly life is subjected to more severe testing:

In harbour the man at the helm cannot yet give sure proof of his skill. . . . I should have no claim to admiration if I did not commit sin only because I was sleeping, or did not get a fall only because I was not wrestling, or was not wounded only because I was not fighting! . . . What am I to do? Nothing is as useless for church government as this inactivity and detachment, which other people regard as a form of self-discipline, but which I have more as a veil for my own worthlessness, using it to cloak most my failings and keep them from becoming obvious. . . . [In pastoral work] all his faults are exposed, and as fire tests metals, so the touchstone of the ministry distinguishes men's souls. (Chrysostom, *On the Priesthood*, Ch. VI, sec. 5, pp. 144-147)

The pastor does well to expect good outcomes under the guidance of divine grace. The distortable theme of positive thinking, rediscovered in the last century by William James and Norman Vincent Peale, was anticipated by Richard Baxter:

If you would prosper in your work, be sure to keep up earnest desires and expectations of success. . . . I have observed that God seldom blesses any one's work so much as one whose heart is set upon the success of it. (Baxter, *RP*, p. 121)*

IV ❧ ON LEAVING THE MINISTRY

The laying on of hands in ordination has been considered, like baptism, an act that occurs only once, that is not repeated, and not reversible once enacted. A distinction recurs in classical pastoral care between between those liturgical acts that are are repeated, and those that are administered only once. The Lord's Supper, preaching, teaching, and prayer are among actions done repeatedly. But baptism, confirmation, and marriage are among the actions ordinarily taken only once, and the commitment is understood or assumed in principle to be once for all. Ordination has usually been placed in this latter category. Thus a debate has ensued as to whether orders are "indelible," i.e., undeletable. The heart of the issue: Once one has been duly called and ordained to the care of souls, how it is possible justly and legitimately to abandon or take leave of it?

The Athanasian Canons stated the rigorist view, that one having taken up ministry shall not leave it:

None shall take upon him this call, that is the priesthood, and despise it. Rather he shall perform his service faithfully, even as did the Levites.

Let none say,"I desire to have nothing to do with the altar, nor do I have time for the ministry." For this cannot be. For the Saviour will say to him, "Either do my law or go forth from my city". . . . If you say, "I take nothing from the altar, and neither do I serve," then think of the parable of the talents, of what God did to the one who had ten pounds and to the other who had one pound and hid it in the earth, and no profit came from it. God took it from him and gave it unto him that had the ten pounds. (*Athanasian Canons*, pp. 36-37)*

Luther and Lutheran scholastics such as Chemnitz took a moderating view that the church does not have the right to remove one called by God to ministry, but it does have the right to remove one not so called:

As long as God lets in the ministry His minister who teaches rightly and lives blamelessly, the church does not have the power, without divine command to remove an unwanted man, namely [if he is] a servant of God. But when he does not build up the church by either doctrine or life, but rather destroys [it], God Himself removes him, 1 Sam 2:30; Hos 4:6. And then the church not only properly can but by all means should remove such a one from the ministry. For just as God calls ministers of the church, so He also removes them through legitimate means. (Chemnitz, *MWS*, Part I, Sec. 31, p. 37)

In the background of the complex debate on indelible orders is the problem of whether it is possible to receive divine gifts from unworthy priests. Augustine had influentially established the point in the controversy with the Donatists that even bad ministers may continue to receive the dignity of the pastoral office when their ordination has been duly authorized. Catherine of Siena made the same point later and with even greater force, that unworthy ministers are due to be revered, since they are not revered for their personal worthwhileness, but for their office. Catherine's striking metaphor is of a tramp bearing kingly gifts:

This reverence should never diminish in the case of priests whose virtue grows weak. . . . This dignity belongs to good and bad alike—all have the Sun to administer, as has been said, and perfect priests are themselves in a condition of light, that is to say, they illuminate and warm their neighbours through their love. And with this heat they cause virtues to spring up and bear fruit in the souls of their subjects. I have appointed them to be in very truth your guardian angels to protect you; to inspire your hearts with good thoughts by their holy prayers, and to teach you My doctrine reflected in the mirror of their life, and to serve you by administering to you the holy Sacraments, thus serving you, watching over you, and inspiring you with good and holy thoughts as does an angel. . . . You know well that if a filthy and badly dressed person brought you a great treasure from which you obtained life, you would not hate the bearer, however ragged and filthy he might be, through love of the treasure and of the lord who sent it to you. His state would indeed displease you, and you would be anxious through love of his master that he should be cleansed from his foulness and properly clothed. This, then, is your duty according to the demands of charity, and thus I wish you to act with regard to such badly ordered priests, who themselves filthy and clothed in garments ragged with vice through their separation from My love, bring you great Treasures. (Catherine of Siena, *A Treatise of Prayer*, pp. 255-257)

The crow is an ancient metaphor of abandonment. In his Table Talk of 1531, Luther compared the abrupt pastoral abandonment of those in one's care to crow deserting their young:

Crows are said to be very heartless in that they desert their young after they have hatched them and fly away. Thereafter God miraculously feeds them (Ps. 147:9). By these crows the false and faithless teachers, and pastors of the church are pictured. For the sake of the belly (*ventris gratia*) or danger, they desert their young ones (*pullos*), that is, the Christians entrusted to their care. (Luther, *Table Talk*, W-T 2, #2154; WLS 1, p. 283)

Ignatius Loyola viewed the authentic choice of priesthood as immutable, binding further choice, for that is the nature of immutable choice. But if the divine call has been misunderstood, one had best not compound one bad choice with another:

There are some things that are the objects of an immutable choice, such as the priesthood, matrimony, etc. There are others in which the choice is not immutable, as for example, accepting or relinquishing a benefice, accepting or renouncing temporal goods.

Once an immutable choice has been made there is no further choice, for it cannot be dissolved, as is true with marriage, the priesthood, etc. It should be noted only that if one has not made this choice properly, with due consideration, and without inordinate attachments, he should repent and try to lead a good life in the choice that he has made. Since this choice was ill considered and improperly made, it does not seem to be a vocation from God, as many err in believing, wishing to interpret an ill-considered or bad choice as a divine call. For every divine call is always pure and clean without any admixture of flesh or other inordinate attachments. (Ignatius Loyola, *Spiritual Exercises*, pp. 83-84)

Luther argued against the strict interpretation of indelibility:

A priest is no longer a priest when he is deposed. But now they have invented *characteres indelebiles* (indelible marks) and prate that a deposed priest is nevertheless something different from a mere layman. They even dream that a priest can nevermore become a layman or be anything else than a priest. All this is mere talk and man-made law. (Luther, "To the Christian Nobility of the German Nation, 1520," WA 6, p. 407; WLS 2, p. 944; cf. LW, 44, p. 129)

Again, Luther:

In this view of the ministry, the so-called "indelible character" vanishes and the perpetuity of the office is shown to be fictitious. A minister may be deposed if he proves unfaithful. (Luther, "Concerning the Ministry, 1523," LW 40, p. 35)

What about pastors who leave parishes and invest their entire time seeking to influence bureaucracies and secondary church organizations? Although it may seem to be only a modern phenomenon, this problem was being debated already at the Council of Chalcedon (451 A.D.). Priests were leaving their parishes to try to influence the bureaucracy at Constantinople, lobbying, scheming, and making trouble:

It has come to the hearing of the holy Synod that certain clergymen and monks, having no authority from their own bishop, and sometimes, indeed, while under sentence of excommunication by him, betake themselves to the imperial Constantinople, and remain there for a long time, raising disturbances and troubling the ecclesiastical state, and turning men's houses upside down. Therefore the holy Synod has determined that such persons be first notified by the Advocate of the most holy Church of Constantinople to depart from the imperial city; and if they shall shamelessly continue in the same practices, that they shall be expelled by the same Advocate even against their will, and return to their own places. (Chalcedon, A.D. 451, Canon XXIII, The Seven Ecumenical Councils, NPNF 2, XIV, pp. 283-284)

Shortly after the Diocletian persecution, the Council of Ancyra rigorously assessed those conditions under which it should not be considered blameworthy to flee from persecution:

Those who have fled and been apprehended, or have been betrayed by their servants; or those who have been otherwise despoiled of their goods, or have endured tortures, or have been imprisoned and abused, declaring themselves to be Christians; or who have been forced to receive something which their persecutors violently thrust into their hands, or meat (offered to idols), continually professing that they were Christians; and who, by their whole apparel, and demeanour, and humility of life, always give evidence of grief at what has happened; these persons, inasmuch as they are free from sin, are not to be repelled from the communion; and if, through an extreme strictness or ignorance of some things, they have been repelled, let them forthwith be re-admitted. (Council of Ancyra, A.D. 314, Canon III, The Seven Ecumenical Councils, NPNF 2, XIV, p. 64)

V ✤ ON HEALING THE CORRUPTIONS OF SACRED MINISTRY

Lapse comes from *lapsare*, to slip, stumble, slide or fall. The stumbling of pastors may occasion the stumbling of many others. Thus the lapsing of clergy (an extension of the analogy of the fall of humanity) has been a recurrent point of debate and analysis for classical pastoral writers.

In this Part we have discussed the pastoral duty to care for oneself, especially as it takes the form of vocational demoralization, burnout, and the temptation of abandonment of ministry. In examining these subjects, the pastoral writers have been intensely aware of *the special corruptions to which ministry is prone*, and have sought alertly to identify, circumvent, and where they occur, reform and heal them.

The pastor, like all others, is liable to stumble along the way, but pastoral stumbling may too quickly elicit a crisis in self-esteem, partly due to the inordinate quality of idealism that sometimes attaches itself to the vocation to ministry. So it is pertinent to ask of the classical writers how they understood the proneness of ministry to fall. This is considered under the category of the pastoral duty to care for oneself because the struggle takes place primarily in the self-consciousness, conscience, and inner life of the pastor.

Some vices or undesirable behavior patterns have been thought to be more directly opposed to the nature and spirit of care of souls than others. Luther thought that two in particular, pride and avarice, were most commonly destructive of the foundation of pastoral service:

> The sum and substance of this epistle is that in a preacher or teacher no vice is more hurtful or harmful than vainglory, although avarice is also an evil trait in them, and both commonly appear together. For the sake of profit—that they may gain more—preachers and teachers want to be something outstanding, special and superior. . . . All other vices are more endurable in a preacher, although, of course, none of them are good; and a preacher should, in fairness, be blameless and perfect, as St. Paul teaches (Titus 1:7). Nor is this surprising, for both vices are naturally and directly opposed to the nature of the ministry. (Luther, WA 17 II, p. 144; WLS 2, pp. 952-953)

On the occasion of his being burned at the stake in Oxford, October 16, 1555, Anglican Bishop Nicolas Ridley of London recounted how repeatedly the ministry has failed the people, and how quickly a corrupted ministry was able to do injury to church and society:

> You that are my kinsfold and countrymen, know that however much the blind, ignorant, and wicked world hereafter shall rail upon my death, they cannot do worse than their fathers did of the death of Christ. . . . Now you also know, my true lovers in

God, my kinsfolk and countrymen, that the cause for which I am put to death is the same sort and condition. . . . For you all know that when the poor true man is robbed by the thief of his own truly-gotten goods, by which he and his household should live, he is greatly wronged. For the thief in stealing and robbing with violence the poor man's goods, offends God, transgresses his laws, and is injurious both to the poor man and to the commonwealth. So I say it is with the Church of England in the cause of my death, as you all know. . . . This Church of England had of late, of the infinite goodness and abundant Almighty God, great substance, great riches of heavenly treasure, great plenty of God's true and sincere word, the true and wholesome administration of Christ's holy sacraments, the whole profession of Christ's religion, truly and plainly set forth in baptism, the plain declaration and understanding of the faith taught in the holy catechism to be learned of all true Christians. . . . But, alas! of late, into this spiritual possession of the heavenly treasure of these godly riches, thieves have entered in who have robbed and spoiled all this heavenly treasure away. I may well complain of these thieves, and cry out upon them with the prophet, saying: "O God, the heathen have set foot in thy domain, defiled thy holy temple, and laid Jerusalem in ruins" (Ps. 79:1)—that is, they have broken and beat down to the ground your holy city. This heathen generation, these thieves of Samaria, these Sabaeans and Chaldeans, these robbers, have rushed out of their dens and robbed the Church of England of all the holy treasure of God. They have carried it away, and overthrown it, and in the place of God's holy Word, the true and right administration of Christ's holy sacraments, as of baptism and others, they mixed their ministry with foolish fantasies, and many wicked and ungodly traditions. (Bishop Ridley, 1555, Confessorsand Martyrs, OCC I, p. 64-67)*

There is no absolute guarantee that once approved and ordained for care of souls, the pastor's integrity will remain inviolable. Tertullian looked to biblical precedent (Saul, David, and Solomon) to show that one could at one time be called and approved of God in performing a special office, and then at a later time fall into abuses:

This again is, I suppose, an extraordinary thing, that one who has been approved should afterwards fall back? Saul, who was good beyond all others, is afterwards subverted by envy. David, a good man "after the Lord's own heart," is guilty afterwards of murder and adultery. Solomon, endowed by the Lord with all

On the Pastoral Obligation to Care for Oneself 23

grace and wisdom, is led into idolatry by women. (Tertullian, *On Prescription Against Heretics*, Ch. III, ANF III, p. 244)

Accountability in caring for souls depends upon something more than formal ecclesiastical approval. Menno Simons, the sixteenth century Anabaptist leader who had suffered so much at the hands of ordained ministers, had good reason to doubt that ordination, once given, would necessarily guarantee its continued authenticity, charity, and fairness. False ministries will be called into account, if not by human, then by divine judgment:

A portion of them are useless, haughty, immoral men; some are avaricious, usurers, liars, deceivers; some are drunkards, gamblers, licentious, open seducers, idolaters, etc., concerning whom it is written that they shall not inherit the kingdom of God if they do not repent (1 Cor. 6:9, 10). Some also are idle profligates, young and haughty, wholly unlearned in the Scriptures, anointed and shaven by Antichrist, just so they have a smattering of Latin, as if the office of God and cure of souls depended not on piety and the gift of grace, but on linguistic attainment. No, my reader, no, we shall have to look deeper than that. . . . It is much worse than I can write. The blind call the blind; the one idolater calls the other; one ungodly man calls the other. The saying of the prophet comes true: deceivers, liars, drunkards, and gluttons are good prophets for this people (Micah 2:11). . . . No doubt it suits perverted fleshly ease to live in luxury here on earth with bodies fat and sleek and with gloved hands putting on airs; to be greeted as doctor, lord, and master by men. But when the messenger of death shall knock at the door of your souls and say: "Give account," you may no longer be stewards. When you must appear before the throne of the eternal majesty and before the poor miserable souls which you have led off the true highway of Christ with your deceiving, false doctrine, idolatrous witchcraft, and wickedly liberal life; when you must be wrenched from your lying mouths, your blind and infidel hearts, and your sleek and lazy bodies, oh, where will you conceal yourselves then from the wrath of God? Then men will cry, ye mountains, fall on us; and ye hills, cover us (Rev. 6:16). Ah, then you will know what kind of calling you had, what office and life you led, that you served no one but your impotent god, the belly, the devil, and your self-seeking evil flesh, that you came without being called, that you have sought nothing but the milk, wool, and flesh of the sheep. (Menno Simons, *Foundations of Christian Doctrine*, 1539, *CWMS*, pp. 162-163)

Ministry is entrusted with power that can greatly harm, as well as help, the community of faith. It is because the people have come to depend so profoundly upon the genuine caring of ministers, that the abuses of ministry become so wrenching. The office of ministry bears special responsibilities, just as physicians or magistrates, which others need not bear. If one had chosen to live a private life without taking a pastoral charge, there would be less grounds for complaint; but ministers have voluntarily accepted and taken on these unique responsibilities:

When reproofs themselves prove so ineffectual, that they are more offended at the reproof than at the sin, and had rather that we should cease reproving than that themselves should cease sinning, I think it is time to sharpen the remedy. . . . To bear with the vices of the ministry is to promote the ruin of the Church, for what speedier way is there for the depraving and undoing of the people, than the depravity of their guides? And how can we more effectually further a reformation, than by endeavouring to reform the leaders of the Church? . . . If thousands of you were in a leaking ship, and those that should pump out of the water, and stop the leaks, should be sporting or asleep, or even but favouring themselves in their labours, to the hazarding of you all, would you not awaken them to their work and call of them labour as for your lives? . . . Neither God nor good men will let you alone in such sins. Yet if you had betaken yourselves to another calling, and would sin to yourselves only, and would perish alone, we should not have so much necessity of molesting you, as now we have; but if you will enter into the office of the ministry, which is for the necessary preservation of us all, so that by letting you alone in your sin, we must give up the Church to loss and hazard, blame us not if we talk to you more freely than you would have us do. If your own body were sick, and you will despise the remedy, or if your own house were on fire, and you will be singing or quarrelling in the streets, I could possibly bear it, and let you alone (which yet, in charity, I should not easily do), but, if you will undertake to be the physician of an hospital, or to a whole town that is infected with the plague, or will undertake to quench all the fires that shall be kindled in the town, there is no bearing with your remissness, how much soever it may displease you. Take it how you will, you must be told of it. (Baxter, *RP*, pp. 39–41)

When the trust offered to the pastoral counselor is abused, as when the counselor has sexual intercourse with a parishioner, the integrity of the whole of the clergy may be thrown in question. That such abuses are ancient is evident in this fourth century account by Socrates Scholasticus. The remedy for such abuses, however, must not itself create greater problems:

A woman of noble family coming to the rite of penitence, made a general confession of those sins she had committed since her baptism. The presbyter urged fasting and prayer continually, that together with the acknowledgment of error, she might have to show works also meet for repentance. Some time after this, the same lady again presented herself, and confessed that she had been guilty of another crime, a deacon of the church having slept with her. When this was proved the deacon was removed from the church; but the people were very indignant, being not only offended at what had taken place, but also because the deed had brought scandal and degradation upon the Church. When in consequence of this, ecclesiastics were subjected to taunting and reproach, Eudaemon a presbyter of the church, by birth an Alexandrian, persuaded Nectarius the bishop to abolish the office of penitential presbyter, and to leave every one to his own conscience with regard to the participation of the sacred mysteries; for in his judgment, only in this way could the Church be preserved from bad repute. . . . My observation to Eudaemon, when he first related the circumstance, was this: "Whether, O presbyter, your counsel has been profitable for the Church or otherwise, God knows; but I see that it takes away from all the means of admonishing one another's faults, and prevents our acting upon that precept of the apostle." (Socrates Scholasticus, *Ecclesiastical History*, Bk. V, Ch. XIX, NPNF 2, II, p. 128)*

Several conclusions may be derived from this vignette: Due to the unique closeness of confessional conversation that brings men and women together on a confidential and personal basis, clergy are brought near the possibilities of sexual irresponsibilities (or more often simply suspicion of sexual misdeeds). However abusable, the answer to potential sexual abuses of confession is not to do away with confession altogether.

Fourth century canon law strictly forbade clergy to do any form of violence to persons. For lay persons become vulnerable in the care of clergy, and put themselves trustfully into the hands of clergy. This rule remains in broad intent still applicable to pastoral counseling relationships—do no harm:

We command that clergy, whether bishop, presbyter or deacon, who resort to violent acts to correct believers, be deprived of their office. They imagine that they are going to terrify people into faith. Yet our Lord has nowhere taught us such things. On the contrary, "when he was abused he did not retort with abuse, when he suffered he uttered no threats" (1 Pet. 2:23). (*Constitutions of the Holy Apostles*, Ecclesiastical Canons, Book VIII, Sec. v, Canon 28, ANF VII, p. 501, NEB)*

There is a strong antinomian temptation almost unique to sacred ministry, which believing that God has especially chosen ministers, consequently tends to view ministers as above or beyond the law. With this false premise, it is difficult to prevent the pastoral office from becoming a cloak for abuses, insensitivities, and deceptions, according to John Chrysostom:

A man who has received an honour beyond his deserving should not use its greatness as a cloak for his faults. He ought rather to use God's abundant favour towards him as a stronger incentive to improvement. But because he has been so highly honoured, he thinks he is allowed to make mistakes, and is determined to prove that the cause of his own sins is the kindness of God. This is always the argument of irreverent men who manage their lives carelessly. We must not be like that. (John Chrysostom, *On the Priesthood*, Ch. IV, sec. 1, p. 106)

This contorted temptation centers on the presumed premise of the lenience of God, as if to say, since God forgives all, why not sin that grace may abound? Such a misguided ministry is candidly likened by Luther to pandering:

In no place have people blasphemed God more and put Him to shame more than in those churches and houses of God, as they were called. Therefore I may well say: It would be better for all churches to be dance halls than churches in which the tomfoolery is preached and practiced with which men rob God of His honor and ruin countless souls. In fact, I would even say more: that such churches are worse than all public houses of ill fame (*alle gemeine Frauenhaeuser*); for there thousands of souls are poisoned and prostituted at once, and the preacher is a thousand times worse than a panderer. He prostitutes so many tender souls by his sermons. (Luther, WA 17 II, p. 342f; WLS 1, #873, p. 298)

According to Tertullian, God the Spirit knew in advance the special vulnerabilities of clergy, that they would be tempted more strongly than others to licence and antinomianism:

The Holy Spirit saw that in the future some would say: "All things are permitted to bishops!" And, in fact, your bishop of Uthina is a case in point: he did not scruple to violate even the edict of Scantinius! And how many bigamists are there who rule in your churches, obviously insulting the Apostle, or at least unembarrassed, even as his words on this subject are read out while they are presiding! (Tertullian, *On Monogamy*, ACW 13, p. 99)

Clergy are capable of elaborate rationalizations. Much more than normal damage can be done under the guise of righteousness. Luther preferred open theivery to deceptive ministry:

There is no more terrible plague, calamity, and misfortune on earth than a preacher who does not preach God's Word. Unfortunately, the world is now full of such preachers. Yet they imagine that they are doing well and are pious. However, they are doing nothing but murdering souls, blaspheming God, and establishing idolatry. It would be far better for them to be robbers, murderers, and the worst rogues; then they would at least know that they are doing wrong. (Luther, WA 10 I, p. 85; WLS 3, p. 1124)

John Donne prayed in his parting days that he be spared those who would abuse the pastoral office:

Keep me back, O Lord, from them who misprofess arts of healing the soul . . . by means not imprinted by thee in the church for the soul. (John Donne, *Devotions*, p. 28)

Every care-giver needs care. The selections of Part One have focussed upon soul care for the care-giver, and the pastoral obligation to care for oneself, to receive due care for one's own soul. Special nourishment is required to transcend despair over the burdens of care for others. Caring for the flock cannot occur unless one first insures that one's own soul is fed. This requires facing the distinctive challenges of pastoral service and the difficulties intrinsic to soul care, so that ministry will not have to be abandoned under fire, and the temptations and corruptions closest to soul care will be resisted.

2 Pastoral Care Through Preaching

PASTORAL CARE HAS BEEN DISJOINED from preaching in modern curricula. In previous periods, pastoral care was thought to include preaching, and preaching was viewed as a task intrinsic to pastoral care. In this Part we will review key texts that make clear the nature of preaching and its integral relation with the care of souls.

I ❦ THE MINISTRY OF THE WORD

In Romans 10:12-15, Paul set forth the primary reason for preaching: "Scripture says: . . . 'Everyone who invokes the name of the Lord will be saved.' How could they invoke one in whom they had no faith? And how could they have faith in one they had never heard of? And how hear without someone to spread the news? And how could anyone spread the news without a commission to do so? And that is what Scripture affirms: 'How welcome are the feet of the messengers of good news!' " Following Paul, the pastoral writers have spoken frequently of the human need for being counseled through the word of preaching. Major classic definitions of soul care, whether of patristic, medieval, or Reformation periods, include proclamation of the gospel. It is not a task that Christianity expects God unilaterally to do for us or without our human voices, as Luther noted:

It would not be surprising if I threw the keys at the Lord's feet and said: Lord, do Your own preaching. No doubt You are able to do better; for we have preached to them, but they will not listen to us. But God wants us to stand fast in our calling and office, to administer them, and to give rebukes. For He wants to rule His church through preachers, through the external word and Sacrament, just as He rules the world through burgomasters, kings, princes, and lords, and punishes the wicked with the sword. (Luther, WA 47, p. 95; WLS 3, p. 1115)

28

As the external, political life of the world needs the ordering provided by government, so does the inner life of the soul need the guidance of preaching. Alan of Lille defined preaching as a highly public activity which nonetheless seeks to reach deeply into the hidden recesses of the soul:

Preaching is an open and public instruction in faith and behavior, whose purpose is the forming of men; it derives from the path of reason and from the fountainhead of the "authorities." Preaching should be public, because it must be delivered openly. That is why Christ says: "What you hear whispered you must shout from the housetops" (Matt. 10:27). For if preaching were hidden, it would be suspect. (Alan of Lille, *The Art of Preaching*, Ch. I, CFS, 23, pp. 16-17, NEB)*

The best pastoral preaching does not focus autobiographically upon the preacher's inward feelings or sentiments, but upon God's own Word addressed through scripture. Martin Chemnitz asked: What is the preacher called to preach about?

Neither his dreams, nor the visions of his heart, nor whatever seemed good or right to him (Jer. 23:16, 25); also not human traditions or ordinances (Is. 29:13; Mt. 15:9). But let him who teaches in the church teach the Word of God (1 Pt. 4:11), so that the heart of the ministry is and remains this, Is. 59:21: "I have put My words in your mouth," and as Augustine aptly says: "Let us not hear in the church: I say this, you say this, he says that; but: Thus says the Lord." (Chemnitz, *MWS*, Part 2, sec. 34, p. 39)

The essential subject matter of preaching is the good news of God's coming to humanity that we might come to share in God's life, as set forth by Anglican theologian Ralph Cudworth:

Though the gospel be not God, as He is in His own brightness, but God veiled and masked to us, God in a state of humiliation and condescendent as the sun in a rainbow, yet it is nothing else but a clear and unspotted mirror of Divine holiness, goodness, purity, in which attributes lies the very life and essence of God Himself. The gospel is nothing else but God, descending into the world in our form and conversing with us in our likeness, that He might allure and draw us up to God and make us partakers of His Divine form. *Theos gegonen anthropos* (as Athanasius speaks) *hina hemas en eauto theopoiese*; "God was therefore incarnated and made man, that He might deify us," that is (as St. Peter expresses

it), "make us partakers of the Divine Nature" (cf. 2 Pet. 1:4). . . .
God Who is absolute goodness cannot love any of His creatures
and take pleasure in them without bestowing a communication of
His goodness and likeness upon them. (Ralph Cudworth, Sermon
Preached Before the House of Commons, 1647, pp. 16-21, *Angl.*,
p. 782)*

The freedom of the pulpit will be maintained only with vigilance. Yet
the free pulpit does not give the preacher the general license to express
any and every private opinion about whatever happens to be of personal
interest. Luther, who did as much as anyone to free the pulpit from
intrusions from state power, argued the case rigorously:

If any man would preach, let him suppress his own words. Let
him make them count in family matters and secular affairs. But
here in the church he should speak nothing except the Word of
this rich Head of the household; otherwise it is not the true
church. Therefore this must be the rule: God is speaking. . . .
That is why a preacher, by virtue of his commission and office, is
administering the household of God and dare say nothing but
what God says and commands. And although much talking is
done which is outside the Word of God, yet the church is not
established by such talk, though men were to turn mad in their
insistence on it. (Luther, WA 47, p. 773f; WLS 1, p. 287)

If Luther is correct, the best pastoral preaching is clear, forceful, relevant exposition of the texts of scripture. That is what distinguishes the
ministry of the Word from editorial opinion on economics, politics and
domestic affairs. Jeremy Taylor, the Anglican defender of religious toleration, warned against the pulpit being used crassly as an arena for
divisive debates, or a platform for the propagation of teachings inconsis-
tent with Christian faith. The guiding rule for what is to be preached is
canonical scripture and ancient ecumenical tradition:

Every minister ought to be careful, that he never expound
Scriptures in public contrary to the known sense of the catholic
Church, and particularly of the churches of England and Ireland,
nor introduce any doctrine against any of the four first general
councils; for these, as they are measures of truth, so also of necessity; that is, as they are safe, so they are sufficient; and besides
what is taught by these, no matter of belief is necessary to salvation.

Let no preacher bring before the people, in his sermons or discourses, the arguments of great and dangerous heresies, though

with a purpose to confute them; for they will much easier retain the objection than understand the answer.

Let not the preacher make an article of faith to be a matter of dispute; but teach it with plainness and simplicity, and confirm it with easy arguments and plain words of Scripture, but without objection; let them be taught to believe, but not to argue. (Jeremy Taylor, *RAC*, sec. 56, *CS*, pp. 18-19)

With wry humor, Luther mused about hyper-creative preachers who imagine that they are called to preach new ideas so as to improve upon the gospel of Christ:

There are some ministers who imagine that they cannot be preachers unless they teach more than Christ and above the level of our preaching. These are the ambitious eccentrics, who forsake our simplicity and rush on with their peculiar wisdom, so that people cast admiring glances at them and exclaim: What a preacher! They should be sent to Athens, where people desired to hear something new every day (Acts 17:21). They seek their own honor, not Christ's, therefore they will also end in shame. Beware of them and stay with Paul, who desired to know nothing save Christ and Him crucified. (Luther, WA 10 II, p. 167f; WLS 3, p. 1116)

II ❧ THE AUTHORITY OF THE WORD

Classic pastoral writers have generally viewed Paul as the key biblical prototype of the ministry of the Word. In his work, *On the Priesthood*, John Chrysostom sought to analyze why this man, who ostensibly had only the fragile power of speech, had such remarkable influence through preaching:

He had a greater power than speech, a power which was able to effect greater results. By his mere presence, and without a word, he terrified the devils. . . . Let a man's diction be beggarly and his verbal composition simple and artless, but do not let him be inexpert in the knowledge and careful statement of doctrine. . . . How did he confute the Grecians? Why was he sent to Tarsus? Was it not because he powerfully prevailed by his words and so far routed them that they were provoked to murder him, not being able to bear their defeat? Then he had not yet begun to work wonders and no one could say that the crowds thought him wonderful because of the fame of his miracles or that the people who opposed him were overthrown by his reputation. For at that time his only power was the power of speech. How did he contend and dispute with those who tried to live like Jews at Antioch? Did not the Areopagite, who belonged to that very superstitious city, follow him with his wife because of his speech alone? How did Eutychus come to fall from the window? Was it not because he was engrossed until midnight in the word of his teaching? What happened at Thessalonica and Corinth? What at Ephesus and Rome itself? Did he not spend whole days and nights continuously in expounding the Scriptures? . . . Why did the Lycaonians believe him to be Hermes? The idea that he and Barnabas were gods was due to their miracles; but the idea that he was Hermes was due not to his miracles but to his eloquence. . . . Listen also to what he says to his disciple in a letter: "Devote your attention to the public reading of the scriptures, to exhortation, and to teaching" (1 Tim. 4:13). And he adds the fruit which develops from this: "For in doing so," he says, "you will further the salvation of yourself and your hearers," and again, "The servant of the Lord must not be quarrelsome, but kindly towards all. He should be a good teacher, tolerant" (2 Tim. 2:24). . . . "Let your conversation be always gracious, and never insipid; study how best to talk with each person you meet" (Col. 4:6). And the command to be ready to give an answer was given to all alike. Writing to the Thessalonians, Paul says, "Fortify one another—as indeed you do." But when he speaks of priests, he says, "Elders who do well as leaders should be reckoned worthy of a double stipend, in particular those who labour at preaching and teaching." (John Chrysostom, *On the Priesthood*, Ch. IV.6-8, pp. 120-125)

Luther was realistically aware that parishioners were not naturally drawn to hear rigorous preaching:

It happened to Ambrosius. He was once told by his parishioners, after they had been admonished to hear the Word and the sermon: The truth is, dear pastor, that if you were to tap a keg of beer in church and call us to enjoy it, we would be glad to come. (Luther, W-T 3, #3663, WLS 1, #890, p. 303)

Nonetheless, since preaching is God's own purpose and intention, God will in due time find listeners for the faithful preacher:

Since God creates people whom He bids to preach, He will no doubt also create and send listeners who will take their teaching to heart. (Luther, WA 46, p. 540; WLS 1, #889, p. 303)

Although the cultural settings in which the Word is proclaimed may be always changing, the Word does not change. Irenaeus contrasted the diversity of false teaching with the fundamental unity of ecumenical teaching amid highly diverse cultures:

The Church, having received this preaching and this faith, although scattered throughout the whole world, yet, as if occupying but one house, carefully preserves it. She also believes these points [of doctrine] just as if she had but one soul, and one and the same heart, and she proclaims them, and teaches them, and hands them down with perfect harmony, as if she possessed only one mouth. For, although the languages of the world are dissimilar, yet the import of the tradition is one and the same. For the Churches which have been planted in Germany do not believe or hand down anything different, nor do those in Spain, nor those in Gaul, nor those in the East, nor those in Egypt, nor those in Libya. . . . Nor will any one of the rulers in the churches, however highly gifted he may be in point of eloquence, teach doctrines different from these. . . . It does not follow because men are endowed with greater and less degrees of intelligence, that they should therefore change the subject-matter [of the faith] itself, and should conceive of some other God besides Him who is the framer, Maker, and Preserver of this universe (as if He were not sufficient for them), or of another Christ, or another Only-begotten. But the fact referred to simply implies this, that one may [more accurately than another] bring out the meaning of those things which have been spoken in parables, and accommodate them to the general scheme of the faith. (Irenaeus, *Against Heresies*, Bk. I, Ch. x, sec. 2-3, ANF I, p. 331)

The authenticity of preaching is to be insured from generation to generation primarily by its accountability to and continuity with the apostolic teaching:

It is within the power of all, therefore, in every Church, who may wish to see the truth, to contemplate clearly the tradition of the apostles manifested throughout the whole world; and we are in a position to reckon up those who were by the apostles instituted bishops in the Churches, and [to demonstrate] the succession of these men to our own times; those who neither taught nor knew of anything like what these [heretics] rave about. For if the apostles had known hidden mysteries, which they were in the habit of imparting to "the perfect" apart and privily from the rest, they would have delivered them especially to those to whom they were also committing the Churches themselves. . . . The faith preached to men. . . . comes down to our time by means of the successions of the bishops. For it is a matter of necessity that every Church should agree with this Church, on account of its preeminent authority, that is, the faithful everywhere, inasmuch as the apostolical tradition has been preserved continuously by those [faithful men] who exist everywhere.

The blessed apostles, then, having founded and built up the Church, committed into the hands of Linus the office of the episcopate. Of this Linus, Paul makes mention in the Epistles to Timothy. To him succeeded Anacletus; and after him, in the third place from the apostles, Clement was allotted the bishopric. . . . Polycarp also was not only instructed by apostles, and conversed with many who had seen Christ, but was also, by apostles in Asia, appointed bishop of the Church in Smyrna, whom I also saw in my early youth, for he tarried [on earth] a very long time, and, when a very old man, gloriously and most nobly suffering martyrdom, departed this life, having always taught the things which he had learned from the apostles, and which the Church has handed down and which alone are true. . . . Suppose there arise a dispute relative to some important question among us, should we not have recourse to the most ancient Churches with which the apostles held constant intercourse, and learn from them what is certain and clear in regard to the present question? For how should it be if the apostles themselves had not left us writings? (Irenaeus, *Against Heresies*, Bk. III, Ch. iii-iv, ANF I, pp. 415-417)

The best pastoral preaching lives out of Holy Writ. The Westminster Confession set forth the complex inward process by which scripture works to transform life, self-evidencing its authority, working in our hearts:

We may be moved and induced by the testimony of the Church to an high and reverent esteem of the holy Scripture; and the heavenliness of the matter, the efficacy of the doctrine, the majesty of the style, the consent of all the parts, the scope of the whole (which is to give all glory to God), the full discovery it makes of the only way of man's salvation, the many other incomparable excellencies, and the entire perfection thereof, are arguments whereby it doth abundantly evidence itself to be the Word of God; yet, notwithstanding our full persuasion and assurance of the infallible truth and divine authority thereof, is from the inward work of the Holy Spirit, bearing witness by and with the

Word in our hearts. . . . All things in Scripture are not alike plain
in themselves, nor alike clear unto all; yet those things which are
necessary to be known, believed, and observed, for salvation, are
so clearly propounded and opened in some place of Scripture or
other, that not only the learned, but the unlearned, in a due use
of the ordinary means, may attain unto a sufficient understanding of them. (Westminster Confession, Ch. I, sec. v-vii, *CC*, pp.
195-196)

This statement concisely defines six common arguments for the inspiration of scripture: (1) its subject matter transcends natural reasoning;
(2) its teachings have good effect; (3) its style is authoritative, as if God
himself were speaking; (4) its various parts, properly understood, agree;
(5) its scope is necessary and sufficient to salvation; and (6) above all the
Holy Spirit bears witness through it that we are children of God.

Using a metaphor of fire igniting fire, Guerric of Igny taught that
inspired preaching comes directly from inspired scripture:

Tongues indeed of fire they were that that fire distributed from
itself and they so set not only the minds but also the tongues of
the Apostles on fire that even now the devout listener is set on
fire by their word. A tongue indeed of fire was Peter's! A tongue
of fire was Paul's! In their utterances there lives even now a perpetual fire which casts its sparks upon our hearts too if we draw
near, if we do not turn our ears or our mind away from their
words. (Guerric of Igny, *Liturgical Sermons*, Vol. 2, Sermon 39,
sec. 1, CFS 32, p. 117)

Alan of Lille used the metaphor of Jacob's ladder to speak of the steps
leading toward effective pastoral preaching. It portrays the intrinsic in-
terconnection of prayer, biblical study and preaching:

Jacob beheld a ladder reaching from earth to heaven, on which
angels were ascending and descending. The ladder represents
the progress of the catholic man in his ascent from the beginning
of faith to the full development of the perfect man. The first
rung of this ladder is confession; the second, prayer; the third,
thanksgiving; the fourth, the careful study of the Scriptures; the
fifth, to inquire of someone more experienced if one comes upon
any point in Scripture which is not clear; the sixth, the expounding of Scripture; the seventh, preaching.

The man who repents his sin then should first set his foot on
the first rung of this ladder by confessing his sin. He should
mount to the second rung by praying to God that grace may be
bestowed on him. The third rung is reached through thanksgiving for the grace which is given. The ascent to the fourth rung is

made by studying Scripture so as to preserve the gift of grace—for Holy Scripture teaches how grace, once given, may be held fast. In this way the fifth rung is seen in sight, when a doubtful point arises, and the reader asks someone senior to help him understand it. The sixth rung is reached when the reader himself expounds Holy Scripture to others. He climbs the seventh rung when he preaches in public what he has learned from Scripture. (Alan of Lille, *The Art of Preaching*, CSS 23, pp. 15-16)

III 🍏 PASTORAL PREACHING

Directness is an elementary rule of preaching:

It is commonly said that these are the three qualifications which mark a good preacher: First, that he step up; secondly, that he speak up and say something (worthwhile); thirdly, that he know when to stop. (Luther, WA 32, p. 302; WLS 3, #3544, p. 1109)

Eloquence, to the pastoral writers, meant expressing oneself with force and fluency. While preaching requires eloquence in this sense, it also requires a strong self-identity that does not depend hungrily upon positive feedback. John Chrysostom, the greatest preacher of the patristic age, noted two principal requirements of effective preaching:

It is impossible to acquire this power [preaching] except by these two qualities: contempt of praise and the force of eloquence. If either is lacking, the one left is made useless through divorce from the other. If a preacher despises praise, yet does not produce the kind of teaching which is "with grace, seasoned with salt" (Col. 4:6), he is despised by the people and gets no advantage from his sublimity. And if he manages this side of things perfectly well, but is a slave to the sound of applause, again an equal damage threatens both him and the people, because through his passion for praise he aims to speak more for the pleasure than the profit of his hearers. . . . So, like a good charioteer, the preacher should have reached perfection in both these qualities, in order to be able to handle both of them as need requires. (John Chrysostom, *On the Priesthood*, Ch. V.2-3, pp. 128-129)

The preacher must first enter deeply into his own feeling process and experience if he is to drive home a point profoundly in the hearts of others. Luther spoke candidly of getting in touch with his anger as an emotive exercise that stimulated and improved his preaching:

If I want to write, pray, preach well, then I must be angry. Then my entire blood supply refreshes itself, my mind is made keen, and all temptations depart. (Luther, W-T 2, #241a; WLS 1, #80, p. 29)

Although preaching may appear easy, it requires great labor and enormous concentration of energies, as Luther wittily observed:

It is true, to ride in armor would be hard work for me. But, on the other hand, I should like to see the horseman who could sit still for an entire day and merely look into a book, even if he had nothing to worry about, to compose, to think, or to read. Ask a writer, preacher, or speaker what labor writing and speaking are; ask a schoolmaster what labor teaching and training boys is. The pen is light, that is true; nor is any tool of any of the trades easier to get than the tool of the writer, for all you need is goose feathers, and plenty of these may be had anywhere for nothing. At the same time, however, the best part of the body (which is the head) and the noblest of its members (which is the tongue) and the highest of its faculties (which is speech) must here bear the burden and do most of the work. In other occupations only the fist or the foot or the back or some other such member has to work. Meanwhile people can cheerfully sing and freely jest, which a writer certainly must forego. Three fingers do the work, people say of writers; but a man's entire body and soul are at work. (Luther, WA 30 II, p. 573; WLS 1, #333, p. 110)

Richard Baxter understood why preaching is such a difficult and subtle task—for it must appeal to both mind and heart, elicit decision, and meet objections, in making the truth plain:

To preach a sermon, I think, is not the hardest part; and yet what skill is necessary to make the truth plain; to convince the hearers, to let irresistible light in to their consciences, and to keep it there, and drive all home; to screw the truth into their minds, and work Christ into their affections; to meet every objection and clearly to resolve it; to drive sinners to a stand. (Baxter, *RP*, p. 70)

The purpose of preaching is misconceived when the congregation becomes the spectator of an aesthetic performance. Sermons are not occasions for literary criticism, but rather a unique moment of expected divine address:

Most of those who are under authority refuse to treat preachers as their instructor. They rise above the status of disciples and assume that of spectators sitting in judgement on secular speech-making.... For most people usually listen to a preacher for pleasure, not profit, like critics of a play or concert. (John Chrysostom, *On the Priesthood*, Ch. V.1, p. 127)*

Popular preachers have regrettably found ways of exploiting preaching to their own benefit. Preaching may become the servant of avarice, celebrity status, and bland civil religion. Socrates of Constantinople (c. 380-450) offered this early account of two cases of the abuse of preaching:

Severian presided over the church at Gabala, a city of Syria, and Antiochus over that of Ptolemais in Phoenicia. They were both renowned for their eloquence; but although Severian was a very learned man, he did not succeed in using the Greek language perfectly; and so while speaking Greek he betrayed his Syrian origin. Antiochus came first to Constantinople, and having preached in the churches for some time with great zeal and ability, and having thus amassed a large sum of money, he returned to his own church. Severian hearing that Antiochus had collected a fortune by his visit to Constantinople, determined to follow his example. He therefore exercised himself for the occasion, and having composed a number of sermons, set out for Constantinople. Being most kindly received by John, to a certain point, he soothed and flattered the man, and was himself no less beloved and honored by him: meanwhile his discourses gained him great celebrity, so that he attracted the notice of many persons of rank, and even of the emperor himself. (Socrates Scholasticus, *Ecclesiastical History*, Bk. VI, Ch. XI, NPNF 2, II, p. 146)

Effectiveness in a church is not measured by size of congregation, but by depth of genuine hearing of the Word of God. Luther urged against trying to collect great numbers of people to preach to:

Great numbers do not make the church ... We must look to the Word alone and judge on the basis of that.... The church is a daughter, born of the Word; she is not the mother of the Word. Therefore, whoever loses the Word and instead eagerly looks to influential persons ceases to be the church and lapses into blindness; neither numbers nor power will do him any good. (Luther, WA 42, p. 334; WLS 1, #844, p. 287)

Hearers cannot be expected to follow a pastor who does not follow his own teachings:

They will think that he does not mean as he speaks, if he does not live as he speaks. They will hardly believe a man that seems not to believe himself. . . .they are more apt to believe their sight than their hearing, as being the more perfect sense of the two. All that a minister does is a kind of preaching. (Baxter, *RP*, pp. 84-85)*

IV ❧ THE GIFT AND CRAFT OF HOMILY

Christian homily (from *homilia*, discourse in an assembly) consists of practical discourse with a view to spiritual edification. The homily originated as a highly personal reappropriation of scriptural wisdom.

There were strong injunctions by some early writers against using materials taken from another in a homily. The prevailing assumption was that a given text or series of texts of scripture was addressing a particular congregation of the faithful at a particular time through a particular preacher who knew the pastoral needs of that congregation at that time. For this reason:

It is as unseemly for teachers to give instruction from notes taken from other men's writings, as it is for painters to take inspiration from other men's compositions. (John Climacus, To the Shepherd, sec. 5, *Ladder of Divine Ascent*, p. 231)

John Chrysostom, whose sermons have been plundered more often than any in the pastoral tradition, deplored the widespread practice of sermonic borrowing:

If it happens that a preacher weaves among his own words a proportion of other men's flowers, he falls into worse disgrace than a common thief. (John Chrysostom, *On the Priesthood*, Ch. V.1, p. 127)

Sermon preparation consists first of all in prayerfully searching the scriptures with utmost inwardness, not pirating nicely turned phrases from popular authors:

Some pastors [rely on commentaries] and other good books to get a sermon out of them. They do not pray; they do not study; they do not read; they do not search the Scripture. It is just as if there were no need to read the Bible for this purpose. They use such books as offer them homiletical helps in order to earn their yearly living; they are nothing but parrots and jackdaws, which learn to repeat without understanding, though our purpose and the purpose of these theologians is to direct preachers to Scripture. (Luther, WA 53, p. 218; WLS 3, #3547, p. 1110)*

Luther, however, did not rule out the use of classical Christian preaching in sermon preparation:

Whoever has no cement must build his wall with mud. . . . If Dr. Martin cannot write such good epistles as St. Paul did to the Romans, or cannot preach as well as St. Augustine did, then it is honorable for him to open the book, to beg a morsel, from St. Paul or from St. Augustine, and to follow the pattern of their preaching. (Luther, WA 51, p. 213; WLS 3, #3511, pp. 1130-1131)

The pastor need not choose between didactic strength and rhetorical appeal, for it is better that both be present in fit proportion:

Dialectic teaches, rhetoric moves; the latter pertains to the will, the former to the intellect. Paul embraces both in Rom. 12:7f: "He that teaches [let him wait] on teaching, or he that exhorteth, on exhortation." And these two constitute the method of preaching. (Luther, W-T 2, #2199a; WLS 3, #3604, p. 1129)

Alan of Lille employed striking metaphor and humor to caution preachers against both excessive fanciness and dullness:

Preaching should not glitter with verbal trappings, with purple patches, nor should it be too much enervated by the hue of colorless words: the blessed keep to a middle way. If it were too heavily-embroidered (the sermon) would seem to have been contrived with excessive care, and elaborated to win the admiration of man, rather than for the benefit of our neighbors, and so it would move less the hearts of those who heard it. Those who preach in this way are to be compared with the pharisees, who made the tassels of their garments long, and wore large phylacteries. . . . He must make it clear that the sermon is not designed to arouse the foolish acclaim of the mob, nor tempered to win popular favor, nor shaped to evoke applause, as in a theatre. It is composed to instruct the souls of the listeners, so that they may concentrate, not on who is speaking to them, but on what he is saying. . . . But let the sermon be brief, in case prolixity should cause boredom. When the preacher sees that his hearers' minds are moved, and that they weep freely, and that their expressions are downcast, he should hold back a little, but not too much, for, as Lucretius says: "Nothing dries up faster than a tear (Cicero, Orat. xvii:57)." (Alan of Lille, *The Art of Preaching*, Ch. 1, CFS 23, pp. 18-19, 21-22)

Jeremy Taylor also warned against the tendency of the novice preacher to use technical or ornate language in sermons:

In your sermons and discourses of religion, use primitive, known, and accustomed words, and effect not new, fantastical, or schismatical terms. Let the Sunday-festival be called the Lord's day; and pretend no fears from the common use of words amongst Christians. For they that make a business of the words of common use, and reform religion by introducing a new word, intend to make a change but no amendment; they spend themselves in trifles, like the barren turf that sends forth no medicinable herbs, but a store of mushrooms. (Jeremy Taylor, *RAC*, sec. 54, *CS*, pp. 17-18)

We sometimes imagine we can change long-established patterns and customs by instantly changing our language about them. The fantasy is that by linguistic revisions we may make actual historical reversals, while in truth we are not looking for signficant amendment but only change (as Kierkegaard's "Rotation Method" in Either/Or, Vol. I, out of boredom hungered constantly for change). Pastoral communication is best when it uses ordinary words known to all.

George Herbert artfully described the diverse means by which the preacher seeks to gain a hearing:

When he preaches, he procures attention by all possible art, both by earnestness of speech, for it is natural that men think that where there is much earnestness there is something worth hearing, and by a diligent and busy cast of his eye on his auditors, without letting them know that he observes who marks and who not. . . . Sometimes he tells them stories and sayings of others, according as his text invites him; for them also men heed, and remember better than exhortations; which, though earnest, yet often die with the sermon, especially with country people; who are thick and heavy and hard to raise to a point of zeal and fervency, and need a mountain of fire to kindle them; but stories and sayings they will well remember. He often tells them, that sermons are dangerous things; that none goes out of church as he came in, but either better or worse; . . . He is not witty or learned or eloquent, but Holy. A character that *Hermogenes* never dreamed of, and therefore he could offer no precepts for it. But it is gained, first, by choosing texts of devotions, not controversy; moving and ravishing texts, of which the scriptures are full. Secondly, by dipping and seasoning all our words and sentences in our hearts before they come into our mouths; truly affecting, and cordially expressing all that we say, so that the auditors may plainly perceive that every word is heart-deep. (George Herbert, *CP*, Ch. vii, CWS, p. 63)*

Although preaching is done by means of human language, under the address of scripture it becomes God's own address:

Let every minister be diligent in preaching the word of God, according to the ability that God gives him: ever remembering, that to minister God's word unto the people is the one half of his great office and employment.

Let every minister be careful that what he delivers be indeed the word of God; that his sermon be answerable to the text; for this is God's word, the other ought to be according to it; that although in itself it be but the word of man, yet by the purpose, truth, and signification of it, it may, in a secondary sense, be the word of God. (Jeremy Taylor, *RAC*, sec. 40-41, CS, p. 14)

Assuming that every word of scripture is understood in relation to the whole witness of scripture, Luther with characteristic hyperbole proposed that a better sermon could be preached on a single biblical word than all human words:

He who has only one word of the Word of God and cannot preach a whole sermon on the basis of this one word is not worthy ever to preach. (Luther, W-T 2, #2287; WLS 3, #3546, p. 1110)

Like a crude barbarian glancing with boredom at an artistic masterpiece—so are our hard-won sermons sometimes received, according to John Chrysostom. Likewise when bad sermons are praised, it is like bad art being superficially admired:

If a painter of first rank who excelled all others in skill, saw the picture he had painted with great care scoffed at by men ignorant of art, he ought not to be dejected or to regard his painting as poor, because of the judgement of the ignorant; just as little should he regard a really poor work as wonderful and charming because the unlearned admired it. . . . So too the man who has accepted the task of teaching should pay no attention to the commendation of outsiders, any more than he should let them cause him dejection. When he has composed his sermons to please God (and let this alone be his rule and standard of good oratory in sermons, not applause or commendation), then if he should be approved by men too, let him not spurn their praise. But if his hearers do not accord it, let him neither seek it or sorrow for it. It will be sufficient encouragement for his efforts, and one much better than anything else, if his conscience tells him that he is organizing and regulating his teaching to please God. For in fact, if he has already been overtaken by the desire for unmerited praise, neither his great efforts nor his powers of speech will be any use. . . . Do you not know what a passion for oratory has recently infatuated Christians? Do you not know that its exponents are respected above everyone else, not just by outsiders, but by those of the household of faith? How, then, can anyone endure the deep disgrace of having his sermon received with blank silence and feelings of boredom, and his listeners waiting for the end of the sermon as if it were a relief after fatigue; whereas they listen to someone else's sermon, however long, with eagerness, and are annoyed when he is about to finish and quite exasperated when he decides to say no more?

Perhaps this seems to you a trifling, negligible matter, because you have no experience of it. Yet it is enough to kill enthusiasm and paralyse spiritual energy, unless a man dispossesses himself of all human passions and studies to live like the disembodied spirits who are not hounded by envy or vain glory or any other disease of that sort. (John Chrysostom, *On the Priesthood*, Ch. V.6-8, pp. 132-135)

John Chrysostom recognized that the preacher will feel extraordinary pressure to perform, to make the public happy, to play for popularity, to please everyone. Just at this point the inner dictates of the true preacher, like those of the true artist, will deliberately resist applause and follow a narrower way.

Preaching well requires living well:

All the week long is little enough, to study how to speak two hours; and yet one hour seems too much to study how to live all the week. [Some preachers] are loath to misplace a word in their sermons, or to be guilty of any notable infirmity (and I blame them not, for the matter is holy and weighty), but they make nothing of misplacing their affections, words, and actions, in the course of their lives. Oh how curiously have I heard some preach; and how carelessly have I seen them live! . . . Those who seemed most impatient of barbarisms, solecisms, and paralogisms in a sermon, seemed to easily tolerate them in their life and conversation. . . . A practical doctrine must be practically preached. We must study as hard how to live well, as how to preach well. We must think and think again how we may so compose our lives as may most tend to men's salvation, as well as to our sermons. (Baxter, *RP*, p. 64)*

The reason why humor in homily has been resisted is that it tends to be used manipulatively to gain approval, or reduce worship to theatre:

Of all preaching in the world (that speaks not stark lies) I hate that preaching which tends to make the hearers laugh, or to move their minds with tickling levity, and affect them as stage-plays do, instead of affecting them with a holy reverence of the name of God. Jerome says, "Teach in thy church, not to get the applause of the people, but to set in motion the groan." (Baxter, *RP*, pp. 119-120)

George Herbert warned against constructing a sermon by dissecting a sentence so that each word becomes the basis of an extended discourse:

The way of crumbling a text into small parts (such as, the person speaking or spoken to, the subject, the object, and the like), has in it neither sweetness nor gravity nor variety. For the words apart are not Scripture, but a dictionary. (George Herbert, *CP*, Ch. VII, CWS, p. 64)*

Those who preach too long make their hearers despise what they are saying:

The Parson exceeds not an hour in preaching, because all ages have thought that a competency, and he that profits not in that time, will less afterwards; the same affection which made him not profit before, making him then weary, and so he grows from not relishing, to loathing. (George Herbert, *CP*, Ch. VII, CWS, p. 64)

V ❧ WORD AND COUNSEL

It is a modern misjudgment to bifurcate preaching and pastoral care, splitting them into two entirely different fields, as they appear in modern theological school curricula. Classical pastoral writers regarded proclamation as a task intrinsic to the nature of pastoral care, and the ministry of the Word through preaching as inextricably interwoven with the ministry of the Word through conversation. Anglican bishop Jeremy Taylor viewed preaching and pastoral care as so closely allied that neither could stand alone without the other:

Let every minister exhort his people to a frequent confession of their sins, and a declaration of the state of their souls; to a conversation with their minister in spiritual things, to an inquiry concerning all the parts of their duty: for by preaching, and catechising, and private intercourse, all the needs of souls can best be served; but by preaching alone they cannot. (Jeremy Taylor, *RAC*, V.68, *CS*, p. 21)

The inward integrity that characterizes good pastoral conversation also characterizes good preaching. Only ministers who have dealt with their own feelings and passions can be trusted to responsibly preach the Word of God, according to Clement:

He who is incapable of speaking what is true respecting himself, is he not much less reliable in what concerns God? (Clement of Alexandria, *The Stromata, or Miscellanies*, Bk. VI, Ch. XVIII, ANF II, p. 519)

Counsel (*nouthesia*, admonition, warning, sometimes translated reproof) has been consistently thought to be a crucial function of the pastor. But this counsel is not to occur only in one-on-one situations, but also in the context of public worship through preaching. However, as Taylor warned, when admonition occurs in a public setting, the pastor must be careful to avoid directing the admonition only to one party instead of to the whole body of hearers. Thus admonitory preaching differs from, yet is closely correlated with, the highly personal level of admonitory conversation. Yet public admonition is not addressed abstractly to "the times," but to the body of actual hearers.

Every minister, in reproofs of sin and sinners, ought to concern himself in the faults of them that are present, but not of the absent; not in reproof of the times: for this can serve no end but of faction and sedition, public murmur and private discontent. Besides this, it does nothing but amuse the people in the faults of others, teaching them to revile their betters, and neglect the dangers of their own souls. . . . Every minister ought to preach to his parish, and urge their duty: St. John the Baptist told the soldiers what the soldiers should do, but did not trouble their heads with what was the duty of the scribes and pharisees. (Jeremy Taylor, *RAC*, IV.44-45, *CS*, p. 15)*

Since preaching constitutes a general act of congregational pastoral care, or a general admonition, it is confusing to direct it toward a particular, small group of scholarly hearers:

When we are in the pulpit, we should nurse people and give them milk to drink; for a new church is growing up daily which needs to know the first principles. Therefore one should not hesitate to teach the Catechism diligently and to distribute its milk. The lofty speculations and matters should be reserved for the wiseacres. I will not consider Drs. Pomeranus, Jonas, and Philipp while I am preaching; for they know what I am presenting better than I do. Nor do I preach to them, but to my little Hans and Elizabeth; these I consider. He must be a harebrained gardener who wants to consider only one flower in a large garden and neglects all the others. Therefore see to it that you preach purely and simply and have regard for the unlearned people. (Luther, W-T 3, #3421; WLS 3, #3610, p. 1130)

It is not sufficient merely to decry sin. Preaching is aimed at spiritual conversion and behavioral transformation:

Publicans and harlots enter heaven sooner than Pharisees because they are sooner convinced of their sin and misery. . . . Although many may seem excellent preachers, and may shout down sin as loudly as others, yet it often amounts to little more than emotive fervency, and too commonly but a mere useless bawling. . . . The perverse preacher may more strongly will the reformation of others than of his own behavior, and hence may show a kind of earnestness in dissuading others from their evil ways. He can preach against sin at an easier rate than he can forsake it. . . . He is like a traitorous commander who shoots nothing against the enemy but powder. His guns may make as great a sound or report as those loaded with bullets. (Baxter, *RP*, pp. 83-84)*

Preaching that perennially elicits doubt is misconceived, since the purpose of preaching is to elicit faith:

If you want to preach to a person in a comforting way, then do it so that he who hears you is certain that he is in God's favor, or be silent altogether. . . . For all preachers who make their hearers doubt are good for nothing. For in the kingdom of God we must be sure that we have a gracious God, forgiveness of sins, and eternal life. (Luther, WA 47, p. 307f; WLS 3, #3566, p. 1116)

Prosper of Aquitaine concisely defined the complex interaction that occurs in preaching between the divine Word, the human word, and the human hearer, so as to awaken behavioral transformation and the regeneration of the fallen will:

Whenever, then, the word of God enters into the ears of the body through the ministry of the preachers, the action of the divine power fuses with the sound of a human voice, and He who is the inspirer of the preacher's office is also the strength of the hearer's heart. Then the food of the word becomes sweet to the soul; the darkness of old is expelled by the new light; the interior eye is freed from the cataracts of the ancient error; the soul passes from one will to another, and although the will that is driven out lingers on for a while, yet the new-born one claims for itself all that is better in man, so that the law of sin and the law of God do not dwell in the same way and together in the same man. (Prosper of Aquitaine, *The Call of All Nations*, Bk. 1, Ch. 8, ACW 14, pp. 38-39)

Alan of Lille viewed the preached word as a precious gift that should not be thrown away miscellaneously to those who might trample on it and abuse it:

Preaching should be withheld from the unworthy and obstinate, for those who reject the word of God make themselves unworthy. . . . (Acts 13:46). He who divulges secrets to the unworthy lessens the greatness of the secrets; and the vessels of the Lord are not to be set before the Babylonians. (Alan of Lille, *The Art of Preaching*, Ch. xxxix, CS 23, p. 146)

VI 🕏 THE HERMENEUTICAL TASK

Since counsel is central to pastoral care, the pastor studies scripture carefully seeking to communicate its message accurately, gauging it properly to speak within concrete situations. The classical pastors wrote so extensively on the interpretation of scripture that the resulting literature has in time become a distinct area of study itself: hermeneutics, the study of interpretation.

The work of interpreting ancient scripture for modern hearers requires careful, responsible study. One aspect of that study hinges on the awareness that oral traditioning has often preceded the written word. Twentieth century scholars of the oral tradition that predates written New Testament documents may think of their studies as completely unprecedented. Yet there is evidence that early pastoral writers were well aware that an oral traditon of preaching existed, for example, prior to the record of the four evangelists:

Perhaps many of the things which were said to them were said to all who virtually believed; for not to the Apostles alone did the saying apply, "Before governors and kings also shall ye be brought for My sake for a testimony to them and to the Gentiles" (Matt. 10:13). . . . "Whosoever shall confess Me," etc. (Matt. 10:31), is said not specially to the Apostles, but also to all believers. According to this, then, through that which was said to the

Apostles an outline was given beforehand of the teaching which would afterwards come to be of service both to them and to every teacher. (Origen, *Commentary on Matthew*, Bk. XII, sec. 16, ANF X, p. 460)

Origen had already grasped in the early third century that an oral tradition preceded the written scriptures. The testimony of this oral tradition was addressed to general audiences of believers in varied cultural settings. The apostles remembered it in an outline form and later wrote it down in order to be of service to those who were not eyewitnesses. Origen nonetheless strongly argued for the historical accuracy of biblical reports of events. Although a few passages are provided for mystical or anagogic interpretation, most are accurate historical accounts. Origen thought the scriptures should be searched for their spiritual meaning wherever a literal truth is not evident:

But that no one may suppose that we assert respecting the whole that no history is real because a certain one is not; and that no law is to be literally observed, because a certain one, (understood) according to the letter, is absurd or impossible; or that the statements regarding the Saviour are not true in a manner perceptible to the senses; or that no commandment and precept of His ought to be obeyed;—we have to answer that, with regard to certain things, it is perfectly clear to us that the historical account is true; as that Abraham was buried in the double cave at Hebron, as also Isaac and Jacob, and the wives of each of them; and that Shechem was given as a portion to Joseph; and that Jerusalem is the metropolis of Judea, in which the temple of God was built by Solomon; and innumerable other statements. For the passages that are true in their historical meaning are much more numerous than those which are interspersed with a purely spiritual signification. . . . The careful (reader), however, will be in doubt as to certain points, being unable to show without long investigation whether this history so deemed literally occurred or not, and whether the literal meaning of this law is to be observed or not. And therefore the exact reader must, in obedience to the Saviour's injunction to "search the Scriptures," (John 5:39), carefully ascertain in how far the literal meaning is true, and in how far impossible; and so far as he can, trace out, by means of similar statements, the meaning everywhere scattered through Scripture of that which cannot be understood in a literal signification.

Since, therefore, as will be clear to those who read, the connection taken literally is impossible, while the sense preferred is not impossible, but even the true one, it must be our object to grasp the whole meaning, which connects the account of what is literally impossible in an intelligible manner with what is not only not impossible, but also historically true, and which is allegorically understood, in respect of its not having literally occurred. (Origen, *De Principiis*, Bk. IV, Ch. I, sec. 19-20, ANF IV, pp. 368-369)

Historical research does not elicit faith. Origen thought explicitly about the extent to which faith may be dependent upon historical research:

Suppose we knew the place in the wilderness, for example, said to be where the children of Israel camped as they were passing through. What use would that be to me, or what progress could it afford to those who read and meditate on the Law of God day and night? (cf. Ps. 1:2). (Origen, Homily XXVII On Numbers, sec. 6, CWS, p. 253)

Origen was aware that scripture is not always self-evident. He recommended that the preacher struggle candidly and non-defensively with difficulties of exegesis. Like many pastoral writers, Origen thought that the scripture was open to debate among serious readers who encountered difficulties in interpreting it, and that it is better to leave some exegetical issues open for continuing theological discussion:

It is fitting to inquire why He now at all commands the disciples that they should not say that He was the Christ? . . . Matthew then, according to some of the manuscripts, has written, "Then He commanded His disciples that they should tell no man that He was the Christ," (Matt. 16:20) but Mark says, "He charged them that they should tell no man of Him;" (Mark 8:30) and Luke, "He charged them and commanded them to tell this to no man" (Luke 9:21). But what is the "this"? . . . The difficulty thus stated seems to me a very real difficulty; but let a solution which cannot be impugned be sought out, and let the finder of it bring it forward before all, if it be more credible than that which shall be advanced by us as a fairly temperate view. (Origen, *Commentary on Matthew*, Bk. XII, sec. 15, ANF X, p. 459)

VII ❧ COMFORTING OTHERS AS GOD HAS COMFORTED US

The assurance of divine care is a prevailing theme of pastoral care. The aim of pastoral preaching is the awakening of awareness that one is loved by God in Christ, freed from sin and death, and given new life. The pastor's task is to help that awareness come into full bloom both in

consciousness and in daily behavior. From this derives the principle connection between pastoral care and preaching: The pastoral preacher
hopes to make plausible the assuring word of divine comfort. The care-
giver seeks to make clear God's own caring.

The pastor seeks daily to enable parishioners to receive the Spirit of
forgiveness, enjoy Christian freedom, pray with boldness, understand
that their being corrected is for their good, as by a loving Father, and
stand assured of their continuing in the divine favor. Main features of
the preaching of assurance were summarized in the Westminster Confession:

All those that are justified God has vouchsafed, in and for his
only Son Jesus Christ, to make partakers of the grace of adoption.
They are taken into the number, and enjoy the liberties and privileges of the children of God; have his name put upon them; receive the Spirit of adoption; have access to the throne of grace
with boldness; are enabled to cry, Abba, Father; are pitied, protected, provided for, and chastened by him as by a father; yet
never cast off, but sealed to the day of redemption, and inherit
the promises, as heirs of everlasting salvation. (Westminister Confession, Ch. XII, *CC*, p. 208)*

While ministers seek deeply to address the feeling processes, they
know that faith is not reducible to an emotion, or to the level of a passing feeling, or to a malleable human experience. Luther argued that
faith is prior to experience, in the sense that faith shapes the life of
feelings, and is not merely shaped by them:

We must not judge by what we feel or by what we see before
us. The Word must be followed, and we must firmly hold that
these truths are to be believed, not experienced; for to believe is
not to experience. Not indeed that what we believe is never to be
experienced but that faith is to precede experience. And the
Word must be believed even when we feel and experience what
differs entirely from the Word. (Luther, WA 40 III, p. 370f; WLS
1, #1539, p. 513)

Having believed the good news, it is quite possible that doubts of its
truthfulness may again invade. This is why the preacher of the good
news will be prepared to continue to nurture the believer in the Christian life subsequent to the first dawning of faith, in order that the
awareness of God's mercy may be sustained through various crises:

Such as truly believe in the Lord Jesus, and love him in sincerity, endeavoring to walk in all good conscience before him, may
in this life be certainly assured that they are in a state of grace,

and may rejoice in the hope of the glory of God, which hope shall never make them ashamed.

This certainty is not a bare conjectural and probable persuasion, grounded upon a fallible hope; but an infallible assurance of faith, founded upon the divine truth of the promises of salvation, the inward evidence of those graces unto which these promises are made, the testimony of the Spirit of adoption witnessing with our spirits that we are the children of God: which Spirit is the earnest of our inheritance, whereby we are sealed to the day of redemption.

This infallible assurance does not so belong to the essence of faith, but that a true believer may wait long, and conflict with many difficulties before he be partaker of it: yet, being enabled by the Spirit to know the things which are freely given him of God, he may, without extraordinary revelation, in the right use of ordinary means, attain thereunto.... True believers may have the assurance of their salvation [in] divers ways shaken, diminished, and intermitted; as, by negligence in preserving of it; by falling into some special sin, which wounds the conscience, and grieves the Spirit; by some sudden or vehement temptation; by God's withdrawing the light of his countenance, and suffering even such as fear him to walk in darkness and to have no light: yet are they never utterly destitute of the seed of God, and the life of faith, that love of Christ and the brethren, that sincerity of heart and conscience of duty, out of which, by the operation of the Spirit, this assurance may in due time be revived, and by the which, in the mean time, they are supported from utter despair. (Westminister Confession, Ch. XVIII, *CC*, pp. 212-213)

Quality pastoral preaching seeks to make credible to the individual hearer the good news of divine forgiveness in Christ. But what if such attempts meet with the objection: "If good works gain no merit, why do them?"

These good works, done in obedience to God's commandments, are the fruits and evidences of a true and lively faith; and by them believers manifest their thankfulness, strengthen their assurance, edify their brethren, adorn the profession of the gospel, stop the mouths of the adversaries, and glorify God, whose workmanship they are, created in Christ Jesus thereunto, that, having their fruit unto holiness, they may have the end, eternal life.... We can not, by our best works, merit pardon of sin, or eternal life at the hand of God, by reason of the great disproportion that is between them and the glory to come, and the infinite distance that is between us and God, whom by them we can neither profit nor satisfy for the debt of our former sins; but when we have done all we can, we have done but our duty, and are unprofitable servants; and because, as they are good, they proceed from his Spirit; and as they are wrought by us, they are defiled and mixed with so much weakness and imperfection that they can not endure the severity of God's judgment.

Yet notwithstanding, the persons of believers being accepted through Christ, their good works also are accepted in him, not as though they were in this life wholly unblamable and unreprovable in God's sight; but that he, looking upon them in his Son, is pleased to accept and reward that which is sincere, although accompanied with many weaknesses and imperfections. (Westminister Confession, Ch. XIV, *CC*, pp. 210-211)

VIII ❦ ENABLING CHRISTIAN FREEDOM

Pastoral preaching intends to enable freedom. It seeks to set the inner self free from guilt, sin and death; free for the neighbor; free for responsible love. Through the ministry of the Word, the pastor seeks to breathe Christian freedom into life, nurture and sustain it. Yet several dilemmas persist concerning what sort of freedom it is to which the Christian is set free.

The liberty which Christ hath purchased for believers under the gospel consists in their freedom from the guilt of sin, the condemning wrath of God, the curse of the moral law; and in their being delivered from this present evil world, bondage to Satan, and dominion of sin, from the evil of afflictions, the sting of death, the victory of the grave, and everlasting damnation; as also in their free access to God, and their yielding obedience unto him, not out of slavish fear, but a child-like love and willing mind. (Westminister Confession, Ch. XX, *CC*, p. 215)

Suppose the good news of freely-given divine grace is met with an attitude of licentious, law-disavowing, anarchism or antinomianism. Then it might seem better not to take the risk of preaching freedom, but soften the promise that faith makes one free. Luther struggled with this dilemma: Which is worse—to preach faith that turns to license, or to fail altogether to preach faith?

If you preach faith, people become lax, want to do no good, serve and help no one. But if you do not preach faith, hearts become frightened and dejected and establish one idolatrous practice after another. Do as you please; nothing seems to help. Yet faith in Christ should and must be preached, no matter what happens. I would much rather hear people say of me that I preach too sweetly and that my sermon hinders people in doing good works (although it does not do so) than not preach faith in Christ at all; for then there would be no help for timid, frightened consciences.

I see and experience this: here is a man who is lax and lazy, who falsely boasts of faith and says that he relies on the grace and mercy of God and that these will no doubt help him even though he clings to sins. But as soon as death comes to him, it appears that he has never really grasped and believed the grace and mercy of God. Therefore one will have enough to do to cheer and comfort him, even though he has not practiced any particular idolatry. But when the message of faith has been extinguished and the heart is completely swamped by sadness, there is neither counsel nor help. Say something about grace to such a heart, and it will answer: You preach much to me about grace and mercy; but if you felt what I feel, you would speak differently. So a frightened, inconsolable heart goes on. I have heard people speak like this when I tried to comfort them. Therefore I should like to have the message of faith in Christ not forgotten but generally known. It is so sweet a message, full of sheer joy, comfort, mercy, and grace. I must confess that I myself have as yet not fully grasped it. We shall have to let it happen that some of our people turn the message into an occasion for security and presumption; but others, the work-righteous, slander us on this account and say that we make people lazy and thus keep them from reaching perfection. Christ Himself had to hear that He was a friend of publicans and sinners (Luke 15:2), that He broke the Sabbath, etc. We shall not fare any better. (Luther, WA 37, p. 394f; WLS 3, #3603, pp. 1128-1129)

Nothing is more deadly for pastoral preaching than unqualified legalisms and endless hortatory harangue. Luther argued that one cannot experience genuine freedom with a good conscience by following many intricate rules and legal maxims, but only by trusting God's reclaiming, freeing Word. He used the metaphor of two persons in love:

When a man and a woman love and are pleased with each other, and thoroughly believe in their love, who teaches them how they are to behave, what they are to do, leave undone, say, not say, think? Confidence alone teaches them all this, and more. They make no difference in works: they do the great, the long, the much, as gladly as the small, the short, the little, and vice versa; and that too with joyful, peaceful, confident hearts, and each is a free companion of the other. But where there is a doubt, search is made for what is best; then a distinction of works is imagined whereby a man may win favor; and yet he goes about it with a heavy heart, and great disrelish; he is, as it were, taken captive, more than half in despair, and often makes a fool of himself.

So a Christian who lives in this confidence toward God, knows all things, can do all things, undertakes all things that are to be done, and does everything cheerfully and freely; not that he may gather many merits and good works, but because it is a pleasure for him to please God thereby, and he serves God purely for nothing, content that his service pleases God. On the other hand, he who is not at one with God, or doubts, hunts and worries in what way he may do enough and with many works move God. (Luther, *Treatise on Good Works*, WML I, p. 191)

Pastoral preaching holds up before the believer the pattern of Christian freedom—God's own freedom to love:

Although the Christian is thus free from all works, he ought in this liberty to empty himself, to take upon himself the form of a servant, to be made in the likeness of men, to be found in fashion as a man, and to serve, help and in every way deal with his neighbor as he sees that God through Christ has dealt and still deals with himself. (Luther, *Treatise on Christian Liberty*, WML II, p. 337)

Luther unpacked stunning metaphors of faith's kingship and priesthood in his preaching of Christian liberty:

This priesthood and kingship we explain as follows: first, as to the kingship, every Christian is by faith so exalted above all things that by a spiritual power he is lord of all things without exception, so that nothing can do him any harm whatever, nay, all things are made subject to him and compelled to serve him to his salvation. Thus Paul says in Rom. 8:28, "All things work together for good to them who are called." And, in 1 Cor. 3:22, "All things are yours, whether. . . . life or death, or things present or things to come, and ye are Christ's." Not as if every Christian were set over all things, to possess and control them by physical power,—a madness with which some churchmen are afflicted,—for such power belongs to kings, princes and men on earth. Our ordinary experience in life shows us that we are subjected to all, suffer many things and even die; nay, the more Christian a man is, the more evils, sufferings and deaths is he made subject to, as we see in Christ the first-born Prince Himself, and in all His brethren, the saints. The power of which we speak is spiritual; it rules in the midst of enemies, and is mighty in the midst of oppression, which means nothing else than that strength is made perfect in weakness, and that in all things I can find profit unto salvation, so that the cross and death itself are compelled to serve me and to work together with me for my salvation. This is a splendid pre-rogative and hard to attain, and a true omnipotent power, a spiritual dominion, in which there is nothing so good and nothing so evil, but that it shall work together for good to me, if only I believe. And yet, since faith alone suffices for salvation, I have need of nothing, except that faith exercise the power and dominion of its own liberty. Lo, this is the inestimable power and liberty of Christians.

Not only are we the freest of kings, we are also priests forever, which is far more excellent than being kings, because as priests we are worthy to appear before God to pray for others and to teach one another the things of God. For these are the functions of priests, and cannot be granted to any unbeliever. . . . Who then can comprehend the lofty dignity of the Christian? Through his kingly power he rules over all things, death, life and sin, and through his priestly glory is all powerful with God, because God does the things which he asks and desires, as it is written, "He will fulfil the desire of them that fear Him; He also will hear their cry, and will save them" (Ps. 145:19). To this glory a man attains, surely not by any works of his, but by faith alone. (Luther, *Treatise on Christian Liberty*, WML II, pp. 324-325)

IX ❧ Preaching the Works of Love

Any pastor who seeks by preaching to enable Christian freedom must also speak often of its corollary, responsible love of the neighbor. Without love, freedom will turn to license. Attentive pastoral preaching seeks to guard against antinomian distortions of Christian freedom. For good works can no more be disjoined from faith than fruit from roots.

He who has right faith yet continues to sin is like a man whose face has no eyes. But he who has no faith, even though he may do some good, is like a man who draws water and pours it into a barrel with holes in it. (John Climacus, *Ladder of Divine Ascent*, Step 26, sec. 51, p. 195)

Opportunities for good works once offered may not be repeated:

Cato says: *"Fronte capillata post est occasio calva."* In front opportunity has hair but it is bald behind. And the statement of Bonaventura is excellent: *"Qui deserit occasionem deseretur ab occasione."* He who neglects an opportunity will be neglected by the opportunity. (Luther, WA 43, p. 348f, WLS 1, #1142, p. 389)

The persistent delay of good works—procrastination—has remained a serious concern of pastoral care and a proper subject of pastoral preaching. Each individual is responsible for the planning and proper use of his or her limited time.

Let him who is still willing to take advice and assistance diligently listen to the helpful counsel of St. Paul that he may yet redeem the time and not sleep away this rich and golden year of God's grace; as also Christ earnestly warns in the parable of the five foolish virgins (Matt. 25:10-11). These, too, might have made their purchase in time, before the coming of the Bridegroom. But since they waited until it was time to meet the Bridegroom, they missed both the market and the wedding.

The poets and sages of old amused themselves with the story about the crickets or grasshoppers. During the winter, when these had nothing more to eat, they went to the ants and besought them to give them something of what they had gathered; and when the ants asked: What did you do in the summer that you did not lay in a supply against the winter? The crickets replied: We sang. Then they had to hear this answer: If you sang away the summer, you must now dance in the winter. (Luther, WA 22, p. 331; WLS 1, #1144, p. 390)

Luther cautioned the faithful about simplistically relying upon God so as to do nothing:

All this is said against those who tempt God, who want to do nothing, and who imagine that God should give and do whatever they desire, without their labor and industry. To them this proverb is proper advice: *"Verlasse dich drauf und backe nicht"* (Rely on it [God's help], and do not bake); again: *"Harre, bis dir ein gebraten Huhn ins Maul fliege"* (Wait until a fried chicken flies into your mouth). . . . The right middle way is not to be lazy and indolent or to rely on one's own work and doing but to work and act and yet expect all success from God alone. (Luther, WA 31 I, p. 436f.; WLS 3, #4830, p. 1495)

Selections in Part Two have focussed upon pastoral care through preaching, and the special forms of pastoral counsel given through public teaching from scriptures. The authority and authenticity of preaching is insured from generation to generation by accountability to the apostolic tradition. The preacher must enter deeply and congruently into his own feeling and experience if he is to drive home a point profoundly in the hearts of others. Although preaching is done by means of human language, under the address of scripture it becomes God's own address. The pastoral preacher seeks to make plausible the word of God's own care for humanity. Christian preaching holds up before the believer the pattern of Christian freedom—God's own freedom to love.

3 Pastoral Care Through Prayer

SOUL CARE OCCURS within a caring community whose primary corporate act is the praise of God's care. It is not incidental that the same pastor who meets persons in one-on-one conversation concerning the health of their souls, also leads the service of worship where life is received with thanksgiving, sins are confessed, divine pardon received, and life consecrated to God. Since the life of prayer holds up before God all dimensions of the nurture of the soul, it is a crucial activity of care of souls. Guidance of the service of common prayer is an indispensable aspect of pastoral guidance.

I ❦ WORSHIP AND THE CARE OF SOULS

In the divine presence one must be prepared to "ransack the heart," according to Joseph Hall, the Anglican divine. Aided by common prayer, scripture and sacrament, the service of worship invites and allows the self to descend into the depths of self-examination. Cleansing prepares for the welcome guest, God himself. One whose heart is cluttered and enmeshed inwardly in ambiguity and sin has little room for the divine guest:

> There are three main businesses wherein God accounts His service here below to consist. The first is our address to the Throne of Grace and the pouring out of our souls before Him in our Prayers; the second is, the reading and hearing His most Holy Word; the third is, the receipt of His Blessed Sacraments; in all of which there is place and use for a settled devotion. . . . What do we in our prayers but converse with the Almighty, and either carry our souls up to Him or bring Him down to us? . . . Descend into thyself therefore, and ransack thy heart, whoever would be a true client of devotion. Search all the close windings of it with the torches of the Law of God, and if there be any iniquity found lurking in the secret corners, drag it out and

58

abandon it. . . . As the soul must be clean from sin, so it must be clear and free from distractions. The intent of our devotion is to welcome God to our hearts; now where shall we entertain Him if the rooms be full, thronged with cares and turbulent passions? (Joseph Hall, The Devout Soul, 1643, Works, VI, pp. 477-79, 485-489; *Angl.*, pp. 618-619)*

Tertullian's early description of what was occurring in Christian worship included corrective pastoral admonition as well as scriptural exposition and intercession for the society:

We are a society with a common religious feeling, unity of discipline, a common bond of hope. We meet in gathering and congregation to approach God in prayer. . . . We pray also for Emperors, for their ministers and those in authority, for the security of the world, for peace on earth, for postponement of the end. We meet to read the books of God—if anything in the nature of the times bids us look to the future or open our eyes to facts. In any case, with those holy words we feed our faith, we lift up our hope, we confirm our confidence; and no less we reinforce our teaching by inculcation of God's precepts. There is, besides, exhortation in our gatherings, rebuke, divine censure. For judgement is passed, and it carries great weight, as it must among those certain that God sees them; and it is a notable foretaste of judgement to come, if anyone has so sinned as to be banished from all share in our prayer, our assembly, and all holy intercourse. Our presidents are elders of proved character, who have reached this honour not for a price, but by character; for nothing that is God's goes for a price. (Tertullian, *Apology*, 39.1-6; NE, sec. 147, p. 174; cf. ANF III, p. 46)*

The soul is nurtured in worship through praise, timely admonition, earnest petition for peace and justice, preaching of the gospel and law, and scriptural study correlated with the emerging needs of the times. The chief means of pastoral care is the living bread that feeds the soul. It was not offered to individuals in isolation, apart from the sacramental community at prayer.

Let no one deceive himself [cf. 1 Cor. 6:9]: unless a man is within the sanctuary, he lacks the bread of God [cf. John 6:33; 1 Cor. 9:13; 10:18]. If the prayer of one or two has such power [cf. Matt. 18:19, 20], how much more does that of the bishop and the whole church? (Ignatius of Antioch, *Letter to Ephesians*, sec. 5, AF, p. 79)

There can be no pastoral care without prayer. The assumption appeared early that communion is received only after confession. The second century Didache stated clearly the connection between penitence, reparation, and the service of Eucharist.

Assemble on the Lord's Day, and break bread and offer the Eucharist; but first make confession of your faults, so that your sacrifice may be a pure one. Anyone who has a difference with his fellow is not to take part with you until they have been reconciled, so as to avoid any profanation of your sacrifice. (*Didache*, sec. 14, ECW, p. 234)

Luther spoke of two elements that cannot be omitted in any service of Christian worship:

A Christian congregation should never gather together without the preaching of God's Word and prayer, no matter how briefly. (Luther, "Concerning the Order of Public Worship, 1523," LW 53, p. 11)

Another perennial pastoral function connected with the life of prayer is the pastoral blessing, not only after the worship service, but in and through ordinary conversations. George Herbert set forth reasons why the pastoral blessing was to be viewed as a standard function of pastoral activity. The pastor looks for ways of expressing pastoral blessings at timely moments of personal interaction:

Now a blessing differs from prayer in assurance; because it is not performed by way of request, but of confidence and power, effectually applying God's favor to the blessed, by yielding interest on that dignity in which God has invested the priest, and by the engaging of God's own power and institution for a blessing. The neglect of this duty in ministers themselves has made the people also neglect it. Now they are so far from craving this benefit from their spiritual father that they often go out of church before he has blessed them. Once the priest's *Benedicite* and his holy water were over-highly valued. Now we are fallen to the clean contrary, from superstition toward coldness and atheism. But the parson first values the gift in himself, and then teaches his parish to value it. And it is observable, that if a minister talks with a great man in the ordinary course of complimenting language, he shall be esteemed as an ordinary complimenter. But if he often interposes a blessing, when the other gives him just opportunity by speaking any good, this unusual form begets a reverence, and makes him esteemed according to his profession. The same is to be observed in writing letters also. To conclude: if all men are to bless upon occasion as it says in Rom 12:14, how much more those who are spiritual fathers. (George Herbert, *CP*, Ch. XXXVI, CWS, p. 111)*

The pendulum had swung in Herbert's time from overestimating to underestimating the role of the pastoral blessing. The pastor whose conversation is willing to settle for routine exchanges and compliments receives its reward. The pastor who finds opportunity to express sincere and heart-felt pastoral blessings finds himself viewed in terms of his calling, not merely in terms of routine sociability.

Thomas Aquinas viewed the sacraments as a series of pastoral remedies for crises, human struggles, and behavioral deficits:

The sacraments of the Church were instituted for two reasons: to perfect man in those things concerned with God's worship in accord with the religion of Christian life, and to be a cure for the evils caused by sin. For both these reasons, seven sacraments are suitable. . . .
The number of sacraments can be gleaned also from their institution as a remedy against the evil caused by sin. For Baptism is intended to remedy the absence of spiritual life; Confirmation remedies the weakness of the recently born soul; the Eucharist remedies the soul's tendency to sin; Penance remedies the actual sin committed after Baptism; Sacrament of the Sick remedies the remainders of sins—of those sins not altogether removed by Penance, whether on account of negligence or ignorance; Order remedies divisions in the community; Matrimony remedies concupiscence in the individual and the numerical deficit brought about by death.
Other people see in the number of sacraments a certain harmony with virtues and evils and punishments for sin. They assert that Baptism harmonizes with faith and is directed to the cure of original sin; Sacrament of the Sick, to hope directed against venial sin; the Eucharist, to charity, directed against the punishment of malice; Order, to prudence directed against ignorance; Penance, to justice, directed against mortal sin; Matrimony to temperance, directed against concupiscence; Confirmation, to fortitude, directed against weakness. (Thomas Aquinas, *Summa Theologica*, IIIa, Q. 65, Art. 1, Vol. III, p. 2375)*

Each sacrament, virtue and vice is treated more fully in the *Summa Theologica*. The sacraments are a complete armamentarium against sin on behalf of the growth of virtue. Accordingly, the pastoral office is primarily concerned with activating the sacramental life through a sacramental ministry. The three theological virtues, faith, hope, and charity, correlate with baptism, unction, and Eucharist. The four primary moral virtues (prudence, justice, temperance, and fortitude) correlate with ordination, penance, matrimony, and confirmation, as follows:

SACRAMENT	REMEDIES VICE	THROUGH VIRTUE
Baptism	original sin	faith
Unction	venial sin	hope
Eucharist	malice	charity
Ordination	ignorance	prudence
Penance	mortal sin	justice
Matrimony	concupiscence	temperance
Confirmation	weakness	fortitude

II ❧ On Preparing the Soul for the Praise of God

The Christian service of worship is a public event, led by the same pastor who quietly and individually cares for each hurt or endangered member of the flock. It requires the forethought, planning, decorum, and organization necessary for a public occasion that bespeaks its importance and its meaning.

If the prayer, praise, proclamation, and sacramental action that occur in Christian worship are as crucial to the health of the soul as the classic pastoral writers allege, then it is to be expected that they will be prepared for carefully. The first element in the preparation of the community for public worship is the pastor's own inward preparation. The Apostolic Constitutions employed the metaphor of the ship's captain readying himself, and the crew and passengers for hazardous voyage:

> Be a builder up, a converter, apt to teach, forbearing of evil, of a gentle mind, meek, long-suffering, ready to exhort, ready to comfort, as one of God. When you call together an assembly of the Church, it is as if you were the commander of a great ship. Set up the enterprise to be accomplished with all possible skill, charging the deacons as mariners to prepare places for the brethren as for passengers, with all due care and decency. (*Constitutions of the Holy Apostles*, Bk. II, Sec. VII, ANF VII, p. 421)*

Luther compared worship preparation to a scaffolding for the construcion of a house. The scaffolding is not an end in itself, but a means:

> We have stuck to founding, building, singing, ringing, to vestments, incense burning, and to all the additional preparations for

divine worship up to the point that we consider this preparation the real, main divine worship and do not know how to speak of any other. And we are acting as wisely as the man who wants to build a house and spends all his goods on the scaffolding and never, as long as he lives, gets far enough along to lay one stone of his house. Guess where that man intends to live when the scaffolding is torn down? (Luther, WA 8, 378; W͇S 1, p. 302)

The best preparation for worship is a life singlemindedly filled with goodness. If one brings to worship a divided heart, it becomes an obstacle to prayer:

For at the beginning God accepted the gifts of Abel, because he offered with singlemindedness and righteousness; but He did not accept the offering of Cain, because his heart was divided with envy and malice, which he cherished against his brother, as God says when reproving his hidden thoughts: "If you do well, you are accepted; if not, sin is a demon crouching at the door. It shall be eager for you, and you will be mastered by it" (Gen. 4:7). God is not appeased by sacrifice. For if any one shall endeavour to offer a sacrifice merely on the strength of outward appearance, albeit discretely, in due order, and according to appointment, while in his soul he does not have that fellowship with his neighbor that is right and proper, nor does he stand in awe of God;—he who thus cherishes secret sin does not deceive God by that sacrifice which is offered correctly as to outward appearance. Such an oblation will profit him nothing; rather only the giving up of that evil which has been conceived within him, so that sin may not the more, by means of the hypocritical action, render him the destroyer of himself. (Irenaeus, *Against Heresies*, Bk. IV, Ch. xviii, sec. 3, ANF I, p. 485)*

God is not fooled by our hypocrisies. External correctness is not noted in God's eyes so much as the correspondence between the inward condition of the heart and the outward justice shown toward the neighbor. The decisive preparation for worship happens inwardly, strictly in the presence of God. No pastoral writer has captured this inwardness more profoundly than the medieval mystic, Ramon Lull, who taught that when one is with God, one is not alone, and that paradoxically when others intrude into the God-and-person dialogue, oddly enough an unexpected aloneness may emerge.

The Lover was all alone in the shade of a fair tree. Men passed by that place and they asked him why he was alone. And the

Lover answered, "I am alone now that I have seen you and heard you. Until now I was in the company of my Beloved." (Ramon Lull, *The Book of the Lover and the Beloved*, sec. 47, p. 24)

Maximus cautioned that if moral self-examination is not stringently honest, it may become an obstacle to prayer:

Examine your conscience with the greatest accuracy, lest because of you your brother may not be reconciled. Do not cheat it, since it knows the hidden things of your heart, accuses you at the time of your passing, and becomes an obstacle in time of prayer. (Maximus the Confessor, *The Four Centuries of Charity*, Ch. 4, sec. 33, ACW, p. 197)

Not everyone is authorized to approach the altar. The *Athanasian Canons* set forth reasons why those whom God has not called and set apart are not to engage in sacred ministry:

The Lord said to Moses: "No mortal man may see me and live" (Ex. 33:20). David knew this when he wrote: "Terrible art thou, O Lord; who can stand in thy presence when thou art angry?" (Ps. 76:7). And the prophet David never ventured to draw near to the Lord or, like a priest, to offer sacrifice, even though he longed so to do. For it is he who wrote: "How dear is thy dwelling-place, thou Lord of Hosts! I pine, I faint with longing for the courts of the Lord's temple" (Ps 84:1-2). His desire to approach the altar and to be a priest was far greater than his desire for the glory of his kingdom. For by no means do all have authority to approach the altar. Rather this is only for those whom the Lord has chosen for this duty. They must then perform his service in fear and trembling. For David had seen how Saul, who without right or authority made a priestly offering, received instead of a blessing a curse, and fell into great grief. For God took from him his glory when he ventured to approach the sanctuary, being not a priest, seeking to take upon himself the office of Samuel, the faithful priest. It was for this reason that God took from him his kingdom and gave it to David, because he approached the altar unfittingly. (*Athanasian Canons*, sec. 1, pp. 4-5)*

The temple into which the Christian worshipper enters is primarily a temple of repentance, faith, and grace, not a temple made by hands:

We come now to the matter of the Temple; and I will show you how mistaken these miserable folk were in pinning their hopes to the building itself, as if that were the home of God, instead of to

God their own Creator. Indeed, they were scarcely less misguided than the heathen in the way they ascribed Divine holiness to their Temple. . . . God is at this moment actually dwelling within us in that poor habitation of ours. How so? Why, the message of His Faith, and in the call of His promise; in the wisdom of His statutes, and the precepts of His teaching; in His own very Presence inwardly inspiring us, and dwelling within us; in His unlocking of the temple doors of our lips, and His gift to us of repentance. It is by these ways that He admits us, the bondsmen of mortality, into the Temple that is immortal. (*The Epistle of Barnabas*, sec. 16, ECW, p. 215)

A powerful approach to contemplative prayer is suggested by Ignatius Loyola. It is a step by step procedure that takes the worshipper through ten commandments, seven cardinal sins, three powers of the soul, and five senses of the body. It is remarkably comprehensive, yet condensed, way of entry into the life of prayer:

The first method of prayer is on the Ten Commandments, the seven capital sins, the three powers of the soul, and the five senses of the body. The purpose of this method of prayer is to provide a method of procedure, and some exercises in which the soul may prepare itself and make progress, thereby making its prayer more acceptable. . . .

1. The Ten Commandments

Method: For the first method of prayer, it is well to consider and to think over the first commandment, how I have kept it, and which I have failed. For this consideration, I will take, as a rule, the time required to recite three times the "Our Father" and the "Hail Mary." If in this time I discover faults I have committed, I will ask pardon and forgiveness for them, and say an "Our Father." I will follow this same method for each of the Ten Commandments. . . .

II. The Capital Sins

Method: Regarding the seven capital sins, after the additional direction, the preparatory prayer is to be made in the manner already prescribed, the only change is that the matter here is the sins which are to be avoided, whereas before it was the commandments to be observed. In like manner the procedure and the rule prescribed above are to be observed, together with the colloquy.

In order to know better the faults committed relating to the capital sins, let the contrary virtues be considered. Thus the better to avoid these sins, one should resolve and endeavor by devout exercises to acquire and retain the seven virtues contrary to them.

III. The Powers of the Soul

Method: The same method and rule that were followed for the commandments should be observed with regard to the three powers of the soul, [memory, understanding, will], with the addition, preparatory prayer, and colloquy.

IV. The Five Senses of the Body

Method: The same method will also be followed with regard to the five senses of the body, only the subject matter is changed. (Ignatius Loyola, *Spiritual Exercises*, pp. 105-6)

III ✞ THE PASTORAL ORDERING OF WORSHIP

It is a pastoral responsibility to seek to insure that the praise of God is fittingly provided for those entrusted to one's pastoral care. If soul care involves the guidance of the community at prayer, then the pastor must give deliberate attention to the right ordering of the service of worship. As early as Clement of Rome it was argued that worship services should proceed with some fixed order, and not in a purely spontaneous way:

There ought to be strict order and method in our performance of such acts as the Master has prescribed for certain times and seasons. Now, it was His command that the offering of gifts and the conduct of public services should not be haphazard or irregular, but should take place at fixed times and hours. (Clement of Rome, *To the Corinthians*, sec. 40, ECW, p. 44)

Luther thought that vigorous pastoral leadership was required to avoid either extremes of excessive piety or exuberance:

We pastors must see to it that ceremonies are made and observed in such a manner that people become neither too disorderly [*wild*] nor too sanctimonious [*zu gar heilig*]. (Luther, W-T 1, No. 882, WLS 1, #904, p. 308)

Paul's injunction to worship God "decently and in order" (1 Cor. 14:40) was taken seriously by the pastoral writers:

But, surely, I fear these men are not more faulty in the one extreme than many Christians are in the other, who place a kind of holiness in a slovenly neglect, and so order themselves as if they thought a nasty carelessness in God's services were most acceptable to Him. . . . For the rectifying of which misconceits and practices, let it be laid down as an undoubted rule,—that it is a thing well-pleasing to God that there should be all outward cleanliness, gravity, reverent and comely postures, meet furniture, utensils, places, used and observed in the service of the Almighty,—a truth, sufficiently grounded upon that irrefragable canon of the Apostle, "Let all things be done decently, and in order" (1 Cor. 14:40); whereof order refers to persons and actions, decency to the things done and the fashion of doing them. (Joseph Hall, Holy Decency in the Worship of God, Works, VI, p. 464; *Angl.*, p. 543)

The *Athanasian Canons* urged pastors to seek to insure a context for worship characterized by quietude, composure, and awe in the presence of God's majesty. Responsibility for a fitting context falls squarely upon the presiding pastor (*presbuteros*):

Shouting children, those who are constantly talkative, those who deliberately refuse instruction, and those who behave themselves in an unseemly way, are not to be in the worship service... in order that the word of God may be glorified and the people hear in quietness, with silence in the whole church, until they finish the word of God with the benediction. If any talk with a loud voice, the blame falls upon the presbyter, in that the deacons have not trained the people. (*Athanasian Canons*, sec. 57, pp. 38-39)*

A gardening analogy—the function of leaves for fruit—was employed by Anglican divine John Bramhall to illumine the relation of religious ceremonies to pastoral care:

Ceremonies are advancements of order, decency, modesty, and gravity in the service of God, expressions of those heavenly desires and dispositions which we ought to bring along with us to God's House, helps of attention and devotion, furtherances of edification, visible instructors, helps of memory, exercises of faith, the shell that preserves the kernel of religion from contempt, the leaves that defend the blossoms and the fruit; but if they grow over thick and rank, they hinder the fruit from coming to maturity, and then the gardener plucks them off. (John Bramhall, *The Consecration and Succession of Protestant Bishops Justified*, Ch. XI, Works, III, p. 170; *Angl.*, pp. 544)*

IV ❦ MODES OF WORSHIP

Assuming the biblical mandate for "decency and order," there have nonetheless emerged over two millenia many liturgies, rites, language-frames, and approaches to worship. These arose as the church met one after another new cultural situation. Considerable tolerance has been shown toward these varieties of forms of worship that have been received as consistent with ancient ecumenical teaching. In different times and places the Christian community has experimented widely with modes of worship. According to the Greek church historian, Socrates Scholasticus (c. 380-450), so diverse were these worship practices by the fifth century that it would be impossible to enumerate them:

> In the same city of Alexandria, readers and chanters are chosen indifferently from the catechumens and the faithful; whereas in all other churches the faithful only are promoted to these offices. . . . I have also known of another peculiarity in Thessaly, which is, that they baptize there on the days of Easter only. . . . At Antioch in Syria the site of the church is inverted; so that the altar does not face toward the east, but toward the west. . . . In short, it is impossible to find anywhere, among all the sects, two churches which agree exactly in their ritual respecting prayers. At Alexandria no presbyter is allowed to address the public: a regulation which was made after Arius had raised a disturbance in that church. At Rome they fast every Saturday. At Caesarea of Cappadocia they exclude from communion those who have sinned after baptism as the Novatians do. . . . The Novatians in Phrygia do not admit such as have twice married; but those of Constantinople neither admit nor reject them openly, while in the Western parts they are openly received. This diversity was occasioned, as I imagine, by the bishops who in their respective eras governed the churches; and those who received these several rites and usages, transmitted them as laws to their posterity. However, to give a complete catalogue of all the various customs and ceremonial observances in use throughout every city and country would be difficult—rather impossible. (Socrates Scholasticus, *Ecclesiastical History*, Bk. V, Ch. 22, NPNF 2, II, p. 132)

This yields the impression of liturgical diversity amid the fairly rigorous doctrinal cohesion that prevailed in the period of the ecumenical councils. There seemed to be room for a tolerable variety of acceptable liturgies. Another passage from Socrates on the "Indifferent Canon" illustrates the embrace of this diversity. It allowed different churches to keep the Easter feast at different times and in different ways according to local practices, without offense to church unity:

> [There was a] disagreement that existed respecting the Feast of Easter. . . . They passed a canon respecting this feast, which they entitled "indifferent," declaring that "a disagreement on such a point was not a sufficient reason for separation from the church;

and that the council of Pazum had done nothing prejudicial to the catholic canon. That although the ancients who lived nearest to the times of the apostles differed about the observance of this festival, it did not prevent their communion with one another, nor create any dissension. Besides that the Novatians at imperial Rome had never followed the Jewish usage, but always kept Easter after the equinox; and yet they did not separate from those of their own faith, who celebrated it on a different day." From these and many such considerations, they made the "Indifferent" Canon, above-mentioned, concerning Easter, whereby every one was at liberty to keep the custom which he had by predilection in this matter, if he so pleased; and that it should make no difference as regards communion, but even though celebrating differently they should be in accord in the church. (Socrates Scholasticus, *Ecclesiastical History*, Bk. V., Ch. XXI, NPNF 2, II, p. 129)

Luther argued that worship may occur anywhere:

The worship of God (*Gottesdienst*) is the praise of God. This should be free at the table, in private rooms, downstairs, upstairs, at home, abroad, in all places, by all people, at all times. (Luther, WA 10 I, 2, 81; WLS 3, p. 1546)

An important summary of the Reformed Protestant understanding of worship practice is found in the Westminster Confession. Scripture instructs the worshipper more fully than nature. One prays in the name of the Son by the power of the Spirit. Preaching is complemented by hearing; the preached-heard Word is complemented by the Sacraments; and Word and Sacrament are complemented by family and private worship, which are complemented by common worship:

The light of nature shows that there is a God, who has lordship and sovereignty over all; is good, and does good unto all; and is therefore to be feared, loved, praised, called upon, trusted in, and served with all the heart, all the soul, and with all the might. But the acceptable way of worshiping the true God is instituted by himself, and so limited to his own revealed will, that he may not be worshiped according to the imaginations and devices of men, or the suggestions of Satan, under any visible representations or any other way not prescribed in the Holy Scripture.... Prayer with thanksgiving, being one special part of religious worship, is by God required of all; and that it may be accepted, it is to be made in the name of the Son, by the help of his Spirit, according to his will, with understanding, reverence, humility, fervency, faith, love, and perseverance; and, if vocal, in a known tongue; ... the reading of the Scriptures with godly fear; the sound preaching; and conscionable hearing of the Word, in obedience unto God with understanding, faith, and reverence; singing of psalms with grace in the heart; as, also, the due administration and worthy receiving of the sacraments instituted by Christ; are all parts of the ordinary religious worship of God. ... God is to be worshiped everywhere in spirit and truth; as in private families daily, and in secret each one by himself, so more solemnly in the public assemblies. (Westminister Confession, Ch. XXI, *CC*, pp. 216-217)

That the essence of worship is to be found everywhere in the human condition is noted by Luther in discussing Adam's simple pattern of worship:

God gave Adam Word, worship, and religion in its barest, purest, and simplest form, in which there was nothing laborious, nothing elaborate. For He does not prescribe the slaughter of oxen, the burning of incense, vows, fastings, and other tortures of the body. Only this he wants: that he praise God, that he thank Him, that he rejoice in the Lord, and that he obey Him by not eating from the forbidden tree. (Luther, "Lectures on Genesis Chapters One to Five, 1535-36," LW 1, p. 106)

The active life of fidelity in human relationships, honesty, responsible sexuality, and preserving of life—that sphere dealt with in the second table of the Decalogue—should not be thought of as separable from worship. For that is where the life of worship takes active shape. The life of worship is best expressed not by perennial withdrawal from the world but by a rhythm of withdrawal and engagement, as expressed by the two tables of law:

To be sure, it is true that the foremost and highest worship of God is preaching and hearing God's Word, administering the Sacraments, etc.,—performing the works of the First Table of the Ten commandments. Nevertheless, also the performance of all the works of the Second Table of the Ten Commandments, such as honoring father and mother, living a patient, chaste, and decent life, is worshiping God. For he who leads such a life is serving and honoring the same God. (Luther, "Sermon on the Gospel of John, Chapter Fifteen, 1537," WA 45, p. 682; WLS 3, p. 1547; cf. LW 24, p. 242)

V   The Pastor and the Sunday Service

Pastoral care through worship comes to its clearest expression for most parishioners in the weekly service on the Lord's Day. Early accounts reveal the essential content and understanding of the Sunday service. Justin, a second century Chrisian martyr, wrote one of the earliest accounts of the primitive Christian liturgy, combining lection, sermon, praise, congregational responsiveness, and Eucharist:

On the day called Sunday there is a meeting in one place of those who live in cities or the country, and the memoirs of the apostles or the writings of the prophets are read as long as time permits. When the reader has finished, the president in a discourse urges and invites [us] to the imitation of these noble things. Then we all stand up together and offer prayers. And, as said before, when we have finished the prayer, bread is brought, and wine and water, and the president similarly sends up prayers and thanksgivings to the best of his ability, and the congregation assents, saying the Amen; the distribution, and reception of the consecrated [elements] by each one, takes place and they are sent to the absent by the deacons. We all hold this common gathering on Sunday, since it is the first day, on which God transforming darkness and matter made the universe, and Jesus Christ our Saviour rose from the dead on the same day. For they crucified him on the day before Saturday, and on the day after Saturday, he appeared to his apostles. (Justin, *First Apology*, sec. 67, LCC I, p. 287)

The order of service was set forth in the Apostolic Constitutions, of Syrian origin:

When there have been two lessons severally read, let some other person sing the hymns of David, and let the people join at the conclusions of the verses. Afterwards let our Acts be read, and the Epistles of Paul our fellow-worker, which he sent to the churches under the conduct of the Holy Spirit, and afterwards let a deacon or a presbyter read the Gospels. . . . While the Gospel is read, let all the presbyters and deacons, and all the people, stand up in great silence. . . . After this, let all rise up with one consent, and looking towards the east, after the catechumens and penitents are gone out, pray to God. . . . As to the deacons, after the prayer is over, let some of them attend upon the oblation of the Eucharist, ministering to the Lord's body with fear. . . . Then let the men give the men, and the women give the women, the Lord's kiss. But let no one do it with deceit, as Judas betrayed the Lord with a kiss. After this let the deacon pray for the whole Church, for the whole world, and the several parts of it, and the fruits of it. . . . After this let the sacrifice follow, the people standing, and praying silently; and when the oblation has been made, let every rank by itself partake of the Lord's body and precious blood in order. (*Constitutions of the Holy Apostles*, Book II, Sec. VII, Ch. lvii, ANF VII, p. 421)

Bread, wine and water are brought in by the laity as fruits of their labors, and received with thanksgiving by the presbyter—essential elements to be consecrated for sacramental use in baptism and holy communion. The service was held on Sunday to celebrate the resurrection. The Christian liturgy is a resurrection liturgy:

On the day of the resurrection of the Lord, that is, the Lord's day, assemble yourselves together, without fail, giving thanks to God, and praising Him for those mercies God has bestowed upon you through Christ. (*Constitutions of the Holy Apostles*, Bk. VII, Sec. II, Ch. xxx, ANF VII, p. 471)

The pastor will be asked: Why shouldn't every day be a day of worship? Luther answered:

Every day should be "Sabbath" for us Christians; for we should hear God's Word every day and should lead our lives in accordance with it. At the same time Sunday has been arranged for the common people, so that everyone may on that day in particular hear and learn God's Word and live in accordance with it. For during the other days of the week the common man must tend to his work and earn a living. And God is content to have him do so, for He has commanded man to work. (Luther, WA 36, p. 331; WLS 3, p. 1331)

George Herbert knew how important to a congregation was the vital piety, demeanor, and sincerity of the chief liturgist, the pastor, whose liturgical duties he described:

No Sermon moves them so much to a reverence (which they forget again when they come to pray), as a devout behavior in the very act of praying. Accordingly his voice is humble, his words treatable, and slow; yet not so slow neither, as to let the fervency of the supplicant hang and die between speaking, but with a grave liveliness, between fear and zeal, pausing yet pressing, he performs his duty. Besides his example, he, having often instructed his people how to carry themselves in divine service, exacts of them all possible reverence, by no means enduring either talking or sleeping or gazing or leaning or half-kneeling or any undutiful behavior in them, but causing them, when they sit or stand or kneel, to do all in a straight and steady posture. . . . (George Herbert, *CP*, Ch. VI, CWS, pp. 60f.)

VI ❦ Continuity in Liturgical Tradition

The pastoral writers were keenly aware of the dangers of constant changes in modes of worship, and sought to set reasonable bounds to the process of revision and reform.

I do not of my own accord like to introduce ceremonies and regulations; for once you begin to do this, there is no end to the practice. (Luther, *Table-Talk*, WA-T 5, #5212; WLS 1, p. 309; cf. LW 54, p. 397)

Since liturgical changes are likely to cause offense, they should be introduced only rarely and with adequate preparation:

Although I must acknowledge that you committed no sin when you touched the sacrament with your hands, nevertheless I must tell you that it was not a good work, because it caused offence everywhere. For the universal custom is, to receive the blessed sacrament directly from the hands of the priest. Why will you not herein also serve those who are weak in the faith and abstain from your liberty? It does not help you if you do it, nor harm you if you do it not.

Therefore no new practices should be introduced, unless the Gospel has first been thoroughly preached and understood, even as it has been with you. (Luther, The Eight Wittenberg Sermons, Fifth Sermon, WML II, p. 414)

There is a temptation to divisiveness in liturgical reforms, however well motivated. Jeremy Taylor thought it was better to educate laity to the received service than change it:

Let no minister of a parish introduce any ceremony, rites, or gestures, though with some seeming piety and devotion, but what are commanded by the Church, and established by law: and let these also be wisely and usefully explicated to the people, that they may understand the reasons and measures of obedience; but let there be no more introduced, lest the people be burdened unnecessarily, and tempted or divided. (Jeremy Taylor, *RAC*, Bk. III, sec. 39, *CS*, p. 14)

VII ❧ ELEMENTS OF PRAYER: ADORATION, THANKSGIVING, CONFESSION, PETITION, AND INTERCESSION

The early pastoral literature developed an analysis of the phases, types, and sequential elements of prayer. The pastor who understands the fundamental structure of prayer, its major modes, and timely ordering, will better lead the congregation in prayer.

Origen (c. 185-c. 254) was among the earliest to analyze this sequence of themes through which Christian prayer appropriately moves— praise, thanksgiving, confession, prayer for healing and pardon, petition, and intercession, concluding with doxology:

It seems to me there are four topics that need to be sketched out and that I have found scattered in the Scriptures, indicating that each one should organize one's prayer according to these topics. This is what they are: In the beginning and the preface of the prayer something having the force of praise should be said of God through Christ, who is praised with Him, and by the Holy Spirit, who is hymned with Him. After this each person should place general thanksgivings, bringing forward for thanksgiving the benefits given many people and those he has himself received from God. After thanksgiving it seems to me that he ought to blame himself bitterly before God for his own sins and then ask, first, for healing that he may be delivered from the habit that brings him to sin and, second, for forgiveness of the sins that have been committed. And after confession, the fourth topic that seems to me must be added is the request for great and heavenly things, both private and general, and concerning his household and his dearest. And, finally, the prayer should be concluded with a doxology of God through Christ in the Holy Spirit. . . . First, giving praise may be found in the following words from Psalm 104:1-3): "O Lord my God, thou art great indeed, clothed with majesty and splendour, and wrapped in a robe of light. Thou hast spread out the heavens like a tent and on their waters laid the beams of thy pavilion; who takest the clouds for thy chariot, riding on the wings of the wind". . . . As for thanksgiving. . . David is amazed at God's gifts and thanks Him for them in these words, "What am I, Lord God, and what is my family, that thou hast brought me thus far?" (2 Sam. 7:18). . . . An example of confession is: .... "My wounds fester and stink because of my folly. I am bowed down and utterly prostrate. All day long I go about as if in mourning" (Ps. 38:5-6).

An example of petition or request is found in Psalm 28:3: "Do not drag me away with the ungodly, with evildoers." Other examples are like this one.

And having begun with praise it is right to conclude the prayer by ending with praise, hymning and glorifying the Father of all through Jesus Christ in the Holy Spirit, to whom be glory forever (cf. Rom. 16:27; Heb. 13:21; Gal. 1:5; 2 Tim. 4:18). (Origen, *On Prayer*, Sec. XXXIII.1-6, CWS, pp. 169-170, NEB)*

John Climacus (c. 570-649) similarly followed this orderly sequence for Christian prayer:

Before all else, let us list sincere thanksgiving first on the scroll of our prayer. On the second line, we should put confession and heartfelt contrition of soul. Then let us present our petition to the King of all. This is the best way of prayer. (John Climacus, *Ladder of Divine Ascent*, Step 28, sec. 7, p. 213)

John of Damascus (c. 675-c. 749) summarized, in a way that has become familiar to subsequent pastoral writers, five phases of the service of worship (adoration, awe, thanksgiving, petition, and confession) as follows:

Worship is a sign of submission. Submission implies abasement and humiliation. There are many different kinds of worship.

The first kind of absolute worship is adoration, which we give to God alone. ... The second kind of absolute worship is the awe and yearning we have for God because of the glory which is His by nature. He alone is worthy to be glorified, but no one can of himself glorify Him, because He himself is the source of all glory, all goodness, unapproachable light, incomparable sweetness, boundless perfection, an abyss of goodness, inscrutable wisdom, infinite power, who alone is worthy in Himself to be admired, worshipped, glorified and desired. The third kind of absolute worship is thanksgiving for all the good things He has created for us. ... The fourth kind of absolute worship is inspired by our needs and hopes for His blessing. Since we realize that without His help we possess no goodness and are able to do nothing, we worship Him, beseeching Him to listen to each one of our needs and desires, that we may be delivered from evil and attain to goodness. The fifth kind of absolute worship is repentance and confession. As sinners we worship and prostrate ourselves before God, begging Him to forgive our sins, as is fitting for servants to do. (John of Damascus, *On Divine Images*, Third Apology, sec. 27-32, pp. 82-83)

Thomas Aquinas carefully delineated the conditions and parts of prayer:

Three conditions are requisite for prayer. First, that the person who prays should approach God Whom he prays: this is signified in the word prayer, because prayer is the raising up of one's mind to God. The second is that there should be a petition, and this is signified in the word intercession. In this case sometimes one asks for something definite, and then some say it is intercession properly so called, or we may ask for something indefinitely, for instance to be helped by God, or we may simply indicate a fact, as in Jo 11:3, "Behold, he whom Thou lovest is sick," and then they call it insinuation. The third condition is the reason for impetrating [beseeching] what we ask for: and this either on the part of God, or on the part of the person who asks. The reason of impetration on the part of God is His sanctity, on account of which we ask to be heard, according to Dan. 9:17,18, "For Thy own sake, incline, O God, Thy ear"; and to this pertains supplication (*obsecratio*), which means a pleading through sacred things, as when we say, "Through Thy nativity, deliver us, O Lord." The reason for impetration on the part of the person who asks is thanksgiving; since through giving thanks for benefits received we merit to receive yet greater benefits, as we say in the collect. Hence a gloss on 1 Tim 2:1 says that "in the Mass, the consecration is preceded by supplication," in which certain sacred things are called to mind; that prayers are in the consecration itself, in which especially the mind should be raised up to God; and that intercessions are in the petitions that follow, and thanksgivings at the end.

We may notice these four things in several of the Church's collects. Thus in the collect of Trinity Sunday the words, "Almighty eternal God" belong to the offering up of prayer to God; the words, "Who has given to Thy servants," etc. belong to thanksgiving; the words, "grant, we beseech Thee," belong to intercession; and the words at the end, "Through our Lord," etc. belong to supplication. (Thomas Aquinas, *Summa Theologica*, II-II, Q. 83, Art. 17, I, pp. 1551-1552)

Izaak Walton (1593-1683), the biographer of many Anglican pastoral writers, noted in his life of George Herbert how useful it is that the pastor make clear to communicants the structure and design of Christian worship:

And that they might pray with understanding, he did usually take occasion to explain not only the Collect for every particular Sunday, but the reasons of all the other Collects and Responses in our Church Service; and made it appear to them that the whole Service of the Church was a reasonable, and therefore an acceptable, sacrifice to God; as namely, that we begin with Confession of ourselves to be vile, miserable sinners; and that we begin so because till we have confessed ourselves to be such, weare not capable of that mercy which we acknowledge we need and pray for. But having in the Prayer of Our Lord begged pardon for those sins which we have confessed, and hoping that as the Priest hath declared our absolution, so by our public confession and real repentance, we have obtained that pardon, then we dare and do proceed to beg of the Lord, to open our lips, that our mouths may shew forth His praise; for, till then, we are neither able nor worthy to praise Him. But this being supposed, we are then fit to say, "Glory be to the Father, and to the Son, and to the Holy Ghost"; and fit to proceed to a further service of our God, in the Collects, and Psalms, and Lauds that follow in the Service. (Izaak Walton, *Life of Rev. George Herbert, 1670*, p. 295; *Angl.*, p. 730)

VIII 🍎 Pastoral Supplication

In petitioning, or asking prayer, the pastor holds up before God the needs of the people.

Clement of Rome provided one of the earliest models of how one might pray pastorally:

Open the eyes of our hearts to know thee, who alone art Highest, amid the highest, and ever abidest Holy amidst the holy. Thou dost bring down the haughtiness of the proud, and scatterest the devices of the people. Thou settest up the lowly on high, and the lofty thou dost cast down. Riches and poverty, death and life, are in thine hand; thou alone art the discerner of every spirit, and the God of all flesh. Thine eyes behold the depths and survey the works of man; thou art the aid of those in peril, the saviour of them that despair, the creator and overseer of everything that hath breath. . . . do thou deliver the afflicted, pity the lowly, raise the fallen, reveal thyself to the needy, heal the sick, and bring home thy wandering people. Feed thou the hungry, ransom the captive, support the weak, comfort the faint-hearted. Let all the nations of the earth know that thou art God alone, that Jesus Christ is thy child, and that we are thy people and the sheep of thy pasture. (Clement of Rome, *To the Corinthians*, sec. 59, ECW, pp. 54-55)

Thomas Traherne, the English metaphysical poet and clergyman, offered a moving example of a prayer for illumination and grace:

As my body without my soul is a carcass, so is my soul without Thy Spirit a Chaos, a dark, obscure heap of empty faculties; ignorant of itself, unsensible of Thy goodness, blind to Thy glory; dead in sins and trespasses. Having eyes I see not, having ears I hear not, having an heart I understand not the glory of Thy works and the glory of Thy Kingdom. O Thou Who art the root of my being and the Captain of my salvation, look upon me. Quicken me, O Thou life-giving and quickening seed. Visit me with Thy light and Thy truth; let them lead me to Thy Holy Hill and make me to see the greatness of Thy love in all its excellencies, effects, emanations, gifts, and operations. O my Wisdom! O my righteousness, Sanctification, and Redemption! Let Thy wisdom enlighten me, let Thy knowledge illuminate me, let Thy Blood redeem me, wash me and clean me, let Thy merits justify me, O Thou Who art equal unto God, and didst suffer for me. Let Thy righteousness clothe me. Let Thy Will imprint the form of itself upon mine; and let my will become conformable to Thine, that Thy Will and mine may be united, and made one for evermore. (Thomas Traherne, Centuries of Meditations, First Century, No. 93, pp. 68f; *Angl.*, p. 776)

From the early liturgies of the ante-Nicene period, we have this example of a supplication to God to accept offertory:

Accept the thank-offerings of those who have presented them this day, as Thou didst accept the gifts of Thy righteous Abel: . . . As Thou didst accept the sacrifice of our father Abraham, the incense of Zacharias, the alms of Cornelius, and the widow's two mites, accept also the thank-offerings of these, and give them for the things of time the things of eternity, and for the things of earth the things of heaven. . . . Be with us, O Lord, who minister unto Thy holy name. Bless our meetings, O Lord. Utterly uproot idolatry from the world. (*Early Liturgies*, ANF VII, pp. 556-557)

Again, a pre-Nicene model of a pastoral supplication:

Deliver the captive; rescue the distressed; feed the hungry; comfort the faint-hearted; convert the erring; enlighten the darkened; raise the fallen; confirm the wavering; heal the sick; and guide them all, good Lord, into the way of salvation, and into Thy sacred fold. Deliver us from our iniquities; protect and defend us at all times. (*Early Liturgies*, ANF VII, pp. 557)

Thomas Aquinas stated reasons why it is fitting to ask God for temporal things as means to lawful ends when we pray:

As Augustine says (*ad Probam, de orando Deum*, Ep. 130:12), "It is lawful to pray for what it is lawful to desire." Now it is lawful to desire temporal things, not indeed principally, by placing our end in them, but as helps whereby we are assisted in tending towards beatitude, in so far as they are the means of supporting the life of the body, and are of service to us as instruments in performing acts of virtue, as also the Philosopher states (Ethics 1:8). Augustine too says the same to Proba (ibid. 6,7) when he states that "it is not unbecoming for anyone to desire enough for a livelihood, and no more." (Thomas Aquinas, *Summa Theologica*, II-II, Q. 83, Art. 6, Vol. I, p. 1541)

Similarly, Thomas considered whether one ought to ask for something definite when one prays:

According to Valerius Maximus (*Fact. et Dict. Memor.* vii.2), Socrates deemed that we should ask the immortal gods for nothing else but that they should grant us good things, because they at any rate know what is good for each one, whereas when we pray we frequently ask for what it had been better for us not to obtain. This opinion is true to a certain extent, as to those things which may have an evil result, and which man may use ill or well, such as riches, by which, as stated by the same authority (ibid.), many have come to an evil end; honors, which have ruined many; power, of which we frequently witness the unhappy results; splendid marriages, which sometimes bring about the total wreck of a family. Nevertheless there are certain goods which man cannot ill use, because they cannot have an evil result. Such are those which are the object of beatitude and whereby we merit it, and these the saints seek absolutely when they pray, as in Ps. 79:4, "Show us Thy face, and we shall be saved", and again in Ps. 118:35, "Lead me into the path of Thy commandments".... Although man cannot by himself know what he ought to pray for, the Spirit, as stated in the same passage, [Romans 8:26] helps our infirmity, since by inspiring us with holy desires, he makes us ask for what is right. (Thomas Aquinas, *Summa Theologica*, II-II, Q. 83, Art. 5, Vol. I, pp. 1540-1541)*

Here is an early pastoral absolution, praying for forgiveness of sin of the penitent:

O Lord Jesus Christ, Son of the living God, Lamb and Shepherd, who takest away the sin of the world, who didst freely forgive their debt to the two debtors, and gavest remission of her sins to the woman that was a sinner, who gavest healing to the paralytic, with the remission of his sins; forgive, remit, pardon, O God, our offences, voluntary and involuntary, in knowledge and in ignorance, by transgression and by disobedience, which Thy all-holy Spirit knows better than Thy servants do. (*Early Liturgies*, ANF VII, p. 550)

This pastoral benediction has survived from the early fourth century:

Going on from strength to strength, and having fulfilled all the divine service in Thy temple, even now we beseech Thee, O Lord our God, make us worthy of perfect loving-kindness; make straight our path: root us in Thy fear, and make us worthy of the heavenly kingdom, in Christ Jesus our Lord, with whom Thou art blessed, together with Thy all-holy, and good, and quickening Spirit, now and always, and for ever. (*Early Liturgies*, ANF VII, p. 550)

Luther commented on what we mean when we say "Amen":

God help us, without doubting, to obtain all these petitions, and suffer us not to doubt that Thou has heard us and wilt hear us in them all; that it is "Yea," not "Nay," and not "Perhaps." Therefore we say with joy, "Amen—it is true and certain." Amen. (Luther, *A Brief Explanation*, WML II, p. 384)

IX ❧ PASTORAL INTERCESSION

While the distinctive stress in supplication is upon the humble entreaty (with the earnestness of an unworthy one who would rightly come before the holy God with a request), the more distinctive stress in intercession is upon entreaty on behalf of others. To intercede is to ask for another. Intercession carries the connotation of acting between two parties so as to reconcile differences. Intercession is thus a pastoral attempt at peacemaking between sinners and God, asking for the benefits of Christ's mediation to be manifested toward particular persons. In pastoral intercession those interceded for may be personally named.

Thomas Aquinas thoughtfully clarified how one might best pray for others:

> When we pray we ought to ask for what we ought to desire. Now we ought to desire good things not only for ourselves, but also for others.... Hence Chrysostom (Hom. 14, in Matth.): "Necessity binds us to pray for ourselves, fraternal charity urges us to pray for others: and the prayer that fraternal charity proffers is sweeter to God than that which is the outcome of necessity."
>
> Reply Obj. 1. As Cyprian says (*De Orat. Dom.*), "We say 'Our Father' and not 'my Father,' 'Give us' and not 'Give me,' because the Master of unity did not wish us to pray privately, that is for ourselves alone, for He wished each one to pray for all, even as He Himself bore all in one." (Thomas Aquinas, *Summa Theologica*, II-II, Q. 83, Art. 7, Vol. II, p. 1542)

Origen argued that it is finally the Spirit who intercedes, not ourselves. We are called to pray for the Spirit's own intercession:

> [Intercession occurs] in the writings of the Apostle, where he quite reasonably assigns prayer to our control, but intercession to that of the Spirit, since He is better and has boldness with the One to whom He makes intercession. What he says is, "For what we should pray for as we ought we do not know, but the Spirit Himself makes special intercession for us to God with sighs too deep for words. And He who searches the hearts knows what is the mind of the Spirit, because the Spirit intercedes for the saints according to the will of God" (Rom. 8:26-27). For the Spirit "makes special intercession" and "intercedes," but we pray. (Origen, *On Prayer*, sec. 4-5, CWS, p. 111)

Augustine recognized a subtle dialectic in prayer—we do not know exactly what we are praying for, since it is not present to us, but we nonetheless pray for the good we cannot rightly envision:

> This blessing is nothing else than the "peace which passeth all understanding" (Phil. 4:7), even when we are asking it in our prayers, we know not what to pray for as we ought. For inasmuch

as we cannot present it to our minds as it really is, we do not know it, but whatever image of it may be presented to our minds we reject, disown, and condemn; we know it is not what we are seeking, although we do not yet know enough to be able to define what we seek.

There is therefore in us a certain learned ignorance so to speak—an ignorance which we learn from that Spirit of God who helps our infirmities. For after the apostle said, "If we hope for what we see not, then do we with patience wait for it," he added in the same passage, "Likewise the Spirit also helpeth our infirmities: for we know not what we should pray for as we ought, but the Spirit itself maketh intercession for us, with groanings which cannot be uttered. And He that searcheth the hearts knoweth what is in the mind of the Spirit, because He maketh intercession for the saints according to the will of God." (Rom. 8:25-27). . . . He therefore makes the saints intercede with groanings which cannot be uttered, when He inspires them with longings for that great blessing, as yet unknown, for which we patiently wait. For how is that which is desired set forth in language if it be unknown, for if it were utterly unknown it would not be desired; and on the other hand, if it were seen, it would not be desired. (Augustine, *Letters*, LXXX, To Proba, NPNF 1, I, p. 468)

John Cosin, the Anglican divine, showed why pastoral intercession for the people is a constant and central pastoral function:

God is more respective to the prayers which they make for the people than ever the people are to the sermons which they make to them. And in this respect are the Priests called God's remembrancers, because they put God in mind of His people, desiring Him to keep and bless them daily with things needful both for their bodies and their souls. . . . It was the office that was appointed the priests in the Law, "He shall make an atonement for the people," not so much to teach and preach to the people (as men now-a-days think all the office lays in doing that), but "to offer sacrifice and incense unto the Lord," which was but a figure of that which the ministers of Christ were to do in the Gospel. Therefore Samuel professes it openly, to the shame of all others, that he should sin no less in neglecting to pray for the people, than he should in leaving off to teach them the right way of God's commandments; both which are needful, but to them that are already converted prayer is more necessary than preaching. . . .

David's diligence in performing his duty for the good of the people was such, as he professes it, "At midnight I will rise up to give thanks unto Thee"; so Paul and Silas rose at midnight to sing praises unto God. It were, therefore well to be wished that the like order were taken in the Church now, and that the Sacrifice of Prayer might be continually offered up unto God among Christians, as well as it was in the synagogues of the Jews. (John Cosin, Works, LACT V, p. 9-11; *Angl.*, p. 629)

The pastor may be asked: If God knows all already, then why are we commanded to let our requests be made known to God?

When the same apostle says, "Let your requests be made known unto God" (Phil. 4:6), this is not to be understood as if thereby they become known of God, who certainly knew them before they were uttered, but in this sense, that they are to be made known to ourselves in the presence of God by patient waiting upon Him, not in the presence of men by ostentatious worship. (Augustine, *Letters*, CXXX, To Proba, Ch. 9, NPNF 1, I, p. 465)

X ✷ EFFECTUAL PRAYER

Instruction in the effective practice of prayer has been a recurrent task of pastoral counsel in the classical tradition. Here is an example of such instruction by Origen:

The person who is about to come to prayer should withdraw for a little and prepare himself, and so become more attentive and active for the whole of his prayer. He should cast away all temptation and troubling thoughts and remind himself, so far as he is able, of the majesty whom he approaches, and that it is impious to approach Him carelessly, sluggishly, and disdainfully; and he should put away all extraneous things. This is how he should come to prayer, stretching out his soul, as it were, instead of his hands, straining his mind toward God instead of his eyes. (Origen, *On Prayer*, Ch. XXXI, sec. 2, CWS, p. 164)

Origen explained why Christian prayer is to the Father through the Son by the power of the Spirit:

Now if we are to take prayer in its most exact sense, perhaps we should not pray to anyone begotten, not even to Christ Him-

self, but only to the God and Father of all, to whom even our
Savior Himself prayed, as we have explained, and to whom he
taught us to pray. For when He heard "teach us to pray," He did
not teach us to pray to Himself, but to the Father by saying "Our
Father in heaven, and so forth" (Lk. 11:1ff; Mt. 6:5ff). . . . We
should pray only to the God and Father of all, yet not without the
High Priest. . . . And so, when the saints give thanks to God in
their prayers, they acknowledge through Christ Jesus the favors
He has done. . . . For you must not pray to the High Priest appointed on your behalf by the Father (cf. Heb. 8:3) or to the Advocate who is charged by the Father with praying for you (cf. 1
John 2:1). Rather you must pray through the High Priest and
Advocate, who is able to sympathize with your weaknesses, since
He has been tempted in every respect as you are, and yet
tempted without sin (Heb. 4:15). (Origen, *On Prayer*, Ch. XV,
sec. 1-4, CWS, pp. 112-114)

Effectual prayer cannot be separated from effective reconcilation with
the neighbor:

For what sort of deed is it to approach the peace of God without peace? the remission of debts while you retain them? How
will he appease his Father who is angry with his brother. . . . Even
if we must be angry, our anger must not be maintained beyond
sunset, as the apostle admonishes. . . . Nor merely from anger,
but altogether from all perturbation of mind, ought the exercise
of prayer to be free, uttered from a spirit such as the Spirit unto
whom it is sent. For a defiled spirit cannot be acknowledged by a
holy Spirit, nor a sad by a joyful, nor a fettered by a free. (Tertullian, *On Prayer*, Ch. XI, ANF III, p. 685)

The very disposition of prayer is itself productive of other goods. The
prayer that comes cleanly and honestly out of unsullied motivation is
bound to be beneficial in some way:

I believe that profit often meets and joins the person who prays
as he ought or who makes every effort to do so as far as he is
able. First, the person who composes his mind for prayer is inevitably profited in some way. Through his very disposition for
prayer he adorns himself as to present himself to God and to
speak to Him in person as to someone who looks upon him and
is present. (Origen, *On Prayer*, Ch. VIII, sec. 2, CWS, p. 97)

Augustine counseled Proba to pray for only one thing:

Whoever desires from the Lord that "one thing," and seeks after it, asks in certainty and in confidence, and has no fear lest when obtained it be injurious to him, seeing that, without it, anything else which he may have obtained by asking in a right way is of no advantage to him. The thing referred to is the one true and only happy life, in which, immortal and incorruptible in body and spirit, we may contemplate the joy of the Lord for ever. All other things are desired, and are without impropriety prayed for, with a view to this one thing. For whosoever has it shall have all that he wishes, and cannot possibly wish to have anything along with it which would be unbecoming. (Augustine, *Letters*, CXXX, To Proba, NPNF 1, I, pp. 467-468)

The power of prayer was attested by Tertullian:

Prayer amplifies grace by virtue, that faith may know what she obtains from the Lord, so as better to understand what she is for God's sake suffering. . . . Prayer has been known to recall the souls of the departed from the very path of death, to transform the weak, to restore the sick, to purge the possessed, to open prison-bars, to loose the bonds of the innocent. Likewise it washes away faults, repels temptations, extinguishes persecutions, consoles the faintspirited, cheers the high-spirited, escorts travellers, appeases waves, makes robbers stand aghast, nourishes the poor, governs the rich, upraises the fallen, arrests the falling, confirms the standing. (Tertullian, *On Prayer*, Ch. XXIX, ANF III, pp. 690-691)*

Augustine examined the paradoxical sense in which we are to pray without ceasing:

It may seem surprising that, although He has forbidden "much speaking," He who knoweth before we ask Him what things we need has nevertheless given us exhortation to prayer in such words as these: "Men ought always to pray and not to faint" (Lk. 18:1); setting before us the case of a widow, who, desiring to have justice done to her against her adversary, did by her persevering entreaties persuade an unjust judge to listen to her, not moved by a regard either to justice or to mercy, but overcome by her wearisome importunity; in order that we might be admonished how much more certainly the Lord God, who is merciful and just, gives ear to us praying continually to Him, when this widow, by her unremitting supplication, prevailed over the indifference of an unjust and wicked judge, and how willingly and benignantly He fulfils the good desires of those whom He knows to have forgiven others their trespasses, when this suppliant, though seeking vengeance upon her adversary, obtained her desire. . . . When we cherish uninterrupted desire along with the exercise of faith and hope and charity, we "pray always." But at certain stated hours and seasons we also use words in prayer to God, that by these signs of things we may admonish ourselves, and may acquaint ourselves with the measure of progress which we have made in this desire, and may more warmly excit ourselves to obtain an increase of its strength. For the effect following upon prayer will be excellent in proportion to the fervour of the desire which precedes its utterance. And therefore, what else is intended by the words of the apostle: "Pray without ceasing," than, "Desire without intermission from Him who alone can give it, a happy life, which no life can be but that which is eternal" . . . Far be it from us either to use "much speaking" in prayer or to refrain from prolonged prayer, if fervent attention of the soul continue. (Augustine, *Letters*, CXXX, To Proba, NPNF 1, I, pp. 464-465)

John Climacus used courtroom and medical analogies to press the awesomeness of prayer:

If you have ever been under trial before an earthly judge, you will not need any other pattern for your attitude in prayer. But if you have never stood before a judge yourself and have not seen others being cross-questioned, then learn at least from the way the sick implore the surgeons when they are about to be operated on or cauterized. (John Climacus, *Ladder of Divine Ascent*, Step 28, sec. 8, p. 213)

XI ❧ THE LANGUAGE AND FORMS OF PASTORAL PRAYER

The pastor is specifically charged to pray for the flock. Pastoral prayer is prayer representatively held up before God on behalf of the people. Corporate or common prayer is therefore distinguished from individual prayer by the fact that a congregation is present and the whole body is being represented in prayer by the pastor. This requires befitting language that appropriately forms the confessions, thanksgivings and petitions of the community into a vocal, corporate act at a particular time and place.

Prayer is two-fold, common and individual. Common prayer is that which is offered to God by the ministers of the church representing the body of the faithful: wherefore such like prayer should come to the knowledge of the whole people for whom it is offered: and this would not be possible unless it were vocal prayer. . . . On the other hand individual prayer is that which is offered by any single person, whether he pray for himself or for others; and it is not essential to such a prayer as this that it be vocal. . . . Vocal prayer is employed not in order to tell God something He does not know, but in order to lift up the mind of the person praying or of other persons to God. (Thomas Aquinas, *Summa Theologica*, II-II, Q. 83, Art. 12, Vol. II, p. 1547)

The gift of pastoral prayer is not reducible to rhetoric, linguistic construction, persuasion, or elocution. One of the most moving descriptions of the qualities needed in representative prayer was offered by Anglican Bishop Joseph Hall:

Some think that a man has the gift of prayer who can utter the thoughts of his heart roundly to God, express himself smoothly in the phrase of the Holy Ghost, and press God with most proper words and passionate vehemence. Surely this is a commendable faculty wherever it is. But this is not the gift of prayer. One might better call it, if you will, the gift of elocution. Do we say that one has the gift of pleading who can talk eloquently at the court of law, who can in good terms loudly and earnestly importune the judge for his client, and not rather he that brings the strongest reason, and quotes his books and precedents with most truth and clearest evidence, so as may convince the jury and persuade the judge? Similarly, do we say one has the gift of preaching who can deliver himself in a flowing manner of speech to his hearers, cite Scriptures or Fathers, please his audience with the flowers of rhetoric? Or rather, does he have the gift of preaching who can divide the word aright, interpret it soundly, apply it judiciously, send it home to the conscience, speaking in the evidence of the Spirit, powerfully convincing the disputants, comforting the dejected, and drawing every soul nearer to heaven? We must say the same thing about prayer. He of whom it may be truly said that he has the gift of prayer is not the one who has the most running tongue, for prayer is not so much a matter of the lips as of the heart. Rather is it he who has the most illuminated apprehension of the God to Whom he speaks, the deepest sense of his own wants, the most eager longings after grace, the most fervent desire of supply from heaven, and in a word, whose heart sends up the strongest groans and cries to the Father of Mercies. (Joseph Hall, The Devout Soul, Works, VI, pp. 477-79; *Angl.*, p. 616)*

Athanasius argued that traditionally received prayers are to be specially revered by the remembering community:

For as much better as the life of the saints is than that of other people, by so much also are their expressions superior to those we construct and, if one were to speak the truth, more powerful as well. For they greatly pleased God in these, and when saying them, as the Apostle put it, "they conquered kingdoms, enforced justice, received promises, stopped the mouths of lions, quenched raging fire, escaped the edge of the sword, won strength out of weakness, became mighty in war, put foreign armies to flight, and women received their dead by resurrection" (Hebr. 11:33-34). (Athanasius, Letter to Marcellinus, sec. 31, ACW 10, p. 127)

It has not ordinarily been left exclusively to the privatized imagination or individual creativity of each pastor to invent the order, design and language of worship in each parish. The repetitive, intergenerational character of common prayer has an educative, upbuilding effect on the soul that is difficult otherwise to achieve. The pastor need not avoid, but should use repetition and form. All divine services need not be alike, but all ought to reflect the apostolic faith:

The prescribing a form in general is more for our edifying, than to leave everyone to do what seems Good in his own eyes, we have the concurrent testimony, experience, and practice of the Universal Church; for we never read or heard of any Church in the world, from the Apostles' days to ours, but what took this course. Though all have not used the same, yet no Church but have used some form or other. And, therefore, for any man to say that it is not lawful, or not expedient, or not to edifying, to use a form of prayer in the public worship of God, is to contradict the general sense of Christianity, to condemn the Holy Catholic Church, and to make himself wiser than all Christians that ever were before him. . . . For we cannot but all find by our own experience how difficult it is to fasten anything that is truly good, either upon ourselves or others; and that it is rarely, if ever, effected without frequent repetitions of it. Whatsoever good things we hear only once, or now and then, though, perhaps, upon the hearing of them, they may swim for awhile in our brains, yet they seldom sink down into our hearts, so as to move and sway the affections, as it is necessary they should do, in order to our being edified by them. (William Beveridge, *A Sermon on the Excellency and Usefulness of the Common Prayer*, Works, Vol. VI, pp. 370-373; *Angl.*, pp. 624-626)

It has been much debated whether public prayer should be in Latin or in a language understood by the people. The case for the vernacular is based on the nature of prayer as an act of the understanding:

It is repugnant to the nature and end of vocal prayer that the same should be exercised in a form of words which people that pray together understand not. For prayer is an ascending of the mind to God; and according to Aquinas and other Schoolmen it is an action of the understanding faculty. (Francis White, A Reply to Jesuit Fisher's Answer to Certain Questions Propounded by His Most Gracious Majesty, King James, 1624, pp. 367f; *Angl.*, p. 634)

XII ❦ THE LORD'S PRAYER AS PATTERN

In the Lord's Prayer, a model is offered for the guidance of all Christian prayer, including pastoral prayer. Believers whose lives are hid in Christ, who live in a new age, under a new law, have been given a new way of praying. In extremely brief scope the Lord's Prayer expresses, as Tertullian argued, the "epitome of the whole gospel":

The Spirit of God and the Word of God, and the Reason of God—Word of Reason, and Reason and Spirit of Word—Jesus Christ our Lord, namely, who is both the one and the other,—has determined for us, the disciples of the New Testament, a new form of prayer; for in this particular also it was needful that new wine should be laid up in new skins, and a new breadth be sewn to a new garment. Besides, whatever had been in bygone days, has either been quite changed, as circumcision; or else supplemented, as the rest of the Law; or else fulfilled, as Prophecy; or else perfected, as faith itself. . . . In the Prayer is comprised an epitome of the whole Gospel. . . . In summaries of so few words, how many utterances of the prophets, the Gospels, the apostles— how many discourses, examples, parables of the Lord, are touched on! . . . . The honour of God in the "Father;" the testimony of faith in the "Name;" the offering of obedience in the "Will;" the commemoration of hope in the "Kingdom;" the petition for life in the "Bread;" the full acknowledgment of debts in the prayer for their "Forgiveness;" the anxious dread of temptation in the request for "Protection." (Tertullian, *On Prayer*, Ch. 1, and Ch. 9, ANF III, pp. 681ff.)

In his treatise on Prayer, Origen set forth an insight that has recently been rediscovered by twentieth century New Testament critics—that prayer to the Father, Abba, was not common in the Old Testament, and may be highly distinctive of the ministry of Jesus. For classical trinitarian thought, this reinforces the notion of the unique and intimate Sonship of Jesus to God the Father:

"Our Father in heaven." It is right to examine what is said in the Old Testament quite carefully to see whether any prayer may be found in it calling God "Father." Up till now, though I have looked as carefully as I can, I have not found one. I do not mean that God was not called Father or that those who are supposed to have believed in God were not called sons of God; but nowhere have I found in a prayer the boldness proclaimed by the Savior in calling God Father. (Origen, *On Prayer*, Ch. XXII, sec. 1, CWS, p. 123)

The Apostolic Constitutions commended saying the Lord's Prayer three times a day:

Pray thus thrice in a day, preparing yourselves beforehand, that ye may be worthy of the adoption of the Father; lest, when you call Him Father unworthily, you be reproached by Him. (*Constitutions of the Holy Apostles*, Bk. VII, Sec. II, ANF VII, p. 470)

Every good prayer is anticipated by the insurmountably good way of praying taught by Jesus, according to Augustine:

If we pray rightly, and as becomes our wants, we say nothing but what is already contained in the Lord's Prayer. And whoever says in prayer anything which cannot find its place in that gospel prayer, is praying in a way which, if it be not unlawful, is at least not spiritual; and I know not how carnal prayers can be lawful, since it becomes those who are born again by the Spirit to pray in no other way than spiritually. For example, when one prays: "Be Thou glorified among all nations as Thou art glorified among us" (Ecclus. 36:4,18), and "Let Thy prophets be found faithful," what else does he ask than, "Hallowed be Thy name"? . . . . When one says: "Order my steps in Thy word, and let not any iniquity have dominion over me" (Ps. 119:133), what else is he saying than, "Thy will be done on earth as it is in heaven"? When one says: "Give me neither poverty nor riches" (Prov. 30:8), what else is this than, "Give us this day our daily bread"? When one says: "Lord, remember David, and all his compassion" (Ps. 132:1 LXX), or, "O Lord, if I have done this, if there be iniquity in my hands, if I have rewarded evil to them that did evil to me" (Ps.

7:3-4), what else is this than, "Forgive us our debts as we forgive our debtors"? When one says: "Take away from me the lusts of the appetite, and let not sensual desire take hold on me" (Ecclus. 23:6), what else is this than, "Lead us not into temptation"? When one says: "Deliver me from mine enemies, O my God; defend me from them that rise up against me" (Ps. 58:1), what else is this than, "Deliver me from evil"? And if you go over all the words of holy prayers, you will, I believe, find nothing which cannot be comprised and summed up in the petitions of the Lord's Prayer. Wherefore, in praying, we are free to use different words to any extent, but we must ask the same things. (Augustine, *Letters*, CXXX, To Proba, Ch. 22, NPNF 1, I, p. 466)

By meditating upon each phrase of the Lord's prayer, Ignatius Loyola proposed an extended spiritual exercise in contemplative prayer:

He should then say, "Father," and reflect upon this word as long as he find meanings, comparisons, relish, and consolation in the consideration of it. He should then continue the same method with each word of the "Our Father," or of any other prayer that he may wish to contemplate in this manner. . . . .
During the contemplation on the "Our Father," if he finds in one or two words good matter for thought, relish, and consolation, he should not be anxious to pass on, even though he spend the entire hour on what he has found. When the hour is over, he will say the rest of the "Our Father" in the usual way. . . . .
The third method of prayer is a rhythmical recitation. . . . . At each breath or respiration, he is to pray mentally, as he says one word of the "Our Father," or any other prayer that is being recited, so that between one breath and another a single word is said. During this same space of time, he is to give his full attention to the meaning of the word, or to the person whom he is addressing, or to his own unworthiness, or to the difference between the greatness of this Person and his own lowliness. He will continue, observing the same procedure and rule, through the other words of the "Our Father" and the other prayers, namely, the "Hail Mary," the "Anima Christi," the "Creed," and the "Hail Holy Queen." (Ignatius Loyola, *Spiritual Exercises*, pp. 107-108)

XIII ❦ PUBLIC PRAYER

The root meaning of the term "parson" is person, in the special sense that an individual has become "the person" of the community representatively in prayer before God. There is a sense in which the parson embodies or "personates" the community, becomes representatively the unified voice of the community at prayer.

So recurrent and crucial is this pastoral act that the pastoral writers have sought to provide reliable guidelines for the public prayer of the pastor. Thus public prayer cannot be separated from the task of soul care. Bishop Gilbert Burnet's guidelines for public pastoral prayer focus upon the heartfelt entry of the pastor into the language of prayer:

He must bring his Mind to an inward and feeling Sense of those things that are prayed for in our Offices: That will make him pronounce them with an equal measure of Gravity and Affection, and with a due Slowness and Emphasis. I do not love the Theatrical way.... And a hasty running through the Prayers, are things highly unbecoming; they do very much lessen the Majesty of our Worship, and give our Enemies advantage to call it dead and formal, when they see plainly, that he who officiates is dead and formal in it. A deep Sense of the things prayed for, a true Recollection and Attention of Spirit, and a holy Earnestness of Soul, will give a Composure to the Looks, and a weight to the Pronunciation, that will be tempered between affectation on the one hand, and Levity on the other. (Burnet, *Of the Pastoral Care*, Ch. VII; *CS*, p. 87)

Philip Doddridge provided this summary instruction for assisting young pastors in improving the gift of prayer:

Converse much with your own hearts, get well acquainted with the state of your souls, attend to your spiritual wants and weaknesses, frequently recollect the mercies you receive from God, and inquire what returns you have made.... In all your prayers avoid the extremes of too mean and too pompous a style. A pompous style shows a mind too full of self, and too little affected with a sense of divine things.... Aim at nothing but pouring out the soul before God in the most genuine language.... The principal parts of prayer are Invocation with Adoration, Confession, Petition, Intercession with Thanksgiving.... Be not too solicitous to introduce novelties into your prayers. Desire not to pray as nobody ever prayed before, or will probably ever pray again. Novelties may sometimes amuse, but in prayer they more frequently disgust. Besides, they have the appearance of too much art, and as new things are generally the product of the imagination, they are not so proper for prayer as preaching, and even in that they must be moderate.

Remember it is the peculiar office of the Spirit of God to help us in prayer. Engage in it, therefore in dependence upon him; and maintain a continual dependence on the intercession and influence of Christ.

I shall now give you some directions which relate more immediately to public prayer.

Begin with a solemn recollection of spirit. Think seriously of the majesty of that Being to whom you are addressing yourselves, and of the importance of the business in which you are engaging. . . . Endeavour to have a unity of design running through your scheme of prayer, and let one petition be connected with another by natural but never laboured transition. . . . Remember the particular cases of your hearers, and the immediate concerns of the congregation. . . . Let the last prayer be agreeable to the sermon; introduce the principal thoughts and heads, but do not turn it into a preaching prayer, nor repeat any peculiarly fine passages of the sermon, lest you should seem too fond of them. (Doddridge, *Lectures on Preaching*, XIII sec. 2-20, pp. 71-76)*

Since truth is one, true prayer seeks simplicity of expression. Origen developed this penetrating argument for short prayers, along with a psychological explanation of our tendency to multiply words:

According to the text of the Gospel only "the Gentiles" heap up empty phrases, since they have no impression of the great and heavenly requests and offer every prayer for bodily and outward things. . . . Truth is one, but lies are many; and true righteousness is one, but there are many ways of counterfeiting it; and the wisdom of God is one, but many are the wisdoms—doomed to pass away—of this age and of the rulers of this age (1 Cor. 2:6); and the word of God is one, but many are the words foreign to God. Therefore, no one will escape sin when words are many; and no one who thinks he will be heard, when words are many, can be heard (cf. Prov. 10:19). (Origen, *On Prayer*, Ch. XXI, sec. 1-2, CWS, p. 122)

The simplicity of this argument makes it easy to miss its profundity: Since there are many ways of lying, there are likewise many ways to dissemble in prayer. Since the truth is one, there is only one way to speak the truth in prayer, and that is with direct, candid simplicity that does not hide behind many words. Thomas Aquinas developed much the same thought in dependence upon Augustine:

Augustine says (*ad Probam Ep. 130*): "It is said that the brethren in Egypt make frequent but very short prayers, rapid ejaculations, as it were, lest that vigilant and erect attention which is so necessary in prayer slacken and languish." . . . As Augustine says (*ad Probam loc. cit.*), "to pray with many words is not the same as to pray long; to speak long is one thing, to be devout long is another. For it is written that our Lord passed the whole night in prayer (Lk. 6:12), and that He 'prayed the longer' in order to set us an example." Further on he says: "When praying say little, yet pray much so long as your attention is fervent. For to say much in prayer is to discuss your need in too many words: whereas to pray much is to knock at the door of Him to whom we pray, by the continuous and devout clamor of the heart. Indeed this business is frequently done with groans rather than with words, with tears rather than with speech." (Thomas Aquinas, *Summa Theologica*, II-II, Q. 83, Art. 14, Vol. I, p. 1549)*

Pray often, not long:

Pray frequently and effectually; I had rather your prayers should be often than long. It was well said of Petrarch. . . . "When you speak to your superior, you ought to have a bridle on your tongue"; much more when you speak to God. (Jeremy Taylor, A Letter to a Person Newly Converted to the Church of England, Works, XI, pp. 206f; *Angl.*, p. 615)

XIV 🌣 THE SPATIAL ORDERING OF THE COMMUNITY AT PRAYER

Since prayer is a public act of soul care—a representative ministry of the most recurrent sort—the pastoral writers discussed many special questions concerning its rightful enactment. Among these are whether there are special dispositions and postures for prayer, particular places for particular prayers, and how the life of prayer is to be placed in time and space.

Our concern here is how care of souls through common prayer seeks to order itself spatially, seeking the appropriate physical place or locus for its fitting enactment. Although this may seem trivial to modern readers, it was taken with great seriousness by the classical pastoral writers. Prayer has been thought to be especially fitting in certain *loci* of time and space. Pastoral care requires reflection on the due placement of common prayer.

Origen offered an ingenious explanation for what he regarded as the most fitting posture for prayer:

The question of disposition must be referred to the soul, that of the posture to the body. Thus, Paul . . . describes the disposition and says that we must pray "without anger or quarreling"; and he describes the posture by the phrase "lifting holy hands" (1 Tim. 2:8). . . . The position with the hands outstretched and the eyes lifted up is to be preferred before all others, because it bears in prayer the image of characteristics befitting the soul and applies it to the body . . . .

Kneeling is necessary when someone is going to speak against his own sins before God, since he is making supplication for their healing and their forgiveness. We must understand that it symbolizes someone who has fallen down and become obedient. . . .

Since there are four directions, north, south, west, and east, who would not immediately acknowledge that it is perfectly clear we should make our prayers facing east, since this is a symbolic expression of the soul's looking for the rising of the true Light. (Origen, *On Prayer*, Ch. XXXI-XXXII, CWS, pp. 164-168)

Only God is to be worshipped, but God may be worshipped through visible images and representations. John of Damascus stated the classic case for a holy place of worship in which visual representations of the holy life (mosaics, paintings, and icons, for example, of the cross) assist the believer toward penitence and faith. While only God is to be worshipped, God may be worshipped relatively or relationally through appointed creaturely means. Seven types are noted:

How many things in Scripture can we find that were worshipped in a relative sense? What are the different ways we offer this relative worship to created things?

First of all, those places where God, who alone is holy, has rested. . . . [Since the saints] partake of the divine nature, they are to be venerated, not because they deserve it on their own account, but because they bear in themselves Him who is by nature worshipful. . . . The second kind of relative worship we give to created things concerns those places and things by which God has accomplished our salvation, whether before the coming of the Lord, or since the dispensation of His incarnation, such as Mount Sinai, and Nazareth, the cave and manger of Bethlehem, the holy mountain of Golgotha. . . . The third kind of relative worship we give to objects dedicated to God, such as the holy Gospel and other books, for they have been written for our instruction. . . . The fourth kind of relative worship is given to those images which were seen by the prophets (for they saw God in the images of their visions). . . . Thus, we venerate the honorable figure of the cross, or the likeness of the physical features of our God, or of her who gave birth to Him in the flesh, and everyone who is part of Him. The fifth kind of relative worship is our veneration of each other, since we are God's inheritance, and were made according to His image, and so we are subject to each other, thus fulfilling the law of love. The sixth kind of relative worship is given to those who have been given authority to rule over us. The apostle says, "pay all of them their due, . . . honor to whom honor is due" (Rom. 13:7). . . . The seventh kind of relative worship is given to masters by their servants, and to benefactors who grant the requests of their petitioners, as was the case when Abraham did reverence to the Hittites, when he bought the cave of Machpelah from Ephron.

It is needless to say that fear, desire, and honor all are signs of worship, as are submission and abnegation. But no one should worship anyone as God. Worship as God only Him who is God by nature. (John of Damascus, *On the Divine Images*, Third Apology, sec. 33-40, NPNF 2, IX, pp. 84-88)

An early interpretation of the positioning of clergy and laity in the bascilica was set forth in the Apostolic Constitutions:

Let the building be long, with its head to the east, with its vestries on both sides at the east end, and so it will be like a ship. In the middle let the bishop's throne be placed, and on each side of him let the presbytery sit down; and let the deacons stand near at hand, in close and small girt garments, for they are like the mariners and managers of the ship: with regard to these, let the laity sit on the other side, with all quietness and good order. (*Constitutions of the Holy Apostles*, Book II, Sec. VII, ch. lvii, ANF VII, p. 421)

XV ❦ THE TEMPORAL ORDERING OF PRAYER

The life of prayer not only exhibits a fit ordering in space, but also a way of ordering time. The pastor is expected to guide the community of faith into an appropriate order of prayer for each day, each week, and each year. Although views differ considerably as to how these are to be ordered, depending upon historical and cultural perspective, it has always seemed important that some order be sought. The Anglican divine, John Cosin, for example, provided a sixteenth century list of regular devotional acts through which laity were guided through time by the pastor. This ordering of time was considered intrinsic to the care of souls:

To observe the Festivals and Holy Days appointed. To keep the Fasting Days with devotion and abstinence. To observe the Ecclesiastical Customs and Ceremonies established, and that without obstinacy or contradiction. To repair unto the public service of the Church for Matins and Evensong, with other Holy Offices at times appointed, unless there be a just and an unfeigned cause to the contrary. To receive the Blessed Sacrament of the Body and Blood of Christ with frequent devotion, and three times a year at least, of which times Easter to be always one. And for better preparation thereunto, as occasion is, to unburden and quit our consciences of those sins that may grieve us, or scruples that may trouble us, to a learned and discreet Priest, and from him to receive advice, and the benefit of Absolution. (John Cosin, *A Collection of Private Devotions*, 1560, Works, LACT II, p. 121; *Angl.*, p. 612)*

The Apostolic Constitutions provided this daily ordering of prayer:

Offer up your prayers in the morning at the third hour, the sixth, the ninth, the evening, and at cock-crowing: in the morning, returning thanks that the Lord has sent you light, that He has brought you past the night, and brought on the day; at the third hour, because at that hour the Lord received the sentence of condemnation from Pilate; at the sixth, because at that hour He was crucified; at the ninth, because all things were in commotion at the crucifixion of the Lord. . . . In the evening, giving thanks that He has given you the night to rest from the daily labours; at cock-crowing, because that hour brings the good news of the coming on of the day. . . . If it be not possible to assemble either in the church or in a house, let every one by himself sing, and read, and pray, or two or three together. (*Constitutions of the Holy Apostles*, Bk. VIII, sec. IV, Ch. xxxiv, ANF VII, p. 496)

Biblical grounds for the three-fold pattern of daily prayer were set forth by Tertullian. He thought that such a daily order would assist in tearing us away from temporal engagements to strengthen communion with God:

The first infusion of the Holy Spirit into the congregated disciples took place at "the third hour." Peter, on the day on which he experienced the vision of Universal Community exhibited in that small vessel, had ascended into the upper parts of the house, for prayer's sake "at the sixth hour" (Acts 10:9). He was going into the temple with John "at the ninth hour" (Acts 3:1) when he restored the paralytic to his health. Even though these practices stand simply without any precept for their observance, still it may be granted that they establish a definite presumption, which may both add stringency to the admonition to pray, and may, as if by command, tear us out from our businesses to such a duty. So we too pray at least three times a day, debtors as we are to Three— Father, Son, and Holy Spirit. So did Daniel pray in accordance with Israel's discipline. (Tertullian, *On Prayer*, Ch. XXV, ANF III, p. 690)*

A model for morning prayer was provided in the Apostolic Constitutions:

O God, the God of spirits and of all flesh, who art beyond compare, and standest in need of nothing, who hast given the sun to have rule over the day, and the moon and the stars to have rule over the night, do Thou now also look down upon us with gracious eyes, and receive our morning thanksgivings. Have mercy upon us. For we have not "spread out our hands unto a strange God" (Ps. 44:20). For there is not among us any new God, but Thou, the eternal God who art without end, who hast given us being through Christ, and given us our wellbeing through Him. Grant us, we pray, eternal life through Him; with whom glory, and honour, and worship be to Thee and to the Holy Spirit for ever. Amen. (*Constitutions of the Holy Apostles*, Bk. IV, sec. IV, Ch. xxxviii, ANF VII, p. 497)*

John Climacus thought that the beginning of the day required a significant spiritual discipline, so as to begin the redeeming and transforming of the rest of the day:

There is an evil spirit, called the forerunner, who assails us as soon as we awake from sleep and defiles our first thought. Devote the first-fruits of your day to the Lord, because the whole day will belong to whomever gets the first start. It is worth hearing what an expert told me: "From my morning," he said, "I know the course of the whole day." (John Climacus, *Ladder of Divine Ascent*, Step 26, sec. 104, p. 177)

Origen reflected on spiritual refreshment through prayer at midday:

Midday denotes those secret places of the heart in which the soul pursues the clearer light of knowledge from the Word of

God; for midday is the time when the sun is at the zenith of its course. . . . God appeared to [Abraham] at the oak of Mambre, as he was sitting at the door of his tent at midday. . . . He will have this midday time within himself; and, being set as it were in the noon through this purity of heart, he will see God as he sits by the oak of Mambre, which means From Seeing.

With regard to the time of vision, then, he "sits at midday" who puts himself at leisure in order to see God. (Origen, *The Song of Songs*, CWS, pp. 225-26)

The Apostolic Constitutions provided a pattern for offering thanks in the evening:

O God, who art without beginning and without end, the Maker of the whole world by Christ, and the Provider for it, but before all His God and Father, the Lord of the Spirit, and the King of intelligible and sensible beings; who hast made the day for the works of light, and the night for the refreshment of our infirmity,—for "the day is Thine, the night also is Thine: Thou has prepared the light and the sun" (Ps. 74:16)—do Thou now, O Lord, Thou lover of mankind, and Fountain of all good, mercifully accept of this our evening thanksgiving. Thou who has brought us through the length of the day, and hast brought us to the beginnings of the night, preserve us by Thy Christ, afford us a peaceable evening, and a night free from sin, and vouchsafe us everlasting life by Thy Christ, through whom glory, honour, and worship be to Thee in the Holy Spirit for ever. Amen. (*Constitutions of the Holy Apostles*, Bk. VIII, sec. IV, Ch. xxxvii, ANF VII, p. 496)

It is fitting that preaching be correlated with the seasons of the Christian year:

Let every preacher in his parish take care to explicate to the people the mysteries of the great festivals, as of Christmas, Easter, Ascension-day, Whitsunday, Trinity Sunday, the Annunciation of the blessed Virgin Mary; because these feasts, containing in them the great fundamentals of our faith, will, with most advantage, convey the mysteries to the people, and fix them in the memories, by the solemnity and circumstances of the day. (Jeremy Taylor, *RAC*, Bk. IV, sec. 61; *CS*, p. 20)

It is a pastoral responsibility to clarify the sequence of events and celebrations of the Christian year. Izaac Walton recalled that George Herbert did this exceptionally well in his exemplary ministry:

He instructed them also what benefit they had by the Church's appointing the celebration of Holy-days, and the excellent use of them; namely, that they were set apart for particular commemorations of particular mercies received from Almighty God; and (as Reverend Mr. Hooker says) to be the landmarks to distinguish times. For by them we are taught to take notice how time passes by us. . . . Namely, at our Christmas, a day in which we commemorate His Birth, with joy and praise; and that eight days after this happy Birth, we celebrate His Circumcision; namely, in that which we call New-year's Day. And that upon that day which we call Twelfth-Day, we commemorate the manifestation of the unsearchable riches of Jesus to the Gentiles. . . . By the Lent-Fast we imitate and commemorate our Saviour's humiliation in fasting forty days; and, that we ought to endeavour to be like Him in purity. And, that on Good-Friday we commemorate and condole His Crucifixion. And at Easter, commemorate His glorious Resurrection. And he taught them, that after Jesus had manifested Himself to His Disciples to be that Christ that was crucified, dead and buried; and by His appearing and conversing with His Disciples for the space of forty days after His Resurrection, He then, and not till then, ascended into Heaven, in the sight of those Disciples,—namely, on that day which we call the Ascension, or Holy Thursday. And that we then celebrate the performance of the promise which He made to His Disciples, at or before His Ascension,—namely, that though He left them, yet He would send them the Holy Ghost to be their Comforter; and that he did so on that day which the Church calls Whitsunday. Thus the Church keeps an historical and circular commemoration of times, as they pass by us, of such times as ought to incline us to occasional praises, for the particular blessings which we do, or might, receive by those holy Commemorations. (Isaac Walton, *Life of Rev. George Herbert*, pp. 295-303; *Angl.*, p. 732)

This sabbath prayer of early Christian communities shows how profoundly the Christian tradition had reappropriated and transmuted the Jewish sabbath:

O Lord Almighty, Thou hast created the world by Christ, and hast appointed the Sabbath in memory thereof, because that on that day Thou hast made us rest from our works, for the meditation upon Thy laws. Thou hast also appointed festivals for the rejoicing of our souls that we might come into the remembrance of that wisdom which is created by Thee. . . . Thou didst enjoin the observation of the Sabbath, not affording them an occasion of idleness, but an opportunity of piety, for their knowledge of Thy power, and the prohibition of evils; having limited them as within an holy circuit for the sake of doctrine, for the rejoicing upon the seventh period. On this account was there appointed one week, and seven weeks, and the seventh month, and the seventh year, and the revolution of these, the jubilee, which is the fiftieth year for remission, that men might have no occasion to pretend ignorance. On this account He permitted men every Sabbath to rest, that so no one might be willing to send one word out of his mouth in anger on the day of the Sabbath. For the Sabbath is the ceasing of the creation, the completion of the world, the inquiry after laws, and the grateful praise to God for the blessings He has bestowed upon men. (*Constitutions of the Holy Apostles*, Bk. VII, sec. I, Ch. xxxvi, ANF VII, p. 474)

Care of souls permits the rest of souls. We rest that God may better work in us:

On the seventh day God rested and ceased from all His works, which He had made. . . . This Sabbath has now for us been changed into the Sunday, and the other days are called work-days; the Sunday is called rest-day or holiday or holy day. . . . This rest or ceasing from labors is of two kinds, bodily and spiritual. . . . The bodily rest is that of which we have spoken above, namely, that we omit our business and work, in order that we may gather in the church, see mass, hear God's Word and make common prayer. . . . For, as we see, the priests and clergy celebrate mass every day, pray at all hours and train themselves in God's Word by study, reading and hearing. For this reason also they are freed from work before others, supported by tithes and have holy-day every day, and every day do the works of the holy-day, and have no work-day, but for them one day is as the other. And if we were all perfect, and knew the Gospel, we might work every day if we wished, or rest if we could. For a day of rest is at present not necessary nor commanded except only for the teaching of God's Word and prayer.

This spiritual rest, which God particularly intends in this Commandment, is this: that we not only cease from our labor and trade, but much more, that we let God alone work in us. (Luther, *Treatise on Good Works*, WML I, pp. 240-241)

XVI ❧ ON MUSIC AND THE CARE OF SOULS

The work of pastoral care through worship has depended significantly upon the gift of music. No period of Christian care of souls has proceeded without music.

Athanasius brilliantly described how music affects the soul. As the ideas of the soul are known through words, the feelings of the soul are expressed through music. The soul becomes united through music. The soul may be moved by the Spirit analogous to a musical instrument being plucked by a musician.

As in music the pluck is used to strike the string, so the human soul may in music become like a stringed instrument completely devoted to the Spirit, so that in all one's members and emotions one is thoroughly responsive to the will of God. The harmonious reading of the Psalms is a figure and type of such undisturbed and calm equanimity of our thoughts. For just as we discover the ideas of the soul and communicate them through the words we put forth, so also the Lord, wishing the melody of the words to be a symbol of the spiritual harmony in a soul, has provided that the odes may be chanted tunefully, and the Psalms recited with song. The desire of the soul is this—to be beautifully disposed, as it is written: "Is anyone among you cheerful? Let him sing praise" (Jas. 5:13). In this way that which is disturbing and rough and disorderly in it is smoothed away, and that which causes grief is healed when we sing psalms. . . .

The melody of the phrases is brought forth from the soul's good order and from the concord with the Spirit. The singers who sing not only with words, but also with understanding may greatly benefit not only themselves but those who hear them. Blessed David, making music in this way for Saul, was himself well pleasing to God. He drove away from Saul the troubled and frenzied disposition, making his soul calm. Similarly, liturgists who are able to sing in this way are summoning the souls of the people into tranquility, and calling them into harmonious accord with those who form the heavenly chorus. Psalms are not recited with melodies merely to make pleasant sounds. Rather, this is a sure sign of the harmony of the soul's reflections. Indeed, the melodic psalmody is a symbol of the mind's well-ordered and undisturbed condition. The praising of God in well-tuned cymbals and harp and ten-stringed instrument was again a figure and sign of the parts of the body coming into natural concord like harp strings. When this happens, the thoughts of the soul become like cymbals. Body and soul then live and move and have their being in unity together through this grand sound, as if through the command of the Spirit, so, as it is written, one overcomes the dying of the body through life in the Spirit. One who sings praise beautifully brings rhythm to the soul. By this means one leads the soul from disproportion to proportion. The result is that the encouraged soul loses fear, thinks on good things, and embraces the future. Gaining composure by the singing of praises, the soul transcends the life of passions, and joyfully beholds according to the mind of Christ the most excellent thoughts. (Athanasius, A Letter To Marcellinus, ACW 10, pp. 124-126)*

By the fourth century, the praise of God was being chanted, and music regarded as a model of proportionality, resonance, harmony, and unity for the soul. The passionate discord of the body is brought into unity through music. The congregation was eschatologically viewed as singing in harmony with the angelic hosts.

There were at least two hypotheses about why music serves the care of souls. One was a purely aesthetic explanation, and the other, preferred by Athanasius, combined an aesthetic with a theological explanation on the relation of the soul and the passions. Athanasius was asking why scriptures are chanted and sung rather than merely read:

It is important not to pass over the question of why words of this kind are chanted with melodies and strains. For some of the simple among us, although they believe indeed that the phrases are divinely inspired, imagine also, on account of the sweetness of sound, that the psalms are rendered musically for the sake of the ear's delight. But this is not so. For Scripture did not seek out that which is pleasant and winning as an end in itself, but this also has been fashioned for the benefit of the soul, for many reasons, but especially two: First, because it is fitting for the Divine Scripture to praise God not in compressed speech alone, but also in the voice that is richly broadened.... The second reason is that, just as harmony that unites flutes effects a single sound, so also, seeing that different movements appear in the soul—including the power of reasoning, eager appetite, high-spirited passion, and the motivations that shape the active parts of the body—the reason intends man neither to be discordant in himself, nor to be at variance with himself.... In order that such confusion not occur in us, the reason intends the soul that possesses the mind of Christ, as the Apostle said, to use music as a guide (1 Cor. 14:15), and by it both to be a master of its passions and to govern the body's members, so as to comply with reason. (Athanasius, A Letter to Marcellinus, ACW 10, pp. 123-124)*

The notion that music has therapeutic value was strongly advanced by Luther. Music fights mightily against the demons of the heart:

Experience testifies that, after the Word of God, music alone deserves to be celebrated as mistress and queen of the emotions of the human heart (of animals nothing is to be said at present). And by these emotions men are controlled and often swept away as by their lords. A greater praise of music than this we cannot conceive. For if you want to revive the sad, startle the jovial, encourage the despairing, humble the conceited, pacify the raving, mollify the hate-filled—and who is able to enumerate all the lords of the human heart, I mean the emotions of the heart and the urges which incite a man to all virtues and vices?—what can you find that is more efficacious than music? (Luther, WA 50, p. 371f; WLS 2, pp. 982-983)

This is why it is pertinent for the pastor to encourage the nurture of souls through music. Izaac Walton wrote of the Anglican pastor and poet, George Herbert:

His chiefest recreation was music, in which heavenly art he was a most excellent master and did himself compose many Divine Hymns and Anthems, which he set and sung to his lute or viol; and, though he was a lover of retiredness, yet his love to music was such that he went usually twice every week on certain appointed days to the Cathedral Church in Salisbury; and at his return would say that his time spent in prayer and Cathedral music elevated his soul, and was his Heaven upon earth. But before his return thence to Bemerton, he would usually sing and play his part at an appointed private music-meeting; and, to justify this practice, he would often say, Religion does not banish mirth, but only moderates and sets rules to it. (Isaac Walton, *Life of Rev. George Herbert*, p. 303; *Angl.*, p. 735)

Since music speaks to human afflictions, it is especially pertinent to pastoral care:

How sweetly doth this music sound, in this dead season! In the day-time, it would not, it could not, so much affect the ear. All harmonious sounds are advanced by a silent darkness.

Thus is it with the glad tidings of salvation. The Gospel never sounds so sweet, as in the night of persecution or of our own private affliction. It is ever the same. The difference is, in our disposition to receive it.

O God, Whose praise it is to give songs in the night, make my prosperity conscionable and my crosses cheerful. (Joseph Hall, Occasional Meditations, 44, Works, XI, p. 94; *Angl.*, p. 763)

Methodius invited all Christians to enter fully into song and music and hear God's own speech through them:

Let every one come, then, and hear the divine song [of the prophets] without any fear. . . . For it is worthy of us to hear such a song as this; and to hear such singers as these seems to me to be a thing to be prayed for. But if one wishes to hear the choir of the apostles as well, he will find the same harmony of song. For the others sang beforehand the divine plan in a mystical manner; but these sing an interpretation of what has been mystically announced by the former. Oh, concordant harmony, composed by the Divine Spirit! Oh, the comeliness of those who sing the mysteries of God! Oh, that I also may join in these songs in my prayer. Let us then also sing the like song, and raise the hymn to the Holy Father, glorifying in the Spirit Jesus, who is in His bosom. Shun not, man, a spiritual hymn, nor be ill disposed to listen to it. (Methodius, *Concerning Free-Will*, ANF VI, p. 356)

Athanasius offered this counsel for singers, a simple but significant contribution to the interpretation of song: Sing out of the depths of oneself, not as though these words addressed to another, but personally to you.

After the prophecies about the Savior and the nations, he who recites the Psalms is uttering the rest as his own words, and each sings them as if they were written concerning him, and he accepts them and recites them not as if another were speaking, nor as if speaking about someone else. But he handles them as if he is speaking about himself. And the things spoken are such that he lifts them up to God as himself acting and speaking them from himself. (Athanasius, A Letter to Marcellinus, ACW 10, sec. 11, p. 110)

Luther speculated on why the prophets practiced music more than any other form of art:

I firmly believe, nor am I ashamed to assert, that next to theology no art is equal to music; for it is the only one, except theology, which is able to give a quiet and happy mind. This is manifestly proved by the fact that the devil, the author of depressing care and distressing disturbances, almost flees from the sound of music as he does from the word of theology. This is the reason why the prophets practiced music more than any art and did not put their theology into geometry, into arithmetic, or into astronomy, but into music, intimately uniting theology and music, telling the truth in psalms and songs. (Luther, "Letters of 1528-1530," WA-Br 5, p. 639; WLS 2, p. 983; cf. LW 49, p. 428)

Can music-haters be trusted?

I am not satisfied with him who despises music, as all fanatics do; for music is an endowment and a gift of God, not a gift of men. It also drives away the devil and makes people cheerful; one forgets all anger, unchasteness, pride, and other vices. I place music next to theology and give it the highest praise. (Luther, W-T 6, #7034; WLS 2, #3091, p. 980)

The Synod of Quinisext was concerned with the quality and kind of music that was employed within the church:

We will that those whose office it is to sing in the churches do not use undisciplined vociferations, nor force nature to shouting, nor adopt any of those modes which are incongruous and unsuitable for the church. (Synod of Quinisext, A.D. 692, Canon LXXV, The Seven Ecumenical Councils, NPNF 2, XIV, p. 398)

Selections in Part Three have focussed upon pastoral care through prayer. Soul care occurs within a caring community whose primary corporate act is the praise of God's care. Guidance of the service of prayer is an indispensable aspect of pastoral guidance. The soul is nurtured in worship through praise, thanksgiving, confession, timely admonition, earnest petition for peace and justice, intercession, preaching of the gospel and law, and scriptural study correlated with the needs of the times. Public worship requires forethought, decorum, and organization necessary for a public occasion that bespeaks its importance and its meaning. Pastoral prayer holds up before God the needs of the people. Instruction in the practice of prayer is a pastoral responsibility, the Lord's Prayer being a primary pattern. The ordering of worship in time and space requires pastoral responsibility in guiding the worshipping community through the seasons of the Christian year, and the maintenance of a proper space for worship. Music is an inestimable dimension of the care of souls.

4 Pastoral Care Through Baptism: The Ministry of Beginnings

CARE OF SOULS precedes baptism in one sense, for much that the pastor does leads up to baptism. Yet in another sense, the care of souls within the Christian community begins with baptism. For in baptism new life in the caring community is visibly manifested. Baptism marks a starting point in the care of a particular person within the community of faith. The personal name traditionally given in baptism marks the receiving of an identity within the healing, redemptive family of God.

Whether pastoral care precedes or follows baptism, there can be no doubt that the ministry of baptism is a central act of pastoral service, a crucial moment in the care of souls. The classical pastoral writers thought carefully about baptism as an act of pastoral care. They understood why the care-giving counselor is also baptizer, and why these two acts belong together. They reflected deliberately about how the pastor is to prepare recipients for baptism, what baptism is, why baptism is essentially a pastoral act, the effects of baptism, and the meaning of confirmation of one's baptism.

I ❧ CARE-GIVER AS BAPTIZER

It is not an incidental point that the same one who offers counsel to troubled souls also serves as liturgical agent to bring, by means of the rite of baptism, souls into the fellowship of believers. The care-giver is baptizer.

Luther thought frequently of his baptism, derived great comfort from it, and commended to others the recollection of their baptism as a central consolation of life in Christ:

It will, therefore, be no small gain for a penitent to lay hold before all else on the memory of his baptism, confidently to call to mind the promise of God. . . . His soul will find wondrous comfort, and will be encouraged to hope for mercy, when he considers that the divine promise which God made to him and which

107

cannot possibly lie, still stands unbroken and unchanged, yea, unchangeable by any sins; as Paul says in 2 Timothy 2:13, "If we are faithless, he keeps faith, for he cannot deny himself." Ay, this truth of God will sustain him, so that if all else should sink in ruins, this truth, if he believe it, will not fail him. For in it he has a shield against all assaults of the enemy, an answer to the sins that disturb his conscience, an antidote for the dread of death and judgment, and a comfort in every temptation,—namely, this one truth,—and he can say, "God is faithful that promised, Whose sign I have received in my baptism. If God be for me, who is against me?" (cf. Rom. 6-8).

The children of Israel, whenever they repented of their sins, turned their thoughts first of all to the exodus from Egypt, and, remembering this, returned to God Who had brought them out. This memory and this refuge were many times impressed upon them by Moses, and afterward repeated by David. How much rather ought we to call to mind our exodus from Egypt, and, remembering, turn back again to Him Who led us forth through the washing of regeneration, which we are bidden remember for this very purpose. (Luther, *The Babylonian Captivity*, WML II, pp. 221-222, NEB)*

If baptism has this high order of importance in the comfort of the soul amid affliction, then the teaching of its recollection surely is a significant task of the pastoral teaching office. Yet what exactly is to be learned from baptism? It is fundamentally such a simple act. Tertullian examined the question of whether the very simplicity of baptism was potentially somewhat misleading:

There is absolutely nothing which makes men's minds more obdurate than the simplicity of the divine works which are visible in the act, when compared with the grandeur which is promised thereto in the effect; so that from the very fact, that with so great simplicity, without pomp, without any considerable novelty of preparation, finally, without expense, a man is dipped in water, and amid the utterance of some few words, is sprinkled, and then rises again, not much (or not at all) the cleaner, the consequent attainment of eternity is esteemed the more incredible. . . . Is it not wonderful, too, that death should be washed away by bathing? But it is the more to be believed if the wonderfulness be the reason why it is not believed. . . . Incredulity, on the other hand, wonders, but does not believe. For the simple acts it wonders at, it views as if they were vain; the grand results, as if they were impossible. And grant that it be just as you think, sufficient to meet each point is the divine declaration which precedes it: "Yet to shame the wise, God has chosen what the world counts folly" (1 Cor. 1:27), and, "What is impossible for men is possible for God" (Luke 18:27). (Tertullian, *On Baptism*, Ch. II, ANF III, p. 669, NEB)*

Faith celebrates the simplicity of baptism as consistent with God's own wisdom. The pastoral writers who have in fact been grasped by the simple mystery of baptism have pondered why something so common as water has become the central sign of entry and initiation into the believing community. Gregory of Nyssa, in defining baptism as cleansing from sin, described the renewal of spirit that accompanies it. He employed a medicinal metaphor, viewing baptism as a two-fold remedy for body and soul:

Baptism is a purification of sins, a remission of transgressions, a cause of renovation and regeneration. By regeneration you must understand a regeneration perceived by thought, not observed by the eyes. . . . For just as the new-born infant is free from accusations and penalties, so too the child of regeneration has no charges to answer, being released from accountability by kingly bounty. It is not the water that bestows this bounty (for then it would be exalted above all creation), but the commandment of God and the intervention of the Spirit, which comes sacramentally to give us liberty. But water has a part to play, by giving an outward sign of the purification. For when our body has been soiled by dirt and mud it is our practice to make it clean by washing in water. We therefore use water in the sacramental action also, signifying, by something perceived by the senses, a shining cleanliness which is not a bodily cleanliness. . . . Man, as we very well know, is composite, not simple: and therefore, for the healing of this twofold and conjunct being, medicines are assigned which suit and resemble his double nature. For his visible body, the sensible water; for his invisible soul, the unseen Spirit, invoked by faith, which comes in a fashion we cannot describe. (Gregory of Nyssa, LCF, p. 161)

Since the human malaise pervades both body and soul, the remedy, baptism, is applied by analogy at two levels, being signified by water, a visible, physical entity, yet what is signified is the renewing activity of the Holy Spirit who enlivens the soul with eternal life. In the Westminster Confession we find a concise Protestant summary of the ministry of baptism. It affirms its divine institution, its elements, meaning, modes, necessity, and effects:

Baptism is a sacrament of the New Testament, ordained by Jesus Christ, not only for the solemn admission of the party baptized into the visible Church, but also to be unto him a sign and seal of the covenant of grace, of his ingrafting into Christ, of regeneration, of remission of sins, and of his giving up unto God, through Jesus Christ, to walk in newness of life: which sacrament is, by Christ's own appointment, to be continued in his Church until the end of the world.

The outward element to be used in this sacrament is water, wherewith the party is to be baptized in the name of the Father, and of the Son, and of the Holy Ghost, by a minister of the gospel lawfully called thereunto.

Dipping of the person into the water is not necessary; but baptism is rightly administered by pouring or sprinkling water upon the person.

Not only those that do actually profess faith in and obedience unto Christ, but also the infants of one or both believing parents are to be baptized.

Although it be a great sin to condemn or neglect this ordinance, yet grace and salvation are not so inseparably annexed unto it, as that no person can be regenerated or saved without it, or that all that are baptized are undoubtedly regenerated.

The efficacy of baptism is not tied to that moment of time wherein it is administered; yet, notwithstanding, by the right use of this ordinance the grace promised is not only offered, but really exhibited and conferred by the Holy Ghost, to such (whether of age or infants) as that grace belongeth unto, according to the counsel of God's own will, in his appointed time.

The sacrament of baptism is but once to be administered to any person. (Westminister Confession, Ch. XXVIII, sec. i-vii, *C*, p. 225)

As the doctrine of the triune God is a summary of Christian teaching, so baptism epitomizes and displays the sum of ecumenical faith. For baptism from its beginnings has been conferred in the name of the Father, the Son, and the Holy Spirit. Early Christian theologies were largely a commentary on the baptismal formula. It was not the other way around, that the theologies were first developed, and then the baptismal formula later summarized them. Rather one can rightly say that Christian theology fundamentally began as a lengthy set of footnotes on the baptismal formula which preceeded all deliberate Christian doctrinal formulation. All the heresies against which early pastoral care had to struggle were essentially offenses against the baptismal formula.

If any bishop or presbyter does not baptize according to the Lord's constitution, into the Father, the Son, and the Holy Ghost, but into three beings without beginning, or into three Sons, or three Comforters, let him be deprived. (*Constitutions of the Holy Apostles*, Ecclesiastical Canons, Bk. VIII, sec. v, Canon 49, ANF VII, p. 503)

Baptism is intrinsically connected with orthodox faith, and definitive of the apostolic witness, according to the Council of Chalcedon:

This is the orthodox faith; this we all believe: into this we were baptized; into this we baptize. (Chalcedon, A.D. 451, Extracts, Session II, The Seven Ecumenical Councils, NPNF 2, XIV, p. 249)

Even though baptism has always been regarded as a solemn event, it has always been equally viewed as an incomparably happy occasion:

Happy is our sacrament of water, in that, by washing away the sins of our early blindness, we are set free and admitted into eternal life! (Tertullian, *On Baptism*, Ch. I, ANF III, p. 669)

Cyril's Catechetical Lectures compared the happiness of baptism with that of a wedding:

Let those souls get themselves ready, that are about to be wed to their spiritual Bridegroom. For lo! "the voice of one crying in the wilderness, Make ready the way of the Lord" (Isa. 40:3). For this wedding is no light matter, nor the usual and undiscriminating union of bodies, but is the election by faith made by "the Spirit that searcheth all things" (1 Cor. 2:10). For the espousals and marriage-contracts of this world are not invariably well-judged, but where there is wealth or beauty there the suitor is quick to give his hand. But in this wedding, it is not physical beauty, but the blameless conscience of the soul that engages. (Cyril of Jerusalem, *The Catechetical Lectures*, Lect. III, sec. 2, LCC IV, p. 90)

Among church fathers who have discussed baptism as a pastoral act with far-reaching implications for soul care, few have been more astute than Tertullian, who astutely sought to avoid misunderstandings of the teaching. One such potential misunderstanding appeared implicit in Paul's writings: If Abraham had faith sufficient without baptism, why cannot we also?

Some say, "Baptism is not necessary for them to whom faith is sufficient. For did not Abraham please God by a sacrament of no water, but of faith?" (cf. Rom. 4:9). . . . Grant that, in days gone by, there was salvation by means of bare faith, before the passion and resurrection of the Lord. But now that faith has been enlarged, and is become a faith which believes in His nativity, passion, and resurrection, there has been an amplification added by means of the sealing act of baptism. It is in some sense like the clothing of the faith that before was bare, and which cannot exist now without its proper law. For the law of baptizing has been imposed, and the formula prescribed: "Go forth therefore," He said, "and make all nations my disciples; baptize men everywhere in the name of the Father and the Son and the Holy Spirit" (Matt. 28:19). (Tertullian, *On Baptism*, Ch. XIII, ANF III, p. 676, NEB)*

Later, Augustine refined the same question, whether baptism is all that is needed for salvation, and whether conversion of the heart nullifies the necessity of baptism:

This all shows that the sacrament of baptism is one thing, the conversion of the heart is another; but the salvation of man is effected by these two. If one is missing, we are not bound to suppose that the other is absent: in an infant, baptism can exist without conversion; in the penitent thief, conversion without baptism. (Augustine, *On Baptism*, Ch. 4, sec. 31, 32, LCF, p. 243; cf. NPNF 1, IV, pp. 461f.)

II ❧ THE RECIPIENTS OF BAPTISM

The pastoral writers have puzzled over the complex interfacing of the divine will and human willing in baptism. It is of great significance to the comfort of the soul, thought Luther, that baptism is primarily God's work, and the human side of the action is primarily receptivity to the divine activity:

It is a work of God, not of man, as Paul teaches. The other works He works through us and with our help, but this one He works in us and without our help.

From this we can clearly see the difference, in baptism, between man the minister and God the Doer. For man baptises and does not baptise: he baptises, for he performs the work, immersing the person to be baptised; he does not baptise, for in that act he officiates not by his own authority, but in the stead of God. . . . This the words themselves indicate, when the priest says: "I baptise thee in the Name of the Father, and of the Son, and of the

Holy Ghost. Amen"—and not: "I baptise thee in my own name." It is as though he said: "What I do, I do not by my own authority, but in the name and stead of God, so that you should regard it just as if our Lord Himself had done it in a visible manner. The Doer and the minister are different persons, but the work of both is the same work, or, rather, it is the work of the Doer alone, through my ministry."... There is much of comfort and a mighty aid to faith in the knowledge that one has been baptised not by man, but by the Triune God Himself through a man acting among us in His name. (Luther, *The Babylonian Captivity*, WML II, pp. 224-225)

Since Paul at one point stated that he had been sent to preach, not to baptize, the question emerged as to why other clergy should not do likewise. Tertullian provided a classical response:

But they roll back an objection from that apostle himself, in that he said, "Christ did not send me to baptize, but to proclaim the Gospel" (1 Cor. 1:17) as if by this argument baptism were done away with! For if so, why did he baptize Gaius, and Crispus, and the house of Stephanas? However, even if Christ had not sent him to baptize, yet He had given other apostles the command to baptize. But these words were written to the Corinthians in regard of the circumstances of that particular time, when schisms and dissensions were agitated among them, while one was attributing everything to Paul, another to Apollos. For this reason the "peacemaking" apostle, for fear he should seem to claim all gifts for himself, says that he had been sent "not to baptize, but to proclaim." For preaching is the prior thing, baptizing the posterior. Therefore the preaching came first, but there can be no doubt that baptism was also authorized to one to whom preaching was authorized. (Tertullian, *On Baptism*, Ch. XIV, ANF III, p. 676, NEB)*

The question of how early baptism may be administered has remained a point of dispute among various interpreters. That the baptism of infants was practiced is seen from the Apostolic Constitutions:

Baptize your infants, and bring them up in the nurture and admonition of God. For says He: "Suffer the little children to come unto me, and forbid them not" (Matt. 19:14). (*Constitutions of the Holy Apostles*, Bk. VI, sec. III, Ch. xv, ANF VII, p. 457)*

Assuming that faith is prior to baptism, Augustine attempted to solve the dilemma of infant baptism by pointing to surrogate faith in the parents:

At this point men are wont to ask what good the sacrament of Christ's Baptism can do to infants, seeing that many of them die after having been baptized but before they can know anything about it. In this case it is pious and right to believe that the infant is benefited by the faith of those who bring him to be consecrated. This is commended by the salutary authority of the Church, so that everyone may realize how beneficial to him is his faith, seeing that one man's faith can be made beneficial for another who has no faith of his own. The son of the widow of Nain could have had no advantage from any faith of his own, for, being dead, he had no faith. But his mother's faith procured him the benefit of being raised from the dead (Luke 7:11ff). (Augustine, *On Free Will*, Bk. III, Ch. xxiii.67, LCC VI, p. 211)

Luther agreed with Augustine. In addressing the issue of the baptism of children, Luther's stress is upon the sovereign power of God to carry out his intention:

In contradiction of what has been said, some will perhaps point to the baptism of infants, who do not grasp the promise of God and cannot have the faith of baptism; so that either faith is not necessary or else infant baptism is without effect. Here I say what all say: Infants are aided by the faith of others, namely, those who bring them to baptism. For the Word of God is powerful, when it is uttered, to change even a godless heart, which is no less deaf and helpless than any infant. Even so the infant is changed, cleansed and renewed by inpoured faith, through the prayer of the Church that presents it for baptism and believes, to which prayer all things are possible. (Luther, *The Babylonian Captivity*, WML II, pp. 236-237)

However simply baptism has sought to manifest the unity of the body of Christ, it has often become a point of sharp controversy. Through successive historical crises, the pastoral tradition sought to define consensually the proper administration of baptism. This passage from Tertullian shows evidence that as early as the second century intense debates about baptism were going on: Who shall be baptized? What is the proper time for baptism? Should baptism be long delayed by penitents?

But they whose office it is, know that baptism is not rashly to be administered. . . . This precept is rather to be looked at carefully: "Give not the holy thing to the dogs, nor cast your pearls before swine" (Matt. 7:6). . . . "But," some say, "Paul too was, in fact, 'speedily' baptized:" for Simon, [sic, Ananias] his host, speedily recognized him to be "an appointed vessel of election" (Acts 9:15). God's approbation sends sure premonitory tokens before it; every "petition" may both deceive and be deceived. And so, according to the circumstances and disposition, and even age, of each individual, the delay of baptism is preferable; principally, however, in the case of little children. . . . The Lord does indeed say, "Forbid them not to come unto me" (Matt 19:14). Let them "come," then, while they are growing up; let them become Christians when they have become able to know Christ. . . . If any understand the weighty import of baptism, they will fear its reception more than its delay. (Tertullian, *On Baptism*, Ch. XVIII, ANF III, p. 677)*

In speaking of Simon, Tertullian apparently confused him with the "Judas" with whom Saul stayed (Acts 9:11); but it was Ananias who recognized him as "an appointed vessel." Tertullian's view on this matter did not become consensually received, but it remained a significant minority view. He argued that, given the hazards of sin after baptism, it is better to delay than hasten baptism. Tertullian also concluded that under conditions of necessity, lay persons could confer baptism, but that it was more fittingly conferred by those duly ordained for its administration:

Even laymen have the right; for what is equally received can be equally given. Unless bishops, or priests, or deacons, be on the spot, other disciples are called, i.e., to the work. The word of the Lord ought not to be hidden by any: in like manner, too, baptism, which is equally God's property, can be administered by all. But how much more is the rule of reverence and modesty incumbent on laymen—seeing that these powers belong to their superiors. . . . "all things are lawful, but not all expedient" (1 Cor. 10:23). Let it suffice assuredly, in cases of necessity, to avail yourself (of that rule), if at any time circumstance either of place, or of time, or of person compels you (so to do); for then the steadfast courage of the succourer, when the situation of the endangered one is urgent, is exceptionally admissible. (Tertullian, *On Baptism*, Ch. XVII, ANF III, p. 677)

Suppose one has already been baptized, yet, having strayed from faith, wishes to be baptized again. How have the pastoral writers responded to the possibility of re-baptism? Tertullian summarized the prevailing view:

We enter, then, the font once: once are sins washed away, because they ought never to be repeated. (Tertullian, *On Baptism*,
Ch. XV, ANF III, p. 676)

This question was framed by a Pre-Nicene anonymous writer:

I observe that it has been asked among the brethren what
course ought specially to be adopted towards the persons of those
who although baptized in heresy, have yet been baptized in the
name of our Lord Jesus Christ, and subsequently departing from
their heresy, and fleeing as supplicants to the Church of God,
should repent with their whole hearts, and only now perceiving
the condemnation of their error, implore from the Church the
help of salvation. The point is whether, according to the most ancient custom and ecclesiastical tradition, it would suffice, after
that baptism which they have received outside the Church indeed,
but still in the name of Jesus Christ our Lord, that only hands
should be laid upon them by the bishop for their reception of the
Holy Spirit, and this imposition of hands would afford them the
renewed and perfected seal of faith; or whether, indeed, a repetition of baptism would be necessary for them, as if they should
receive nothing if they had not obtained baptism afresh, just as if
they were never baptized in the name of Jesus Christ. (Anonymous, *A Treatise on Re-Baptism*, s c. I, ANF V, p. 667)

An ongoing controversy accompanied the question of rebaptism. The
sharp distinction between person and office of the pastor helped Luther
conceptually with the issue:

Do not rebaptize children, as, it is true, Cyprian did. He had
the false idea that he could not consider the Baptism of heretics a
valid Baptism. Therefore he rebaptized them. But this reasoning
is wrong, for we must distinguish office from person. A public
sinner is also not in the unity of the Christian Church, and yet
the office he holds in the church is not to be despised on this
account. The reason: The office is not his but the Lord Jesus
Christ's. However, if he intended to break the command of Christ
and wanted to baptize, preach, and administer the Sacrament in
a way different from that commanded by Christ, then we would
have reason to reject his Baptism, his preaching, and other activities. But if he changes nothing that Christ has ordained, the fact
that he is personally wicked and sinful does not detract anything
from the office. (Luther, WA 52, p. 310f; WLS 2, pp. 933-934)

III ⚕ The Sign of Baptism

Some imagine a lack of sophistication concerning comparative cultural anthropology and the history of religions among classical pastoral writers. Yet there is considerable evidence that, within the boundaries of the knowledge available to them, they were thinking resourcefully and significantly about how common elements of nature and human culture become symbolically used in the history of revelation.

The symbolism of water is a case in point. Tertullian argued that we can easily see in the history of religions an abundant use of water as a cleansing or purifying analogy. He did not hesistate to view Christian baptism as standing in continuity with that history. This typological reflection is not unlike what Jung would later call an archetypal mode of consciousness. For Tertullian, water symbolized the primordial state of creation:

> We proceed to treat the question: "How foolish and impossible it is to be formed anew by water. In what respect, we ask, has this material substance merited a role of such high dignity?" I suppose it useful to examine the symbolic authority of the liquid element. It is found in abundance, and has been from the very beginning. For water is one of those things which, before all the furnishing of the world, were quiescent with God in a yet unshapen state. "In the beginning of Creation," says the Scripture, "when God made heaven and earth, the earth was without form and void, with darkness over the face of the abyss, and a mighty wind that swept over the surface of the waters" (Gen. 1:1,2). The first thing, O mortal man, that you must respect is the age of the waters, in that their very substance is ancient. The second thing you must respect is their dignity, in that they were the seat of the Divine Spirit, more pleasing to Him, no doubt, than all the other then existing elements. . . . [Others may ask:] "But do not the nations who are strangers to all understanding of spiritual powers also ascribe to their idols the imbuing of waters with the self-same efficacy?" Indeed they do. . . . For washing is the channel through which they are initiated into sacred rites—of some notorious Isis or Mithras. The gods themselves they similarly honor by washings. (Tertullian, *On Baptism*, Ch. III, IV, V, ANF III, p. 670-671, NEB)*

However universal the mystical symbolism of water may be, Tertullian warned against focussing upon water as such in teaching about baptism:

If I go forward in recounting universally from that time forward, or at more length, the evidences of the "authority" of this element, adducing how great is its power or its grace, how many ingenious devices, how many functions, how useful an instrumentality, it affords the world, I fear I may seem to have collected rather the praises of water than the reasons of baptism. Nonetheless I would be thereby teaching all the more fully that it is not to be doubted that God has made the material substance which He has disposed throughout all His products and works obey Him also in His own peculiar sacraments; and that the material substance which governs terrestrial life acts as agent likewise in the celestial.

But it will suffice to have thus called at the outset those points in which that primary principle of baptism is recognized—which was foreordained by the very attitude assumed for a type of baptism,—that the Spirit of God, who hovered over (the waters) from the beginning, would continue to linger over the waters of the baptized. (Tertullian, *On Baptism*, Ch. III-IV, ANF III, p. 670)

Water is a recurrent, multivalent biblical symbol embracing such diverse themes as primordial creation, deliverance, and purification:

Now if anyone is eager to learn why baptismal grace is given by means of water, and not by any other of the elements, he will find the answer if he takes up the Scriptures. For water is a great subject and the fairest of the four visible elements of which the world is made. . . . As water was the foundation of the world, so Jordan was the foundation of the Gospel. Israel was set free from Pharaoh by means of the sea, and the world was freed from sins "with the washing of water by the (divine) word" (Eph. 5:26). . . . The high-priest first washes and then offers the incense, for Aaron first washed with water and after that was invested as high-priest. How indeed could he properly intercede for others if he had not first been cleansed with water? (Cyril of Jerusalem, *The Catechetical Lectures*, Lect. III, sec. 5, LCC IV, pp. 92-93)

The death and resurrection theme was central for Luther in his discussion of the sign of baptism, what it signifies, and the relation of faith and baptism as follows:

The second part of baptism is the sign, or sacrament, which is that immersion into water whence also it derives its name; for the Greek *baptizo* means I immerse, and *baptisma* means immersion. For, as has been said, signs are added to the divine promises to represent that which the words signify, or, as they now say, that which the sacrament "effectively signifies." We shall see how much of truth there is in this. The great majority have supposed that there is some hidden spiritual power in the word or in the water, which works the grace of God in the soul of the recipient. Others deny this and hold that there is no power in the sacraments, but that grace is given by God alone, Who according to His covenant aids the sacraments He has instituted. Yet all are agreed that the sacraments are effective signs of grace. . . . Even so it is not baptism that justifies or benefits anyone, but it is faith in the word of promise, to which baptism is added. This faith justifies, and fulfils that which baptism signifies. For faith is the submersion of the old man and the emerging of the new. . . . Baptism, then, signifies two things—death and resurrection; that is, full and complete justification. The minister's immersing the child in the water signifies death; his drawing it forth again signifies life. Thus Paul expounds it in Romans 6:4, "By baptism we were buried with him, and lay dead, in order that, as Christ was raised from the dead in the splendour of the Father, so also we might set our feet upon the new paths of life." This death and resurrection we call the new creation, regeneration, and the spiritual birth. (Luther, *The Babylonian Captivity*, WML II, pp. 226-230, NEB)*

The pastor may be asked whether it is water in itself that is the source of regeneration and renewal. Luther answered:

It is not the water indeed that does them, but the word of God which is in and with the water, and faith, which trusts such word of God in the water. For without the word of God the water is simple water and no Baptism. But with the word of God it is a Baptism, that is a gracious water of life and a washing of regeneration in the Holy Ghost. . . . What does such baptizing with water signify? Answer: It signifies that the old Adam in us should, by daily contrition and repentance, be drowned and die with all sins and evil lusts and, again, a new man daily come forth and arise, who shall live before God in righteousness and purity forever. (Luther, *Small Catechism*, Sec. III, IV, WA 30 I, p. 285f; WLS 1, pp. 43-44)

IV ❧ PREPARATION FOR BAPTISM

Those being prepared for baptism were called catechumens (those receiving rudimentary instruction). A program of instruction was provided by pastors, called *catechesis*, or catechetical instruction, from which derives our word catechism. *Catechesis* was regarded by classical pastoral writers as a regular pastoral duty.

Tertullian's description of preparation for baptism was written in a period in which martyrdom was often the price paid for one's baptism:

> They who are about to enter baptism ought to pray with repeated prayers, fasts, and bendings of the knee, and vigils all the night through, and with the confession of all bygone sins, that they may express the meaning even of the baptism of John: "They were baptized," says the Scripture, "confessing their own sins" (Matt. 3:6). To us it is matter for thankfulness if we do now publicly confess our iniquities or turpitudes. For by doing so we at the same time are making satisfaction for our former sins by mortification of our flesh and spirit, and secondly we are laying the foundation of defences against the temptations which will closely follow. . . . Together with your brethren, ask from the Father, ask from the Lord, that His own specialties of grace and distributions of gifts may be supplied you. "Ask," Jesus says, "and ye shall receive" (Matt. 7:7). Well, you have asked, and have received; you have knocked, and it has been opened to you. Only, I pray that, when you are asking, you be mindful likewise of Tertullian the sinner. (Tertullian, *On Baptism*, Ch. XX, ANF III, pp. 678-679)

Baptismal instruction may be of benefit not only to those considering baptism, but also to those whose baptismal faith has remained for some time unexamined.

> A treatise on this matter will not be superfluous. It should instruct not only those who are just becoming newly formed in the faith, but also those who have been resting contentedly with having simply believed, yet without having fully examined the grounds of the traditions, who are trying to carry on, yet somewhat ignorantly, in an untried though probable faith. (Tertullian, *On Baptism*, Ch. I, ANF III, p. 669)*

An elementary outline of a systematic theology was provided by the Apostolic Constitutions in the proposed list of issues for examination in baptismal instruction. Such instruction apparently touched upon creation, providence, anthropology, Christology, and eschatology:

> Let the catechumens learn the order of the several parts of the creation, the sequential acts of providence, and the different dis-

pensations of the laws. Let them be instructed on why the world was made, and why human beings were appointed to be citizens in it. Let them also know of their own human nature, of what sort it is. . . . And how God still took care of and did not reject humanity. . . . Let those who offer themselves to baptism learn these and similar things during the time that they are catechumens. . . . And after this thanksgiving, let him instruct them in the doctrines concerning our Lord's incarnation, and in those concerning His passion, his resurrection from the dead, and his assumption. (*Constitutions of the Holy Apostles*, Bk. VII, sec. III, Ch. xxxix, ANF VII, pp. 475-476)*

Cyril of Jerusalem stressed the incomparable opportunity of early and sound catechetical teaching:

Think of this as being the season for planting young trees. If we do not now dig and set them deep in the earth, when can we find another opportunity for planting well what has been once planted badly? (Cyril of Jerusalem, *The Catechetical Lectures*, Procatechesis, sec. 11, LCC IV, p. 72)

The pastor is never to baptize without teaching. For the command to baptize and to teach are intrinsically welded together. Athanasius argued that bad theology has frequently emerged out of an inadequate understanding of baptism. Each heresy is, properly understood, a baptismal heresy. He illustrated this principle by viewing Arianism essentially as a baptismal heresy:

The Arians do not baptize into Father and Son, but into Creator and creature, and into Maker and work. And as a creature is other than the Son, so the Baptism, which is supposed to be given by them, is other than the truth, though they pretend to name the Name of the Father and the Son, because of the words of Scripture. For not he who simply says, "O Lord," gives Baptism; but he who with the Name has also the right faith. On this account therefore our Saviour also did not simply command to baptize, but first says, Teach; and then "Baptize into the Name of Father, and Son, and Holy Ghost" (Matt. 287:19); that the right faith might follow upon learning, and together with faith might come the consecration of Baptism. (Athanasius, *Discourses Against the Arians*, II, Ch. XVIII, sec. 17, NPNF 2, IV, p. 368)

The baptismal supplication found in the Apostolic Constitutions provides a glimpse of how the early church prayed for the Spirit to empower the act of baptism, so that the believer might through it share in the life, death and resurrection of Jesus:

Look down from heaven, and sanctify this water, and give it grace and power, so that he who is to be baptized, according to the command of Thy Christ, may be crucified with Him, and may die with Him, and may be buried with Him, and may rise with Him to the adoption which is in Him, that he may be dead to sin and live to righteousness. (*Constitutions of the Holy Apostles*, Bk. VII, sec. IV, Ch. xliii, ANF VII, p. 477)*

Should baptism be administered at certain seasons of the year?

The Passover affords a more than usually solemn day for baptism. For it was during the Passover that our Lord's Passion, into which we are baptized, was completed. . . . After that, Pentecost is a most joyous space for conferring baptisms. For it was at Pentecost that the resurrection of the Lord was repeatedly demonstrated among the disciples. . . . However, every day is the Lord's; every hour, every time, is apt for baptism. If there is a difference in the solemnity, there is no distinction in the grace. (Tertullian, *On Baptism*, Ch. XIX, ANF III, p. 678)*

V ❧ THE ACT OF BAPTISM

One of the earliest accounts of how the pastor confers baptism is found in the first century *Didache*. It is evident from this source that a number of issues were being debated very early that continued to be debated for many centuries: whether by immersion or sprinkling, whether by running or still water, whether fasting is presupposed:

The procedure for baptizing is as follows. After rehearsing all the preliminaries, immerse in running water "In the Name of the Father, and of the Son, and of the Holy Ghost." If no running water is available, immerse in ordinary water. This should be cold if possible; otherwise warm. If neither is practicable, then sprinkle water three times on the head "In the Name of the Father, and of the Son and of the Holy Ghost." Both baptizer and baptized ought to fast before the baptism, as well as any others who can do so; but the candidate himself should be told to keep a fast for a day or two beforehand. (*Didache*, Part 2, sec. 7, ECW, pp. 230-231)

Hippolytus (c. 170-c. 236) provided a fairly detailed account of the act of baptism:

And when they are chosen who are set apart to receive baptism let their life be examined, whether they lived piously while catechumens, whether "they honoured the widows" (1 Tim. 5:3), whether they visited the sick, whether they have fulfilled every good work.

If those who bring them bear witness to them that they have done thus, [then] let them hear the gospel. . . . [And] let those who are to be baptised be instructed to wash and cleanse themselves on the fifth day of the week. . . . Those who are to receive baptism shall fast on the Friday and on the Saturday. And on the Saturday the bishop shall assemble those who are to be baptised in one place, and shall bid them [all] to pray and bow the knee. . . . And they shall spend all the night in vigil, reading the scriptures [to them] and instructing them. . . . And at the hour when the cock crows they shall first [of all] pray over the water.

[When they come to the water, let the water be pure and flowing.]

And they shall put off their clothes.

And they shall baptise the little children first. And if they can answer for themselves, let them answer. But if they cannot, let their parents answer or someone from their family. . . . And when the presbyter takes hold of each one of those who are to be baptised, let him bid him renounce saying:

I renounce thee, Satan, and all thy service and all thy works.

And when he has said this let him anoint him with the Oil of Exorcism saying:

Let all evil spirits depart far from thee.

And also turning him to the East, let him say:

[I consent to Thee, O Father and Son and Holy Ghost, before whom all creation trembleth and is moved. Grant me to do all Thy wills without blame.]

Then after these things let him give him over to [the presbyter] who stands at the water [to baptise];

[And a presbyter takes his right hand and he turns his face to the East. Before he descends into the water, while he still turns his face to the East, standing above the water he says after receiving the Oil of Exorcism, thus: I believe and bow me unto Thee and all Thy service, O Father, Son and Holy Ghost. And so he descends into the water.]

And let them stand in the water naked. And let [a] deacon likewise go down with him into the water.

And let him say to him and instruct him: Dost thou believe in one God the Father Almighty, and His only-begotten Son Jesus Christ our Lord and our Saviour, and His Holy Spirit, Giver of life to all creatures, the Trinity of one Substance, one Godhead, one Lordship, one Kingdom, one Faith, one Baptism in the Holy Catholic Apostolic Church for life eternal [Amen]? And he who is baptised shall say [again] thus: verily, I believe.

And [when] he [who is to be baptised] goes down to the water, let him who baptises lay hand on him saying thus:

Dost thou believe in God the Father Almighty? And he who is being baptised shall say: I believe. Let him forthwith baptise him once, having his hand laid upon his head. And after [this] let him say: Dost thou believe in Christ Jesus, the Son of God, Who was born of Holy Spirit and the Virgin Mary, Who was crucified in the days of Pontius Pilate, And died, [and was buried] And rose the third day living from the dead And ascended into [the] heaven[s], And sat down at the right hand of the Father, And will come to judge the living and the dead? And when he says: I believe, let him [baptise him] the second time. And again let him say: Dost thou believe in [the] Holy Spirit in the Holy Church, And the resurrection of the flesh? And he who is being baptised shall say: I believe. And so let him [baptise him] the third time. And afterwards when he comes up [from the water] he shall be anointed by the presbyter with the Oil of Thanksgiving saying: I anoint thee with holy oil in the Name of Jesus Christ. And [so] each one drying himself [with a towel] they shall [now] put on their clothes, and after this let them be together in the assembly. (Hippolytus, *The Apostolic Tradition*, pp. 30-38)

This is among the most important documents of the pastoral tradition, showing the intricate confluence of liturgy, teaching, pastoral care, spiritual formation, and primitive systematic theology in the baptismal act. Instruction, fasting, cleansing and all night vigil preceeded baptism, an early morning rite, featuring the renunciation of Satan, anointment with oil, and the affirmation of the rule of faith.

Similar features were present in the baptismal order of the Apostolic Constitutions:

Let, therefore, the candidate for baptism declare thus in his renunciation:

I renounce Satan, and his works, and his pomps, and his worships, and his angels, and his inventions, and all things that are under him. And after his renunciation let him in his consociation say: And I associate myself to Christ, and believe, and am baptized into one unbegotten Being, the only true God Almighty, the Father of Christ, the Creator and Maker of all things, from whom are all things; and into the Lord Jesus Christ, His only begotten Son, the First born of the whole creation, who before the ages was begotten by the good pleasure of the Father, by whom all things were made, both those in heaven and those on earth, visible and invisible; who in the last days descended from heaven, and took flesh, and was born of the holy Virgin Mary, and did converse holily according to the laws of His God and Father, and was crucified under Pontius Pilate, and died for us, and rose again from the dead after His passion the third day, and ascended into the heavens, and sitteth at the right hand of the Father, and again is to come at the end of the world with glory to judge the quick and the dead, of whose kindgom there shall be no end. And I am baptized into the Holy Ghost, that is, the Comforter, who worked in all the saints from the beginning of the world, but was afterwards sent to the apostles by the Father, according to the promise of our Saviour and Lord, Jesus Christ; and after the apostles, to all those that believe in the Holy Catholic Church; into the resurrection of the flesh, and into the remission of sins, and into the kindgom of heaven, and into the life of the world to come. And after this vow, he comes in order to the anointing with oil. (*Constitutions of the Holy Apostles*, Bk. VII, sec. IV, sec. xl-xli, ANF VII, p. 476)*

The renunciation of Satan, three-fold baptism in the name of the triune God, and the sharing in Christ's death, burial and resurrection, were also major features of Ambrose's account of the baptismal rite:

He asked you, "Do you renounce the devil and his works?" What did you reply? "I renounce." "Do you renounce the world and its pleasures?" What did you reply? "I renounce." Remember what you said, and never let the terms of your bond slip from your mind. . . ." You were asked: "Do you believe in God the Father Almighty?" You said: "I believe," and you dipped; that is, you were buried. Again you were asked: "Do you believe in our Lord Jesus Christ, and in his cross?" You said: "I believe," and you dipped, therefore you were "buried with Christ". . . . A third time you were asked: "Do you believe also in the holy Spirit?" You said: "I believe," and you dipped for the third time, so that the threefold confession might cancel the fall of your earlier life. (Ambrose, *The Sacraments*, LCF, pp. 182-183)

Although Luther argued that immersion was the preferable mode, he did not insist upon it as a required mode for valid baptism:

Baptism (*Die Taufe*) is *baptismos* in Greek, and *mersio* in Latin, and means to plunge something completely into water, so that the water covers it. Although in many places it is no longer customary to thrust and dip infants into the font, but only with the hand to pour the baptismal water upon them out of the font, nevertheless the former is what should be done. (Luther, *The Holy and Blessed Sacrament of Baptism*, 1519, LW 35, p. 29)

Again, in *The Babylonian Captivity*:

I would have those who are to be baptized completely immersed in the water. . . . Not that I hold this to be necessary (*non quod necessarium arbitrer*). But it were well to give to so perfect and complete a matter a perfect and complete sign. (Luther, *The Babylonian Captivity*, WA 6, p. 534; WLS 1, p. 58)

This solemn prayer for the efficacy of baptism followed the ante-Nicene rite:

And after this, when he has baptized him in the name of the Father, and of the Son, and of the Holy Ghost, he shall anoint him with ointment, and shall add as follows:—
O Lord God, who art without generation, and without a superior, the Lord of the whole world, who hast scattered the sweet odour of the knowledge of the Gospel among all nations, do Thou grant at this time that this ointment may be efficacious upon him that is baptized, so that the sweet odour of Thy Christ may continue upon him firm and fixed; and that now he has died with Him, he may arise and live with Him. . . . After this let him stand up and pray that prayer which the Lord taught us. . . .
[Then the newly baptized shall] pray thus after the foregoing prayer, and say: O God Almighty, the Father of Thy Christ, Thy only begotten Son, give me a body undefiled, a heart pure, a mind watchful, an unerring knowledge, the influence of the Holy Ghost for the obtaining and assured enjoying of the truth, through Thy Christ, by whom glory be to Thee, in the Holy Spirit, forever. Amen. (*Constitutions of the Holy Apostles*, Bk. VII, sec. IV, Ch. xliv-xlv, ANF VII, p. 477)

VI ❧ The Effects of Baptism

For almost two millenia, pastors have been baptizing persons into the unity of faith. The act of baptism seeks to manifest that triune-grounded unity. Despite this, baptism remains a point of deep division in Christianity. There remain many questions about the effects of baptism, what actually occurs in baptism, whether it can be judged by its effects, and about the relation of new birth and baptism.

For example, does spiritual illumination accompany baptism? Justin Martyr's description indicates that such was an early Christian belief:

We learned from the apostles this reason for this [rite]. At our first birth we were born of necessity without our knowledge, from moist seed, by the intercourse of our parents with each other, and grew up in bad habits and wicked behavior. So that we should not remain children of necessity and ignorance, but [become sons] of free choice and knowledge, and obtain remission of the sins we have already committed, there is named at the water, over him who has chosen to be born again and has repented of his sinful acts, the name of God the Father and Master of all. . . . This washing is called illumination, since those who learn these things are illumined within. The illuminand is also washed in the name of Jesus Christ. . . . We, however, after thus washing the one who has been convinced and signified his assent, lead him to those who are called brethren, where they are assembled. They then earnestly offer common prayers for themselves and the one who has been illuminated and all others everywhere, that we may be made worthy, having learned the truth, to be found in deed good citizens and keepers of what is commanded, so that we may be saved with eternal salvation. (Justin Martyr, *First Apology*, sec. 61-65, LCC I, pp. 282-285)

Similarly Clement of Alexandria spoke of the expectation of a gift of new vision, an illumination accompanying baptism:

When we are baptized, we are enlightened; being enlightened, we become adopted sons; becoming adopted sons, we are made perfect; and becoming perfect, we are made divine. . . . Like those suffering from some blinding eye-disease who meanwhile receive no light from the outside and have none themselves, but must first remove the impediment from their eyes before they can have clear vision. In the same way, those who are baptized are cleansed of the sins which like a mist overcloud their divine spirit and then acquire a spiritual sight which is clear and unimpeded and lightsome, the sort of sight which alone enables us to behold divinity, with the help of the Holy Spirit who is poured forth from heaven upon us. (Clement of Alexandria, *Christ the Educator*, Bk. I, Ch. 6.26-28, FC 23, p. 26-28)

Sin after baptism was held to be unthinkable by many pastoral writers of the pre-Nicene period:

Beloved, be it known to you that those who are baptized into the death of our Lord Jesus are obliged to go on no longer in sin; for as those who are dead cannot work wickedness any longer, so those who are dead with Christ cannot practise wickedness. We do not therefore believe, brethren, that any one who has received the washing of life continues in the practice of the licentious acts of transgressors. (*Constitutions of the Holy Apostles*, Bk. II, sec. III, sec. vii, ANF VII, p. 398)

Luther employed a stunning political metaphor to speak of the invalidation of sin through baptism:

The jurisdiction, authority, and rights of a prince are not impaired because he has many faithless and disobedient subjects in his principality. Even so in Baptism: Once we have received it, we are included and received by it into the number of those who shall be saved, and God makes an eternal covenant of grace with us. That we thereafter often stumble and fall does not render this blessed Baptism futile. (Luther, WA 37, p. 668; WLS 1, p. 58)

What if baptism should result in no behavioral change?

If the "birth from above" is a refashioning of man's nature, we must ask what change is made to bring the grace of regeneration to perfection. . . . If the life after initiation is of the same quality as the uninitiated life, then, though it may be a bold thing to say, I will say it without flinching; in the case of such people the water is merely water, for the gift of the Holy Spirit in no way shows itself in what takes place. (Gregory of Nyssa, LCF, p. 160)

It is an ancient practice associated with Christian baptism that its recipient receives a name, and thus symbolically receives an identity in the family of God:

The Educator and Teacher is there naming us little ones, meaning that we are more ready for salvation than the worldly wise who, believing themselves wise, have blinded their own eyes. (Clement of Alexandria, *Christ the Educator*, Bk. I, Ch. 2.32, FC 23, p. 31)

One's baptism is not made less real by one's neglect of it, according to Luther's metaphor of the gift refused:

It is terrible to hear that people venture to slander God's work by saying: The trouble is that if he who receives Baptism does not believe, the Baptism is no good. If a person were given a hundred gulden but refused to take them, the hundred gulden would certainly retain their value, would they not? The fact that the fellow does not want the money does not in any way harm the gold. The same principle applies in the case of Baptism. (Luther, WA 46, p. 154; WLS 1, p. 55)

VII ❧ DOES A BAD PASTOR NULLIFY A GOOD SACRAMENT?

The Donatist controversy forced Augustine to sharpen a careful distinction between the sacrament itself and its effects, which has been widely received by subsequent pastoral writers. This distinction helped solve the question of whether an unworthy minister may confer a worthy sacrament, and whether the very validity of a sacrament is finally determined by its behavioral results:

The reason why the blessed Cyprian and other eminent Christians . . . decided that Christ's baptism could not exist among heretics or schismatics was that they failed to distinguish between the sacrament and the efficacy or working out of a sacrament. Because the efficacy and working out of baptism, in freedom from sins and in integrity of heart, was not found among heretics, it was supposed that the sacrament itself did not exist there. But if we turn our eyes to the multitude within the fold, it is clear that those within the unity of the church who are perverse and lead wicked lives can neither give nor have the remission of sins. Nevertheless the pastors of the Catholic Church spread through the whole world were quite clear that such men had the sacrament of baptism and could confer it; and through them the original custom was afterwards established by the authority of a plenary council. Even when a wandering sheep has received the Lord's brand-mark at the hands of dishonest robbers, and then comes into the security of Christian unity, it is restored, freed, and healed; but the Lord's brand-mark is recognized, not disallowed. . . . The recipient of a schismatic's baptism may receive it to his salvation, if he himself is not in schism. (Augustine, *On Baptism*, Ch. IV, sec. 1, LCF, p. 241; cf. NPNF 1, IV, pp. 446ff.)

This maxim, that one schismatically baptized may not be in schism, has profound modern ecumenical significance. It helps those who understand themselves not to be in schism with ancient apostolic ecumenical faith to experience their link with orthodox and catholic traditions that would regard their baptism as schismatic. Augustine was not the first, but among the most influential, to argue that baptism is not polluted by being administered by polluted ministers:

The water over which the name of God is invoked is not profane and polluted, even if that name is invoked by profane and polluted men; for neither God's creation nor God's name can be polluted. The baptism which is consecrated by the words of Christ in the Gospels is holy, even when conferred by the polluted, and on the polluted, however shameless and unclean they may be. This holiness is itself incapable of contamination, and the power of God supports his sacrament, whether for the salvation of those who use it aright, or the doom of those who employ it wrongly. The light of the sun, or of a lamp, is not defiled by contact with the filthy on which it shines: so how can Christ's baptism be defiled by the wickedness of any man? (Augustine, *On Baptism*, Ch. III, sec. 15, LCF, p. 242; cf. NPNF 1, IV, p. 441)

Nor does unworthily partaking nullify the validity of the sacrament:

Judas, to whom the Lord gave the piece of bread, gave the devil his chance to enter him, not by receiving something evil, but by receiving something in an evil way. So when a man receives the sacrament of the Lord unworthily the result is not that the sacrament is evil because he is evil, not that he has received nothing at all because he has not received it for his salvation. It is just as much the Lord's body and blood when a man "eats and drinks judgement to himself" (1 Cor. 11:29) by partaking unworthily. (Augustine, *On Baptism*, Ch. V, sec. 9, LCF, p. 246; cf. NPNF 1, IV, p. 467)

Centuries later the Anglican Thirty-nine Articles affirmed that the sacrament remains good even when administered by evil men:

Although in the visible Church the evil be ever mingled with the good, and sometimes the evil have chief authority in the Ministration of the Word and Sacraments, yet forasmuch as they do not the same in their own name, but in Christ's, and do minister by his commission and authority, we may use their Ministry, both in hearing the Word of God, and in receiving the Sacraments. Neither is the effect of Christ's ordinance taken away by their wickedness, nor the grace of God's gifts diminished from such as by faith, and rightly, do receive the Sacraments ministered unto them; which be effectual, because of Christ's institution and promise, although they be ministered by evil men. (Anglican Thirty-nine Articles of Religion, Ch. XXVI, CC, p. 275)

Calvin pressed the point even further:

If some Epicurean, inwardly grinning at the whole performance, were to administer the Supper to me according to the command of Christ and the rule given by him, and in due form, I would not doubt that the bread and the cup held forth by his hand are pledges to me of the body and the blood of Christ. (Calvin, *Antidote to Council of Trent*, SW, p. 216)

VIII ❧ CONFIRMATION OF ONE'S BAPTISM

If baptism is the seal of God's promise, confirmation celebrates that promise as having been consciously and deliberately received. In confirmation, one receives that grace which confirms, consummates and completes the sacrament of baptism, and one thereby assumes personal responsibility for one's baptismal vows. In the service of confirmation, the church prays that confirmands will be empowered by the Spirit to service, and that grace shall increase in them all the days of their lives. Only the baptized can be confirmed, and only then at the age of sufficient accountability to understanding fully the implications of their baptism. Hence this pastoral act is an important part of soul care of young people and of persons newly entering into full and deliberate participation in the Christian community.

That confirmation of baptism was a very ancient rite is clear from this prayer from Hippolytus (c. 170-235):

The bishop shall lay his hand upon them invoking and saying;
O Lord God, who did count these Thy servants worthy of the forgiveness of sins by the washing of regeneration, make them worthy to be filled with Thy Holy Spirit and send upon them Thy grace, that they may serve Thee according to Thy will. For to Thee is the glory, to the Father and to the Son with the Holy Ghost in the holy Church, both now and ever and world without end. Amen.

After this, pouring the consecrated oil from his hand and laying his hand on his head, he shall say:

I anoint thee with holy oil in God the Father Almighty and Christ Jesus and the Holy Ghost.

And sealing him on the forehead, he shall give him the kiss of peace and say:

The Lord be with you.

And he who has been sealed shall say: And with thy spirit. And so he shall do to each one severally. (Hippolytus, *The Apostolic Tradition*, Ch. xxii, "Confirmation," sec. 1-4, pp. 38-39)*

Young persons are not to come to communion without instruction—a pre-Reformation maxim sustained by the Reformation:

When a child has been well enough instructed to pass the Catechism, he is to recite solemnly the sum of what it contains, and also to make profession of his Christianity in the presence of the Church.

Before this is done, no child is to be admitted to receive the Supper; and parents are to be informed not to bring them before this time. For it is a very perilous thing, for children as for parents, to introduce them without good and adequate instruction. (John Calvin, *Draft Ecclesiastical Ordinances*, 1541, SW, p. 240)

It is the nature of confirmation to confirm one's baptism, hence to learn what baptism means, and to enter into its covenant voluntarily. The Anglican pastor, John Cosin, provided this definition:

The ancient custom of the church of Christ was, after that persons were once baptized, to add unto their Baptism Imposition of hands, with earnest prayer for the gifts of God's graces to be bestowed upon them, whereby they might be confirmed and strengthened in that holy profession which, in the Sacrament of Baptism, they had first begun to make. (John Cosin, Correspondence, Part II, pp. 69-72; *Angl.*, p. 443)

The purpose of confirmation is distortable in the form of superstitious excess or the opposite defect of negligence:

Besides that extraordinary act of laying on the hand for curing of diseases and infirmities, practised by Our Blessed Saviour and His Apostles and for conveying the Holy Ghost in a miraculous way, in the Primitive Times there were three occasions and usages of Imposition of Hands,—in cases of 1. Confirmation; 2. of Ordination; 3. of Absolution and Readmission of Penitents. . . . It has been the lot of this sacred rite [i.e. of Confirmation] to fall into ill hands and to be foully wronged by a double extreme; the one, of Excess, the other, of Defect. The Excess, in a superstitious over-doing and over-valuing it; the Defect, in a neglective disestimation. (Joseph Hall, Apostolic Institution of Imposition of

Hands for Confirmation Revived, Sec. 2-5, Works, X, pp. 442-447; *Angl.*, p. 445)*

Baxter described how the practice of confirmation had fallen into abuse in his boyhood, lacking serious instruction:

When I was a schoolboy about fifteen years of age, the Bishop coming into the country, many went to him to be confirmed. We that were boys ran out to see the bishop among the rest, not knowing anything of the meaning of the business. When we came there, we met about thirty or forty in all, of our own stature and temper, that had come for to be "bishopped," as then it was called. The Bishop examined us not at all in one article of the Faith; but in a churchyard in haste we were set in a rank, and he passed hastily over us, laying his hands on our head, and saying a few words, which neither I nor any that I spoke with, understood; so hastily were they uttered, and a very short prayer recited, and there was an end. But whether we were Christians or infidels, or knew so much as that there was a God, the Bishop little knew nor inquired. And yet he was esteemed one of the best Bishops in England. And though the Canons require that the Curate or Minister send a certificate that children have learned the Catechism, yet there was no such thing done, but we ran of our own accord to see the Bishop only; and almost all the rest of the country had not this much. This was the old, careless practice of this excellent duty of Confirmation. (Richard Baxter, *Confirmation and Restauration*, Works, XIV, pp. 481f; *Angl.*, p. 449-450)

George Herbert argued against a specific age for receiving confirmation and first Eucharist. One is ready to receive when one understands the difference between Bread and bread:

The time of everyone's first receiving is not so much by years, as by understanding; particularly the rule may be this: When any one can distinguish the Sacramental from common bread, knowing the Institution, and the difference, he ought to receive, of what age soever. (George Herbert, *CP*, Ch. XXII, CWS, p. 86)

Selections in Part Four have focussed upon pastoral care through baptism, the ministry of beginnings—how baptism is understood and defined, to whom administered, its elements, modes, necessity, enactment, and effects, whether a bad pastor can nullify a good sacrament, and how it is confirmed.

5 Confession and Communion Counsel

Two subjects are joined in Part Five which have in the modern period become separated: confessional preparation for holy communion on the one hand, and on the other the ministry of holy communion as the pastoral act *par excellence*. The modernization, secularization, and psychologization of pastoral care has resulted in a form of confession that appears to bear little relationship to classical confessional prior to communion. But upon closer inspection, it may be that the form of communication in modern "pastoral psychotherapy" is a partial, unconscious reappropriation of classical communion counsel, largely unaware of its roots.

I ❧ The Hard Remedy of Confession

Our first step is to clarify the meaning of penitential confession generally, its intrinsic connection with Christian pastoral care, its trenchant challenge to the human spirit, its leading to pardon, and the role of restitution in serious confession. Only then will we be ready to move more directly into the subject of the ministry of holy communion as the epitome of pastoral care.

Anglican bishop Francis White concisely stated the four purposes of confession: instructing, admonishing, comforting, and readying for communion.

> The true ends of private Confession are these which follow: First, to inform, instruct, and counsel Christian people in their particular actions. Secondly, if they be delinquents, to reprove them and make them understand the danger of their sin. Thirdly, to comfort those that are afflicted, and truly penitent, and to assure them of remission of sins by the word of Absolution. Fourthly, to prepare people to the worthy receiving of the Holy Communion. (Francis White, A Reply to Jesuit Fisher's Answer to Certain Questions Propounded by His Most Gracious Majesty,

King James, 1624, pp. 187-189; *Angl.*, p. 515)

Despite the abuses that Martin Luther felt were distorting auricular confession in his time, he strongly commended to Christian laity the continued practice of private confession to a trusted pastor. The human need is great for talking through the struggles of conscience. From the pastor's side, the door to confession must always be open:

Private confession should be retained in the church, for in it consciences afflicted and crushed by the terrors of sin lay themselves bare and receive consolation which they could not acquire in public preaching. We want to open up confession as a port and refuge for those whose consciences the devil holds enmeshed in his snares and whom he completely bewitches and torments in such a way that they cannot free or extricate themselves and feel and see nothing else but that they must perish. For there is no other greater misery in this life than the pains and perplexities of a heart that is destitute of guidance and solace. To such, then, an approach to confession should be opened up so that they may seek and find consolation among the ministers of the church. (Luther, "Lectures on Genesis Chapters 31 to 37, 1544," LW 6, pp. 297-298; cf. WA 44, 221)

Yet the human heart is prone to resist asking forgiveness or receiving counsel. Where is the courage to confess secret sins to be found?

This cannot be done without discovering the nakedness and blemishes of the soul, and there is shame in that, and therefore men are unwilling to do it. But, to that I answer, that it is very unreasonable that should be a hindrance. . . . Indeed there were shame in it, yet as long as it may be a means to cure both your trouble and your sin too (certainly godly and faithful counsel may tend much to both) that shame ought to be despised; and it is sure it would, if we loved our souls as well as our bodies. For in bodily diseases, be they never so foul or shameful, we count him a fool who would rather miss the cure than discover it; and then it must here be so much a greater folly, by how much the soul is more precious than the body. (Anonymous, *The Whole Duty of Man*, 1684, Sunday III, sec. 23, p. 90; *Angl.*, p. 514)

Persons today often resist therapy because they do not want to be viewed or known as sick. In earlier times of pastoral care, parishioners resisted confession because they did not want to be viewed by themselves or others as sinners. These resistances are distinguishable. The metaphor of sickness does not take fully into account the distorted will, as does the basic idea of sin. In confession of sin, one deliberately takes responsibility for one's own distortions, and asks for divine forgiveness. The pastor's purpose is not only to hear confession, but to provide counsel for understanding the dynamics of whatever is welling up within it so as to direct one toward reparation, and at the crucial time to pronounce the word of divine pardon.

Confession can occur non-verbally, as in the case of Peter:

It was true of Peter, whose tears over his denial we know, although we do not read of other satisfaction or of confession. Whence Ambrose on Luke (22:62) says of this very denial by Peter and of his weeping: "I do not find what he said; I find that he wept. I read of his tears; I do not read of his satisfaction. Tears wipe away a wrong which it is disgraceful to confess with one's voice and weeping guarantees pardon and shame. Tears declare the fault without dread, they confess without prejudicing shame. Tears do not request pardon but deserve it. I find why Peter was silent, namely lest by asking for pardon so soon he should offend more." (Peter Abelard, *Ethics*, p. 101; cf. Ambrose, Exposition on Luke, x.88, CCL 45, p. 371; cf. MPL 15. 1825B-1826A)*

As nature provides animals with remedies for injury, so does grace provide the wounded human soul the remedy of confession (*exomologesis*) and communion:

Since you know that in *exomologesis* you have a second safeguard against hell which backs up that first line of defense, the Lord's Baptism, why do you abandon the means of salvation which is yours? Why are you slow to take hold of something which will restore you to health? Even dumb, irrational animals recognize, in due season, remedies supplied to them by God. When a stag is transfixed by an arrow, it knows that it must eat dittany in order to expel the arrowhead with its barbs projecting backwards from the wound. If a swallow blinds her young, she has learned to restore their sight with her own peculiar herb, the celandine. (Tertullian, *On Penitence*, ACW 28, p. 36)

Tertullian anticipated the psychoanalytic principle that repression drives psychological dysfunction ever more deeply into unawareness:

Confession lightens an offense as much as concealment aggravates it, for confession is counseled by satisfaction and concealment by impenitence. (Tertullian, *On Penitence*, ACW 28, p. 31)

Baxter concisely defined the therapeutic function of confession:

Unpardoned sin will never let us rest or prosper, though we be at ever so much care and cost to cover it: our sin will surely find us out, though we find not it out. The work of confession is purposely to make known our sin. . . . (Baxter, *RP*, p. 39)

The Benedictine rule urged full confession:

Confess to the abbot every unlawful thought as it arises in the heart, and the hidden sins we have committed. The Scripture advises this, saying: "Reveal your way to God and hope in him" (cf. Ps. 37:5): and again: "Confess to God because he is good: for his mercy endureth for ever" (cf. Ps. 106:1). And in the prophet: "I have made known my sin to thee, and have not covered my iniquities. I have said, I will declare to God my own iniquities against myself: and thou hast forgiven the wickedness of my heart" (Ps. 32:5). (Benedict of Nursia, Rule, LCC, IX, p. 303)

It may seem awkward in terms of our present communion practices for pastors to think of making themselves available on the days before communion for private confession to prepare parishioners for communion. It is not clear precisely how the ancient practice of communion confession might be practically restored. It does seem clear, however, that there was a crucial connection between confession and communion in the earliest centuries of pastoral care. We have lived through a century of evolutionary optimism that has taught us that humanity is good and history is getting better and better. These phrases have washed over us so many times that it is difficult to take the confession of sin seriously. But modern collective consciousness at a hidden level remains deeply and wretchedly concerned with the analysis and thwarted confession of sin, though it is seldom called by that name. Nonetheless, what takes place in much good secular psychotherapy is structurally similar to that close examination of conscience of classical communion counsel lacking its moral and sacramental dimensions.

As early as the *Didache*, a close relationship was assumed between confession and a right spirit in prayer:

In church, make confession of your faults, and do not come to your prayers with a bad conscience. That is the Way of Life. (*Didache*, sec. 4, ECW, p. 229)

Ambrose understood that a special opportunity for soul care is offered when one is in despair, "bottoming out" from a life wretchedly lived. He described that soul who is most ready for confession:

It is the soul who hears that she will not gather the fruit of her seeds, and, in losing the harvest, will find no strength for herself;

who hears that she will press the olive but will not find the oil of gladness or drink the wine of pleasure. It is the soul who finds that the deeds of the flesh are full of violence, full of deception, cheating, and fraud, empty shows of affection and calculated guile, and all those of her own house her enemies. (Ambrose, *Letters*, 45, To Horontianus, FC 26, pp. 238-239)*

Luther recognized, out of his own personal struggle, how difficult it is to comfort the terrorized conscience:

The man who has been humbled by God cannot forget the wound and the pain, for a hurt lingers in the memory far longer than a benefaction. Children illustrate this truth. Although a tender mother tries to quiet a child which she has chastised with the rod by giving it toys and other allurements, yet the pain so lingers in the memory that the child cannot hold back frequent sighs and bitter sobs. (Luther, "Lectures on Genesis Chapters Six to Fourteen, 1536," WA 42, 364; WLS 1, p. 322; cf. LW 2, p. 145)

Early Anglican writers followed the scholastic demarcation between venial sins (offenses against God not serious enough to cause the loss of sanctifying grace), and mortal (deadly) sins which trouble conscience so deeply that they require confession and absolution:

Venial sins that separate not from the grace of God need not so much to trouble a man's conscience; if he hath committed any mortal sin, then we require Confession of it to a Priest, who may give him, upon his true contrition and repentance, the benefit of Absolution. (John Cosin, Works, LACT, V, p. 163f; *Angl.*, p. 516)

II ❧ COMMUNION COUNSEL: PREPARING FOR THE LORD'S TABLE

The point seems to have been mislaid by modern pastoral writers that the context in which pastoral counsel is most pertinent, most valued, and most profoundly called for, is shortly before holy communion. Protestants sometimes imagine that this is a medieval scholastic idea. But the following texts show that this was a theme shared by patristic and Reformation writers. Here is a widely-read seventeenth century Anglican statement of the need to search out a discreet and godly minister to receive spiritual counsel before communion:

I shall add but one thing more concerning the things which are to be done before the Sacrament [i.e., Holy Communion], and that is an advice, that if any person upon a serious view of himself cannot satisfy his own soul of his sincerity, and so doubts whether he may come to the Sacrament, he does well not to rest wholly on his own judgement in the case. . . . In the midst of so many dangers which attend one's mistaking of himself, I would, as I said before, exhort him not to trust to his own judgement, but to make known his case to some discreet and godly Minister, and rather be guided by his judgement, who will probably (if the case be duly and without any disguise discovered to him) be better able to judge of him than he of himself. This is the counsel the Church gives in the Exhortation before the Communion, where it is advised that if any by other means already mentioned "cannot quiet his own conscience, but require further counsel and comfort, then let him go to some discreet and learned Minister of God's Word and open his grief, that he may receive such spiritual counsel, advice, and comfort that his conscience may be relieved, etc." (Anonymous, *The Whole Duty of Man*, 1658, Sunday III, sec. 21-23, pp. 87-90; *Angl.*, p. 513)*

An Anglican promulgation, the Irish Canons of 1634, set forth the desired procedure for inviting and hearing confession prior to communion:

The minister of every parish, and in Cathedral and Collegiate Churches some public minister of the Church, shall the afternoon before the said administration give warning by the tolling of the bell or otherwise, to the intent that if any have any scruple of conscience, or desire the special ministry of reconciliation, he may afford it to those that need it. And to this end the people are often to be exhorted to enter into a special examination of the state of their own souls. Those who find themselves either extremely dull or much troubled in mind, may resort to God's ministers to receive from them advice and counsel for the quickening of their dead hearts and the subduing of those corruptions to which they have become subject, as well as the benefit of Absolution likewise for the quieting of their consciences, by the power of the keys which Christ has committed to His ministers for that purpose. (The Irish Canons of 1634, Canon XIX, *Concilia Magnae Britanniae et Hiberniae*, Vol. IV, p. 501; cf. *Angl.*, pp. 516-517)*

Luther strongly commended private confession as an unparalleled remedy for the distressed conscience:

There is no doubt that confession is necessary and commanded of God. Thus we read in Matthew 3:6, "They were baptised of John in Jordan, confessing their sins." And in 1 John 1:9-10: "If we confess our sins, he is faithful and just to forgive us our sins. If we say that we have not sinned, we make him a liar, and his word is not in us." If the saints may not deny their sin, how much more ought those who are guilty of open and great sins to make confession! But most effectively of all does Matthew 18:15-17 prove the institution of confession, in which passage Christ teaches that a sinning brother should be rebuked, haled before the Church, accused and, if he will not hear, excommunicated. But he hears when, heeding the rebuke, he acknowledges and confesses his sin.

Of private confession, which is now observed, I am heartily in favor, even though it cannot be proved from the Scriptures; it is useful and necessary, nor would I have it abolished—nay, I rejoice that it exists in the Church of Christ, for it is a cure without an equal for distressed consciences. For when we have laid bare our conscience to our brother and privately made known to him the evil that lurked within, we receive from our brother's lips the word of comfort spoken by God Himself; and, if we accept it in faith, we find peace in the mercy of God speaking to us through our brother. (Luther, *The Babylonian Captivity*, WML II, p. 249-252)

Clement of Rome in the late first century had urged that faults be openly confessed:

So let us beg forgiveness for all our misdoings. . . . If men are really living in the fear and love of God, they would sooner endure affliction themselves than see their neighbours suffer, and would prefer reproach to fall on them rather than on the tradition of peaceful harmony which has been so proudly and loyally handed down to us. It is better for a man to admit his faults frankly than to harden his heart. (Clement of Rome, *To the Corinthians*, sec. 51, ECW, p. 50)

Yet, despite its benefits, confession remains for most people extremely difficult. Why?

All people are so minded that they do not want themselves and their dealings to become publicly known. All can bear to have us say that God is benevolent, and who in the world would deny that

God is just and always right when we judge Him? Yet people cannot bear to be rebuked. No one wants to be a homicide, thief, or miser before the world, nor be stained with gross vices. Who, then, is the man who hates the light? All of us! For not one of you would want his story written on his forehead. All of us still gladly hear people praise and honor us. No one thinks: Ah, God be gracious to me; for if the sins of which I am conscious in my heart were evident to the world, I should deserve to be hanged. To be sure, the world honors me; but if it knew who I am, it would spit at me.—But if we realized this, it would serve to humble us before God. . . . The proverbial saying is not meaningless: More souls go to heaven from the gallows than from the cemetery.—For those hanged on the gallows are forced to confess their sins and say: Lord, I am a wicked fellow, Thou art just.—Another man, however, dies on his bed but covers up his sin. . . . Everyone is so constituted that he does not want the sin he commits to be considered sin. He wants it to be called righteousness before the world and before God. However, it is also true that no one should betray and expose himself before the world, but everyone should cover his sins and ask God to forgive them; and you should be reconciled with those whom you have injured. (Luther, "Sermons on the Gospel of John Chapters Three and Four, 1529," WA 47, pp. 122f., WLS 1, pp. 327-328; cf. LW 22, pp. 403-404)

Luther argued that believers other than clergy may *in extremis* hear confession and point to God's pardon:

And so I advise these children, brethren and sisters: If your superiors are unwilling to grant you permission to confess your secret sins to whomever you wish, then take them to whatever brother or sister you will and confess them, receive absolution, and then go and do whatever you wish and ought to do; only believe firmly that you are absolved, and nothing more is needed. (Luther, *An Open Letter to the Christian Nobility*, WML II, p. 124)

The state does not have any just or legitimated power to ask a pastor to tell what was heard in confession:

Within the church's sphere of authority we deal in secret with the conscience and do not take its jurisdiction from the civil estate. Therefore people should leave us undisturbed in our sphere of authority and should not drag into their jurisdiction what we do in secret. (Luther, WA-T 4, #5179; WLS 1, p. 333)

III ⁊ Soul Care to Penitents

Repentance may be immediately preceded by an experience of despair over oneself, bemoaning the recent course of one's life, accompanied by a new hunger for gracious empowerment and resolution to begin afresh. These processes of intense behavioral reversal, which have intrigued contemporary psychologists, have been of perennial interest to the writers of the pastoral tradition. Long before William James, classical writers studied carefully the dynamics of penitence, the psychology of *metanoia*—turning one's personal direction around, breaking through inner imprisonment, starting on the road to healing. These and other dynamics must be dealt with in soul care of the penitent.

Tertullian strongly commended the cartharic values of a searching, highly personal, *exomologesis* (confession). The future health of the soul depends upon making open what had been emotively concealed:

> *Exomologesis*, then, is a discipline which leads a man to prostrate and humble himself. . . . Therefore, in humbling a man it exalts him. When it defiles him, he is cleansed. In accusing, it excuses. In condemning, it absolves. In proportion as you have had no mercy on yourself, believe me, in just this same measure God will have mercy upon you. Most men, however, shun this duty as involving the public exposure of themselves, or they put it off from day to day, thinking more about their shame, it seems to me, than about their salvation. They are like men who have contracted some disease in the private parts of the body, who conceal this from the knowledge of the physicians and thus preserve their modesty but lose their lives. (Tertullian, *Exomologesis*, sec. 9-10, ACW 28, pp. 31-32)

With characteristic realism, Luther described the crunch of the heart that yearns for divine mercy:

> To repent means to feel the wrath of God in earnest because of one's sin, so that the sinner experiences anguish of heart and is filled with a painful longing for the salvation and the mercy of God. (Luther, "Lectures on Genesis Chapters 26 to 30, 1542," WA 43, p. 534; WLS 3, p. 1210; cf. LW, 5, p. 154)

Repentance begins in guilt and ends in hope of reconciliation:

> Repentance is begun when we acknowledge our sins and are sincerely sorry for them; it is completed when trust in the mercy of God comes to this sorrow and hearts are converted to God and long for the forgiveness of sins. (Luther, Erlangen edition, Vol. 24, p. 482; WLS 3, p. 1210)

Shall confession occur only in the presence of the pastor, or before the congregation, or in solitude before God, or with a Christian brother or sister? Luther proposed a way of looking at all these levels of confession:

> In the first place, There is a confession which is founded on the Scriptures; namely, when some one commits a sin publicly, or with other men's knowledge, and is accused before the congregation. If he abandons his sin, they intercede for him with God. . . . Secondly, A confession is necessary for us, when we go away in a corner by ourselves, and confess to God Himself and pour out before Him all our faults. . . . Thirdly, There is also a confession when one takes another aside, and tells him what troubles him, so that he may hear from him a word of comfort. . . . I will let no man take private confession away from me, and I would not give it up for all the treasures in the world, since I know what comfort and strength it has given me. No one knows what it can do for him except one who has struggled much with the devil. Yea, the devil would have slain me long ago, if the confession had not sustained me. For there are many doubts which a man cannot resolve by himself, and so he takes a brother aside and tells him his trouble. (Luther, The Eight Wittenberg Sermons, Eighth Sermon, WML II, pp. 422-424)

The Reformed tradition viewed penitence as a highly personalized act, in addition to stressing the value of public penitence and common prayer:

> Repentance unto life is an evangelical grace, the doctrine whereof is to be preached by every minister of the gospel, as well as that of faith in Christ. . . . Although repentance be not to be rested in as any satisfaction for sin, or any cause of the pardon thereof, which is the act of God's free grace in Christ; yet is it of such necessity to all sinners that none may expect pardon without it. As there is no sin so small but it deserves damnation, so there is no sin so great that it can bring damnation upon those who truly repent.
>
> Men ought not to content themselves with a general repentance, but it is every man's duty to endeavor to repent of his particular sins particularly. As every man is bound to make private confession of his sins to God, praying for the pardon thereof, upon which, and the forsaking them, he shall find mercy; so he that scandalizeth his brother, or the Church of Christ, ought to be willing, by a private or public confession and sorrow for his

sin, to declare his repentance to those that are offended, who are thereupon to be reconciled to him, and in love to receive him. (Westminister Confession, Ch. XV, sec. 1-6, *CC* p. 209-210)

Bonaventure described three steps of penance: contrition, confession and satisfaction:

The integral parts of this sacrament are: contrition in the soul, oral confession, and actual satisfaction. Out of these penance is integrated when the sinner, after having perpetrated mortal sin, asserts the same by deed, accuses himself by word, and detests his sin within his soul, proposing never to repeat the sin. After these things have been done in the required manner together with absolution given by one with orders, the key, and the jurisdiction, man is absolved from sin, reunited with the Church, and reconciled with Christ through the medium of the priestly key. (Bonaventure, *Breviloquium*, p. 201)

They are blessed who mourn their misdeeds, because they are visited richly and often with the spirit of divine consolation. Hence do not be surprised if you find the wise believer ever attentive to his or her own inward sins:

Although the wise man sometimes deserves consolation so as to be mindful no longer of his sorrows, those, that is, for which he receives consolation, yet in order to make room for fresh consolations he is always looking for fresh causes of sorrow in himself. He does not immediately flatter himself that he is just in all respects. But he more searchingly accuses and judges himself the more he has begun to be enlightened; the more strictly, the more he has begun to be justified. To such a man, if I am not mistaken, the Spirit of consolation comes often, for he already anticipates his own coming; that is, he comes to accord consolation but he anticipates by teaching to mourn.

Devout and religious mourning occupies the first place and is outstanding in usefulness in the spirit's teaching. It is the highest wisdom of the saints, the safeguard of the just, the sobriety of the moderate, the first virtue of beginners, the spur of the proficient, the crown of the perfect, the salvation of those who are perishing, the harbor of those in danger: in a word it promises consolations in the present and joys in the future. (Guerric of Igny, *Liturgical Sermons*, Vol. 2, CFS 32, Sermon 39, sec. 6, pp. 121-122)

After enduring an extended period of martyrdom, persecution, and schism, the Church of the late fourth century had the pastoral task of healing its wounds, and bringing back into the fold many of the wandering flock. Here is the report of the First Council of Constantinople on how that ministry of reconciliation was managed and understood:

Those who from heresy turn to orthodoxy, and to the portion of those who are being saved, we receive according to the following method and custom: Arians and Macedonians, and Sabbatians, and Novatians, who call themselves Cathari or Aristeri, and Quarto-decimans or Tetradites, and Apollinarians, we receive, upon their giving a written renunciation (of their errors) and anathematize every heresy which is not in accordance with the Holy, Catholic, and Apostolic Church of God. Thereupon, they are first sealed or anointed with the holy oil upon the forehead, eyes, nostrils, mouth, and ears; and when we seal them, we say, "The Seal of the gift of the Holy Ghost." . . . On the first day we make them Christians; on the second, catechumens; on the third, we exorcise them by breathing thrice in their face and ears; and thus we instruct them and oblige them to spend some time in the Church, and to hear the Scriptures; and then we baptize them . . .

Our persecutions are but of yesterday. The sound of them still rings in the ears alike of those who suffered them and of those whose love made the sufferers' pain their own. It was but a day or two ago, so to speak, that some released from chains in foreign lands returned to their own churches through manifold afflictions; of others who had died in exile the relics were brought home; others again, even after their return from exile, found the passion of the heretics still at the boiling heat, and, slain by them with stones, as was the blessed Stephen, met with a sadder fate in their own than in a stranger's land. Others, worn away with various cruelties, still bear in their bodies the scars of their wounds and the marks of Christ. Who could tell the tale of fines, of disfranchisements, of individual confiscations, of intrigues, of outrages, of prisons? In truth all kinds of tribulation were wrought out beyond number in us, perhaps because we were paying the penalty of sins, perhaps because the merciful God was trying us by means of the multitude of our sufferings. For these all thanks to God, who by means of such afflictions trained his servants and, according to the multitude of his mercies, brought us again to refreshment. We indeed needed long leisure, time, and toil to restore the church once more, that so, like physicians healing the body after long sickness and expelling its disease by gradual treatment, we might bring her back to her ancient health of true re-

ligion. (Council of Constantinople, A.D. 382, The Synodical
Letter, The Seven Ecumenical Councils, NPNF 2, XIV, pp. 185,
188)

IV ❧ THE MINISTRY OF PARDON

God's pardon is promised to those who sincerely confess sin. The offering of absolution is a crucial moment of pastoral activity. This occurs in
every well-ordered service of Christian worship. The pastor is not the
only one who can point to divine forgiveness, but by the inner address
of God and the outward appointment of the church through vocation,
the pastor is called and appointed to represent the people liturgically
before God in petition, and to represent the good news of God's par-
doning care by means of absolution to penitents.

Although a general absolution is fitting for common prayer, the ministry of pardon becomes all the more personalized at times in pastoral
conversation. Pardon need not always be overtly articulated, and may be
effectively communicated non-verbally. As any experienced pastor can
attest, it can be an incomparably powerful pastoral act.

In the early period of the church's history, the pardon of penitents
was not taken lightly, as may be seen from this early Christian instruction:

Our Saviour Himself earnestly petitioned His Father for those
who had sinned, as it is written in the Gospel: "Father, forgive
them; they do not know what they are doing" (Luke 23:34).
When the penitent comes in, an examination shall be made as to
the sincerity of penitence, and whether one is ready to be received again into the church, having fasted according to the degree of one's offense, whether two, three, five, or seven weeks. If
so, set free his conscience. Say whatever is fitting to him by way
of admonition, instruction, and exhortation to a sinner for his
reformation, that so he may continue privately in his humility,
and pray to God to be merciful to him, saying: "If Thou, O
Lord, shouldest keep account of sins, who, O Lord, could hold up
his head? But in thee is forgiveness, and therefore thou art
revered" (Ps. 130:3, 4). (*Constitutions of the Holy Apostles*, Bk. II,
sec. III, ANF VII, p. 402, NEB)*

When in common prayer the people confess and receive absolution
together, does everyone receive forgiveness equally? Does absolution
bear weight because the minister asks it, or the people so earnestly desire it, or because God wishes to make it effective in us? The Anglican
via media took a centrist route through long-standing ecclesial controver-

sies by combining aspects of all three of these views of absolution: that it assumes or requires the petition of the penitent, that it is a declaratory application of God's promise to the penitent, and that it derives its power from God yet utilizing the human voice and language of the representative minister:

There are three opinions concerning Absolution. The first, entertained by a few, conceive it optative, precarious, or by petition only, as praying for the pardon of the sins of the penitent. The second think it declaratory only, that it, pronouncing the penitent absolved, by applying God's promises to the signs of his contrition. Lastly, some contend that it is authoritative, as deriving power and commission from God, not to declare the party absolved, but for the priest to do it in words denoting the first person. All these three opinions our Church seems in part to favour. The first under these words, "Almighty God have mercy upon you, pardon and deliver you," etc. (Absolution for the Communion). The second under these words, "Hath given charge and command to His Ministers, to declare and pronounce to His people, being penitent, the absolution and remission of their sins." The last by these words, "I absolve thee." Such an authoritative Absolution is proper at this point. For where the priest absolves in his own person, his Absolution is not fitly applicable to any but such as have given him evident tokens of hearty sorrow for their sins, such as Divine chastisement usually elicits. Extendible it is not to whole congregations (as in the former instances) where the confession is too general to be conceived in all real; and a confession at large can at most but pretend to an Absolution at large, effectual only to such a truly and sincerely repent. (Hamon L'Estrange, *Alliance of Divine Offices*, LACT, pp. 448f.; *Angl.*, p. 520)*

John Climacus urged promptness of confession and untardy reparation, so as to move through penitence to a lively awareness of genuine pardon. Otherwise the scrupulosity of confession may become a poisonous syndrome of self-recrimination:

An anchorite who remembers wrongs is an adder hidden in a hole, which carries about within itself deadly poison. The remembrance of Jesus' sufferings cures remembrance of wrongs, which is mightily shamed by His forbearance. Worms grow in a rotten tree, and malice finds a place in falsely meek and silent people. He who has cast it out has found forgiveness, but he who clings to it is deprived of mercies. Some, for the sake of forgiveness, give

themselves up to labours and struggles, but a man who is forgetful of wrongs excels them. If you forgive quickly, then you will be
generously forgiven. The forgetting of wrongs is a sign of true
repentance. But he who dwells on them and thinks that he is repenting is like a man who thinks he is running while he is really
asleep. (John Climacus, *The Ladder of Divine Ascent*, Step 9, sec.
13-17, p. 88-89)

There is a time for pardon—not too early, not too late. Too early it
may accelerate wrongdoing. Too late it may fester in self-pity. Numerous pitfalls and potential misunderstandings may accompany the un-
timely ministry of pardon. Augustine found that pardon sounds exactly
like license to those who are wrongly predisposed to interpret it as such:

This happened to St. Augustine. He preached the article of the
forgiveness of sins, highly extolled God's grace, and taught that a
man is justified and saved out of the pure grace and mercy of
God, promised and won through Christ, without any merit or
worthiness of his own. . . . Then he had to hear the Pelagians accuse him of being a harmful teacher and preacher, who could do
no more than make people lax and lazy and keep them from doing good works and attaining perfection. Then St. Augustine
had to defend himself by writing against these slanderers. He
pointed out that he was not hindering perfection although he was
preaching the forgiveness of sin, but that the message of the forgiveness of sins and of grace was helping people to attain true
perfection. . . . There are many among us who understand the
message of the Gospel in such a way as to imagine that they now
need do no good, suffer nothing, and give nothing. (Luther, *Ascension Day Sermon*, 1534, WA 37, pp. 393f.; WLS 2, pp. 741-742)

When the pastor pronounces pardon, it always runs the risk of antinomian misunderstanding. This is why the timing of pardon in pastoral
conversation is critical. There is no formal answer to the question of
seasonable pardon that can be passed on in a formula. What is required
is wisdom and prudent judgment to know when to pardon in such a
way as not to encourage license.
Luther wrote of the ecstatic joy he experienced after having heard
the counsel of Staupitz on true penitence as the love of God's righteousness:

This word of thine stuck in me like a sharp arrow of the
mighty, and from that time forth I began to compare it with the
texts of Scripture which teach penitence. Lo, there began a joyous game! The words frollicked with me everywhere! They

laughed and gamboled around this saying. Before that there was
scarcely a word in all the Scriptures more bitter to me than "penitence," though I was busy making pretences to God and trying
to produce a forced, feigned love; but now there is no word
which has for me a sweeter or more pleasing sound than "penitence." (Luther, Letter to Staupitz, WML I, p. 40)

Luther, who had personally struggled mightily with the ambiguities of
assurance of his own forgiveness, thought it possible to hear God's forgiveness spoken directly through the mouth of the confessor:

If any one is wrestling with his sins and wants to get rid of
them and looks for some assurance from the Scriptures, let him
go and confess to another in secret; and accept what is said to
him there as if God himself had communicated it through the
mouth of this person. (Luther, The Eight Wittenberg Sermons,
Eighth Sermon, WML II, p. 424)*

V ❧ On Cheap Grace: Forgiveness Without Responsiveness

When Pastor Dietrich Bonhoeffer spoke amid the Nazi regime of
"cheap grace" that was willing to receive God's pardon without significant behavioral transformation in response to it, he was reappropriating
a familiar theme of the classical pastoral writers. It has long been recognized that confession and pardon are profound pastoral acts, but easily distortable toward license, apathy, or quietude. Gregory the Great
thought carefully about proper pastoral counsel targeted to those who
lament sins but do not abandon them:

When the sow takes a bath in its muddy wallow, it makes itself
even filthier. So, too, he who bewails his sins but does not abandon them, subjects himself to punishment for a more grievous sin.
For he despises the pardon which he could have obtained by his
tears. . . . They who lament their sins but do not abandon them
are to be admonished to consider carefully that, for the most
part, evil men are moved in vain by compunction to righteousness, just as, for the most part, the good are tempted to sin without harm. (Gregory the Great, *Pastoral Care*, Part III, Ch. 30,
ACW 11, pp. 204-205)

Forgiveness is not offered in order to open the door to new sin:

When God, through His grace, grants us forgiveness of sins
without our merit, so that we need not purchase it or earn it our-

selves, we are at once inclined to draw this reassuring conclusion and to say: Well, so we need no longer do good!—Therefore, in addition to teaching the doctrine of faith in His grace, God must constantly combat this notion and show that this is not at all His meaning. Sins are assuredly not forgiven in order that they should be committed, but in order that they should stop; otherwise it should more justly be called the permission of sins, not the remission of sins. (Luther, *Sermon on Romans, Chapter 8*, WA 22, p. 132; WLS I, p. 520)

The question of whether one could truly repent and still continue in sin was rigorously debated among the Ante-Nicene Fathers during the period of persecution:

Examine your own conscience, and, as far as you are able, heal your wounds. But you must not think, since your offenses are removed by God's grace, that a licence is given you for sinning. . . . To repent is nothing else than to profess and to affirm that one will sin no more. . . . No one can be without fault as long as he is burdened with a covering of flesh, the infirmity of which is subject to the dominion of sin in a threefold manner—in deeds, in words, and thoughts. (Lactantius, *The Divine Institutes*, Bk. VI, Ch. XIII, ANF VII, p. 178)*

Tertullian recognized that the opportunity of penitence once offered might not be offered again:

If the indulgence of the Lord favors you with what you need for the restoration of that which you lost, be grateful for His repeated, nay rather, for His increased beneficence. For to give back is a greater thing than to give. . . . When a disease recurs the medicine must be repeated. You will prove your gratitude to the Lord if you do not refuse what He offers you anew. (Tertullian, *On Penitence*, ACW 28, p. 29)

Yet to repent repeatedly for the same sin was tantamount to not repenting at all. One had better gain new footing in that case:

[The penance] which is required of us and which brings us back to favor with the Lord, must never, once we have known and embraced it, be violated thereafter by a return to sin. In this case, no plea of ignorance excuses you. . . . He repudiates the giver when he abandons the gift; he rejects the benefactor when he dishonors the benefaction. How can God Himself be pleasing to a man who takes no pleasure in His gift?. . .

The man who began to satisfy the Lord by repenting his sin will satisfy the devil by repenting his repentance, and he will be as hateful to the Lord as he is dear to his adversary.

Some say, however, that God is satisfied if He be honored in heart and mind, even though this be not done externally. Thus they sin, yet lose not reverential fear and faith. That is to say, they lose not chastity and commit adultery! They lose not filial piety and poison a parent! . . . A wonderful example of wrong-headedness. (Tertullian, *On Penitence*, ACW 28, p. 22, 23)

The soul guide must strive for balanced judgment between two extremes: inordinate laxity in response to God's grace; and being too hard on those who fall short. There are indeed examples of times when the community of faith has made excessive judgments on one side or the other. There is no better place to go for an example than the desert ascetics, among whom St. Anthony exercised moderating judgment:

It happened one day that one of the brethren in the monastery of Abba Elias was tempted. Cast out of the monastery, he went over the mountain to Abba Anthony. The brother lived near him for a while and then Anthony sent him back to the monastery from which he had been expelled. When the brothers saw him they cast him out yet again, and he went back to Abba Anthony saying, "My Father, they will not receive me." Then the old man sent them a message saying, "A boat was ship-wrecked at sea and lost its cargo; with great difficulty it reached the shore; but you want to throw into the sea that which has found a safe harbour on the shore." When the brothers understood that it was Abba Anthony who had sent them this monk, they received him at once. (Anthony the Great, sec. 21, *Sayings of the Desert Fathers*, pp. 4-5)

VI ❧ RESTITUTION

One of the points at which behavior modification theories and "responsibility therapies" are most akin to the classical pastoral tradition is in their seriousness about attempts to restore damages done, to make reparation for misdeeds. In behavior change strategies that follow the modern pattern of Alcoholics Anonymous, for example, this reparative concern is integral to the process of reconciliation. It is one of the most familiar themes in classical pastoral care.

Gregory the Great chided those who would pretend to quit sin, but fail to make any concrete or meaningful reparation:

Those who desist from sinning but do not lament their sins are to be admonished not to suppose that their sins are forgiven on the mere plea that they have not been repeated, if they have not been cleansed by tears. A writer, for instance, who has given up writing, has not deleted what he has written, just because he has not added anything. So, too, one does not make reparation for insults offered, merely by holding one's peace, for, in truth, it is necessary that he abjure the words of his former pride by expressions of subsequent humility. Nor, again, is a debtor discharged, merely because he incurs no further debts, if he has not paid the debts already incurred. So, too, when we sin against God, we certainly do not make reparation merely by ceasing from evil. (Gregory the Great, *Pastoral Care*, Part III, Ch. 30, ACW 11, p. 206)

Thomas Aquinas used a legal analogy to define restitution:

Restitution is opposed to taking away. Now it is an act of commutative injustice to take away what belongs to another. Therefore to restore it is an act of that justice which directs commutations. . . . Even as the term commutation has passed from such like things to those actions and passions which confer reverence or injury, harm or profit on another person, so too the term restitution is applied, to things which though they be transitory in reality, yet remain in their effect; whether this touch his body, as when the body is hurt by being struck, or his reputation, as when a man remains defamed or dishonored by injurious words. (Thomas Aquinas, *Summa Theologica*, II-II, Q. 62, Art. 1, Vol. II, pp. 1455-1456)

The pastor is called to guide the process of restitution according to the rule of proportionality, i.e., restitution should be reasonably equal in value to whatever has been harmed, taken away, or injured, if possible. Restitution does not require more than compensation for damages. Thomas further developed this legal analogy:

Restitution re-establishes equality where an unjust taking has caused inequality. Now equality is restored by repaying the exact amount taken. Therefore there is no obligation to restore more than the exact amount taken. . . . The judge can exact more by way of damages. . . . Restitution belongs to justice, because it re-establishes equality. But if one were to restore what one did not take, there would not be equality. . . . Loss is so called from a man having less than his due. Therefore a man is bound to make restitution according to the loss he has brought upon another. . . .

Restitution must be made to the person from whom a thing has been taken. . . . If the person to whom restitution is due is unknown altogether, restitution must be made as far as possible, for instance by giving alms for his spiritual welfare (whether he be dead or living): but not without previously making a careful inquiry about his person. If the person to whom restitution is due be dead, restitution should be made to his heir, who is looked upon as one with him. . . . Whoever is cause of an unjust taking is bound to restitution. This happens in two ways, directly and indirectly. Directly, when a man induces another to take. . . . Indirectly, when a man does not prevent another from evil-doing (provided he is able and bound to prevent him), either by omitting the command or counsel which would hinder him from thieving or robbing, or by omitting to do what would have hindered him, or by sheltering him after the deed. . . . Not only is he bound to restitution who commits the sin, but also he who is in any way cause of the sin, whether by counselling, or by commanding, or in any other way whatever. (Thomas Aquinas, *Summa Theologica*, II-II, Q. 62, Art. 3-7, Vol. II, pp. 1457-1461)

Three levels of positive effects accompany acts of reparation:

Exterior penances are performed principally to produce three effects:
a. To satisfy for past sins.
b. To overcome ourselves, so that sensuality will be obedient to reason and our lower inclinations be subject to higher ones.
c. To seek and find some grace or gift that we wish to obtain, as for instance . . . the solution of some doubt that is troubling us. (Ignatius Loyola, *Spiritual Exercises*, pp. 62-63)

Repentance becomes a hollow, feigned act, without restitution.

How very many indeed do we daily see dying, groaning deeply, reproaching themselves greatly for usuries, plunderings, oppressions of the poor, and all kinds of injuries which they have committed, and consulting a priest to free them from these faults. If, as is proper, the first advice given to them is this, that selling all they have, they restore to others what they have taken—in accordance with Augustine: "If something which belongs to another is not returned when it can be returned, repentance is not done but is feigned"—instantly by their reply they declare how hollow is their repentance for these things. (Abelard, *Ethics*, pp. 79, 81)

VII ❦ THE MINISTRY OF EUCHARIST

To shepherd is to feed the flock. The quintessential Christian pastoral act is one of feeding: eating and drinking, receiving spiritual nourishment for our souls. All that we have said thus far about confession is prologue to the ministry of Eucharist.

No pastoral act is more central to the care of souls than the Supper where the resurrected Christ himself is present at the table. If all acts of pastoral care were stopped except Eucharist, the work of pastoral care would remain vital and significant. Graham Greene's novel, *The Heart of the Matter*, has precisely that premise: an unworthy priest is being chased by a tyrannical government in the hills—the last priest who can offer holy communion to the people. Even though he can care for the flock only in one way and that rather poorly, nonetheless his ministry has moving significance to those who receive the living Christ in the bread and wine under conditions of tyranny.

What is this power of the Eucharist to care for souls? Why is the ministry of the Eucharist so central to pastoral care? How does God's own care meet us in the Eucharist? Christ's broken body becomes truly present to the community through the broken bread:

> What the Lord did not endure on the cross [the breaking of his legs] he submits to now in his sacrifice for his love of you: he permits himself to be broken in pieces that all may be filled. (John Chrysostom, *Homilies on First Corinthians*, Homily 24, LCF, pp. 174-175)

The death and resurrection of Jesus is not only proclaimed through the sacramental act but is embodied to the believing community:

> We proclaim the death, in the flesh, of the only-begotten Son of God, Jesus Christ, and acknowledge his return to life from the dead and his ascension into heaven, and as we do this we perform the bloodless sacrifice in the churches: and thus we approach the consecrated gifts of the sacrament, and are sanctified by partaking of the holy flesh and the precious blood of Christ, the Saviour of us all. (Cyril of Alexandria, *Epistles*, Epistle 17, To Nestorius, sec. 3, LCF, p. 267)

The benefits of Christ's death and resurrection are conveyed to the believer through the supper in a way analogous to food, providing nourishment for the soul:

> Our Lord Jesus, in the night wherein he was betrayed, instituted the sacrament of his body and blood, called the Lord's Supper, to be observed in his Church, unto the end of the world; for

the perpetual remembrance of the sacrifice of himself in his death, the sealing all benefits thereof unto true believers, their spiritual nourishment and growth in him, their further engagement in, and to all duties which they owe unto him; and to be a bond and pledge of their communion with him, and with each other, as members of his mystical body. . . . The Lord Jesus hath, in this ordinance, appointed his ministers to declare his word of institution to the people, to pray, and bless the elements of bread and wine, and thereby to set them apart from a common to an holy use; and to take and break the bread, to take the cup, and (they communicating also themselves) to give both to the communicants; but to none who are not then present in the congregation. (Westminister Confession, Ch. XXIX, sec. 1-3, *CC*, p. 225)

"Set-apart" ministry consecrates the set-apart elements of communion for holy use. The pastoral effect of the reception of the supper is to seal in our hearts the promise of the gospel:

Our Lord, therefore, instituted the Supper, first, in order to sign and seal in our consciences the promises contained in his gospel concerning our being made partakers of his body and blood, and to give us certainty and assurance that therein lies our true spiritual nourishment, and that having such an earnest, we may entertain a right reliance on salvation. (John Calvin, *Short Treatise on the Holy Supper of Our Lord Jesus Christ*, Sec. 6, SW, p. 510)

The whole body of Christ is communicated through the Eucharist, according to Catherine of Siena. She used the conflated metaphors of a broken mirror whose fragments reflect perfectly, a single light that illumines many, and candles of varied sizes lit from a single flame, to express the essential unity and paradoxical equality of all faithful recipients of communion:

When you break a mirror the reflection to be seen in it is not broken; similarly, when the host is divided God and man are not divided, but remain in each particle. . . . If you have a light, and the whole world should come to you in order to take light from it—the light itself does not diminish—and yet each person has it all. . . . Suppose that there are many who bring their candles, one weighing an ounce, others two or six ounces, or a pound, or even more, and light them in the flame, then in each candle, whether large or small, is the whole light, that is to say, the heat, the colour, and the flame; nevertheless you would not judge that he whose candle weighs an ounce has less of the light than he whose candle weighs a pound. Now the same thing happens to those who receive this Sacrament. Each one carries his own candle, that is the holy desire, with which he receives this Sacrament, which of itself is without light, and lights it by receiving this Sacrament. (Catherine of Siena, *A Treatise of Prayer*, pp. 230-231)*

The authenticity and apostolicity of the Eucharist must be guarded in order to maintain the unity of the body:

Make certain, therefore, that you all observe one common Eucharist; for there is but one Body of our Lord Jesus Christ, and but one cup to union with His Blood, and one single altar of sacrifice—even as also there is but one bishop, with his clergy and my own fellow-servitors the deacons. This will ensure that all your doings are in full accord with the will of God. (Ignatius of Antioch, *To the Philadelphians*, sec. 4, ECW, p. 112)

The sense in which Christ is mystically present in the Supper has been repeatedly discussed by the pastoral tradition, but there is little question that Christ is truly present. This centrist statement shows the difficulty of articulating the mystery of Christ's presence in the sacrament:

The opinion of Zwingli which the Divines of Zurich tenaciously maintained and defended, namely that "Christ is present in the Eucharist only by the contemplation of faith; that there is no place to be given here to a miracle, since we know in what way Christ is present to His Supper, namely, by the quickening Spirit, spiritually and efficaciously; that Sacramental union consists wholly in signification," etc., is by no means to be approved, since it is most clearly contrary to Scripture and the common opinion of all the Fathers. . . .

The holy Fathers . . . most firmly believed that he who worthily receives the mysteries of the Body and Blood of Christ really and actually receives into himself the Body and Blood of Christ, but in a certain spiritual, miraculous, and imperceptible way. . . .

The opinion of those Protestants and others seems to be most safe and most right who think, nay, who most firmly believe, that the Body and Blood of Christ are really and actually and substantially present and taken in the Eucharist, but in a way which the human mind cannot understand and much more beyond the power of man to express, which is known to God alone and is not revealed to us in the Scriptures,—a way indeed not by bodily or oral reception, but not only by the understanding and merely by faith, but in another way known, as has been said, to God alone, and to be left to His omnipotence. (William Forbes, *Considerationes Modestae*, Bk. I, Ch. I.2ff.; *Angl.*, p. 471)

Luther argues that sacrament of holy communion profoundly personalizes pastoral care:

When I preach the death of Christ, I am delivering a public sermon in the congregation. In it I am not giving to any person in particular; he who grasps the saving truth grasps it. But when I administer the Sacrament, I am applying it to him in particular who is taking it; I am giving him Christ's body and blood that he (personally) may have the forgiveness of sins, purchased through Christ's death and preached in the congregation. This is something more than the ordinary sermon. (Luther, "The Sacrament of the Body and Blood of Christ Against the Fanatics, 1526," WA 19, p. 504; WLS 3, p. 1242; cf. LW 36, p. 348)

VIII ❧ The Invitation to the Lord's Table

Who are the rightful recipients of holy communion, under what conditions are they invited to the Lord's table, and how are they to receive the curative sacrament?

In one sense *all* are invited, and the supper is for *all*, even though all may not faithfully receive it, as John Chrysostom sought to clarify:

"Thus Christ also was once offered" (Heb. 9:28). By whom? By himself, to be sure. Here the author shows that [Christ] is not only a priest, but also victim and sacrifice. Then he gives the reason for his being offered: "Offered once to bear the sins of many." Why "many" and not "all"? Because all did not believe. He, for his part, did indeed die for all, to save all; for his death was equivalent to the death of all. (Chrysostom, *Homilies on Hebrews*, Homily 17, LCF, p. 173)

The supper has relevance for all humanity, and is intended for all, as Christ's death and resurrection is for all; yet regrettably not all come to believe, partake and participate in Christ's death and resurrection.

Those are best prepared for holy communion who are instructed in its meaning and seek to live out its implications in their lives.

According to custom, urge that each one of the people individually should take his part. One's own conscience is best for choosing carefully or turning aside. It provides a firm foundation for the upright life, provided it has suitable instruction. But the imitation of those who have already been tested and who have led upright lives is most excellent for the understanding and practice of these commandments. "It follows that anyone who eats the bread or drinks the cup of the Lord unworthily will be guilty of desecrating the body and blood of the Lord. A man must test himself before eating his share of the bread and drinking from the cup" (1 Cor. 11:27-28). (Clement of Alexandria, *The Stromata, or Miscellanies*, Bk. I, Ch. I, ANF II, p. 300, NEB)*

Serious moral self-examination accompanies the preparation and approach to holy communion. The ill-prepared may be harmed by unworthy reception, according to Catherine of Siena:

It gives life and adorns the soul with every grace, in proportion to the disposition and affection of him who receives It; similarly It gives death to him who receives It unworthily. (Catherine of Siena, *A Treatise of Discretion*, p. 66)

It need not be assumed that we must present ourselves as morally perfected in order to merit the gift of communion with the Lord. Much more, according to Luther, should we be aware of our inability to merit that communion which the cross merits:

He who has not felt the battle within him, is not distressed by his sins nor has a daily quarrel with them, and wishes no protector, defender and shield to stand before him, is not yet ready for this food. This food demands a hungering and longing man, for it delights to enter a hungering soul, one that is in constant battle with its sins and eager to be rid of them. . . . This is what Christ did, when He prepared to institute the blessed sacrament. He brought anguish upon His disciples and trembling to their hearts when He said that He would go away from them, and again they were tormented when He said: One of you shall betray me. Think you not that that cut them to the heart? Truly, they received the word with all fear, and sat there as though they were all traitors to God. And after He had made them all tremble with fear and sorrow, then only did He institute the blessed sacrament as a comfort, and consoled them again. For this bread is a comfort for the sorrowing, a healing for the sick, a life for the dying, a food for all the hungry, and a rich treasure for all the poor and needy. (Luther, The Eight Wittenberg Sermons, Sixth Sermon, WML II, p. 418-419)

The pastor may be asked by those who feel unworthy to receive the sacrament whether they do best to stay away until they feel worthy. Isaac Barrow answered:

What unworthiness should hinder us from remembering Our Lord's excessive charity towards us, and thanking Him for it, from praying for His grace, from resolving to amend our lives? Must we, because we are unworthy, continue so still, by shunning the means of correcting and curing us? Must we increase our unworthiness, by transgressing our duty? (Isaac Barrow, *Brief Exposition*, Works, V, p. 608; *Angl.*, p. 505)

Menno Simons argued of excommunication not that it was the church's act of barring a member from the table, but rather the member's own self-determined absence from communication, or choice to remain separated:

No one is excommunicated or expelled by us from the communion of the brethren but those who have already separated and expelled themselves from Christ's communion either by false doctrine or by improper conduct. For we do not want to expel any, but rather to receive; not to amputate, but rather to heal; not to discard, but rather to win back; not to grieve, but rather to comfort; not to condemn, but rather to save. (Menno Simons, *A Kind Admonition on Church Discipline*, 1541, *CWMS*, p. 413)

In order to insure the proper administration of communion duly grounded in apostolic teaching, Ignatius stressed that the supper be celebrated only by one duly called and elected who stands faithfully in the apostolic tradition:

The sole Eucharist you should consider valid is one that is celebrated by the bishop himself, or by some person authorized by him. Where the bishop is to be seen, there let all his people be; just as wherever Jesus Christ is present, we have the world-wide Church. Nor is it permissible to conduct baptisms or love-feasts without the bishop. (Ignatius of Antioch, *Letter to Polycarp*, sec. 8, ECW, p. 121)

The connection with the bishop signified to Ignatius the connection with the authorized apostolic teaching of Christ's ministry. In the absence of a minister, can a lay person, even a child, serve the Eucharist in an emergency, under the guidance of an absent presbyter? Eusebius reports a letter from Dionysius of Alexandria concerning an unusual event of a child's providing emergency communion:

"I will give you this one example which occurred among us. There was with us a certain Serapion, an aged believer who had lived for a long time blamelessly, but had fallen during the times of persecution. He asked frequently to be restored, but no one gave heed to him, because he had sacrificed idolatrously. But he became sick, and for three successive days continued speechless and senseless. Having recovered somewhat on the fourth day he sent for his daughter's son, and said, 'How long do you detain me, my child? I beg you, make haste, and absolve me speedily. Call one of the presbyters to me.' And when he had said this, he became again speechless. And the boy ran to the presbyter. But it was night and the presbyter was sick, unable to come. But as I had commanded that persons at the point of death, if they requested it, and especially if they had asked for it previously, should receive remission, that they might depart with a good hope, he gave the boy a small portion of the Eucharist, telling him to soak it and let the drops fall into the old man's mouth. The boy returned with it, and as he drew near, before he entered, Serapion again arousing, said, 'You have come, my child, and the presbyter could not come; but do quickly what he directed and let me depart.' Then the boy soaked it and dropped it into his mouth. And when he had swallowed a little, immediately he gave up the ghost. Is it not evident that he was preserved?" (Eusebius, *Church History*, Bk. VI, Ch. XLIV, sec. 2-6, NPNF 2, I, p. 290)

IX ❧ THE BREAKING OF BREAD

If the act which epitomizes soul care is Supper with the resurrected Lord, it behooves the pastor to look carefully at the language of the eucharistic event to see how the ancient pastoral writers interpreted its meaning. The eucharistic prayers and rubrics yield the deepest insight. One of the earliest of such prayers is found in the *Didache*:

At the Eucharist, offer the eucharistic prayer in this way. Begin with the chalice: "We give thanks to thee, our Father, for the holy Vine of thy servant David, which thou hast made known to us through thy servant Jesus." *"Glory be to thee, world without end."* Then over the particles of bread: "We give thanks to thee, our Father, for the life and knowledge thou hast made known to us through thy servant Jesus." *"Glory be to thee, world without end."* "As this broken bread, once dispersed over the hills, was brought together and became one loaf, so may thy Church be brought together from the ends of the earth into thy kingdom." *"Thine is the glory and the power, through Jesus Christ, for ever and ever."* No one is to eat or drink of your Eucharist but those who have been baptized in the Name of the Lord; for the Lord's own saying applies here, "Give not that which is holy unto dogs" (Matt. 7:6).

When all have partaken sufficiently give thanks in these words: "Thanks be to thee, holy Father, for thy sacred Name which thou hast caused to dwell in our hearts, and for the knowledge and faith and everlasting life which thou hast revealed to us through thy servant Jesus." *"Glory be to thee for ever and ever."* "Thou, O Almighty Lord, hast created all things for thine own Name's sake; to all men thou hast given meat and drink to enjoy, that they may give thanks to thee, but to us thou hast graciously given spiritual meat and drink, together with life eternal, through thy Servant. Especially, and above all, do we give thanks to thee for the mightiness of thy power." *"Glory be to thee for ever and ever."* "Be mindful of thy church, O Lord; deliver it from all evil, perfect it in thy love, sanctify it, and gather it from the four winds into the kingdom which thou hast prepared for it." *"Thine is the power and the glory for ever and ever."* "Let His Grace draw near, and let this present world pass away." *"Hosanna to the God of David."* "Whosoever is holy, let him approach. Whoso is not, let him repent." *"O Lord, come quickly. Amen."* (Charismatists, however, should be free to give thanks as they please.) (*Didache*, sec. 9-10, ECW, pp. 231)

The Eucharist is a free act. It cannot be coerced:

We are to force no one to believe, or to receive the Sacrament, nor to fix any law, time, or place for it, but so to preach that they will be urged of their own accord, without our law, and will, as it were, compel us pastors to administer the Sacrament. (Luther, *Small Catechism*, Introduction, WA 30, I 264f; WLS 1, p. 118)*

On the frequency of holy communion, Anglican Isaac Barrow wrote:

The primitive Christians did very frequently use it, partaking in it, as it seems, every time they met for God's service. It is said of them by St. Luke that "they continued steadfastly in the Apostles' doctrine and communion, and in breaking of bread, and in prayers," (Acts 2:42) and "When you meet together, it is not (as according to the intent and duty of meeting it should be) to eat the Lord's Supper" (1 Cor. 11:20) said St. Paul. And Justin Martyr in his Second Apology, describing the religious service of God in their assemblies, mentions it as a constant part of it. And Epiphanius reports it a custom in the Church, derived from Apostolical institution, to celebrate the Eucharist three times each week, that is, so often as they met to pray and praise God." (Isaac Barrow, *A Brief Exposition of the Lord's Prayer and Decalogue*, Works, V, pp. 606-608; *Angl.*, p. 504)*

Luther wrote a Maundy Thursday discourse in 1521 which included this prayer for preparation for holy communion:

Lord, it is true that I am not worthy for you to come under my roof, but I need and desire your help and grace to make me godly. I now come to you, trusting only in the wonderful words I just heard, with which you invite me to your table and promise me, the unworthy one, forgiveness of all my sins through your body and blood if I eat and drink them in this sacrament. Amen. Dear Lord, I do not doubt the truth of your words. Trusting them, I eat and I drink with you. Do unto me according to your words. Amen. (Luther, *Sermon on the Worthy Reception of the Sacrament*, 1521, LW 42, p. 174)

Can beer or some other substitute be canonically offered instead of wine?

If any bishop or presbyter, otherwise than our Lord has ordained concerning the sacrifice, offer other things at the altar of God, as honey, milk, or strong beer instead of wine. . . . let him be deprived. (*Constitutions of the Holy Apostles*, Ch. XLVII, sec. 3, ANF VII, p. 500)

How are the bread and wine consecrated?

Do you wish to know how it is consecrated by heavenly words? Hear what those words are—the priest says: "Make for us this oblation ratified, reasonable, acceptable, because it is the figure of the body and blood of our Lord Jesus Christ." (Ambrose, *On the Mysteries*, Ch. IV, sec. 21, NPNF 2 X, 319; LCF, p. 184)

The crucial moment of the service, when the bread and wine are consecrated, was carefully set forth by John Chrysostom:

Christ is now also present. He who adorned that table [of the Last Supper] is he who now also adorns this. It is not man who makes the gift of the oblation to become the body and blood of Christ, but Christ himself, who was crucified. The priest stands, fulfilling the original pattern, and speaks those words; but the power and grace come from God. "This is my body" (Matt. 26:26; Mk. 14:22; Lk. 22:19), he says. This statement transforms the oblations. (Chrysostom, *De prod. Jud. 1.6*, IV.a; LCF p. 173)

The *epiklesis*, or invocation, is the prayer following and completing the consecration of the bread and wine, which calls upon God to pour out the Holy Spirit upon the bread and wine that their recipients may be filled with grace. Especially important in Eastern liturgies, its dramatic significance was set forth by John Chrysostom:

When the priest stands before the Table, holding up his hands to heaven, and invokes the Holy Spirit to come and touch the elements, there is a great silence, a great stillness. When the Spirit gives his grace, when he descends, when he touches the elements, when you see the sacrifice of the lamb completed; do you then indulge in uproar, riot, quarrelling or abuse? (John Chrysostom, *De coemet.*, IV.a; LCF, p. 173)

Hippolytus offered this account of the words spoken to accompany the fraction of the bread:

And when he breaks the Bread in distributing to each a fragment (*klasma*) he shall say: The Bread of Heaven in Christ Jesus. And he who receives shall answer: Amen. (Hippolytus, *The Apostolic Tradition*, XXIII.5-6, p. 41)

Thomas Aquinas set forth three reasons why the laity need the ministry of the eucharist, and why it is viewed as a pastoral remedy:

Sacraments are necessary unto man's salvation for three reasons. The first is taken from the condition of human nature which is such that it has to be led by things corporeal and sensible to things spiritual and intelligible. Now it belongs to Divine providence to provide for each one according as its condition requires. Divine wisdom, therefore, fittingly provides man with means of salvation, in the shape of corporeal and sensible signs that are called sacraments.

The second reason is taken from the state of man who in sinning subjected himself by his affections to corporeal things. Now the healing remedy should be given to a man so as to reach the part affected by disease. Consequently it was fitting that God should provide man with a spiritual medicine by means of certain corporeal signs; for if man were offered spiritual things without a veil, his mind being taken up with the material world would be unable to apply itself to them.

The third reason it taken from the fact that man is prone to direct his activity chiefly towards material things ... It follows, therefore, that through the institution of the sacraments man, consistently with his nature, is instructed through sensible things. (Thomas Aquinas, *Summa Theologica*, III, Q. 61, Art. 1, Vol. II, p. 2352)

Widely debated since the sixteenth century is the question of whether or to what extent a sacrifice is being offered in the mass. Here is a fourth century statement by Eusebius that combines the themes of mystery, memorial, and divine sacrifice:

We have received a memorial of this offering which we celebrate on a table by means of symbols of His Body and saving Blood.... Here it is plainly the mystic Chrism and the holy Sacrifices of Christ's Table that are meant, by which we are taught to offer to Almighty God through our great High Priest all through our life the celebration of our sacrifices, bloodless, reasonable, and well-pleasing to Him.... These were Isaiah's "wonders," the promise of the anointing with ointment of a good smell, and with myrrh made not to Israel but to all nations.... So, then, we sacrifice and offer incense: On the one hand when we celebrate the Memorial of His great Sacrifice according to the Mysteries He delivered to us, and bring to God the Eucharist for our salvation with holy hymns and prayers; while on the other we consecrate ourselves to Him alone and to the Word His High Priest, devoted to Him in body and soul. (Eusebius, *The Proof of the Gospel*, Bk. I, Ch. 10, sec. 4-5, pp. 60-62)

The Westminster Confession concisely stated the classical Reformed view of sacrament:

Sacraments are holy signs and seals of the covenant of grace, immediately instituted by God, to represent Christ and his benefits, and to confirm our interest in him: as also to put a visible difference between those that belong to the Church and the rest of the world; and solemnly to engage them to the service of God in Christ, according to his Word.

There is in every sacrament a spiritual relation or sacramental union, between the sign and the thing signified; whence it comes to pass that the names and the effects of the one are attributed to the other.

The grace which is exhibited in or by the sacraments, rightly used, is not conferred by any power in them; neither does the efficacy of a sacrament depend upon the piety or intention of the one who administers it, but upon the work of the Spirit, and the word of institution, which contains, together with a precept authorizing its use, a promise of benefit to worthy receivers.

There be only two sacraments ordained by Christ our Lord in the gospel, that is to say, Baptism and the Supper of the Lord; neither of which may be dispensed by any but by a minister of the Word lawfully ordained. (Westminister Confession, Ch. XXVII, sec. i-v, *CC*, pp. 223-224)*

The selections of Part Five have focussed upon confession and communion counsel. God's pardon is promised to those who sincerely confess sin. The offering of absolution is a crucial moment of pastoral activity. Holy communion is the fitting context for acts of contrition, confession, satisfaction, pardon, and restitution. The quintessential Christian pastoral act is one of feeding: eating and drinking, receiving spiritual nourishment for our souls in the Eucharist.

6 Pastor as Educator of the Soul

"APTNESS TO TEACH" (*didaktikos*, 2 Tim. 2:24) is requisite to the call to soul care. The pastor is not only preacher, liturgist, and empathic listener, but also to a significant degree teacher of the soul.

Soul care is education. The soul-friend is life-crisis mentor. The caregiving agent is also an agent of teaching of the truth. If the care of souls is a pedagogy of the inner life, then the pastor must develop the art of teaching.

I ❧ MINISTRY TO INQUIRERS

Each new generation will inquire with its own particular questions into the truth of Christianity. There is no standard format or predictable mode of inquiry. In each new culture and historical situation, the apostolic teaching seeks to be presented in ways that that emergent consciousness can understand and assimilate. Effective mission depends upon high competencies in teaching. Although laity in a given parish have many gifts for teaching that need to be channeled and utilized, the central burden of ordering, planning, and authenticating the teaching ministry in the parish falls primarily upon the pastor.

Yet the "pastor-knows-everything" syndrome may fail to understand the crucial function of doubt in faith. Consciousness of doubt is a preconditioning phase in which the truth can be constructively taught. The classical pastoral writers have welcomed unfettered, honest inquiry into the truth of Christianity. The following sayings, attributed to Peter in the pre-Nicene Clementine literature, demonstrate an early teaching style:

[They asked Peter]: "What will others think if they see you, like Socrates, pretending ignorance? . . . For if someone sees even you hesitating and doubting, then truly he will think that no one has knowledge of the truth." To this Peter answered: "Let us not concern ourselves about this. If indeed it is fitting that he enter the

166

gate of life, God will afford a fitting opportunity. Then the beginning shall be from God and not from man"....

[They asked Peter]: "Is it permitted to one to ask a question, if he wishes it? Or is silence enforced, after the manner of the Pythagoreans?" Then said Peter: "We do not compel those who come to us either to keep silence continually, or to ask questions; but we leave them free to do as they will, knowing that those who are anxious about their salvation, if they feel wounded in any part of the soul, that pain does not permit them to remain silent." (Clementina, *Recognitions of Clement*, Bk. X, Ch. IV, ANF VIII, p. 193)*

Although the Socratic method of "pretended ignorance" was not the standard method of early Christian teaching, it was available as a part of its teaching armamentarium. This imaginative recollection (presumably by Clement of Peter, but written much later) portrays the apostle as astutely fielding questions of inquirers, not anxious about the pretence of knowing everything, and willing to allow God time to plant and nurture the seeds of understanding in God's own time. There is an unusual degree of nondefensive freedom (to ask or not ask, to speak or keep silent) in this recollection.

Should special guidance be given to the best, so as to neglect the less advanced pupils?

There is no credit in spending all your affection on the cream of your pupils. Try rather to bring the more troublesome ones to order, by using gentleness. Nobody can heal every wound with the same unguent; where there are acute spasms of pain, we have to apply soothing poultices. So in all circumstances "be wary as serpents," though always "innocent as doves" (Matt. 10:16). (Ignatius of Antioch, *Letter to Polycarp*, sec. 2, ECW, p. 127, NEB)*

Clement of Alexandria, on the other hand, urged more pastoral attention to those who excel:

The Shepherd, then, cares for each of his sheep; and his closest inspection is given to those who are excellent in their natures and are capable of being most useful. (Clement of Alexandria, *The Stromata, or Miscellanies*, Bk. VI, Ch. XVII, ANF II, p. 577)

Some will come to Christian instruction with dubious motives or ambiguous intentions. Cyril showed high tolerance for various motivations to attend classes of inquiry into the Christian faith:

It is quite what might happen, that a man should be wanting to advance his suit with a Christian woman, and to that end has come here. And there is the like possibility the other way round. Or often it may be a slave that wanted to please his master, or a person that comes for the sake of his friend. I accept this as bait for the hook, and I welcome you as one who shall be saved, by a good hope, in spite of having come with an unsound intention. It may well be that you did not know where you were coming or what sort of a net it is that is taking you. And now you are inside the ecclesiastical fishnets. Let yourself be taken, do not make off, for Jesus is angling for you, not to make you die, but by his having died, to make you live. (Cyril of Jerusalem, *The Catechetical Letters*, Procatechesis, sec. 5, LCC, IV, p. 68)

Jewish pedagogy was greatly admired by some Christian pastoral writers:

During the Ten or Twelve years of their Education, their Youth are so much practised to the Scriptures, to weigh every word in them, and get them all by heart, that it is an Admiration to see how ready both Men and Women among them are at it; their Rabbis have it to that perfection that they have the concordance of their whole Bible in their memories. (Burnet, *Of the Pastoral Care*, Ch. VIII, p. 157)

The catechism seeks to bring the whole range of Christian teaching into a concise statement for elementary instruction in the faith:

The Catechism is an epitome and brief transcript of the entire Holy Scripture. (Luther, WA 30 I, p. 128; WLS 1, p. 124)

The usual practice was for the pastor to prove catechetical instruction of young people and inquirers at least once per year:

Great care must be taken in the Instruction of the Youth: The bare saying the Catechism by Rote is a small Matter; it is necessary to make them understand the weight of every Word in it: And for this end, every Priest, that minds his Duty, will find that no Part of it is so useful to his People, as once every year to go through the whole Church Catechism, Word by Word, and make his People understand the Importance of every Tittle in it. . . . By this means his people will come to have all this by heart; they will know what to say upon it at home to their children; and they will understand all his sermons the better when they have once had a clear notion of all those terms that run through them. (Burnet, *Of the Pastoral Care*, Ch. VIII, p.161; cf. *CS*, pp. 88-89)

Baxter argued that Christian education best proceeds through families under pastoral guidance:

It will be very necessary that we give one of the catechisms to every family in the parish, whether rich or poor, that so they may be without excuse: for if you leave it to themselves to buy them, perhaps the half of them will not get them. . . . As to the delivery of them, the best way is for the minister first to give notice in the congregation, that they shall be brought to their houses, and then to go himself from house to house and deliver them, and take the opportunity of persuading them to the work; and, as he goes round, to take a list of all the persons who have come of years of discretion in the several families, that he may know whom he has to take care of and instruct, and whom he has to expect when it cometh to their turn. . . . take the people in order, family by family, beginning a month or six weeks after the delivery of the catechisms, that they may have time to learn them. (Baxter, *RP*, pp. 235-236)

Cyril of Jerusalem, in speaking to inquirers into Christian truth (catechumens soon to be baptized), distinguished speaking and whispering in order to illustrate the difference between noisy den of elementary education toward the mystery of God's presence, and the solemn conclusion of that process—veritable baptismal entry into the living immediacy of that presence:

You were called catechumen, which means one into whom something is dinned from without. You heard of some hope, but you did not know what. You heard mysteries without understanding anything. You heard scriptures without plumbing their depth. It is not dinned in, any more, but whispered. (Cyril of Jerusalem, *The Catechetical Lectures*, Procatechesis, sec. 6, LCC, IV, p. 68)

Plain speaking is required more than fine theological distinctions in teaching young people of the faith:

All our teaching must be as plain and simple as possible. This best suits a teacher's ends. He that would be understood must speak to the capacity of his hearers. Truth loves the light, and is most beautiful when most naked. It is the sign of an envious enemy to hide the truth, but a work of a hypocrite to do this under pretence of revealing it. . . . There is no better way to make a good cause prevail than to make it as plain, and generally and thoroughly known as we can. . . . It is, at best, a sign that one has not well digested the matter himself, if one is not able to deliver it plainly to others. (Baxter, *RP*, pp. 115-116)*

Even deep points of truth can be patiently elicited from anyone, even a "silly tradesman" (as in Plato's *Meno*), if one learns to put the right question, as did Socrates:

Many say the catechism by rote, as parrots, without ever piercing into the sense of it. . . . The catechiser . . . will draw out of ignorant and silly souls even the dark, and deep points of religion. Socrates did thus in philosophy, who held that the seeds of all truths lay in every body; and accordingly, by questions well ordered, he found philosophy in silly tradesmen. (George Herbert, *CP*, Chap. XXI, CWS, pp. 83–84)

The Socratic method, drawing the truth out by questioning the learner, takes this form in Baxter:

When you perceive that they do not understand the meaning of your question, you must draw out their answer by an equivalent, or expository question; . . . I have often asked some very ignorant people, "How do you think that your sins, which are so many and so great, can be pardoned?" And they tell me, "By repenting, and amending their lives.". . . If you find them at a loss, and unable to answer your questions, do not drive them too hard, or too long, with question after question, lest they conceive you intend only to puzzle them, and disgrace them; but when you perceive that they cannot answer, step in yourself, and take the burden off them, and answer the question yourselves; and do it thoroughly and plainly, and give a full explanation of the whole truth to them. . . . (Baxter, *RP*, pp. 242-243)

II 🎗 THE PASTOR AS PEDAGOGUE

The nature of pedagogy is the central concern of Clement of Alexandria's major treatise, *Christ the Educator (paidagogos)*. Its theme: how Christ teaches and guides the soul. The soul-guide mediates Christ's own guidance on the pathway toward behavioral excellence (virtue).

In a thoughtful description of what psychologists today call "neonate responsiveness" (the capacity of children to be immediately in touch with their own feelings), Clement clarified the sense in which the best learners are like children, and why "becoming a child" (an "uncontaminated lover of the horn of the unicorn") is a desirable quality of consciousness:

We define education as a sound training from childhood in the path of virtue. Be that as it may, the Lord once very clearly revealed what He means by the name "little child": A dispute having arisen among the Apostles as to which of them was greater, Jesus made a little child stand among them, saying: "Let a man humble himself till he is like this child, and he will be the greatest in the kingdom of Heaven" (Matt. 18:4). Therefore, He does not mean by "little child" one who has not yet reached the use of reason because of his immaturity, as some have thought. When He says: "Unless you turn round and become like children, you will never enter the kingdom of Heaven" (Matt. 18:3), we must not foolishly mistake His meaning. We are not little ones in the sense that we roll on the floor or crawl. . . . Children are those who look upon God alone as their father, who are simple, little ones, uncontaminated, who are lovers of the horn of the unicorn. . . . The name "little one" is not used in the sense of lacking intelligence. Childishness means that, but "little one" really means "one newly become gentle." (Clement of Alexandria, *Christ the Educator*, Bk. I, FC 23, pp. 17-19, NEB)*

Athanasius was among the first to recognize that God's way of teaching is by empathic participation in our limited situation—through incarnation:

He deals with them as a good teacher with his pupils, coming down to their level and using simple means. St. Paul says as much: "Because in the wisdom of God the world in its wisdom knew not God, God thought fit through the simplicity of the News proclaimed to save those who believe" (1 Cor. 1:21). . . . The Saviour of us all, the Word of God, in His great love took to Himself a body and moved as Man among men, meeting their senses, so to speak, half way. He became Himself an object for the senses. (Athanasius, *On the Incarnation*, sec. 15, p. 25)

The intriguing analogy between incarnation and empathic teaching was firmly grasped by the pastoral writers:

When Christ wished to attract and instruct men, He had to become a man. If we are to attract and instruct children, we must become children with them. (Luther, WA 19, p. 78; WLS 1, p. 447)

Ignatius did not despise the premise that the teacher is a fellow student who needs constantly to be taught by his students:

I am not giving you commands as if I were someone. For even though I am in bonds for the Name, I am not yet perfect in Jesus Christ; for now I am beginning to be a disciple, and I speak to you as my fellow students. For I needed to be anointed by you with faith, instruction, endurance, patience. But since love does not let me be silent about you, I have undertaken to exhort you [cf. Philem. 9], so that together you may run your race in accordance with God's purpose. For Jesus Christ, our inseparable life, is the expressed purpose of the Father, just as the bishops who have been appointed throughout the world exist by the purpose of Jesus Christ. (Ignatius of Antioch, *Letter to the Ephesians*, sec. 3:1-2, AF, p. 78)

Jesus taught the disciples through gradual stages of development, according to Origen. Education is a developmental process. It does not happen all at once:

[Christ] wished first to give catechetical instruction as it were to those of the Apostles who were to hear the name of Christ, then to permit this, so to speak, to be digested in the minds of the hearers, that, after there had been a period of silence in the proclamation of something of this kind about Him, at a more seasonable time there might be built up upon the former rudiments "Christ Jesus crucified and raised from the dead," which at the beginning not even the Apostles knew.... For our Saviour wished, when He enjoined the disciples to tell no man that He was the Christ, to reserve the more perfect teaching about Him to a more fitting time, when to those who had seen Him crucified, the disciples who had seen Him crucified and risen could testify the things relating to His resurrection. For if the Apostles, who were always with Him and had seen all the wonderful things which He did, and who bore testimony to His words that they were words of eternal life, were offended on the night on which He was betrayed,—what do you suppose would have been the feelings of those who had formerly learned that He was the Christ? To spare them, I think, He gave this command. (Origen, *Commentary on Matthew*, sec. 17, ANF X, pp. 460-461)

At one point in *Paedogogos*, Clement of Alexandria described the teaching method of his own teachers. The account is shaped by two metaphors: bees gathering pollen from widely diverse sources, and good seeds being carefully planted.

Now this work of mine in writing is not artfully constructed for display; but my memoranda are stored up against old age, as a remedy against forgetfulness, truly an image and outline of those vigorous and animated discourses which I was privileged to hear, and of blessed and truly remarkable men.

Of these the one, in Greece, an Ionic; the other in Magna Graecia: the first of these from Coele-Syria, the second from Egypt, and others in the East. The one was born in the land of Assyria, and the other a Hebrew in Palestine.

When I came upon the last (he was the first in power), having tracked him out concealed in Egypt, I found rest. He, the true, the Sicilian bee, gathering the spoil of the flowers of the prophetic and apostolic meadow, engendered in the souls of his hearers a deathless element of knowledge.

Well, they preserving the tradition of the blessed doctrine derived directly from the holy apostles, Peter, James, John, and Paul, the sons receiving it from the father (but few were like the fathers), came by God's will to us also to deposit those ancestral and apostolic seeds. (Clement of Alexandria, *The Stromata, or Miscellanies*, Bk. I, Ch. I, ANF II, p. 301)

No names are mentioned, although Tatian, Theodotus and Pantaenus were probably among them. The principal feature of the teaching was the transmission of tradition through effective seed-planting (from which comes the word "seminary") of genuine, undistorted apostolic teaching.

III ⚡ COHERENCE IN EDUCATING THE SOUL

The better pastor is the one more ready to respond to emergent situations that require particular insights into the larger body of Christian teaching. Hence it is commended that the pastor study the whole range of Christian teaching as an internally consistent witness. Good teaching proceeds in a definite order, through sequential development, with internal congruity. Early pastoral writers sought a meaningful order for instruction in the faith that would correspond with scriptural requirements and manifest the intuitive coherence found in the apostolic witness.

Stone must follow stone in the appointed order, and corners be turned in each successive course. Unevennesses must be levelled off, so that the building may rise without fault. So we are proffering to you, as it were, building-stones of knowledge. You have to be told about the living God, you have to be told about the judgement, you have to be told about Christ, you have to be told about the resurrection. There are many things to be said, and in their proper order. As they are being said, they appear casual, but afterwards they present themselves as all connected together. (Cyril of Jerusalem, *The Catechetical Lectures*, Procatechesis, sec. 11, LCC, IV, p. 72)

Cyril understood that even though the pastor might seem to be contextually applying scriptural teaching to various situations, such insight can only emerge out of a deep inward grasp of a congruent whole. The practice of ministry needs both a sense of the integrity of the whole and the specificity of its application. Martin Luther thought that the surest and simplest way to organize the whole range of Christian teaching was to adhere closely to the primary texts of the Lord's Prayer, the Apostles' Creed and the Ten Commandments. All of these texts were memorized by every believer in Luther's time:

The ordinary Christian, who cannot read the Scriptures, is required to learn and know the Ten Commandments, the Creed, and the Lord's Prayer; and this has not come to pass without God's special ordering. For these three contain fully and completely everything that is in the Scriptures, everything that ever should be preached, and everything that a Christian needs to know, all put so briefly and so plainly that no one can make complaint or excuse, saying that what he needs for his salvation is too long or too hard to remember.

Three things a man needs to know in order to be saved. First, he must know what he ought to do and what he ought not to do. Second, when he finds that by his own strength he can neither do the things he ought, nor leave undone the things he ought not to do, he must know where to seek and find and get the strength he needs. Third, he must know how to seek and find and get this strength.

When a man is ill, he needs to know first what his illness is,— what he can do and what he cannot do. Then he needs to know where to find the remedy that will restore his health and help him to do and leave undone the things he ought. Third, he must ask for this remedy, and seek it, and get it or have it brought to him. In like manner, the Commandments teach a man to know his illness, so that he feels and sees what he can do and what he cannot do, what he can and what he cannot leave undone, and thus knows himself to be a sinner and a wicked man. After that the Creed shows him and teaches him where he may find the remedy,—the grace which helps him to become a good man and to keep the Commandments; it shows him God, and the mercy which He has revealed and offered in Christ. In the third place, the Lord's Prayer teaches him how to ask for this grace, get it, and take it to himself, to wit, by habitual, humble, comforting prayer; then grace is given and by the fulfilment of God's commandments he is saved. (Luther, *Brief Explanation*, WML II, pp. 354-355)

The first three commandments of the decalogue correlate with the petitions of the Lord's Prayer in a way that constitutes a reliable introduction to Christian teaching. Luther summarized:

See, therefore, what a pretty, golden ring these three Commandments and their works naturally form, and how from the First Commandment and faith the Second flows on to the Third, and the Third in turn drives through the Second up into the First. For the first work is to believe, to have a good heart and confidence toward God. From this flows the second good work, to praise God's Name, to confess His grace, to give all honor to Him alone. Then follows the third, to worship by praying, hearing God's Word, thinking of and considering God's benefits, and in addition chastising oneself, and keeping the body under.... Thus faith goes out into the works and through the works comes to itself again.... This order of good works we pray in the Lord's Prayer. The first is this, that we say: "Our Father, Who art in heaven"; these are the words of the first work of faith, which, according to the First Commandment, does not doubt that it has a gracious Father in heaven. The second: "Hallowed be Thy Name," in which faith asks that God's Name, praise and honor be glorified, and calls upon it in every need, as the Second Commandment says. The third: "Thy kingdom come," in which we pray for the true Sabbath and rest, peaceful cessation of our works, that God's work alone be done in us, and so God rule in us as in His own kingdom, as He says, Luke 17:21, "Behold, God's kingdom is nowhere else except within you." The fourth petition is "Thy will be done"; in which we pray that we may keep and have the Seven Commandments of the Second Table, in which faith is exercised toward our neighbor; just as in the first three it is exercised in works toward God alone. (Luther, *Treatise on Good Works*, WML I, pp. 248-250)

The extent to which catechectical teaching should pursue the meaning of the triune teaching was discussed by Cyril in his pre-baptismal lectures:

Every grace is given by the Father, through the Son, who also acts together with the Holy Spirit. There are not some graces that come from the Father, and different graces from the Son, and others again from the Holy Spirit. There is but one salvation, one giving of power, one faith, and yet there is one God the Father, our Lord, his only-begotten Son, and one Holy Spirit, the Paraclete. Let us be content with this knowlege and not busy ourselves with the questions about the divine nature or hypostasis. I would have spoken of that had it been contained in Scripture. Let us not venture where Scripture does not lead, for it suffices for our salvation to know that there is Father, and Son, and Holy Spirit. (Cyril of Jerusalem, *Catechetical Lectures*, Lecture XVI, sec. 24, LCC, IV, p. 173)

Luther warned against constantly revising and changing the curricular resources for catechetical study:

The minister should above all things avoid the use of different texts and forms of the Ten Commandments, the Lord's Prayer, the Creed, the Sacraments, etc. Let him adopt one form and adhere to it, using it one year as the other; for young and ignorant people must be taught one certain text and form, and will easily become confused if we teach thus today and otherwise next year, as if we thought of making improvements. In this way all effort and labor will be lost. This our honored fathers well understood, who all used the Lord's Prayer, the Creed, the Ten Commandments in one and the same manner. Therefore we also should so teach these forms to the young and inexperienced as not to change a syllable, nor set them forth and recite them one year differently from the other. (Luther, *Small Catechism*, 1529, Introduction, WA 30, I p. 263f.; WLS 1, p. 117-118)

IV ❧ TRUE TEACHING

The first responsibility of the educator of the soul is to have reasonable knowledge of the subject matter—the health of the soul. One cannot guide others in a path never taken. One cannot teach what one does not know:

Who can defend that which he has not learned, or make clear to others that which he himself does not know? (Lactantius, *On the Workmanship of God*, Ch. XX, ANF VII, p. 299)

Not only must the teacher know what he teaches, but also follow his own teaching. Merely intending to do so is not enough. Lactantius distinguished the effective from the defective teacher largely by behavioral fruits:

If any one should diligently inquire into their [false teachers'] character, he will find that they are passionate, covetous, lustful, arrogant, wanton, and, concealing their vices under a show of wisdom, doing those things at home which they had censured in the schools.

Perhaps I speak falsely for the sake of bringing an accusation. Does not Tullius both acknowledge and complain of the same thing? "How few," he says, "of philosophers are found of such a character, so constituted in soul and life, as reason demands! how few who are obedient to themselves, and submit to their own decrees! We may see some of such levity and ostentation, that it would be better for them not to have learned at all; others eagerly desirous of money, others of glory; many the slaves of lusts, so that their speech wonderfully disagrees with their life." Cornelius Nepos also writes to the same Cicero: "So far am I from thinking that philosophy is the teacher of life and the completer of happiness, that I consider that none have greater need of teachers of living than many who are engaged in the discussion of this subject. For I see that a great part of those who give most elaborate precepts in their school respecting modesty and self-restraint, live at the same time in the unrestrained desires of all lusts." Seneca also, in his Exhortations, says: "Many of the philosophers are of this description, eloquent to their own condemnation: for if you should hear them arguing against avarice, against lust and ambition, you would think that they were making a public disclosure of their own character, so entirely do the censures which they utter in public flow back upon themselves. . . . It makes no difference with what intention you act, when the action itself is vicious; because acts are seen, the intention is not seen.". . . Tullius rightly gives the preference, above teachers of philosophy, to those men employed in civil affairs, who govern the state, who found new cities or maintain with equity those already founded, who preserve the safety and liberty of the citizens either by good laws or wholesome counsels, or by weighty judgements. For it is right to make men good rather than to give precepts about duty to those shut up in corners, which precepts are not observed even by those who speak them. . . . They who merely teach without acting, of themselves detract from the weight of their own precepts; for who would obey, when they who give the precepts themselves teach disobedience? . . . Since they are the advisers of actions, and do not themselves act at all, they are to be regarded as mere talkers. (Lactantius, *The Divine Institutes*, Bk. III, Ch. XV, ANF VII, pp. 84-85)

Athanasius set forth Jesus as exemplar of one who taught so as to embody his teaching:

He not only taught, but also accomplished what he taught, so that everyone might hear when he spoke, and seeing as in an image, receive from him the model for acting, hearing him say, "Learn from me, for I am gentle and lowly in heart" (Matt. 11:29). A more perfect instruction in virtue one could not find than that which the Lord typified in himself. For whether the issue is forbearance of evil, or love of mankind, or goodness, or courage, or compassion, or pursuit of justice, one will discover all present in him, so that nothing is lacking for virtue to one who considers closely this human life of his. Cognizant of this, Paul said, "Be imitators of me, as I am of Christ" (1 Cor. 11:1). (Athanasius, A Letter to Marcellinus, ACW 10, p. 112)

Should a lecherous teacher be entrusted to teach children?

Aristippus, the master of the Cyrenaics, had a criminal intimacy with Lais, the celebrated courtesan; and that grave teacher of philosophy defended this fault by saying, that there was a great difference between him and the other lovers of Lais because he himself possessed Lais, whereas others were possessed by Lais. O illustrious wisdom, to be imitated by good men! Would you, in truth, entrust your children to this man for education, that they might learn to possess a harlot? . . . Nor was it enough to live in this manner, but he began also to teach lusts; and he transferred his habits from the brothel to the school, contending that bodily pleasure was the chief good. (Lactantius, *The Divine Institutes*, Ch. XV, ANF VII, p. 84)

Are there restrictions on the laity in teaching of Christian doctrine?

It does not benefit a layman to dispute or teach publicly, thus claiming for himself authority to teach, but he should yield to the order appointed by the Lord, and to open his ears to those who have received the grace to teach, and be taught by them divine things; for in one Church God has made "different members," according to the word of the Apostle: and Gregory the Theologian, wisely interpreting this passage, commends the order in vogue with them saying: "This order brethren we revere, this we guard. Let this one be the ear; that one the tongue, the hand or any other member. Let this one teach, but let that one learn." And a little further on: "Learning in docility and abounding in cheerfulness, and ministering with alacrity, we shall not all be the tongue which is the more active member, not all of us Apostles, not all prophets, nor shall we all interpret" (cf. 1 Cor. 12:29-30). And again: "Why dost thou make thyself a shepherd when thou art a sheep? Why become the head when thou art a foot? Why dost thou try to be a commander when thou art enrolled in the number of the soldiers?" And elsewhere: "Wisdom orders, Be not swift in words; nor compare thyself with the rich, being poor; nor seek to be wiser than the wise." (Synod of Quinisext, A.D. 692, Canon LXIV, The Seven Ecumenical Councils, NPNF 2, XIV, p. 394; quotations from Gregory of Nazianzus, *Theological Orations*, First Oration, Against Eunomians, NPNF 2, VII, p. 286)

V ❧ FALSE TEACHING

Wherever Christian instruction proceeds, it must deal with alternative views of history, God, humanity, reality, and ethics. These views may come from within the Christian community or from the culture it confronts. A *heterodox* opinion is other than that received in ecumenical teaching, while *hairesis* simply means an opinion self-chosen in opposition to the received teaching. The task of differentiating authentic from inauthentic teaching does not end with any given generation. True teaching must distinguish itself in each new cultural situation from its spurious or dubious alternatives.

Pastoral writers thought that an unintended providential purpose was at work in false teaching: to challenge, test out, and improve true teaching.

The character of the times in which we live is such as to call forth from us even this admonition, that we ought not to be astonished at the heresies which abound, neither ought their existence to surprise us. For it was foretold that they should come to pass. Nor need we be surprised that they subvert the faith of some, for their final purpose is, by affording a trial to faith, to give it also the opportunity of being approved. . . .

The Lord teaches us that many "ravening wolves shall come in sheep's clothing" (Matt. 7:15). Now, what are these sheep's clothings other than the external surface of the Christian profession? Who are the ravening wolves but those deceitful senses and spirits which are lurking within to waste the flock of Christian? . . . Heresies, at the present time, will no less rend the church by their perversion of doctrine, than will Antichrist persecute her at that day by the cruelty of his attacks, except that persecution makes martyrs while heresy makes only apostates. And therefore "dissensions are necessary if only to show which of your members are sound" (1 Cor. 11:19), both those who remained steadfast under persecution, and those who did not wander out of their way into heresy. . . . It was owing to the prospect of the greater evil that Paul readily affirmed the meaning of the lighter ones; and so far indeed was he from believing, in the face of evils of such a kind, that heresies were good, that his object was to forewarn us that we ought not to be surprised at temptations of even a worse stamp, since (he said) they tended to "show which of your members are sound" (1 Cor. 1:19). (Tertullian, *Prescription Against Heretics*, Ch. I, IV-V, ANF III, pp. 243, 245, NEB)*

This does not make *hairesis* good as such, but only divinely permissible within the frame of reference of God's purpose of freedom and redemption. Both heresy and persecution test the mettle of the believing church. These false teachings, however, win only temporary victories over true teaching. Where do heresies derive their strength? Believers who have to face repeatedly the buffetings of false teachers may become like a boxer with lowered morale:

False teachings would have less power if everyone would cease to be amazed at their alleged potency. . . . In a combat of boxers and gladiators, generally speaking, it is not simply because a man is physically strong that he gains the victory, or loses it because he is not strong, but often because he vanquished a smaller man. And sometimes it happens that this very conqueror, when afterwards matched against a really powerful man, actually retires crest-fallen from the contest. In precisely the same way, heretical teachings derive such strength as they have from the infirmities of individuals. They have no strength whatever when they encounter a really powerful faith. (Tertullian, *Prescription Against Heresies*, Ch. II, ANF III, pp. 243, 244)*

Hippolytus provided an account of how the motives, internal consistencies, and scriptural grounds of false teachings might be critically examined, as in the case of Noetus:

Some others are secretly introducing another doctrine, who have become disciples of one Noetus, who was a native of Smyrna, and lived not very long ago. This person was greatly puffed up and inflated with pride, being inspired by the conceit of a strange spirit. He alleged that Christ was the Father Himself, and that the Father Himself was born, and suffered, and died. You see what pride of heart and what a strange inflated spirit had insinuated themselves into him. From his other actions, then, the proof is already given us that he did not speak with a pure spirit; for he who blasphemes against the Holy Spirit is cast out from the holy inheritance. He alleged that he was himself Moses, and that Aaron was his brother. When the blessed presbyters heard this, they summoned him before the Church, and examined him. But he denied at first that he held such opinions. Afterwards, however, taking shelter among some, and having gathered round him some others who had embraced the same error, he wished thereafter to uphold his dogma openly as correct. And the blessed presbyters called him again before them, and examined him. But he stood out against them, saying, "What evil, then, am I doing in glorifying Christ?" And the presbyters replied to him, "We too know in truth one God; we know Christ; we know that the Son suffered even as He suffered, and died even as He died, and rose again on the third day, and is at the right hand of the Father, and cometh to judge the living and the dead. And these things which we have learned we allege." Then, after examining him, they expelled him from the Church. And he was carried to such a pitch of pride, that he established a school. (Hippolytus, *Against the Heresy of One Noetus*, sec. 1, ANF V, p. 223)*

It was not an incidental error (claiming oneself to be Moses, confusing the Father and the Son, blaspheming the Holy Spirit). The case of Noetus showed very early in the pastoral tradition that there was an orderly procedure for the examination of idiosyncratic, unecumenical, unorthodox, unworthy pastors who teach heresy but call it Christian faith. Later Jeremy Taylor would warn that Christian education does not invite in all opinions equally so as to pretend or appear to be merely a debating society:

Receive not the people to doubtful disputations: and let no names of sects or differing religions be kept up amongst you, to the disturbance of the public peace and private charity: and teach not the people to estimate their piety by their distance from any opinion. (Jeremy Taylor, *RAC*, Bk. III, sec. 29; *CS*, p. 11)

Some highly controversial (yet widely received) Christian teachings, like predestination and divine foreknowledge, need to be taught cautiously in such a way as not to lead to the abuse of other teachings:

We should not make predestination an habitual subject of conversation. If it is sometimes mentioned we must speak in such a way that no person will fall into error, as happens on occasion when one will say, "It has already been determined whether I will be saved or lost, and in spite of all the good or evil that I do, this will not be changed." As a result, they become apathetic and neglect the works that are conducive to their salvation and to the spiritual growth of their souls.

In like manner, we must be careful lest by speaking too much and with too great emphasis on faith, without any distinction or explanation, we give occasion to the people to become indolent and lazy in the performance of good works, whether it be before or after their faith is founded in charity.

Also in our discourse we ought not to emphasize the doctrine that would destroy free will. We may therefore speak of faith and grace to the extent that God enables us to do so, for the greater praise of His Divine Majesty. But, in these dangerous times of ours, it must not be done in such a way that good works or free will suffer any detriment or be considered worthless. (Ignatius Loyola, *Spiritual Exercises*, p. 141)

It is not only the clergy who have responsibility to recognize, judge, and reject false teaching, but the laity as well:

To recognize and judge doctrine behooves each and every Christian, so much so that he is accursed who infringes upon this right by as little as a hairsbreadth. For Christ Himself has established this right by various and unassailable statements, such as Matt. 7:15: "Beware of false prophets, which come to you in sheep's clothing." He is certainly speaking this word to the people in opposition to those who teach, and He commands them to avoid false teachings. But how can they avoid them if they do not recognize them? And how can they recognize them if they do not have the right to judge them? (Luther, WA 10 II, p. 217; WLS 1, p. 418)

False teaching should be approached by persuasion, not by persecution. However skewed the false teaching, it should not be resisted by coercion:

We should vanquish heretics with books, not with burning; for so the ancient fathers did. If it were a science to vanquish the heretics with fire, then the hangmen would be the most learned doctors on earth. (Luther, *An Open Letter to the Christian Nobility*, WML II, p. 142)

Selections of Part Six have focussed upon the pastor as educator of the soul, the aptness to teach required of ministry, the pedagogy of the inner life. The soul-guide mediates Christ's own guidance on the pathway toward behavioral excellence. God teaches by empathic participation in the limited situation of the learner. True teaching must distinguish itself in each new cultural situation from its spurious alternatives, under the guidance of apostolic teaching.

7 Care of the Community

Pastors do not direct their soul care exclusively to individuals within the Church. Their care is also extended to the congregation as a body, and beyond the congregation to the secular sphere, the world. The pastor's care within the domestic order and economic order are treated in another volume of this series on *Crisis Ministries*. In this Part we will deal with four ever-widening circles of community to which the pastor is responsible: church institutions, inter-institutional relationships, the political order, and the world.

First, curacy requires the nurture of institutional processes within the Church that they may better serve the education and growth of souls effected by them. Modern seminary courses of study call these tasks by various names: church and ministry, church management, and "church administration." We prefer to call it, "administry," or that which leads to and prepares for ministry. Secondly, curacy involves dealing with other pastors, and with alternative church structures that interface in various inter-institutional relationships. In earlier periods this part of the pastoral task was sometimes called "pastoral etiquette," which referred to the maintenance of cordial relationships with others in Christian ministry. Third, curacy involves dealing with economic and political structures that confront and affect the lives of Christian communicants, and the society at large. The church has thought long and hard about the extent of the pastor's involvement in political activities. This task involves the political ethics of the pastor. Fourth, curacy is called to care more largely for the *saeculum*, the world, the structures of secularity given to the church by God at a particular time, for service, intercession, responsible love, and the search for justice. There are varied interpretations of the relationship of the church to the world.

I ❦ Administry: Pastoral Care Through Institutions

"Administry" is an old English word derived from the Latin *administrare*, to manage as a steward. Administry is literally "toward ministry," or do-

184

ing that which one must do to enable ministry. Ministry cannot proceed without administry, without working patiently with institutions and group processes seeking to elicit responsiveness to the church's mission of care.

From the earliest centuries, the pastor has been called to be steward not only of the mysteries of God but also of the temporal life of the congregation. The pastor will expend much time and energy in planning which seeks to avert future problems, scarcities, or needless limitations upon Christian mission:

But you, O steward, who receive all offerings that come from the churches, conceal nothing from the bishop. In the same spirit, the bishop must set aside nothing for himself personally. But the management of resources of the Lord shall be under the steward and the seals under the bishop. . . . And the treasuries of the house of the Lord you are charged with keeping filled, because scarcity may befall the city or its outlying district. (*Athanasian Canons*, sec. 89, p. 55)*

A letter from Theonas of Alexandria to Lucianus shows how important the pastoral writers thought it was to keep accurate accounts and properly designate fiscal accountability:

Keep every thing in an exact reckoning. He should be ready at any time to give an accurate account of all things. He should note down everything in writing, if it is at all possible, before giving money to another. He should never trust such things to his memory, which, being drawn off day by day to other matters, readily fails us, so that, without writing, we sometimes honestly certify things which have never existed; neither should this kind of writing be of a commonplace order, but such as easily and clearly unfolds all things, and leaves the mind of the inquirer without any scruple or doubt on the subject. This will easily be effected if a distinct and separate account is kept in writing of all receipts, and of the time when, and the person by whom, and the place at which they were made. (Theonas of Alexandria, *Epistle to Lucianus*, sec. IV, ANF VI, p. 159)

Clement of Rome thought that the willingness voluntarily to give up leadership roles, and to put oneself at the disposal of others, was the key to integrity in pastoral leadership:

Is there any man of noble mind among you? A man who is compassionate? A man overflowing with love? Then let such a one say, "If it is I who am the cause of any disorder, friction, or division among you, I will remove myself. I will go away, any-

where you wish, and I will do anything the congregation says."
(Clement of Rome, *To the Corinthians*, sec. 54, ECW, p. 51)

Baxter suggested a deliberate principle of time distribution for pastoral priorities:

A preacher must be oft upon the same things, because the matters of necessity are few. We must not either feign necessaries, or fall much upon unnecessaries, to satisfy them that look for novelties. . . . As Gregory Nazianzen and Seneca often say, "Necessaries are common and obvious; it is superfluities that we waste our time for, and labour for, and complain that we attain them not." Ministers, therefore, must be observant of the care of their flocks, that they may know what is most necessary for them, both for matter and for manner; and usually the matter is to be first regarded, as being of more importance than the manner. (Baxter, *RP*, p. 114)

Jeremy Taylor, a moderate Anglican defender of toleration, argued that the pastor must provide leadership, and not simply follow a perceived consensus:

Let not the humours and inclinations of the people be the measures of your doctrines, but let your doctrines be the measure of their persuasions. Let them know from you what they ought to do; but if you learn from them what you ought to teach, you will give but a very ill account at the day of judgment of the souls committed to you. He that receives from the people what he shall teach them is like a nurse that asks of her child what physic she shall give him. (Jeremy Taylor, *RAC*, Bk. III, sec. 43; *CS*, p. 15)

Luther, concerned about the quality of governance of church institutions, advised that such institutions should not be continued that cannot be well managed:

Of spiritual power we have much; but of spiritual government nothing or little. Meanwhile may he help who can, that endowments, monastic houses, parishes and schools be well established and managed. . . . It is much better that there be no monastic house or endowment than that there be evil government in them, whereby God is the more provoked to anger. (Luther, *Treatise on Good Works*, Sec. VIII, WML II, p. 259)

Lay persons may justly withhold money from corrupted clergy.

Now our prelates are perverted on the side of the devil, not so sustaining the poor by hospitality, but rather secular lords and tyrants, who do not need such alms, but are commonly gorged with inhuman and gluttonous feasts, and yet are satiated sumptuously without a qualm from the goods of the poor.... From these considerations the faithful conclude that when a curate is notoriously negligent in his pastoral office, they as subjects should, yea, ought, to withdraw offerings and tithes from him and whatever might offer occasion for the fostering of such wickedness.... In all such cases it is permitted to the parishioners wisely to withdraw their alms, lest they seem to defend and foster the obstinacy of such a so-called pastor. (John Wyclif, *On the Pastoral Office*, sec. 4, 8, 17, LCC XIV, pp. 35, 38, 45-46)*

Pastors often seem to be found promoting community events, encouraging persons to get together, eat together, celebrate occasions, enjoy processions and feasts, and experience themselves as a community. George Herbert is one of the few pastoral writers who thought deliberately about the theological-liturgical rationale for this sort of activity:

The Country Parson is a Lover of old Customs, if they be good and harmless; and the rather, because Country people are much addicted to them; so that to favour them therein is to win their hearts, and to oppose them therein is to deject them. If there be any ill in the custom, which may be severed from the good, he pares the apple, and gives them the clean to feed on. Particularly, he loves Procession, and maintains it; because there are contained therein four manifest advantages. First, a blessing of God for the fruits of the field; secondly, justice in the Preservation of bounds; thirdly, Charity in loving, walking and neighborly accompanying one another, with reconciling of differences at that time, if there be any; fourthly, Mercy relieving the poor by a liberal distribution and largess, which at that time is, or ought to be used.... and sometimes where he knows there hath been or is a little difference, he takes one of the parties, and goes with him to the other; and all dine or sup together. There is much preaching in this friendliness. (George Herbert, *CP*, Ch. XXXV, CWS, p. 109)

In order to maintain contact with the parish through regular visitation, the pastor may have to make rigorous choices about the distribution of his time. Richard Baxter offered this practical suggestion:

Before we undertook this work [of pastoral visitation] our hands were full, and now we are engaged to set apart two days every week, from morning to night, for private catechizing and instruction; so that any man may see that we must leave undone all that other work that we were wont to do at that time: and we are necessitated to run upon the public work of preaching with small preparation, and so must deliver the message of God so rawly and confusedly, and unanswerably to its dignity and the need of men's souls, that it is a great trouble to our minds to consider it, and a greater trouble to us when we are doing it. And yet it must be so; there is no remedy: unless we will omit this personal instruction. . . . [If we] set apart two whole days a week for this work, it will be as much as we shall be able to do, to go over the parish once in a year (being about 800 families). Otherwise we would be forced to cut it short, or do it less effectually. We have above fifteen families a week to deal with. And, alas! how small a matter is it to speak to a man only once in a year. (Baxter, *RP*, pp. 183–184)*

The number of people in the church is hardly an accurate indicator of its spiritual strength. Salvian the Presbyter (c. 400–c. 480) worried about the overemphasis upon numbers:

When the people in the faith are multiplied, their faith is weakened. When the children are growing, their mother sickens. You, the Church, have become weaker as your fertility has progressed. You fall back as you go forward, and, as it were, you are weaker by reason of your strength. Indeed, you have spread throughout the whole world members who bear the name of Christians, but who do not possess the force of religion. Thus, you have begun to be rich in number and poor in faith. The richer you are in multitudes, the more needy you are in devotion. The bigger your body, the more limited your soul. You are, so to speak, both greater in yourself and lesser in yourself. You increase and decrease at the same time by a new and almost unheard of progression and recession. (Salvian the Presbyter, *The Four Books of Timothy to the Church*, Bk. 1, sec. 1, FC 3, p. 270)

Luther also urged the pastor not to allow numbers to become a special preoccupation of ministry, but rather to focus primarily upon being faithful to the Word:

The point of importance is not whether many or few people believe or do not believe, are damned or saved. On the contrary, the point of importance is what God has commanded or forbidden, what is His Word or what is not His Word. To this one should look, and about this one should think; and one should ignore the entire world. (Luther, *Sermon on Matthew* 7, 1532, WA 30 II, p. 192; WLS III, p. 1208)

The pastor has a duty to oversee the physical caring for the church building. The biblical grounding of this task was set forth by George Herbert as follows:

The Country Parson has a special care of his Church, that all things there be decent, and befitting his Name by which it is called. Therefore, first, he takes order, that all things be in good repair; as walls plastered, windows glazed, floors paved, seats whole, firm and uniform, especially that the Pulpit, and Desk, and Communion table, and Font be as they ought, for those great duties that are performed in them. . . . And all this he does not as out of necessity, or as putting a holiness in the things themselves, but because he desires to keep the middle way between superstition and slovenliness, and to follow the Apostle's two great and admirable Rules in things of this nature; the first of which is, *Let all things be done decently and in order*, and the second, *Let all things be done to edification* (1 Cor. 14:[26,40]). For these two rules comprise and include the double object of our duty, God and our neighbor; the first being for the honor of God, the second for the benefit of our neighbor. (George Herbert, *CP*, Ch. XIII, CWS, pp. 74f.)*

The Synod of Quinisext prohibited the use of church property for the making of money:

It is not right that those who are responsible for reverence to churches should place within the sacred bounds an eating place, nor offer food there, nor make other sales. For God our Saviour teaching us when he was tabernacling in the flesh commanded not to make his Father's house a house of merchandise. (Synod of Quinisext, A.D. 692, Canon LXXVI, The Seven Ecumenical Councils, NPNF 2, XIV, pp. 398-399)

II ❦ THE PASTOR'S RELATION TO OTHER PASTORS

The pastor is charged with a flock and a parish, which traditionally was defined as a distinct geographical area. Most of the pastoral tradition has assumed that there would only be one pastor in charge of a parish. The term parish derives from *para oikos*, beside the house, i.e., nearby the pastor's residence, or within a day's walk of the church. From the outset there has been an assumption of territoriality of ministry. Potential conflicts between clergy may emerge when this sense of territory has been upset, intruded, or challenged. The notion of a parish antedated the explosion of denominations after the Protestant Reformation, which itself intensified and complicated the problem of territoriality of ministry. The pastoral writers have had a long-standing concern about how to avert, adjudicate, and deal with conflicts between ministers.

Let no preacher envy any other who has a greater audience, or more fame in preaching, than himself; let him not detract from him or lessen his reputation directly or indirectly; for he that cannot be even with his brother but by pulling him down, is but a dwarf still; and no man is the better for making his brother worse. (Jeremy Taylor, *RAC*, Bk. III, sec. 60; *CS*, p. 19)*

The Second Council of Constantinople urged that pastors gather together often to discuss their mutual pastoral tasks and needs:

For although the grace of the Holy Spirit abounded in each one of the Apostles so that no one of them needed the counsel of another in the execution of his work, yet they were not willing to define on the question then raised touching the circumcision of the Gentiles, until being gathered together they had confirmed their own several sayings by the testimony of the divine Scriptures. (Second Council of Constantinople, A.D. 553, The Sentence of the Synod, The Seven Ecumenical Councils, NPNF 2, XIV, p. 306)

Yet it is no simple matter to cross over these territorial lines and still maintain good relationships:

Entertain no persons into your assemblies from other parishes unless upon great occasion, or in the destitution of a minister, or by contingency and seldom visits, or with leave; lest the labour of your brother be discouraged, and you yourself be thought to preach Christ out of envy, and not of good-will. (Jeremy Taylor, *RAC*, Bk. III, sec. 37; *CS*, p. 13)*

Earlier the Apostolic Constitutions had recognized the problem of territoriality in episcopal administration:

A bishop ought not to leave his own parish and leap to another. (*Constitutions of the Holy Apostles*, Ecclesiastical Canons, sec. 14, ANF VII, p. 501)

Nor should clergy wander from parish to parish without the advice and consent of the bishop:

If any presbyter or deacon, or any one of the catalogue of the clergy, leaves his own parish and goes to another, and, entirely removing himself, continues in that other parish without the consent of his own bishop, him we command no longer to go on in his ministry, especially in case his bishop calls upon him to return, and he does not obey, but continues in his disorder. However, let him communicate there as a layman. (*Constitutions of the Holy Apostles*, Ecclesiastical Canons, sec. 15, ANF VII, p. 501)

The First Council of Nicaea was similarly concerned about wandering, unattached ministries:

Neither bishop, presbyter, nor deacon shall pass from city to city. And if any one, after this decree of the holy and great Synod, shall attempt any such thing, or continue in any such course, his proceedings shall be utterly void, and he shall be restored to the Church for which he was ordained bishop or presbyter. . . . Such presbyters or deacons as desert their own Church are not to be admitted into another, but are to be sent back to their own diocese. (First Council of Nicea, A.D. 325, Canon XV; Ancient Epitome of Canon XVI, The Seven Ecumenical Councils, NPNF 2, XIV, pp. 32, 35)

Yet it was thought to be proper for the church of a well-resourced region to send missionary personnel and free-will gifts to a region that lacks resources:

News has come to me that, in response to your prayers and your loving sympathy in Christ Jesus, peace now reigns in the church at Antioch in Syria. It would therefore be very fitting for you, as a church of God, to appoint one of your deacons to go there as God's ambassador, and when they are all assembled together to offer them your felicitations and give glory to the Name. The man whom you think suitable for such a mission will have the blessing of Jesus Christ. (Ignatius of Antioch, *To the Phillipians*, sec. 10, ECW, p. 114)

Clergy from other parishes are to be received with dignity and mutuality:

If a presbyter comes from another parish, let him be received to communion by the presbyters; if a deacon, by the deacons; if a bishop, let him sit with the bishop, and be allowed the same honour with himself; and thou, O bishop, shalt desire him to speak to the people words of instruction: for the exhortation and admo-

nition of strangers is very acceptable, and exceeding profitable.... Thou shalt also permit him to offer the Eucharist.
(*Constitutions of the Holy Apostles*, Bk. II, Sec. VII, lviii, ANF VII,
p. 422)

Strong measures were proposed by the Council of Ancyra against one
bishop invading another's territory:

If any who have been constituted bishops, but have not been received by the parish to which they were designated, shall invade
other parishes and wrong the constituted (bishops) there, stirring
up seditions against them, let such persons be suspended from
office and communion. (Council of Ancyra, A.D. 314, Canon
XVIII, The Seven Ecumenical Councils, NPNF 2, XIV, p. 71)

The Council of Chalcedon (451 A.D.) provided measures to prevent
one group of clergy from conspiring against other clergy:

The crime of conspiracy or banding together is utterly prohibited even by the secular law, and much more ought it to be forbidden in the Church of God. Therefore, if any, whether
clergymen or monks, should be detected in conspiring or banding together, or hatching plots against their bishops or fellow-
clergy, they shall by all means be deposed from their own rank.
(Council of Chalcedon, A.D. 451, Canon XVIII, The Seven Ecumenical Councils, NPNF 2, XIV, p. 281)

It is not beyond the reach of pastoral care to seek also to heal the
divisions of the church. Here is a seventeenth century form of the ecumenical vision:

That is necessary to us as we are fellow-labourers in the same
work; and that is this, we must be very studious of union and
communion among ourselves, and of the unity and peace of the
churches that we oversee. We must be sensible how needful this is
to the prosperity of the whole, the strengthening of our common
cause, the good of the particular members of our flock, and the
further enlargement of the kingdom of Christ. And, therefore,
ministers must smart when the Church is wounded, and be so far
from being the leaders in divisions, that they should take it as a
principal part of their work to prevent and heal them. Day and
night should they bend their studies to find out means to heal
such breaches. They must not only hearken to motions for unity,
but propound them and prosecute them; not only entertain an
offered peace, but even follow it when it flies from them. They

must, therefore, keep close to the ancient centre of catholic unity. (Baxter, *RP*, p. 123)

III ❧ THE POLITICAL ETHICS OF THE PASTOR

An entire book could be justifiably written of the classical pastoral tradition on this theme alone. For ministry exists always within some political order, and the relation of ministry and statecraft has fascinated the pastoral writers. We will limit our observations primarily to those that seek to define the boundary between pastoral care and care of the *polis* (the city, the political order).

Luther argued that the church's responsibility to temporal and political authority is not absolute, and that there are limits of legitimate civil power:

But if it should happen, as it often does, that the temporal power and authorities, as they are called, should urge a subject to do contrary to the Commandments of God, or hinder him from doing them, there obedience ends, and that duty is annulled. Here a man must say as St. Peter says to the rulers of the Jews: "We ought to obey God rather than men" (Acts 5:29). . . . Thus, if a prince desired to go to war, and his cause was manifestly unrighteous, we should not follow nor help him at all; since God has commanded that we shall not kill our neighbor, nor do him injustice. (Luther, *Treatise on Good Works*, sec. XXI, WML III, p. 271)

The search for justice is doubly difficult, first to find, then to preserve:

It is a problem to find where justice lies, and it is hard not to pervert it when found. . . . Many of those who have suffered wrong hate those who cannot help them just as much as those who did the wrong. (John Chrysostom, *On the Priesthood*, Ch. III, sec. 18, p. 101)

Luther defined the legitimacy and limits of pastoral authority in the political sphere in this way:

Although governmental authority is an ordinance of God, God has nonetheless reserved for Himself the right to rebuke its faults. And so government, too, is to be censured that the possessions of the lower classes may not be drained by usury and because of bad supervision. But it is not proper for a preacher to want to prescribe regulations to government concerning the price of bread and meat and the manner of imposing taxes. (Luther, *Table Talk*, W-T 5, #5258; WLS 3, p. 1114)

The extent to which church bodies and leaders may rightly and prudently enter into the political sphere has been much debated. The Westminster Confession stated a majority Reformed opinion in urging caution:

Synods and councils are to handle or conclude nothing but that which is ecclesiastical: and are not to intermeddle with civil affairs which concern the commonwealth, unless by way of humble petition in cases extraordinary; or by way of advice for satisfaction of conscience, if they be thereunto required by the civil magistrate. (Westminister Confession, Ch. XXXI, sec. v, *CC*, p. 228)

Shall the pastor seek political office and influence?

To be able clearly to distinguish between these two kingdoms is a great art, for few people make the proper distinction. This is what commonly happens: the temporal lords want to rule the church, and, conversely, the theologians (*die Geistlichen*) want to play the lord in the town hall. Under the papacy mixing the two was considered ruling well, and it is still so considered. But in reality this is ruling very badly. When bishops were still pious, they observed the distinction well, took care of the churches, and let the emperor do his ruling. But their descendants subsequently mixed the two, grabbed for the sword, and turned into worldly lords. The same thing is happening today: noblemen and young lords want to rule consciences and issue commands in the church. And someday, when the theologians get back on their feet, they will again take the sword from the temporal authorities, as happened under the papacy. (Luther, *Christmas Day Sermon on Luke 2*, WA 34 II, p. 502; WLS 1, pp. 294-295)

Elsewhere, Luther stated forthrightly:

A minister must not go in for politics. Christ was the sole Lord, and yet He said to Pilate: You are My lord (cf. John 19:10f). (Luther, *Table Talk*, W-T 1, #181; WLS 2, p. 937)

Athanasius thought that one of the most heinous aspects of the Arian heresy is that it sought to coerce belief through political force:

Our fathers called an Ecumenical Council, when three hundred of them, more or less, met together and condemned the Arian heresy, and all declared that it was alien and strange to the faith of the Church. Upon this its supporters, perceiving that they were dishonoured, and had now no good ground of argument to insist upon, devised a different method, and attempted to vindicate it by means of external power. . . . . If anyone so much as speaks against them, he is dragged before the Governor or the General. . . . .

The other heresies also, when the very Truth has refuted them on the clearest evidence, are wont to be silent, being simply confounded by their conviction. But this modern and accursed heresy, when it is overthrown by argument, when it is cast down and covered with shame by the very Truth, forthwith endeavours to coerce by violence and stripes and imprisonment those whom it has been unable to persuade by argument. (Athanasius, *History of the Arians*, sec. 66,67, NPNF 2, IV, pp. 294-295)

Ministry and statecraft are generally thought to be distinguishable caring functions, alike in their office of governance, but different in their sphere of operation:

I admonish you who are someday to become the instructors of consciences and of Christian churches to see to it that you continue to observe the difference [between church and state]. For nothing good comes of a mixing of these two. And this mixing takes place as soon as the prince says: Listen, you preacher, I want you to teach in this and that way on my behalf; do not criticize and rebuke in the way you are doing. Conversely, it is also wrong for a preacher to propose: Listen, you government officials or judges, you are to pass judgment according to my will. (Luther, *Exposition of John 2*, 1538, WA 46, pp. 184f.; WLS 2, p. 937)

How does pastoral care of the church differ from the prince's care of the *polis*?

The spiritual power is to reign only over the soul, seeing to it that it comes to Baptism and the Sacrament of the Altar, to the Gospel and true faith, over which matters emperors and kings have no jurisdiction. . . . Power over temporal affairs has not been committed to us (clergymen). The spiritual ban, which Christ preached and used, belongs to us. Beyond this ban we must not go, nor should we arrogate to ourselves the ban which belongs only to the government and the executioner. (Luther, *Sermon on Matthew 18*, WA 47, p. 284; WLS 1, p. 294)

Allan of Lille provided this penetrating instruction on how governmental authorities are to be counseled by pastors:

O prince, if you wish to judge the earth rightly, judge rightly the earth of your own body. For there is a three-fold earth: the earth which we tread, the earth which we live in, and the earth which we seek. The earth we tread is the material earth, which is to be trampled on; the earth which we live in is the earth of our own body, which must be tended; the earth which we seek is everlasting life, which must be cultivated. . . . What will your spirit say to you then, O prince of the earth, when it, a pauper, will judge you on the Day of Judgement, if you have ruled your sphere ill, and unjustly judged the poor? (Alan of Lille, *The Art of Preaching*, Ch. xlii, CFS 23, pp. 154-155)

There is no reason for the spiritual guide to quake with fear in the presence of governmental power. Among many accounts of kings visiting pastors, this one of St. Severin is outstanding:

Batavis is the name of a town situated between the two rivers, Inn and Danube. There blessed Severin had built a monastery for a few monks in his usual manner because he was often asked by the citizens to come to that place, especially in view of the frequent invasions of the Alamanni, whose king, Gibuldus, greatly honored and loved him. At one time the king, wishing ardently to see Severin, even went there to see him. The saint, fearing that the king's coming might be a burden to the city, went outside to meet him. He addressed the king so firmly that the latter began to tremble vehemently in his presence; after they had parted, the king declared to his army that never before, either in battle or in any peril, had he been shaken by such trembling. When he gave the servant of God his choice to demand of him what he wanted, the wise teacher asked him that, in his own interest, he should restrain his people from the devastation of Roman territory, and that he should graciously release those who were being held prisoners by his men. (Eugippius, *The Life of Saint Severin*, 5, Memorandum, 19.1-3, FC 55, p. 77)

IV ❦ CARE OF THE SAECULUM

The world is the object of God's care (John 3:16). In this light, the pastor cares not only for the church, but also for the world, the *saeculum*, the whole secular sphere. Augustine made a distinction between the heavenly city characterized by the selfless love of God, and the earthly city characterized by the godless love of self. These two cities interact in this world. Wheat and tares are mixed together in the visible church. The pastor has primary responsibility for the nurture and guidance of the flock and the eliciting of virtue and the health of the soul. But pastoral responsibility also reaches out to the world, to whatever extent possible.

Augustine thought that the city of God was a universal human community embracing all languages and cultures:

This heavenly city, then, while it sojourns on earth, calls citizens out of all nations, and gathers together a society of pilgrims of all languages, not scrupling about diversities in the manners, laws, and institutions whereby earthly peace is secured and maintained, but recognising that, however various these are, they all tend to one and the same end of earthly peace. It therefore is so far from rescinding and abolishing these diversities, that it even preserves and adapts them, so long only as no hindrance to the worship of the one supreme and true God is thus introduced. (Augustine, *The City of God*, Bk. XIX, sec. 17, p. 696)

John Chrysostom argued that the parish ministry that engages in the rough and tumble life of the world is not inferior to that ministry that withdraws from the world to a life of prayer. The double metaphor is that of a ship at sea and at anchor:

For just in the same way as the man who is always at anchor in harbor, is not the man who requires his ship to be fitted out, and who needs a pilot and a crew, but he who is always out at sea; so is it with the man of the world and the monk. The one is entered as it were into a waveless harbor, and lives an untroubled life, and far removed from every storm; whilst the other is ever on the ocean, and lives out at sea in the very midst of the ocean, battling with billows without number. (John Chrysostom, *Homilies on Ephesians*, XX, NPNF 1, XIII, p. 155)

The Epistle of Diognetus viewed the Christian life as existing in a paradoxical relation to the world.

The difference between Christian and the rest of mankind is not a matter of nationality, or language, or customs. Christians do not live apart in separate cities of their own, speak any special dialect, nor practise any eccentric way of life. The doctrine they profess is not the invention of busy human minds and brains, nor are they, like some, adherents of this or that school of human thought. They pass their lives in whatever township—Greek or foreign—each man's lot has determined; and conform to ordinary local usage in their clothing, diet, and other habits. Nevertheless, the organization of their community does exhibit some features that are remarkable, and even surprising. For instance, though they are residents at home in their own countries, their behaviour there is more like that of transients; they take their full part as citizens, but they also submit to anything and everything as if they were aliens. For them, any foreign country is a motherland, and any motherland is a foreign country. . . . They obey the prescribed laws, but in their own private lives they transcend the laws. . . . They repay calumny with blessings, and abuse with courtesy. For the good they do, they suffer stripes as evildoers; and under the strokes they rejoice like men given new life. (*The Epistle to Diognetus*, sec. 5, ECW, pp. 176-177)

The Christian community's relation to the world is something like the relation of soul and body:

To put it briefly, the relation of Christians to the world is that of a soul to the body. As the soul is diffused through every part of the body, so are Christians through all the cities of the world. The soul, too, inhabits the body, while at the same time forming no part of it; and Christians inhabit the world, but they are not part of the world. The soul, invisible herself, is immured within a visible body; so Christians can be recognized in the world, but their Christianity itself remains hidden from the eye. The flesh hates the soul, and wars against her without any provocation, because she is an obstacle to its own self-indulgence; and the world similarly hates the Christians without provocation, because they are opposed to its pleasures. All the same, the soul loves the flesh and all its members, despite their hatred for her; and Christians, too, love those who hate them. The soul, shut up inside the body, nevertheless holds the body together; and though they are confined within the world as in a dungeon, it is Christians who hold the world together. The soul, which is immortal, must dwell in a mortal tabernacle; and Christians, as they sojourn for a while in the midst of corruptibility here, look for incorruptibility in the heavens. Finally, just as to be stinted of food and drink makes the soul's improvement, so when Christians are every day subjected to ill-treatment, they increase the more in numbers. Such is the high post of duty not to shrink from it. (*The Epistle to Diognetus*, sec. 6, ECW, pp. 177-178)

Selections in Part Seven have focussed upon the ever-widening circles of community in and to which the pastor is responsible: church institutions, inter-institutional relationships, the civic and political order, and the world. Curacy requires the upbuilding of institutional processes both within the church and society on behalf of the health of souls. The pastor must learn to deal with other pastors, and with para-church structures to elicit improved contexts for soul care. Curacy, although distinguishable from civic and political office, requires dealing with economic and political structures that effect the lives of communicants. The pastor guides not only individual souls but the redemptive community as a body in the hope that the Christian community may enter into a responsible, intercessory, prophetic, and healing relationship to the world.

8 On Enabling Support and Limiting Abuse

THE WORK OF MINISTRY requires the confidence and support of laity. If this support system is not consistent with everything else that ministry says about itself, its integrity is suspect. Consequently the pastoral writers have paid careful attention to better and worse means of funding and resourcing pastoral care, rejecting fees for service, and urging voluntary contributions from the laity on the basis of biblical imperatives. They have also thought carefully about how abuses of ministry are properly to be corrected, with due process, amid conflicting interests.

I 🌣 REJECTION OF FEES FOR PASTORAL SERVICE

Unlike pastors in the classical tradition, some modern "pastoral counseling" has looked toward an excessively professionalized medical realm as a model for financial support. Professional pastoral counselors have been happy to provide the counseling services clients want, receive fees for those services, and call the whole operation "pastoral care." Few objections have been raised by theologians to this dubious procedure. Yet such practice demonstrates a lack of awareness of the support systems for pastoral care as conceived and sustained for almost two millenia.

There is no traditional objection to receiving *fees for services other than pastoral care*. The problem arises when one borrows the term "pastoral" from ministry and calls such services *pastoral* care or *pastoral* psychotherapy, tending toward a misunderstanding of the adjective "pastoral." It tends to separate the individual from the caring community, to disjoin the pastor from the apostolic witness, and to provide services primarily for those who can pay for them, thus reinforcing class differences rather than seeking to reconcile them. It is appropriate, therefore, in connection with the discussion of abuses of the pastoral office, to state the time-tested reasons why the classical pastoral writers have so persistently rejected the fee-for-service conception of support for ministry.

In professions other than ministry, the pastoral writers have voiced no objection to the reception of reasonable fees. Thomas Aquinas in fact

200

provided a solid argument in defense of the justice of physicians and attorneys receiving fees:

Augustine says that an advocate may lawfully sell his pleading, and a lawyer his advice. . . . A man may justly receive payment for granting what he is not bound to grant. Now it is evident that an advocate is not always bound to consent to plead, or to give advice in other people's causes. Wherefore, if he sells his pleading or advice, he does not act against justice. The same applies to the physician who attends on a sick person to heal him, and to all like persons; provided, however, they take a moderate fee, with due consideration for persons, for the matter in hand, for the labor entailed, and for the custom of the country. (Thomas Aquinas, *Summa Theologica*, Pt. II-II, Q. 71, Art. 4, II, p. 1499)

Criteria here applied to the assessment of a just fee are fairness, moderation, contextual needs of the client, amount of work, and custom. The classical pastoral writers' objection is not to the idea of fees, but to the application of the fee system to pastoral acts that are presumably based on the idea of service. Freely bestowed gifts for the support of the church's ministry are not to be thought of as analogous to just payments for services rendered:

These gifts are not prices, purchases, or sales. We must have our daily sustenance, food and drink; but absolution is not paid for with these. For who would be able to pay it? What are 100 or 1,000 guldens in comparison with the incalculable gift of the forgiveness of sins?

Therefore when we receive sustenance from the church, it is not a price equivalent to this gift, which is worth so much that the wealth of the whole world cannot pay for it. But because this stupendous and incalculable gift cannot be administered except by men who need food and clothing, it is necessary to nourish and support them. This, however, is not payment for the gift; it is payment for the service and the work. (Luther, "Lectures on Genesis Chapters 21 to 25," LW 4, p. 204; cf. WA 43, 282)

Giving freely to support ministry is not an attempt to pay for the services pastors offer, for a price cannot be put on the mediation of God's forgiveness. Support for ministry is not primarily to be viewed as an act of economic justice, but an act of thanksgiving, love, and the praise of God. Gifts are given in gratitude for God's goodness which is manifested through duly called, well-prepared and well-performed pastoral service. But when these are put on a monetary scale of regularized expectation, such as a per hour figure, the whole basis of the relationship is essentially distorted.

Over a millenium before Luther, Tertullian had clarified the reasoning behind a free, voluntary offering, rejecting the contractual fee-for-service conception:

There is no buying and selling of any sort in the things of God. Though we have our treasure-chest, it is not made up of money paid in entrance fees, as if religion were a matter of contract. Everyone once a month brings some modest coin—or whenever he wishes, and only if he does wish, and if he can; for nobody is compelled; it is a voluntary offering. You might call them the trust funds of piety. For they are not spent upon banquets nor drinking-parties nor thankless eating-houses; but to feed the poor and to bury them, to supply the wants of boys and girls destitute of means and parents, and for slaves grown old and ship-wrecked mariners; and if there happen to be any in the mines, or banished to the islands, or shut up in the prisons for no reason except their fidelity to the cause of God's church. These are among those who shall receive support from the confessing church. (Tertullian, *Apology*, 39. 1-6, Loeb, pp. 175-177; cf. ANF I, p. 46)*

Early canon law especially provided that fees were not to be associated in any way with the giving and receiving of holy communion:

That no one, whether bishop, presbyter, or deacon, when giving the immaculate Communion, shall exact from him who communicates fees of any kind. For grace is not to be sold, nor do we give the sanctification of the Holy Spirit for money; but to those who are worthy of the gift it is to be communicated in all simplicity. (Synod of Quinisext, A.D. 692, Canon XXIII, The Seven Ecumenical Councils, NPNF 2, XIV, p. 376)

Menno Simons argued that pastoral services are unpriceable, and therefore not to be viewed primarily as residing within the realm of fees. Nonetheless, voluntary support for ministry to the poor is welcomed and urged:

As they had received the knowledge of the kingdom of God, the truth, love, and Spirit of God, without price, so they were again prepared to dispense it diligently and teach it without price, to their needy brethren. And as for the temporal necessities of life, the begotten church was sufficiently driven by love, through the Spirit and Word of God, to give unto such faithful servants of Christ and watchers of their souls all the necessities of life, to assist them and provide for them all such things which they could not obtain by themselves. O brethren, flee from avarice! (Menno Simons, Brief and Clear Confession, 1544, *CWMS*, p. 443)

Fully attentive "watchers of souls" (pastors) cannot be part-time tradesmen. The Word which was freely given cannot be bought and sold. Those who are unconditionally stewards of sacred mysteries cannot also be entrepreneurs. A pastoral service contingent upon a direct fee may tend to distort or trivialize the pastoral relationship. Nonetheless, the church's ministry needs the support of all who have benefited by it, who understand it and wish to share it. As early as the fourth century, in the Clementine literature, this sort of rationale was provided to lay persons for pastoral support:

[The pastor] having given himself up wholly to labour for you, and needing sustenance, and not being able to attend to his own affairs, how can he procure necessary support? Is it not reasonable that you are to take forethought for his living, not waiting for his asking you, for this is the part of a beggar? But he will rather die of hunger than submit to do this. . . . Let no one say: Is, then, the word sold which was freely given? Far be it. . . . If he who has not takes support in order to live—as the Lord also took at supper and among His friends, having nothing, though He alone is the owner of all things—he sins not. Therefore suitably honour elders, catechists, useful deacons, widows who have lived well, orphans as children of the Church. But wherever there is need of any provision for an emergency, contribute all together. (Clementina, *Homilies*, Hom. III, Ch. LXX, ANF VI, p. 251)*

Since Jesus was willing to sit down at the table of many sorts of people and receive food, it was reasoned, so are Christian pastors called upon to accept support for worthy ministry.

Some sort of surveillance may be required in order to prevent fee-for-service support of ministry. If we examine pastoral practice in the Church of England in 1635, we find Archbishop Laud asking annually in each episcopal visitation to a congregation whether any pastor had abused the pastoral office by taking any extraordinary (i.e., outside of the due ordering of ministry) fees for services:

Do you know, or have you heard, that any ecclesiastical judge, officer, or minister, has received or taken any extraordinary fees, or other rewards or promises, by any ways or means, directly or indirectly, from any person or persons whatsoever? (William Laud, Visitation Articles, 1635, sec. 4; *Angl.*, p. 714)*

There have doubtless been in most periods of the church's history incidental exceptions to the rule against reception of fees for pastoral services. This would apply to occasional events such as weddings, etc., upon which the minister's livelihood does not fundamentally depend, but which have been thought in some cultures to be occasions in which token acts of gratitude are considered appropriate, especially if the proceeds are directly to poor relief. But it is quite a different matter when monetary entanglements, billings, payments, or compensations begin fundamentally to preoccupy the pastor or become central or conditional to the offering of pastoral services. Bishop Jeremy Taylor sought to distinguish between more and less fitting forms of pastoral engagement in business affairs:

Let not the name of the Church be made a pretence for personal covetousness. . . . Never exact the offerings, or customary wages, and such as are allowed by law, in the ministration of the sacraments; nor condition for them, nor secure them beforehand: but first do your office, and minister the sacraments purely, readily, and for Christ's sake and when that is done, receive what is your due. . . . Let every minister be careful to live a life as abstracted from the affairs of the world as his necessity will permit him; but in no way immersed and principally employed in the affairs of the world. (Jeremy Taylor, *RAC*, Bk. IV, sec. 6-12; *CS*, pp. 6-8) *

The Anabaptist left wing of Protestantism was especially determined to resist the practice of receiving fees for pastoral service:

One is a hireling who has hired himself out as a servant at certain wages and a stipend. This stands contrary to the example of Christ and of all the true messengers who have been sent by Him. (Menno Simons, Reply to Gellius Faber, 1554, *CWMS*, p. 648)*

Even voluntary gifts to the church's mission to the poor are subject to abuse by those who might deceitfully raise money or peddle influence. Among the charges that Appolonius made against Montanus (c. 211) were self-aggrandizement, deception, and a kind of advertising mentality that abused voluntary offerings. Note the full list of charges:

But who is this new teacher? His works and teaching tells who he is. This is the one who taught the dissolution of marriage; who inculcated fasting; who called two small towns of Phrygia "Jerusalem" (they were Peruga and Tymius), because he wanted to bring people there from all about the country!; who set up exactors of money; who craftily contrived the taking of gifts under the name of voluntary offerings; who even granted stipends to those who would publish his doctrine abroad. (Apollonius, *Concerning Montanism*, sec. 1, ANF VIII, p. 775)*

Thus as early as the third century we find the church having to deal with those who abused ministry in order to make a profit. This appears to be an extraordinarily bold scam based on misrepresentation of facts, not wholly unlike some modern television ministry practices that focus on collecting money, engendering intense enthusiasms, and sometimes taking offerings under false pretenses. On the contrary, learning contempt for riches was thought by Ambrose to be a crucial precondition for becoming a good counselor:

Is it not better that the clergy know how not to be excited at the thought of money, have a contempt for riches, and look down as if from a higher vantage point upon the human passions? . . . It is more fitting that the clergy be superior in soul rather than treasures, and in willing service to friends. . . . But if it is desirable to have one's soul free from this failing, how much more desirable is it to gain the love of the people by liberality which is neither too freely shown to those who are unsuitable, nor too sparingly bestowed upon the needy. . . . The highest kind of liberality is to redeem captives, to save them from the hands of their enemies, to snatch men from death, and most of all, women from shame, to restore children to their parents, parents to their children, and to give back a citizen to his country. (Ambrose, *Duties of the Clergy*, Bk. II, Ch. XIV-XV, sec. 66-70, NPNF 2, X, pp. 53-54)*

II ❧ Pastoral Disengagement from Worldly Preoccupations

It is a common assumption of pastoral writers that upon entry into curacy, the care-giver will systematically disengage from business activities in order to give undivided attention to soul care. The Athanasian Canons stated the point succinctly:

No priest shall sell in the market. (*Athanasian Canons*, sec. 38, p. 33)

The rationale for this restriction hinged largely upon the notion of set-apartness, of priestly separation, purity and the life of holiness:

O thou levitical priest, to what purpose do you sell or buy? For to you is given the first fruits of all. . . . The priests are chosen that they may be more holy than the people and that unto them the offerings may be given, that they may be holy, praying for the people, entreating for their sins, even as Moses said of them that they are those whom "the Lord God hath chosen" (Deut. 18:1-5). And when the priest shall sin like the people, who then will intercede for them? (*Athanasian Canons*, sec. 3, p. 8)*

Although Paul served as a tentmaker for temporal support during portions of his ministry, in subsequent centuries more definite restrictions were placed upon the secular employment of *presbuteroi* who were expected to offer full and undivided energies to the life of prayer and proclamation:

Shake off all the cares of life, being neither a bondsman, nor an advocate, nor involved in any other secular business. For Christ does not wish to appoint you either a judge or an arbitrator in business, or negotiator of the secular affairs of the present life, lest, being confined to the present cares of men, you should not have leisure by the word of truth to separate the good. . . . from the bad. (Clementina, *Epistle of Clement to James*, Ch. V-VI, ANF VIII, p. 219)*

In the Apostolic Constitutions the practice by clergy of usurious lending was rigorously constricted:

Let a bishop, or presbyter, or deacon who requires usury of those he lends to either leave off to do so, or let him be deprived. (*Constitutions of the Holy Apostles*, Ecclesiastical Canons, Canon 44, ANF VII, p. 502)

With the specific exception of business activities necessary to care for the poor, widows and minors, and of assigned ecclesiastical business, clergy were not permitted by the Council of Chalcedon to engage in entrepreneurial management of businesses:

It has come to (the knowledge of) the holy Synod that certain of those who are enrolled among the clergy have, through lust of gain, become hirers of other men's possessions, and make contracts pertaining to secular affairs, lightly esteeming the service of God, and slip into the houses of secular persons, whose property they undertake through covetousness to manage. Wherefore the great and holy Synod decrees that henceforth no bishop, clergyman, nor monk shall hire possessions, or engage in business, or occupy himself in worldly engagements, unless he shall be called by the law to the guardianship of minors, from which there is no escape; or unless the bishop of the city shall commit to him the care of ecclesiastical business, or of unprovided orphans or widows and of persons who stand especially in need of the Church's help, through the fear of God. (Chalcedon, A.D. 451, Canon III, The Seven Ecumenical Councils, NPNF 2, XIV, p. 269)

Ministry is to be freed from temporal affairs in order to study and serve:

Sirach says, 38:24-26: "The wisdom of a scribe (namely for the kingdom of heaven) requires opportunity for leisure; and it is necessary for him to be free of other matters, who wants either to obtain that wisdom for himself or impart it to others. For how can he deal with wisdom, who must hold the plow and drive oxen, etc.?" The office of a minister of the church therefore is that he diligently study the holy Scriptures and give himself to reading them (1 Ti 4:13), moreover, that he labor in the Word and doctrine (1 Ti 5:17), that he feed the flock of Christ and the church of God (1 Ptr 5:2; Acts 20:28); that is, he is to serve the church with the preaching of the Word and administration of the Sacraments and the use of the keys. As Origen aptly writes on Lev. 8: "These two are works of a priest: First, that he learn of God by reading the Holy Scriptures and frequent meditation, and that he teach the people, but that he teach the things that he himself has learned from God. There is also another work, which Moses does: he does not go to war, but prays for the people." (Chemnitz, *MWS*, Part 2, sec. 33, p. 38)

Wherever the pastor becomes preoccupied with financial affairs, Luther thought, the caring tasks easily become displaced. It is better that the pastor entrust temporal support to the laity and live without complaint on whatever resources are available:

A true minister of Christ should not be concerned about money and creature comforts (*deliciis*), which are a cause of avarice, but about the care which he exercises in his actual calling. And money is not worth arguing about, because it makes proud and does this only for a little while; it does not go with us when we die. (Luther, W-T 2, #2796; WLS 2, pp. 940-941)

More dangerous, according to Menno Simons, was the temptation of clergy to neglect the poor in pursuing their own economic interest:

O preachers, dear preachers, where is the power of the Gospel you preach? Where is the thing signified in the Supper you administer? Where are the fruits of the spirit you have received? And where is the righteousness of your faith which you dress up so beautifully before the poor, ignorant people? Is it not all hypocrisy that you preach, maintain, and assert? Shame on you for the easygoing gospel and barren bread-breaking, you who have in so many years been unable to effect enough with your gospel and sacraments so as to remove your needy and distressed members from the streets, even though the Scripture plainly teaches and says, "But if a man has enough to live on, and yet when he sees his brother in need shuts up his heart against him, how can it be said that the divine love dwells in him?" (1 John 3:17). Also Moses said: "There will never be any poor among you if only you obey the Lord your God" (Deut. 15:4). (Menno Simons, Reply to False Accusations, 1554, *CWMS*, p. 559)

III Support of Ministries

It is clear from the above selections that the pastoral writers rejected direct fee support from individuals for pastoral services contingent upon payment. Some might therefore prematurely conclude that the pastoral writers rejected all regularized arrangements for the support of ministries, but this is not the case. Proper means of temporal support of soul care has been a much-debated question from New Testament times to the present. It is now useful to set forth the reasons why the mainstream pastoral tradition has appealed not to individual fees for services, but to a biblically and theologically grounded system of support for ministry in which gratitude, stewardship, and mutually shared responsibility are interrelated themes. They appealed to earlier Hebraic traditions of tithing and first-fruits in their reasoning about support of Christian ministries. Thomas Aquinas drew together much of this reasoning in his treatise on tithes:

"It is a duty to pay tithes, and whoever refuses to pay them takes what belongs to another" [Augustine, Append. Serm. cclxxiv]. I answer that: In the Old Law tithes were paid for the sustenance of the ministers of God; hence it is written (Malachi 3:10): "Bring the tithes into the treasury, all of them; let there be food in my house." Hence the precept about the paying of tithes was partly moral and instilled in the natural reason; and partly judicial, deriving its force from its divine institution. Natural reason dictates that the people should administer the necessities of life to those who minister the divine worship for the welfare of the whole people even as it is the people's duty to provide a livelihood for their rulers and soldiers and so forth. Hence the Apostle proves this from human custom, saying (1 Cor. 9:7): "Did you ever hear of a man serving in the army at his own expense? or planting a vineyard without earning the fruit of it?". . . For ten is, in a way, the perfect number (being the first numerical limit since the figures do not go beyond ten but begin over again from one), and therefore he that gave a tenth, which is the sign of perfection, reserving the nine other parts for himself, acknowledged by a sign that imperfection was his part, and that the perfection which was to come through Christ was to be hoped for from God. . . . The right to receive tithes is a spiritual thing, for it arises from the debt in virtue of which the ministers of the altar have a right to the expenses of their ministry, and temporal things are due to those who sow spiritual things. This debt concerns none but the clergy who have care of souls, and so they alone are competent to have this right. (Thomas Aquinas, *Summa Theologica*, Pt. II-II, Q. 87, Art. 1-3, II, pp. 1562-1565, NEB)*

Several pivotal principles undergird Thomas' interpretation: temporal support is pertinent to and needed for those who offer spiritual gifts; the fruits of tithing are intrinsically connected with the idea of caring for souls; both mystical significance and moral reasoning have become attached to the idea of a tenth. For giving the first tenth and keeping the remainder meant that one was giving the perfect to God and withholding the imperfect for oneself. One of the earliest Christian writings, the Didache, appealed to the tradition of offering first-fruits as tithe. It assumed that one gives the first and best quality of the ten parts, not the last or least:

Take the first products of your winepress, your threshing-floor, your oxen and your sheep, and give them as firstfruits to the charismatists, for nowadays it is they who are your "High Priests." If there is no charismatist among you, give them to the poor. And when you bake a batch of loaves, take the first of them and give it away, as the commandment directs. Similarly when you broach a jar of wine or oil, take the first portion to give to the charismatists. So, too, with your money, and your clothing, and all your possessions; take a tithe of them in whatever way you think best, and make a gift of it, as the commandment bids you. (*Didache*, sec. 13, ECW, p. 234)

The same texts were appealed to in the Apostolic Constitutions:

You shall give a tenth of your produce to the orphan and to the widow, and to the poor, and to the stranger. The first-fruits of your hot bread, your barrels of wine, oil, honey, nuts, grapes, and the first-fruits of other things you shall give to the *presbuteroi*. But those of silver, and of garments, and of all sort of possessions, give to the orphan and to the widow. (*Constitutions of the Holy Apostles*, Bk. VII, Sec. II, Ch. XXIX, ANF VII, p. 471)*

Distributions to the poor were to be made through the office of ministry. Origen argued that it is proper that Christian *presbuteroi*—analogous to priests in the Levitical tradition—should live from the freely-given voluntary support of laity, in order to devote undivided energies to the care of souls:

The levites and priests, on the other hand, have no possessions but tithes and first fruits. . . . The same is the case with those who approach Christian studies. Most of us devote most of our time to the things of this life, and dedicate to God only a few special acts, thus resembling those members of the [non-Levitical] tribes. . . . But those who devote themselves to the divine word and have no other employment but the service of God may not unnaturally . . . be called our levites and priests. . . . Now our whole activity is devoted to God, and our whole life, since we are bent on progress in divine things. (Origen, *Commentary on John*, sec. 3-4, ANF X, p. 298)

The Apostolic Constitutions coalesced the ox-muzzling, levitical, and first-fruits analogies:

It is written, "You shall not muzzle an ox while it is treading out the corn" (Deut. 25:4). . . . The ox that labours in the threshing-floor without a muzzle does indeed eat but does not eat up everything. Similarly, you who labour in the threshing-floor, that is, in the Church of God, feed from the resources of the Church. This was also the case of the Levites, who served in the tabernacle of the testimony, which was in every way a type of the Church. Furthermore its very name implied that the earlier tabernacle was providentially given as a testimony to the Church. Levites who attended the tabernacle received those things that were offered to God by all the people—gifts, offerings, first-fruits, tithes, sacrifices, and oblations. . . . Those who exercise care for the Church ought to be maintained by the Church as similar to priests, Levites, presidents, and ministers of God. It is written in the book of Numbers concerning the priests: "I give you all the choicest of the oil, the choicest of the new wine and the corn, the firstfruits which are given to the Lord. The first-ripe fruits of all produce in the land which are brought to the Lord shall be yours" (Numbers 18:12,13). (*Constitutions of the Holy Apostles*, Bk. II, Sec. IV, Ch. XXV, ANF VII, p. 409, NEB)*

Diaconal, presbuteral and episcopal support begins with gifts gratefully and freely given by the laity. The supported ministries are then thought to be responsible to God to administer resources faithfully, mercifully and fairly:

Give to the priest that which is due, the first-fruits of your harvest, of your wine-press, and sacrificial offerings, as if he were mediating between God and those who stand in need of purgation and forgiveness. It is your duty to give and his to administer, since he is the steward and disposer of churchly matters. You are not in a position to call your bishop to account, or watch his administration, how he does what, when, to whom, or where, or whether he does it well or poorly or indifferently. For the bishop already has Another who will call him sufficiently to an account, the Lord God, who put this administration into his hands, and thought him worthy of an office of such great importance. (*Constitutions of the Holy Apostles*, Bk. II, sec. IV, Ch. XXXV, ANF VII, p. 413)*

Funds assigned to Christian ministry are not to be diverted for private use:

Let the bishop have the care of ecclesiastical revenues, and administer them as in the presence of God. But it is not lawful for him to appropriate any part of them to himself, or to give the things of God to his own kindred. (*Constitutions of the Holy Apostles*, Bk. VIII, Sec. V, Ch. XLVII, ANF VII, p. 502)

The Athanasian canons warned against left-over, second-rate, or tawdry offerings for the support of soul care. The bread is to be "fresh and whole," for it is God's own mission and ministry that one is supporting:

All the first-fruits of corn, wine and beasts of burden shall be given to the priests of the church, and from it there shall be taken a choice offering into the sanctuary; and what remains the servants of the Lord shall eat. An offering that remains over from yesterday shall not be offered, nor any offering that has already been divided into pieces previously in any church. Rather use bread that is warm, fresh and whole. (*Athanasian Canons*, sec. 63-64, p. 42)*

The pastor to whom is given the task of serving the poor shall be willing to share in their poverty:

If you shall still say that you cannot live so meanly as poor people do, I further ask whether your parishioners can better endure damnation than you can endure want and poverty. . . . Should you not rather beg your bread than put to risk or disadvantage so great a matter as salvation? . . . This poverty is not so intolerable and dangerous a thing as it is pretended to be. If you have but food and rainment, must you not be content? . . . "A man's life consisteth not in the abundance of the things that he possesseth" (Luke 12:15). If your clothing be warm, and your food be wholesome, you may be as well supported by it to do God's service as if you had the fullest satisfaction to your flesh. (Baxter, *RP*, pp. 92-94)*

Appeals were made to encourage laity in the sharing of God's ministry to the world, but with a solemn awareness that both wealth and lack of it stand equally reduced before the majesty of God:

What good is what we possess if we do not make God a sharer in what we possess? If there is someone poor like Elias' widow, or sick like the lame man who received alms, he shall be honored as one who is making an offering of himself to God. And even if what he offers is small, yet shall it be a remembrance of himself. For not only is he remembered who gives gold to the sanctuary, but he that gives an earthen cup or bread or a little wine or a water-vessel, or who fills up a tankard with water as a gift. God remembers him as much as another who gives out of his riches. (*Athanasian Canons*, sec. 84, p. 51)*

Clergy as well as laity are called upon to offer tithes:

It it fitting not only for the laity to give tithes, but the clergy also, from the bishop to the door-keeper. (*Athanasian Canons*, sec. 83, p. 50)*

IV ❧ ANSWERING CRITICS

Since the pastor is in a highly visible public office which cannot altogether avoid criticism, it is necessary to learn to face conflicts, hear out critics, assess them appropriately, and answer proportionally. It is better that the pastor not compulsively ignore criticism, but promptly respond, before the imagination of greater error grows in the minds of the doubtful:

The right course is neither to show disproportionate fear and anxiety over ill-directed abuse (for the president will have to put up with unfounded criticism), nor simply to ignore it. We should try to extinguish criticisms at once, even if they are false and are levelled at us by quite ordinary people. . . . We should leave nothing untried that might destroy an evil report. (John Chrysostom, *On the Priesthood*, Ch. V, sec. 3, p. 129)

Pastors do better to utilize limited energies defending the Word than focussing upon their own personal integrity:

If anyone undeservedly persecutes, slanders, and curses my person, I should and will say *Deo gratias* (thank God) for this, because God will richly bless me for suffering such injustice. But if anyone assails the Baptism, Sacrament, and ministry committed to me by God and thus does not attack me but God, it does not become me to be silent, merciful, and friendly; then I must maintain the office committed to me and "use argument, reproof, and appeal," as St. Paul says, "with all the patience that the work of teaching requires" (2 Tim. 4:2), in season and out of season, for those who do not teach and believe correctly or do not amend their lives, no matter who they may be or how they may like it. (Luther, WA 22, pp. 62ff.; WLS 3, pp. 1113-1114)*

John Chrysostom, in his analysis of challenges distinctive to ministry, correctly realized that defects tend to be exceptionally long remembered:

Men are so made that they overlook their neighbour's successes, however many or great; yet if a defect comes to light, however commonplace and however long since it last occured, it is quickly noticed, fastened on at once, and never forgotten. So a trifling and unimportant fault has often curtailed the glory of many fine achievements. (John Chrysostom, *On the Priesthood*, Ch. V, sec. 5, p. 131)

Chrysostom noted a special temptation in pastoral service to love and desire applause overmuch. This may make clergy especially sensitive to even the hint of censure, or more subtly, the lack of being constantly praised:

We should not be much elated by their praise nor much dejected by their censure, when we get these things from them out of season. This is not easy, my friend, and I think it may be impossible. I do not know whether anyone has ever succeeded in not enjoying praise. If he enjoys it, he naturally wants to receive it. And if he wants to receive it, he cannot help being pained and distraught at losing it. People who enjoy being wealthy take it hard when they fall into poverty, and those who are used to luxury cannot bear to live frugally. So, too, men who are in love with applause have their spirits starved not only when they are blamed off-hand, but even when they fail to be constantly praised. (John Chrysostom, *On the Priesthood*, Ch. V, sec. 4, p. 130)

One who tells the truth may as well expect resistance:

The truth is something men do not like; they become angry with him who tells them the truth. (Luther, W-T 6, #6784; WLS 3, p. 1169)

Luther regarded his greatest temptation the wish to remain at peace and uncondemned by everyone:

I know that if my cause is just, it must be condemned on earth, and approved only by Christ in heaven; for all the Scriptures show that the cause of Christians and of Christendom must be judged by God alone. Such a cause has never yet been approved by men on earth, but the opposition has always been too great and strong. It is my greatest care and fear that my cause may remain uncondemned, by which I should know for certain that it was not yet pleasing to God. (Luther, "An Open Letter to the Christian Nobility," WML II, p. 164)

Some decry mostly those who excel them. Thus it may happen ironically that the higher quality of one's work may be attested by the lower quality of one's detractors. In defending a theological master like Origen from his less-gifted critics, the Constantinopolitan Church historian, Socrates (c. 380-450) wrote:

Worthless characters, and such as are destitute of ability to attain eminence themselves, often seek to get into notice by decrying those who excel them. And first Methodius, bishop of a city in Lycia named Olympus, labored under this malady; next Eustathius, who for a short time presided over the church at Antioch; after him Apollinaris; and lastly Theophilus. This quaternion of revilers has traduced Origen. . . . But I affirm that from the censure of these men, greater commendation accrues to Origen. (Socrates Scholasticus, *Ecclesiastical History*, Ch. XIII, VI. 13, NPNF 2, II, p. 147)

Jerome was sadly aware of the temptation of some persons in ministry to gain public favor by discrediting others. In writing Augustine

(402 A.D.) on an issue that might have divided them, he pleaded for a spirit of mutual correction, and reflected upon the spirit of divisiveness:

Far be it from me to presume to attack anything which your Grace has written. For it is enough for me to prove my own views without controverting what others hold. But it is well known to one of your wisdom, that every one is satisfied with his own opinion, and that it is puerile self-sufficiency to seek, as young men have of old been wont to do, to gain glory to one's own name by assailing men who have become renowned. I am not so foolish as to think myself insulted by the fact that you give an explanation different from mine; since you, on the other hand, are not wronged by my views being contrary to those which you maintain. But that is the kind of reproof by which friends may truly benefit each other, when each, not seeing his own bag of faults, observes, as Persius has it, the wallet borne by the other. Let me say further, love one who loves you, and do not because you are young challenge a veteran in the field of Scripture. I have had my time, and have run my course to the utmost of my strength. It is but fair that I should rest, while you in your turn run and accomplish great distances; at the same time (with your leave, and without intending any disrespect), lest it should seem that to quote from the poets is a thing which you alone can do, let me remind you of the encounter between Dares and Entellus, and the proverb, "The tired ox treads with a firmer step." With sorrow I have dictated these words. Would that I could receive your embrace, and that by converse we might aid each other in learning! (Jerome, To Augustine, in Augustine, *Letters*, LXVIII, NPNF 1, I, p. 324-325)

Hugh Latimer, burned with Ridley at the Oxford stake in 1555, had to defend himself against false and absurd charges that viciously blamed him for consequences which he did not cause. In this case, he had been falsely accused of preaching rebellion. He adroitly examined the *non sequitur* of his accusers:

It is we preachers that trouble England. We preached against covetousness last year in Lent, and the next summer followed rebellion. Ergo, preaching against covetousness was the cause of the rebellion! A fine argument!

Here now I remember an anecdote of Master More's (Lord-Chancellor Sir Thomas More) set forth in a book he wrote against Bilney. I will tell you the pleasant tale. Master More was once sent in commission into Kent, to find out if he could what might be the cause of movement of the Goodwin Sands, and the shelf that stopped up Sandwich haven. Along came Master More, and called out from around the country such as were thought to be men of experience, who could most likely reason with him concerning the stopping of the movement of Sandwich haven. Among others there came before him an old man with a white head who was thought to be little less than a hundred years old. When Master More saw this aged man, he thought it expedient to hear him speak his mind in this matter; for, being so old a man, it was likely that he knew most of any man in that company. So Master More called this old aged man unto him, and said, "Father, tell me, if you can, what is the cause of this great rising of the sands and shelves here about this haven, which stop it up so that no ships can arrive here? You are the oldest man that I can find in all this company, so that if any man can tell any cause of it, you it is likely can say most in it, or at least more than any other man here assembled." "Yea, forsooth, good master," said this old man, "for I am well-nigh a hundred years old, and no man here in this company is anything near to my age." "Well, then," said Master More, "how say you in this matter? What think you are the causes of these shelves and flats that stop up Sandwich haven?" "Forsooth, sir," said he, "I am an old man; I think that Tenterden steeple is the cause of Goodwin Sands. For I am an old man, sir," said he, "and I may remember the building of Tenterden steeple, and I remember when there was no steeple at all there. And before that Tenterden steeple was built, there was no speaking of any flats or sands that stopped the haven, and therefore I think that Tenterden steeple is the cause of the destroying and decay of Sandwich haven." Thus said this old man, and even so to my purpose is preaching of God's Word the cause of rebellion, as Tenterden steeple was the cause that Sandwich haven is decayed!" (Hugh Latimer, Defense, OCC I, pp. 57-58)*

V ❦ Dealing with False Accusations

When ministry is under unjust attack by those who would seek to discredit it, it is fitting to respond proportionally in a way that is consistent with everything else that the care of souls stands for. This may require astute efforts to preserve the community from devisiveness. From Jesus' ministry to the present, the care of souls has had to deal with serious challenges from determined detractors. Nothing is more salutary, under such circumstances, than to reflect fundamentally upon the nature of the church as a redemptive community:

Jesus was called a winebibber, a blasphemer, and one possessed of the devil. Paul was called mutinous and an apostate Jew, etc. Behold, thus in their time the mission of the faithful servants of the Lord, nay, of the Lord and Messiah Himself, was despised, although bolstered by many miracles. How much more then shall we be despised, who are such weak and insignificant instruments, and come to a seven fold more wicked and evil world than theirs was. Inasmuch then as we are so reviled by our opponents, the learned ones, that we are not called of a church of God, but of false prophets, or a false church, therefore I would briefly admonish the reader to weigh well with the Scriptures who, how, and what the church of God is. It is not a collection of proud, avaricious, usurers, pompous, drunkards, and impenitent as the church of the world is, of whom the learned ones are called, but a gathering or congregation of saints, as the Holy Scriptures and the Nicene Creed clearly teach and present, namely, those who through true faith are regenerated by God unto Christ Jesus and are of a divine nature, who would gladly regulate their lives according to the Spirit, Word, and example of the Lord, who are actuated by His Spirit, and are willing and ready patiently to bear the cross of their Lord Jesus Christ. (Menno Simons, Reply to Gellius Faber, 1554, *CWMS*, pp. 666-667)*

False accusations against the pastor are best answered through a life lived in congruence with one's teachings. Those who make such accusations should be brought to realize that they may cause great harm, as happened in the suffering of Menno Simons, who for many years was hunted down as an outlaw on the basis of false accusations by ordained ministers:

Some alas, from a perverted heart, say that I eat more roasted than they do seethed; and that I drink more wine than they do beer. My Lord and Master, Jesus Christ, was also called a winebibber and a glutton by the perverse. I trust that through the grace of the Lord I am innocent in this matter, and stand acquitted before God. He who purchased me with the blood of His love, and called me, who am unworthy, to His service, knows me, and He knows that I seek not wealth, nor possessions, nor luxury, nor ease, but only the praise of the Lord, my salvation, and the salvation of many souls. Because of this, I with my poor, weak wife and children have for eighteen years endured excessive anxiety, oppression, affliction, misery, and persecution. At the peril of my life I have been compelled everywhere to drag out an existence in fear. Yes, when the preachers repose on easy beds and soft pillows, we generally have to hide ourselves in out-of-the-way corners. When they at weddings and baptismal banquets revel with pipe, trumpet, and lute; we have to be on our guard when a dog barks for fear the arresting officer has arrived. When they are greeted as doctors, lords, and teachers by everyone, we have to hear that we are Anabaptists, bootleg preachers, deceivers, and heretics, and be saluted in the devil's name. In short, while they are gloriously rewarded for their services with large incomes and good times, our recompense and portion must be fire, sword, and death. (Menno Simons, Reply to Gellius Faber, 1554, *CWMS*, pp. 673-674)

Calvin often had to deal with accusations that were fabricated out of whole cloth. Here are some of his reflections on why these stories seem so delicious to his detractors:

Because I affirm and maintain that the world is managed and governed by the secret providence of God, a multitude of presumptuous men rise up against me, and allege that I represent God as the author of sin. This is so foolish a calumny, that it would of itself quickly come to nothing, did it not meet with persons who have tickled ears, and who take pleasure in feeding upon such discourse. But there are many whose minds are so filled with envy and spleen, or ingratitude, or malignity, that there is no falsehood, however preposterous, yea, even monstrous, which they do not receive, if it is spoken to them. . . . Others circulated ridiculous reports concerning my treasures; others, of the extravagant authority and enormous influence which they say I possess; others speak of my delicacies and magnificence. . . . And if there are some whom I cannot persuade whilst I am alive that I am not rich, my death at length will prove it. I confess, indeed, that I am not poor; for I desire nothing more than what I have. All these are invented stories, and there is no colour whatever for any one of them, but many nevertheless are very easily persuaded of their truth, and applaud them; and the reason is, because the greatest part judge that the only means of cloaking their enormities is to throw all things into disorder. (John Calvin, Preface to Psalms, SW, pp. 30-32)

Innocent pastors have a right to be defended, and to have their rights protected by ecclesiastical due process and civil guarantees. As bishop, Augustine often came to the defense of pastors falsely accused, as in the case of Boniface:

Let me therefore say in a few words to your Charity, that the presbyter Boniface has not been discovered by me to be guilty of any crime, and that I have never believed, and do not yet believe, any charge brought against him. How, then, could I order his name to be deleted from the roll of presbyters? . . . As a bishop, I ought not rashly to suspect him; and as being only a man, I cannot decide infallibly concerning things which are hidden from me. (Augustine, *Letters*, LXXVII, NPNF 1, I, p. 345)

Nonetheless, Augustine argued that a magnanimous resignation could be exceedingly honorable in cases where it might serve to protect the unity and peace of the church:

It is a far more magnanimous thing to have resigned the onerous responsibilities of the bishop's dignity in order to save the Church from danger, than to have accepted these in order to have a share in her government. He truly proves that he was worthy of holding that office, had the interests of peace permitted him to do so, who does not insist upon retaining it when he cannot do so without endangering the peace of the Church. . . . In laying down that ministry of stewardship of the mysteries of God, he was not deserting his duty under the pressure of some worldly desire, but acting under the impulse of a pious love of peace, lest, on account of the honour conferred upon him there should arise among the members of Christ an unseemly and dangerous, perhaps even fatal, dissension. (Augustine, *Letters*, LXIX, sec. 1, NPNF 1, I, p. 325)

Among principle values under such conditions of conflict are the tranquility and cohesion of the caring community. John Chrysostom went further in arguing that it is not always a disgrace to be expelled from an order of ministry. Rather under some circumstances it could be an extraordinary badge of honor:

"Blessed are ye" says our Lord, "when men shall reproach you and persecute you, and say all manner of evil against you falsely for my sake. Rejoice and be exceeding glad; for great is your reward in heaven" (Matt. 5:11-12). This is surely true even when anyone is expelled by men of his own order, either through envy or to please others or through enmity or any other wrong motive. But when he gets this treatment from his enemies, I do not think any argument is needed to prove how great a benefit they confer on him by their wickedness. (John Chrysostom, *On the Priesthood*, Ch. III, sec. 11, p. 81)

Great pastors have handled conflicted periods in imaginative ways. An amazing story is told by Palladius concerning Athanasius, who patiently waited for seven years for an opposing tyrannical Arian regime to fold, willing to risk scandal in order to persist in his mission:

In Alexandria I knew a virgin whom I met when she was about seventy years old. All the clergy confirmed that when she was a young maiden of about twenty she was exceedingly pretty and really to be avoided because of her beauty, lest one be suspected of having been with her. Now it happened that the Arians were in conspiracy against Saint Athanasius, the Bishop of Alexandria, working through Eusebius while Constantius was Emperor. They were bringing false charges and accusing Athanasius of unlawful deeds, and he fled to avoid the risk of being judged by a corrupt court. He trusted his person to no one, not to relative, friend, cleric, or anyone else. But when the prefects came suddenly into the bishop's palace looking for him, he fled in the middle of the night, taking only his tunic and cloak, and went to the maiden. She was astonished and frightened by this.

He told her: "Since the Arians are searching for me and have informed on me unjustly, I made up my mind to flee so that I might not get a bad reputation and be the cause of a crime by those who want to punish me. Just this night now God made it clear to me that I will be saved by no one but you."

With great joy then she cast all doubts to the wind and became an instrument of the Lord. She hid the most holy man for six years, until the death of Constantius. She washed his feet and cared for all his bodily needs and his personal affairs, obtaining the loan of books for his use. During these six years no one in Alexandria knew where Saint Athanasius was spending his time.

When news of the death of Constantius reached him, he got dressed and appeared in the church at night. All were amazed and looked on him as one risen from the dead. (Palladius, *The Lausiac History*, Ch. 63, sec. 1-4, ACW 34, pp. 144-145)

Palladius is the source of another case study of an unjust accusation by and toward clergy. The lector of this story was innocently accused. His ministry under these entangled conditions focussed upon a redemptive attempt to help those who had been harmed, and to appeal in prayer to divine mercy and justice:

A maiden, daughter of a priest in Caesarea of Palestine, fell, and she had been coached by her despoiler to accuse a certain lector in the city. And as she was now pregnant and her father was asking questions, she put the blame on the lector. The bishop called the priests together and had the lector called in also. The whole matter was investigated and the lector, upon being questioned, did not confess—for how could he admit something which had never happened?

The bishop was vexed and spoke to him severely: "You will not confess, you wretched and miserable man, glutted with impurity?"

The lector replied: "I told you that it was not of my doing. I am innocent of any design upon her. But if you insist on hearing something, even if it is not true, then I did it."

When the lector said this, the bishop deposed him. Then he came to the bishop and said: "Well, since I have made a mistake, command her to be given to me in marriage, for I am no longer a cleric, nor is she a maiden."

Then he gave her over to the lector, supposing that the young man would stay by her and could not help but continue his relations with her. But the young man took her from the bishop and her father and entrusted her to a monastery of women. He enjoined the deaconess of the sisterhood there to care for her until it was time for the child to be born.

It was not long before it was the time for her to give birth. The decisive hour had come. Sighs, pangs, labors, visions of the underworld—and still the child was not born!

Then passed the first, the second, the third day, a week—the woman, in hell with her pain, did not eat, drink, or sleep, but kept calling out, saying: "Miserable me, I am in danger for having accused this lector falsely."

They hurried off and told this to her father. He was afraid of being condemned as an informer and kept his peace for two more days. The young lady did not die, but she also did not deliver her child. As they could no longer bear her outcries, they ran and told the bishop: "This woman has confessed, crying out for days now that she falsely accused the lector."

Then the bishop sent deacons to the lector with a message for him: "Pray that the woman who accused you falsely may deliver her child."

He gave them no answer, he did not even open the door, but he had been praying to God from the day he went inside.

Again the father went to the bishop and prayers were recited in church—and still she did not give birth. Then the bishop got up and went to the lector, knocked on the door, went in, and said to him: "Eustathius, arise, and open the door you have closed."

At once the lector knelt down with the bishop and the woman was delivered of the child. His prayer and persistence had prevailed both to show the chicanery and to teach a lesson to the one who had made the false accusation. From this we may learn to devote ourselves to prayer and to know its power. (Palladius, *The Lausiac History*, No. 70, sec. 1-5, ACW 34, pp. 151-152)

With his usual generosity and wisdom, George Herbert commented on the varied ways that pastors may respond to those who hold them in contempt:

The Country Parson knows well, that,—both for the general ignominy which is cast upon the profession, and much more for those rules which out of his choicest judgment he hath resolved to observe, and which are described in this book,—he must be despised. . . . Nevertheless, according to the apostle's rule, he endeavors that none shall despise him; especially in his own parish he suffers it not, to his utmost power, for that, where contempt is, there is no room for instruction. . . . He that will be respected, must respect; . . . when any despises him, he takes it either in an humble way, saying nothing at all; or else in a slighting way, showing that reproaches touch him no more than a stone thrown against heaven, where he is and lives; or in a sad way, grieved at his own and others' sins. (George Herbert, CP, Ch. XXVIII, CWS, p. 95)

VI 🐟 Inquiry into Pastoral Abuses

When abuses of the pastoral office have been charged, circumspect inquiry is required. Careful procedures have been worked out over the course of much historical experience to seek to protect the conflicting rights of various parties. Efforts at reconciliation must come first, which if unsuccessful, must be followed by rigorous efforts at equity.

Polycarp, Bishop of Smyrna (c. 69-c. 155), a direct link between the apostlic age and the second century writers, set a moderating pattern.

He thought it inappropriate to be harsh on clergy who have fallen. He plead for serious efforts at reconciliation rather than a hasty, judgmental attitude:

I feel the deepest sorrow for that man [Valens] and his wife; may the Lord grant them real repentance. You too, for your part, must not be over severe with them, for people of that kind are not to be looked on as enemies; you have to restore them, like parts of your own person that are ailing and going wrong, so that the whole body can be maintained in health. Do this, and you will be promoting your own spiritual welfare at the same time. (Polycarp, *To the Philippians*, ECW, pp. 148-149)

The motive of accusers requires careful analysis. Justin Martyr (c. 100-c. 165), stated an early form of the protection of the rights of the accused:

If anyone brings an accusation and proves that the men referred to have done anything contrary to the laws, you will assign penalties in accordance with the character of the offenses. But you must certainly take the greatest care, that if anyone accuses any of these people merely for the sake of calumny, you will punish him with severe penalties for his offense. (Justin Martyr, *First Apology*, sec. 68, LCC I, pp. 288-289)

Accusations were to be supported by more than one or two witnesses, to protect against personal invective:

There shall no accusation be received against any man that is reckoned of the priesthood, from the bishop unto the doorkeeper, except it be with three witnesses. (*Athanasian Canons*, sec. 53, p. 37)

In Augustine's struggle with the Donatists, he chided them for their lack of interest in dialogue, and for their neglect of due process and abuse of fair procedures:

Some of your predecessors, in whose impious schism you obstinately remain, delivered up to persecutors the sacred manuscripts, and the vessels of the Church (as may be seen in municipal records), . . . [and] condemned others without a hearing. . . . Let your bishops answer these questions to your laity at least, if they will not debate with us; and do you, as you value your salvation, consider what kind of doctrine that must be about which they refuse to enter into discussion with us. If the wolves have prudence enough to keep out of the way of the shepherds, why have the flock so lost their prudence, that they go into the dens of the wolves? (Augustine, *Letters*, LXXVI, sec. 3-4, NPNF 1, I, p. 344)

In seeking to sustain a high ethic of ministry, Calvin's *Draft Ecclestical Ordinances* set forth a list of possible charges against clergy, and an order for guaranteeing due process:

To obviate all scandals of living, it will be proper that there be a form of correction to which all submit themselves. It will also be the means by which the ministry may retain respect, and the Word of God be neither dishonoured nor scorned because of the ill reputation of the ministers. For as one is to correct those who merit it, so it will be proper to reprove calumnies and false reports which are made unjustly against innocent people.

But first it should be noted that there are crimes which are quite intolerable in a minister, and there are faults which may on the other hand be endured while direct fraternal admonitions are offered.

Of the first sort are:

heresy, schism, rebellion against ecclesiastical order, blasphemy open and meriting civil punishment, simony and all corruption in presentations, intrigue to occupy another's place, leaving one's Church without lawful leave or just calling, duplicity, perjury, lewdness, larceny, drunkenness, assault meriting punishment by law, usury, games forbidden by the law and scandalous, dances and similar dissoluteness, crimes carrying with them loss of civil rights, crime giving rise to another separation from the Church.

Of the second sort are:

strange methods of treating Scripture which turn to scandal, curiosity in investigating idle questions, advancing some doctrine or kind of practice not received in the Church, negligence in studying and reading the Scriptures, negligence in rebuking vice amounting to flattery, negligence in doing everything required by his office, scurrility, lying, slander, dissolute words, injurious words, foolhardiness and evil devices, avarice and too great parsimony, undisciplined anger, quarrels and contentions, laxity either of manner or of gesture and like conduct improper to a minister. (John Calvin, *Draft Ecclesiastical Ordinances*, 1541, SW, p. 232)

Augustine thought that it would not be good order if a minister in disrepute in one diocese should be readily welcomed and well-received by another:

If you come to us while debarred from communion with the venerable bishop Aurelius, you cannot be admitted to communion with us; but we would act towards you with that same charity which we are assured shall guide his conduct. Your coming to us, however, should not on this account be embarrassing to us, because the duty of submission to this, out of regard to the discipline of the Church, ought to be felt by yourself, especially if you have the approval of your own conscience, which is known to yourself and to God. (Augustine, *Letters*, LXIV, NPNF 1, I, p. 321)

The early church synods sought to guarantee the right of appeal and to protect pastors against the wrath of irrascible bishops. The presumption of innocence was assumed:

If some bishop is perchance quick to anger (which ought not to be the case) and, moved hastily and violently against one of his presbyters or deacons, decides to cast him out of the Church, provision must be made that an innocent man be not condemned or deprived of communion. Therefore let him that is cast out be authorized to appeal to the neighbouring bishops and let his case be heard and examined into more diligently. For a hearing ought not to be denied one who asks it. (Council of Sardica, A.D. 343 or 344, Canon XIV, The Seven Ecumenical Councils, NPNF 2, XIV, p. 428)

The principle of assuming innocence was clearly operative in this concluding epistle by Augustine. He argued that clergy under charges should not be prematurely barred from Christian community:

Even in secular affairs, when a perplexing case is referred to a higher authority, the inferior judges do not presume to make any change while the reference is pending. Moreover, it was decreed in a Council of bishops that no clergyman who has not yet been proved guilty be suspended from communion, unless he fail to present himself for the examination of the charges against him. (Augustine, *Letters*, LXXVIII, sec. 4, NPNF, I, p. 346)

The selections of Part Eight have sought to show reasons why ministry is better supported by free gifts than by contracted fees for services, and why ministry has traditionally been regarded as a full-time calling requiring disengagement from worldly occupations and temporal affairs. In the event of accusations of conduct unbecoming to a minister, the classic pastoral tradition has provided guidelines for fair hearing, due process, and the presumption of innocence.

Conclusion

EIGHT CONCLUSIONS FOLLOW from these selections on soul care in the classical pastoral literature:

(1) Pastors owe a duty not only to care for the flock, but to care for themselves, since caring for the flock cannot occur unless one first cares for oneself, in the sense of feeding and nurturing one's own soul. Pastors are enjoined by scripture to "keep watch over yourselves" (Acts 20:28), as a prior condition to watching over the flock.

(2) Pastoral care occurs not only in individuated conversation but also through preaching, a public task intrinsic to the care of souls.

(3) Soul care occurs within a caring commuity whose primary corporate act is the praise of God's care. The worshipping community is the necessary spiritual matrix for individual care of souls. Guidance of the community at prayer is an indispensable aspect of pastoral guidance.

(4) Soul care is mediated powerfully through sacramental actions, the first of which is a ministry of beginnings—baptism—a decisive starting point in the care of a particular person within the community of faith.

(5) The quintessential Christian pastoral act is one of feeding: eating and drinking, receiving spiritual nourishment for our souls. No pastoral act is more central to the care of souls than the Supper where the resurrected Christ is present at table with the community. Confession is intrinsically connected with holy communion. The pastor attends the communicant through penitential confession with its trenchant challenge to the human spirit, through pardon to restitution.

(6) The pastor is a teacher of the soul, educating the soul toward behavioral excellence. The soul-friend is a life-crisis mentor, and reliable teacher of the good life. If care of souls is a pedagogy of the inner life, then the pastor must develop the art of teaching.

(7) The care of souls occurs not only individualistically, but extends to institutional nurture and accountability, and beyond the parameters of the congregation to the nurture of community in the parish, the civil sphere, the *polis*, and ultimately to the world.

(8) Soul care requires the support of the laity through voluntary gifts grounded in biblical imperatives, rather than on a fee-for-service basis, which tends to separate the individual from the caring community, to

disjoin the pastor from the apostolic witness, and to provide services primarily for those who can pay for them. When pastoral abuses occur, they require rigorous inquiry which presumes innocence and seeks procedures for fair hearing and due process.

Abbreviations

ACW   Ancient Christian Writers. Edited by J. Quasten, J. C. Plumpe, and W. Burghardt. 44 Vols. New York: Paulist Press, 1946–1985.

AF   *The Apostolic Fathers.* Edited by J. N. Sparks. New York: Thomas Nelson, 1978.

AF-Ltft   The Apostolic Fathers. Edited by J. B. Lightfoot, revised by J. R. Harmer, London, New York: Macmillan, 1907.

ANF   Ante-Nicene Fathers. Edited by A. Roberts and J. Donaldson. 10 vols. 1866–1896. Reprint ed., Grand Rapids: Eerdmans, 1979.

Angl.   *Anglicanism: The Thought and Practice of the Church of England, Illustrated from the Religious Literature of the Seventeenth Century.* Edited by P. E. More and F. L. Cross. London: S.P.C.K., 1935.

BCP   *Book of Common Prayer* (1662 unless otherwise noted). Royal Breviar's edition. London: S.P.C.K., n.d.

BPR   *Book of Pastoral Rule.* Gregory the Great, NPNF 2nd X, pp. 1–94.

CC   *Creeds of the Churches.* Edited by John Leith. Richmond: John Knox Press, 1979.

CFS   Cistercian Fathers Series. 44 vols. Kalamazoo, MI: Cistercian Publications, 1968ff.

COCL   Classics of the Contemplative Life. Edited by J. M. Hussey. 8 vols. London: Faber and Faber, 1960ff.

CS   *The Curate of Souls.* Edited by John R. H. Moorman, London: S.P.C.K., 1958.

CSS   Cistercian Studies Series. 68 vols. Kalamazoo, MI: Cistercian Publications, 1968ff.

CWMS   *Complete Writings of Menno Simons* (c. 1496–1561). Edited by John C. Wenger, Scottdale, PA: Herald Press, 1956.

CWS   Classics of Western Spirituality. 37 vols. to date. Edited by Richard J. Payne et al. New York: Paulist Press, 1978ff.

ECF   *Early Christian Fathers.* Edited by H. Bettenson. London: Oxford University Press.

ECW   Early Christian Writers: The Apostolic Fathers. Translated by Maxwell Staniforth. London: Penguin Books, 1968.

FC   Fathers of the Church. Edited by R. J. Deferrari. 73 vols. Washington, DC: Catholic University Press, 1947ff.

FER   The Fathers for English Readers. 15 vols. London: S.P.C.K., 1878–1890.

Inst.   Institutes of the Christian Religion, by John Calvin. LCC, vols. 21–22. Philadelphia: Westminster Press, 1960.

KVJ   King James Version, 1611 (also called the Authorized Version).

LACT   Library of Anglo-Catholic Theology. 99 vols. Oxford University Press, 1841–63.

LCC   Library of Christian Classics. 26 vols. Edited by J. Baillie, J. T. McNiell, and H. P. Van Dusen. Philadelphia: Westminster Press, 1953–61.

LCF   *Later Christian Fathers.* Edited by H. Bettenson. London: Oxford University Press, 1970.

LF   A Library of Fathers of the Holy Catholic Church. Edited by E. B. Pusey, J. Kebel, J. H. Newman, and C. Marriott. 50 vols. Oxford: J. H. Parker, 1838–88.

Loeb   Loeb Classical Library. Edited by Page, Capps, Rouse. Cambridge, MA: Harvard University Press, 1912ff.

LPT   Library of Protestant Thought. Edited by John Dillenberger. 13 vols. New York: Oxford University Press. 1964–72.

LW   Luther's Works. Edited by J. Pelikan and H. T. Lehmann. 54 vols. St. Louis: Concordia, 1953ff.

MPG   J. B. Migne, ed., Patrologia Graeca. 162 vols. Paris: Migne, 1857–76.

MPL   J. B. Migne, ed., Patrologia Latina. 221 vols. Paris: Migne, 1841–1865. General Index, Paris, 1912.

MPLS   J. B. Migne, ed., Patrologia Latina: Supplementum. 4 vols. Edited by A. Hamman, Turnhout, Belgium: Editions Brepols.

MWS   *Ministry of Word and Sacrament: An Enchiridion,* by Martin Chemnitz (1595). St. Louis: Concordia, 1981.

NE   *A New Eusebius: Documents Illustrative of the History of the Church to A.D. 337.* Edited by J. Stevenson (based on B. J. Kidd). London: S.P.C.K., 1957.

NEB   New English Bible.

NIV   New International Version.

NPNF   A Select Library of the Nicene and Post-Nicene Fathers of the Christian Church. 1st Series, 14 vols; 2nd series, 14 vols. Edited by H. Wace and P. Schaff. New York: Christian, 1887–1900.

OCC   Our Christian Classics, ed. James Hamilton. London: Nisbet, 1858.

PW   Practical Works, Richard Baxter. 23 vols. London: James Duncan, 1830.

RAC   *Rules and Advices to the Clergy of the Dicocese of Nown and Connor*, by Jeremy Taylor (1661), Works, ed. R. Heber, 1839, vol. xiv.

RD   *Reformed Dogmatics*. Edited by J. W. Beardslee. Grand Rapids: Baker, 1965.

RSV   Revised Standard Version.

SC   *Spiritual Conferences* (1628), St. Francis de Sales. Westminster MD: Newman, 1943.

SCG   Summa contra Gentiles, On the Truth of the Catholic Faith, Thomas Aquinas. 4 vols. New York: Doubleday, 1955–57.

SED   Standard English Divines. 19 multi-volume series. Oxford: Parker, 1855ff.

SSW   *Selected Sacred Writings*, Hugh of St. Victor. London: Faber and Faber, 1962.

ST   Summa Theologica, Thomas Aquinas. Edited by English Dominican Fathers. 3 vols. New York: Benziger, 1947–48.

SW   *John Calvin, Selections from His Writings*. Edited by John Dillenberger. Missoula, MT: Scholars' Press, 1975.

TCL   Translations of Christian Literature. Edited by Sparrow Simpson and Lowther Clarke. London: S.P.C.K., 1917ff.

TPW   Taylor's Practical Works, by Jeremy Taylor. 2 vols. London: H. G. Bohn, 1854.

WA   "Weimarer Ausgabe," D. Martin Luthers Werke. Kritische Gesamtausgabe, Weimar, 1883ff.

W-Br.   Weimarer Ausgabe, D. Martin Luther, Briefwechsel, Kritische Gesamtausgabe, Weimar, 1930ff., Letters.

WLS   What Luther Says. Edited by E. Plass. 3 vols. St. Louis: Concordia, 1959.

WML   Works of Martin Luther. Philadelphia Edition. 6 vols. Philadelphia: Muhlenberg Press, 1943.

WA-T   Weimarer Ausgabe. D. Martin Luther, Tischreden, Kritische Gesamtausgabe, Table Talk, 1912ff.

WSD   *Writings on Spiritual Direction*, ed. J. M. Neufelder, and Mary C. Coelho. New York: Seabury Press, 1982.

Acknowledgments

THE AUTHOR IS GRATEFUL to the following for the use of the selections listed below in the four volumes of this series.

Benziger Bros., Inc.: Thomas Aquinas, *Summa Theologica*.

Catholic University of America: R. J. Deferrari, ed., Fathers of the Church Series.

Cistercian Publications, Inc., Kalamazoo, MI: Cistercian Studies Series, Cistercian Fathers Series.

Concordia Press: J. Pelikan, ed., Martin Luther, *Luther's Works;* E. Plass, ed., *What Luther Says*.

Faber and Faber, Inc.: Classics of the Contemplative Life Series.

Herald Press: Menno Simons, *Complete Writings of Menno Simons*.

Holy Transfiguration Monastery Press: John Climacus, *Ladder of Divine Ascent*.

Muhlenberg Press: Works of Martin Luther.

Oxford University Press: John Dillenberger, ed., Library of Protestant Thought; and E. B. Pusey et al., eds., A Library of Fathers of the Holy Catholic Church; Library of Anglo-Catholic Thought.

Paulist Press: Richard J. Payne, ed., Classics of Western Spirituality; and J. Quasten et al., eds. Ancient Christian Writers Series.

Scholars Press and the American Academy of Religion: John Dillenberger, ed., *John Calvin: Selections from His Writings*.

S.P.C.K.: S. Simpson and L. Clarke, eds., Translations of Christian Literature, The Fathers for English Readers; and P. W. Moore and F. L. Cross, eds., *Anglicanism*.

Thomas Nelson: Jack Sparks, ed., *The Apostolic Fathers: New Translations of Early Christian Writings*.

University of Michigan Press: John Donne, *Devotions Upon Emergent Occasions*.

Viking-Penguin Inc.: *Early Christian Writings: The Apostolic Fathers,* trans. Maxwell Staniforth.

Westminster Press: J. Baille, J. T. McNeill, and H. P. Van Dusen, eds., The Library of Christian Classics.

How to Keep Control
of Your Life after 50

WITHDRAWN

In Memoriam

Congressman Claude Pepper

Cynthia Northrop, R.N., Esq.

*Two shining examples of what love, dedication, and commitment
can do to improve the lives of millions,
now and in the years to come.*

How to Keep Control of Your Life after 50

A Guide for Your
Legal, Medical, and Financial Well-Being

TERESA SCHWAB MYERS

Lexington Books

D.C. Heath and Company • Lexington, Massachusetts • Toronto

Library of Congress Cataloging-in-Publication Data

Myers, Teresa Schwab
How to keep control of your life after fifty.

Includes index.
I. Aged—Legal status, laws, etc.—United States.
2. Estate planning—United States.   3. Aged—Medical
care—United States.   4. Aged—United States—Finance,
Personal.   I. Title.
KF390.A4M97 1989   346.7301'3   88-45305
                          347.30613
       ISBN 0-669-19457-3 (pbk.: alk. paper).

Published simultaneously in Canada
Printed in the United States of America
International Standard Book Number: 0-669-19457-3
Library of Congress Catalog Card Number: 88-45305

The paper used in this publication meets
the minimum requirements of American National Standard
for Information Sciences—Permanence of Paper
for Printed Library Materials, ANSI Z39.48-1984.

Year and number of this printing:

90 91 92 8 7 6 5 4 3 2 1

Contents

PART 1
Planning Ahead

PART 2
Staying in Charge in a Hospital or Nursing Home

PART 3
When Someone Can No Longer Make Decisions

PART 4
Conclusion

Getting Attention and Influencing a Particular Program

Acknowledgments

T HERE is, I think, a certain ineffable excitement that surrounds specific events in our lives. They are events, in this case the writing of this book, that, for lack of a better word, summon up the commitment that lies deep within each one of us. If one is very lucky, then perhaps a few such events will occur in a single life span.

This book seemed blessed from the beginning: the publisher was excited by it; the outline fell together readily enough, waiting to be fleshed into chapters; and, most importantly, top experts in the field agreed to consult on each chapter. Each one, I believe, felt that excitement mentioned earlier—each one was committed to the success of this project. They worked for far less than their usual compensation, made countless excellent suggestions, rearranged already busy schedules, and reviewed all materials quickly and thoroughly. They did so because they care—because this subject, and the offering of clear and usable information to the elderly and their families, is as important to them as it is to me. I have noticed that there are certain topics, and this is one of them, that pull so strongly at the hearts and minds of the people involved that they will outdo themselves in their efforts to make a better world. Anyone who believes that "no one cares about the elderly" has never met these people.

There are a few people who deserve special mention: my mother, who, in addition to giving regular and welcome doses of moral and maternal support, acted as a lay reader of this book and helped to organize the glossary; chapter consultants Susan Pettey, Bill Benson, David Schulke, Tom Jazwiecki, Marshall Kapp, John Fears, John Laster, David Chavkin, Penelope Hommel, Barbara Mishkin, and Cynthia Northrop, who went more than a few "extra miles" to help out; Amy Cohen, who, as my assistant, was industrious, cheerful, and efficient; and Margaret Zusky, of Lexington Books, who without fail remained all that an editor should be—enthusiastic, intelligent, interested, and caring.

Lastly, this book is dedicated to my parents, Joan and Gerald Schwab, who have always urged me to find the best within myself; and to David, who makes all of that worthwhile.

Introduction

Why Plan Ahead?

Why plan ahead? In order to properly use this book, it is necessary to understand why planning ahead is important in the first place. To do that, it is also useful to know why the society we live in makes it vital that we plan ahead for our own illness, infirmities, and death.

In the United States, we have the luxury of holding life to be the most sacred of all things. It is a luxury that does not exist in many poorer, less developed nations, where living is much harder and dying much easier. In those countries, the moral, ethical, and legal questions we face when we make decisions to refuse lifesaving medical treatment simply do not apply. In such countries there are too many other problems to tackle to spend a great deal of time worrying about whether an elderly person should undergo another operation, be put on life-support systems, or be allowed to die.

So life in the United States is a luxury made possible by our standard of living and by our medical and technological knowledge. But it is a luxury that now acts as a double-edged sword. If life is perceived as preeminent, then what about the people who don't want to continue living with illness, or who simply want to be able to control what happens to their bodies?

We are at a crossroads now. Our ability to extend and prolong life has run smack up against our own questions of whether life should always be extended and prolonged. Until society makes some very hard choices, elderly individuals can maintain control over their own life-and-death decisions only by making plans and arrangements before, or shortly after, they become ill—before medicine, technology, doctors, and lawyers take over and decide for them.

The purpose of this book is not to tell anyone to refuse medical treatment, nor is it to tell anyone to demand it. All it sets out to do is simply offer the knowledge and the tools necessary for elderly people to get what they want—in their medical treatment, their finances, and their right to maintain control over their own lives.

Hopefully, it will also help families and friends carry out the wishes of their elderly if they are too ill or frail to do so themselves.

The Consequences of Not Planning Ahead

Some three out of every four Americans die without having written a will. A survey conducted in 1982 by Louis Harris and Associates showed that only about a third of respondents had given instructions to someone about how they would like to be treated if they became too ill to make decisions about health care. Of those who had given instructions, only one-fourth had put those instructions into writing.

By not planning ahead, elderly people who become too ill to decide for themselves place a great burden on their families, their friends, and their caretakers. Few people welcome the responsibility of making such important decisions for others, yet millions of people must make those judgments every year. The decisions these people must make include whether or not to put ailing elderly persons into nursing homes, how to take care of their finances, how they would want to live if ill, and how they would want to die.

If no instructions are left to them and no legal documents are drawn up telling them what to do, those people must try to figure out what their elderly relatives and friends would have wanted. If their religious, moral, and personal beliefs are different from those of the elderly people in their care, they will then have to face the struggle between following their own wishes and following those the elderly individuals may have had. Not only are such decisions difficult; in many cases they could be avoided by a little advance planning.

Planning ahead is also more likely to result in elderly people's wishes being respected. For example, an elderly person may know that a particular friend is more able than a relative to understand and follow his or her wishes. While still healthy, the elderly person can legally plan for that friend to be in charge of making the necessary decisions if the elderly person becomes too sick to do so. If, however, the elderly person becomes very ill before planning ahead, a court might appoint a relative (and not the friend) to make decisions because it is unaware of what the elderly person would have wanted.

Planning ahead by appointing someone to make decisions might also stop a hospital or nursing home from going to court to fight a particular decision.

Why don't we plan ahead? The reasons behind not doing so are understandable: illness and death are not pleasant subjects to think about; many people fear having to go through a complicated (and expensive) legal process; they think their families and their doctors will know what to do; and perhaps most common of all, it's something that just gets put off until it's too late.

Illness and death are frightening for everyone—the patient, the family, and the doctor. The stress and fear and pain that all of us face at these times can be greatly eased by the presence of a few plans and instructions. If an elderly person is already too sick to make decisions for himself or herself, then maybe this book can help his or her family make those decisions. Maybe it will also assist families to plan ahead for themselves.

Enough people have become concerned about these issues that there now exist many ways to plan ahead—some are complicated, expensive, and require a lawyer; some are much simpler, cheaper, and can be done with little if any professional help. Some people don't consult with a lawyer or doctor at all but still manage to do some advance planning. Different ways to plan ahead are described in this book. Hopefully, it will help elderly people or their family members find out what they need to know, who they need to talk to, and what questions to ask.

Patients are not the only ones unfamiliar with the ways to plan ahead. Often, legal and health care professionals are just as ignorant of the options for pre-planning health care. It is important to make sure that the elderly person's doctor, nurse, social worker, and lawyer are aware of the person's plans, and if they are unfamiliar with the planning mechanism chosen by the patient, they will need to be educated. Maybe they should be given this book.

How Best to Use This Book

This book is divided into four parts to help readers easily locate the information they need.

1. Part 1, "Planning Ahead," contains chapters on wills, trusts, and joint accounts; purchasing "Medigap" and long-term care insurance policies; paying for nursing home care; writing a living will; and the various legal tools elderly people can use to appoint someone else to make decisions for them should they become too sick to do so themselves.

2. Part 2, "Staying in Charge in a Hospital or Nursing Home," discusses how elderly people or their families can maintain control of their own medical care in a hospital or nursing home setting. It has chapters on what people should know before they agree to medical care, patient rights, what to do if the hos-

pital releases a patient too early, what to do about problems or complaints, and how to work through the maze of Medicare and Medicaid regulations.

3. Part 3, "When Someone Can No Longer Make Decisions," deals with the problems faced by the families and friends of elderly people who can no longer make decisions for themselves. It has chapters on mental competence and incompetence, guardians and conservators, what to do if Social Security payments should go to a family member or friend, and the limits on the decisions made for someone else.

4. Part 4, the book's conclusion, presents various ways to get results by involving government agencies, the media, and politicians. It also discusses how every individual can help mold and define the important decisions our society must make in how to deal with the problems of the elderly and their families.

Each chapter explains a specific issue and answers the questions and concerns that may be raised by it. Chapters are broken down into individual segments that address particular points of each issue.

The appendixes at the back of this book are designed to accompany each chapter and contain a series of charts, sample forms, additional materials, and addresses that should assist readers in identifying their relevant state laws, understanding what documents they will need to fill out, and locating specific state and national agencies, boards, and commissions from which to request further information or assistance. Also at the end of the book are glossary terms to help readers understand some of the medical and legal language used in the chapters and a list ("Additional Reading") of sources providing more information on specific topics.

This book does not claim to have all the answers, but it does provide the basic information necessary to fight a problem, find an answer, and know where to go for further help. The problems discussed here are among the most important issues facing society today. This book is designed to explain the issues and help the people who need it most—the elderly and their families—to resolve the problems.

Planning Ahead

1

Wills, Trusts, and Joint Accounts
Using Them Now

Overview

Writing a will is one of the many ways that an individual can plan ahead. It is an important topic, one that might better be served by a whole book rather than a single chapter. Nevertheless, several legal tools—including wills—that can be used to transfer money and property to others before (as well as after) death deserve to be examined here.

Wills are flexible tools that allow individuals to control all their assets during life and then dispose of them after death. *More important for the purpose of this book, there are alternatives to wills that*

greatly assist elderly individuals in transferring their financial responsibilities to friends or family members when they become too ill to manage these things themselves; and

help everybody concerned avoid the cost and trauma of getting court-appointed guardians or conservators to take care of the affairs of an incapacitated elderly individual (for more information, see chapter 12). In short, they provide another way to plan ahead.

Wills and How They Work

Often, an individual dies without ever having written a will. The reasons for this omission are varied. An individual may

have little or no property left to give anyone;

die suddenly and without warning by a stroke or in an accident;

gradually become unable to think for himself or herself and therefore be unable to write a will at a certain point; or

simply not want to think about his or her own death, and avoid writing a will until it's too late.

A will controls the property that an individual owns in his or her own name at the time of death. If a person does not own something when he or she dies, the will normally will have no effect. For example, if Mr. X gives his stock in General Motors to his daughter (so that General Motors thinks the daughter owns it) and then leaves it in his will to his son, there is no stock for the son to inherit.

When an individual dies, it is important to find out if he or she had a will. Wills are supposed to be filed right after someone dies, but certainly within three months after the death. *Anyone who has the will of a deceased person can file it by taking it to the registry of wills (or a similar office) in the local courthouse. It is a crime to hide or destroy someone else's will.* After the will is filed, anyone who might have an interest—such as family members, creditors, or friends who might have been left something—files a petition with the probate court asking that someone be appointed to *administer,* or manage, the estate.

Administering a will or estate involves filing all the appropriate papers with the court; taking charge of all the deceased individual's property, such as bank accounts; and performing such tasks as paying taxes, closing houses, caring for pets, paying creditors, and finding heirs. Usually the person who wrote the will has included the name of an *executor* (male) or *executrix* (female) to administer his or her estate (other terms that mean more or less the same thing are *personal representative* and *administrator*). Usually, the court will appoint the person mentioned in the will. The main reasons a court might not appoint that person are that someone opposes the appointment and the court agrees with his or her reasons or the person is not a resident of a state that requires executors to be residents.

If someone dies with no will or if the person named in the will can't administer the estate because he or she has died or become disabled, the law determines who is entitled to administer. There are set lists of people whom the court prefers to appoint to administer an estate. A typical list would start with the deceased person's spouse (and, if no spouse is available), the person's parents (and, if no parents are available), the person's adult children, and so on.

The will directs much, but not all, of what will happen during the administration of the estate, in a process called *probate*.

During probate, the will's instructions are carried out, and the *bequests*, or gifts listed in the will, are given to the appropriate people or organizations. For example, if Mr. X's will states that $1,000 of his estate should go to his close friend, then the administrator will do that. Or, if Mr. X wants to donate $5,000 to his synagogue, church, or favorite charity, then the administrator will do that. Mr. X might also use his will to "forgive" a debt of $10,000 borrowed by his son, so that the son does not have to pay that amount back into his father's estate.

Other kinds of bequests that an individual might want to make include china, silverware, jewelry, or an autographed baseball. The person writing the will has to decide in advance who will receive those items.

Wills often also include instructions about taxes. For example, in his will Mr. X leaves china and silverware worth $10,000 to his niece, who is both extraordinarily kind and extremely poor. If Mr. X lives in a state that has an inheritance tax, his niece might have to pay a tax for the privilege of inheriting property from Mr. X. If in this state the tax is 10 percent, she would have to pay $1,000. To avoid this situation, Mr. X could request that the tax be paid from money in his estate.

Then, too, Mr. X might prefer *not* to have his estate pay for taxes on the gift to his niece, so as to leave more money for his children, who are inheriting the rest of his estate. Very often, people say that they want their estate to pay all inheritance taxes without thinking through what that means. Of course, if the person receiving the china is the same person receiving the rest of the money, the issue makes much less difference. *All individuals thinking about writing a will should strongly consider consulting a lawyer about taxes and other matters.* Doing so is particularly important if the estate is worth a substantial amount, yet even someone with a smaller estate, who still wants to leave a will, should also consider getting a lawyer's advice. Many lawyers offer a low, set fee to write uncomplicated wills, and it is worth calling several different lawyers or legal clinics to find out what services are offered.

The State Unit on Aging (see appendix 20 for addresses) should have a legal services developer who can direct callers to the appropriate low-cost legal aid office or clinic. Also, almost all states have an Information and Referral (I&R) hot line for older people or the general public in need of services, and this resource can also provide guidance. Local senior citizens' centers should have the I&R telephone number.

If Mr. X has young children, he might want to name the person with whom those children should live after he dies. If Mr. X has young children or grandchildren to whom he would like to leave money, he might want to place the money *in trust* for them. This means that some adult would watch over the money and invest it until the children or grandchildren reach a certain age specified in Mr. X's will. There are two reasons to think about a trust for young children or grandchildren: (a) many are unable to manage or spend the money responsibly until they are older, and (b) children cannot sign for the money (even if they have learned to write), because they are minors. When children sign documents, it has less legal effect than when adults do (more information on trusts is included later in this chapter).

A will can also be used to ensure that the intended *beneficiaries,* or heirs, receive as much as possible. For example, Congress allows each individual to give away $600,000 during his or her lifetime (or upon his or her death) without having to pay federal estate taxes. Moreover, people can give unlimited amounts of money to a spouse without being taxed at the time of death or at the time of the gift. A person who has more than $600,000 (including the value of his or her house, life insurance, pension benefits, and so on) will benefit from a will that sets up his or her estate in such a way as to minimize the overall tax. If Mr. and Mrs. X have $900,000 worth of property, all of which is passed to Mrs. X upon her husband's death, there is no federal estate tax, because spouses can give unlimited amounts to each other. However, when Mrs. X dies (assuming that she has not spent the excess over $600,000), there will be a substantial estate tax, thus reducing what ultimately passes to Mr. and Mrs. X's children. Had Mr. and Mrs. X planned ahead, they might have eliminated the tax altogether, thus increasing the amount that passed to their children.

A will can make it easier to administer a person's estate. Some state laws, for example, forbid an administrator from selling real estate without a court order; usually this means that the administrator has to hire a lawyer to get the court order, and the lawyer has to be paid. In other states, however, a person's will can authorize the administrator to sell the real estate without having to go to court. Interested individuals should talk with a lawyer to find out the laws of their state.

Precise definitions in a will can also help the administrator. For example, if

Mr. X wants his adopted grandchild to share in the money given to his children, he should say so.

State laws differ on how a will can be written. For example, it is almost always difficult to omit, or leave out, a spouse, but in most (not all) states, it is possible to omit a child.

States also have varying laws on what makes a will legal. In some states, a will must be signed and witnessed by at least two disinterested people (not heirs). In other states, a will can be in the person's own handwriting and signed by him or her without witnesses. Still other states require three witnesses. Again, interested individuals should check with a lawyer to find out the laws in their state.

Usually, special legal language is unnecessary to the writing of a will. The important thing is to be very clear. In one case, a woman wanted to leave money to her daughter, but if her daughter did not survive her, she wanted her sister to have the money. She wrote, "To my sister, if my daughter does not survive. . . ." While it was clear that she meant for her sister to have the money if her daughter did not survive, several insurance companies thought it was not clear that she wanted her daughter to have the money if the daughter did survive!

Advantages and Disadvantages of Wills

There are many advantages and few disadvantages to making a will. The principal advantage is that individuals can make their wishes known—which itself can be an act of great love for the surviving family members and friends. Moreover, writing a will can save a great deal of money in taxes, as well as aggravation in administration.

The principal disadvantage is that writing a will usually costs money. While it is possible to write one's own will in most states, it is often advisable to go to a lawyer or a legal clinic. Again, the State Unit on Aging's legal services developer can make suggestions (see appendix 20), as can the state's I&R hot line, whose number should be available from local senior citizens' centers. Another option is to purchase computer software to assist in the writing of a will (some recommendations for books and software appear in the "Additional Reading" section at the back of this book). None of these options is right or wrong—it is the individual's personal situation and preferences that should determine which option is used.

Dying without a Will

When people die *intestate,* that means they have died without leaving a will. For people who owned property at the time they died intestate, the state legislature "writes" a will, its structure determined by the state's intestacy law. Frequently, states' intestacy laws divide people's assets somewhat by compromise. Often, the compromise that the state has written into law is exactly what those people wanted anyway. For example, the law might provide that one-half (or one-third) of someone's property go to the surviving spouse, while the other one-half (or two-thirds) go to the surviving children. Particularly in the case of second marriages, one-third may not be enough to support the surviving spouse, although two-thirds would go to any children from the individual's first (and second) marriage.

Intestacy laws often treat the person's spouse and parents equally. If there are no close blood relatives, then distant relatives or the state may inherit the property. Close friends are not included in state intestacy laws. Thus, any individual who has definite ideas about who should inherit what items, should either write a will or take advantage of one of the will substitutes, or alternatives.

The only advantages to intestacy are that it is the least expensive way for people to pass on their estates and that it requires no thought or planning whatsoever. Individuals might choose not to leave a will if they were sure that (a) the state's intestacy law would divide the property in an acceptable way or (b) administration would not be more difficult for survivors than if a will or will substitute had been left.

Why Alternatives Are Needed

Before examining any alternatives, it is important to look at why people might want to do more than leave a will, which simply passes their property to other individuals at the time of death. Death is rarely a neat, quick, uncomplicated event. More often, people become ill, then more ill, sliding slowly toward death. Some may remain alert and mentally healthy throughout this process, but many become confused by pain and painkillers, or illness may rob them of the ability to think clearly (as in Alzheimer's disease). *When people can no longer think for themselves, many personal, medical, and financial decisions have to be made for them while they are still alive. Most people, if given the opportunity, would like to have some way of remaining in control of their own lives even after they are unable to think for themselves, and the only way to do this is to leave advance instructions.*

A great deal of information on these topics is available in the various chapters of this book; however, the thumbnail definitions below should make it a little easier to understand this chapter and determine what alternatives are appropriate in a particular situation.

Competence. A competent individual is one who is able to make informed choices and understand the consequences of his or her decisions. A person who is unable to do so is termed *incompetent* or *incapacitated.* Although mental disability is usually what triggers a guardianship proceeding, physical incapacity can sometimes be grounds for such a proceeding as well.

Guardian or conservator. An individual appointed by the court to make decisions for someone who is incapacitated. Usually a guardian is appointed to make personal and medical decisions, and a conservator to make financial decisions. However, a guardian may be given responsibility for an incapacitated person's finances, just as a conservator may be responsible for an individual's personal and medical decisions.

Ward. An incapacitated individual who has been put under the care and decision-making authority of a guardian or conservator.

Principal. A person who uses a power of authority (defined below) to appoint someone else to take care of his or her affairs and make decisions for him or her.

Agent or attorney-in-fact. A person appointed in a (durable) power of attorney to make decisions for and handle the affairs of the principal before and/or after the principal becomes incapacitated.

Power of attorney. A legal tool to permit decision-making authority by one competent individual (the agent) for another (the principal) while the principal is still competent. There are several varieties—including durable power of attorney and springing durable power of attorney—that allow the agent to start or continue making decisions after the principal becomes incapacitated or even incompetent.

Living will. A document that specifies someone's preferences regarding medical care and treatment decisions. It is most often used when that person is terminally ill and imcompetent, and is unable to express himself or herself, or direct his or her own care and treatment.

For more information on determining whether an individual can make decisions, see chapter 11. To understand who else can make decisions, see chapters 4, 5, and 12. And to understand the restrictions on such decisions, see chapter 14.

Alternatives to Wills

Different legal tools can be used to avoid many of the problems faced by the elderly and their families. The information that follows focuses on alternatives to wills, or will substitutes. *These tools, properly used, may make it possible for an individual to*

avoid the expense of writing a will;

protect his or her family from incurring the cost and trauma of getting a court-appointed guardian or conservator; and

leave behind instructions for someone else to carry out in the event that he or she becomes incompetent.

Among the most common of these alternatives are living wills, which are used to give advance directions for medical decisions, and durable powers of attorney, which appoint an agent who can be left advance instructions on how an incompetent individual's financial and medical decisions should be made. These are important issues, best described in separate chapters (see chapters 4 and 5, respectively). *Both these tools may be useful alternatives or adjuncts to guardianship.*

Tools for Managing Money and Property

If future concerns about an individual's competence revolve primarily around making arrangements for money or property control, there are several alternatives to consider. Any of these might be used with a durable power of attorney.

- Direct-deposit banking of regular income, such as Social Security or pension payments, can usually be arranged with the individual's bank. The check is sent directly to the bank and credited to the specific account. This arrangement can be extremely helpful for those who tend to forget or misplace their checks or have physical disabilities that prevent them from getting to the bank.

- Some banks have automatic banking services to pay regular bills, such as mortgages or utilities. Again, this service can be very helpful for the person who manages well on a daily basis but can no longer easily handle paperwork. The charge for this service varies from bank to bank.
- A personal money manager or bill-paying service can be hired or is sometimes available through a trust department of a bank, if the individual has adequate income. These services are usually staffed by bonded professionals (often certified public accountants) who keep track of income, pay bills, and may prepare tax returns. Some charge flat fees (such as $40 per month), while others charge a percentage of the individual's monthly income.
- A representative payee can also be appointed to manage an individual's Social Security benefits. (This topic is covered in chapter 13.)

Joint Property Arrangements and Joint Bank Accounts

An elderly individual who is ill or has trouble moving around may also want to add the name of a spouse, adult child, or friends to his or her checking or savings account or other financial asset. In addition to making banking transactions easier, this action can in some cases take the place of a will. By using a special kind of account, the *joint tenant* (joint owner) will receive, on the death of the elderly individual, what is left in the account without having to go to court for it.

It is important to understand the differences between accounts offering *joint tenants with right of survivorship* and those offering only *tenants in common*. Both are joint tenant accounts (that is, two or more names are on a single account), but only the one offering right of survivorship allows one joint tenant to automatically receive the assets after the other joint tenant dies. Some states require that automatic rights of survivorship be specified; however, any bank manager can explain what options are available.

Some joint accounts allow either owner to transact business and sign checks; others require the signature of all joint owners for all transactions; and still others restrict the ability of one or another owner to withdraw funds. Law and local bank practices determine which choices are possible.

The following examples should serve to illustrate some general points about joint tenancies with right of survivorship. If Mr. X puts all his money in an account with his son, who has right of survivorship, and then leaves his daughter $10,000 in his will, there is nothing for the daughter to get. The instant Mr. X dies, his son owns the whole account "by operation of the law."

Another example is if Mr. X opens a checking account by himself, and without any joint tenant with right of survivorship, at his local bank. Under the terms of the account he has opened, the bank will honor only checks with his signature. If there is still money in the account when Mr. X dies, the bank will freeze the account and not release any of the money until a court appoints someone to manage Mr. X's estate.

Even if Mr. X has signed a power-of-attorney card at the bank, allowing his daughter to sign checks as well, her legal authority to do so ends when Mr. X dies (or when she knows he has died). Once again, the bank will freeze the account until the court appoints someone to handle the estate.

Joint ownership arrangements—of bank accounts, certificates of deposit, U.S. savings bonds, stocks, homes, cars, and other assets—are also commonly used tools in estate planning. They avoid the difficulties of transferring power from an incompetent individual to a competent one. State laws differ as to the conditions and consequences of joint property arrangements and the right of survivorship. Interested individuals should have a lawyer verify that joint ownership will provide the desired results.

Joint ownership is an important and useful tool, but it can also be a double-edged sword. Its advantages include the fact that it costs little or nothing to establish for most assets, and can be done quickly and easily. For real estate, the deed must be filed with the recorder or registrar of deeds; for bank accounts, a new bank card or form must be signed; and for stock registered in one name, a transfer must be performed.

If a person is physically ailing, placing funds in a joint account is an easy way for a trusted friend or family member to make deposits and withdrawals for the disabled person. Sometimes joint ownership can avoid the delays and problems of putting an individual's will in probate (the process of carrying out the instructions left in the will, paying creditors from the estate, and so on), should one of the signers die. When the circumstances are right, a joint account can be useful for those people who are mentally or physically unable to handle their own finances.

Still, great care must be taken to choose an honest, responsible joint owner. Remember, while one joint tenant can use funds in an account to take care of the other joint tenant, he or she can also use them for personal gain. A dishonest co-owner could misuse funds in the account at any time. Also, the incompetent owner could withdraw funds and use them unwisely.

Depending on the kind of joint ownership, one person may not be able to withdraw some of the assets without the other person's signature. By the time a problem arises with a joint ownership arrangement, it may be too late to undo it. First, it doesn't do any good to end a joint ownership if the other person has already removed all the money in the account. Second, creditors of one of the joint owners may be able to seize the account, even if the money in it belongs to the other person. Third, it is impossible to undo joint ownership of some assets—U.S. savings bonds, corporate stocks, homes, and other real property—with only one signature. In addition, if one joint owner becomes ill or incompetent, court assistance may be necessary to help the other owner transfer or sell an asset at all.

Finally, in some states, when officials are determining someone's eligibility for Medicaid, the entire joint account is considered part of the individual's property. This stipulation may make someone ineligible, even though the funds in the joint account may belong to the other account owner. (For more information on Medicaid eligibility requirements, see chapters 3 and 10.)

Here is a short list of some of the important estate-planning features of joint ownership:

- Creating a joint asset may mean "giving" a gift that could have gift, estate, and income tax implications.
- Placing real estate into joint ownership or removing it from joint ownership may result in transfer and recordation taxes.
- Placing a home into joint ownership could put an unnecessary income tax burden on survivors. Principal residences, in particular, have special treatment under federal income tax laws.

Although establishment of joint assets might avoid the need for a court-appointed guardian or conservator to manage an incompetent or incapacitated individual's financial matters, joint assets do not completely take the place of a will. Through a will, an individual can plan for many more possibilities than through a joint asset. Once one of the joint tenants dies, the other one owns the asset outright. If that person dies, the asset will be controlled either by that person's will or by the intestacy law if no will exists.

Trusts

A trust is a common legal device used by one person to authorize another person to handle assets. It is the most flexible and versatile tool for arranging assets, and it can be tailored to fit specific needs. During a person's lifetime, a trust can substitute for court guardianship or conservatorship proceedings. If properly written, it can sometimes help an aging or ill person qualify for medical and housing benefits that depend on his or her income and assets. A trust can also act as a will in directing how an individual's assets should be divided upon his or her death. Its principal disadvantages is that it usually costs more to set up than the other options do.

Trusts are good planning tools, and more people ought to think about using them. A trust is like a corporation—a kind of legal entity that can own property; buy, sell, and manage it; invest money or spend it; or use it in whatever way is required to meet someone's living expenses.

Basically, a trust is an arrangement in which property is transferred by one person (the *grantor, settlor,* or *trustor*) to benefit himself or someone else (the *beneficiary*). It is managed by another person (the *trustee*) and is limited by whatever restrictions the grantor (or *testator,* in the case of a testamentary trust) included in the trust agreement. There are two kinds of trusts:

1. A *testamentary* trust, created within a will, which does not take effect until the testator (the person whose will it is) dies.
2. An *inter vivos,* or *living,* trust, which goes into effect while the grantor is still alive. An inter vivos trust can be revocable (changed or canceled by the grantor at a later time) or irrevocable (permanent and unchangeable once the trust has begun).

For the purposes of this book, the information that follows concerns inter vivos, or living, trusts.

To illustrate what happens without one, suppose that Mrs. X goes to her bank to open a checking account. The bank requires that she fill out a signature card. Upon having her signature, the bank will honor Mrs. X's checks for as long as she is able to sign them. If she becomes incapacitated or dies, the bank will not cash her checks signed by anyone else. In either case, the bank will not normally release Mrs. X's money until someone comes forward with the required authority. If Mrs. X becomes incompetent and has asked no one else to act for her under a durable power of attorney, the bank will require that someone be appointed by a court as her guardian or conservator. If Mrs. X dies, the bank will require that someone be appointed by a court as the administrator of her estate.

Now, suppose that Mrs. X has set up the "Mrs. X Trust," in which she is the trustee and beneficiary and her brother is the successor trustee. In this case, Mrs. X opens her bank account in the name of the Mrs. X Trust, and the bank might ask for a copy of the agreement establishing the trust. If Mrs. X becomes unable to sign checks, her brother will show the bank that Mrs. X is incapacitated (for example, by showing the bank a doctor's letter) or dead (by showing the bank a death certificate), and the bank will then honor checks written by the brother. No court papers are needed, and from this point on, the brother can act for the trust as long as necessary.

This example shows two advantages of the living trust: it makes going to court unnecessary if an individual becomes incapacitated, and it can transfer money to the individual's beneficiaries without court action if he or she dies.

Trusts can be set up so that they go into effect only if the grantor becomes incapacitated, in order to ensure that the grantor is well cared for and that his or her finances are handled properly. They are also sometimes combined with a durable power of attorney.

To set up a good living trust, individuals need

one or more beneficiaries;

a trustee, along with a successor or cotrustee;

property and money in the name of the trust; and

a trust agreement that tells the successor or cotrustee what to do with the trust property for the benefit of the beneficiary or beneficiaries.

The individual who sets up the trust might be its lifetime beneficiary, but other beneficiaries (those people Mrs. X wants to provide for during her lifetime) can be listed as well. Mrs. X can also name who would get the trust property after her death. In this way, a trust functions as a will: Mrs. X can specify that the other beneficiaries will receive her money and property as soon as possible after her death, or she can direct that the money be held in trust for them after her death because, for whatever reason, they cannot manage that money themselves.

A trustee can be anyone Mrs. X chooses—herself while she is capable of managing her own affairs, a relative, lawyer, friend, business partner, or even a corporation like a bank or trust company.

The property of the trust is whatever property an individual chooses to put in it. It can be all that is owned or selected property; it can be a home or income-producing property; or it can be bonds or long-term appreciation property.

Like all options, trusts have advantages and disadvantages. *The main advantages are that they provide a relatively seamless plan for dealing with an individual's incapacity, incompetence, or death; avoid court involvement to determine an individual's competence; and avoid the delay and expense associated with estate administration if the individual dies.* Another advantage is that assets can be professionally managed, regardless of whether the grantor becomes ill, dies, or simply finds the problems of management too complex. Also, if a trust is revocable, it allows the grantor control as long as possible, while allowing smooth management when her or she is no longer interested in or able to manage the trust. For the upper-income person, there can be tax advantages to a trust. All interested individuals should consult a lawyer or financial planner when considering setting up a trust.

A trust's primary disadvantage is its cost. Stocks, real estate, and other property may require a great deal of paperwork to put them into trust. If there is a professional trustee (such as a bank), there will be fees. Also, many banks or financial institutions are reluctant to accept responsibility as the professional trustee of a trust that is worth less than $50,000 to $100,000. Moreover, a trust may not be possible unless the grantor has friends or family members who are willing to assume the responsibility of being a trustee for little or no pay. Sometimes, a simple power of attorney may be an equally efficient (and less expensive) way of achieving the same results. A trust does not eliminate the need for either a will or a power of attorney, although these documents can be far simpler when they accompany a trust than when they are the sole means for planning the management of an individual's estate.

Another use of trusts is linked to Medicaid, the federal and state program that pays for long-term care in an Intermediate Care Facility (ICF) nursing home (one that provides some medical care) when people's income and assets are insufficient to meet the costs of nursing home care. Since trusts can legally own property, some people plan to transfer their assets to a trust so that they, individually, can qualify for Medicaid.

When Medicaid officials are considering someone's eligibility, they want to know about any trusts established by him or her or for his or her benefit. Depending on the type of trust and all the relevant dates that show when the trust was set up, they might deny or delay that individual's application. It may be possible for some irrevocable living trusts to allow individuals to qualify for Medicaid if they enter a nursing home, thereby safeguarding the rest of their assets for other beneficiaries; however, *the law changes regularly in this area, and no one should attempt this action without fully exploring its Medicaid* and *tax consequences.*

Trusts also require some expertise with estate and tax planning, as there may be tax disadvantages if a large trust is not carefully set up. If properly established, trusts can achieve all the estate tax savings that a will can, and will have no effect on income tax while the grantor is alive.

If an individual plans to put his or her home into a trust, there are at least two points to remember. First, some banks require that the home be solely owned by that individual, and will not lend money if the house is owned by a trust. Second, some states impose a transfer tax when the home is put into a trust.

Gifts

Giving away assets to one's spouse, children, or others is another way to handle assets. Such giving can be extremely beneficial in estate planning. It also has one obvious serious drawback: once an individual gives away his or her money or assets, he or she no longer has that money or those assets. The individual who gives the gifts (the *donor*) could become dependent on the goodwill of the person or persons to whom the gifts were given (the *donee* or *donees*).

Gifts are not income to the donee. Giving away large amounts, however, may eventually result in higher income taxes for the donee (since the money, once in the donee's hands, will make money). Such giving may also deprive the donor and the donees of important tax benefits.

Giving is easy to do, although sometimes gift tax returns need to be filed. Its principal disadvantage is that it requires an individual to give up control of his or her assets while he or she is still alive. Interested individuals should always consult a lawyer and/or financial planner before choosing this option.

2

"Medigap" and Long-Term Care Insurance Policies

T HIS chapter is organized into two parts. The first focuses on "Medigap" and Medicare supplemental insurance policies, designed to cover bills (or parts of bills) left unpaid by Medicare. The second treats long-term care insurance policies, designed to pay policyholders for the long-term care or nursing home services not covered by Medicare. Concluding the chapter is a section—applicable to both parts—on what to do if a problem or complaint arises.

Medigap Policies

Overview

Medicare was not designed to cover all the health care costs of the elderly. Instead, it pays for only those medical services needed by someone suffering from an acute, or serious, illness or accident. As a result, elderly patients still face numerous bills for medical services either not covered by Medicare or covered only in part. These costs, known as out-of-pocket expenses, must be paid by the elderly themselves. In 1986, for example, Medicare paid only 48 percent of the average cost of its beneficiaries' health care bills, leaving the beneficiaries to pay the remaining 52 percent, an average of $17,000, per person that year.

To combat the problem of these out-of-pocket medical expenses, nearly two-thirds of elderly persons have purchased "Medicare supplemental" or "Medigap" insurance policies. These policies are sold by private companies, not the federal government, and are designed to pay for the cost of services not covered by Medicare. Such policies often don't work in an ideal fashion, however, so consumers need to look carefully at whether or not they really need to buy a supplemental policy, and if so, which one best suits their needs.

When Might It Be Necessary to Purchase Medigap Insurance?

The first step in buying Medigap insurance is to understand what Medicare does and does not pay for in the first place (see appendix 1 for a description of services covered by Medicare Part A and Part B). Only by knowing what isn't covered by Medicare can consumers know whether they need another policy, and if so, which one to purchase.

Not everyone needs Medigap insurance, but people without any health care coverage other than Medicare should probably consider buying a supplemental policy. People thinking about buying Medigap insurance should keep the following points in mind.

- *Medicaid.* Elderly persons covered by Medicaid do not need to purchase Medigap policies because Medicaid pays almost all of their health care costs.

- *Employee Group Health Insurance.* Many employed persons may continue to use their group health insurance or, when they reach age sixty-five, convert it to a Medicare supplemental policy. When group coverage is continued, the items it covers are often reduced or the premium to be paid is increased. Some people may have coverage through a working spouse. *These options should be checked with the employer before retirement.* Under a new law, in 1989 and 1990 any employer who currently provides to an employee or a retired former employee health benefits that duplicate at least 50 percent of Medicare's Part A and Part B benefits must provide either (a) additional benefits that are at least equal to the value of the duplicated benefits or (b) a refund to the employee or retired former employee.

- *Health Maintenance Organizations (HMOs).* HMOs offer prepaid health insurance plans that provide all acute medical services that policyholders may need. Medicare is encouraging HMOs to provide services to older people, and more and more HMOs are enrolling people over sixty-five years of age into their programs. Coverage may be expensive, however, and often subscribers or policyholders must use physicians selected by the HMO.

- *Major medical insurance.* Major medical insurance is supposed to cover large medical bills, and so it may have a high deductible (the out-of-pocket amount that patients spend before the insurance company begins to pay). A major medical insurance policy therefore probably won't cover deductibles and coinsurance for Medicare. If it does cover those costs, its premium, or annual purchase price, is likely to be quite high.

If consumers decide to buy supplemental or Medigap insurance, such policies should cover the gap

of "deductibles," or the out-of-pocket amount that patients spend before Medicare begins to pay;

of "coinsurance," or the balance of the bill after Medicare has paid;

between the amount that Medicare will pay for a specific treatment or health care service and the amount that the doctor, hospital, nurse, or other health care provider will charge for the same treatment or service; and

left by those items which Medicare does not cover at all.

Unfortunately, Medigap policies usually focus only on deductibles and coinsurance, although some policies address the other gaps as well. *Most Medigap policies do not cover services that Medicare doesn't cover, such as*

skilled or specialized nursing home care that is not already covered by Medicare;

intermediate or custodial nursing home care;

private-duty nursing care;

drugs not already covered for hospital or hospice patients;

care received outside the United States, except under certain specific instances in Mexico and Canada; and dental care, routine health care, eye examinations and glasses, hearing aids, and cosmetic surgery such as face-lifts.

A Word of Caution

Elderly consumers need to shop carefully for the Medigap policy that will give them the extra coverage they need; otherwise, they may waste their money. It may not always be possible to get coverage for all out-of-pocket expenses. Many consumers have purchased policies that simply duplicate one another—which doesn't help much—or that cover only one specific disease.

A special note is in order about insurance policies that cover only one illness, also known as *dread disease policies.* Consumers would have to buy many of these single-disease policies to get the same coverage they would receive by purchasing a single, more complete or comprehensive policy. Single-disease policies are usually expensive, often not very valuable to the consumer, and not really designed to fill in the gaps in the Medicare system.

Medigap insurance companies that pretend to represent the federal government or that knowingly sell insurance that duplicates Medicare coverage are breaking the law and are subject to heavy fines. They should be reported to government officials in the state insurance department (see appendix 2 for a state-by-state listing of these departments).

Consumers also should be wary of being sold "replacement" policies to take the place of the policies they already own. New policies often won't pay right away for *preexisting conditions,* illnesses consumers have at the time they buy a replacement policy. Instead, such policies require that the consumers themselves pay the bills for these preexisting conditions for a certain period of time, when the same conditions may already be covered under the first policy. Preexisting conditions might even be excluded completely from a new policy, meaning that the insurance company will never pay for them.

Because insurance agents are licensed by the state, consumers should ask for some proof of an agent's license that also shows the name of the company where the agent is employed. Payment for a policy should be by check, money order, or bank draft and made payable only to the insurance company. Consumers should never pay cash for a policy, nor should they make out a check in the agent's name.

The New Legal Requirements for Medigap Insurance Policies

Although state insurance departments must approve all policies being sold in a state to ensure compliance with specific state laws, those laws do vary from state to state and have different levels of protection for consumers. In recent years, most states have followed the standards set by the National Association of Insurance Commissioners (NAIC), which were also recommended by Congress in 1981.

At the end of 1989, however, the NAIC modified its standards to be consistent with the changes in Medicare under the repeal of the Congressional Catastrophic Care Act. The 1990 NAIC standards require the following:

- Individual and group Medicare supplemental policies are prohibited from containing benefits that duplicate those of Medicare.
- Miminum benefit standards in 1990 are to include:

  Coverage of Part A Medicare-eligible expenses for hospitalization that are not covered by Medicare from the 61st through the 90th day of hospitalization (up to $148 a day in 1990);

  Part A hospital deductible (meaning that policies must pay all of the deductible, or none at all; they cannot pay only part of it. In 1990, the deductible is $592);

  Coverage of Part A Medicare-eligible expenses incurred as daily hospital charges during the patient's use of Medicare's lifetime 60 hospital-inpatient-reserve days (up to $296 per day in 1990);

  90 percent of all Part A Medicare-eligible expenses for hospitalization, not covered by Medicare after patient uses all of the 60 Medicare lifetime-inpatient-reserve days, up to a lifetime maximum of an additional 365 days;

  Approximately $75 for the first 3 units of whole blood unless the patient has not paid the annual Medicare Part A hospital deductible ($592 in 1990);

  20 percent copayment of Part B expenses, up to a maximum out-of-pocket amount, not including outpatient prescription drugs and subject to the Medicare part B deductible ($75 in 1990);

  First three units of whole blood under Part B (for patients who did not receive blood while in the hospital), subject to the 20 percent coinsurance amount on Medicare Part B and the Medicare deductible.

- Duplication of services now covered by Medicare is prohibited. There is no maximum benefit amount, but payments are subject to a deductible ($75 in 1990).

In its new standards, NAIC also retained several earlier requirements. For example:

- Payment must be made for treatment or services received six months after a policy is issued, whether or not a claim is related to a preexisting condition (one the policyholder already had at the time he or she bought the policy).
- Buyers can cancel policies without penalty for thirty days after purchase.
- The terms of the policy must be disclosed clearly.
- Benefit payments must represent at least 60 percent of the money taken in through premiums. This percentage, called a *loss ratio,* is 60 to 65 percent for individual policies (depending on the state) and 75 percent for group policies. Under a new federal law, insurers offering Medigap policies are required to report to the state insurance commissioners information on the actual ratio of benefits provided to premiums collected.
- After January 1, 1989, companies that issue Medicare supplemental policies must submit their advertising files to the state insurance commissioner to see if their marketing practices comply with state law.

In addition, there are special provisions to protect beneficiaries who dropped their Medicare supplemental policies in 1989. Insurers must offer to reinstitute their previous coverage with no penalties, such as excluding pre-existing conditions or requiring new screenings or physicals. These reissued policies must be based on same rate in effect at the time that the policy was dropped, although the premiums may not be exactly the same.

Under the new NAIC rules, companies had to notify consumers by January 30, 1990, regarding their offer of renewed coverage. Interested individuals were to have decided on renewing their coverage by February 1, 1990. Contact the State Insurance Department (see Appendix 2) if this offer of renewed coverage was never received.

Only policies meeting these standards can be sold as Medigap or Medicare supplemental policies. However, these standards do not apply to major medical, catastrophic, dread disease, or long-term care policies.

Questions to Ask the Insurance Agent

Elderly people buying or thinking about buying a Medigap or supplemental insurance policy might want to ask insurance agents the following questions.

1. Is there a clearly worded and understandable summary or outline of the policy for the buyer to review?
2. What does the policy cover? Does it cover deductibles? coinsurance? services beyond what Medicare covers? only specific diseases? costs not covered by the amount Medicare would pay were the health provider to charge more than the amount allotted by Medicare?
3. What is the annual premium (yearly price) of the policy?
4. Does the premium increase with age? If so, how often—every year? every five years?
5. Are there exclusions or waiting periods for payments on preexisting conditions?
6. What is the policy's loss ratio, or minimum level of benefits the insurance company expects to pay out?
7. Does the policy offer riders or other optional coverage?
8. Is there a maximum amount of benefits payable under the policy? in dollars? in days covered?
9. Under what circumstances can the company refuse to renew a policy?
10. Is the policy approved by the state insurance department?
11. What is the company's rule regarding prompt delivery of the policy?
12. What is the company's rule regarding refunds?
13. Does the company allow a "free look" for thirty days or longer to review the policy?

Long-Term Care Insurance Policies

Overview

As noted in the first part of this chapter, even Medigap policies may leave large gaps in coverage for health care services. Perhaps the most significant of these gaps is payment for *long-term care*, a phrase that usually refers to a long stay in a nursing home for "intermediate" or "custodial," rather than "acute," care. One example would be patients with Alzheimer's disease who can no longer be cared for in their homes but require almost round-the-clock supervision to make sure they don't wander off or hurt themselves. Another example would be patients who have a stroke and need extensive care and rehabilitation in a nursing home for a period of time before they can return to their homes.

Medicare pays for only about 2 percent of all nursing home care and only 4 percent of home health care in the United States. Fifty percent of all nursing home care costs are paid for, out-of-pocket, by patients or their family members. Most patients who run out of money become eligible for Medicaid, which pays about 42 percent of all nursing home care costs in the United States.

To fill this gap, private insurance companies offer policies to protect consumers against the cost of long-term care. These policies are designed to pay for the care needed by people with a chronic illness or disability that lasts a long time and leaves them unable to care for themselves. Thus, while Medicare and Medigap policies focus on skilled or specialized nursing care, these long-term care policies include intermediate or custodial care and usually also offer more generous home care benefits. Some insurance companies are also beginning to cover such services as "adult day care" and "respite care," both of which offer temporary (half-day or day-long) care up to several times a week for individuals who are being cared for in their homes by family members or friends.

Policy premiums range from about $200 to $1,200 or more per year, depending on age, amount, duration of benefits, and deductible or "elimination periods," such as waiting periods for coverage of a preexisting condition.

When Might It Be Necessary to Purchase Long-Term Care Insurance?

Statistics show that most older people's greatest insurance risk is their need for long term care services not covered by Medicare. Approximately one out of every five elderly people has a chronic illness or disability, and about four out of every ten elderly people will enter a nursing home at some time in their lives. Some 20 percent of older people living in the community rely on friends, neighbors, or family members to help them with some important activity of daily living, such as eating, bathing, or buying groceries.

The cost of nursing home services for these people can be very high—as much as $20,000 to $40,000 a year. Almost two-thirds of elderly people living alone who enter nursing homes run out of money to pay for them after only thirteen weeks of care. More than a third of elderly married couples over age sixty-five will run out of money in thirteen weeks if one of them needs nursing home care.

Obviously, people need financial protection from these expenses. A national policy debate is under way over whether the federal government or private insurance companies should provide more long-term care coverage.

Just like Medigap and Medicare supplemental insurance policies, policies for long-term care should be studied carefully to make sure they meet the needs of the people buying them.

Probably the biggest factor for most people deciding whether to purchase long-term care coverage is the cost of these policies. As coverage increases, so do premium prices, and a number of good policies are likely to be too expensive for many older people living on fixed incomes. Although initially these policies may not have been well designed financially for the people who need them most, they are now improving and may be a better buy for consumers.

An important element to look for in a long-term care policy is a good inflation adjustment (an increase in the amount paid for benefits that corresponds with the country's rising costs of medical care); otherwise purchasing one may not be worthwhile. For people who have a substantial income, a long-term policy may offer good protection of both their health and their assets. People who have a modest income and modest assets, however, may not be as interested in this type of insurance, because if they suffered from a long-term illness they would quickly run out of money and would qualify for Medicaid to pay for their care.

What to Look For in Buying Long-Term Care Insurance

Insurance companies use medical and other information in deciding whether or not to issue a long-term care insurance policy. They may refuse to sell coverage, or they may charge higher premiums to high-risk individuals likely to need and use more services. Before buying a policy, consumers need to understand a number of features of long-term care insurance.

- *Index for inflation.* Most policies provide *indemnity benefits,* wherein they pay a fixed amount per day for the illnesses and disabilities they cover. By 1990, many policies began indexing for inflation, or raising the amount they agree to pay to match the rising costs of medical care. In such cases, policies may increase their payments by a certain percentage each year for a given number of years. *Consumers with policies not indexed for inflation may be paid a smaller percentage of the actual bill for services if the cost of those services has risen due to inflation. Some newer policies now pay a fixed percentage of service costs, or they index benefits for inflation.*

- *Limitations on renewability.* Usually the insurance company has the right to cancel or not renew someone's policy even if the person is paying the premiums. Premiums may have one of four types of renewability provisions:

  1. *Optionally renewable.* This means the policy is renewable only by the decision of the insurance company. This kind of policy offers the least amount of protection for the consumer.

  2. *Conditionally renewable.* Here, the insurance company can decide not to renew policies for people in certain classes of coverage, or because of where they live, or for a number of reasons other than the policyholder's increased illness.

  3. *Guaranteed renewable.* In this type of policy, the insurance company cannot cancel or refuse to renew a policy for any reason, but it can change the amounts of the premiums for similar groups or classes of coverage (for example, requiring substantial increases as groups of subscribers become older).

  4. *Noncancelable.* This means the insurance company cannot cancel (or refuse to renew) a policy or increase its premiums. This kind of policy offers the most protection for the consumer.

- *Exclusions of certain conditions.* Most policies exclude, or refuse to pay for, specific conditions or illnesses in their coverage. The most common of these excluded conditions are alcohol and drug-related diseases, treatment received outside the United States, and nervous and mental disorders that cannot be proved to result from an organic, or physical, problem. *Policy exclusions for mental and nervous disorders do not meet the insurance needs of patients with Alzheimer's disease, because there is currently no medical test that can positively diagnose Alzheimer's disease in a living person. Even policies covering mental and nervous disorders or an organic nature may be a problem because the insurance company may require diagnosis by a brain biopsy or autopsy, which can be done only after death.*

- *Exclusions of preexisting conditions. Many insurance companies have rules against paying for treatments or services related to an illness or condition consumers had before they bought their current insurance policy. This usually means that the insurance companies won't pay for claims from a preexisting condition until a certain amount of time has passed.* Insurance companies often define how long policyholders must have had an illness or condition for it to be called preexisting, and how long a policyholder must wait after buying a policy before benefits are paid on that preexisting illness or condition.

- *Prior hospitalization requirement. Many policies require individuals to stay in a hospital before benefits will be paid for their stay in a nursing home. This requirement severely limits the coverage of these policies and makes them even more restrictive than Medicare, which does not require prior hospitalization for home health benefits.* This restriction has been removed from some of the newer policies being sold.

- *Skilled nursing care.* Many policies follow Medicare's example in paying only for nursing home care and home care that are "skilled," or specialized. Such policies will pay, for example, for home health aide service only if patients need skilled nursing care or another skilled therapy (speech therapy, physical therapy, or occupational therapy). *A policy that defines and covers skilled nursing care the way Medicare does is likely to be of little use. Consumers should seek policies that cover intermediate and custodial or personal care at home or in a nursing home.*

- *Limits on duration of services.* Nearly all policies have a maximum length of time for which they will pay benefits. *True long-term care insurance policies should offer at least twelve consecutive months of benefits.*

- *Waiting periods.* Many policies will not pay benefits to patients until they have waited a specified period of time or have already paid out-of-pocket for a specified number of home care visits or days in a nursing home.

Long-term care policies are still quite new, and the insurance agents themselves may not understand the policies they are selling. Don't rely on what agents say; stick with what is clearly written in the policy summary.

Legal Requirements for Long-Term Care Insurance Policies

While the federal government sets standards for Medigap policies, it does not do so for long-term care policies. Instead, these policies must meet the requirements of state insurance departments, whose rules and regulations vary from state to state.

The National Association of Insurance Commissioners (NAIC) has drafted a model act, or set of proposed standards, that tries to encourage the sale of long-term care policies and still protect the people buying them. Under this act, insurance companies can require policyholders to stay in a hospital before they are eligible for nursing home benefits or can insist that policyholders receive skilled nursing care before they receive intermediate, custodial, or home care benefits. The act also:

- requires clear descriptions of benefits, coverage, major exclusions, restrictions, limitations, and renewal provisions;
- requires a "right to look" provision, allowing policyholders to return a policy and receive a refund within ten days after purchasing it (buyers approached by the insurance company, instead of initiating the purchase themselves, would have thirty days to return the policy for a refund);
- prohibits companies from not covering specific health conditions;
- prohibits companies from offering much greater benefits for skilled nursing care than for intermediate or custodial care;
- requires policies to be of the guaranteed renewable type, although some state insurance commissioners may allow companies to cancel their policies under special circumstances;
- *prohibits companies from not covering Alzheimer's disease, although policies are not required to specify that the disease is covered.*
- requires some inflation protection;
- prohibits requiring a skilled level of care before covering a lower level of care, or prohibits requiring that care be provided by a registered nurse; and
- protects against the cancellation of policies due to incomplete information provided on the application form—*policies must contain clear and unambiguous questions about the health of the applicant, and must also warn that incorrect answers may result in policies being cancelled unless they are guaranteed issue.*

By mid-1989, Arizona, Arkansas, California, Connecticut, Delaware, Florida, Georgia, Hawaii, Idaho, Illinois, Iowa, Indiana, Kansas, Louisiana, Maine, Massachusetts, Michigan, Minnesota, Montana, Nebraska, Nevada, New Hampshire, New Mexico, North Carolina, North Dakota, Ohio, Oklahoma, Oregon, Rhode Island, South Carolina, South Dakota, Tennessee, Vermont, Virginia, Washington, West Virginia, Wisconsin, and Wyoming had adopted either the model act, or a more stringent version of it. Alaska, New Jersey, Oregon, and Pennsylvania were considering adopting it.

Questions to Ask the Insurance Agent

Elderly people buying or thinking about buying a long-term care insurance policy might want to ask insurance agents the following questions.

1. How much does the policy cost per month? per year?
2. What does the policy cover? Does it cover skilled nursing home care? Intermediate or custodial care in a nursing home? Home health care, including skilled nursing, home health aides, personal care, and other services? Adult day care? Respite care? Other services?
3. How many days or years will the benefits last for each of the services listed above?
4. Does the policy cover nervous or mental disorders such as Alzheimer's disease?
5. Does the policy premium always stay at the same amount? If not, under what circumstances can the insurance company raise it? How often can the premium be increased?
6. Under what circumstances can the insurance company cancel or refuse to renew a policy? Does the company guarantee it will renew the policy as long as the policyholder pays the premium on time?
7. What are the elimination or deductible periods before benefits begin to be paid?
8. What is the waiting period for preexisting conditions?
9. Is a prior hospital stay required for benefits to be paid for nursing home care? If so, how many days of hospitalization are required? Is a prior hospital or nursing home stay required for benefits to be paid for home care or other noninstitutional services?
10. Are there any other limits or exclusions?
11. Will the policy premium be waived if the policyholder is residing in a hospital or nursing home?
12. Are benefits paid on an indemnity basis (a specific dollar amount per day) or as a percentage of the costs of care?

13. Are benefits indexed for inflation? If so, what index is used and how often are benefits adjusted?

14. Will the policy pay even if the policyholder is covered by Medicare or Medigap policies?

15. What is the maximum age at which a person can apply for coverage? Will the premium continue to be based on the age of the person at the time he or she first purchased the policy?

16. Is there a maximum benefit amount a person can receive in his or her lifetime? If so, how much is that maximum amount?

17. Is there a maximum time during which a policyholder can collect benefits? If so, how long is that maximum time?

What to Do if a Question or Problem Arises

The Health Insurance Association of America has a toll-free telephone number for questions about health insurance policies, including long-term care policies. The association can be reached at 1–800–828–0262.

Complaints can be filed with state insurance departments, which are usually responsible for regulating policies sold in their state (see appendix 2, for a list of addresses). These departments should also be contacted if insurance agents claim to represent the government or try to sell Medigap policies that duplicate Medicare coverage.

3

Paying for Nursing Home Care

T HIS chapter focuses on patients who will probably live out the rest of their lives in a nursing home. (For patients who need temporary care in a nursing home, see chapter 2; for people who are confused about how to make their way through the Medicare and Medicaid systems, more information can be found in chapter 10.)

Overview

Paying for nursing home care is something most people would rather not think about, much less plan for in the future. Often, it is not the cost that is so frightening as the idea of living out one's life in a nursing home. No one wants to grow old, lose independence, and have a restricted life-style. Yet, for those unfortunate enough to need a nursing home, paying for it can become a confusing and emotional experience for them and their families.

For most people, there may be only two practical options: (a) paying for nursing home services out-of-pocket, from personal savings and resources, or (b) relying on Medicaid for financial assistance. In reality, it is generally a combination of these two options that pays for most nursing home care in the United States today.

The costs of nursing home care vary significantly from state to state and also depend on the amount and type of services needed by the patient. These services define the two main categories of nursing homes:

1. *Skilled Nursing Facilities (SNF)* provide specialized medical and nursing care. SNF residents include those who are more seriously ill or disabled. These patients need frequent medical and intensive skilled nursing services but do not need to stay in a hospital to receive it.

2. *Intermediate Care Facilities (ICF)* provide patients with a limited level of medical and nursing care, as well as custodial, or general, care. ICFs might be used by those patients who need additional time to recover after leaving a hospital but who will eventually be able to return to their own homes. Patients who have broken bones or who have had surgery often fall into this group. Other ICF residents might include elderly people who can no longer care for themselves and have no family members they can live with, or those with Alzheimer's disease who need more constant supervision than can be given them at home.

Daily rates for nursing home services may range from $45 to $75 for ICF residents and may reach $100 or more for SNF residents. Such costs can easily exceed $25,000 or $30,000 a year, depending on each patient's care needs and medical services. This is a significant amount, and sadly, most of it has to be paid from the savings of elderly individuals. In 1984, more than $12.5 billion was spent out-of-pocket on nursing home care in the United States.

Many elderly people mistakenly believe that Medicare will protect them from the costs of long-term care or nursing home services. Almost 80 percent of people responding to a 1984 survey conducted by the American Association for Retired Persons (AARP) believed that Medicare would pay for their nursing home care if such care became necessary. Nothing, however, could be further from the truth. *The fact is that individual Medicare coverage for nursing home care is highly restricted by bureaucratic regulations, and, by all accounts, Medicare payment for these services is severely limited for qualifying beneficiaries.* Overall, Medicare pays for less than 2 percent of all nursing home costs and, more important, was never intended to pay for general nursing home care at all.

Currently, about 50 percent of all nursing home costs are financed by people's personal resources or savings. Less than 30 percent of nursing home residents, however, are able to pay the full cost of such services solely out-of-pocket. Those who can pay generally cannot afford to do so for more than a year or two. A recent Harvard Medical School study of people age seventy-five or older who live alone concluded that almost half of them would have "spent down," or exhausted their savings, after only thirteen weeks in a nursing home. Only 25 percent of the people studied would not have been impoverished by the end of the first year of living in a nursing home.

Public assistance under Medicaid is available to pay for nursing home care, but this assistance is available only after an individual's personal savings and resources have been spent down to poverty levels. Approximately 70 percent of all nursing home residents depend on Medicaid to help pay for their care.

Private long-term care insurance, while increasing in popularity, still pays only for less than 2 percent of nursing home costs at this time (see chapter 2). Veterans' care and various other public assistance programs pay for the remaining 4 percent of nursing home costs.

Unless someone is independently wealthy, even those who may have planned ahead for their retirement and general health care needs are likely to find the cost of long-term nursing home care to be more than they can afford. In many cases, elderly individuals may face impoverishment or the depletion of most of their available financial resources when having to pay for long-term care needs.

Medicare as a Resource

Medicare, a national health insurance program funded by the federal government, is available to most individuals age sixty-five or older. Although it pays for medical care for the elderly, Medicare is primarily intended to cover hospital care and doctor's services.

Medicare is actually two insurance programs in one: Hospital Insurance (HI) is provided under Part A of Medicare, and Supplemental Medical Insurance (SMI) is provided under Part B. The HI program pays for inpatient and outpatient hospital services, home health care services, and to a limited extent SNF services. The SMI program requires Medicare beneficiaries to pay a monthly premium. (For more information, see chapter 10.)

Medicare's skilled nursing benefit currently pays for a maximum of 100 days of skilled care in a Medicare-certified nursing home but also requires that patients be hospitalized for at least three days beforehand in order to qualify for the benefit. Improved Medicare benefits that were passed under the Catastrophic Coverage Act of 1988 were later repealed by Congress as of January 1, 1990. This repeal reduced Medicare's skilled nursing benefit back to its original level of coverage, passed in 1965.

To qualify for Medicare SNF coverage, patients must require around-the-clock skilled nursing or have the potential to recover sufficiently to be able to return to the community as a result of receiving this specialized care. It is rare for patients to receive the full 100 days of SNF coverage benefits, as the requirements for skilled nursing and rehabilitation are strictly enforced. In fact, should one ever qualify for Medicare's SNF benefit, the covered length of stay in a nursing home would probably be less than thirty days.

If and when patients qualify for skilled nursing care, Medicare requires that they pay a *coinsurance* amount—or portion of the fee out of their own pocket—from the twenty-first to the hundredth day of their stay in the SNF. As of January 1, 1990, Medicare patients were required to pay a coinsurance amount of $74.00 a day from the twenty-first to the hundredth day of a covered stay in an SNF. Depending on how the billing arrangements are set up, Medicare payments can be made directly to the doctor, the hospital, or the patient.

Medicare utilization figures show just how restricted the skilled nursing benefit actually is: in 1984, Medicare paid benefits on behalf of more than 18.7 million individuals for doctors' services, 6.2 million individuals for hospitalization, and less than 300,000 individuals for SNF services they received. To make matters worse, Medicare does not pay for ICF or other nursing home services that are considered primarily custodial (general) in nature.

Limited Part B benefits under Medicare's SMI program pay for such services as doctors' visits, medical supplies, and certain durable medical equipment (like wheelchairs) and prosthetic devices (like artificial limbs) for nursing home residents. Payment under Part B is made either (a) directly to doctors or medical suppliers by assignment or (b) as a direct reimbursement to Medicare beneficiaries after they submit itemized bills for services. *If doctors or suppliers are paid by Medicare under the assignment approach, patients cannot be billed for any amount greater than what Medicare has agreed to pay.*

Local Social Security offices can answer questions about Medicare benefit eligibility (to find local offices, look in the "Government" section of the phone directory). Interviews can be arranged with the local representative for guidance and information on Medicare benefits. In addition, nursing homes should have admissions or social services directors who can assist those nursing home applicants and their families who request information on Medicare eligibility and coverage.

If patients or their families have questions about individual Medicare coverage denials and nursing home claims payments, they should contact the office of the Medicare intermediary handling the claim (that information can be found on the Medicare claim form). They may also wish to contact the health care facility or group that provided the service in the first place. In addition, individuals can contact their local Social Security office for assistance and advice on how to proceed. Other options for "fighting back" include legal services programs for the elderly, funded by the Older Americans Act; legal services programs for the poor, funded by the Legal Services Corporation Act; lawyers willing to work for reduced fees; and some legal clinics or programs associated with law schools. (Also see chapter 10.)

To find appropriate, low-cost legal aid, contact the State Unit on Aging (see appendix 20, for a state-by-state list) and talk with the legal services developer. Also, almost all states have an Information and Referral (I&R) hot line for older people or the general public in need of services, and this resource can provide the same information; local senior citizens' centers should be able to furnish the I&R hot line number.

Medicaid as a Resource

Medicaid is the chief public assistance program that pays for nursing home care. It is a state-administered program, funded by both federal and state government. Medicaid essentially offers financial assistance to certain low-income individuals who cannot pay for their medical care. Most (two out of every three) nursing home residents are dependent on Medicaid to help pay for their care.

Individuals living in long-term care facilities that are not licensed as nursing homes, such as board and care homes and domiciliary care facilities, are not eligible to receive assistance under the Medicaid program. These facilities are not licensed to provide nursing care and instead provide only custodial or domiciliary care services. Personal and residential care facilities may offer limited nursing services, although such services are usually provided and paid for under a separate arrangement between the resident and the facility.

Medicaid programs are administered by each state's government. Each one has its own eligibility and coverage rules, which vary a great deal from state to state. The result is fifty-one different Medicaid programs (all states plus the District of Columbia), all with different standards and a different scope and depth of coverage benefits. People eligible for Medicaid assistance to help pay for nursing home care in one state may not be eligible for such assistance in another state. The same is true of other specific coverage benefits.

Qualifying for medical assistance payments to help pay for nursing home services under Medicaid is a bit more complicated than doing so under Medicare. Medicaid must judge first that individuals applying for assistance actually need nursing home services and second that they are unable to pay for those services themselves. Generally speaking, people who are eligible to recieve Medicaid include

individuals receiving Aid to Families with Dependent children (AFDC);

individuals under the age of twenty-one who receive general relief payments;

individuals age sixty-five or older whose income and financial resources are below the established minimum state resource levels (state Medicaid offices, listed in appendix 34, or nursing home administrators will have this information);

blind adults or children whose income and financial resources are below the established minimum state resource levels; and

residents of nursing homes whose income does not meet the cost of care.

People qualify for Medicaid if they are "categorically needy," or, in many states, "medically needy." Medicaid staff have specific criteria to help them judge who qualifies as categorically needy. These criteria—based on income and financial resource levels—are generally linked to financial limitations for AFDC recipients, federal supplemental security resources, or federal Supplemental Security Income (SSI).

The criteria for being medically needy are based on an individual state's requirements for programs serving the medically needy. Not all states have programs for the medically needy, because such programs are not required by the federal government (again, local Medicaid offices or nursing home administrators can assist individuals interested in this information). Medically needy individuals are people who meet the definition of categorically needy in a somewhat different way—they may have a higher income but also large out-of-pocket medical expenses, such as payments for nursing home care.

This process of contrasting individual income against personal medical expenses to qualify for Medicaid eligibility is called *spend down.* It is through this spend-down process that most middle-income individuals are able to become eligible for Medicaid assistance in paying for nursing home care.

Each state has its own maximum amount of *allowable resources,* that is, the amount of money the state allows individuals to keep. This amount is not large in any state, usually a few thousand dollars. Each state allows individuals a limited amount of personal "protected" income for personal use, such as buying a newspaper or getting a manicure or permanent wave. Although the amount varies by state, it is usually in the range of $25 to $30 per month.

The financial resource and income standards that determine whether people are eligible for Medicaid are quite strict. Medicaid was really intended to serve only those very poor who could not afford basic medical care. While the program has been expanded to help the elderly pay for nursing home care, its requirements often force middle-income individuals to become impoverished in order to qualify for its benefits. To make matters worse, all joint assets and income from married couples are considered in the eligibility determination if a couple was living together at the time one of them was admitted into a nursing home. This stipulation can have frightening results, in that a spouse who is not ill can also become impoverished and will have to survive on very little money or apply for public assistance as well. *However, a change in legislation in 1988, introduced by Congresspersons Mikulski, Mitchell, and Kennedy, provides limited financial protection for elderly couples. It permits the healthy spouse, who is still living in the community, to keep a "resource allowance" and restricts Medicaid from including this amount in its determinations. This allowance ranges between a minimum of $12,000 and a maximum of $60,000.* All these rules and regulations make it especially important for the elderly to plan ahead, well in advance, with professional legal and financial advisers who can help ward off the financial impact of a serious and long-term illness.

To qualify for Medicaid, individuals should first contact the appropriate local Medicaid office—usually located in the county welfare department, health department, or social services department—and request an appointment to process a Medicaid eligibility application. This application can usually be made by a competent (mentally healthy) family member or by a legal guardian, if applicants have one. While each state has a specific Medicaid agency that determines program requirements and policy guidelines, the application process is generally handled at the local level. The telephone number and address for such offices can usually be found in the telephone book under "Government Offices—County." A county Medicaid claims representative can discuss the application process and provide additional information about local Medicaid requirements. Application forms range in length from just a few pages to many pages, requiring detailed information about financial assets, as well as income and expense statements. Generally, the type of information requested in the application includes:

- proof of income and earnings, including alimony, estate or trust income, annuities, dividends, interest income, capital gains, and retirement or government pensions;
- information on checking accounts, savings accounts, stocks, bonds, individual retirement accounts (including Keogh and 401-K plans), pension funds, trust funds, and other financial assets;

- information on real property, including personal residences and any recent real property transfers;
- information about life insurance policies, including the face value of the insurance policies and their cash surrender values;
- information on burial plots and burial trusts;
- a Social Security card;
- a Medicare card and information about any other health or disability insurance;
- a birth certificate; and
- a driver's license or other proof of identification.

Individuals thinking about admitting a relative into a nursing home should request a copy of the state's application form well in advance of the proposed admission date. Doing so will allow for a review of the type of detailed information required to process a Medicaid application. Gathering all the information in time for the appointment with the local Medicaid office will help hasten the application process.

Most Medicaid application forms will also inquire about or request information on any recent transfers of financial assets and gifts made by the applicant during the previous two to three years. Such transfers or gifts might still be counted as assets for the applicant and could also postpone the person's eligibility for Medicaid. In some cases, states can refuse to grant Medicaid assistance to people who have transferred or given away their assets two to three years prior to applying for Medicaid. States can also refuse to grant Medicaid assistance to people who have sold their assets at less than fair market value, if the real value of those assets would have made the individual ineligible for Medicaid. People facing these issues should talk with a lawyer or financial adviser who is familiar with Medicaid eligibility requirements before they submit their Medicaid applications. When individuals have substantial assets, any property transfers or gifts made as part of their estate and financial planning should be done well in advance of entering a nursing home.

Everyone who applies for Medicaid deserves a polite and complete explanation of his or her eligibility status. Those who do not receive explanations or who disagree with determinations should ask to speak with the claim representative's supervisor. If an issue cannot be resolved, applicants are entitled to a departmental appeal or hearing on the matter (see chapter 10).

People applying for Medicaid either for themselves or for a relative do not have to muddle through this process alone (again, see chapter 10). Most nursing home admissions or social services directors are both qualified and willing to assist family members in the process of applying for Medicaid eligibility. Frequently, nursing home staff have working relationships with Medicaid claim representatives and can be of great help in this process. *It would also be wise to seek the advice of a lawyer if it appears that an appeal will be necessary.*

What Medicaid actually pays to a nursing home will depend on the facility's Medicaid reimbursement rate and on the eligible individual's income. The eligible individual's income, minus a small amount for personal needs (usually $25 to $30), is paid to the facility; the rest is paid by Medicaid. For example, assume that Mrs. X, an eighty-year-old nursing home resident, has a monthly income of $800 from Social Security and a private insurance annuity. Also assume, in this case, that Medicaid's reimbursement rate for the nursing home is $45 a day and that the state Medicaid allowance for personal needs is $25 a month. The nursing home charges $1,395 each month for caring for Mrs. X ($45 per day for a thirty-one-day month). Mrs. X will pay $775 from her personal income each month ($800 minus $25 for personal needs) and Medicaid will pay the rest—$620 per month—for a total of $1,395.

Nursing homes would prefer to admit only *private-pay patients* (those who have the financial resources to pay for their own care) rather than Medicaid-eligible individuals, because in most states Medicaid nursing home payment rates are significantly below the rates charged to private-pay patients. In several states, Medicaid payment rates are simply not high enough for the nursing home to provide quality services. Most nursing homes use the extra money paid by private-pay patients to offset low Medicaid payment rates. While this practice might seem unfair to the private-pay patients, a negative effect on nursing home quality and care standards could result if the two rates were kept at the same level. At least two states—Minnesota and Connecticut—do restrict private-pay charges to the same amount as Medicaid rates.

While some nursing homes require that financially responsible individuals other than patients sign the admission contracts, such contracts are illegal in some states and generally are not legally enforceable. It is also illegal for a nursing home to request private funds from Medicaid patients or their relatives as a condition of admission and/or of keeping patients. Facilities that attempt any of these actions can be criminally prosecuted under federal law. Those who suspect a facility of engaging in any of these practices should contact their local Medicaid office to complain, or call the office of the Inspector General at the U.S. Department of Health and Human Services. A toll-free number (1-800-368-5779) is available for this purpose.

Veterans' Benefits and Other Resources

Veterans' benefits are available to all eligible veterans, with priority given to veterans with disabilities resulting from their military service. Veterans who require nursing home care may be entitled to receive such care through Veterans Administration (VA) nursing facilities or in private nursing homes. In addition, disabled veterans who are capable of caring for themselves but require minimal medical support in a therapeutic living environment may qualify for domiciliary care.

The VA provides a significant amount of long-term care services, even though those services are limited to veterans. Some 115 nursing homes owned and operated by the VA serve more than 20,000 patients nationwide. The VA also contracts and pays for nursing home and long-term care services in more than 3,000 private community nursing homes throughout the country. In 1985, the VA paid for more than 38,000 veterans to receive care in private nursing homes.

Veterans, their families, or legal representatives can contact the local VA office to discuss eligibility for VA nursing home assistance. Telephone numbers for the local VA office can be found in the "Government" section of the telephone book.

Other ways to finance nursing home care include private long-term care insurance and "Medigap" insurance policies. These options are discussed in chapter 2.

The Importance of Planning Ahead

Overall, America's elderly are fairly well insured against the costs of health care except when it comes to paying for nursing home and other long-term care services. The greatest amount of money spent by the elderly for medical services goes to nursing home care.

Unless people plan ahead, paying for nursing home care can be an upsetting and confusing experience. Hopefully, this problem will never occur, but the older people are, the more likely they are to need long-term care services. By the time individuals become seriously ill, it is probably too late to begin effective financial planning to meet the costs associated with nursing home and long-term care needs. Without insurance, payment for nursing home care is likely to come from either out-of-pocket funds or Medicaid. Serious illness and the cost of nursing home care are as much financial issues as medical ones. Planning to meet the costs of a long-term illness should become an estate- or financial-planning requirement for everyone, not just the elderly.

4

Is a Living Will a
Good Idea for You?

Overview

Planning ahead has a simple purpose: it allows individuals to say in advance what they want done regarding their medical treatment and/or estate before they become ill and unable to make those decisions themselves. Without that forethought—that planning ahead—those and many other decisions will be made by other people, people who may not know what the individuals would have wanted (or might disagree with it if they did know). The previous chapters have focused on ways to plan ahead for estate or financial decisions—by writing a will, creating a trust or joint account, purchasing the right kind of health insurance, and considering ways to pay for nursing home care. This chapter, on living wills, examines one way to plan ahead for health care.

Before looking at ways to plan ahead, it is important to understand that "advance directives," like living wills and powers of attorney (the latter are covered in the next chapter), are not new legal rights. The courts have long recognized the rights of individuals to direct their own medical care. *What these advance directives do is extend people's opportunity to direct such care to a time when they may be too ill to make and understand decisions.*

As noted in the Introduction, there are many reasons for planning ahead. Perhaps the two most important ones that individuals have are to

make sure their wishes are followed; and

relieve family members and health care professionals of the burden of having to make those difficult decisions for them.

Thinking about illness and death and trying to understand and plan for all the different treatment options can be difficult and confusing, but only the individuals themselves fully know what they want and don't want in the way of medical care. And although such planning might mean making some hard decisions, many people feel that having their wishes followed at a time when they're unable to express themselves makes it all worthwhile. *A living will is a document that gives people the ability to record those treatment decisions so that no one will ever have to guess what they'd want when they are no longer able to speak for themselves.* Unlike a regular will that directs where people's property should go after their death, a living will states what medical care people want while they are still alive but unable to speak for themselves.

What Can Be Put in a Living Will?

Definitional problems can arise over a living will. A particular medical treatment may not be clearly defined as *extraordinary care* (which can be refused) but instead might be seen as *supportive care* (which might not be refused). Or the patient's doctor might see as supportive treatment that the patient's family finds extraordinary.

Some examples of what individuals may wish to include in their living wills are

refusal or acceptance of a respirator or mechanical ventilator;

refusal or acceptance of artificial feeding and hydration tubes, depending on state law (this issue is more fully described later in this chapter);

antibiotic therapy, chemotherapy, or radiotherapy; and

invasive surgery.

Does a Living Will Constitute Suicide?

Most state laws that permit the use of living wills also specify that the refusal of life-prolonging treatment does not, for insurance or other purposes, constitute suicide.

People's personal and religious views on suicide may be another matter, but the law does not view as suicide a death that is the result of instructions in a living will. People who have questions about the religious nature of using a living will should consult with a knowledgeable representative of their religious order.

How and When Does a Living Will Work?

Most often, a living will is effective only in case of a terminal illness. It states that if death is near, the patient does not want to prolong the process of dying but does want the care necessary to maintain comfort and dignity until the fatal illness takes it natural course. At the same time, a living will does not *have* to be used to refuse treatment; it can also request medical care or list treatments that the person does want.

The Problem of Defining *Terminally Ill*

Directions contained in a living will do not usually take effect until two doctors have stated, in writing, that the patient is terminally ill (in a few states, only one such opinion is necessary). However, because there is no clear definition of when a patient is "terminally ill," getting that diagnosis is not without problems. *Some doctors believe the label* terminally ill *applies to patients expected to live six months; others feel that patients with only a month or a week left to live are terminally ill; and still others believe that patients are terminally ill* only *when they will die in a few days, no matter what treatment is given.* To put it another way, some doctors may diagnose a patient as terminally ill when certain diseases are first discovered, while others may use the same label only after the disease has spread or a relapse occurs after treatment.

How doctors define terminal illness *is important. Anyone using a living will should interview his or her doctors in advance and find out their definitions of terminal illness and their views on refusing life-supporting treatment.* Once a patient-doctor relationship has formed and a patient's illness has already progressed to a serious stage, it may be too late for the patient (or his or her family members) to comfortably consider switching to another doctor with more compatible views on such matters.

Remember, if a doctor believes that a patient is terminally ill only when death is imminent or around the corner, then directions contained in the patient's living will might not take effect until the last few days or weeks of life. Patients who are victims of serious accidents or strokes and are in an irreversible coma called a *persistent vegetative state* typically are not considered terminally ill even if they would not wish to be kept alive were recovery impossible. Family members of a patient in an irreversible coma should know that his or her living will might be accepted anyway; moreover, there are other options available to get life-prolonging treatment halted (see chapters 12 and 14).

Another drawback is that in some states patients can execute and sign a living will only after being diagnosed as terminally ill. For patients in these states who are too ill, too confused by heavy sedatives or painkillers, or too senile by the time they are diagnosed as terminally ill, a living will would not be an option. They would be unable to make the decisions necessary to a living will at the time they most need one.

When terminally ill patients are able to execute a living will, some states permit them to talk about what they want and don't want in the presence of witnesses who then sign a written version.

Writing a Valid Living Will

Different states have different laws surrounding living wills, and so what is legal in one state might not be legal in another. This situation poses several problems. *If individuals execute living wills that are valid for the state in which they live, those same documents may not be valid if those individuals become ill and hospitalized in another state.*

Most states provide a form to make it easier to write a living will, but will accept variations if individual state requirements are met. A sample form for a living will is provided in appendix 3. In addition, organizations like the Society for the Right to Die in New York City, can provide current forms that take state variations into account. (The Society for the Right to Die, 250 West Fifty-seventh Street, New York, N.Y., 10107, [212] 246-6973, will mail the appropriate form on request.)

All states require that living wills be signed in the presence of two adult witnesses. While the rules vary from state to state, most states restrict certain persons from acting as legal witnesses—for example, relatives and potential heirs of the person executing the living wills, anyone paying for that person's health care, and anyone responsible for taking care of him or her. Changing laws make it impossible to print a checklist of state variations. Contact the Society for the Right to Die, at the above address, for current information on state laws.

Some states require that one witness be the nursing home ombudsman, or patient advocate, when a nursing home resident signs a living will. Others require that living wills be notarized. Still others require that they be filed with a government office, or reviewed and reaffirmed after a certain number of years. The rules and regulations do not stop there: many states limit when a living will can be used, often barring its use by pregnant women, and others prohibit individuals from refusing food and fluids as a part of their living will (again, contact the

Society for the Right to Die, at the address on page 46, for information on individual state laws. Also see appendix 4 and the section entitled ''The Issue of Artificial Feeding and Hydration'' in this chapter).

Living wills written without a lawyer's assistance cost nothing at all. If a lawyer helps to prepare and draw up the document, the cost will usually depend on the lawyer's hourly fees. Although drawing up a living will should not take an excessive amount of time, interested individuals should ask their lawyer in advance how many hours the task is likely to take and how much experience the lawyer has in writing living wills. *A lawyer who is experienced in writing living wills will almost certainly be able to give far better advice, and will probably have more knowledge of state laws surrounding living wills.*

How to Make a Living Will Work

Most state laws require that individuals (or their families) notify their doctors that they have a living will. The doctors are then required to attach a copy of the living will to the appropriate medical records. Ideally, living wills are drawn up by patients before, or soon after, they become ill, thereby allowing sufficient time for discussion and an exchange of opinions before the document goes into effect. Yet even under the best of circumstances, there is no guarantee that everything will proceed smoothly once patients are too ill to speak for themselves.

At the time living wills go into effect, patients might not be under the care of their regular doctors. Patients who are hospitalized in another state, or undergo emergency surgery are likely to experience this problem. Patients and families alike must be alert to this situation and ensure that any new doctors are aware of the existence and contents of their living wills.

Extra copies of living wills should also be kept in a safe place to ensure that if the original is lost, the directions contained in it will still be available to the doctor. However, a safe deposit box is not a good place for a living will as access to the box may not be possible when its owner is hospitalized.

How to Change or Revoke a Living Will

Individuals can change the directions in their living will anytime they want to, as long as they comply with their state's laws about witness requirements. To change directions, they either need to revoke, or cancel, any previously written living wills and then write up new ones; or add a codicil, or additional directions to their existing living will. In either case, individuals must have them witnessed, and file them according to the laws of their state.

A living will can be canceled simply by someone's stating that it is no longer valid; however, to be on the safe side, doctors or nursing administrators in possession of a patient's living will should be told that it has been revoked. The same is true for living wills registered in government offices in compliance with some states' laws. *It is against the law for anyone to produce a fake living will, to lie about a living will's having been revoked when it is still valid, or to hide the fact that an existing living will has been revoked by the patient.*

The Limits of Living Wills

Most states have enacted natural-death legislation that recognizes living wills as legal documents representing a patient's choices. *Even states without such laws, however, do not necessarily ignore the presence of living wills or other advance directives.* Courts in some of these latter states, such as New York and New Jersey, have recognized living wills as evidence of a patient's wishes and have agreed that such instructions may be followed by a doctor. Moreover, all states permit durable powers-of-attorney agreements that can be used for health care purposes and that allow for the same kind of advance planning as living wills do (see chapter 5 for more information). In any event, it is likely that if the question was brought before them, courts in all states would accept a living will as clear and convincing evidence of a patient's wishes.

Generally, a doctor or health care provider may accept a living will as evidence of a patient's wishes, and may follow the directions contained in it, unless the patient's family members disagree over whether or not to refuse a particular treatment. When family members do disagree, the patient has far less chance of having his or her wishes obeyed, at least without a court hearing on the matter.

If the patient is terminally ill, if the treatment is considered extraordinary, and if the living will clearly refuses such treatment, the doctor must either comply with the living will or transfer the patient to a doctor who will comply with it. If the treatment is considered ordinary, the doctor has the right to provide it. If the living will is unclear regarding a particular treatment, different people may interpret it differently. In such instances, a hospital or nursing home ethics committee might review the case, or it might go to court so that a judge could decide whether or not a patient should receive a particular treatment.

The biggest barrier to having one's written wishes followed is the doctor's fear of being sued by a family member or some other individual for failing to provide proper care. These fears are very strong, even if they are mistaken.

Sadly, it took only one case—later dismissed by the court—to raise these unrealistic fears. In 1983, two California doctors were charged for removing, with the family's consent, life-support equipment from a terminally ill, comatose patient. One court convicted them, but the doctors appealed and the higher court ruled that the doctors, with the family's consent, had the right to withdraw life-sustaining treatment even if the patient did not have a living will. *Doctors do have the right to discontinue treatment that will not improve the patient's chances for recovery, and no doctor has ever been punished for withholding or withdrawing treatment based on a patient's written, signed directive or on the agreement of next of kin.*

Those facing a situation in which a doctor does not want to follow a terminally ill patient's written wishes or the wishes of the patient's family should keep the following in mind:

- *Doctors who use treatments that prolong life against the patient's or family's wishes can be sued for wrongful treatment and for battery.*
- *Natural-death laws specifically protect health care providers from civil and criminal liability if they withhold or withdraw life-prolonging treatment in accordance with a living will.*
- *In most states, a doctor who doesn't want to conform to a patient's advance directive must try to transfer that patient to another professional who is willing to do so. Failure to conform or to transfer the patient can result in charges of unprofessional conduct or in a misdemeanor.*
- *Patients and their families always have the right to choose a different doctor or transfer to a different hospital or nursing home.*

How Federal Health Care Facilities View Living Wills

Changes in legislation may affect how Federal health care facilities view living wills, and individuals should check the practices of particular facilities when entering them. Health care facilities operated by the air force, the navy, the Indian Health Service, and Hansen's Disease Center all recognize living wills as legal documents. These facilities will follow the wishes set forth in living wills as long as those wishes comply with the laws of the state in which the facility is located.

Although the army does not have a policy about living wills, patients who can still speak for themselves always have the right to decide what medical treatment they do or don't want. And while facilities operated by the Veterans Administration don't recognize living wills as legal documents, they will add them to patients' medical records and consider them when deciding what to do.

Further, the Clinical Center at the National Institutes of Health will accept living wills prepared in any state as long as the patient is an adult and the document was witnessed and signed by two other adults; the center does not require that a living will be notarized.

The Issue of Artificial Feeding and Hydration

The issues surrounding the artificial feeding and hydration of patients (the giving of food and water to them) are highly complex and pose special legal, ethical, emotional, and definitional problems for patients with living wills. The question that has raised these problems is, simply, Can artificial nourishment and hydration be withdrawn from a terminally ill or comatose patient?

The reason such food and water are termed *artificial* is that the patients receiving them are unable to eat or drink for themselves. Instead, nasogastric feeding tubes, which enter the stomach through the patient's nose, or gastrostomy tubes, which are inserted directly into the stomach, or intravenous solutions, which are dripped into a patient's veins, are used.

Many courts have said that these artificial means of providing food and water are no different from other types of artificial life-support devices, such as the mechanical ventilator or respirator that permits a patient to breathe with the assistance of a machine. Therefore, if a terminally ill patient has specifically requested that food and water be withdrawn, it may be possible to do so.

Yet this is by no means an easy task. Many states do not allow individuals to request in their living wills that food and water be removed (see appendix 4). Also, many doctors and nurses are upset by the request and have occasionally refused to honor it. Such cases, where removal of feeding and hydration is permitted by the state, may end up in court.

The removal of food and water is no trivial matter. Many comatose patients who will never recover can be kept alive for years, even decades, through artificial feeding and hydration. There is no evidence that these patients suffer either hunger or thirst, yet their families can easily use up all their savings paying for this treatment, even if the patient would not have wanted it. If individuals want to refuse artificial feeding and hydration in their living wills, it is probably wise to seek a lawyer's advice on state laws and on how to write their living will to reflect this desire (for more information on this topic, see chapter 14).

5

Powers of Attorney and
Other Ways to Plan Ahead

Overview

As discussed in the preceding chapter, a living will is one way to plan ahead for decisions about medical care. But there are other ways to plan ahead for financial, personal, and medical decisions. This chapter considers several ways that allow people to appoint specific individuals—spouses, adult children, relatives, trusted friends—to make decisions for them.

There may be many reasons why older individuals might want to give up their rights to make certain decisions and let others make decisions for them now or at some time in the future. These *surrogate decision-makers,* as they are called, can be identified in advance by elderly people or, in cases where those people are already too ill to do so, by a court (see chapter 12). In this chapter, only those surrogate decision-makers who are appointed by people capable of making their own decisions are discussed.

Who decides whether individuals are competent, or capable of making decisions? This evaluation is often made informally by the family, friends, colleagues, doctors, or lawyers of elderly people (for more information, see chapter 11). Some state laws may require the evaluation to be made by two doctors. It is also a judgment that can be made formally by a court, when there is disagreement about an individual's ability to make rational decisions and appreciate their consequences. A court is *petitioned,* or asked by those concerned with the situation, to decide whether or not an elderly person is competent or incompetent—that is, able or unable to make rational decisions. (Courts may also be asked by concerned individuals to review the authority of family members making decisions for an incompetent person; see chapter 14).

All the laws applying to adult protective services, such as those provided by the county or state departments of aging or social services, require that services be accepted voluntarily if elderly people are competent to make such a decision. Accepting these decision-making services can thus be simply a matter of an elderly person agreeing to receive the services being offered.

Whether or not adult protective services are needed or are being used, older persons may want to give up some or all of their decision-making responsibilities on a temporary or permanent, immediate or future, basis. This action is called a *transfer of decision-making powers.*

Appointing a Guardian to Make Decisions

One way to transfer decision-making powers in advance is for elderly people in declining health to ask the court to appoint particular guardians. Guardians can also be appointed by a court to take on the decision-making powers of already incompetent individuals. (This topic is important and is the subject of chapter 12.)

Using a Power of a Attorney to Transfer Decision-Making Responsibilities

Perhaps the most common way to transfer power or appoint others to make decisions is through a written document called a *power of attorney. Briefly, power-of-attorney documents require two people, a* principal *who wants to appoint someone and an* agent *who is being appointed.* Agents are usually close friends or relatives, lawyers, business associates, or financial advisers who are authorized to sign documents or conduct business for principals. *Principals can decide exactly how much or how little authority to give agents and can end, or revoke, these agreements at any time. These agreements must be canceled in writing. If they are canceled, principals should notify all businesses with which their agents deal on their behalf, even though the businesses have a duty to continually verify the agents' authority, such notification is still a good idea.* (Appendix 6 contains a sample state power-of-attorney form, and appendix 7 a general power-of-attorney form.)

While these agreements can be written by principals and agreed to by agents, it is usually wise to have lawyers draw them up. Doing so can avoid many unforeseen or unintended problems that might arise. Lawyers usually charge by the hour to do such work; however, legal clinics for the elderly often offer these services at a lower cost. These agreements are legal everywhere in the United States.

A power of attorney can be *executed*, or written up, and used only during the period of time that principals are competent. *If at any time a principal becomes incompetent to make decisions, the power-of-attorney agreement is automatically ended. Thus, this agreement is really designed for the convenience of elderly people who could make decisions but for some reason do not want to do so.* If others suspect that a principal is not competent to decide that he or she wants a power of attorney, they can challenge such agreements in court. If the court agrees that the principal was imcompetent when the power of attorney was written or that the principal is no longer competent, the court will revoke the agreement.

Because a power of attorney is useless as soon as the principal dies or becomes incompetent, it also poses another problem: *at the time principals most need agents to make decisions, it is no longer legal for the agents to do so.*

Durable Powers of Attorney

To address the problem outlined above, a different kind of legal tool is available: a *durable power of attorney.* Like the regular power of attorney, this agreement involves principals and agents, and once again the principals can decide how much or how little power they want their agents to have. Principals can also decide to appoint several agents, who must act either unanimously (or by majority vote) or individually but only on specific tasks. *The basic difference between a regular power of attorney and a durable power of attorney is that the durable one doesn't stop being legal when principals become incompetent.* Durable powers of attorney are available in every state in the country and the District of Columbia.

As with the regular power of attorney, agents are usually spouses, adult children, siblings, close friends, or advisers—people who principals believe understand and will act on what they would want. Because these documents may be used for health care decisions, it is not a good idea for principals to appoint as agents their doctors, nurses, home health aides, or other primary paid health care workers. Doing so could cause problems, as it might be considered a conflict of interest.

There are two types of durable power-of-attorney agreements. *First, a* springing durable power of attorney *means that agents are not allowed to make decisions until principals are incompetent to make them on their own.* The advantage of this type of document is that it can be executed by competent principals who still want to make their own decisions but are looking ahead and planning for the time when they might become incompetent. (Appendix 9 contains a sample springing durable power-of-attorney form.) *Second, an* immediate durable power of attorney *means that agents may start making decisions as soon as the document is written up, and continue to do so after principals become incompetent.* The advantage of this type of document is that principals can transfer decision-making powers to an agent while they are still competent and do not have to worry about what will happen if they later become incompetent.

Durable powers of attorney can save a lot of lawyers' fees and court costs that might have to be paid if an elderly person becomes incompetent before appointing agents and the court has to do it for the person. (For more information on situations in which a court might need to appoint a surrogate decision-maker, see chapter 14.) *These agreements do not require that the agent be legally supervised, licensed, or bonded, but different states have different witness, agent, and notarization requirements that must be satisfied before the durable power-of-attorney document is considered legal.* Because this is a fast-changing area of the law, it is difficult to compile a complete chart of state requirements for durable power-of-attorney documents. A partial list is included in appendix 5 to illustrate what kinds of rules a state may impose; however, *all interested individuals should consult with a knowledgeable lawyer to find out the laws of their state, or ask the Society for the Right to Die, 250 West 57th Street, New York, NY 10107, for forms valid in thier state.*

If people other than the principals or agents are concerned about these agreements or the decisions being made, they can ask a court to review the matter. *A durable power of attorney can be ended or revoked, usually in writing, at any time before the principal becomes incompetent.* Again, to be on the safe side, a principal who cancels such an agreement should notify all businesses with which the agent is doing business on his or her behalf. And again, although these agreements can be written up without a lawyer, it is probably wise to use one; lawyers can structure these agreements to avoid unintended and unanticipated problems.

Lawyers usually charge an hourly fee for these services, but interested individuals should also contact legal clinics that specialize in working for the elderly, as such clinics might do the same thing for a lower cost. To find low-cost legal aid, contact the legal services developer of the State Unit on Aging (see appendix 20 for addresses), who should be able to make some recommendations. Also, almost every state has an Information and Referral (I&R) service for older people or for the general public in need of services. Local senior citizens' centers should be able to provide the area I&R telephone number.

In the past, regular and durable power-of-attorney agreements were normally used by principals who wanted agents to take care of their financial estate and assets. There does not seem to be any legal reason, however, why the durable power of attorney could not also be used by agents to make decisions about the medical care of principals. Indeed, *a few state laws specifically allow durable power-of-attorney agreements to be used for medical care decisions.*

Durable Power-of-Attorney Agreements for Health Care

A few states have special provisions for documents called *durable power of attorney for health care. In actuality, though, the regular durable power-of-attorney documents accomplish the same purpose in almost all cases.* The more specific documents are designed to let principals appoint agents to make health care decisions for them. One advantage such documents might have is to calm the collective worries of doctors, lawyers, hospital administrators, and family members making decisions— especially life-and-death decisions—for incompetent patients.

The durable power of attorney for health care allows principals to state, in detail, what kinds of medical care or life-sustaining treatments are acceptable to them. This kind of advance planning can save a great deal of grief and uncertainty on the part of agents.

Like the regular durable power of attorney, these documents can be executed by filling out a standard form and following the laws of one's state. It is probably a good idea for principals to discuss the form with a doctor who can explain the different kinds of medical problems and treatments that principals might want to include in the document. A sample form is provided in appendix 8.

If there are problems with the medical care decisions being made, they generally surround life-and-death decisions, such as taking a patient off life-support machines or removing nasogastric feeding and hydration tubes. There is growing support among lawyers, judges, and state legislators to allow durable power-of-attorney agreements to be used for making critical medical decisions for principals.

Why Use a Durable Power of Attorney?

Durable power-of-attorney documents are often considered stronger, more flexible documents than living wills because they provide for competent agents who can make and enforce decisions for incompetent principals. There are several advantages to using a durable power of attorney.

- Principals, while still competent, can decide exactly which persons they most trust to make decisions for them. For example, although principals might know that certain friends most clearly understand their wishes, a judge faced with appointing agents might instead select family members.

- Agents will not lose their legal right to make decisions once principals become incompetent.

- Principals can decide whether they want an agent to start making decisions immediately or whether they want the agent to wait until they become incompetent.

- Principals who want agents to start making decisions immediately have only one document to execute, instead of writing up first a power-of-attorney agreement and then a second document to appoint a surrogate decision-maker who could take over if the principal were to become incompetent.

- Durable power-of-attorney documents can save the lawyers' fees and court costs incurred when judges must appoint surrogate decision-makers for incompetent people who have not already done so.

- Because these documents are valid across the country, a durable power of attorney written in one state is likely to be honored in another state if a principal becomes ill and hospitalized outside his or her home state.

Further advantages of durable power-of-attorney documents include the following:

- They apply to many different kinds of health care decisions—such as whether incompetent nursing home residents should have cataract surgery—not just decisions about accepting or refusing life-prolonging treatment.

- They can be used by individuals who want life-prolonging treatment continued, as well as by those who wish to refuse such treatment.

- Unlike living wills, which do not necessarily (but could) appoint agents, durable power-of-attorney agreements always appoint agents who can act as advocates or defenders of principals' wishes. This way, agents can enforce principals' preferences for medical care and ensure that those preferences are not forgotten or ignored by other family members, doctors, hospital administrators, or staff.

- The presence of agents means that principals do not need to anticipate all possible treatment choices. Agents are expected to make decisions for the principal on the basis of *substituted judgment* (that is, to the best of their ability, agents are to make the same decisions principals would have made).

- Clearly identified agents provide health care facilities with a measure of legal protection and certainty not currently provided by either a living will or the informal consent of unappointed but available family members (except in states with clear family consent laws. For more information, see chapter 14).

- The presence of appointed agents makes it much less likely that hospital and nursing home administrators—who are afraid of being sued, or doing the wrong thing, when making important medical decisions for incompetent patients—will take cases to court so that judges can review the decisions being made.

How to Create a Durable Power of Attorney

Durable power-of-attorney documents can be created either with or without the help of lawyers. As noted earlier, principals can decide to give their agents many areas of responsibility, only a few areas, or even just one. The document can cover any financial, personal, and health care decisions, although it may be a good idea to execute a separate durable power-of-attorney document for the latter.

Depending on the state in which principals live, durable power-of-attorney agreements may need to list each specific task to be undertaken by agents. Some states have a *statutory short form power of attorney* that gives broad authority to agents by listing one or more of a number of categories—for example, real estate transactions; chattel and goods transactions; bond, share, and commodity transactions; business operating transactions; banking transactions; insurance transactions; estate transactions; claims and litigation; personal relationships and affairs; benefits from military service; records, reports, and statements; and all other matters.

Following are tasks that, in general, agents may perform for principals under a durable power-of-attorney agreement. In states without the short form described above, principals may have to specify in the agreement each of the tasks agents should perform. (To read more about these tasks, see the first entry for this chapter in the "Additional Reading" section at the back of this book.)

Property Management
To make deposits and withdrawals from checking and savings accounts.

To sell, lease, borrow, and invest assets.

To sign tax returns and represent, or arrange for representation of, the principal in a tax audit. (In these cases, use the IRS's own power-of-attorney forms, and limit the agent's power to specific years.)

To work on retirement plans, pay IRA contributions, handle rollovers, elect payout options, and so on.

To fund a previously created living trust (see chapter 1).

To administer life insurance policies, including buying additional coverage and borrowing against policies when necessary.

To collect or forgive debts, complete charitable pledges, and pay salaried employees.

To redirect mail and to cancel or continue credit cards and charge accounts.

To start, settle, appeal, or dismiss legal proceedings.

To update or reform estate-planning documents other than wills.

To nominate a conservator for estate purposes and a guardian for any minor children.

To resign from public and private offices and positions.

Personal Management

To establish or change residence (for example, when the principal moves into a nursing home).

To arrange transportation, travel, and recreation.

To buy, store, repair, and dispose of clothing, food, household goods, furnishings, and personal items.

To arrange for advance funeral and burial arrangements and for anatomical gifts.

To arrange for the care or disposition of pets.

To employ, pay, or fire paid servants, companions, and other nonmedical personnel.

To arrange for spiritual or religious needs.

To provide for companionship.

To nominate a guardian for any minor children.

Health Care

To have access to and disclose medical records and other personal information.

To employ and discharge health care personnel.

To give or withhold consent regarding medical treatment.

To give or withhold consent regarding psychiatric care.

To authorize relief from pain.

To grant releases to medical personnel and others.

(For more information on making critical care decisions, such as terminating life-support systems or removing artificial feeding and hydration tubes, see chapter 14. This is an important topic, one best dealt with in a separate chapter.)

A durable power-of-attorney agreement can be written by filling out a standard form and checking to see whether all the relevant state laws are followed (see appendixes 5, 6, 7, 8, and 9 for some special state requirements and forms). *Nevertheless, it is a good idea to have all durable power-of-attorney agreements witnessed and notarized, no matter what the relevant state laws may be.* Doing so is particularly important when agreements written in states that do not require notarization end up being used in states that do require it.

It's also a good idea to appoint more than one agent in case the only appointed individual is unavailable. This situation is more likely to occur when couples appoint each other and then are both seriously injured in a single accident. Both partners will then need an agent but may have appointed only each other. Had they each left instructions that, for example, their daughter should become their agent if their spouse could not, then someone would still exist to act on their behalf.

Legal Status and Other Points to Remember

While a great deal can be said in favor of durable power-of-attorney agreements, they are not without a few problems. As mentioned earlier, although these documents are generally accepted for use in health care decisions, their validity for that use can be questioned. *It is essential that the agents' authority to make medical decisions be clearly defined in the durable power of attorney.* However, the tougher the decisions—such as whether to remove life-support systems from an incompetent patient—the more likely are the agreements to be scrutinized, and possibly rejected, by caregivers in favor of receiving "sue-proof" court judgments on those decisions.

Another problem lies with the fact that individuals may not be psychologically ready to execute these documents before, or at the start of, a progressive illness that may afflict them at a relatively early age.

One of the most difficult problems faced by agents, health care facilities, and even courts may be determining when principals are no longer competent to make decisions. This is particularly true when agents have a springing durable power of attorney that goes into effect only when principals become incompetent. (For more information, see chapter 11.) Sometimes this determination seems obvious, but not always. Some elderly people with progressive illnesses may be intermittently competent, with periods of time when they are lucid, rational, and capable of making decisions for themselves. Others may be less competent than they once were, yet still competent enough to make at least some decisions.

Many lawyers recommend that those individuals who have not executed such an agreement but who are stricken with Alzheimer's disease or another illness that slowly robs them of their competence be brought to an attorney for explanations and signatures during times when they are relatively clearheaded and lucid.

Many banks and lending institutions are not familiar with durable powers of attorney and may not accept them as legal proof that principals' finances are now under the control of other individuals, unless the institutions' own forms are used. For those who executed a springing durable power of attorney that took effect when they became incompetent, this poses an impossible situation, as they are no longer competent to sign bank forms.

Yet another problem with these agreements is that their power can potentially be abused. While most elderly people assign these powers to trusted relatives or friends, it is certainly possible that elderly people could be forced or pressured into appointing agents who do not have the people's best interests at heart. For this reason, it is important that the courts be allowed to review decisions being made by agents if other concerned individuals bring the matter to the courts' attention.

Limits on Decisions and Why a Decision Might Not Be Followed

There may be many reasons that agents' decisions are not followed. The reasons may be simple—for example, that doctors don't agree with agents' choices—or more complex. Contributing to the current legal, medical, ethical, and moral confusion over the right of surrogates to make critical care decisions are

the uneasy relationship between law and medicine;

the actual and perceived authority of doctors;

the existence of new life-prolonging technologies;

arguments about the patient's quality of life;

an increasing reliance on and fear of lawsuits;

the public's growing awareness of the individual's right to refuse treatment; and

the growing numbers of incompetent elderly patients.

These problems may also contribute to agents' decisions not being honored without a court battle.

Limits to the rights of agents to make decisions tend to apply on a case-by-case and decision-by-decision basis. As with most things in life, agents' decisions are less likely to be questioned if the other concerned individuals agree with them. Most often, questions and limits arise over end-of-life decisions—decisions made to refuse life-prolonging treatment—and they can be imposed by a number of different people and institutions.

Limits may be imposed by state laws that define what may be refused in an advance directive. Limits may also be imposed by health care facilities if for religious or policy reasons they do not want to permit patients or agents to refuse treatment (in these cases, facilities should assist agents in finding another facility agreeable to their decision, and should transfer the patients in question). Limits may also be imposed by doctors or nurses who don't agree with agents' decisions and force the issue to be taken to court. The same is true of other friends or family members who do not agree with agents' decisions on behalf of principals.

Discussing and Registering the Document
with Health Care Professionals

Doctors and other health care professionals who provide care to competent elderly people can recommend that these patients execute a durable power of attorney. Doctors can also be excellent sources of information in the writing up of these agreements—they can explain medical treatments to principals and help them anticipate and plan for medical decision-making by their agents.

Unfortunately, many health professionals are ignorant of the legal tools—such as living wills and durable power-of-attorney documents—that can help elderly people and their families plan ahead. They may also feel uncomfortable discussing medical treatments and refusals with patients and their families. *It is important to raise these issues with doctors, nurses, and even administrators so that they become aware of the preferences of patients and their agents.* If these health professionals are unaware of what patients wanted when competent, they may be more reluctant to follow their wishes when expressed by agents.

Once durable power-of-attorney agreements are written, it is important that they be given to, or registered with, the doctors, nurses, hospitals, nursing homes, and other facilities that care for principals. The agreements won't do any good if no one knows about them, and if known about in advance, their mere existence may help to avoid some potential problems. Copies of agreements should be available to these professionals, who will want to know the extent and validity of the agents' powers. Principals or agents should also discuss these documents with each concerned individual. Obviously, others will want to ensure that agents are not making medical decisions when they are authorized only to make financial ones.

Every nursing home should have a written policy about how it views living wills and durable power-of-attorney documents. Some nursing homes even request that competent patients execute a durable power of attorney upon admission, so that in the event patients become incompetent, facilities will know who should be making decisions.

Staying in Charge in a Hospital or Nursing Home

6

Saying Yes to Medical Care
What You Should Know First

Overview

When illness strikes, people's everyday lives (and those of their family's) are suddenly thrown into confusion and uncertainty. Terribly important decisions must often be made quickly, and patients and their families may have few chances to really think things through. Medical terms, proposed treatments, and their statistics for patient recovery can be frightening and upsetting. Making a decision to either undergo or refuse surgery, chemotherapy, radiotherapy, or other treatments may have life-or-death results. At the same time, quality-of-life arguments must also be considered. At the very point when people feel the most helpless, they are asked to make some of the most crucial decisions of their lives.

Some steps can be taken in advance—steps that may make the immediate burdens of illness a little lighter when the time comes—and these are of the utmost importance before deciding to say yes to medical care. These steps range from the careful selection of doctors to the questions that should be asked before treatment decisions are made.

Selecting a Doctor

If at all possible, select a doctor before a serious illness develops that requires medical attention or hospitalization. Except in emergencies when people become ill and must be hospitalized while away from home, this is a useful bit of advance planning. In most cases, however, elderly people already have a doctor they regularly see for checkups, minor aches and pains, or problems they had in the past.

A person's regular doctor should be someone who understands the needs of the ill person in particular and the needs of the elderly person in general. Family doctors, internists, and general practitioners may be the best choices. Specialists should be reserved for more complicated needs, such as kidney failure or cancerous growths. Regular doctors can call in specialists as consultants if and when the need arises, and they can also refer patients to those specialists if cases become too complicated for them.

The process of selecting a doctor or of interviewing one's regular doctor to make sure he or she is suitable is important. The last problem patients want to face while gravely ill is finding out that their doctor has a fundamental disagreement with how they want to be treated and how they view their life and death.

How to Find a Doctor

For people who are in the process of selecting a doctor for the first time, a number of steps can be taken to ensure finding one who meets their particular needs. New doctors may have to be found when a person's regular doctor retires or when patients are dissatisfied with a doctor's response to their illness. Also, many elderly people retire to sunnier climates and in so doing lose the services of doctors they have grown used to seeing. When any of these situations occurs, there are several ways to find a new doctor:

- Directories of doctors are available in public libraries, telephone books, and state medical societies.
- Individuals who move to another area can ask their current doctor for recommendations or suggestions about what doctors to use in a new location.
- Friends, family members, nurses, pharmacists, and social workers may all have useful information about and experience with doctors they can recommend.
- Area hospitals and medical centers can suggest individual doctors.
- Individuals who have not yet retired can sometimes tap into the resources of their workplace, such as the company benefits manager.
- Retired individuals who receive pensions can ask their company for lists of doctors and their specialties.

What to Look For in a Doctor

Many factors can go into the choosing of a new doctor. Male patients may feel more comfortable with male doctors, and female patients may prefer female doctors, depending on the types of problems they are experiencing. No one should be embarrassed about interviewing potential doctors, for doctors play an important role in the life of every patient. It's wise to find out in advance whether a particular doctor will suit the needs of an individual patient.

The *American Medical Association's Family Medical Guide* (listed in the "Additional Reading" section at the back of this book) recommends four areas that can act as rough clues to a doctor's performance and a patient's satisfaction with his or her care:

1. *How well organized is the doctor's practice?* A well-organized practice allows for effective follow-up, accurate record-keeping, a minimum of waiting time before appointments, and adequate time for the doctor to spend with each patient.

2. *How does the doctor treat his or her patients?* Does the doctor take enough time to truly examine or evaluate a problem? Are his or her examinations done carefully and with adequate respect for a patient's privacy? Does the doctor explain both what is wrong and what the treatment is in such a way that the patient can understand it? Does the patient feel comfortable asking the doctor questions?

3. *Is the doctor willing to consult with other doctors if a patient's problem is out of his or her area of expertise or appears to be particularly complex?* The doctor should explain why a consultation is needed and should provide the second doctor with adequate information so that he or she can evaluate the patient's situation.

4. *Is the doctor willing to discuss any questions a patient may have about treatment, especially when a disease has been treated for a long time without apparent progress?* The doctor should also discuss other options or different treatments the patient could choose. He or she should tell the patient what choices are available and the advantages and disadvantages of each one.

Other helpful clues can be obtained by asking and observing the following:

- Is the doctor knowledgeable? What are his or her credentials? Has the doctor completed medical school, an internship, and a residency? Is he or she board certified? Has the doctor conducted and published any research?

- Is the doctor experienced in caring for elderly people?

- Has the doctor kept current on new procedures and treatments? How conservative is he or she in recommending treatment? (Individuals will have to decide for themselves whether they want a very conservative, cautious doctor; a more radical one; or someone whose approach is somewhere in between.)

- Is the doctor available for over-the-phone questions? Is he or she willing to make house calls if necessary?

- Does the doctor have someone who will attend to his or her patients if the doctor is out of town or unavailable? Does that second doctor have access to patients' medical records?

- Does the doctor have privileges to practice in one or more area hospitals (*privileges* means that a hospital's medical staff has reviewed the doctor's credentials and abilities and permitted him or her to practice in the facility)? What is the reputation of the hospital(s) in which the doctor has privileges? What services are offered in that hospital(s)?

- What arrangements does the doctor have for being paid? Does he or she accept Medicare or Medicaid payment as payment-in-full for services, or is the patient expected to pay additional money? Individuals should check their health insurance coverage to find out what doctor's services are included.

An excellent book to read on this subject is *How to Choose and Use Your Doctor,* by Marvin Belsky and Leonard Gross (see the ''Additional Reading'' section at the back of this book). When meeting with a doctor, these authors say that individuals have the following rights:

- To be fully informed. Information and medical terms should be explained in a way that can be understood by patients.

- To expect and receive the doctor's ongoing abilities.

- To be treated with compassion.

- To have their privacy respected and to have their records and medical information be a private and confidential matter between patient and doctor.

- To know everything about a doctor that might influence his or her decisions about treatment.
- To be educated about medical treatments.
- To question the doctor, make suggestions, and be critical when appropriate.
- To have their medical records sent to another doctor on request (whether they are leaving one doctor for another or are receiving a consultation from a second doctor).

Remember, it is always possible for individuals to change doctors if they are unhappy with the care they receive. People who are dissatisfied with a doctor should tell him or her the reasons behind their decision to switch to another doctor. They should also ask that their records be forwarded to the new doctor. (This request may involve signing a release form, although the new doctor's office might be able to handle the process instead.)

Selecting a Hospital

Individuals who select a doctor who has privileges to admit patients into one or more hospitals have in effect already selected (or narrowed down their search for) a hospital. Therefore, it's a good idea to find out where a doctor has privileges and to check out those hospitals before selecting the doctor.

Individuals can arrange to take a look at hospitals in which a doctor they like has privileges. After seeing those facilities, they might also want to check out other hospitals that have good reputations or that seem worth the effort. A hospital's administrator or a member of its community relations department can usually arrange such a visit. When planning to visit a hospital, make a note to ask questions about the food, rooms, personnel, policies, and services offered.

A handy book for such an exercise is Charles Inlander's *Take this Book to the Hospital with You* (see the "Additional Reading" section). It has a complete checklist of questions to ask when visiting a hospital. Other questions to ask are as follows:

- Is the hospital licensed by the state?
- Is it accredited by the Joint Commission on Accreditation of Health Care Organizations?

- Are a wide variety of services available, such as outpatient, surgery, hospice, ambulatory, and home care services? Which services would be available in the individual's particular area? (See appendix 10 for a list of possible hospital services.)
- Does the hospital have ways of evaluating and ensuring quality care?
- Is the hospital affiliated with a university or school?

Also helpful is the American Hospital Association's (AHA) *Guide to the Health Care Field.* This annual directory, which can be found in public libraries, lists AHA-registered hospitals, all U.S. hospitals, U.S. government hospitals located in foreign countries, accredited long-term care or nursing home facilities, and those hospitals accredited by the Joint Commission on Accreditation of Health Care Organizations. Included in every hospital's listing is the name of the administrator, services, facilities, type of hospital, number of beds, number of staff, payroll size, and a great deal of other information. The directory also lists Peer Review Organizations (PROs), state health planning and development agencies, state departments of health and welfare, health care coalitions, and statewide health coordinating councils.

Individuals should also review their insurance policies to identify what hospital services are covered. Some insurance companies require prior permission before they will pay for certain services. Health permitting, individuals should contact their insurance companies to receive permission before agreeing to use such services.

Other health care facilities can be inspected as well. Individuals should find out what is available in their area, such as home care, nursing home, and health maintenance organizations (HMOs). Whenever possible, visit these organizations, ask to speak with their representatives, and review their brochures.

How to Get the Most out of the Doctor-Patient Relationship

Any relationship has to be worked at if it's going to be good. Once a doctor (and a hospital) is chosen, attending to a few matters will help both the doctor and the patient to make the most of their time together.

Patients should make a list of their medical problems or complaints and take it to the doctor's office; trying to remember everything in the doctor's office does not always work. Patients should also have regular appointments and should set a schedule for seeing the doctor based on his or her recommendations.

Patients should be sure to ask the doctor what to do in case of an emergency—should patients call first, go the an emergency room first, or have the doctor call the emergency room in advance? *Because a doctor's privileges are limited to certain hospitals, he or she cannot admit or see patients in just any emergency room. Patients entering the emergency room of a hospital in which their doctors do not have privileges will be assigned another doctor by the hospital.*

Honesty between doctor and patient is essential. Even though some information may be embarrassing to reveal, it is important that the doctor know about it anyway. Appropriate diagnosis and treatment are impossible if the doctor doesn't know all the facts. *The information that a patient gives a doctor is strictly confidential.*

The patient's medical records should be located at the doctor's office, or at the hospital while the patient is hospitalized. Records are also kept by health maintenance organizations, nursing homes, and any other medical services in which the patient is enrolled. These records include previous hospitalizations, previous doctor's records, X-ray and laboratory records, and records of specialists and other consultants who provided the patient with medical care in the past. *A patient has the right to see and copy his or her medical records. The only person who can give permission for these records to be transferred to someone else is the patient. If records need to be sent elsewhere, the doctor or hospital will ask the patient to sign a form agreeing to the transfer.* (For more information, see chapter 7.)

How Patients Can Help

Patients can greatly assist their doctors in helping them to get well by becoming actively involved in the doctor-patient relationship. There are several specific ways for patients to do this:

- Be honest and cooperative. After examining a patient or diagnosing a problem, the doctor will outline a *treatment plan* that may include medications, changes in diet, exercise, medical therapy, or other treatments to improve the patient's condition. Patients should help shape their treatment plan by telling the doctor if there are parts of it they are unwilling to follow or will find difficult to follow.

- Discuss details or information that may not be clear when first explained by the doctor.

- Discuss medical tests before they are ordered, and find out about any associated risks; ask whether tests are absolutely necessary and what they cost (patients always have the right to refuse tests; for more information, see chapter 7).

- Keep track of test results, and review them with the doctor.

- If hospitalization is recommended for a specific procedure, ask if it can be done outside the hospital (for example, same-day surgery, tests at outpatient departments, or treatment at home or in a hospice).

In some states when doctors prescribe drugs, they can indicate whether pharmacists may use generic substitutes that cost a great deal less than brand-name drugs but have the same effect. Also available in some states are programs that pay for drugs for eligible elderly individuals. Interested persons should check with theit State Unit on Aging, doctor, or pharmacist for this information.

Emergency Room Treatment and Hospitalization

Sometimes hospitalization is inevitable. But whenever possible, it is a good idea for individuals to know some self-care and first-aid skills for dealing with emergencies—for example, knowing how to give cardiopulmonary resuscitation (CPR) for someone who stops breathing suddenly, or how to stop a wound from bleeding. Local American Red Cross organizations and fire departments often offer such courses.

When hospitalization is a necessity, it can be for many different reasons and take several different forms. While emergency rooms (ER) are for emergencies, patients can sometimes get faster medical attention by calling their doctors with urgent requests. Other ER-type alternatives may be available in some communities; independent centers for minor accidents and abrasions or for similarly urgent but nonemergency needs are an example.

When admitted to an emergency room, a patient will be assigned a doctor unless his or her regular doctor is available, can respond, and has privileges to practice in that hospital. Patients should always tell hospitals the name of their doctors in any event.

State and federal laws prohibit hospitals and their emergency personnel from refusing to admit someone in immediate need of hospitalization. Care cannot be denied on the basis of an individual's inability to pay, and hospitals that attempt to do so can be fined and found guilty of a misdemeanor; licensed personnel can be disciplined by the state. Further, a patient can be transferred, rather than admitted to a facility, only if (a) his or her condition is stabilized according to medical opinion, (b) the hospital does not have the proper equipment or personnel, or (c) the hospital does not have any beds available immediately or in the reasonable future.

Individuals may also be hospitalized for nonemergency medical needs, such as the observation and treatment of heart, lungs, kidneys, or other health problems, or to evaluate changes in symptoms or chronic illnesses. Other reasons for hospitalization include treatments such as cardiac care, renal dialysis, and psychiatric and mental health services.

Patients should always ask whether the same results can be achieved at home, through home care. For terminally ill patients, the doctor may recommend pain medications or antibiotic therapy. Once again, patients and their families should ask if this could be done in home care, through a hospice, or at an extended care facility.

Surgery

Being hospitalized for surgery involves a whole new group of medical personnel—a surgeon, an anesthesiologist or nurse anesthetist—and settings, such as a special care unit, an operating room, a recovery room, and possibly the critical care unit of a hospital.

The person who is to undergo surgery is responsible for selecting his or her surgeon. Often a patient's regular doctor can help by recommending several surgeons to contact and interview. Just as important as finding a surgeon, however, is determining whether surgery is really necessary. *Individuals facing surgery should always get a second opinion on the need for surgery.* It has been estimated that about one-quarter of all surgical procedures recommended by one doctor are not recommended by the second doctor.

If surgery is necessary, it is a good idea to find out the surgeon's views and plans depending on what he or she finds while the patient is on the operating table. *Before any surgery takes place, the patient should always make sure that the surgeon knows his or her views on quality of life after surgery, as well as what is and is not wanted. Patient should also ask if the surgeon is board certified in surgery* (two ways to find out without asking the surgeon are to check in the local library for a directory of medical specialists and to write the American College of Surgeons, 55 East Erie Street, Chicago, Illinois 60611). (For more information on what to do before agreeing to surgery, see chapter 7.)

Individuals are also responsible for deciding who will anesthetize them for the surgery. Here, the surgeon may recommend someone whom he or she is famiiar with and has worked with before. There are two types of specialists educated to give anesthesia: (a) anesthesiologists, who are specially trained doctors, and (b) nurse anesthetists, who are nurses who have taken advanced courses in giving anesthesia. Individuals should always know whether the person giving anesthesia is a doctor or a nurse. *If choosing a nurse anesthetist, individuals should ask if there will be an anesthesiologist (doctor) physically available during surgery in case any problems arise.*

It is also important to ask if the chosen surgeon will be the person actually doing the surgery. In hospitals that act as teaching facilities, a medical resident or intern may be doing the surgery with a surgeon present. *Individuals have the right to know who will be operating on them.*

Patients also have specific legal rights surrounding surgical treatment, including informed consent and refusal. This is an important topic, best dealt with in a separate chapter; see chapter 7.

Before Entering the Hospital

Before agreeing to enter a hospital, individuals should ask several basic questions:

- Why is it necessary to enter a hospital?
- What will be done in the hospital?
- How long is the stay likely to be?
- What will be the result of entering the hospital?
- What will be the result of not entering the hospital?

Upon agreeing to be admitted into a hospital, individuals should take the following items or written information with them:

- Diagnoses the doctor has made.

- Lists of allergies to foods, medicines, and other substances.

- Names and types of medications being taken, doses, directions for their use, and the name of the doctor who prescribed them.

- Special needs, such as eyeglasses, hearing aids, and dentures.

- Valuables (not jewelry) that are needed in the hospital.

- Names and phone numbers of one's regular doctor, family members, and friends.

- A bag of personal items, such as toothbrush, toothpaste, cosmetics, hairbrush, nightgown or pajamas, robe, and slippers. Patients might also want to take along something familiar (and inexpensive).

- A medical insurance card.

(For more information on the above and on entering a hospital in general, see Belsky and Gross, *How to Choose and Use Your Doctor,* listed in the "Additional Reading" section.)

Being Admitted into the Hospital

Entering a hospital usually means a lot of forms to fill out, arrangements to consider, and decisions to make. It also means a frightening upheaval of the daily chores and activities that can sometimes be as familiar and comforting as they are irritating. When people are sick, taken out of their home surroundings, put through upsetting tests on strange equipment, and made to wear hospital gowns and eat unappetizing meals at strange hours of the day, they are likely to feel depressed, anxious, intimidated, and dependent. To make matters worse, hospitals are filled with doctors, medical residents or interns, administrators, and nurses, most of whom seem too busy to explain what is going on with the patients. *It's important for patients and their family members to fight against feeling intimidated or dependent in the face of all this authority and expertise.*

Patients and family members should avoid feeling that they "shouldn't raise a fuss" by asking questions or requesting a certain level of treatment. Although some things, like mealtimes, can't be changed, other matters, such as nonsmokers unhappily sharing rooms with smokers, usually can be corrected. Besides, accidents and mistakes do happen in hospitals from time to time. *The best way for patients to recognize and avoid any of these problems is to ask about—and know—what is supposed to happen: what medication, and how much of it, they are supposed to receive; what time of day they are supposed to be operated on; whether or not they are supposed to receive X-rays or specific treatments; and so on.*

Hospital stays can also be much easier when patients have an advocate, someone (usually a family member or friend) who is looking out for them. Patients who do not feel up to the task of asking questions, getting results, and explaining their needs should choose someone who is willing to do these things for them. Patients with and without their own advocates should, if they need help, ask whether the hospital has patient representatives or patient advocates—that is, people employed by the hospital to act on patients' behalf.

Patients who are dying might not want to stay in a hospital for their last days or weeks. A hospital is a place that focuses on saving lives, and there are many patients who—when death is around the corner and impossible to fight against any longer—would prefer to die without further interference or "help." Some patients may be happier staying at home and using private-duty nurses and home care services as necessary. Other patients may prefer to enter a hospice, a special facility that cares for dying patients and provides them with painkilling medication or assists them in being cared for in their own homes. Medicare and many other health insurance policies now pay for hospice care.

If patients do need or want to stay in a hospital, they will have to make several decisions, including the following:

- Whether to get a private room (which costs more than a shared room) and whether their insurance will pay for it.

- Whether to request private-duty nursing services (those involving nurses who are hired to give the patient additional care) and whether their insurance will pay for them.

- Whether special dietary needs are understood by the hospital. (Such needs include special diets ordered by a doctor, foods that for religious reasons cannot be eaten, and food allergies.)

- Whether or not to get a telephone or television in the room.

Patients will also have to sign admission forms agreeing to enter the hospital and receive the general care provided. *By signing these forms, patients are* not *agreeing to specific medical or surgical treatments; at a later time patients will be asked to sign separate consent forms for such treatments* (for more information, see chapter 7).

Other forms that require a patient's signature include those regarding insurance coverage. The forms signed give the hospital permission to share any information they have about the patient with that patient's insurance company.

Once admitted, patients will then be taken to their rooms or to a laboratory for tests. Because there are so many people working in a hospital, all of them wearing white clothing, the various ranks and titles can be confusing. Here is a list to help patients make sense of it all:

clerks

housekeeping staff

technicians from various hospital departments (the laboratory, X ray, radiation therapy, and so on)

registered nurses (RNs) or staff nurses, who coordinate a patient's nursing care

licensed practical nurses (LPNs), licensed vocational nurses (LVNs), or practical nurses (PNs), all of whom, along with the RNs, monitor and observe the patient, give care, carry out a doctor's orders, and give medication and treatments

charge nurses, nursing supervisors, and nursing administrators, who supervise the nursing staff

nursing assistants, orderlies, and aides, who assist the nurses in carrying out the patient's needs

nursing students (if the hospital is associated with a nursing school), who are there to learn about nursing and who are supervised by nursing instructors

the patient's doctor, who supervises and coordinates that patient's medical care

attending doctors, who supervise interns and residents working on a patient

residents (medical school graduates who have completed their internships in a particular medical specialty), who also examine and work on the patient interns (medical school graduates with one or two years of experience), who may examine and work on the patient

medical school students (especially in teaching hospitals or hospitals associated with a university medical school), who are there to learn

specialists or consultants (doctors trained in a particular specialty), depending on a patient's illness

fellows (doctors in the process of being trained in a particular specialty), depending on a patient's illness

discharge planners and social workers, who work to place the patient in a nursing home, if necessary, or to arrange for home care or other special services that will be needed after a patient leaves the hospital

religious representatives

While in the Hospital

A doctor should visit his or her hospitalized patients daily to evaluate their progress and write medical orders for the nurses. Patients should talk with their doctor, be kept up-to-date on their treatment plans, and understand what the doctor has ordered of the nursing staff. Only by knowing this information will patients or their family members be able to make sure that the various staff members remember to do what is asked of them. Patients can easily call their doctors from the hospital, just as they would from their homes.

If all goes well, patients will recover sufficiently to be discharged (for information on what to do if a patient is being discharged before he or she feels ready, see chapter 8). Surrounding a patient's discharge is a process called a *utilization review,* that includes a Peer Review Organization (PRO) made up of doctors and nurses who review all patients' cases and agree or disagree with the length of time a patient is to stay in the hospital. The PRO must agree to a patient's extended stay in a hospital.

How long a patient stays in the hospital determines how much money the hospital makes or loses in caring for that particular patient. Medicare and other health insurance groups pay a particular amount to the hospital for each patient with a particular disease. Diseases—and the amount paid for their coverage—are categorized into Diagnostic Related Groups (DRGs). Every diagnosis has an average length of hospital stay connected to it. The hospital is paid the same amount of money whether a patient leaves before that average stay is up or after it (under certain circumstances, more will be paid to the hospital if the patient requires a longer stay). Hospitals make money on a patient who leaves early because they stop having to provide the person with expensive space and services, and hospitals lose money on a patient who receives more services than are covered by the insurance money paid to them.

When Mistakes or Accidents Occur in the Hospital

Despite the fact that hospitals are places that treat patients and attempt to return them to a healthy condition, mistakes and accidents do happen that can make a patient worse. These include

falls;

errors in medication (too much or too little of the right medication is given, or the wrong medication is given);

failure to monitor a patient's progress and notice changes in his or her condition;

failure of the doctor or nurse to communicate about a patient's progress;

nosocomial infections (bacteria- or virus-caused infections that develop as a result of the patient's staying in the hospital);

surgical errors, such as sponges being mistakenly left in the site of a patient's operation; and

iatrogenic diseases or disorders (conditions that result from medical personnel, treatment, or diagnostic procedures or simply through the patient's being exposed to the hospital's environment).

Negligence and *malpractice* mean more than that the hospital has made a mistake; they mean that the mistake has led to harm or caused injuries to the patient. The behavior and actions of a doctor, nurse, or hospital are judged on the basis of standards of care. The legal standard of care is that the doctor, nurse, and hospital must be reasonable and prudent under the circumstances; the standard is measured by what other doctors, nurses, and hospitals would do under similar circumstances.

If mistakes do happen, patients should be told about them by their doctor or a hospital administrator. If patients realize a mistake has been made, they should tell a doctor or nurse that they wish to meet with the supervisor and the hospital's patient advocate or representative who should be present at such meetings.

When mistakes occur, patients or their family members might first try to resolve the problem within the facility. If that doesn't work, there is always the option of suing the doctor, nurse, or facility responsible for the problem. Individuals should call a reliable lawyer to discuss their complaint before making any decisions of this kind.

Most hospitals have many different ways of ensuring quality of care and guarding against malpractice and patient injury. Hospitals and their staff don't want to make mistakes, but a mistake does happen occasionally. Hospitals have committees that review the credentials and abilities of the people who practice and have admitting privileges in them. Many also have set procedures for resolving patient grievances or complaints related to injuries, accidents, treatments, or events that may result in the patient suing the hospital.

In some states, hospitals must also educate their staff about

patient safety;

injury prevention;

the legal aspects of patient care;

causes of malpractice claims or lawsuits;

improved communication with patients; and

the responsibility to report professional misconduct.

In addition, licensing authorities in some states oversee hospitals and also require them to report certain incidents, such as

patient's deaths or disabilities due to circumstances other than those related to the natural course of illness, disease, or proper treatment;

fires in the hospital that disrupt patient care services or harm patients and staff;

equipment failures that occurred during treatment or diagnosis of a patient and that harmed or could have harmed a patient or staff member;

poisoning occurring within the hospital;

strikes by hospital staff;

emergency situations outside the hospital that affect the hospital's activities; and

termination of any services necessary to the continued safe running of the hospital or to the health and safety of its patients and staff (including such things as the anticipated or actual termination of telephone, gas, electric, fuel, water, heat, air-conditioning, rodent- or pest-control, laundry, food, or other services).

7

Patients Have Rights, Too

Overview

Our entire society is based on the idea that every person has a number of inherent rights. Children have the right to be protected from abuse, employees have the right to work in a healthy environment, and patients have rights, too. As with all rights, the simple fact that they exist does not mean they are always respected. Rights occasionally have been fought for, and people who abuse those rights may need to be reminded that doing so is illegal.

Explored at length in this chapter are the many rights of patients, as well as the methods for demanding that those rights be observed.

A number of professional associations, hospitals, and nursing homes have come up with their own list of patient rights. The most widely used is the bill of rights of the American Hospital Association (AHA) (see Appendix 11). Under state and federal law, AHA's bill of rights must be posted and made available to patients as a condition of the hospital's being reimbursed under Medicare.

States have also passed laws and regulations on the rights of patients in hospitals and of residents in nursing homes (appendix 12 contains a sample state bill of rights for hospital patients). Further, many states have defined the rights of mentally ill and mentally disabled patients. And even the federal government has its own series of regulations on the rights of patients in health care facilities run by the Veterans Administration (see appendix 13). Moreover, both the federal and the state legal systems have become involved in this issue. Courts make decisions about the rights and responsibilities of patients, doctors, and hospitals. The law views hospitals as corporations that have certain duties to their patients, including the supervision of staff and nonemployee activities.

The extent of laws, rules, regulations, and declarations is not really a surprise. This topic is significant and a formal framework is required to protect patients—often among the most helpless of individuals—from being abused. The importance of the issue has also resulted in a number of excellent books written in language easily understood by any patient or family member. Because these books focus solely on patient rights, they have the luxury of going into much more depth than can be done here. They have been used as the foundation for this chapter and are strongly recommended to all interested individuals. These books are cited throughout this chapter and are listed in the "Additional Reading" section. It may take some effort to become educated on the issues, but doing so is certainly worthwhile.

All Relationships Carry a Price

It must be remembered that patients are not the only ones with rights in a medical situation. Hospitals and doctors have their own rights as well, and they, too, must be respected. The different groups involved in the health care situation each have privileges and responsibilities, all of them intersecting to define the relationships among the various groups.

There is an old saying that cuts to the heart of the matter: "My right to hit you stops at the tip of your nose." In other words, a person's right to do something stops short of violating another person's rights—in this case, the right not be hit.

Hospitals have legal advisers, and doctors are taught the legal boundaries of patient care. Patients are the ones who are most likely to be ignorant of the extent and limits of their rights. In order to enter the doctor-patient relationship on equal footing, individuals must be aware of their own rights and of the responsibilities of doctors to people in their care. (Some excellent information on these issues—explained in brief in the sections that follow—can be found in *How to Talk to Your Doctor: Getting Beyond the Medical Mystique,* by Dr. Janet Maurer; *Take This Book to the Hospital with You,* by Charles Inlander; and *Medical Care Can Be Dangerous to Your Health,* by Eugene Robin.)

The Patient's Rights in the Doctor-Patient Relationship

In the doctor-patient relationship, patients have the right to have as much information as they wish about their illness;

be educated about treatment options and the consequences of refusing treatment;

refuse treatment;

be allowed adequate time to ask questions and state concerns about medical problems;

have privacy and confidentiality;

have continuity of care;

have reasonable access to the doctor;

participate in major decisions about their care;

refuse to participate in research;

know the doctor's availability outside of regular office hours and the provisions the doctor has made for coverage of patients during those hours;

determine who other than the doctor shall have access to information about their health;

know in advance the approximate amount of the bill and possible arrangements for payment;

be seen within a reasonable time of the scheduled appointment;

change doctors if a breakdown in the doctor-patient relationship occurs; and

have medical records permanently transferred to another doctor.

For more information on these issues, see chapter 6.

The Patient's Responsibilities

Rights carry with them certain responsibilities. In the doctor-patient relationship, these responsibilities often aid the doctor in correctly diagnosing an illness or prescribing a treatment. The responsibilities of patients are to

tell the doctor all the information that relates to their illnesses or conditions;

keep office appointments or cancel them well in advance;

plan their visit with the doctor (for example, patients might write down their questions and concerns rather than trying to remember them all in the doctor's office);

stop the doctor when they don't understand his or her explanation of a problem, and ask for a simpler explanation;

ask questions;

follow the doctor's advice;

quickly report to the doctor any adverse reactions to drugs or therapy, as well as any complications from tests or worsening symptoms;

limit phone calls to the doctor between visits except to report the problems listed above or other agreed-upon matters; and

pay agreed-upon bills promptly or in a way that is acceptable to both parties.

The Doctor's Responsibilities

Doctors have specific obligations to people in their care. These obligations are governed by the law and by the doctor's personal code of ethics and good practice. The responsibilities of a doctor are to

thoroughly discuss with the patient his or her diagnoses, laboratory test results, therapy, and prognosis (what is likely to happen in the course of a given disease), in language that the patient can understand;

tell the patient of alternative and generally accepted approaches to therapy or diagnostic procedures, even if the doctor does not agree with them;

recommend to the patient what the doctor considers the best approach and why;

allow adequate time, on at least one occasion, to answer the patient's questions and discuss the patient's concerns;

provide adequate follow-up and emergency care, and make the patient aware of these provisions;

ask a specialist to consult on the patient's case or refer the patient to another doctor for a second opinion if uncertain about a diagnosis;

assist the patient in getting needed social or rehabilitative services;

keep complete patient medical records;

assist in a smooth transition for the patient to another doctor when the relationship has ended; and

make available to the patient a list of charges for the services performed.

The Right of Informed Consent

While all patient rights are important, the right of *informed consent* deserves a close look. *Informed consent simply means that an individual has all the necessary information that he or she needs—in language that he or she understands—to agree to or refuse treatment. Informed consent must be obtained before any medical work can be done. Whoever is actually going to order or perform the treatment or procedure is responsible for giving the patient all necessary information and obtaining his or her informed consent.*

Informed consent applies to medical treatment—from tests to decisions about using life-prolonging technology or treatments. Patients will be asked to sign a consent form agreeing to have surgery or undergo treatment. But before doing anything, patients have the right to understand what they are agreeing to if they sign the form. They should ask the person who will perform the procedure to explain it, along with its risks, benefits, alternatives, and consequences.

Consent forms can be altered to reflect exactly what the patient has agreed to with his or her doctor, surgeon, anesthesiologist, or nurse anesthetist. The form should be correctly dated; it should include the specific procedure that is planned; and the patient's signature should be witnessed (usually by a nurse).

Consent forms should be signed before the patient takes or is given medication to prepare him or her for the operation or procedure in question. The patient should review and sign the form only when thinking clearly.

The Right to Information

The cornerstone of a patient's informed consent is his or her access to information. Without all the necessary knowledge, truly informed consent is impossible. Some excellent books, listed in the "Additional Reading" section, form the basis for the information that follows. Books of particular use in the writing of this chapter were *The Patient's Guide to Medical Tests,* by Cathey and Edward Pinckney;

Medical Care Can Be Dangerous to Your Health, by Eugene Robin; *Take This Book to the Hospital with You,* by Charles Inlander; and *How to Talk to Your Doctor: Getting Beyond the Medical Mystique,* by Dr. Janet Maurer.

A patient's access to information about his or her disease or condition should cover not only the disease itself but all aspects related to it. It is important to use the rights listed below to determine what questions need to be asked of doctors.

Individuals undergoing medical tests have the right to

know the cost of proposed tests;

be accurately tested;

have tests correctly performed by trained and prepared personnel, on properly maintained and precisely calibrated equipment;

know and understand the purpose, need, and rationale for each test;

know how each test is performed;

know and understand each test's dangers and complications;

know what the results of each test will mean;

know how precise each test is;

have tests repeated to ensure accuracy;

know the risks and benefits of each test, including whether it involves an invasion of the patient's body, pain, or a significant risk of harm;

understand the consequences of taking or not taking each test;

know of any alternatives to each test and the consequences of taking or not taking them; and

know and understand all test results.

About the diagnosis, patients have the right to know

how certain the doctor is about his or her diagnosis;

whether there is a possibility that the diagnosis is incorrect;

whether there is any way to confirm the diagnosis; and

whether a second opinion is indicated.

About the cause and nature of the disease, patients have the right to know

what bodily organs are involved in the disease and in what way;

how or why the disease started;

whether the disease will be passed on to, or is likely to be present in, any children; and

how contagious the disease is and what protections to take against other people catching it.

About the course of the disease, patients have the right to know

the prognosis, or likely course the disease will take;

whether the disease is limited to certain organs or whether it will spread;

whether the involved organs will get progressively worse, and if so, how;

what complications may arise and at what stage of the illness;

what symptoms or changes the patient should be concerned about;

whether there are any symptoms that other people should watch for in the patient; and

the names of any organizations that can provide information about the illness or help with problems resulting from it.

About the treatment for the disease, patients have a right to know

what medications are available to control the disease;

how often the doctor has treated this particular illness and with what success;

the risks and benefits of taking the medication at the current stage of the illness;

what the medication is supposed to accomplish;

whether there are alternative therapies if the patient is unable to tolerate the medication or if it proves ineffective;

whether hospitalization will be needed to start the medication;

how to judge whether the treatment is working and how long it will be needed;

whether surgery is an alternative to the treatment, and when or if it would be recommended;

what dietary changes or other measures could lessen the effects of the disease;

how frequently the doctor will have to be seen;

how to contact the doctor in an emergency;

whether any home monitoring of the illness can be done to reduce the need for office visits; and

the cost of the treatment.

About the influence of the disease and treatment on family, social, and work life, patients have the right to

know if they will be able to continue in their jobs;

know if they are likely to have many days when they are too sick to work;

know if the illness will affect their ability to get life or health insurance;

ask if they can continue to be involved in specific hobbies, sports, family, or social activities;

know any limitations on travel, or travel to certain areas;

know if any drugs being prescribed will interact with alcohol or the ability to have sex; and

know if the illness or the treatment will be disfiguring.

About surgery, patients have the right to

get a second opinion on whether the surgery is necessary;

know at what hospital the doctor operates and what kinds of facilities it has to support the operation;

know if the surgeon is board certified in surgery;

know how often the surgeon has performed the operation in question;

know what the usual result of the operation is;

know what will happen during the course of the operation;

know the risks and benefits of the operation;

know if they will be disfigured by the operation, and if so, how;

know what will happen if no surgery is performed;

know how long a recovery period to expect;

know what daily activities, such as cooking, shopping, bathing, and so on, will be more difficult after the operation and for how long;

know how long they will need to be hospitalized after the operation;

know whether they will need any specialized care after surgery, and if so, for how long;

know whether the necessary care can be provided at home.

Knowing one's rights to information but not asking any questions to get it is useless. Patients have the right to know because they need to know. Ask questions—it is the doctor's responsibility to answer them in a way that is understandable to the patient.

Patients' Rights and Medical Records

According to state law and hospital policies, a patient has the right to see and copy his or her medical records. Specific rules on this issue vary, but generally a patient can see his or her own record by notifying the appropriate doctor or hospital. The hospital may ask to see the request in writing, or it may require a patient to be with his or her doctor or a medical records staff member when reviewing records.

Rarely, a doctor will decide that it will harm a particular patient to know what is contained in his or her record. This judgment is known as the doctor's *therapeutic privilege.* In such instances, the patient might instead be offered a summary of his or her record or be asked to identify someone else who could see the record.

In some states, a patient who doesn't agree with what is said in the record can amend it by inserting his or her own statements. Usually the patient is charged a reasonable fee to copy a chart, but if he or she is unable to pay the fee, the hospital must make the chart available anyway.

A hospital record is a legal document kept by a business (the hospital). It has many uses, including ensuring continuity of care, recording a patient's response to treatment, and creating a history of what treatments have been tried and their outcomes.

Hospitals do audits of their records to ensure quality of care, and researchers use the records to study particular diseases, drugs, and treatments. A patient's permission must be obtained before his or her record can be seen by a researcher, unless all identifying information (name, address, social security number, and so on) is removed from it and the patient's privacy is ensured. Insurance companies review records as a basis of paying for health services rendered; government agencies review records to ensure that standards are met. Lastly, a patient's medical record has legal applications as well—it can be used as evidence of care in a malpractice lawsuit or as evidence of a patient's mental status in a lawsuit over a patient's estate or will.

In cases in which a patient changes to another doctor, seeks a second opinion, or consults with a specialist, he or she will be asked to sign a form agreeing to release the record to that other person. A patient can limit the permission on the release of his or her records by requesting that only certain information be released (such as only those records which pertain to a patient's most recent heart attack). A patient can also require that his or her records be sent to a specific person, to be used only for a specific purpose.

The Right to Be Free of Restraints and Abuse

Patients have the right to be free of restraints and abuse. There are very specific state laws and regulations governing patient abuse. Health care providers, including doctors and nurses, are required to report patient abuse to the state. Under no circumstances does anyone have the right to abuse a patient.

A patient can be restrained, but only if his or her safety (or the safety of others) requires doing so. This means that the use of restraints must be related to a patient's specific therapeutic needs and be an essential part of his or her treatment plan.

Restraints are not allowed to be applied as a punishment or for the convenience of the staff or facility. The least restrictive methods of restraining a patient must be tried first. Only if less restrictive measures are inadequate to protect the safety of the patient, or of others around the patient, can more restrictive methods be applied.

Restraints can be ordered only by the patient's doctor, except in emergency cases wherein a registered nurse can temporarily order the use of physical restraints.

Hospitals have written policies that must be followed by staff members when they apply restraints. These policies include written doctor's orders specifying the length of time restraints should be applied and the type of restraints to be used (some types, such as leather straps, are prohibited). When restraints are applied, the nursing staff has a duty to closely monitor the patient, remove the restraints periodically (some policies require that they be removed at least once every two hours), and remove them completely when they are no longer needed.

Patients' Right to Leave a Hospital

A competent (mentally healthy) patient has the right to leave the hospital, even if doing so goes against his or her doctor's opinions and wishes (for more information, see chapter 11). Similarly, any patient who disagrees with his or her doctor or with the proposed treatment plan can leave the hospital. A patient may be asked to sign a form stating that he or she is being discharged against medical advice, but the patient is not legally required to do so. *If a patient is kept against his or her will, the hospital can be sued for false imprisonment. A patient may leave even if his or her bill is not paid.*

Hospitals are not allowed to keep patients against their will unless a patient is thought to be a danger to himself or herself or others. If that is the medical opinion and the patient wants to leave anyway, the hospital and the doctor must institute an involuntary commitment proceeding.

State laws specify rules about involuntary commitment (such as requiring that two doctors state that a patient should be held for up to seventy-two hours for observation and evaluation). A patient is entitled to legal representation and due process (a notice and a hearing on the case) in these instances. When this happens, a patient's health status and situation are reviewed by a court, which decides whether the patient should be committed for treatment or released.

Even patients who are involuntarily committed have the right to refuse certain treatments, such as medications.

Rights and More Rights: What They Mean for Patients

Many people may understand that they have specific rights but are unsure how those rights translate into particular situations (some excellent material on this matter—illustrated briefly below—can be found in *Take This Book to the Hospital with You,* by Charles Inlander; *The Rights of the Critically Ill,* by John Robertson; and *The Rights of Hospital Patients,* by George Annas, all of which are listed in the "Additional Reading" section). A quick guide to other patient rights is as follows:

- *Contrary to popular belief, most individuals do not have a legal right to medical care.* (Prisoners and the involuntarily committed mentally ill, however, do have a legal right to health care.)

- *An individual has the right to hear the truth about his or her illness or condition.* A doctor is required to give an honest diagnosis and prognosis to every patient. A doctor who fails to do so in cases in which such failure leads to patient injury can be sued for malpractice. A doctor who fails to tell a patient the whole truth—particularly if asked—can be sued for breach of contract. And a doctor who withholds information that affects the medical, financial, or personal decisions made by a patient can be held liable for any damages. (Two exceptions to this right exist when a patient asks not to be told the truth and when a doctor has a reason to believe that the patient would be harmed by hearing the truth.)

- *A competent (mentally healthy) patient has the right to full information about his or her condition, even if his or her family members object to the patient's hearing the truth.*

- *An individual has the right to keep his or her condition a secret from family members.* A doctor must go along with the decision made by the patient in this matter. (An exception exists in cases in which the information is necessary to prevent harm or to protect others from catching a contagious disease.)

- *A competent patient has a right to continued treatment if he or she can pay for it.* This is true whether or not the patient's family members want the care continued. If a patient is terminally ill and unconscious or comatose, then the family members are more likely to be consulted about the patient's wishes.

- *A competent adult patient has the right to refuse medical care, even when it is life prolonging.*

- *A patient has the right to consent to (or refuse) the donation of his or her organs or tissues.* The hospital must ask if the patient would like to be a donor, not just assume that he or she intends to be one. In some cases, the patient's family members may be able to consent to or refuse the donation on a patient's behalf.

- *In some instances, a patient may be asked if he or she wants life-sustaining treatment, such as cardiopulmonary resuscitation (CPR).* Usually, what is being asked is whether the patient wants to be revived if his or her heart fails. Patients do have the right to make these decisions.

- *A doctor can refuse to treat a patient who is unable to pay but cannot stop treating a patient who can't pay.* Once treatment has started, the doctor must continue it for as long as the patient wants it, benefits from it, or decides to stop receiving it. (An exception to this right exists if the doctor has told the patient in advance that he or she must pay for treatment in order to receive it.)

- *A patient cannot be thrown out of a hospital if he or she can no longer pay for care or treatment.* A patient whose condition has stabilized can be transferred out of one hospital and into another. If a patient is discharged because of his or her inability to pay and then gets worse or suffers additional problems, the patient can sue the hospital for abandonment.

- *If a patient asks to be referred to another doctor for a second opinion or expert consultation, his or her doctor is not legally required to make the referral.* Making the referral is, however, commonly regarded as a good and ethical practice. If a doctor refuses to do so and incorrectly treats and harms the patient, the doctor can be sued for negligence.

- The relationship between the doctor and the patient can end only if both individuals want it to end, the doctor is no longer needed, or the doctor gives the patient sufficient notice that he or she will no longer handle the patient's case. A doctor who does not give the patient sufficient notice can be sued for abandonment.

- *A patient can refuse to be examined by a medical student, intern, resident, or anyone else in a hospital setting.*

- A cancer patient does not have the right to demand to be treated with laetrile (a controversial anticancer drug), even in those states in which laetrile is legal. If a patient wants to try laetrile but his or her doctor refuses to prescribe it, the patient can always seek another doctor who is willing to use it.

Making a Complaint

A patient can complain about the violation of his or her rights. In most instances, the problem can be taken up with the doctor or hospital staff and be resolved that way. In other cases, a patient may feel more comfortable taking a complaint to authorities outside the hospital (see chapter 9).

Two places outside the hospital that may be of help are the medical and nursing licensing agencies and the hospital licensing agencies (see appendix 34 for addresses). These agencies can receive and investigate confidential or anonymous reports about doctors', nurses', or hospitals' care of patients.

Rights Are Not Absolute

Patient rights are not absolute. The right to refuse treatment, for example, can, under very few circumstances, be overridden by important state interests, including the following:

- The protection of innocent third parties. For example, patients may not be allowed to refuse treatment of contagious diseases that threaten the health of the public. Similarly, individuals may be required to receive vaccinations if the danger to the community is severe. This exception applies even if the treatment goes against the wishes or religious convictions of the patients involved.

- The preservation of life. For example, a woman who wishes to refuse a blood transfusion may be overruled if the transfusion is the only way to save her life and she has an infant to look after. Cases to which this exception might apply are decided on a case-by-case basis, and patients (or their family members) should always seek the advice of a lawyer if a refusal of treatment is not honored by the hospital.

- The prevention of suicide. This exception does not include terminally ill or comatose patients; *in those cases, the courts have determined that the refusal of treatment is not the same as suicide.* Insurance companies must follow the court in these matters and are prohibited from classifying as suicide cases those terminal or comatose patients who refuse treatment.

- The maintenance of the ethical integrity of the medical profession. For example, in one case a Massachusetts court decided that a hospital did not have to honor a patient's refusal of treatment but did have to assist the patient in transferring to another hospital that would honor the refusal. In New Jersey, however, a court upheld a patient's right to refuse treatment but refused to order the patient's transfer; in that case, the original hospital had to comply with the patient's decision to refuse treatment.

When patients refuse treatment, complex ethical, legal, and practical problems can arise. Hospitals should have specific policies to guide them in these areas. Ethics committees, case conferences, and careful medical and legal evaluations can usually provide an answer on how to proceed. Equally important, patients themselves can avoid many of the potential complications that surround their refusal of treatment by preparing in advance written documents that specify their wishes (for more information, see chapters 4 and 5).

8

If the Hospital Tells You
to Go Home Too Early

*L*IKE *many other chapters in this book, the information here is addressed both to patients and the family members of those patients who may be too ill to speak for themselves. This chapter details the necessary steps in fighting an early discharge from the hospital; and patients who may or may not be able to carry out the suggestions herein should try to arrange for their family members or friends to read this material. Nevertheless, as in most situations in which the patient is too sick to take charge personally, it is always useful to have a written document—such as a durable power of attorney with health care decision-making authority—from the patient that appoints a family member or friend to act on the patient's behalf if and when the patient is unable to do so (see chapter 5 for more information).*

Patients and family members should also be prepared to discuss with the doctor whether or not a patient wants to receive life-sustaining treatment (including resuscitation). These discussions, held in advance, can save much trauma and hurt during emergency situations.

Overview

Recent stories in newspapers, in magazines, and on television about patients being "dumped," or released from hospitals too early to fend for themselves, have raised new fears among patients and their family members. Entering a hospital for treatment can be frightening, and the possibility of not being allowed to stay can make the prospect even worse. These fears are particularly pronounced for the elderly, who even when healthy may face a host of day-to-day problems. If forced to leave a hospital before they can return home to their normal routine, elderly patients must either temporarily enter another health care facility (such as a nursing home) or be cared for at home by friends, family members, or hired professionals.

Why are stories of patients being released too early surfacing now? Were we simply unaware of a practice that always existed, or is the problem a new one? In fact, it is a new problem. And in order to understand how to combat it, patients and their families should first understand why it is happening in the first place.

Individual patients and their families are not the only ones feeling the pinch of rising hospital care costs. For a number of years now, the federal government, which pays specific medical bills for individuals eligible for Medicare, has also found itself paying out more and more money for hospital care. The government (like its individual taxpayers) cannot easily afford to pay ever-increasing hospital care costs.

However, the problem was, and is, bigger than the government's money woes. While medical costs rose higher and higher, reports began to surface that hospitals were running unessential (and sometimes risky) tests on patients and keeping them longer than necessary. These extra tests represented extra income, because Medicare used to pay for each additional day of hospital care. At the same time, many hospitals threatened to close down unless they were adequately paid for their services. The question was how to contain costs without hospitals either shutting down—which would be a disastrous public health problem—or recommending more services to make up for less funding.

By 1983, the government decided what to do about the situation. That year, Medicare instituted a new payment system for hospitals. It was part of a series of reforms designed to keep Medicare itself from going bankrupt.

The New Medicare System

Under the new system, Medicare categorized all health problems into Diagnostic Related Groups (DRGs). It then decided to pay hospitals a fixed amount of money for each Medicare patient in a particular DRG. *The amount of money paid by Medicare for each DRG is based on the average cost of care of treating a patient for a specific (or similar) disease, condition, or problem.*

To discourage hospitals from keeping patients too long so as to receive more federal funds, Medicare does not pay for a certain number of days of care per patient; rather, it pays only that one fixed amount associated with a specific disease or condition. The hospital, in return, must keep caring for patients as long as they need acute, or specialized, hospital care.

Medicare pays higher DRG rates across the board to hospitals with unavoidably higher costs, such as teaching hospitals and those serving large numbers of poor and elderly patients, those in urban areas, and those with higher labor costs. These higher DRG payments apply to all Medicare patients treated by a hospital that meets government criteria as a high-cost institution.

Medicare has several safety-valve mechanisms for recognizing extraordinary situations in which an individual needs more hospital care than the average patient does. Medicare will make additional payments to a hospital, beyond the regular DRG payment, for the continuing care of an individual patient under the following conditions:

- *The patient needs continued hospital care for much longer than the average stay of a person with a similar diagnosis, and care for the patient at another kind of institution would be inadequate.*
- *The patient needs such expensive hospital treatment that it costs the hospital more to treat him or her than it does to treat the average patient with a similar diagnosis.*
- *The patient needs skilled nursing home care, but no skilled nursing home will accept him or her.*

What the New System Means for Hospitals

Under the old system, hospitals had a good reason to give patients the kind of care that could have been provided at home or in a nursing home—they generally could get Medicare to pay for it. As a result, both patients and health care professionals began to rely on hospitals for services that could have been provided more cheaply somewhere else.

The new system gives hospitals a strong incentive to provide no more services than are medically necessary, because for most patients the average payment is all the hospital will receive from Medicare. The hospital can lose money on patients whose care costs more than the fixed payment.

What does all this mean for hospitals? They can respond to the new system with good management that cuts costs while preserving quality care, or they can cut corners that result in poor quality care. *In the end, the most effective way for hospitals to reduce services and costs is to reduce the amount of time a patient spends in the hospital.*

There are two legitimate ways for hospitals to cut a patient's length of stay:

1. Hospitals can ask doctors to perform some or all diagnostic tests and other treatments before admitting a patient into the hospital, and to wait until it is medically necessary to admit him or her.

2. Hospitals can discharge a patient as soon as he or she no longer requires special equipment and around-the-clock medical care.

While these cost-cutting strategies could cause various problems for patients and their families, the most serious problems occur because patients are discharged too early. There are two ways in which this problem shows up:

1. Patients are discharged while their condition is so unstable that hospital care and supervision by doctors and nurses are still needed. Medicare program managers report that this problem occurred in about 1 percent of all Medicare hospital cases in late 1984 and early 1985. Congress has created a national network of Peer Review Organizations to catch hospitals that discharge patients prematurely. (The role of these organizations is described more fully later in this chapter.)

2. Patients who do not require continued hospital care but still need continued nursing care are discharged before preparations are completed for their necessary after-hospital nursing care or supportive services. This problem seems to be more common than the early discharge of patients who still require hospital care, although there are no figures to show just how common—or rare—it may be. Congress has imposed strict new requirements on hospitals to ensure that discharge planning is improved to correct this problem.

While the government has taken action to prevent these problems from occurring, they still do happen. Patients (and their family members) can protect themselves by understanding the system and by knowing whom to call for help.

What the New System Means for Patients

It's not always easy, even for doctors and nurses, to know the right time to discharge a patient. *The decision of when to release a patient is a judgment call that* involves both the medical situation and the social situation of each patient. Patients and families can influence this decision.

Patients who still feel ill and weak may wonder whether they should be discharged at the time the hospital wants them to leave. Many patients think they should stay in the hospital until they are fully recovered; however, Medicare and private insurance companies see the matter differently.

Medicare views hospital care as only one part of a patient's medical treatment. Medicare wants to move patients—as soon as it is safe to do so—to less costly settings in which a lower level of care can be provided (for example, patients' homes or nursing homes). Even dying patients may have little need for hospital care and may be moved back into their homes, nursing homes, or hospices.

Yet, just because patients or family members do not understand Medicare's rules does not mean they should always leave the discharge decision up to the professionals. Remember, the professionals, too, are often making a judgment call. For example, while doctors and hospitals usually agree on a date of discharge, they may also disagree. And patients, family members, and friends can certainly disagree with the decision being made as well.

Medicare has contracts with Peer Review Organizations (PROs). These organizations are made up of groups of doctors and nurses who are asked to resolve disagreements and ensure that patients receive all the hospital care they require (but no more than is medically necessary).

In cases in which the doctor and hospital disagree, a hospital may ask the PRO to decide whether the patient should be discharged over the objection of the patient's doctor. By law, if the hospital asks the PRO to review the case to overrule the attending physician, the hospital must inform the patient that it has done so. Because hospitals are often reluctant to upset the doctor and patient, they rarely ask the PRO to overrule a patient's doctor. For this reason, having one's doctor on one's side of the argument can be crucial.

Patients and their families may also argue against a proposed discharge by appealing to the PRO. If successful, a patient may be allowed to stay longer in the hospital or may receive a better discharge plan from the hospital (see appendix 16 for a list of state PROs).

In any event, there is no substitute for the patient having an advocate—someone on the patient's side of the argument, such as a doctor, friend, or family member—who can help argue the case. Some hospitals employ patient advocates or representatives to work on behalf of patients that need their help. A call to the hospital switchboard or its social services department can determine whether a given hospital offers this service.

Helping to Plan Your Own
(or a Family Member's) Discharge

The time to prepare for a patient's discharge is before his or her admission into the hospital. Since emergencies do happen, certain steps should be taken before any hospital care is needed. The following steps can help.

- Patients should talk with reliable friends and family members who would be willing and able to assist them in getting to and from the hospital, if someday they should need care.

- Patients should share this book with family members or friends who are willing to help; such persons may need to use it to assist patients who are feeling too ill to handle matters themselves.

- Patients should consider executing a durable power of attorney that authorizes someone to make health care decisions if patients are unable to do so themselves. This way, patients can make sure that a trusted friend or relative will be in charge either temporarily or permanently. (For more information, see chapter 5.)

- Patients who discuss their upcoming treatment with friends who have had similar treatments or procedures should also find out from their own doctor whether their experience is likely to be the same as or different from their friends'.

- Before entering a hospital for a scheduled (nonemergency) treatment or procedure, patients should talk with their doctor to find out how their lives might be temporarily or permanently changed as a result of the upcoming surgery or medical care. This includes asking what daily activities, such as cooking, walking, climbing stairs, eating, dressing, and bathing, might be more difficult after leaving the hospital and for how long those tasks would be more difficult to perform.

- Patients should also ask their doctors which agencies will provide them with formal medical or nursing care following discharge from the hospital. If patients will need nursing home care, they should check the institutions' reputations with the Long Term Care Ombudsman Program (see appendix 19 for the addresses of state ombudsman program offices; for more information about the program itself, see chapter 9).

What to Do on Admission into a Hospital

Upon admission to the hospital, eligible patients should be given a copy of *An Important Message from Medicare.* (This document is reprinted in appendix 14.) Patients should then put this message in a safe place where they and their family members or friends can find it. (Patients who do not receive a copy or who lose the one they have should request one from the hospital admissions department. *Under federal law, patients have the right to have this information.* The message from Medicare briefly describes some, but not all, of the rights of patients under Medicare. It also lists the name and telephone number of the local Medicare PRO. *The PRO will investigate immediately if told that the patient is being discharged too early or lacks proper arrangements for posthospital nursing care.*

As soon as possible after being admitted into the hospital, patients or family members should ask to speak with a hospital discharge planner. This person may be a social worker or a nurse; he or she should meet with patients (or family members) and doctors to determine whether a patient should have a formal discharge plan. *Under federal law, patients have the right to have the hospital, upon request, formally evaluate their need for a discharge plan.*

- *Patients should not* assume *that a discharge plan is being prepared; if they don't request one, the hospital may decide they don't need one.*
- Preparing a discharge plan can take a few hours or a few days, depending on how busy the discharge planner is and how long patients are expected to stay in the hospital. *Although discharge planners are usually very busy, patients who need a discharge plan should not leave the hospital without one.*

The best discharge plan is developed with patients and, if possible, the people (spouses, siblings, adult children) who will care for them after they leave the hospital. Everyone involved with the care of patients leaving the hospital should arrange to be available at the same time and place to talk with the discharge planner, if he or she feels that would be helpful. Questions to raise when meeting with the discharge planner should be the same ones that were asked of the doctor—for example, the ease or difficulty with which the patient will be able to perform daily tasks after discharge from the hospital, and who or what will be available to assist the patient on a day-to-day basis.

Organizations such as the American Association of Retired Persons, the American Hospital Association, and the National Association for Home Care have developed complete guidelines for good discharge planning (see appendix 15 for guidelines written by the American Hospital Association).

When It's Time to Be Discharged

How a discharge is handled by both hospitals and patients is important. Often a doctor or hospital representative will tell patients—or family members, if patients are unable to understand—the date they are to be discharged. Because patients or family members might not be given a written notice, they should write down the name of the person who informs them of the discharge, the date and time of the conversation, and the date and time of the proposed discharge.

A hospital may bill Medicare patients who stay past the date of their scheduled discharge; at the customary rate, this fee could amount to $500 a day or more. *However, it is against federal law for a hospital to bill Medicare patients for services provided past their date of discharge unless the hospital has given patients a written notice of their discharge date and of their right to appeal the discharge.* It is also important to remember that under federal law,

- *it is the hospital's responsibility to give the patient a written discharge notice, not the patient's responsibility to ask for one;*

- *the hospital cannot bill the patient for care provided before the third day after giving the patient a written discharge notice (except, of course, for the annual Medicare hospital deductible); and*

- *the patient must receive the written discharge notice before he or she can appeal the proposed date to the PRO.*

By law, the hospital's written discharge notice must contain certain information and must not mislead patients into thinking that Medicare will pay only for a certain number of days in the hospital. Patients will be asked to sign a form indicating that they have received the written notice.

Model discharge notices for situations in which (a) the doctor and hospital agreed with the proposed discharge and (b) the PRO overruled the patient's objections to the proposed discharge can be found in appendix 17.

Receiving a Written Discharge Notice

Once patients receive a written discharge notice, they have until noon of the following working day (weekends are excluded) to decide whether they want to appeal it. There are several ways patients and their family members and friends can respond to the written notice.

First, they must decide if they want to fight the proposed discharge. In deciding this issue, patients should consider whether they are recovering as the doctor expected, whether the doctor and discharge planner have answered all their questions, and whether all their necessary posthospital care has been arranged for in the discharge plan.

If patients do not feel ready to be discharged, they should discuss it as soon as possible with their doctor and the discharge planner. *Remember, if patients and family members are assertive and have good reasons for objecting to the discharge date, they can be very effective in getting it changed without any formal or legal process.*

Some patients and family members have also gotten discharge dates changed with what might be considered extreme behavior. Family members have been known to refuse to leave a doctor's offices and have even threatened to barricade themselves in the patient's room until the doctor approved a necessary extra day or two. This sort of action may not be for everyone, but if the situation is severe, it might be worth a try as a last-resort tactic.

Another way of working with doctors and discharge planners to change a discharge date involves a useful tool known as a *quality screen,* a device developed by Medicare to identify possible cases of premature discharge. A quality screen poses a series of medical questions, the answers to which can help determine whether or not patients should be released.

One difficulty with using a quality screen is that patients would need to read and understand their medical records. Also, the screen asks for information that the doctor may not yet have at the time a patient is first notified of an impending discharge, such as the pulse or blood pressure of the patient twenty-four hours before discharge. Because quality screens were designed for use by doctors and nurses, the best way to use one is to make it available to one's doctor or discharge planner and to discuss it with them item by item (a copy of a Medicare quality screen can be found in appendix 18).

Remember, the quality screen is only a tool that can help patients or family members discuss the situation with a doctor or discharge planner. It is not the final word on whether or not patients should be discharged on a particular day.

Deciding Whether to Appeal a Discharge Decision to the Medicare Peer Review Organization

If the doctor and the discharge planner continue to believe that a patient should be released when the patient or the patient's family continue to disagree with that proposal, the case can be appealed to the PRO. Here, some simple dos and don'ts can help the patient or family member who is considering an appeal to the PRO.

- *Do call the PRO and appeal the decision if the doctor or discharge planner will not agree to discuss the case with the patient by the morning of the next working day after the patient has received a written discharge notice. The PRO must be called by noon of that day to ensure that patients will not to be charged by the hospital for extra days if the appeal is turned down.*

- *Do call the PRO and appeal if the discharge plan fails to address a patient's serious problem or personal need; if the hospital does not provide convincing evidence that the problem is resolved; or if the discharge plan does not meet the standards of the discharge-planning guidelines listed in appendix 15.*

- *Do call the PRO and appeal if the patient's medical condition is unstable. The Medicare quality screen can assist individuals in recognizing possible problems (see appendix 18). Remember, try to discuss these issues with the doctor before assuming they mean trouble.*

- *Don't call and appeal unless a patient's health and safety will be jeopardized by the proposed discharge. If the PRO decides that the appeal is unnecessary and that the patient or family member knew it was unnecessary when they appealed, the PRO may let the hospital bill the patient for any delay in the scheduled discharge.*

Appealing to the Peer Review Organization

Once patients have decided to appeal to the PRO, received a written discharge notice from the hospital, and called the PRO by noon of the working day after receiving the notice, the appeal process is set in motion.

The PRO representative, who is usually a registered nurse, will ask patients why they think the discharge date is unsafe or inappropriate. *Patients (or the people appealing a discharge) should be ready to answer these questions when the initial telephone call is made.* Thus, it's a good idea before making the call to compose a written list of reasons that the discharge is being appealed.

The PRO will try to complete its work quickly and decide on the appeal so that even if patients lose, they will still have time to leave without being billed for noncovered hospital days or services.

Losing an Appeal

Hospitals may bill a patient for staying beyond a proposed discharge date beginning with services provided on the third day after they have given the patient a written discharge notice and a notice of his or her right to appeal. *If, however, the PRO takes longer than two days to decide the appeal and the patient receives the answer on, or later than, the third day after receiving the written discharge notice, the patient is not liable for the cost of the continued stay until noon of the day after he or she has been informed that the appeal was turned down. This extra time at no charge is allowed only if (a) patients filed their appeals by noon of the working day after they received their written discharge notice and (b) the PRO believes that patients were unaware that their continued stay was not medically necessary.*

Oddly enough, Medicare instructions indicate that the PRO may decide that written discharge notices are sufficient evidence that patients knew that any further stay was not medically necessary; however, if patients agreed with the decision, they obviously would not be appealing it. Therefore, until the rules change, patients should be prepared to convince the PRO that their continued stay is medically necessary.

If patients lose their appeals, it is up to the hospitals to collect any money owed. *Patients or family members might be able to convince a hospital to waive the charges if they leave promptly after receiving notice of the PRO's decision.*

Lost appeals can also be taken a step further. Patients can ask the PRO for instructions on how to file a further appeal. This next level of appeal, however, will take too long for patients to remain in the hospital while it is being decided.

Discharge Dates and Supplemental Insurance

Patients should not assume that any "Medigap" or Medicare supplemental insurance policies they carry will pay for their continued stay in a hospital after the discharge date. Many patients wrongly believe that these policies will pay for any continued hospitalization that Medicare won't cover. In fact, all insurance companies use standards similar to those of Medicare to decide whether patients require additional hospitalization. Like Medicare, they will not cover days in the hospital that are not medically necessary. (For more information, see chapter 2.)

Hospital managers are aware that these supplemental policies will not cover continued hospitalization that is not medically necessary. They are reluctant to accept patients' offering them as evidence of upcoming payment because they generally find they cannot collect on these accounts. Patients should be prepared to pay if they stay long after their appeal is lost.

9

What to Do if You Have a Problem or Complaint

L IKE many chapters in this book, this one is worthwhile reading for residents of nursing homes and other facilities, their families, and their friends. When residents are unable to effectively resolve a complaint by themselves, it is often these other people who become involved in trying to correct the situation. Although this chapter primarily addresses problems and complaints that arise in nursing homes, it also discusses what to do when similar difficulties occur with or in other types of health care facilities.

The picture painted here of nursing homes is not always pretty, but it should be remembered that nursing homes range in quality from very poor to excellent, and not all nursing homes treat their residents in such a way that problems and complaints arise frequently. Whether a nursing home or other health care facility is good, bad, or in between, this chapter should give readers an idea of how to get their problems and complaints taken care of—which should make for a more comfortable stay in any health care facility.

Overview

It is probably unnecessary to say that the nursing home industry has been plagued by scandals, horror stories, abuses, and poor quality. These are not private problems, they have been splashed across everybody's television screens, newspapers, magazines, and—thankfully—government agendas.

Numerous studies and reports were commissioned that basically said the same thing: many nursing homes do not give appropriate or sufficient care to their residents, abuses do exist, and the systems of inspection and enforcement of standards are inadequate to solve the problem. The bad publicity surrounding nursing homes in the late 1960s and early 1970s resulted in many laws being passed, and supervisory programs started, at both federal and state levels of government. These laws and programs have dealt with quality-of-care issues, enforcement of standards, and nursing home complaint resolution. As a result, there has been considerable improvement in the quality of care that residents receive in nursing homes.

People who are residents of a nursing home—either for a temporary stay or for the rest of their lives—may face a lot of potential concerns, disputes, and problems. These problems can be trivial and are frequently a matter of residents preferring one thing over another. But they can also be serious and affect the quality of care residents receive or their basic rights. Problems can affect one particular resident, all residents, or even the entire population of nursing home residents in a single state.

Many of the problems experienced by nursing home residents, their families, and their friends are for the most part due to the nature of life in an institution. The typical nursing home is large (a hundred residents or more) and may have only one nurse's aide to take care of fifteen to twenty residents or more. As a result, nursing homes usually make decisions based on how they can most easily deal with a large number of residents and limited staff. These decisions include when and what meals are served, when residents must sleep, when residents must bathe, and so on. Nursing homes try to treat everyone the same, and have them follow the same routine, even though the residents themselves may be very, very different from one another. This is a real problem all by itself, because some residents may be much younger than others, some may be extremely confused while others are still mentally alert, and some may be severely disabled while others are quite physically fit.

Nursing home staffs usually have a heavy work load. Few facilities have a registered nurse on duty around the clock, and it is extremely rare to have a doctor present on a regular basis. Nursing homes also rarely have enough employees, and those they do have are usually underpaid, overworked, and too often lacking in the skills needed to do their jobs. Almost 80 percent of all direct resident care is provided by nursing assistants who have no medical background and often receive little if any training.

Recently, federal laws were passed that will require all nursing assistants in the approximately 15,000 federally certified facilities to complete a training program and skills evaluation.

Demands on the existing staff's time mean that a minimal amount of attention is paid to an individual resident's preferences and interests; his or her concerns can easily be overlooked, ignored, or denied. This situation may also mean poor-quality care and, worse, inappropriate or inadequate care. When this happens, it's important to remember the old saying "The squeaky wheel gets the grease." *Residents, their family members, and their friends have to be aware that the best way to receive needed care or desired attention is to ask for it and, if necessary, to insist on it.* If that fails, it may be necessary to take those concerns elsewhere to insist that they be handled.

The best way to ensure that residents receive appropriate care and attention is to make sure they are visited frequently by people outside the facility. Unfortunately, a great many residents do not have any visitors—many have outlived their families and friends—and may have to depend on the more formal mechanisms available to residents as a way to handle their complaints.

Nursing Homes and Other Types of Institutions

As mentioned earlier, the focus of this chapter is on residents of nursing homes, but many of the options are applicable to other health care institutions, such as hospitals and related settings, for example, board and care homes.

The phrase *nursing home* is used to cover almost all health care facilities that provide services related to health care in a residential or long-term care setting. They may be licensed or categorized as *Skilled Nursing Facilities (SNF)*, which provide extensive medical and skilled nursing services; *Intermediate Care Facilities (ICF)*, which provide some medical services; or other names, depending on the state in which they are located.

Board and care homes include a number of different types of facilities, such as those which provide "residential care," "domiciliary care," and "assisted-living care." These facilities don't provide medical care but do house many chronically ill or frail elderly people who may require supervision and assistance with things like bathing, grooming, and eating.

It is important that residents of a particular facility, as well as their family members, know and understand the category into which their facility falls. Wherever possible, this chapter will note which issues, options, and programs for resolving complaints apply to which type of facility.

Choosing a Facility

There are many fine nursing homes whose top priorities include high-quality medical care and respect for the wishes of residents. Careful shopping for a facility is probably the best way to avoid problems in the first place, but unfortunately, such shopping is not always possible.

Where shopping for a nursing home or other residential care facility is possible, family members (and, health permitting, the people who are going to reside in the nursing home) should do the following:

- Visit a number of facilities. Many federal, state, and local agencies and organizations publish excellent guides on how to select a nursing home. These guides offer sound, practical advice on what to look for while visiting a nursing home and what factors to consider in choosing a facility. A good place to start in obtaining a guide is the state department of health or aging (see appendix 34 for a list of addresses by state).
- Talk with residents, staff, and any available visitors.
- Request and examine the following information, most of which is public information, available on nursing homes:

  Medicare and Medicaid certification inspection or survey reports

  state licensure inspection reports

  "statement of deficiencies" reports

  "plans of correction" for problems

  complaint investigation reports (depending on state laws)

  cost reports showing what money is spent on food, nursing, and other key categories

This kind of information is available to people who request it from state medical and nursing licensure and certification agencies, which are generally part of a state's department of health (see appendix 34); some local Social Security offices; and the Health Care Financing Administration (HCFA). HCFA is preparing to publicly distribute information on facility deficiencies or problems noted during annual surveys.

- Speak with people who visit facilities on a regular basis, including those who serve as patient advocates. In particular, speak with representatives of state and local offices of the Long Term Care Ombudsman Program, which was established and authorized under the federal Older Americans Act to "investigate and resolve complaints made by or on behalf of older individuals who are residents of long-term care facilities." Ombudsman program offices should have copies of inspection reports or be able to direct people on how to get them (see appendix 19 for the addresses of ombudsman program offices by state).

- Speak with community advocacy and citizen action committees or organizations; they are often very knowledgeable about the nursing homes and other health care facilities in their area.

- For facilities that do not participate in the Medicare or Medicaid programs, check with the state licensure agency, usually located in the state department of health, or with the local groups mentioned above to see what information must by law be made available and where to get it (see appendix 34 for a listing of state addresses).

Obtaining information about individual facilities requires determination and some legwork, but it's worth it. If individuals know about deficiencies identified by federal, state, and local agencies, such knowledge can provide helpful clout when dealing with problems arising in a particular facility. Nonetheless, no matter how much information is available, residents may still encounter problems.

Types of Problems Occurring in Residential Facilities: Medical, Financial, and Personal

In many cases, the need to enter a nursing home may be a sudden event that doesn't allow residents or family members the time to visit and compare many facilities. A common problem is that many nursing homes don't have enough beds for the residents who want to fill them. This problem is worse for residents who must rely on Medicaid to pay their bills, since not all facilities accept Medicaid residents and many don't accept them very willingly (for more information, see chapters 3 and 10). Too often, people who need to find a nursing home in a hurry have to accept the first bed in the first institution that has an opening.

For the frail and ill elderly people who lack family and friends to assist them in looking for a nursing home—and who are therefore dependent on busy strangers to place them in a facility—this problem is particularly severe.

Yet even residents who have the funds to pay for their care, as well as those who rely on Medicaid, may still face problems or have complaints, even in the best of facilities. Although the types of problems that occur in a residential facility vary tremendously, the following indicates the kinds of medical, financial, and personal problems that may arise:

Medical problems

- *Inappropriate use of restraints and chemical sedatives.* Residents are "tied up" or "doped up" for the convenience of other residents and staff; restraints are too restrictive or are left on for too long; doctors don't order restraints for residents who need them; residents are restrained without doctor's orders.

- *Inappropriate medical care.* Residents develop decubitus ulcers (that is, bedsores and pressure sores); insufficient care is given for decubitus ulcers, severe bowel impactions, or extreme constipation; sudden and significant losses of weight are not acknowledged or treated; overdrugging occurs; potential drug reactions and interactions are not taken into account (for example, the impact of a particular dosage of a drug may differ greatly in a frail eighty-two-year-old woman and in a healthy sixty-year-old man); infections develop or spread; contractures (permanent shortenings of muscle, tendon, or tissue that produce deformity or distortion and are caused by lack of exercise, therapy, or movement) form and are inadequately treated.

- *Inattention.* Residents are left for too long on the toilet or in the bath, resulting in falls, broken bones, and other injuries; residents are left in one position too long or not turned often enough, resulting in bedsores and pressure sores; residents are left sitting or lying in their own feces or urine for extended periods of time.

- *Therapy.* Therapy, such as speech and physical therapy, is not provided regularly or is not provided at all.

Financial problems

- *Coverage of care and eligibility for care.* Residents are bumped from one level of care to another; residents are denied certain forms of therapy, care, or treatment; residents are denied coverage under Medicare or Medicaid.

- *Billing.* Residents and families are charged for services not received or are charged for services that should be paid by insurance or health care coverage (such as hospital gowns); families are not refunded for services not received if a resident is discharged or dies early in a month for which they have already paid.

- *Financial discrimination.* Residents who cannot pay for themselves but who are covered by Medicaid are discriminated against in admission procedures; residents are discriminated against in the types of care received and where it is received (such as in a separate "Medicaid wing" of the facility).

- *Mishandling of funds.* Facilities use inappropriate accounting, combine resident funds with facility funds, misuse funds, or occasionally steal funds from residents.

Personal problems

- *Food* (probably the most common category of complaints in long-term care facilities). Inappropriate diets are given to diabetic and hypoglycemic residents (or those with other conditions); food given lacks in choice, variety, or amount; food is unappetizing or cold when served; the facility is insensitive to patients' cultural and religious preferences.

- *Privacy.* Residents are exposed to view while on the toilet, in the bath, and being cared for in bed; residents experience lack of privacy while making personal calls or receiving personal visits from spouses, relatives, friends, and patient advocates.

- *Roommates.* Personality conflicts occur between roommates; mentally incompetent residents share rooms with alert residents; residents are put in rooms with abusive or noisy roommates.

- *Recreation and education.* Residents have inadequate recreational and educational activities—or none at all.

- *Abuse.* Residents suffer from physical, verbal, and mental abuse; they are yelled at or struck by staff or other residents; residents are ignored, belittled, and even sexually assaulted.

- *Transfers.* Residents are moved from one room to another or from one floor to another; residents are sometimes required to leave the facility as a form of retaliation.

- *Disability discrimination.* Residents are discriminated against in admission procedures when they require a great deal of care or could be disruptive to other residents and staff.

- *Racial discrimination.* Residents are discriminated against in admission and care procedures because of their race.

- *Theft* (a severe problem in many facilities). Residents have personal items, such as TVs, radios, clothes, and mementos, stolen from their rooms.

- *Patient rights.* Many resident rights, as stated in the "Federal Patients' Bill of Rights" and in numerous states' resident rights laws, are violated, as shown by this list of problems (see chapter 7 for more information). Residents are denied the right to share a room with their spouses; to meet with and participate in social, religious, and community group activities; to organize and participate in resident groups in the facility; and to express grievances about the facility's quality of care or lack of care provided.

What to Do When There Is a Problem

Problems are most easily pursued by people who have organized and factual information on the issue(s) of concern. The following checklist should provide some ideas about the kind of information that will be helpful in pursuing a complaint.

- How serious is the problem, how important is the problem, and how far is the person raising the complaint willing to go to get it resolved?

- Will complaining about the problem make future communications more difficult, cause retaliation against a resident, or result in the individual and resident concerned being labeled troublemakers?

- Decide what remedy or resolution would solve the problem, what would be an ideal solution, and what would be a reasonable one—know one's "bottom line."

- Be as specific as possible about the problem, determining what specific incident or issue is the subject of the complaint.

- Gather the facts, including the date and time the problem occurred (or did not occur, as in when a resident did not receive therapy), who was involved, if there were any witnesses who can corroborate what happened, why the incident was inappropriate, and any evidence or other information that can support the existence of a problem or basis for a complaint.

- Determine whether the matter was an isolated incident or has happened before to this particular resident or other residents; whether there is a pattern to the problem; whether it has been raised before (by oneself or others); whether anything was done or promised when the problem occurred at other times, and if so, what was done or promised; and whether the situation or a recurrence of it could adversely affect other residents.

- Determine why the situation occurred and whether there were any unusual or mitigating circumstances.

- Determine whether there is any legal basis for concern or any patient rights' that were violated, whether any terms of the resident's admission agreement were breached, whether a specific patient right was violated, whether the incident breached federal or state laws or facility policies, and whether it involved a potential criminal violation.

- Determine who would be helpful, or even necessary, in order to involve others in getting assistance.

- Identify who is the most appropriate person to resolve the problem, who is likely to resolve it most quickly, who is likely to find a long-term solution, and who is most likely to permit individuals to comfortably express their complaints (the answers to these questions do not all necessarily lead to the same person).

In other words, know as much as possible about the complaint or incident before bringing it to the attention of the authorities. It is particularly useful to know whether any legal, procedural, or contractual rights have been violated or are at stake. It is also important to decide how far one is willing to go in resolving the complaint.

The nursing home industry is large, complex, and highly regulated by policies, laws, and government agencies. There are a considerable number of things that can go wrong in nursing homes—and an equally large number of places to take a complaint.

Pursuing the Matter within the Facility

Most people wish to resolve their problems in the quickest manner possible, with the least amount of conflict. This can usually be done by expressing the grievance to facility employees—the staff person directly involved with the problem, the one who oversees it (such as the food services director, if the problem is about food, or the head nurse, regarding a care problem), or the facility's administrator. If this doesn't work, the next step may be to go to the facility's owners or governing board. If the facility is part of a large chain, there may be regional staff who can be approached. At least one national chain established its own toll-free telephone line for consumer complaints. Many facilities have specific grievance procedures; in most instances, it is appropriate to follow the suggested procedures until the problem is solved or the options in it exhausted. Then take the problem elsewhere.

It may be useful to work with a facility's social services staff member or social worker, if it has one. A new federal law will require that facilities with more than 120 beds employ at least one full-time social worker with at least a bachelor's degree or similar professional qualifications to either provide social services or direct residents and families in getting them (individual states may have a similar requirement). The role, training, and orientation of such workers are to solve problems, and they could be very helpful. They may not always be effective in tackling problems that are not the fault or responsibility of the nursing home (such as denials of eligibility, or coverage of medical devices under the state's Medicaid program). Another facility employee who can be of use is the activities director. Again, it all depends on the type of problem.

Many facilities have residents' councils that may participate in the grievance procedure. A council may be a place to express a problem and provide a way to solve it—particularly if the problem is experienced by other residents as well. It may be worthwhile finding out what kinds of authority and independence the council actually has, before taking the problem to its members. Positive signs are

its ability to meet without facility staff being present;

the presence of individuals from outside the facility who may participate at meetings and advise the council; and

the presence of individuals from outside the facility who may act as members of the council.

Other vehicles for resolving complaints are family councils, or committees made up of the families and friends of the facility's residents. Such councils can be very useful in dealing with resident problems. If a council is not reasonably independent or open to outside participation, there is a danger (as with some residents' councils) that it may be a time-consuming dead end for the airing of complaints.

Some facilities, usually good ones, have established community advisory committees made up of knowledgeable and concerned citizens from the local area. Again, depending on the makeup of the community council and the loyalty and dedication of its members, this group could be an effective ally in pursuing a grievance.

Federal law gives people the right to express grievances about treatment and care that are or are not received, without discrimination or retaliation for doing so. It also gives people the right to urge the facility to solve the problem, even if the problem has to do with the behavior of other residents. Further, the law insists on the rights of residents to organize and participate in resident councils, and of family members to meet in the facility with the families of other residents in the facility.

Complaints about Hospital Care

For complaints about hospital care, many of the same principles apply, especially with regard to speaking with appropriate staff, following the facility's suggested grievance procedures, and working one's way up the chain of command.

In addition, hospitals usually have patient advocate or patient relations offices that are intended to respond to patient-related problems and grievances. Growing numbers of hospitals are beginning to provide long-term care by buying or building nursing homes, converting empty hospital beds into nursing home beds, or converting whole sections of hospitals into nursing facilities. If the nursing home part of a hospital is not a separate facility, it is important to find out what state nursing home laws apply to it. The existence of a hospital patient relations office or staff could be helpful in dealing with problems related to the nursing home part of the operation.

When to Seek Outside Assistance to Resolve a Complaint

Sometimes, residents, friends, or family members voicing a complaint are dissatisfied with a facility's response to it. There also are times when taking grievances to facility personnel is not desirable or even appropriate. When either of these two circumstances arises, it is probably best to take the problem outside the facility.

Taking the complaint to the facility's management may not be wise if past complaints have been ignored or have been met with hostility. Doing so may also be inappropriate in situations in which the administrator, key personnel, or owners are the subject of the complaint—for example, when there is possible misuse of funds or suspected fraudulent billing, or when essential medications were not provided and harmful results occurred. In the latter case, if the matter were brought to the facility authorities, they could change resident medical charts to indicate that the medication had been given.

In matters that may involve a serious risk to the resident's health, safety, or welfare, or that may involve possible fraud or other criminal behavior, individuals must consider the possibility that discussing the matter with facility personnel could lead to destruction of evidence or some other form of cover-up. This is not to say that all nursing home personnel act in an unethical or criminal manner; however, for unscrupulous people, the prospect of civil fines, suspension or loss of professional licenses, suspension or termination from Medicare or Medicaid, facility closure or a forced sale, loss of business, civil litigation, criminal indictments, and related bad press and community relations can provide a powerful incentive to alter the facts.

Individuals raising problems should strongly consider seeking the advice of an attorney or other knowledgeable authority if the matter

is serious;

involves violations of the law;

is symptomatic of other serious problems; or

adversely affects the health, safety, or welfare of the resident involved (or has the potential to do so).

Typically, however, individuals are likely to seek outside assistance for the following reasons:

- To obtain objective guidance and advice.
- To find out more about the issue of concern and the options available to resolve it.
- To find a witness to meetings with facility administrators.
- To get moral support (for example, arguing with a tough, seasoned head nurse can be an intimidating experience).
- To mediate a dispute.

- To argue the case and negotiate on behalf of the resident or the person raising the complaint.

- If the issue reflects a violation of public law or regulation, is contrary to public policy, or should be noted in the public record to spur change or help ensure that fewer similar incidents happen in the future. (For example, persistent staff shortages not only violate the law and are harmful to all the facility's residents; they may also reflect significant underlying problems with the facility, its corporate management, and public policies regarding nurse shortages and inadequate reimbursements in public financing programs).

If the problem is a minor one—such as a resident's being cold and needing another blanket—then the options chosen should be simple ones, such as asking the nursing assistant or aide for a blanket. If the problem is serious and could affect a resident's health, safety, and rights; if it is a recurring problem; or if the specific problem is just a symptom of other major difficulties, then solving it might require some real creativity and persistence. Problem solving is often much easier when people other than residents are involved, for complaints expressed by residents are frequently dismissed as confusion, imagination, or hostility.

Options for seeking outside assistance are varied, and which one is used can be strongly influenced by the nature of the problem.

Where to Go for Outside Assistance

There are a wide variety of options, available in nearly every community, to help people resolve complaints. The subject and severity of the complaint will often determine what measures are appropriate. In some cases, a variety of actions may be necessary to appropriately resolve a complaint. The range of actions taken is limited only by the determination, resources, and creativity of the person trying to solve the problem. The following list does not include all the options that may be available in a specific community, but it does give ideas of where to go for assistance.

Private resources
- Facility administration, board of directors, or owners, if necessary.
- Facility-based grievance committees, including residents' councils and family councils.

- Nursing home industry-based grievance mechanisms.

- Private attorneys for pro bono or free services, or attorneys paid by the hour or on a contingency-fee basis. Often used in malpractice and personal injury cases, *contingency fees* mean that lawyers don't charge the client unless they win the case; if they do win the case, they are paid a predetermined percentage of the settlement.

- Small-claims courts.

- Unions representing facility personnel.

- The media. This is probably the option that facilities fear most, as negative stories in newspapers, in magazines, and on television can greatly harm their reputations and, as a result, their profits. (For more information, see chapter 15.)

Public resources

- Ombudsman programs (for more information, see the next section, entitled "The Long Term Care Ombudsman Program," and see appendix 19 for a list of ombudsman program offices).

- Citizen or community-based advocacy programs, typically operating under such names as the Bay Area Advocates for Nursing Home Reform (in San Francisco) and Kansans for the Improvement of Nursing Homes.

- State and local organizations and agencies that deal with issues affecting older Americans, such as the Gray Panthers, the Older Women's League, and the local Area Agency on Aging. The State Unit on Aging (see appendix 20) can also direct interested individuals to their nearest resources.

- State nursing home licensure and certification officials, who have responsibilities for licensing, certifying, and regulating nursing homes, as well as for investigating problems that arise in them (see appendix 34 for addresses).

- Officials with licensure and certification responsibilities over various professionals who provide care in nursing homes, such as nursing home administrators, doctors, hospitals, nurses, nursing assistants, psychologists, and therapists (check with the licensing and certification division or the consumer affairs department of the area agency on aging for this information).

- Federally funded Peer Review Organizations (PROs) that can evaluate care being provided in a facility (see appendix 16 for a list of state addresses).

- Law enforcement agencies, such as the police, district attorneys, and state offices of the attorney general (including their Medicaid fraud and abuse divisions).

- The U.S. Department of Health and Human Services' Office of the Inspector General and Office of Civil Rights, located in Washington, D.C.

- State civil rights investigative authorities.

- Publicly funded legal aid offices, including legal programs for the elderly—often funded by the Older Americans Act. (To find low-cost legal aid, contact the State Unit on Aging, whose addresses are listed in appendix 20, and talk to the legal services developer.) Also, almost every state has an Information and Referral (I&R) hot line for the elderly or the general public in need of services; local senior citizens' centers should have the telephone number of this resource.

- Judges or other officials, such as public guardians, who have authority over guardianship and conservatorship proceedings and practices (it is strongly recommended that interested individuals consult with an ombudsman or lawyer in these instances).

- State or local consumer protection agencies (look under "Consumer Protection" or "Consumer Affairs" in the telephone directory, or check with the Area Agency on Aging or the State Unit on Aging, whose addresses are listed in appendix 20).

- State and local mediation and dispute resolution agencies (again, check with the Area Agency on Aging or the State Unit on Aging).

- Special state or local commissions and investigative groups, particularly those with experience in examining nursing home and other elder-individual issues (to find these groups, check with the area ombudsman; addresses are listed in appendix 19).

- Officials in state or local welfare agencies and protective services agencies with responsibility for investigating elder-abuse complaints. (Check "Social Services Agencies" under the "State Agencies" or "County Agencies" section of the telephone directory. Or ask the area ombudsman; see appendix 19 for addresses.)

- Financing sources for nursing home coverage, such as insurance companies, Medicare intermediaries, and state Medicaid agencies (check with the area ombudsman for these listings).

- Local agencies and organizations that place or help to place elderly people into long-term care facilities. These would include home health care agencies, visiting nurse associations, family services agencies, hospital discharge planners, and county welfare and protective services workers (again, check with the area ombudsman for these listings).

- Federal, state, and local elected officials and legislative committees such as the committees on aging in the U.S. Senate and House of Representatives and their state equivalents.

The Long Term Care Ombudsman Program

One of the best and most widely available resources to call upon when faced with a problem in a nursing home is the Long Term Care Ombudsman Program (LTCOP). Under the Older Americans Act, each state is required to have an ombudsman program (see appendix 19 for addresses of each state's program).

The program is free of charge. It is responsible for investigating and resolving complaints made by or on behalf of older individuals who are residents of long-term care facilities. It also permits the ombudsmen themselves to raise concerns or initiate complaints on behalf of residents. Specifically, the problems they investigate are those which may adversely affect the health, safety, welfare, or rights of residents relating to the action, inaction, or decisions of (a) providers of long-term care or their representatives, (b) long-term care services, (c) social services agencies, or (d) public agencies. Examples of problems ombudsmen would normally investigate include the following:

- Denial of home health care or adult day care that would allow residents to move out of the nursing home into a less restrictive setting.

- Failure of a nursing home licensing agency to fully or quickly investigate problems in a facility or to only minimally penalize them when stronger sanctions would seem more appropriate.

- Failure of guardians to provide appropriate resources or clothing to their wards in nursing homes.

- A Medicaid agency determination that residents are not eligible for coverage or should be moved out of a facility.

- A Medicaid agency denial of Skilled Nursing Facility (SNF) coverage.

- Inappropriate placement of residents by a community social services agency, such as into a facility with a poor record or into one that is too restrictive for the particular needs of the residents in question.

The program was designed to provide a way to respond to residents' complaints, both on an individual basis and as a way to bring about changes in the entire nursing home system. Many states have very strong programs, with solid state laws governing them. *The programs are generally statewide, and their services should be available to residents in all nursing homes and in certain board and care or residential facilities.*

The state ombudsman program is usually a part of the State Unit on Aging, often known as the state department or Agency on Aging. Some states, however, have the program located elsewhere.

Most state ombudsman programs have local program offices, known as substate programs. Most of the activity related to investigating and solving complaints is done at the substate level. There are now nearly seven hundred substate programs throughout the country, located in such places as legal services offices, area agencies on aging, social services agencies, community nursing home reform groups, county departments, and various senior citizens' organizations. To find the nearest substate ombudsman office, contact the state ombudsman program office (see appendix 19 for addresses); nursing homes should also be able to provide this information.

Ombudsmen can be invited by residents to visit a facility, investigate a particular complaint, or speak at a residents' or family council meeting. Most ombudsmen programs, particularly the substate ones, depend on volunteers to visit facilities and investigate complaints. Volunteer ombudsmen are usually older individuals with diverse backgrounds who are trained before they begin responding to problems.

Ombudsmen frequently get to know local facilities and their personnel, residents, family members, and other visitors. This kind of familiarity often makes residents and family members feel easier about discussing problems or filing complaints. The regular presence of the ombudsman in a facility is also important because most residents would be reluctant to use the facility's pay phone—often located by the nurse's station—to make a long-distance or even a toll-free call to the state's nursing home regulatory agency or the attorney general's office.

Ombudsmen are allowed to see residents' medical and social records, if they receive written permission from residents or their legal guardians. Many states already have strong laws to enforce the ombudsman's right to see such records.

Ombudsmen rarely have any power to punish facilities—they cannot levy fines, suspend Medicaid funds, issue citations, or otherwise force actions to be taken. For the most part, ombudsmen must rely on their knowledge, credibility, persistence, negotiating skills, and other tactics to solve a problem or, if necessary, bring it to the public's attention.

Ombudsmen are also effective in advising residents and other concerned individuals on the most appropriate and desirable strategy to solve a problem. They are knowledgeable about the realities, limitations, and consequences of taking a particular problem to any of the public and private resources listed earlier in this chapter.

The ombudsman's only purpose is to work on behalf of the rights and interests of current and potential nursing home residents. Ombudsmen are not dependent on or under the authority of any other groups having conflicting interests. They will also not reveal the identity of people making complaints unless they receive written permission to do so (or are so ordered by a court).

It is against the law for nursing homes to retaliate or punish residents or employees who file complaints or provide information to an ombudsman. Some states have passed other laws involving ombudsmen, including requiring them to act as witnesses when residents sell or transfer property at less than fair market value to anyone related to the nursing home, or when residents write a living will (see appendix 4 for a checklist of state laws regarding living wills). In Minnesota and California, for example, ombudsmen may provide services to hospital patients under certain conditions.

Ombudsman programs, particularly at the substate level, are often understaffed and underfunded. Ombudsman services are available to people who need them, however, and ombudsmen are obligated to respond to complaints. People have a right to go to ombudsmen for their services and to expect them to act quickly and effectively. Once again, the old saying "the squeaky wheel gets the grease" may come in handy. Insist on their assistance.

While the ombudsman program is certainly not the only place to go for help, it's often a good place to start. If ombudsmen can't help directly, they can offer reliable advice and guidance on where to go next or concurrently. Ombudsmen act as brokers of problems, leading concerned individuals everywhere they need to go to correct a situation. If indi-

viduals are going to go to only one place to make a complaint, it ought to be the ombuds-man program or the state licensing authority (see appendixes 19 and 34 for state addresses for these groups).

Regulatory and Licensure Agencies for Nursing Homes

In each state are a variety of state regulatory and licensure agencies and boards that address concerns related to health care. The most widely known among them is the state health department's licensure and certification agency (or division). Another commonly used group, the Peer Review Organization (PRO), is also responsible for examining complaints about quality of care provided to Medicare patients in nursing homes (for more information on PROs, see chapter 8).

The federal government and state governments are both responsible for making sure that nursing homes comply with their requirements and for overseeing nursing home quality. States are also responsible for licensing nursing homes. Nursing homes are inspected at least once every fifteen months, more often if the state believes circumstances warrant it. These inspection surveys specifically include interviews with residents and others to elicit their comments about their care and treatment in the facility.

More typically, however, complaints would be made directly to the regulatory agency when an incident occurs (rather than waiting for the inspection). The actual procedures used to investigate complaints vary from state to state. To find out the procedures for a particular state, interested individuals can consult the area ombudsman. Also, each nursing home should have posted information about the filing of complaints with the licensing and certification agency.

As previously stated, only complaints that involve violations of federal and state laws and standards governing nursing home care—particularly those which have adversely affected or may adversely affect, the health, safety, welfare, and rights of residents—are appropriately brought before the state's nursing home regulatory agency. These regulatory and licensing agencies can penalize nursing homes in a variety of ways, such as removing a facility's license to operate or decertifying a facility from participating in Medicare and Medicaid programs. Such penalties are not often invoked, however, as they are severe, and too many individuals need nursing home beds to easily close a facility. Instead, less severe penalties, such as levying fines or requiring new management of a facility, may be used. (See appendix 34 for a list of state medical and nursing licensure agencies.)

Regulatory and Licensure Agencies for Other Health Care Facilities

In addition to regulating nursing homes, a wide range of other facilities related to health care are regulated by the states or are required to meet federal and/or state standards. Hospitals are typically licensed by the state's health department— usually the same entity that licenses nursing homes.

As mentioned earlier, long-term care facilities for the elderly and disabled that do not provide health or medical services are generally known as board and care homes. Some states regulate these homes, and some do not. Some states also regulate clinical laboratories that conduct a wide variety of tests, while others provide minimal oversight at best.

Increasing numbers of states are not only licensing home health care agencies but also taking seriously the need to investigate problems associated with this kind of care. Nevertheless, when problems arise with these types of facilities and others, it is essential to find out who has reponsibility for overseeing quality in them and what the appropriate procedures are for filing complaints. Again, the area ombudsman should be helpful in this regard.

Regulatory and Licensure Agencies for Health Care Professsionals

States provide for licensure of a wide variety of professionals, a number of whom may interact with nursing home residents. These include, but are not limited to, nursing home administrators, nurses, doctors, pharmacists, social workers, psychiatrists, psychologists, and physical therapists. Inevitably, certain types of problems that arise in the nursing home (or hospital or health care setting) will involve questions about the quality of care or treatment by various health care professionals.

For example, if a nursing home resident develops severe decubitus ulcers (bedsores) that become infected, it raises questions not only about the nursing home's compliance with federal and state standards but also about the competence or professionalism of the following: the nursing home administrator (for not selecting appropriate staff or for not taking appropriate action if the problem is brought to his or her attention), the facility's medical director and/or the resident's doctor (for not adequately supervising the care or treatment of the resident), the nursing staff (for allowing the sores to develop and become infected and possibly for not quickly alerting the doctor to the problem), and the nursing assistants or aides (for possibly failing to turn the resident appropriately or provide other preventive measures, or for failing to bring the problem to the attention of other staff on a timely basis). Depending on the circumstances, each of these professionals could merit a complaint about the care given.

Generally, the agencies that license and regulate health care professionals have few ways to penalize professionals short of suspending or revoking their licenses, reprimanding professionals for the public record, and making their licenses conditional. Few of these agencies have the staffing or resources to conduct extensive investigations, and most people do not file complaints with them anyway. Even when complaints are filed, many of these agencies are run by professionals who are reluctant to police their own.

Nonetheless, a threat to the license of an administrator, doctor, nurse, or other health care professional is a serious threat to his or her professional standing and economic well-being. Federal law requires that nursing home administrators meet certain standards under Medicare and Medicaid. As a result, each state has a licensure agency for nursing home administrators (see appendix 34 for a list of addresses). Typically, complaints can be brought to the attention of these agencies for investigation and the imposition of standards, as appropriate.

Getting Help from Law Enforcement Agencies

The role that law enforcement agencies can play in dealing with certain nursing home or other complaints related to health care can be considerable. Local police can, and should, be brought in anytime there is a potential violation of criminal law. Although theft of residents' personal goods is a large problem in some nursing homes, the police are rarely brought in to investigate such events. Nursing home personnel often hate the idea of police in their facilities, but police are the people best equipped to investigate theft and other criminal acts. The mere presence of police can also act as a deterrent for future acts of theft. Assaults on residents and other forms of physical abuse against residents are criminal acts, and it is certainly appropriate to involve police in these matters.

District attorneys have an important role to play in investigating and prosecuting criminal acts. It is important to remember that district attorneys do more than address traditional criminal acts (such as theft, assault, and possible drug misuse by facility personnel). They also address violations of civil law, including enforcing consumer protection laws and fair business practices statutes. Facility practices that limit admissions to a nursing home, price-fixing, billing fraud, overcharging for services, and many other practices could be matters that a local district attorney's office would be interested in investigating.

At the state level, the attorney general can and should play an important role in taking on a wide variety of matters related to nursing homes, including situations that may have broad or statewide implications. Also, under federal law, states establish Medicaid fraud and abuse units to investigate and prosecute a range of activities that can occur in nursing homes (they can also investigate Medicaid providers, such as doctors, nurses, hospitals, and other groups). These units would investigate, for example, fraudulent billing of families and the government, as well as instances in which nursing homes seek or receive additional amounts in the form of ''donations'' or ''gifts'' to consider individuals for admission.

Getting Help from Lawyers and the Courts

Residents and their families can also seek the assistance of lawyers. To find low-cost legal aid, interested individuals should contact the legal services developer within the State Unit on Aging (see appendix 20 for addresses). Also, nearly all states have an Information and Referral (I&R) hot line for the elderly or for the general population in need of services; local senior citizens' centers should have the telephone number of this resource.

The most typical types of cases that legal services programs deal with are public entitlement cases involving disputes and problems concerning Medicare and Medicaid eligibility and coverage (for more information, see chapter 10). Other cases, more rarely, may involve personal injury and malpractice, as well as class action suits.

Small-claims courts are another option to pursue. These courts are inexpensive, conduct cases quite quickly, and do not use lawyers to represent either side. They are primarily used to settle disputes involving limited amounts of money, and the disputes are settled by the presiding judge (juries are not involved). These courts are especially effective in recovering the cost of residents' personal items that have been stolen or lost in a facility, but they can also be useful in recovering funds from billing disputes and other problems.

Other Avenues to Pursue

Other avenues to pursue in resolving problems and complaints are outlined below.

- Community advocacy and consumer organizations that focus on nursing homes and other matters related to senior citizens can be of great help. Each state and region should have at least one group that can either directly assist or make referrals to other appropriate bodies.

- Federal, state, and local government agencies that may be able to assist with certain types of problems are too numerous and diverse to discuss here. When consulting knowledgeable individuals about particular problems, ask what agencies might be useful to involve.

- Mediation and arbitration services are also a possibility for resolving complaints. These programs typically use an objective third party to try to help resolve disputes. The mediator, or arbitrator, will usually propose a settlement that may or may not (depending on the kind of mediation) be accepted by either or both individuals or groups involved in the dispute.

- Each state has a protection and advocacy system designed to protect the developmentally disabled and the mentally ill. Such programs typically operate at the state level and respond to complaints made by or on behalf of their constituencies, many of whom reside in nursing homes and other long-term care facilities. A great many nursing home residents have significant mental health problems and therefore qualify for these services. Protection and advocacy groups generally address problems that affect many of their clients, rather than solve individual problems.

- Finally, the media and elected officials are two other options that may be useful in resolving disputes. For more information see chapter 15.

10

The Medicare/Medicaid Maze

I T would be impossible to provide a clear understanding of everything that Medicare and Medicaid programs do and do not pay for in the confines of this chapter. Entire books have been written to explain the details of these programs' eligibility and reimbursement policies. To answer specific questions about specific claims, interested individuals will have to do some necessary extra reading and work on the telephone. This chapter has a different purpose—to outline the most basic services and intentions of each program and, more important, to discuss where to go for help when there is a problem.

Several excellent books have formed the basis for much of the information that follows. Specifically, they are *Understanding Alzheimer's Disease: What It Is, How to Cope with It, Future Directions,* by Miriam Aronson, and *Losing a Million Minds: Confronting the Tragedy of Alzheimer's Disease and Other Dementias,* by the Office of Technology Assessment. Highly recommended to interested individuals, both works are listed in the "Additional Reading" section at the back of this book, as are other publications that are useful aids in explaining the rules and regulations of Medicare and Medicaid. In addition more information on these programs can be found in chapters 2 and 3.

Overview

Anytime a bureaucracy as large as Medicare or Medicaid is responsible for matching millions of claims against an enormous number of rules and regulations, there's bound to be trouble. And while few people enjoy the challenge of "fighting City Hall" when healthy, most people really dislike doing so when ill. Often, the process of applying for eligibility or of arguing over a denied claim can seem like an endless series of false starts, closed doors, and mysterious answers. In short, it seems like a maze with no directions about how to get out.

Medicare and Medicaid both have a vast number of restrictions, limitations, and requirements that must be met before any medical costs are paid or reimbursed. To start with, there are complex eligibility requirements and puzzling service coverages. Public misconceptions about each program and the sometimes inept and often overworked employees who work in them exacerbate the situation.

Bluntly put, the multiple rules and regulations can be as confusing to Medicare and Medicaid employees—who often misinterpret them and unfairly deny people their benefits—as they are to applicants and beneficiaries. To make matters worse, program administrators have no real reason to grant claims or applications, because they are often penalized for giving benefits to ineligible individuals but are not penalized for denying benefits to eligible ones.

Key Components of the Maze

When faced with the problem of looking for available benefits, it is helpful to understand what programs exist, who funds or administers them, what they are meant to do, and a few other key words or phrases that can help individuals make order out of chaos:

Medicare. A government-funded health insurance program for individuals usually over the age of sixty-five or those who have been entitled to Social Security disability benefits for twenty-four months. It pays for certain medical care costs of the people who are eligible to receive it, but it usually does not pay for long-term care or nursing home services. Eligibility is administered through the Social Security Administration; services and reimbursement issues are handled by the Health Care Financing Administration of the U.S. Department of Health and Human Services (HHS).

Medicaid. A federal- and state-funded social welfare program that pays for certain medical care costs of the people who are eligible to receive it. In most states, eligible individuals include elderly persons who either receive Supplemental Security Income (SSI) or need nursing home care. Medicaid will often pay for long-term care or nursing home services.

General Public Assistance (GPA), general assistance or *home relief.* A social welfare program funded only by states or counties, not by the federal government. It gives financial aid to indigents, that is, poor people who have no other income.

Social Security Disability Income (SSDI). A social insurance program that provides financial assistance to people who, because of a physical or mental disability, can no longer work. It is administered by the Social Security Administration of HHS.

Supplemental Security Income (SSI). A social welfare program that provides financial aid to poor people over the age of sixty-five and those who are blind or totally and permanently disabled. This program is also administered by the Social Security Administration of HHS.

Entitlement program. Any program that provides financial or other kinds of assistance to all persons who meet specific eligibility requirements.

Health care providers. Any persons or organizations that provide health care— doctors, hospitals, home care services, "meals on wheels," and so on. The services they provide may or may not be covered by entitlement programs, depending on specific program rules and regulations.

Benefits. The money paid by an entitlement program to reimburse patients or pay doctors, hospitals, or other health care providers.

Beneficiary or recipient. A person who is eligible for the benefits paid by any of the entitlement programs.

Claim. The bill for the medical care or service that the beneficiary wants reimbursed by an entitlement program.

Case manager. An individual whose job it is to manage, plan for, and arrange continuing health care services for ill individuals. Case managers are employed by hospitals, social service agencies, local health departments, and other agencies and occasionally by families directly.

Food stamp program. A social welfare program for low-income persons that provides vouchers redeemable for food items at grocery stores. The program is administered by the U.S. Department of Agriculture through state or county welfare offices.

How to Get Through the Maze

As is the case with most mazes, people who persist despite the dead ends will eventually get through. Some initial frustrations can be avoided by doing a little background research. Choosing the appropriate entitlement program is one way to start. When evaluating any of the entitlement programs listed on page 137, it is important to ask a series of questions to find out who would be eligible in the first place:

- Who is eligible for the program?

- What are the requirements for eligibility?

- What benefits do recipients receive?

- Does the program make cash payments, offer services, or reimburse health care providers?

- What government agencies pay the benefits to recipients?

- Is the program administered by the federal, state, or county government or by some other group?

- What are the program's requirements for continued eligibility?

All entitlement programs have printed information about who is eligible. To receive this information, individuals should contact the programs themselves. The district Social Security Administration office should have information on SSI, SSDI, and Medicare. Other program information should be available through the county welfare agency. Look under the ''Government'' section of the telephone directory.

Once individuals know which program or programs they might be eligible for, the next step is to apply. *If turned down, individuals should not automatically assume they are ineligible.* Remember, all mazes have a way out; finding it requires a little persistence, determination, and stubbornness. Sadly, elderly ill people often don't have the energy to keep battling a bureaucracy and may have to depend on the efforts of a social worker or case manager. Those with family members or friends may be lucky enough to have someone who is willing to do it for them. Whoever does the work, the reward for making a successful effort can be substantial and worth all the effort involved.

Many applicants for benefits are initially turned down, even if they deserve the benefits.

A recent study of federal welfare benefits showed that of the people who are wrongfully turned down, less than 5 percent ever challenge the denial. In light of rising costs, increased claims, and tighter budgets, there is no motivation for these programs to initially grant benefits. If people successfully appeal negative decisions, then the agency only ends up giving out money it was required by law to pay in the first place. If negative claims are not appealed, the agency saves money.

Persons denied eligibility can appeal the decision within the program itself. Each program has set procedures for this, as well as numerous employees who generally do nothing but review appeals. Usually, the notice sent to individuals informing them that they have been denied eligibility will include information on how to appeal the decision.

A skilled guide is always useful in an appeal. *Happily, there are many ways individuals and their family members can get assistance in pursuing or appealing claims that are wrongfully denied:*

- *The Older Americans Act funds legal services programs for the elderly.*

- *The Legal Services Corporation funds legal services programs for the poor.*

- *Some lawyers will pursue such claims for less than their regular fee.*

- *Some legal clinics or programs associated with law schools may also provide such services for little or no cost.*

There are several ways to locate low-cost legal help. Interested individuals can contact the State Unit on Aging (see appendix 20 for addresses); the legal services developer there should be able to recommend where to get assistance. Also, almost all states have an Information and Referral (I&R) hot line for older people or for the general public in need of services; local senior citizens' centers should have the area INR telephone number. Finally, each state's legal system has a bar association whose referral service can provide this information as well.

Thumbnail Sketches of Each Program and How They Work

As previously mentioned, each program has its own criteria for determining eligibility, along with its own set of procedures for individuals to appeal either a refusal of eligibility or a denied claim. Thumbnail sketches of the programs and their procedures are provided below.

Social Security Disability Income (SSDI)

This social insurance program is designed to protect wage earners who can no longer be gainfully employed. It is the major program available to people under the age of sixty-two who are disabled by dementia (such as those who have Alzheimer's disease). Applicants must have worked a certain amount of time before becoming disabled and must not wait too long before applying for disability benefits after becoming disabled. Applicants must also be prevented from being gainfully employed because of a "medically determinable physical or mental impairment" that can be expected to last for at least a year.

If turned down after reviewing all the eligibility requirements and making an application, individuals have the options listed below. *First, though, they should remember that many applicants for SSDI benefits are turned down the first time they apply. Benefits may never be granted unless the applicant*

files a request for reconsideration and, if that also denies eligibility,

requests a hearing before an administrative law judge and, if that also yields the same negative result,

requests an Appeals Council review and, if that is unfavorable,

petitions for judicial review.

A *reconsideration* consists of a review of existing paperwork and applications by someone not previously involved in denying eligibility. During the reconsideration, applicants can submit additional medical documentation to support their cases.

The *hearing* provides another opportunity for someone not previously involved in denying eligibility to review appealed cases. Oral and written testimony can be presented at this stage of the appeals process, and the applicants can be assisted by family members, friends, lawyers, or paralegals.

The *Appeals Council* and the *judicial review* are two more levels of review. They allow less participation by applicants and other interested individuals.

It is important to note that about half of all denials are overturned, and benefits granted, at the administrative hearings stage. However, less than 10 percent of the people denied benefits at the earlier stages ever appeal in the first place.

Medicare

Since Medicare almost automatically covers individuals age sixty-five and older, there are fewer problems with people being refused eligibility (coverage often depends on an individual's eligibility for Social Security old-age and disability benefits). Once eligible for Medicare, a beneficiary is eligible for benefits under Parts A and B of the program. (For more information on Medicare, see appendix 1.)

- Part A's major benefit is that it pays for all hospitalization costs of Medicare beneficiaries after the patient pays a single annual deductible ($560 in 1989). In 1989, under the recently passed congressional catastrophic care bill, a supplemental premium is imposed based on a beneficiary's federal income tax liability, up to $800 per enrollee. Under very limited circumstances, Part A benefits will also pay part of the cost for a patient to stay in a Skilled Nursing Facility (SNF), a special nursing home that provides a substantial amount of medical care, for up to 150 days. The SNF coinsurance amount a patient is required to pay is 20 percent of the nationwide average per-day cost for eight days ($25.50 a day in 1989). (For more information on using Medicare to cover SNF costs, see chapter 3 and appendix 1.)

  Under certain conditions, Part A also pays for home health care, including physical and speech therapy, and hospice care for terminally ill beneficiaries.

- Part B's major benefit is that it pays for 80 percent of the approved fee for doctors' services. If a doctor charges more than the amount set aside by Medicare for the service, the beneficiary must pay the remaining 20 percent of the approved fee and the rest of the full amount charged by the doctor. However, Medicare will pay for covered Part B expenses after the first $1,370 of out-of-pocket costs in 1990. The monthly premium for Part B is $27.90 in 1989 and will increase thereafter.

  Part B also covers outpatient hospital services, home health visits under certain conditions, and other medical and health services, such as ambulance transportation, home dialysis equipment, independent laboratory tests, and oral surgery.

Neither Part A nor Part B covers custodial (general) nursing home care, personal care, day care, respite service (except for eighty hours per year), or less specialized nursing care. Medicare beneficiaries do, however, have the opportunity to appeal denials of other specific claims in Part A or Part B. If claims are denied and then appealed, many beneficiaries do end up receiving coverage for at least a portion of the service (or bill) that was originally denied. Once again, all it takes is determination.

An individual who disagrees with a decision regarding his or her eligibility for Medicare has the same appeal rights as under the SSDI program. These rights include the opportunity for an appeal to an administrative law judge (ALJ) and the right to judicial review of an ALJ decision.

A beneficiary who disagrees with a denial, in whole or in part, of a claim submitted under Part A of Medicare can request reconsideration by the fiscal intermediary. If the amount in question is $100 or more, the beneficiary is entitled to a hearing before an ALJ. The beneficiary can also seek judicial review of the ALJ's decision, if the amount in question is $1,000 or more.

A beneficiary who disagrees with a denial, in whole or in part, of a claim submitted under Part B of Medicare can request reconsideration by the carrier. If the amount in controversy is $500 or more, the beneficiary is entitled to a hearing before an ALJ. The beneficiary can also seek judicial review of the ALJ's decision if the amount in controversy is $1,000 or more.

It is important to refer to the Medicare denial notices for each claim, as they will indicate a time limit for appealing decisions. These time limits are ordinarily strictly enforced.

Medicaid

Most people become eligible for Medicaid in one of three ways. First, many people establish eligibility for Medicaid through receipt of Supplemental Security Income (SSI) benefits. Another group of people establish eligibility when they enter a nursing home and have insufficient income and resources to pay for their costs of care. These first two classes of recipients are referred to as *mandatory* and *optional categorically needy,* respectively.

The third group of recipients is referred to as the *medically needy.* Approximately two-thirds of the states have a program for the medically needy that assists at least some persons whose high medical care costs offset a higher than usual amount of allowable income. Resources may still not ordinarily exceed approximately $2,000.

Being determined eligible for Medicaid does not mean that the services people need are covered under each state's program. States have wide discretion in deciding which services will be reimbursed. Most states provide a mix of inpatient and outpatient services, however, including hospital care, nursing home care, physician services, and prescribed drugs.

It is nearly impossible to give any hard-and-fast rules about appealing eligibility and services under Medicaid, because each state runs its own program and has its own rules. There are some common characteristics, however, since all states must comply with federal law.

Medicaid recipients have a right to appeal decisions by requesting an administrative hearing (called a *fair hearing*). This hearing is requested from the agency administering the Medicaid program in that state. Ordinarily, a decision must be rendered within ninety days of the date of the request for a hearing. Dissatisfied recipients may then seek further administrative review, in some states, or may seek judicial review.

Several years ago, statistics showed that fewer than 5 percent of all recipients appealed to Medicaid in cases in which their coverage was wrongfully withheld, ended, or denied. Sadly, a state can be penalized by the federal government for paying too much or for paying for an uncovered service but not for wrongfully paying too little or denying service in the first place. The system does not provide any motivation for Medicaid program employees to grant benefits.

When Someone Can No Longer Make Decisions

11

Competence and Incompetence
What They Mean

Overview

People must make decisions almost from the time they are born. They start out simply—what game to play, what to eat for lunch, what to wear—and then progress to much harder decisions about marriage, career, and finances. The one constant that ties all these things together is that they are decisions that have to be made. Normally, people are able to make their own decisions, choosing the personal or professional options that make them happiest. But what happens when people are no longer able to make decisions? And who is qualified to decide that people can no longer make decisions?

These are not simple questions. And in most cases, there are no simple answers. Adult children may have witnessed their parents' increased senility or inability to understand decisions that need to be made. They may instinctively know that their parents are incapable of making decisions, but that does not mean the adult children have an instant legal right to make decisions for them (in some states, certain family members are given an automatic right to make certain medical decisions for incompetent relatives; for more information, see chapter 14). Besides, who is to say that the parents aren't still able to make some decisions? Or that they are able to make decisions but in a less sophisticated manner than their children expect? Also, people are often less willing to accept the same "silly" or "foolish" decision from elderly people that they would from younger adults. The problem is that elderly people are faced with some of the most difficult decisions of all, decisions of life and death, and they need to be competent to make those decisions—or have guardians or other representatives to make decisions for them.

Competence and incompetence are legal terms for someone's ability—or inability—to make informed, rational decisions. Elderly individuals are more likely than the rest of the adult population to have difficulty making decisions. They may become so because of depression, grief, loneliness, the effects of prescribed drugs or pain-killers, or a particular disease. *Dementia,* a medical term for the slow loss of brain function that gradually makes people incompetent, affects up to 10 percent of people over age sixty-five, and 20 percent of people over age eighty. Dementia can be caused by more than seventy illnesses (the most common of which is Alzheimer's disease); its symptoms include memory loss, inability to remember words, inability to care for oneself, personality and behavioral changes, and a confusion over time and place. There is no cure for Alzheimer's disease or for some other illnesses that cause dementia, and often no available drugs that work without making patients confused and incompetent. Despite that, problems keep presenting themselves, and decisions must be made, whether people are competent to make them or not.

When individuals are no longer able to make decisions, there are a number of legal tools that can give their decision-making power to other people. These tools, including living wills, durable powers of attorney, guardianships, conservatorships, and representative payee appointments, are explained in other chapters in this book. To know when these tools should go into effect, however, it is important to understand competence and incompetence and the situations in which they are likely to matter.

The Kinds of Decisions That May Need to Be Made for an Individual

Financial, medical, and personal decisions are the three most important categories of decisions that may need to be made for an individual. These categories are briefly discussed below. It is difficult to give any hard-and-fast rules, or even suggestions, for making decisions about them, because each case is unique. Other problems arise because different patients may have different levels of ability to make decisions, or different levels of incompetence, as discussed later in this chapter.

Financial Decisions

Bills don't stop arriving when people become too ill or confused to pay them. Car payments, monthly rent checks or mortgage payments, insurance premiums, and credit card debts still need to be paid. When people become unable to manage their own finances, the surest and least complicated way to have other people take over is to have planned ahead. Obviously, such planning should be done before an individual becomes incompetent (for more information, see chapters 5 and 12).

When no advance planning has been done, putting others in charge can be more difficult and more expensive. The reasons for the difficulty (and the expense) are simple: the law tries to protect people from being taken advantage of, or from having their money stolen by corrupt or unethical people. Often, when people who have not planned ahead become confused or forgetful, their closest relatives or friends start to make decisions for them on an informal basis. Patients' Social Security checks can be assigned to others under the representative payee system (see chapter 13). Bankers, lawyers, and stockbrokers, however, may be less willing to simply accept that people other than their original clients are now in charge (see chapter 14).

Decisions about Medical Treatment, Nontreatment, and Experimental Treatment

Obviously, the most important decisions that can be made for other persons are those affecting their life and death. Usually, in the case of sick and elderly individuals, these decisions must be made in hospitals or nursing homes. One possible treatment decision is *nontreatment,* or a decision to withhold or withdraw treatment, a decision that can result in permitting death to occur.

Deciding against certain treatments can frighten and upset everybody: family members, friends, doctors, nurses, lawyers, judges, and hospital and nursing home administrators. Such decisions may also pose serious legal problems, and individual states, courts, hospitals, and nursing homes often have their own rules about accepting a request for nontreatment. Too, individual state laws must be consulted. Some states have family consent laws that automatically allow family members of incompetent patients to make certain medical decisions for them (see chapter 14).

Another highly personal medical decision that may have to be faced is whether or not patients should participate in scientific research experiments that may eventually lead doctors to find a cure for their illnesses. This is a difficult decision, particularly because it's unlikely that any cure, if eventually found, will arrive in time for patients to benefit from it. *By law, only competent patients or patients with guardians or other legally authorized representatives can make the decision to be part of a research experiment, and both federal and state laws must be consulted on this matter* (interested individuals should discuss this issue with their lawyers). Many states, however, do not have laws prohibiting people from making decisions about someone else's research participation, and so it is a difficult question for both the decision makers and the research groups. Like most decisions, this one is best made while patients are still competent.

Many people believe that patients who cannot themselves weigh the risks and benefits of research should probably not participate in it. Yet research is vital to finding cures. If research participation is a possibility and patients are incompetent to agree to it, the following questions need to be answered:

- Is the research dangerous, painful, or physically difficult?
- What are the benefits to patients if they participate?
- Are the possible benefits, either to patients or to society, important enough for others to agree to it on behalf of patients?
- Is it what the patients would have wanted?

For more information, see chapter 14.

Personal Decisions

Personal decisions that need to be made are as varied as the people making them. Briefly, they include where to live, what to wear, whom to befriend or associate with, whether to vote, whom to marry, whether to drive a car, what activities or groups to join, whether to donate one's bodily organs after death, and so on.

The Concept of Competence

If people are considered mentally competent, they are assumed to have a particular set of mental skills and abilities. In a strictly legal sense, people are presumed competent unless they are legally declared incompetent, in the same way that those accused of a crime are presumed innocent until proven guilty.

Basically, doctors and judges call patients *competent* if they are

aware of who they are (their name);

aware of time (what day and year it is);

aware of place (where they are);

capable of understanding the diagnosis of their illness;

capable of understanding how their illness is likely to progress;

capable of making a choice between real options;

able to make reasonable, thoughtful decisions based on rational reasons and to appreciate the consequences of those decisions.

Levels of Competence and Incompetence

Competence to make decisions is not like a light switch that turns on or off. Many elderly people may be partially competent, that is, able to make some decisions but not others. Or they may be intermittently competent—more lucid or clearheaded on some days than on others.

In making medical decisions, the competence of patients to agree to (or refuse) treatment could be evaluated in terms of how fully they understand the information about their treatment options. Here, patients fall roughly into three categories in their abilities to agree to or refuse treatment:

1. *Some patients are completely incompetent to consent to or refuse treatment. The most obvious case would be patients in a coma or those who are otherwise unaware of their surroundings.* Some patients may be able to recognize certain people or things but still be unable to make or communicate decisions. If treatments were suggested, patients either could not answer at all or would not make sense when they did answer.

2. *Other patients are partially competent. They may be able to answer some simple questions but probably not any complex ones.* They may understand that they are being asked a question, and they may answer it, but they aren't likely to fully understand their treatment options and thus cannot give an informed opinion or answer to the question. Good examples of this state would be patients who cannot repeat back much of the information given them about their treatment options and patients who refuse all treatment but have no understanding that they are ill.

3. *Still other patients are competent to agree to or refuse treatment. They understand and appreciate the possible risks and benefits of various treatment options, as well as how*

the information applies to them. Simply understanding (or repeating back) the information is not enough; they must also grasp the realities of their situation.

It is important to remember that competence is not a simple matter of patients agreeing with proposed treatments, nor is incompetence the same as a difference of opinion. *Patients are much more likely to have their competence questioned if they disagree with what their doctors or families want to do, and it is important to keep this factor in mind. Just because patients disagree does not automatically mean they are incompetent to make decisions.*

Finally, out of respect for patients and their rights and dignity, they should be encouraged and helped to make as many decisions as possible, for as long as possible.

Competence to Make Specific Decisions

Another way of looking at competence is to make it *decision-specific,* or to ask the question, Is this person competent to make this specific decision? In this way, decisions can be roughly broken down into the following categories:

- *Trivial decisions,* such as what to eat, what to wear, and what to do.
- *Minor decisions,* such as what clothing to buy, whether to agree to less important treatments, and whether to participate in certain activities.
- *Important decisions,* such as whether to have surgery, whether to take medications that may have strong side effects, whether to take part in research experiments, whether to make large financial investments, and whether to sell property.
- *Major decisions,* such as whether to enter or leave a nursing home or other health care facility and whether to appoint a guardian or other decision maker.
- *Life-and-death decisions,* such as whether to agree to risky surgery, medications, or other treatments and whether to refuse treatment or discontinue life-prolonging treatments.

De Facto Incompetence and De Facto Surrogates

Ideally, everyone should be allowed to stay in control and make the decisions he or she is capable of making until the time he or she dies. Partially competent people, for instance, would make those decisions they are competent to make, and intermittently competent people would make decisions when they were capable of making them. But real life does not always follow the ideal, or even the rules of the court, and many people are judged and treated as incompetent by their doctors, family members, and friends without ever having been examined by a psychiatrist or declared legally incompetent.

Most clearly incompetent patients never go through a court hearing for a formal determination of their incompetence. Instead, their doctors and family members decide they are incompetent and the family begins making decisions for them. These patients are *de facto incompetent,* and their family members become *de facto surrogates.* Court guardianship hearings that determine whether patients are incompetent—and if so, appoint guardians for them—can be expensive, upsetting, and time-consuming for both families and patients. Such hearings are therefore often avoided. (For more information on guardianship hearings, see chapter 12.) The alternative explained above works well in many cases, and disagreements between the family and the health care facility can usually be resolved without anyone's needing to go to court.

De facto surrogates can, however, run into problems if courts have not declared patients incompetent, or appointed individuals to make their decisions. Problems are more likely to arise if de facto surrogates want patients taken off life-support systems or if they refuse life-prolonging treatments. *In other words, the more controversial the decisions, the more likely that hospitals, nursing homes, and family members who disagree with the proposed decisions will insist that decision makers be formally appointed by a durable power of attorney, a court, or that a court formally agree with the decision being made.* The reverse is also true, and family members can take health care facilities to court over decisions with which they disagree.

How Health Care Professionals Can Help
Determine a Patient's Competence

Health care professionals taking care of elderly patients can and should be involved with determining whether those patients are competent to make decisions or are incompetent and in need of a guardian or some other type of surrogate decision-maker. Although such involvement regularly occurs as a practical matter, only the courts can legally declare people incompetent. Because health care professionals work with many patients, they are often able to use their experience to help them decide if patients are competent or not. Often, questions about the competence of patients first arise when discussing a proposed treatment.

When health care professionals and family members fear that patients are incompetent, they should remember that competence and incompetence are not divided by a definite line. Patients may be more or less competent depending on the time or day, where they are, temporary medical problems, their reaction to medication they are receiving, and the presence or absence of people who may be trying to pressure them into making a particular decision. *Giving patients the same information under different circumstances—such as in their own homes instead of doctors' offices or during different times of the day—may help. Changing or temporarily lessening their medication may also make a difference. Also, patients who take a long time to decide should not automatically be viewed as incompetent; it may simply take them a while to come to a decision.*

If patients do not have a durable power of attorney, are thought to be incompetent, and are the focus of strong disagreements about how to treat them, then guardians may have to be appointed by a court for them. This is particularly true if family members and health care professionals cannot agree on how to proceed.

When courts are asked to appoint a guardian, health care professionals are often asked to evaluate the patient in question and to give information and opinions on whether or not the patient is incompetent and in need of a guardian. Courts may also ask other experts to evaluate patients. Normally, experts would be doctors or psychiatrists, although nurses may also have a great deal of information and insight based on their contact with patients.

Policies for Evaluating a Patient's Competence

There is no precise medical test that proves patients are competent or imcompetent. When patients are called *incompetent,* that label is really based on the personal and expert opinions of the family, the doctor, and other individuals. Some states have legislation defining incompetence and listing those persons capable of determining it; and many nursing homes and hospitals have general guidelines or written policies to help them evaluate patients' abilities to make decisions. Those guidelines or policies should include

who in the institution has the responsibility for deciding if patients are competent or incompetent;

how such decisions should be made; and

what kinds of questions patients should be asked.

An institution's policy should require that several different kinds of experts participate in the decision. Although the patients' doctors are usually the ones in charge of such an evaluation, other health professionals and family members can and should help them in making the decision. Nurses or nurse's aides, for instance, may have noticed behavior changes, and family members and friends can tell if patients are acting strangely or are making decisions that don't match their lifelong opinions.

The use of family members, friends, doctors, and other experts to decide whether patients are incompetent is also important in other ways—it gives institutions a justification for deciding whether patients are competent or incompetent without going to court for a formal decision.

The Geriatric Mental Status Examination

The evaluation of patients by medical experts should begin with a complete *geriatric mental status examination*. This examination should include observations about the patients and answers to the types of questions listed below. (Much of the following information is taken from Marshall Kapp's *Preventing Malpractice in Long Term Care: Strategies for Risk Management*, listed in the "Additional Reading" section.)

1. How does the patient dress?
2. Is the patient clean?
3. Does he or she make eye contact?
4. How does the patient talk?
5. How does he or she move or walk?
6. Does the patient make any unusual movements?
7. What is the mood of the patient?
8. Is the patient's mood normal for his or her situation?
9. Does the patient's ability to think match his or her level of education?
10. Does the patient's knowledge match his or her career or work experience?

11. Can the patient remember things that just happened?

12. Does he or she remember things that happened a short time ago?

13. Does he or she remember things that happened a long time ago?

14. Is the patient acting in a dangerous or self-destructive way?

15. Does the patient understand his or her problems?

16. Does the patient know the date?

17. Is the patient aware of where he or she is?

18. Does the patient know who he or she is?

19. Does the patient recognize specific people?

20. Does the patient have any delusions, hallucinations, or illusions?

When trying to decide if patients are competent to agree to or refuse particular medical treatments, other questions need to be asked. In these cases, patients should be asked what they think will happen if they decide to accept or refuse treatment, and whether they understand. (Much of the information that follows is based on the article "Competence to Refuse Medical Treatment: Autonomy vs. Paternalism," by George Annas and Joan Densberger, listed in the "Additional Reading" section.)

1. What is their present physical condition?

2. What treatment is being suggested?

3. What does the doctor think will happen if treatment is refused?

4. What does the doctor think will happen if treatment is accepted?

5. What are the other available treatments?

6. What is likely to happen if those other treatments are accepted?

Competence and incompetence are, as shown in this chapter, not always clear-cut; and the people involved with determining an individual's ability to make decisions should proceed with all the care and caution necessary to taking such a grave, and usually irrevocable, step. *In addition, it should be remembered that a person may be able to make health care decisions even if he or she is legally incompetent to do other things, such as handle business affairs.*

12

Guardians and Conservators

When, If, and How

Overview

One of the most significant concerns of older people is the potential need for others to make financial and personal decisions for them in the event they become unable to make such decisions themselves. Some elderly individuals reach a point when, because of either disease or accident, they experience mental confusion or physical limitations that prevent them from attending to everyday needs, such as paying bills, shopping, or cooking.

The court's appointment of guardians or conservators is the most common legal mechanism for putting in place the needed surrogate decision-makers, or people who make decisions on behalf of other individuals. It is also, however, the most dramatic and restrictive form of legal intervention that can be imposed on aged individuals.

The state statutes and court decisions governing guardianship vary significantly from state to state. Even within each state, practices may vary greatly depending on the statute under which a guardianship proceeding is begun. In some states, different guardianship statutes exist for incapacitated adults, minors, and developmentally disabled or retarded individuals. Other variables include the beliefs and practices of individual judges that influence the nature and results of the proceedings. Because of all these variations and uncertainties, this chapter does not attempt to describe the laws or procedures as they apply to any one region or courthouse. Rather, it describes, in general terms, the process and consequences of having a guardianship or conservatorship imposed.

No one likes the idea of not having the capacity or right to make the decisions that shape his or her life. Even so, by understanding the purpose and uses of guardianship and alternatives to it, older individuals and their family members can often plan ahead to keep as much of their individual autonomy, or freedom to make their own decisions, as possible. Sometimes individuals may be able to use legal tools other than guardianship that still provide for their personal and property management. Better yet, with a little advance planning, elderly people can arrange for these surrogate decisions to be made according to directions they have written in the event they become incapacitated (these legal alternatives are best described in separate chapters; see chapters 4 and 5).

What Are Guardianship and Conservatorship?

Guardianship and conservatorship are really just two sides of the same coin; the two words are often used interchangeably. The term *guardianship* generally refers to the court's appointment of someone (the *guardian*) to make decisions for and handle the affairs of another person (the *ward*) whom the court has found to be incapacitated or incompetent, that is, unable to make rational decisions and understand their consequences. (For more information, see chapter 11.) Although the formal terms vary from state to state, generally speaking there are two forms of guardianship:

1. *The term* guardian *refers to someone with the legal authority to make decisions regarding the ward's "person."* For example, the guardian has the power to determine where the ward will live, what medical treatment he or she may receive, and other life-style matters. A guardian is appointed only after the court has decided that a person is incompetent.

2. *The term* conservator *generally refers to someone with the legal authority to make decisions regarding the ward's property.* For example, the conservator has the power to manage property, make investments, and pay bills. In some states, the appointment of a conservator does not depend on the court deciding that someone is incompetent. Similarly, in some states a conservatorship can be requested by the individual in need of assistance as well as by other interested persons.

Other terms used to describe the two types of guardians include *guardian of the person, guardian of the estate, conservator of the person, conservator of the estate, curator,* and *committee. For the purposes of this chapter, unless otherwise stated the term* guardian *or* guardianship *is used to refer to legal decision-making authority over another individual's "person." Conservator or conservatorship is used to refer to legal decision-making authority over another individual's property and estate.*

A Few Legal Terms and Their Definitions

Because this chapter concerns legal issues, there is no way to get around using legal terms. Thus, some additional terms and definitions are included here to help the reader fully understand the chapter's content. (These terms are also listed in the Glossary.)

Competence; capacity. Terms referring to an individual's ability to think clearly, make rational decisions, and understand their consequences. People who are unable to do so may be termed *incompetent* or *incapacitated* (see chapter 11 for a more complete explanation.)

Probate court. The court involved in handling guardianship and conservatorship petitions in most states (although the name does vary). There is usually a probate court and a probate judge in each county.

Guardian ad litem. A court-appointed individual (not necessarily a lawyer) authorized to represent the ward in a specific matter being heard by the court (or by another official forum that can make decisions affecting the rights of the ward). A guardian *ad litem* has a very limited function and should not be confused with an individual's legal representation by a lawyer.

Hearing. The proceeding in which a judge reviews a petition, hears the evidence, and decides whether someone is competent or incompetent and in need of a guardian or conservator.

Petition. A legal form that must be obtained from a court to start proceedings requesting the appointment of a guardian or conservator. The petition must be completed by stating why a guardian or conservator may be needed and by giving facts about the incapacity or incompetence of the person in question.

Petitioner. The individual who files a petition and requests that a guardianship or conservatorship hearing be held by the court. The petitioner is usually a family member or another person who wants to become the ward's guardian, but it can also be a hospital, nursing home, or social service agency that is asking the court to determine who is responsible for the person in question. Most states allow "any interested party" to act as petitioner.

Ward or respondent. The individual who either has a guardian or is the subject of a guardianship hearing. The term *ward* is typically used after a guardian has been appointed; *respondent* is used during the court process to determine the need for guardianship.

The Implications of Guardianship

Guardianship takes away from wards many important and basic civil rights. Depending on the state, such rights may include the loss of the right to marry, to sue and be sued, to hold licenses (such as a driver's license), to decide where to live, and—in some states—to vote. (In most states, guardians have the same rights and duties toward wards that parents have to minor children.) *Perhaps the most important and basic right that wards lose is the right to self-determination, that is, the ability to make choices about their lives and determine where their own interests lie. In light of these serious losses, guardianship is a drastic action that may be an emotionally painful experience for everyone involved.*

Before initiating guardianship proceedings, one should be convinced that they are truly necessary. Considering the extreme nature of guardianship, it is essential before filing a petition to first explore alternatives, such as trusts, living wills, and durable powers of attorney (see chapters 1, 4, and 5).

Full versus Limited Guardianship Arrangements

Guardianship typically refers to *full,* or *plenary, guardianship,* wherein the guardian has very broad and general powers (the right to make almost all decisions) over the ward.

Some states now allow *limited guardianships,* which means that if a judge finds the respondent to be totally incapacitated, a full/plenary guardianship will be imposed; however, if the judge finds that the respondent can partially take care of himself or herself, a limited guardianship may be imposed. Under a limited guardianship, the powers and duties of the guardian are expressly limited by the court and the ward keeps all the rights and powers that are not turned over to the guardian.

Most states also have even more limited forms of guardianship, such as *temporary* or *emergency guardianship,* when a particular situation requires someone other than the person in question to be able to make immediate decisions. *Single-transaction guardianship,* for one event only (such as the sale of the ward's home), is also possible depending on the state. Sometimes these more limited forms of guardianship may be all that are necessary.

Public Guardianship Programs

The phrase *public guardian* is used very loosely. It often means a guardian of last resort who is paid by public funds, whether that guardian is a government employee or simply some person or organization known to the court to be available to provide such services for a fee.

Some state agencies have public guardianship programs that serve as guardians for people who have no one else able or willing to fill that role (see appendix 21 for a list of states with limited or statewide programs). Public guardians have the same responsibilities as other court-appointed guardians—they decide where wards will live, agree to or refuse medical treatment, determine how wards' assets are used, and so on. In these instances, public guardians are state or county employees who are paid a salary and therefore do not need to charge a fee for services; however, some programs do charge a fee, which is taken out of the ward's estate.

Public guardianship programs, generally understaffed and overworked, are not without problems. Some have been criticized for neglecting wards, sending wards to nursing homes for the sake of convenience, and occasionally misusing funds. Yet they also fill an important need, as incompetent people without guardians must have someone reviewing their cases and making decisions for them.

Recently, a few private nonprofit organizations under state contract have been established to perform the same duties as those of the state-administered programs. Some churches and other nonprofit groups offer these services as well, on a case-by-case basis, generally being paid on an hourly basis. There are also private for-profit agencies that offer, for a fee paid out of the ward's estate, to act as guardians; they take a fee or percentage of assets as payment for services.

When Is Guardianship Necessary and What Triggers a Petition?

Unless an individual has done advance planning and established a durable power of attorney, a trust, or some other mechanism for handling personal affairs and property, a guardianship becomes necessary only when the person is no longer competent.

It is difficult to generalize about the many situations that may result in the filing of a petition for guardianship. Sometimes an individual has lost all capacity to function or communicate (for example, following a severe stroke or a serious accident). Perhaps more typically, an individual experiences no sudden or severe medical problem and retains some ability to function and communicate but may still need someone to help make decisions for him or her.

Four factors usually trigger the filing of a petition for guardianship:

1. *The petitioner believes that the individual is behaving in an unreasonable manner.*

2. *The individual is unwilling or unable to change the behavior that the petitioner sees as unreasonable.*

3. *The unreasonable behavior threatens some facet of the person's life that the petitioner thinks is important.*

4. *The unreasonable behavior is apparent to the outside world.*

For purposes of guardianship, the term *incompetence* has a precise legal meaning. While specific legal standards defining incompetence differ from state to state, they basically involve a two-part test. First, the person must be mentally incapable of giving *informed consent* (that is, be unable to understand the consequences of his or her decisions). Second, as a result of the inability to give informed consent, the person must be incapable of handling his or her own affairs.

When thinking about legal incompetence and the need for guardianship, one must separate the idea of informed consent from subjective terms like *rational* and *reasonable* (for more information on informed consent, see chapter 11). To assess someone's competence based on one's personal views can lead to inappropriate guardianship and the loss of individual rights. After all, what is a rational or reasonable decision for one person with one set of values could be an irrational or unreasonable decision for another person with another set of values.

Before guardianship can be imposed, legal incompetence or incapacity must be proved in court; however, with some of the other alternatives, such as durable powers of attorney, it may not be necessary to go before a judge at all.

Advantages and Disadvantages of Guardianship

The primary advantage of guardianship is that at its best, it appoints an honest and concerned individual to make decisions for an incapacitated person and provides some court oversight. The amount of actual court supervision available to oversee this protection, however, is often limited. For a well-meaning family with a totally incapacitated member, guardianship may be the best solution to an unhappy situation.

There are a number of disadvantages to guardianship. One is the social stigma that some people attach to the phrase *legally incompetent.* If a person's condition is temporary and he or she is able to recover from an illness, accident, or stroke, it may be traumatic to have been previously declared legally incompetent.

Then too, guardianship does not have many practical means of protecting the ward from a corrupt or unethical guardian. Once the ward is declared legally incompetent, he or she is often denied the right to hire a lawyer to get the guardianship order overturned. Decisions to appoint a guardian are often made quickly and without a great deal of evidence being presented. In short, it is not a process designed to give maximum protection to the rights of the ward.

Guardianship is sometimes a last-ditch solution occurring because there has been no adequate advance planning. The incapacitated person's wishes may be better served by one or more of the alternatives listed in chapters 4 and 5.

Although most guardians and conservators do a good job, there is the possibility for abuse if the person appointed does not really have the ward's best interests at heart. Even when states require that financial accountings and personal status reports be provided, abuse or neglect of the ward can and does occur because the overburdened court system does not have the time or the personnel to carefully review these reports. Depending on state laws, guardians may have to file a report each year.

The Duties and Responsibilities of a Guardian

The general boundaries of a guardian's authority to make decisions are set out in state law, case law, and court rules. For any particular case, obligations and/or limitations are spelled out in the court's *order of appointment,* the judge's ruling of how much authority the guardian shall have. (See appendix 26 for a sample order.) In some states, the guardian has only those powers specifically noted in the order. In others, the guardian may be given almost unrestricted authority (though even in these cases, a guardian may have to seek the court's approval for certain serious decisions that strongly influence the life and death of the ward).

In general, a guardian must keep enough contact with the ward to be aware of his or her current condition and needs. Specifically, a guardian may have any or all of the following powers, rights, or duties:

- To determine where and with whom the ward will reside.
- To see to the care, comfort, and maintenance of the ward. (This may include the duty to obtain services for the ward and seeing to the care of the ward's belongings.)
- To consent to medical and professional treatment of the ward. (Such decisions run the gamut from physical examinations, dental examinations, and vaccinations to surgery, after-death organ donation, experimental treatments, and withholding or withdrawing of life-supporting treatment. Depending on state laws and the individual case, guardians may need to get prior court approval to make some of these decisions.)
- To maintain a lawsuit on behalf of the ward.
- To receive and apply any of the ward's money or property to his or her current needs for support and care. (In some places, the guardian must get the court's approval before spending any money. While this arrangement is meant to protect the ward, it can backfire, as when a nursing home demands payment and threatens to discharge the ward before the court gets around to approving the expense.)
- To conserve any of the ward's excess money for his or her future needs.
- To report the condition of the ward and his or her estate to the court.

Some states have additional duties, responsibilities, and restrictions for guardians. *For example, depending on state law and the court orders in a particular case, a guardian may or may not be allowed to place a ward in a nursing home against his or her wishes; in order to do so, the guardian may have to get the court's prior approval.* Some states also require that guardians provide reports on the personal status of wards (see appendix 22 for a list of states that have this requirement).

At What Point Is Conservatorship Necessary?

When an individual becomes incapable of caring for or managing his or her own property and estate, a court-appointed conservator may be necessary if alternatives have not been established through advance planning. As previously noted, in some states conservatorship is not linked to a formal ruling on a person's incompetence. (Sometimes the term *conservatee* is used instead of *ward,* but for the purposes of this chapter, *ward* will be used.)

Also, some states allow an individual in need of assistance to petition the court for conservatorship on his or her own behalf and to nominate the person he or she would like to have serve as conservator.

Advantages and Disadvantages of Conservatorship

The primary advantage of conservatorship is that at its best, it protects the ward from an inexperienced, foolish, or dishonest conservator by imposing court supervision and review of reports and financial accountings.

Unfortunately, many courts do not have the time or staff necessary to monitor conservators and to review their reports as carefully as they should. There are some serious problems with conservators misusing their ward's assets, as was shown recently in a study done by the Associated Press.

Legally, a conservator does not have any power over the ward's "person." However, in having control over a ward's funds, the real powers of a conservator over the ward are substantial.

The Duties and Responsibilities of a Conservator

A conservator is entrusted with the duty to protect, preserve, and wisely invest the ward's property. Most states also require conservators to post a bond (put up their own money) as a financial guarantee that the duties will be performed faithfully. *A conservator is not permitted to gain any personal profit or advantage from dealing with the ward's property or estate.* Some states also require conservators to provide annual or periodic accountings of wards' estates (see appendix 23 for a list of states that have these requirements).

Like the duties of a guardian, the duties of a conservator vary from state to state and depend on the exact amount of authority granted by the court (see appendix 26 for a sample of a court order for conservatorship). In general, a conservator may have the powers, rights, and duties to

invest funds of the estate;

collect, hold, retain, or dispose of assets;

continue or participate in the operation of a business;

handle banking transactions on behalf of the ward;

make ordinary or extraordinary repairs, alterations, or improvements to real estate;

enter into leases either as the lessee or the lessor;

engage in securities transactions on behalf of the ward;

pay the expenses and debts of the ward;

settle or contest a claim;

pay taxes owed by the ward or the ward's estate;

employ persons to assist in the administration of the ward's estate; and

use funds for the support of dependents of the ward.

The Process of Petitioning for Guardianship

The guardianship process begins with the filing of a petition for guardianship in the appropriate court (see appendix 25 for a sample petition). Who can petition a court to hold a guardianship hearing depends on individual state laws, and concerned individuals should ask a lawyer to explain the guardianship statutes in their state. In many states, anyone can file such a petition. Most of the time, however, petitioners are the people who want to become guardians.

Petitioners are usually relatives. About 75 percent of the time a family member serves as the ward's guardian, although the petitioner also can be a social service agency, such as a county health department, Catholic Charities, a senior citizens' center, the visiting nurse association, or "meals on wheels." Social service agencies act as petitioners when they discover people in the community who they believe can't take care of themselves and who refuse offered services. Social service agencies, both because their role is to protect people and because of their own fears of liability if they don't, will often initiate proceedings. Hospitals and nursing homes may also file guardianship petitions (a) just because a patient is old, (b) to determine who is legally responsible for paying an individual's bills, and (c) to find out who is legally authorized to agree to or refuse treatment on behalf of a patient.

Some, but not all, states have preprinted forms that must be completed to petition for guardianship. These forms can usually be found by contacting an organization listed under "Legal Forms" or "Legal Stationers" in the telephone directory.

No matter who files for a hearing or why, all petitions for guardianship must allege (state that the petitioner believes) that the proposed ward is incapable of properly caring for himself or herself or of managing his or her estate. Once the petition has been filed with the appropriate court, a date for a hearing will be set. In many states, a guardian *ad litem* must be appointed by the court to protect the potential ward's interests throughout the legal proceedings.

The court will then send a notice to various individuals, depending on the state. All states except Alabama, Louisiana, and Mississippi require that the proposed ward receive notice of the time and place of the hearing, regardless of his or her mental state. Generally, the guardianship statutes also require that notice be given to a third person, usually a relative. This requirement is to help protect the ward both from his or her own confusion and from a possibly dishonest or unethical petitioner. If the ward is too confused to understand the notice, the third person might ensure that the ward's interests are protected. If the proposed ward wishes to protest the petition, then the notice allows him or her to begin to take steps to fight the proceeding.

Unfortunately, the notices are often inadequate, in that they do not convey what is at stake, what defenses may be raised, or that the proposed ward has the right to be present, hire a lawyer, present evidence, and cross-examine witnesses. Whatever rights prospective wards do have are meaningful only if they are asserted.

When individuals receive such a notice, they should seek the assistance of a lawyer or a trusted friend, insist on being present at the hearing, and make arrangements to do so. Even if people want a guardian or know they need one, they may still want a say in who that person will be and in what areas that person will be authorized to make decisions. Their presence at the hearing will ensure that they can express their opinions and their preferences.

The right to a lawyer, or counsel, at a guardianship hearing depends on the laws of each individual state (see appendix 24 for a list of state requirements for the legal representation of wards). If an individual can afford to personally pay for and hire a lawyer, he or she can always have one. If the individual does not have the money or the mental ability to enter into a lawyer-client relationship, then it is up to state law as to whether the court has to appoint a lawyer for that individual and as to how the lawyer will be paid. *There is no constitutional right to have a court-appointed lawyer at a guardianship hearing. A potential ward should always ask the court to appoint a lawyer if he or she is without one and wishes to contest the need for guardianship.*

Hearings are frequently held very quickly after a petition is filed. Most statutes do not specify the amount of time that must pass between the notice and the hearing, but it is often less than ten days. This short period does not allow much time for the proposed ward to plan a defense.

Hearings are usually held in the absence of the proposed ward. While proposed wards have the right to attend, they may not realize they do or may not understand the importance of attending. They may even believe that a guardian cannot be appointed in their absence. Although some states do require that proposed wards be present at these hearings, even in those states many courts routinely waive the requirement in the belief that it will not help the wards and might aggravate their condition to attend. *The specific rules and regulations surrounding such hearings vary; however, most hearings are held without the proposed ward unless he or she insists on being present.*

Often, no witnesses are called and the court thus makes its decision based on affidavits (sworn statements by individuals) and written doctors' reports. In 1987 the Associated Press conducted a study of 2,200 guardianship hearings, finding that approximately 30 percent of them did not require that medical evidence be presented.

Decisions in these hearings are usually made by a judge, not a jury, in a probate court. In some cases, a jury is allowed only on request. Each state has a different *standard of proof,* that is, type of evidence required before a judge can decide that someone is incompetent and in need of a guardian. In some states, the standard is simply what the judge feels has a 51 percent weight, or likelihood of being true—legally called *preponderance of evidence.* Other states have more restrictive laws that demand clear and convincing evidence. *Ordinarily, a decision is made at the end of the hearing.*

Guardians (and conservators) are paid according to state law. It is not unusual for them to receive, each year, a certain percentage of disbursements (the amount the guardian or conservator has paid out of the ward's estate on the ward's behalf). They also may receive a percentage of the remaining estate when the guardianship or conservatorship ends, usually on the death of the ward.

The cost of a guardianship proceeding is generally taken out of the estate of the proposed ward—whether guardianship is granted or not and whether the proposed ward wants it or not. The cost will vary from case to case but will almost always include fees for the petitioner's lawyer and the guardian *ad litem,* bond costs, court costs, and, depending on the case, the lawyer for the proposed ward. It is not unusual to pay $2,000 to $4,000 for a normal guardianship hearing. In contested cases, in which disagreements are expressed by the ward or other individuals, the fees can run very high indeed. If no estate exists, then the cost is paid for out of public funds or by the petitioner.

The Process of Petitioning for Conservatorship

The process of petitioning for conservatorship is similar to that for guardianship. It typically requires the filing of a petition with the probate court in the county in which the potential ward lives. In some states, the court process, notice requirements, and so on, are the same as those for guardianship. In other states, the law does not require that a person be declared incompetent in order to appoint a conservator; rather, the court must find that the person is in need of protection because he or she cannot manage his or her own financial matters. Because this latter situation is considered less serious than being declared incompetent is, many of these states have fewer notice requirements and other procedural protections for wards for conservatorship than for wards for guardianship.

As with guardianships, some states have preprinted forms that need to be completed to petition for conservatorship. These forms can be found by contacting an organization listed under "Legal Forms" or "Legal Stationers" in the telephone directory.

Finally, some states allow for *voluntary conservatorship,* in which the individual who wants assistance petitions the court for the appointment of a conservator.

Removing a Guardian and Terminating a Guardianship Arrangement

At any point during a guardianship or conservatorship, most states allow any interested person to ask the court for an order removing a guardian or conservator. In some cases, the court itself may initiate action to dismiss a guardian.

A guardian may be dismissed for several reasons, such as the mismanagement or waste of the ward's assets, or the fact that the guardian has become physically or mentally unable to continue serving as guardian. Similarly, guardians (and conservators) can always petition the court if it is no longer possible for them to continue in that position; in such cases, the court will appoint a new guardian. A guardianship may also be completely ended if a ward recovers sufficiently to handle his or her own affairs.

To fully understand the seriousness of imposing a guardianship, one needs to examine the restoration process required for the courts to find a ward healthy enough not to need a guardian. This process usually has to be initiated by formal procedures, involving petitioning the court that granted the guardianship in the first place. Although notice to interested individuals is usually required, the ward has even fewer legal safeguards in this process than during the appointment of a guardian. As previously noted, once the ward is declared legally incompetent, he or she may lose the ability to hire a lawyer. The restoration hearing is generally considered more of a review of current medical judgment than a fight between the guardian and the ward.

Some statutes allow for partial as well as complete restoration of the rights of the ward. Many statutes barely address the restoration process at all, probably because of the unfounded belief that individuals rarely recover enough to be considered competent. As a result, the statutes generally do not specify the period that must pass between additional petitions for restoration if the first petition is denied. In addition, the appeals procedure is not clearly defined. Finally, it should be noted that even where the restoration petition is successful, there is usually no way to erase the social or professional stigma of the ward's having been declared incompetent in the first place. In short, a guardianship is not an easy matter to undo.

The Importance of Considering Alternative Methods

With advance planning, there are a number of alternatives for handling the affairs of a mentally or physically incapacitated person. Without such planning, the choices are few, and guardianship may be the only real option. For more information on options that can be used instead of guardianship, see chapters 1, 4, and 5.

13

When Social Security Payments
Go to Someone Else

Overview

Most people who receive Social Security payments are able to manage and spend their money as they see fit. However, when disease or confusion makes it impossible for an individual to handle a bank account, pay bills, or make financial decisions, someone else usually takes over those responsibilities for him or her. In the case of Social Security benefits, there is a specific term for people who are appointed to manage and supervise money paid to Social Security recipients—they are called *representative payees,* or just *payees.*

Payees have a very important position, and their honesty is perhaps the most crucial aspect of it. Payees are in charge of other people's money at a time when those people are unable to make their own financial decisions or even to protect themselves from a payee's misuse of their money. There are laws surrounding how these funds can and should be used, but in order to understand them, it is necessary first to understand the system.

A payee is an individual or an institution, such as a nursing home, board and care home, or mental hospital, that is *designated* or appointed, to receive Social Security payments on behalf of the *beneficiary,* or the person who would ordinarily receive them. Once designated, the payee is the only person (or institution) who has the legal right to spend the beneficiary's money.

While this situation works well most of the time, it is not without problems. A 1983 study evaluating payees showed that nearly 20 percent of them performed unsatisfactorily and/or misused the benefit checks they received. The study, conducted by the Social Security Administration (SSA), did not evaluate parents or spouses who acted as payees, and so it is possible that the real number of problems could be even greater than 20 percent.

Among other protections designed to combat the misuse of funds is that payees are now required to submit a report every year showing how they have spent beneficiaries' money. This reporting requirement was instituted in 1987, after a court forced SSA to review how beneficiaries' monies were being spent.

This chapter focuses on when individuals may need a payee, how to get one appointed, and how payees should handle beneficiaries' money.

When Does the Social Security Administration Designate Representative Payees?

The SSA has the right to designate a payee whenever it appears that a beneficiary would be helped by having one. *A beneficiary does not have to be legally declared incompetent, that is, unable to make rational decisions and understand their consequences, before a payee can be appointed* (for more information, see chapter 11), *and by law, the SSA must appoint a payee for any beneficiary who is diagnosed as an alcoholic or a drug addict.*

SSA has guidelines for determining whether or not to designate a payee. SSA believes that payees are needed for

individuals who are legally incompetent or mentally incapabable of managing their benefits;

individuals who are physically incapable of managing their benefits; and

beneficiaries under the age of eighteen, unless they receive Social Security benefits in their own name, are serving in the military, are living alone and supporting themselves, are parents and are capable of supporting themselves, or are four months away from being age eighteen.

Qualifying to Be a Representative Payee

When the SSA designates a payee, it certifies benefit payments to that individual. It is important that a payee be carefully investigated because the beneficiary must depend on him or her for the purchase of food, clothing, and shelter. Although the investigation should be completed before the payee is certified, the law requires that the investigation be completed no later than forty-five days after certification. Information used in selecting a payee, as well as SSA's preferred order of selection, can be found in appendix 28.

The SSA assigns a high preference to guardians to act as payees, although in rare instances it will appoint someone other than the guardian. A few states have public guardianship programs that fulfill the same purpose as payees (see appendix 21 for a list of states with public guardianship programs).

Under SSA policy, the person who wants to be considered for the position of payee must complete an application that covers his or her qualifications to be a payee, his or her relationship to the beneficiary, the availability of other potential payees, and how he or she would spend the benefits if appointed payee. The application also requires the potential payee to state that he or she is aware of reporting requirements and understands his or her legal liability for the deliberate misuse of funds. A copy of the application appears in appendix 27.

Once the application is completed, the potential payee must be interviewed by an SSA field office. This interview, which usually takes place in person, is a way for the SSA to evaluate an applicant's qualifications and explain the responsibilities of being a payee. *Sometimes the SSA will decide to contact other individuals who know the beneficiary and who are aware of the situation. This is likely to happen when there is more than one applicant, when the beneficiary does not live with the applicant, or when the SSA thinks that other individuals may have important information about the beneficiary or the applicant.*

The SSA prefers to appoint as a payee someone who lives with or has responsibility for the beneficiary. If more than one person qualifies as payee, the SSA will try to appoint the person who demonstrates the most concern and responsibility for the beneficiary's health and well-being.

In most instances, the SSA will contact the beneficiary directly, which allows the beneficiary to state a preference for who should be his or her payee. The SSA is required to contact the beneficiary if he or she lives alone, is in a facility that is not approved by either Medicare or Medicaid, and is not in close contact with the potential payee. These requirements allow the SSA to better determine the applicant's qualifications.

When an application is submitted, the SSA sends a written notice about the proceedings to the beneficiary (and his or her legal representative, if one exists). One notice is sent before the SSA appoints a potential payee, thereby giving the beneficiary a chance to object or to submit more information. A second notice is sent after the appointment has been made. *The beneficiary (or his or her legal representative) has the right to appeal both the SSA's decision that a payee is needed and the appointment of a specific payee.* Only a beneficiary who is declared legally incompetent, is diagnosed as an alcoholic or drug addict, or is a minor is not allowed to appeal the need for a payee.

If the SSA believes that a payee's use of funds needs to be carefully tracked, it will review the payee's performance within four months. A special review also takes place if the payee receives a large lump-sum payment, which may happen when a beneficiary wins an appeal for disability payments or waits a long time before filing a disability claim. In such instances, special payee evaluation procedures go into effect and the SSA field office monitors the payee's performance more closely than usual.

Institutional Payees: Rules and Regulations

A federal, state, or private institution can also be appointed as the payee for a patient in its care. Obviously, this situation can pose problems, since the institution is in charge of deciding what care to provide, providing it, and then paying itself for it. Federal and state institutions, such as nursing homes or mental hospitals, are investigated and monitored by the SSA through its on-site review program. Private institutions, such as room and board homes, are investigated and monitored by the SSA in the same way as individual applicants for payee positions are; however, because many room and board homes are not regulated by any federal or state law, it may not be wise to designate one as a payee.

An institutional payee must deduct its normal fee from the benefit check it receives on behalf of a particular patient. This fee must go toward only the care of the patient who is the beneficiary and must be written down in an *earnings record* or statement of how the patient's money is being used. The earnings record is then submitted to the SSA for review every year. An institution that receives Medicaid funds and Social Security checks for a specific patient is allowed to use the latter only for that patient's personal needs.

Responsibilities of Payees

Payees can easily be confused by all the possible uses for a beneficiary's Social Security checks. *Generally, the SSA believes that benefits should be spent on a beneficiary's maintenance care, such as rent, food, clothing, and medical treatment. Payees should not use benefit checks to pay for any of a patient's old debts; under federal law, money from benefit checks is exempt from collection agencies or any of the patient's creditors.*

If any money from the benefit checks is left over after the patient's current care needs are paid for, it should be kept in a separate account that is held in trust for the beneficiary.

Payee Misuse of Funds

Before 1987, the SSA was not responsible for requiring or reviewing a payee's accounting statements of how a beneficiary's money was spent. In the past, such monitoring was done only in special circumstances. *However, a lawsuit over the possible misuse of funds resulted in the Supreme Court's requiring all individual payees to submit annual accounting statements to the SSA. To comply with the court, the SSA now sends out accounting forms to be filled out by each payee.*

The Social Security Disability Benefits Reform Act of 1984 used to exempt parents and spouses of beneficiaries from submitting accounting statements. As a result of court actions, however, they, too, must now submit annual accounting statements. By law, the SSA must request these accounting statements from all payees except for those federal and state institutions which are reviewed under the SSA's on-site review program.

The SSA's internal studies show that these annual accounting statements are useful not only for finding and investigating the misuse of funds but also for educating and monitoring payees on their use of beneficiaries' funds. Payees who do not submit accounting statements are usually those who misuse benefit checks. While the misuse of funds can be investigated and proved through reports submitted by people other than payees, the annual signed accounting form is helpful to the SSA in successfully prosecuting payees for fraud.

Payees are legally liable for any intentional misuse of benefit funds. Punishment for the misuse of funds can include large fines and even prison sentences. Payees who are first-time offenders in misusing funds may receive one-year prison sentences and be fined $5,000; second-time offenders may face five years in prison and $25,000 in fines. In addition, offenders may have to repay beneficiaries all the money that was misused.

Accounting Procedures for Payees

At least once a year, payees are asked to complete a "representative payee report," an accounting form (see appendix 29 for a sample form). This relatively short accounting form comes with the SSA's full instructions on how to complete it. It asks payees for information on beneficiary custody, how much involvement payees have with beneficiaries, the use of benefits, the amount spent on beneficiaries' personal needs, and the amount and investment of any money left over from benefit checks. The SSA then reviews the report and checks it against SSA guidelines for how payees should use benefit funds. If the report is accepted, nothing more happens until payees fill out the next report (which, in turn, is also reviewed).

If payees don't seem to understand how to complete the form or if they leave out some of the more important information, the SSA will try to contact them directly to resolve the problem. If the SSA is unable to get in touch with these payees or cannot resolve the problem by discussing it with them, then the SSA field office will fill out a "representative payee evaluation report" (see appendix 30 for a sample evaluation form). This report is also used if the regular short accounting form is missing important information or if payees do not submit the regular accounting forms.

Evaluation reports request a much more detailed accounting of the use of all benefit funds and also include an SSA interview with the payee in question. The SSA field office is then responsible for checking and evaluating in writing all the information obtained in these reports. The field office is also responsible for initiating any follow-up actions that may be necessary. For example, the field office may directly contact beneficiaries or their custodians in order to verify all payee statements.

On-Site Review of Federal and State Institutions

The law requires that all state institutions covered by the SSA's on-site review program be audited at least once every three years. The review program is designed to evaluate the performance of state institutions that serve as payees. The SSA's general policies and procedures for on-site reviews are as follows:

- The ten SSA regional offices are responsible for conducting on-site reviews in states that fall under their region. In conducting reviews, the SSA staff must discuss specific payee procedures with institutional staff, audit patient accounts, interview the caretaking staff, and observe beneficiaries in the institution.

- The SSA conducts an in-depth review of how an institution uses patient benefits and checks to see whether SSA policies for the use of funds are being followed. Institutions under the on-site review program do not need to complete individual accounting forms for each patient, which minimizes their paperwork.

- Once the review is completed, a report on the SSA's findings is given to state health officials. During the review process, officials from the institution or the state may ask SSA staff to meet with them and discuss SSA recommendations.

Information obtained from the accounting process or other sources may lead the SSA to conduct a more thorough investigation of an institutional payee's performance. It may also lead the SSA to question whether or not the institution is suited to be a payee. These investigations may result in the SSA's replacing the payee or prosecuting the institution for the misuse of funds.

Replacing a Payee

Replacing a payee is always an alternative, and a new payee may be appointed even if no misuse of beneficiary funds has occurred. Payees may be replaced when

they do not comply with SSA guidelines for the use of beneficiary funds;

there is sufficient evidence that they have misused funds;

they die or are unable to fulfill the responsibilities of a payee; or

they fail to cooperate with the SSA or do not provide accounting statements, evidence, or other information.

Whenever a payee is replaced, the SSA tries to get back any savings left over from a beneficiary's checks, as well as any misused funds from the former payee. All funds that the SSA gets back are then given to the new payee for use on behalf of the beneficiary. In cases in which funds have been misused, a payee is almost always replaced.

If the SSA decides that funds have been misused, it notifies the Office of the Inspector General (OIG) of the U.S. Department of Health and Human Services. The OIG then reviews all misuse cases. If after reviewing a case the OIG believes it does not have enough evidence to prove the misuse of funds (or doubts it will be able to find enough evidence to prove misuse), it closes the case. If there is sufficient evidence, the OIG conducts another investigation before deciding whether to pass the case to the Justice Department for prosecution of the payee. If the OIG or the Justice Department does not recommend prosecution, the OIG tries to get back all misused funds from the payee.

If the Justice Department does prosecute, it tries to get back any misused funds or court-ordered fines directly from the payee. It also works to enforce prison sentences. When payees are prosecuted, the OIG acts as the go-between for the Department of Health and Human Services and the Justice Department.

A Closing Word

Because of the vulnerability of beneficiaries, it is obvious that a fair, efficient, and carefully monitored program is needed when Social Security checks go to someone else.

Beneficiaries who are unable to manage their own money are at the mercy of the people who handle it for them. Most payees are conscientious and do a good job for the beneficiaries they represent. Still, inasmuch as nearly $2 billion is paid each year to some five million payees of beneficiaries, precise monitoring, investigation, and accounting procedures are extremely important.

14

Limits on Decisions
Made for Someone Else

Overview

Up to this point, this book has focused on how individuals can maintain control over their own lives and continue to make the decisions important to them even after they have become too ill or confused to speak for themselves. It has also dealt with how, when necessary, other people can step in and take over the making of decisions for seriously ill or senile individuals.

Whether decisions are made in advance by individuals who later become ill or by people with the responsibility of making decisions for others, there may be limits on the decisions being made. Some of the limits are legal ones, imposed by the state. Some are emotional ones, imposed by doctors and by hospital or nursing home administrators who either fear being sued or simply disagree with the decisions being made and decide to fight them.

Much of the information about the limits on decisions is contained in chapters that deal with decision-making tools or decision makers. Interested individuals should read chapters 4, 5, and 12. A short review of the issue of limits on decisions, however, is worthwhile.

Decision-Making Tools: A Review

As discussed in earlier chapters, there are legal tools available to individuals who want to leave directions about how they should be treated in the event they become incompetent, that is, unable to make decisions and understand their consequences.

One of the more common tools is a *living will,* a document that can be written by individuals on their own (and witnessed by a number of other people) or with the assistance of a lawyer. *Living wills provide elderly individuals with a way to make some of their medical decisions in advance.* Basically, they allow individuals to express their preferences on the kinds of medical treatments they do or do not want to have in the future, if they become terminally ill. By stating these desires in advance, individuals who become too ill to speak for themselves still have written instructions that their doctors can follow. For example, individuals may decide that they do not want to be revived if they suffer a bad heart attack on top of an already serious illness. Or they may not want to be put on a respirator to be kept alive if they are already terminally ill. Or they may want to be given only painkilling drugs, and not antibiotics or chemotherapy, once they reach a certain point of illness. All these contingencies could be written into a living will.

Living wills are not automatically enforceable—but if doctors do not wish to comply with the directions in living wills, judges petitioned to review these cases will almost certainly use living wills as strong evidence of what patients wanted. Since patients have the right to determine the outcome of their own lives, courts will usually decide that the choices expressed in living wills should be followed. Doctors and health care institutions, such as hopsitals or nursing homes, can be sued for refusing to follow the wishes of their patients. Doctors can safely rely on living wills without having to go to court.

Living wills have to be written carefully. Sometimes states will have already written into law certain decisions that they believe cannot be made in advance by patients. It is important to find out any state limitations on directions that can be left in living wills. For more information, see chapter 4.

Another common legal tool is the *durable power of attorney,* which permits individuals to authorize other people to make decisions for them after they have become incompetent or too ill to speak for themselves (see chapter 11). Unlike living wills, durable powers of attorney are not limited to medical decisions.

One of the advantages of durable powers of attorney over living wills is that the ill individuals have left behind more than just a set of written instructions; they have also put into place people who are authorized to make decisions and argue that those decisions be followed. Some, but not all, states permit living wills to appoint such a person (a *proxy*). Often, people with durable power-of-attorney documents will discuss their preferences and future instructions with the individuals they appoint. This way, not only are their wishes known, but their rights to make those decisions in advance can be protected by the authorized individuals.

As with living wills, decisions made (or instructions followed) by the authorized individuals still have to comply with state laws. Once again, interested individuals must take the time to find out the limits imposed by their state legislatures and courts. For more information on powers of attorney, see chapter 5.

Decision Makers and De Facto Surrogates

There are a number of different ways people can be authorized or appointed to become *surrogate decision makers*—people who make decisions for those unable to do so for themselves. These surrogates can go by various names, depending on how they were appointed to their positions of authority.

Surrogates appointed by judges are called *guardians* or *conservators.* They are appointed after the individuals in question are declared incompetent and in need of a surrogate decision-maker (see chapter 12). Guardians have the most legal authority to make decisions for others, but even they may have to seek court approval to make certain serious decisions.

Surrogates appointed by a durable power-of-attorney document are called *agents* or *attorneys-in-fact.* Their decisions are limited to whatever categories (medical, financial, personal) are listed in the documents. *While durable power-of-attorney documents are not guarantees against agents having to go to court to enforce the wishes of* principals *(those who execute durable power-of-attorney agreements), the existence of such documents can certainly lessen those risks and give added weight to the decisions made by agents.*

Still others become informal or *de facto surrogates,* people, usually family members, who are not formally appointed or authorized to make decisions but are the only ones available to do so. Many people become de facto surrogates when individuals around them become ill. They begin taking over those individuals' personal care and making decisions and arrangements for it. They begin monitoring an individual's finances, making sure that bills get paid and checks get deposited into the correct accounts. Finally, they are looked to for instructions and decisions by doctors taking care of the individuals in question. This arrangement is commonplace, particularly between spouses and between elderly parents and their adult children.

De facto surrogates are the people to whom the decisions fall either when individuals have not planned ahead and authorized someone to be their agent or when no court hearing takes place to formally appoint guardians for them. *Often, this system works well enough—if there are no disagreements with the decisions being made.*

If family members disagree over the use of finances or about what kind of medical treatment the people in question should receive, then there can be trouble for de facto surrogates. Because they have no legal standing—no formal appointment or authorization—their decisions can easily be challenged both in courts and in hospitals and nursing homes. *Actually, de facto surrogates have only as much decision-making power as is allowed them by other interested parties (doctors, lawyers, bankers, other family members, and so on).*

The more controversial the decisions being made, the more likely it is that people may have to go to court to get them approved or enforced. This is true whether or not ill individuals have authorized agents, the courts have authorized guardians, or de facto surrogates have simply stepped in to make decisions that must be made; *however, those with legal authority to make decisions are far less likely to have their decisions challenged.*

All decisions made by all surrogates must comply with the laws of their states. These laws usually surround the making of critical care decisions—those which can prolong or permit the death of the ill people in question.

Family Consent Statutes

Several states have provided another way for families to make health care decisions on behalf of individuals who become incompetent without having appointed a surrogate. Instead of requiring families to petition a court to select a guardian, or letting them become de facto surrogates, these states have automatically authorized them to make health care decisions for incompetent patients (see appendix 31 for a list of states). In six of these states, family members are allowed to make all health decisions for incompetent patients; in the other nine, they are allowed to make decisions if patients are diagnosed as terminally ill (for more information on doctors' views of when patients are considered terminally ill, see chapter 4).

These *family consent statutes,* as they are called, vary somewhat from state to state. Some states have their own order of preference for which family members should be allowed to make decisions, while others list no priority at all. Some specifically authorize family members to make critical care decisions, including the withholding or withdrawing of life-prolonging treatment, for terminally ill or comatose patients. Others name specific conditions for which consent is not valid, such as abortion, sterilization, and mental health care (see appendix 32 for specific provisions included in family consent laws). If the incompetent individuals have already authorized agents or been given court-appointed guardians, they—not the family member named in the statute—would have the legal priority to make decisions in these states.

In states without family consent laws, doctors and hospitals usually decide to rely on the informal consent of families or require families to have formal guardians appointed for the individuals in question.

The Kinds of Medical Care Decisions
That Need to Be Made

A number of different kinds of medical care decisions may need to be made for incompetent patients—ranging from routine care to critical care, or life-and-death, decisions. Each kind of decision is accompanied by different requirements in the decision-making process. The categories and their requirements, discussed briefly below, are taken from the American Health Care Association's statement on health care decision making in long-term care facilities.

1. *Routine treatment decisions.* These decisions include changing medications for such chronic problems as blood pressure and diet or prescribing more exercise or physical therapy. Often, the general consent form signed by patients (or their family members) when they enter hospitals or nursing homes is enough to authorize these kinds of decisions. Such facilities should, however, try to inform agents, guardians, or family members of every routine decision to give them the opportunity to consent or object. Often, nurses can do this communicating after discussing treatment decisions with doctors.

2. *Nonroutine treatment decisions.* These decisions include surgery and invasive tests. In these cases, doctors should be the ones to discuss the proposed treatment with agents, guardians, or family members. In some instances, doctors can simply note on a patient's chart that they have received consent; in other instances (depending on state law), doctors will need written consent.

3. *Life-and-death treatment decisions.* Life-and-death decisions include whether or not to take patients off respirators when they aren't expected to be able to

breathe for themselves, agreeing to or refusing surgery or chemotherapy that might prolong life, and removing or retaining equipment for artificial feeding and hydration.

Facilities should, but are not likely to, have set procedures that allow surrogates to have treatments withheld (not started) or withdrawn (stopped). *It should be noted that both the courts and other professional groups have stated that there is no real difference between withholding and withdrawing treatment, and that legally authorized surrogates have the right to make either of those kinds of decisions on behalf of the patients they represent.* Once again, de facto surrogates may be able to make such decisions as well, as long as the decisions are agreed to by the doctors, hospitals, or nursing homes involved in the case. (See appendix 33 for the American Medical Association's statement on withholding or withdrawing life-prolonging medical treatment.)

Procedures and guidelines used by facilities to help them through the decision-making process include the following:

- Doctors of incompetent patients will usually be the ones to explain life-and-death situations and the need for medical decisions to family members, agents, guardians, and so on. They will also obtain informed consent or refusal of treatment from the surrogate decision-maker(s). (For more on informed consent, see chapter 7.)

- *Facilities may require that patients be diagnosed as terminally ill before such decisions can be made, or that the expected burdens (pain, nausea, weakness) of the treatments be greater than the expected benefits (improvement, longer life, less pain) before surrogates can refuse such treatment.*

- *When facilities (and family members) evaluate decisions, they should pay attention to how the burdens of proposed treatments compare with the benefits.* For example, if surgery is not expected to prolong life but is expected to relieve great pain, it may be appropriate, but if surgery will prolong life a little for people who will remain in great pain, then it might not be appropriate. This kind of comparison can help put some perspective into making life-and-death decisions.

- The existence of living wills, durable powers of attorney, and other legal documents that show patients' wishes is important. If none exists, then a review of prior decisions made by patients while still competent is also of great value. Such decisions can give considerable insight into what patients would have wanted.

The Decision to Remove Feeding and Hydration Tubes

One kind of life-and-death decision merits special notice: the removal of feeding and/or hydration tubes from incompetent patients who are comatose or terminally ill. The crux of the issue is whether or not food and water, supplied by tubes that enter through patients' noses, esophagi, or stomachs, are considered medical treatment or ordinary care. (These patients are unable to eat either by themselves or with assistance by the normal spoon-to-mouth technique.)

If these tubes are considered medical treatment, then surrogates have a greater legal right to refuse them. If, however, they are considered ordinary care, then surrogates cannot refuse them on behalf of patients. Some surrogates who refuse the use of life-support systems will also want to refuse feeding and hydration tubes. When writing a living will or a durable power-of-attorney document, individuals should discuss this issue with their lawyers to find out whether refusal is specifically permitted in their states. *However, it is likely that refusal by a competent person or a surrogate would be permitted if a clear directive is given in advance in a living will or durable power of attorney.* However, all surrogates, including guardians, may have to go to court to have these kinds of decisions enforced.

This issue is highly controversial, and individuals must be prepared to face the emotional and legal toll of making it. Many doctors, hospitals, and nursing homes are opposed to the removal of food and water and may be willing to challenge in court a decision to refuse such treatment or care.

The Decision to Donate Organs

Individuals may decide, while still competent, that they wish to donate their organs for use after they die. They may express this wish by filling out organ donation cards or by writing the request into their living wills or durable powers of attorney.

When no cards or documents have been signed, family members of a deceased individual may authorize organ donations on his or her behalf. The order of preference in which family members may make such decisions is

the spouse;

any adult child;

either parent;

any adult sibling;

the guardian; and

other authorized agents.

No family members are allowed to authorize organ donations if they are aware that the deceased patient (or other individuals with a higher priority in the decision-making process) would not have wanted them to do so.

The Decision to Participate in Medical Research

In most states, individuals and their legal representatives may decide whether or not patients should participate in research experiments. Such participation is something they should decide and arrange to do while still competent. Individuals may include these wishes in their living wills or durable powers of attorney. Guardians can consent to research participation as well. It is possible that family members, too, can make these arrangements in cases in which patients have said that they wished to participate in research experiments but did not document those statements. This is a sensitive subject, however, and the decision is probably best left to still-competent patients.

Financial and Personal Decisions

Medical decisions are not the only ones that carry restrictions and limitations, but they are probably the most common ones. Financial and personal decisions can be limited as well, either by the terms of a durable power of attorney or guardianship order or by other interested individuals who challenge such decisions in court.

Once again, formally appointed or authorized conservators and agents are less likely to be challenged in their decisions than de facto surrogates are. Conservators have their decision-making limits set by the courts, which, if asked, will review the decisions being made to ensure that they are appropriate. The same is true of agents, whose decision-making powers are determined in durable power-of-attorney documents. Challenges to agents may also be brought to court by other interested persons.

Standards for Making Decisions

Two standards are involved in making decisions on behalf of others.

1. *When individuals write durable power-of-attorney documents authorizing specific agents to make decisions for them, those agents are expected to use the* standard of substituted judgment, *which means they are to make, to the best of their ability, the same decisions as they think the incompetent patient in question would have made (even if they disagree with those decisions).*

2. *Guardians may use either the standard of substituted judgment or the* best-interests standard. *This second standard means that the decisions made by a guardian should serve, in the guardian's opinion, the best interests of the incompetent patient.*

What to Do When Decisions Are Challenged or Ignored

When guardians, conservators, agents, or de facto surrogates make decisions that are challenged or ignored, they have four basic responses available to them. They can

review and change a decision that seems inappropriate on second thought;

go to the doctor or individual disputing the decision;

go to the facility disputing the decision; or

go to court.

Whenever possible, it is probably best for decision makers to try to resolve their problems with the family members, friends, doctors, or nurses raising the complaints. If problems concern medical decisions and cannot be resolved by the people involved, decision makers can always go a step further—to hospital or nursing home administrators. Often health care facilities have their own sets of procedures for resolving problems, and it is usually worthwhile following them to see if the problems can't be worked out through the normal channels. Such facilities may also have special groups of people that review controversial medical decisions and may be helpful in the solving of problems; an example is an institutional ethics committee, made up of health care professionals, religious representatives, philosophers, and ethicists.

The fourth possibility, usually a last resort, is to go to court. Courts can resolve disputes over medical, personal, and financial decisions. They are also more expensive than the other options, as they involve lawyers' fees and court costs. Anyone can take cases to court. For example, if a hospital disagrees with a guardian's decision to remove a patient from a respirator, the hospital can petition the court to review the decision. Similarly, the guardian (or the agent or the de facto surrogate) could also take the case to court to get the court's approval to remove the patient from the respirator.

There are several places individuals can go for legal assistance in resolving problems:

- *The Older Americans Act funds legal services programs for the elderly.*
- *The Legal Services Corporation funds legal services programs for the poor.*
- *Some lawyers will pursue such claims for less than their regular fee.*
- *Some legal clinics or programs associated with law schools provide such services for little or no cost.*

Making important decisions is never easy, and it can be doubly painful if those decisions are challenged or ignored. While surrogates need to make the best decisions possible for the people they represent, *surrogates' responsibilities are greater than just the making of decisions—they include working to make sure those decisions are enforced or approved. People who can no longer speak for themselves depend on surrogates to speak for them, and there is perhaps no greater gift or sign of respect that can be given to elderly individuals than to stand up for their rights, their wishes, and their choices when they are unable to do so themselves.* (For more information on resolving problems, see chapters 7 and 9.)

Conclusion

15

People Will Listen—*If* You Talk

Overview

This book examines a great many issues and, hopefully, answers a great many questions. If it has served its purpose, it will provide both the reasons and the incentive for readers to plan ahead and avoid potential medical, financial, and legal problems. If nothing else, this book should have given enough information and ideas to its readers that they will know where to go next for help in dealing with a particular problem.

But what happens when an issue can't easily be solved or when individuals become so immersed in a situation that they want to make a difference not only in their own lives but also in the lives of others? Our very system of government depends on professional advocates and on individuals who see a problem to call it to the attention of their community, their state, and their nation.

If a problem can't be resolved by working directly with a hospital, a nursing home, a lawyer, or a federal or state agency, there are other options. Individuals can always take additional steps by going to the media; to local, state, or national advocacy groups and government bodies; and even to elected officials.

Getting Involved

Individuals who are dissatisfied with the results of working directly with a health facility or other group may wish to continue their fight. One way to do so is to become an advocate or activist on a particular issue. There is not only a place but also a tremendous need for community, state, and national involvement by people who have firsthand experience with the problems of the elderly.

Individuals who really know and understand these problems are valuable assets to many organizations and coalitions seeking change. Their involvement opens the door not only to providing advice based on personal experience but also to providing services. Many people frustrated by the care and advice received by their elderly relatives or friends have become volunteer ombudsmen, "Medigap" insurance counselors, and members of family councils or committees working with nursing homes to improve conditions. Accountants who have had problems with a parent in a nursing home would be welcomed into any number of groups that need financial advice not only for their own organizations but also for evaluating how money is spent by nursing homes or other groups they are in charge of monitoring. The same is true for people who have experience in fund-raising, public relations, secretarial work, and any number of other occupations.

It is also possible to participate on boards, commissions, committees, and groups such as the county or regional advisory committee on aging or the board of examiners for nursing homes. Many of the people sitting on these boards are political appointees, not professionals who have specialized in this kind of work—get appointed. In any particular state or community, both individuals and groups are working to improve a given problem or situation—find them, join them, and get involved.

Getting involved has several benefits: it is one of the best ways to force change within the system, it is an avenue into which frustrations can be channeled in a positive way, and it is an excellent link to the people who can sometimes do the most good—legislative authorities. Those who are putting on federal, state, or public hearings of one kind or another are usually eager to find people with personal experiences they're willing to share. Regular citizens *can* change national policy.

Getting Involved in the Political Arena

Opportunities for involvement and change exist at all levels of local, state, and federal government. In choosing which way to go, individuals should figure out which level is likely to have the most power and authority to address the particular problem they want to attack. If a problem involves a single nursing home, then it is probably better to deal with state and local officials. If the problem is wider reaching and involves federal law or policy, then federal officials are likely to be able to do the most good. Whatever the problem, having the support of local and state officials is likely to result in more people taking notice of the problem and more changes being made.

There's sometimes a tendency on the part of the public to believe that politicians and elected officials don't accomplish much or work very hard. The fact of the matter is that whether these people work hard or not, individuals who want to get their attention will have to be persistent and intelligent about getting it. Officials should be told that a particular situation is not the only one of its kind—that there are other people who are experiencing the same problem and who will also get involved if the problem is not solved.

Many officials at all levels are grateful to have bright, capable people to work with them on a particular problem. It's likely that individuals trying to get something done will have to do a lot of the work themselves. For example, if individuals need to have a letter from an official sent on their behalf, they should provide the official with a draft of that letter. Chances are it will get done faster that way anyway, and it's likely that the letter will be used word for word. If individuals are capable of working and fighting for something, they allow officials to free up their time to do the work for people who can't do it themselves.

Getting Attention and Influencing a Particular Problem

When approaching officials about a particular problem, explain it to them in *specific* terms. Don't drop in on elected or appointed officials unannounced, unless doing so is a deliberate tactic or a last resort. They are busy, too. Treat them as professionals, make appointments, insist on meeting with a particular person who is knowledgeable about—or at least familiar with—the problem to be presented. Individuals should send the person they are going to meet a history of the problem, as well as any other available background material. This kind of competent and determined display of action will let people know that the problems (and the individuals providing the information) are not going to go away.

When calling an official or staff member for the first time, understand that the person may not have much time to talk. If the subject requires a long time to explain, let the person know and offer to make an appointment at a time convenient to him or her. Ask what he or she would prefer. All people are entitled to the services of elected officials and government workers; they are elected, appointed, or employed to work on problems. It is reasonable to expect good service and if necessary, to insist on it.

If more than one official needs to be approached at the same time, do so directly and in a personalized fashion. If one letter is sent to six individuals, they may all think that someone else is going to take care of the problem. Write or call each one individually. Do any necessary homework before approaching a government official. For example, if one of the two senators in a state concentrates only on defense issues and is not known for dealing with human services, calling him or her might not do much good (unless the senator is a friend or relative). But if the second senator in the state is better known for his or her involvement with elder issues, then that is the person to contact. Find out the official's committee assignments and what legislation he or she has proposed—it's a matter of public record.

Be brief but clear, and prepare information in advance. Well-organized presentations of specific problems are going to get faster results. Offer to provide more detailed information if the person wants it, and set up an appointment to do so. Above all, have a sense of what changes are appropriate and necessary. Giving officials a sense of what can actually be done will save them a lot of time.

Don't underestimate the importance of working with an official's staff members—it's often an important part of getting changes made. The more important officials are, the less time they have to get directly involved. Senators and representatives have a great many issues to work on, so talk with their staff and get them interested and involved with specific problems. Don't dismiss the influence of the official's staff members; they are likely to have much more time, energy, and even expertise to devote to the subject and will be advising the official on what to do. Persistence and determination do pay off, as long as the problem is presented in an intelligent, thoughtful way.

Individuals should not expect that public officials or their staff know a great deal about a particular issue. That may be frustrating, but it is important to remember that they have a lot of subjects to deal with and may not be up-to-date on a particular problem. Take the opportunity to educate them.

When approaching an official, individuals can do more than simply explain the problem. They can offer to be a witness at a hearing or can suggest that the official hold a hearing on a particular subject. Offer to work with the official's staff on holding that hearing by supplying witnesses and background information. Above all, be professional when approaching officials—they are wary of people who seem to have an axe to grind or a chip on their shoulder. It's both necessary and important to be tenacious, tough, and determined—but individuals should use their anger to motivate what they do, not how they do it.

Involving the Media

Another option that can be used to get results is to involve the media. This can be done instead of or in addition to getting involved with an advocacy group or official body. Television and newspaper journalists are interested in getting stories; if individuals have a story to tell, they should do so. There are several advantages to getting the media involved. First of all, it can produce quick results. Media involvement is often what a health care facility or public agency fears most; exposure and bad publicity are both embarrassing and bad for business.

The problems of the elderly are often tailor-made for human interest stories and news—people who are fighting guardianship, people who are released too early from hospitals or abused in nursing homes, people whose money has been misused by their representative payees, and other stories can all attract the interest of the media. Sometimes just the threat of going to the media or of having a reporter come to a meeting can have immediate positive effects.

Letters to the editor and newspaper editorials can also force positive solutions to particular problems. Locate other people facing the same problem and try to get an appointment with the editorial board of a newspaper. Ask the board to consider writing an editorial or publishing a feature story on the problem.

Remember that many groups and individuals are as eager to get good publicity as they are to avoid bad publicity. When talking with officials or staff members who have been particularly helpful, make sure they know that their name (or their boss's name) will be mentioned to the press. Elected officials and their staffs, particularly, will respond to this gesture, as it is important to their ability to get reelected.

Whether approaching low- or high-ranking officials, the media, or bureaucrats, it is important to let them know, in a professional and polite way, that this problem is not going to go away. Individuals should be clear and firm that they are not going to give up, that they know what they're talking about, and that they know what they want done about it.

A Final Word

Many elderly people feel they have to accept what's been given to them—that they shouldn't make a fuss or upset the applecart. However, arguing for one's rights and the rights of others is an important part of the democratic process.

Forcing a particular problem into the spotlight and demanding that it be changed are not only okay; they're often the only way to get things done.

Above all, remember that there are many ways to get things done. Direct contacts with health facilities, lawyers, advocacy groups, elected officials, and the media are options to be considered. Wherever possible, however, it's wise to plan ahead and avoid the problem in the first place.

Appendixes

Appendix 1
Coverage under Medicare
Parts A and B

What Is Medicare?

Medicare is a Federal health insurance program for people 65 or older, people of any age with permanent kidney failure, and certain disabled people. It is administered by the Health Care Financing Administration. Local Social Security Administration offices take applications for Medicare, assist beneficiaries in claiming Medicare payments, and provide information about the program.

Medicare has two parts—hospital insurance and medical insurance. Hospital insurance helps pay for inpatient hospital care and certain follow-up care. Medical insurance helps pay for your doctor's services and many other medical services and items.

Hospital insurance is financed through part of the payroll (FICA) tax that also pays for Social Security. Voluntary medical insurance is financed from the monthly premiums paid by people who have enrolled for it and from general Federal revenues.

Who Is Eligible for Hospital Insurance

You are eligible for Medicare hospital insurance at 65 if:

you are entitled to monthly Social Security or railroad retirement benefits, or

you have worked long enough to be insured under Social Security or the railroad retirement system, or

you have worked long enough in Federal, State, or local government employment to be insured for Medicare purposes.

Source: Adapted for 1990 from *Medicare,* U.S. Dept. of Health and Human Services, Social Security Administration, SSA Publication No.: 05–10043, January 1989.

You are eligible before age 65 if:

> you have been entitled to Social Security disability benefits for 24 months, or

> you have worked long enough in government employment and meet the requirements of the Social Security disability program.

Under certain conditions, your spouse, divorced spouse, widow or widower, or dependent parents may be eligible for hospital insurance at age 65. Also, disabled widows and widowers under 65, disabled surviving divorced spouses under 65, and disabled children 18 or older may be eligible. For more information, contact a Social Security office.

You are eligible at any age if you need maintenance dialysis or a kidney transplant for permanent kidney failure and:

> you are insured or are getting monthly benefits under Social Security or the railroad retirement system, or

> you have worked long enough in government employment.

Your wife, husband, or child may be eligible if she or he needs maintenance dialysis or a transplant. Only the family member who has permanent kidney failure is eligible for Medicare protection.

If you are entitled to a railroad disability annuity or railroad retirement benefit based on disability, contact a railroad retirement office to find out if you are eligible for hospital insurance.

How You Get Hospital Insurance Protection

Some people have to apply for hospital insurance protection before it can start. For others, hospital insurance protection starts automatically.

If You Are Nearing 65

You do not have to retire to have hospital insurance protection at 65. But if you plan to keep working, you will have to file an application for hospital insurance in order for your protection to begin. You should apply at a Social Security office about 3 months before you reach 65.

If you are receiving Social Security or railroad retirement checks, your hospital insurance protection will start automatically at 65.

If you are a government retiree who is eligible for Medicare on the basis of government employment, you will have to apply for hospital insurance in order for it to begin at 65. Contact a Social Security office about 3 months before your 65th birthday to file your application.

If you aren't eligible for hospital insurance at 65, you can buy it. The basic premium is $176 a month for 1990. To buy hospital insurance, you also have to enroll and pay the monthly premium for medical insurance. If you are an alien, you must be a permanent resident and must reside in the U.S. for 5 years before you can buy Medicare. You can apply at any Social Security office.

If You Are Disabled

If you are under 65 and disabled, you will have hospital insurance protection automatically when you have been entitled to Social Security disability benefits for 24 months.

If you are a widow or widower between 50 and 65 and have been disabled at least 2 years but haven't applied for disability benefits because you are already getting other Social Security benefits, you may be eligible for hospital insurance. Contact a Social Security office for more information.

If you are a government employee and you become disabled before age 65, you may be eligible for Medicare on the basis of your government employment. Generally, there is a 29-month waiting period before your hospital insurance protection can start. But, you should contact a Social Security office as soon as you become disabled.

If You Have Permanent Kidney Failure

If you, your spouse, or your dependent child needs kidney dialysis or a kidney transplant, contact a Social Security office to apply for Medicare. You can apply by phone, or a representative can visit you to take an application if you are unable to go to the office.

If you are eligible for Medicare, your protection will start with the 3rd month after the month you actually begin maintenance dialysis treatments. Under certain conditions, your coverage can start earlier. The people in the Social Security office can tell you exactly when your protection will begin.

Who Is Eligible for Medical Insurance

Almost anyone who is 65 or older or who is eligible for hospital insurance can enroll for Medicare medical insurance. You don't need any Social Security or government work credits to get medical insurance.

Aliens 65 or older who are not eligible for hospital insurance must be permanent residents and must reside in the U.S. for 5 years before they can enroll in medical insurance.

How You Can Get Medical Insurance Protection

If you want medical insurance protection, your premium is $28.60 a month in 1990. Some people are automatically enrolled in medical insurance. Others must apply for it.

Automatic Medical Insurance Enrollment

If you are receiving Social Security benefits or retirement benefits under the railroad retirement system, you will be automatically enrolled for medical insurance—unless you say you don't want it—at the same time you become entitled to hospital insurance.

People Who Must Apply for Medical Insurance

You will have to apply for medical insurance if you:

plan to continue working past 65,

are 65 but aren't eligible for hospital insurance,

have permanent kidney failure,

are a disabled widow or widower between 50 and 65 who isn't getting disability benefits,

are eligible for Medicare on the basis of government employment, or

live in Puerto Rico or outside the U.S.

Contact your local Social Security or railroad retirement office for detailed information about medical insurance enrollment.

Your Medical Insurance Enrollment Period

There is a 7-month initial enrollment period for medical insurance. This period begins 3 months before the month you first become eligible for medical insurance and ends 3 months after that month.

If you enroll during the first 3 months of your enrollment period, your medical insurance protection will start with the month you are eligible. If you enroll during the last 4 months, your protection will start 1 to 3 months after you enroll.

If you don't take medical insurance during your initial enrollment period, you can sign up during a general enrollment period—January 1 through March 31 of each year. But if you enroll during a general enrollment period, your protection won't start until the following July. Also, your monthly premium will be 10 percent higher than the basic premium for each 12-month period you could have been enrolled but were not.

Special rules apply to workers and their spouses age 65 or older and to disabled people under 65 who have employer group health coverage. (See Employer Group Health Plans.)

Hospital Insurance Benefits

Medicare hospital insurance can help pay for inpatient hospital care, inpatient care in a skilled nursing facility, home health care, and hospice care.

Inpatient Hospital Care

If you need inpatient care, hospital insurance pays for unlimited approved care in a Medicare-certified hospital after you pay a deductible. The deductible is $592 in 1990. If you pay the hospital deductible in December, you may not have to pay it again if you are still a patient in January or are readmitted for inpatient care during January.

Covered services include semiprivate room, all meals, regular nursing services, operating and recovery room costs, hospital costs for anesthesia services, intensive care and coronary care, drugs, lab tests, X rays, medical supplies and appliances, rehabilitation services, and preparatory services related to kidney transplant surgery.

Skilled Nursing Facility Care

If you need inpatient skilled nursing or rehabilitation services and meet certain other conditions, hospital insurance helps pay for up to 100 days per spell of illness in a Medicare-certified skilled nursing facility. In 1990, patients must pay a coinsurance amount of $74 per day, for days 21–100 of their stay in a skilled nursing facility.

Covered services include semiprivate room, all meals, regular nursing services, rehabilitation services, drugs, medical supplies, and appliances.

Home Health Care

If you are confined to your home and meet certain other conditions, hospital insurance can pay the full approved cost of home health visits from a participating home health agency. There is no limit to the number of covered visits you can have.

Covered services include part-time skilled nursing care, physical therapy, and speech therapy. If you need one or more of those services, hospital insurance also covers part-time services of home health aides, occupational therapy, medical social services, and medical supplies and equipment.

Hospice Care

Under certain conditions, hospital insurance can help pay for hospice care for terminally ill beneficiaries, if the care is provided by a Medicare-certified hospice.

Special benefit periods apply to hospice care. Hospital insurance can pay for a maximum of two 90-day periods and one 30-day period. There is no limit to the amount of time hospital insurance will pay for hospice services, as long as the patient's need for such services is certified by a doctor.

Covered services include doctors' services, nursing services, medical appliances and supplies including outpatient drugs for pain relief, home health aide and homemaker services, therapies, medical social services, short-term inpatient care including respite care, and counseling.

Hospital insurance pays part of the cost of outpatient drugs and inpatient respite care. For all other covered services, hospital insurance pays the full cost.

Medical Insurance Benefits

Medicare medical insurance helps pay for your doctor's services and a variety of other medical services and supplies that are not covered by hospital insurance. Most of the services needed by people with permanent kidney failure are covered only by medical insurance.

Each year, as soon as you meet the annual medical insurance deductible, medical insurance generally will pay 80 percent of the approved charges for covered services you receive during the rest of the year. In 1990, the annual deductible is $75.

Doctors' Services

Medical insurance covers doctors' services no matter where you receive them in the United States. Covered doctors' services include surgical services, diagnostic tests and X rays that are part of your treatment, medical supplies furnished in a doctor's office, services of the office nurse, and drugs which are administered as part of your treatment and cannot be self-administered.

Outpatient Hospital Services

Medical insurance covers outpatient hospital services you receive for diagnosis and treatment, such as care in an emergency room or outpatient clinic of a hospital.

Home Health Visits

Medical insurance can cover an unlimited number of home health visits if all required conditions are met.

Other Medical and Health Services

Under certain conditions or limitations, medical insurance covers other medical services and supplies. Some examples are: ambulance transportation; home dialysis equipment, supplies, and periodic support services; independent laboratory tests; oral surgery; outpatient physical therapy and speech pathology services; and X rays and radiation treatments.

What Medicare Does Not Cover

Medicare provides basic protection against the high cost of illness, but it will not pay all of your health care expenses. Some of the services and supplies Medicare cannot pay for are: custodial care, such as help with bathing, eating, and taking medicine; dentures and routine dental care; eyeglasses, hearing aids, and examinations to prescribe or fit them; long-term care (nursing homes); personal comfort items, such as a phone or TV in your hospital room; prescription drugs and patent medicines; and routine physical checkups and related tests.

In certain situations, Medicare can help pay for care in qualified Canadian and Mexican hospitals. Otherwise Medicare cannot pay for hospital or medical services you receive outside the U.S. (Puerto Rico, Guam, American Samoa, the Virgin Islands, and the Northern Mariana islands are considered part of the U.S.)

If You Have Other Health Insurance

Many private health insurance companies point out that their policies for people who have Medicare are designed to coordinate their coverage with Medicare. They recommend that their policy holders sign up for Medicare medical insurance to have full protection.

If you have other health insurance, it may not pay for some of the services that are covered by Medicare medical insurance. You should get in touch with your insurer or agent to discuss your health insurance needs in relation to Medicare protection. This is particularly important if you have family members who are covered under your present policy. Also, in planning your health insurance coverage, remember that long-term care (or nursing home care) is not usually covered by medicare or most private health insurance policies.

If you have health care protection from the Veterans Administration (VA) or under the CHAMPUS or CHAMPVA program, your health benefits may change or end when you become eligible for Medicare. You should contact the VA, the Department of Defense, or a military health benefits advisor for information before you decide not to enroll in Medicare medical insurance.

If you have health care protection from the Indian Health Service, a Federal employees' health plan, or a State medical assistance program, the people there probably can help you decide whether it is to your advantage to have Medicare medical insurance.

For your own protection, be sure not to cancel any health insurance you now have until the month your Medicare coverage begins.

Buying Supplemental Health Insurance

If you want help in deciding whether to buy private supplemental insurance, ask at any Social Security office for the pamphlet, "Guide to Health Insurance for People with Medicare," or the fact sheet, "Should You Buy A Supplement to Medicare?"

Employer Group Health Plans

Employers with 20 or more employees are required to offer their workers age 65 or older the same health benefits that are provided to younger employees. They also must offer the spouses age 65 or older of workers of any age the same health benefits given younger employees.

If you are 65 or older and continue working or are the spouse 65 or older of a worker and you accept the employer's health plan, Medicare will be the secondary health insurance payer. If you reject the employer's health plan, Medicare will be the primary health insurance payer. The employer is not allowed to offer you Medicare supplemental coverage if you reject his or her health plan.

Also, if you work past 65 or are a spouse 65 or older and are covered under an employer health plan, you can wait to enroll in Medicare medical insurance during a special enrollment period. You won't have to pay the 10 percent premium surcharge for late enrollment, if you meet certain requirements.

If you are under 65 and disabled, Medicare will be the secondary payer if you choose coverage under your employer's health plan or a family member's employer health plan. This provision applies only to large group health plans. A large group health plan is any plan that covers employees of at least one employer that has 100 or more workers. But, you have the same special enrollment period and premium rights under Medicare medical insurance that workers 65 or older have. For more information about these special rules, contact your employer.

If you are under 65, are entitled to Medicare solely on the basis of permanent kidney failure, and have an employer group health plan, Medicare will be the secondary payer for an initial period of up to 12 months. At the end of the 12-month period, Medicare becomes the primary payer.

Any Questions

If you have any questions about enrolling in Medicare, please call your local Social Security office, or contact the Health Care Financing Administration at 1–800–888–1998 toll-free or contact the Medicare carrier in your area. Other phone numbers should be listed in your telephone book under "Social Security Administration" or "U.S. Government."

Appendix 2
State Insurance Departments

Alabama
Insurance Commissioner
135 South Union Street
Montgomery 36130–3401
205/269–3550

Alaska
Director of Insurance
333 Willoughby Avenue
9th Floor
P.O. Box D
Juneau 99811–0800
907/465–2515

American Samoa
Insurance Commissioner
Office of the Governor
Pago Pago 96797
684/633–4116

Arizona
Director of Insurance
3030 N. 3rd Street, Suite 1100
Phoenix 85012
602/255–5400

Arkansas
Insurance Commissioner
400 University Tower Building
12th and University Street
Little Rock 72204
501/371–1325

California
Commissioner of Insurance
100 Van Ness Avenue
San Francisco 94102
415/557–9624

or

3450 Wilshire Boulevard
Los Angeles 90010
213/736–2572

Colorado
Commissioner of Insurance
303 West Colfax Avenue
5th Floor
Denver 80204
303/620–4300

Source: National Association of Insurance Commissioners, 1989.

Connecticut
Insurance Commissioner
165 Capitol Avenue
State Office Building
Room 425
Hartford 06106
203/297–3801

Delaware
Insurance Commissioner
Rodney Building
841 Silverlake Boulevard
Dover 19901
302/736–4251

District of Columbia
Superintendent of Insurance
613 G Street, NW, 6th Floor
Washington 20001
202/727–7424

Florida
Insurance Commissioner
State Capitol
Plaza Level 11
Tallahassee 32399–0300
904/488–3440

Georgia
Insurance Commissioner
2 Martin L. King, Jr. Drive
Floyd Memorial Building
704 West Tower
Atlanta 30334
404/656–2056

Guam
Insurance Commissioner
855 West Marine Drive
Agana 96910
011–671/477–5106

Hawaii
Insurance Commissioner
1010 Richards Street
Honolulu 96813
808/548–5450

Idaho
Director of Insurance
500 South 10th Street
Boise 83720
208/334–2250

Illinois
Director of Insurance
320 West Washington Street
4th Floor
Springfield 62767
217/782–4515

or

State of Illinois Center
100 W. Randolph Street
Suite 15–100
Chicago 60601
312/917–2420

Indiana
Commissioner of Insurance
311 West Washington Street
Suite 300
Indianapolis 46204–2787
317/232–2386

Iowa
Insurance Commissioner
Lucas State Office Building
6th Floor
Des Moines 50319
515/281–5705

Kansas
Commissioner of Insurance
420 S.W. 9th Street
Topeka 66612
913/296–7801

Kentucky
Insurance Commissioner
229 West Main Street
P.O. Box 517
Frankfort, 40602
502/564–3630

Louisiana
Commissioner of Insurance
950 North 5th Street
Baton Rouge 70801–9214
504/342–5328

Maine
Superintendent of Insurance
State Office Building
State House, Station 34
Augusta 04333
207/582–8707

Maryland
Insurance Commissioner
501 St. Paul Place
Stanbalt Building
7th Floor South
Baltimore 21202
301/333–2520

Massachusetts
Commissioner of Insurance
280 Friend Street
Boston 02114
617/727–7189

Michigan
Insurance Commissioner
611 West Ottawa Street
2nd Floor North
Lansing 48933
517/373–9273

Minnesota
Commissioner of Insurance
500 Metro Square Building
5th Floor
St. Paul 55101
612/296–6848

Mississippi
Commissioner of Insurance
1804 Walter Sillers Building
Jackson 39205
601/359–3569

Missouri
Director of Insurance
301 West High Street 6 North
Jefferson City 65102–0690
314/751–2451

Montana
Commissioner of Insurance
126 North Sanders
Mitchell Building
Room 270
Helena 59601
406/444–2040

Nebraska
Director of Insurance
Terminal Building
941 O Street, Suite 400
Lincoln 68508
402/471–2201

Nevada
Commissioner of Insurance
Nye Building
201 South Fall Street
Carson City 89701
702/885–4270

New Hampshire
Insurance Commissioner
169 Manchester Street
Concord 03301
603/271–2261

New Jersey
Commissioner of Insurance
20 West State Street CN325
Trenton 08625
609/292–5363

New Mexico
Superintendent of Insurance
P.O. Drawer 1269
Santa Fe 87504–1269
505/827–4500

New York
Superintendent of Insurance
160 West Broadway
New York 10013
212/602–0429
or
Agency Building #1
Albany 12257
518/474–6600

North Carolina
Commissioner of Insurance
Dobbs Building
430 Salisbury Street
Raleigh 27611
919/733–7349

North Dakota
Commissioner of Insurance
600 E. Boulevard
Bismarck 58505–0320
701/224–2440

Ohio
Director of Insurance
2100 Stella Court
Columbus 43266–0566
614/644–2658

Oklahoma
Insurance Commissioner
1901 North Walnut
Oklahoma City 73105
405/521–2828

Oregon
Insurance Commissioner
21 Labor and Industries Building
Salem 97310
503/378–4271

Pennsylvania
Insurance Commissioner
Strawberry Square, 13th Floor
Harrisburg 17120
717/787–5173

Puerto Rico
Commissioner of Insurance
Fernandez Juncos Station
1607 Ponce de Leon Avenue
Santurce 00910
809/722–8686

Rhode Island
Insurance Commissioner
233 Richmond Street, Suite 237
Providence 02903–4237
401/277–2246

South Carolina
Chief Insurance Commissioner
1612 Marion Street
Columbia 29201
803/737–6117

South Dakota
Director of Insurance
Insurance Building
910 E. Sioux Avenue
Pierre 57501
605/773–3563

Tennessee
Commissioner of Insurance
Volunteer Plaza
500 James Robertson Parkway
Nashville 37219
615/741–2241

Texas
Commissioner—State Board of Insurance
1110 San Jacinto Boulevard
Austin 78701–1998
512/463–6464

Utah
Commissioner of Insurance
160 E. Third Street
Heber M. Wells Building
Salt Lake City 84111
801/530–6400

Vermont
Commissioner of Insurance
State Office Building
Montpelier 05602
802/828–3301

Virginia
Commissioner of Insurance
700 Jefferson Building
1120 Bank Street
Richmond 23209
804/786–3741

Virgin Islands
Commissioner of Insurance
Kongens Gade #18
St. Thomas 00802
809/774–2991

Washington
Insurance Commissioner
Insurance Building AQ21
Olympia 98504
206/753–7301

West Virginia
Insurance Commissioner
2019 Washington Street East
Charleston 25305
304/348–3394

Wisconsin
Commissioner of Insurance
123 West Washington Avenue
Madison 53707
608/266–0102

Wyoming
Commissioner of Insurance
Herschler Building
122 West 25th Street
Cheyenne 82002
307/777–7401

Appendix 3
Sample Living Will

**Society for the
Right to Die**
250 West 57th Street
New York, NY 10107

Living Will Declaration

INSTRUCTIONS
Consult this column for help
and guidance.

To my Family, Doctors, and All Those Concerned with
My Care

This declaration sets forth your
directions regarding medical
treatment.

I, _____, being of
sound mind, make this statement as a directive to be
followed if I become unable to participate in decisions
regarding my medical care.

If I should be in an incurable or irreversible mental or
physical condition with no reasonable expectation of
recovery, I direct my attending physician to withhold or
withdraw treatment that merely prolongs my dying. I
further direct that treatment be limited to measures to
keep me comfortable and to relieve pain.

You have the right to refuse
treatment you do not want,
and you may request the care
you do want.

These directions express my legal right to refuse treatment. Therefore I expect my family, doctors, and
everyone concerned with my care to regard themselves
as legally and morally bound to act in accord with my
wishes, and in so doing to be free of any legal liability
for having followed my directions.

You may list specific treatment you do not want. For example:

    Cardiac resuscitation
    Mechanical respiration
    Artificial feeding/fluids
        by tubes

Otherwise, your general statement, top right, will stand for your wishes.

I especially do not want: _____

_____

_____

_____

_____

_____

_____

You may want to add instructions for care you do want— for example, pain medication; or that you prefer to die at home if possible.

Other instructions/comments: _____

_____

_____

_____

If you want, you can name someone to see that your wishes are carried out, but you do not have to do this.

Proxy Designation Clause: Should I become unable to communicate my instructions as stated above, I designate the following person to act in my behalf:

Name _____

Address _____

If the person I have named above is unable to act in my behalf, I authorize the following person to do so:

Name _____

Address _____

Sign and date here in the presence of two adult witnesses, who should also sign.

Signed: _____ Date: _____

Witness: _____ Witness: _____

Keep the signed original with your personal papers at home. Give signed copies to doctors, family, and proxy. Review your declaration from time to time; initial and date it to show it still expresses your intent.

Appendix 4
Some State Laws
Regarding Living Wills
& Feeding Tubes

T he charts that follow provide information on which states have living will statutes, as well as their views relating to artificial feeding and hydration tubes. It is impossible, within the context of this book, to include the important details of each state's law. Therefore, interested individuals should consult with a reliable lawyer who is familiar with the individual provisions of their state's living will law. Remember, these provisions are important and may mean the difference between a living will's being considered valid or invalid at the time it is most needed. Additional information, as well as living will forms for each state, can be obtained by writing the Society for the Right to Die, 250 West Fifty-seventh Street, New York, New York 10107, or by calling (212) 246–6973.

The information that follows is copyrighted by and reprinted with permission from the Society for the Right to Die.

The following terms are defined for persons interested in writing a living will:

Declaration. A living will. Living will declarations must be executed voluntarily by an adult of "sound mind" to express treatment choices in the event of that adult's terminal condition and inability to participate in decision making.

Declarant. The person writing, or executing, the living will.

Statute. The state law authorizing the use of living wills.

Source: Society for the Right to Die, 1989.

- A *qualified patient* is typically one who is in a terminal condition with no prospect of recovery (some states specifically include patients in a persistent vegetative state (PVS), or permanent coma, although the absence of this provision does not necessarily exclude PVS patients from being qualified).

- *Terminal condition* may be a condition that will cause death "imminently," or "within a short time," if life-sustaining procedures are not used. It may also be a condition in which death will occur with or without life-sustaining procedures.

- *Life-sustaining procedures* that can be withheld or withdrawn are defined as mechanisms that only prolong dying; may specifically include or exclude artificial feeding and hydration; may not specifically mention and may therefore permit withdrawal of this kind of treatment; or may be unclear about withdrawing such treatment if not needed for a patient's comfort.

- Revocation (cancellation) procedures are simple, often merely requiring a patient to state that the living will is no longer valid.

- A qualified patient's expressed wishes take precedence over any prior declaration.

- People who are not allowed to act as witnesses to a living will declaration include any *interested party* such as any of the patient's relations by blood or marriage, any heirs to the patient's estate, and anyone professionally or financially responsible for the patient's medical care. Where a special witness is required for a living will declaration made by a nursing home patient, that person is usually, but not always, a state-appointed ombudsman or patient advocate.

- A living will declaration has no effect on a patient's life insurance or medical benefits.

- There are penalties for hiding, forging, or intentionally destroying a living will declaration or its revocation.

- A living will declaration is presumed valid.

- A state's living will law does not condone suicide, aided suicide, euthanasia, or homicide.

Living Will Legislation

Enacted State Laws: Alabama, Alaska, Arizona, Arkansas, California, Colorado, Connecticut, Delaware, District of Columbia, Florida, Georgia, Hawaii, Idaho, Illinois, Indiana, Iowa, Kansas, Louisiana, Maine, Maryland, Minnesota, Mississippi, Missouri, Montana, Nevada, New Hampshire, New Mexico, North Carolina, North Dakota, Oklahoma, Oregon, South Carolina, Tennessee, Texas, Utah, Vermont, Virginia, Washington, West Virginia, Wisconsin, and Wyoming.

1989 Living Will Bills Introduced   Massachusetts, Michigan, Nebraska, New Jersey, New York, Ohio, Rhode Island, South Dakota.

States With No Living Will Laws in 1989   Kentucky, Pennsylvania

Artificial Tube Feeding Laws

Alabama	5	Montana	3
Alaska	3	Nebraska	
Arizona	1, 6	Nevada	5
Arkansas	3	New Hampshire	6
California*	1, 5	New Jersey	1
Colorado*	1, 3	New Mexico	5
Connecticut**	1, 4	New York	1
Delaware	5	N. Carolina	5
District of Columbia	5	N. Dakota	1, 3
Florida*	1	Ohio	2, 3
Georgia*	1, 4	Oklahoma	4
Hawaii	1, 6	Oregon	3
Idaho	3	Pennsylvania	1
Illinois	3	Rhode Island	1
Indiana	6	S. Carolina	6
Iowa	6	S. Dakota	
Kansas	5	Tennessee***	3
Kentucky		Texas	5
Louisiana	5	Utah	6
Maine*	1, 4	Virginia*	1, 5
Maryland****	6	Vermont	5
Massachusetts	1	Washington	2, 5
Michigan	1	W. Virginia	6
Minnesota	3	Wisconsin	4
Mississippi	5	Wyoming	6
Missouri	2, 4		

Notes

1.   Court decisions indicate it is permissible to withhold or withdraw tube feeding.

2.   Court decisions prohibit withholding or withdrawing tube feeding under certain conditions.

3.   Statutes authorize withholding or withdrawing tube feeding.

4.   Statutes require tube feeding in some cases (Oklahoma), or permit withholding and withdrawing of some forms of life support but specifically exclude tube feeding from these.

5.   Jurisdictions with statutes that permit removal of life support in general, but don't mention tube feeding. Withholding or withdrawing tube feeding is implicitly permissible (except in Washington) when the patient's condition is covered by the act.

6.   Further interpretation is needed to decide if tube feeding may be withheld or withdrawn. Statutes usually associate tube feeding with comfort care, suggesting that it may be withheld or withdrawn if not necessary for comfort.

*   Courts here have held that patients have the right to have tube feeding withheld regardless of the terms of state statutes.

**   Court decisions interpreted the act to permit withdrawing tube feeding, despite language that would seem to prohibit it.

***   Interpreted by the attorney general to forbid the withdrawal of tube feeding when the "result would be death by starvation or dehydration."

****   Interpreted by the attorney general to permit withholding or withdrawing of tube feeding.

Appendix 5
State Law Governing Durable Power of Attorney, Health Care Agents, Proxy Appointments, and Special Requirements for Creating Durable Powers of Attorney

Alabama	5	Louisiana	4
Alaska	2	Maine	1
Arizona	3	Maryland	3
Arkansas	4	Massachusetts	5
California	1	Michigan	5
Colorado	2, 3	Minnesota	4
Connecticut	5	Mississippi	5
Delaware	4	Missouri	5
District of Columbia	1	Montana	5
Florida	4	Nebraska	5
Georgia	5	Nevada	1
Hawaii	3	New Hampshire	5
Idaho	4	New Jersey	3
Illinois	1	New Mexico	2
Indiana	4	New York	3
Iowa	3	N. Carolina	2
Kansas	5	N. Dakota	5
Kentucky	5	Ohio	1

Oklahoma	5	Utah	4
Oregon	1	Virginia	4
Pennsylvania	2	Vermont	1
Rhode Island	1	Washington	2
S. Carolina	5	W. Virginia	5
S. Dakota	5	Wisconsin	5
Tennessee	5	Wyoming	4
Texas*	1, 4		

Notes

1. Jurisdictions with Durable Power of Attorney statutes that permit agents to make medical decisions, specifically including decisions to withdraw or withhold life support. The agent can act when the patient loses the ability to make his or her own medical decisions.

2. States with Durable Power of Attorney statutes that positively authorize consent to medical treatment but make no mention of authority to withdraw or withhold life support.

3. States with Durable Power of Attorney statutes that, through court decisions, Attorney Generals' Opinions or other statutes, have been interpreted to permit agents to make medical decisions, including those to withhold or withdraw life support.

4. States that authorize proxy appointments through their living will or natural death acts. Proxies are permitted to make decisions authorized by the act when the patient is in a medical condition covered by the act (usually "terminal" as defined in the act).

5. States with general Durable Power of Attorney statutes that make no mention of medical decisions.

* Proxy decision making in Texas is also authorized by a provision in its Natural Death Act and by court interpretations.

Source: Society for the Right To Die, 1989.

Special Requirements for Creating Durable Powers of Attorney

State	Notary Required	Filing Required	Other
Arkansas	Yes (or approval of Probate Court)	Probate Court	
California*	Yes (or signed by two witnesses)		If patient is in nursing home, one witness must be patient advocate or ombudsman. Must be accompanied by statutory notice or signed by an attorney.
Connecticut	Yes		Must be accompanied by statutory notice.
Florida	No		Only a spouse, parent, adult child, sibling, niece or nephew may be appointed.
Minnesota	Yes		
Missouri	Yes	Recorder of deeds	
New York	Yes		Must be accompanied by statutory notice.
North Carolina	Yes	Register of deeds (copy with clerk of Superior Court)	
Oklahoma	No	Clerk of State District Court	Must be approved by judge of state District Court.
Rhode Island*	No		At least one witness must not be related by blood, marriage or adoption and must not be entitled to any part of the maker's estate.
South Carolina	Yes	Register of Mesne Conveyance	Requires three witnesses.
Wyoming	No	Clerk of District Court (copy with clerk of county court where principal resides)	Must be approved by judge of state District Court

*California and Rhode Island have statutory forms for durable powers of attorney for health care which include a notice or warning to persons executing the document.

Source: B. Mishkin, *A Matter of Choice: Planning Ahead for Health Care Decisions*, Senate Special Committee on Aging, 1986.

Appendix 6
Sample State Power-of-Attorney Form

Statutory Form of Power of Attorney
(Minnesota)

§523.23. Statutory short form of general power of attorney; formal requirements; joints agents.

Subdivision 1. Form.

The use of the following form in the creation of a power of attorney is lawful, and, when used, it shall be construed in accordance with the provisions of sections 523.23 and 523.24:

Notice: The powers granted by this document are broad and sweeping. They are defined in section 523.24. If you have any questions about these powers, obtain competent advice. The use of any other or different form of power of attorney desired by the parties is also permitted. This power of attorney may be revoked by you if you later wish to do so. This power of attorney authorizes the attorney-in-fact to act for you but does not require that he or she do so.

Know All Men by These Presents, which are intended to constitute a Statutory Short Form Power of Attorney pursuant to Minnesota Statutes, section 523.23:

That I

(insert name and address of the principal) do hereby appoint

(insert name and address of the attorney-in-fact, or each attorney-in-fact, if more than one is designated) my attorney(s)-in-fact to act (jointly):

Note: If more than one attorney-in-fact is designated and the principal wishes each attorney-in-fact alone to be able to exercise the power conferred, delete the word "jointly." Failure to delete the word "jointly" will require the attorneys-in-fact to act unanimously.)

First: In my name, place, and stead in any way which I myself could do, if I were personally present, with respect to the following matters as each of them is defined in section 523.24:

[To grant to the attorney-in-fact any of the following powers, make a check or "x" in the line in front of each power being granted. To delete any of the following powers, do not make a check or "x" in the line in front of the power. You may, but need not, cross out each power being deleted with a line drawn through it (or in similar fashion). Failure to make a check or "x" in the line in front of the power will have the effect of deleting the power unless the line in front of the power of (O) is checked or x-ed.] Check or "x"

(A)   real property transactions;
(B)   tangible personal property transactions;
(C)   bond, share, and commodity transactions;
(D)   banking transactions;
(E)   business operating transactions;
(F)   insurance transactions;
(G)   beneficiary transactions;
(H)   gift transactions;
(I)   fiduciary transactions;
(J)   claims and litigation;
(K)   family maintenance;
(L)   benefits from military service;
(M)   records, reports, and statements;
(N)   all other matters;
(O)   all of the powers listed in (A) through (N) above.

Second: [You must indicate below whether or not this power of attorney will be effective if you become incompetent. Make a check or "x" in the line in front of the statement that expresses your intent.]

This power of attorney shall continue to be effective if I become incompetent. It shall not be affected by my later disability or incompetency.

This power of attorney shall not be effective if I become incompetent.

Third: [You must indicate below whether or not this power of attorney authorizes the attorney-in-fact to transfer your property directly to himself or herself. Make a check or "x" in the line in front of the statement that expresses your intent.]

This power of attorney authorizes the attorney-in-fact to transfer property directly to himself or herself.

This power of attorney does not authorize the attorney-in-fact to transfer property directly to himself or herself.

In Witness Whereof I have hereunto signed my name this _____ day of _____, 19____.

(Signature of Principal)

(Acknowledgment)

Specimen Signature of Attorney(s)-in-Fact

Appendix 7
Sample General
Power-of-Attorney Form

KNOW ALL PEOPLE by these presents that I, (name of principal), Social Security Number _____, permanently domiciled in (residence of principal—city and state), do hereby make, constitute, and appoint my (relationship of attorney-in-fact to principal), (name of agent or attorney-in-fact), presently of (residence—city and state only—of attorney-in-fact), as my true and lawful attorney-in-fact to act in my name, place and stead, for my use and benefit, and to exercise or perform any act, power, duty, right or obligation whatsoever that I now have or may hereafter acquire relating to any person, matter, transaction or property, real or personal, tangible or intangible, now owned or hereafter acquired by me, including, by way of example and not by way of limitation, the powers set out in this power of attorney. If (s)he cannot or will not so serve, then I appoint my (relationship of substitute attorney-in-fact), (name of substitute attorney-in-fact), presently of (residence—city and state—of substitute attorney-in-fact), to serve in his/her stead.

Article I—Powers

My [agent or] attorney-in-fact shall have, by way of illustration and not by way of limitation, the following powers:

Section 1. To ask, demand, sue for, collect and receive each and every sum of money, including, but not limited to, wages, checking or savings account(s), debts, legacies, bequests, money-market accounts, Treasury bills, interest, dividends, certificates of

Source: *Guardianship and Alternative Legal Interventions: A Compendium for Training and Practice*, The Center for Social Gerontology, Inc.

deposit, annuities, demands, pensions or government benefits, now or hereafter due, owing, or payable, to which I have a claim; to take any lawful means for the recovery of the same; to execute and deliver a satisfaction or release, together with the right and power to compromise or compound any claim or demand;

Section 2. To perform any and all banking business including, by way of example and not by way of limitation: to draw, make, sign in my name, accept or deliver notes, checks, drafts, orders, receipts and to otherwise make withdrawals from any checking or savings account in which I may have any interest, solely or jointly with any other persons, in any financial institution; to endorse, negotiate and deliver checks, certificates of deposit, notes, drafts, money-market instruments or any other instrument for the payment of money and to deposit same as check or for collection and cash into any savings or checking account in which I may have an interest, solely or jointly with other persons, in any financial institution; to have access to any safe deposit box of which I am tenant or co-tenant and to exercise any rights I might have with regard to that safety deposit box and the contents thereof.

Section 3. To contract for, buy, sell, exchange, transfer, and in any legal manner deal with personal property, tangible or intangible, including but not limited to goods, wares and merchandise, choses in action and all other property in possession or in action; and to mortgage, transfer in trust, or otherwise encumber the same to secure payment of a negotiable or non-negotiable note or the performance of any obligation or agreement;

Section 4. To contract for, purchase, receive and take possession of real property, or any interest in or building on real property, and of evidence of title thereto; to lease the same for any term and for any lawful purpose; to sell, exchange, grant or convey the same with or without warranty; and to mortgage, transfer in trust, or otherwise encumber the same to secure payment of a negotiable or non-negotiable note for the performance of any obligation or agreement; it being expressly intended to permit my attorney-in-fact to act on my behalf with respect to all transactions related to my residence at [*], and any such other real property as I may own or acquire; it being further intended that my attorney-in-fact may record or cause to be recorded upon public land records any such act or transaction authorized above;

Section 5. To borrow or lend money, and to execute and deliver or receive negotiable or non-negotiable notes, with or without security as my attorney-in-fact shall deem proper;

Section 6. At my attorney-in-fact's sole discretion, to make such gifts as my attorney-in-fact may deem proper, either outright or in trust, including charitable gifts and

---

*It is appropriate to insert the address *and* legal description of any real property so that it is clear that the attorney-in-fact has authority to act with regard to that property. This also facilitates recording the power of attorney with the register of deeds.

pledges; provided, however, that no gifts to a single donee shall in any one calendar year exceed the amount of Ten Thousand Dollars ($10,000.00);

Section 7. To prepare, execute and file, by way of illustration and not by limitation, reports, returns, declarations, forms and statements of all and any kinds for tax purposes including, but not limited to, federal, state, local, income, gift, real estate, personal property, business, and intangibles taxes and any other kind of tax whatsoever; to receive any and all information whatsoever bearing upon my obligations to pay taxes, to adjust, settle, pay and compromise any and all claims regarding my tax liabilities; to appear for me and represent me in connection with any tax matter; and to receive any tax refunds due me;

Article II—Durability

Section 1. This power of attorney shall not be affected by my subsequent disability or incapacity, and all acts done pursuant to its terms shall be as fully effective as if I were competent and were myself so acting or causing others to act. This declaration of durability is made as an expression of my intent, and I ask that my intent be honored, if necessary, pursuant to any law of any other jurisdiction that may have an interest in the proceeding in question, whether the law is now in effect or later enacted to authorize powers of attorney which survive the incompetence of the principal.

Section 2. If for any reason this power is determined not to be legally binding, I ask that it be honored to the fullest extent possible.

Section 3. In executing this general durable power of attorney, it is my intent to avoid the necessity of ever having to seek judicial appointment of a guardian of my person and/or for my estate; however, should I ever be adjudged incapacitated or incompetent by a court, I hereby nominate my attorney-in-fact to be appointed as the guardian of my person and/or my estate.

Article III—Discretion in the Exercise of Duties

Section 1. I give and grant to my attorney-in-fact full power and authority to do and perform all and every act and thing whatsoever required, necessary or appropriate, to be determined solely in his/her discretion, to be done as fully to all intents and purposes as I might or could do if personally present, hereby ratifying all that my attorney-in-fact shall do or cause to be done by virtue of this power of attorney. The power and authority hereby conferred upon my attorney-in-fact shall be applicable to all matters relating to my financial and business matters, as well as to other matters, as fully as I may decide such matters myself if competent and present.

Section 2. My attorney-in-fact may retain, compensate, and make such use of agents to assist in acting under this power as my attorney-in-fact may deem advisable; and my attorney-in-fact may designate another person as the joint or successor attorney-in-fact either temporarily or permanently, under this power of attorney if for any reason my attorney-in-fact is unable or unwilling to act individually pursuant to the other provisions of this power of attorney but my attorney-in-fact has no duty to appoint a joint or successor attorney-in-fact and it would be contrary to my wishes and intent for any person to require that my attorney-in-fact do so or to require that my attorney-in-fact obtain the consent of any other person for any determination which my attorney-in-fact makes.

Section 3. My attorney-in-fact has sole discretion to determine the time when, purpose for, and manner in which any power herein conferred upon my attorney-in-fact shall be exercised, and the conditions to be accepted or waivers to be granted incident thereto.

Section 4. The powers delegated under this power of attorney are separable, so that the invalidity of one or more powers shall not affect any others.

Article IV—Revocation

Section 1. This general durable power of attorney revokes any previous powers of attorney granted by me.

Section 2. This general durable power of attorney may be voluntarily revoked by me at any time, either by my written revocation delivered to the last known address of my attorney-in-fact or by my written revocation entered of record in the deed of records of _____ County, _____ (State).

Article V—Third Party Reliance

Section 1. Third parties may rely upon the representation of my attorney-in-fact as to all matters relating to any power granted herein.

Section 2. For the purpose of inducing any third party to act in accordance with the grant of powers in this Power of Attorney, I and my successors, assignees, heirs and legal representatives agree to indemnify and hold harmless from any loss suffered or liability incurred by said third party by it acting in good faith in accordance with the Power of Attorney prior to said third party's receipt of written notice of termination of this Power of Attorney.

I have signed and delivered this Durable Power of Attorney consisting of _____ pages this _____ day of _____, 19_____.

_____
(name of principal)

(name of principal), the Principal named in the foregoing instrument, signed this instrument, on the _____ day of _____, 19_____. At that time, (s)he declared that the instrument reflects his/her will and intent with respect to his/her financial affairs and all other matters contained herein. At the request of (name of principal), in the presence of (name of principal) and in the presence of each other, each of us believing (name of principal) to be now competent, we have signed our names as witnesses. [Note: The attorney-in-fact should not act as a witness, as that may cause third parties to question the authenticity of the document.]
Witnesses:

_____

_____

_____

State of _____)SS.
          _____)
County of _____

On the _____ day of _____, 19_____, before me, the undersigned, a Notary Public in and for (jurisdication of signing), personally appeared (name of principal), known to me to be the person whose name is subscribed to the within instrument, and acknowledged that (s)he executed the same. Witness my hand and official seal.

(Seal) _____
       Notary public in and for
       (jurisdiction of signing)

My Commission expires   _____

Drafted by:
(Name of attorney
address
telephone number)

Appendix 8
Sample Durable Power of Attorney for Health Care Forms

Generic Short Form

I, _____
hereby appoint:

_____
name

_____
home address

_____

_____
home telephone number

_____
work telephone number

as my agent to make health care decisions for me if and when I am unable to make my own health care decisions. This gives my agent the power to consent to giving, withholding or stopping any health care, treatment, service, or diagnostic pro-cedure. My agent also has the authority to talk with health care personnel, get information, and sign forms necessary to carry out those decisions.

If the person named as my agent is not available or is unable to act as my agent, then I appoint the following person(s) to serve in the order listed below:

1. _____
   name

   _____
   home address

   _____

   _____

   _____
   home telephone number

   _____
   work telephone number

Source: Barbara Mishkin, Hogan and Hartson, Washington, D.C.

2. _____
name

_____
home address

_____

_____

_____

home telephone number

_____
work telephone number

By this document I intend to create a power of attorney for health care which shall take effect upon my incapacity to make my own health care decisions and shall continue during that incapacity.

My agent shall make health care decisions as I direct below or as I make known to him or her in some other way.

(a) Statement of desires concerning life-prolonging care, treatment, services, and procedures:

_____

_____

_____

_____

_____

(b) Special provisions and limitations:

_____

_____

_____

_____

_____

_____

_____

Appendix 8 (continued)

Sample State Durable Power of Attorney
for Health Care Decisions Form

(California Civil Code Sections 2410–2443)

Warning to Person Executing This Document

This is an important legal document. It creates a durable power of attorney for health care. Before executing this document, you should know these important facts:

1. This document gives the person you designate as your attorney-in-fact the power to make health care decisions for you. This power is subject to any limitations or statement of your desires that you include in this document. The power to make health care decisions for you may include consent, refusal of consent, or withdrawal of consent to any care, treatment, service, or procedure to maintain, diagnose, or treat a physical or mental condition. You may state in this document any types of treatment or placements that you do not desire.

2. The person you designate in this document has a duty to act consistent with your desires as stated in this document or otherwise made known or, if your desires are unknown, to act in your best interests.

3. Except as you otherwise specify in this document, the power of the person you designate to make health care decisions for you may include the power to consent to your doctor not giving treat-ment or stopping treatment which would keep you alive.

4. Unless you specify a shorter period in this document, this power will exist for seven years from the date you execute this document and, if you are unable to make health care decisions for yourself at the time when this seven-year period ends, this power will continue to exist until the time when you become able to make health care decisions for yourself.

5. Notwithstanding this document, you have the right to make medical and other health care decisions for yourself so long as you can give informed consent with respect to the particular decision. In addition, no treatment may be given to you over your objections, and health care necessary to keep you alive may not be stopped if you object.

6. You have the right to revoke the appointment of the person designated in this document to make health care decisions for you by notifying that person of the revocation orally or in writing.

Source: *A Matter of Choice: Planning Ahead for Health Care Decisions,* AARP, Washington, D.C.

7. You have the right to revoke the authority granted to the person designated in this document to make health care decisions for you by notifying the treating physician, hospital, or other health care provider orally or in writing.

8. The person designated in this document to make health care decisions for you has the right to examine your medical records and to consent to their disclosure unless you limit the right in this document.

9. This document revokes any prior durable power of attorney for health care.

10. *If there is anything in this document that you do not understand, you should ask a lawyer to explain it to you.*

1. Designation of Health Care Agent

I, _____

_____
(Insert your name)

do hereby designate and appoint:

Name: _____

Address: _____

_____

Telephone Number: _____

as my attorney-in-fact to make health care decisions for me as authorized in this document.

(Insert the name and address of the person you wish to designate as your attorney-in-fact to make health care decisions for you. None of the following may be designated as your attorney-in-fact: (1) your treating health care provider, (2) an employee of your treating health care provider, (3) an operator of a community care facility, or (4) an employee of an operator of a community care facility.)

2. Creation of Durable Power of Attorney for Health Care

By this document I intend to create a durable power of attorney by appointing the person designated above to make health care decisions for me as allowed by Sections 2410 to 2443, inclusive, of the California Civil Code. This power of attorney shall not be affected by my subsequent incapacity.

3. General Statement of Authority Granted

In the event that I am incapable of giving informed consent with respect to health care decisions, I hereby grant to the attorney-in-fact named above full power and authority to make health care decisions for me before, or after my death, including: Consent, refusal of consent, or withdrawal of consent to any care, treatment, service, or procedure to maintain, diagnose, or treat a physical or mental condition, subject only to the limitations and special provisions, if any, set forth in Paragraph 4 or 6.

4. Special Provisions and Limitations

(By law, your attorney-in-fact is not permitted to consent to any of the following: Commitment to or placement in mental health treatment facility, convulsive treatment, psycho-surgery, sterilization, or abortion. If there are any other types of treatment or placement that you do not want your attorney-in-fact to have authority to give consent for or other restriction you wish to place on his or her attorney-in-fact's authority, you should list them in the space below. If you do not write in any limitations, your attorney-in-fact will have the broad powers to make health care decisions on your behalf which are set forth in Paragraph 3, except to the extent that there are limits provided by law.)

In exercising the authority under this durable power of attorney for health care, the authority of my attorney-in-fact is subject to the following special provisions and limitations:

_____

_____

_____

_____

_____

_____

_____

5. Duration

I understand that this power of attorney will exist for seven years from the date I execute this document unless I establish a shorter time. If I am unable to make health care decisions for myself when this power of attorney expires, the authority I have granted my attorney-in-fact will continue to exist until the time when I become able to make health care decisions for myself.

I wish to have this power of attorney end before seven years on the following date: _____.

6. Statement of Desires

(With respect to decisions to withhold or withdraw life sustaining treatment, your attorney-in-fact must make health care decisions that are consistent with your known desires. You can, but are not required to, indicate your desires below. If your desires are unknown, your attorney-in-fact has the duty to act in your best interests; and, under some circumstances, a judicial proceeding may be necessary so that a court can determine the health care decision that is in your best interests. If you wish to indicate your desires, you may initial the statement or statements that reflect your desires and/or write your own statements in the space below.)

(If the statement reflects your desires, initial the box next to the statement.)

1. I desire that my life be prolonged to the greatest extent possible, without regard to my condition, the chances I have for recovery or long-term survival, or the cost of the procedures. (_____)

2. If I am in a coma which my doctors have reasonably concluded is irreversible, I desire that life sustaining or prolonging treatments or procedures *not* be used.   (_____)

3. If I have an incurable or terminal condition or illness and no reasonable hope of long-term recovery or survival, I desire that life sustaining or prolonging treatments *not* be used.   (_____)

4. I do not desire treatment to be provided and/or continued if the burdens of the treatment outweigh the expected benefits. My attorney-in-fact is to consider the relief of suffering, the preservation or restoration of functioning, and the quality as well as the extent of the possible extension of my life.   (_____)

(If you wish to change your answer, you may do so by *drawing* an "X" through the answer you do not want, and circling the answer you prefer.)

Other or additional statements of desires:

_____

_____

_____

_____

_____

_____

_____

_____

7. Designation of Alternate Attorney-in-Fact

(You are not required to designate any alternative attorney-in-fact but you may do so. Any alternative attorney-in-fact you designate will be able to make the same health care decisions as the attorney-in-fact designated in Paragraph 1 above in the event that he or she is unable or unwilling to act as your attorney-in-fact. Also, if the attorney-in-fact designated in Paragraph 1 is your spouse, his or her designation as your attorney-in-fact is automatically revoked by law if your marriage is dissolved.)

If the person designated in Paragraph 1 as my attorney-in-fact is unable to make health care decisions for me, then I designate the following persons to serve as my attorney-in-fact to make health care decisions for me as authorized in this document, such persons to serve in the order listed below:

A. First Alternative Attorney-in-fact

Name: _____

Address: _____

_____

Telephone Number: _____

B. Second alternate Attorney-in-fact

Name: _____

Address: _____

_____

Telephone Number: _____

8. Prior Designations Revoked

I revoke any prior durable power of attorney for health care.

(You must date and sign this power of attorney).

I sign my name to this Statutory Short Form Durable Power of Attorney for Health Care on _____

_____ at

(Date)

_____,

(City)

_____.

(State)

_____

(Signature)

(This power of attorney will not be valid for making health care decisions unless it is either (1) signed by at least two qualified witnesses who are person-ally known to you and who are present when you sign or acknowledge your signature or (2) acknowledged before a notary public in California.)

Certificate of Acknowledgment of Notary Public

(You may use acknowledgment before a notary public instead of the statement of witnesses.)

State of California _____)

_____)SS.

County _____) of

On this _____ day of _____,
in the year _____, before me,

_____

(here insert name of notary public)

personally appeared

_____

(here insert name of principal)

personally known to me (or proved to me on the basis of satisfactory evidence) to be the person whose name is subscribed to this instrument, and acknowledged that he or she executed it. I declare under penalty of perjury that the person whose name is subscribed to this instrument appears to be of sound mind and under no duress, fraud, or undue influence.

Notary Seal _____

(Signature of Notary Public)

Statement of Witnesses

(You should carefully read and follow this witnessing procedure. This document will not be valid unless you comply with the witnessing procedure. If you elect to use witnesses instead of having this document notarized, you must use two qualified adult witnesses. None of the following may be used as a witness:

(1) A person you designate as the attorney-in-fact,

(2) A health care provider,

(3) An employee of a health care provider,

(4) The operator of a community care facility,

(5) An employee of an operator of a community care facility.

At least one of the witnesses must make the additional declaration set out following the place where the witnesses sign.)

I declare under penalty of perjury under the laws of California that the principal is personally known to me, that the principal signed or acknowledged this durable power of attorney in my presence, that the principal appears to be of sound mind and under no duress, fraud, or undue influence, that I am not the person appointed as attorney-in-fact by this document, and that I am not a health care provider, an employee of a health care provider, the operator of a community care facility, nor an employee of an operator of a community care facility.

Signature: _____

Print Name: _____

Residence Address: _____

Date: _____

Signature: _____

Print Name: _____

Residence Address: _____

_____

_____

Date: _____

(At least one of the above witnesses must also sign the following declaration.)

I declare under penalty of perjury under the laws of California that I am not related to the principal by blood, marriage, or adoption, and to the best of my knowledge I am not entitled to any part of the estate of the principal upon the death of the principal under a will now existing or by operation of law.

Signature: _____

Signature: _____

Special Requirements

(Special additional requirements must be satisfied for this document to be valid if (1) you are a patient in a skilled nursing facility or (2) you are a conservatee under the Lanterman-Petris-Short Act and you are appointing the conservator as your agent to make health care decisions for you.)

1. If you are a patient in a skilled nursing facility (as defined in Health and Safety Code Section 1250(c)) at least one witness must be a patient advocate or ombudsman. The patient advocate or ombudsman must sign the witness state-

ment *and* must also sign the following declaration.

I declare under penalty of perjury under the laws of California that I am a patient advocate or ombudsman as designated by the State Department of Aging and am serving as a witness as required by sub-division (a) (2)A of Civil Code 2432.

Signature: _____

Print Name: _____

Residence Address: _____

_____

_____

_____

Date: _____

2. If you are a conservatee under the Lanterman-Petris-Short Act (of Division 5 of the Welfare and Institutions Code) and you wish to designate your conservator as your agent to make health care decisions, you must be represented by legal counsel. Your lawyer must sign the following statement:

I have advised my client _____
(Name)
concerning his or her rights in connection with this matter and the consequences of signing or not signing this durable power of attorney and my client, after being so advised, has executed this durable power of attorney.

Signature: _____

Print Name: _____

Residence Address: _____

_____

Date: _____

Copies: You should retain an executed copy of this document and give one to your attorney-in-fact. The power of attorney should be available so a copy may be given to your health care providers.

Appendix 9
Sample Springing (Durable)
Power-of-Attorney Form

A springing power of attorney should be carefully drafted to ensure that the power does not take effect either too early or too late. One possible version is presented below. Any definition and test of disability may be used so long as they provide the principal with adequate protections considering the facts of his or her particular situation.

KNOW ALL PEOPLE by these presents that I, (name of principal), Social Security Number _____, permanently domiciled in (residence of principal—city and state), do hereby make, constitute, and appoint my (relationship of attorney-in-fact to principal), (name of attorney-in-fact), presently of (residence of attorney-in-fact), as my true and lawful attorney-in-fact to act in my name, place and stead, for my use and benefit, and to exercise or perform any act, power, duty, right or obligation whatsoever that I now have or may hereafter acquire relating to any person, matter, transaction or property, real or personal, tangible or intangible, now owned and hereafter acquired by me, including, by way of example and not by way of limitation, the powers set out in this power of attorney. If (s)he cannot or will not so serve, then I appoint my (relationship of substitute attorney-in-fact), (name of substitute attorney-in-fact), presently of (residence of substitute attorney-in-fact), to serve in his/her stead.

Source: *Guardianship and Alternative Legal Interventions: A Compendium for Training and Practice,* The Center for Social Gerontology, Inc.

Article 1—Powers

My attorney-in-fact shall have, by way of illustration and not by way of limitation, the following powers:

Section 1. To ask, demand, sue for, collect and receive each and every sum of money, debt, account, legacy, bequest, interest, dividend, annuity, demand and government benefit (now or hereafter due, owing, or payable) to which I have a claim, and to take any lawful means for the recovery of the same, and to execute and deliver a satisfaction or release, together with the right and power to compromise or compound any claim or demand;

Section 2. To contract for, purchase, receive and take possession of real property, or any interest in or building on real property, and of evidence of title thereto; to lease the same for any term and for any lawful purpose; to sell, exchange, grant or convey the same with or without warranty; and to mortgage, transfer in trust, or otherwise encumber or hypothecate the same to secure payment of a negotiable or non-negotiable note for the performance of any obligation or agreement; it being expressly intended to permit my attorney-in-fact to act on my behalf with respect to all transactions related to my residence at [   ], and any such other real estate as I may own or acquire; it being further intended that my attorney-in-fact may record or cause to be recorded upon public land records any such act or transaction authorized above;

Section 3. To contract for, buy, sell, exchange, transfer, and in any legal manner deal with personal property, tangible or intangible, including goods, wares and merchandise, choses in action and all other property in possession or in action; and to mortgage, transfer in trust, or otherwise encumber or hypothecate the same to secure payment of a negotiable or non-negotiable note or the performance of any obligation or agreement;

Section 4. To borrow or lend money, and to execute and deliver or receive negotiable or non-negotiable notes, with or without security as (s)he shall deem proper;

Section 5. To create, amend, supplement, make additions to, withdraw and receive the income or corpus of, and terminate a trust and to instruct and advise the trustee of any trust of which I may have or will have an interest; to take any action with respect to stock, stock rights, dividends, distributions and bonuses which I, whether as owner or claimant or otherwise, could take; and to compound, compromise, adjust, settle and satisfy any obligation, secured or unsecured, owing by or to me, and to give or accept any property or money whether or not equal to or less in value than the amount owing in payment, settlement or satisfaction thereof;

Section 6. To continue or complete any gifts or gift programs of mine with any of my real estate or personal property to my spouse, any of my children, their spouse, or their descendents, or to any charitable organizations;

Section 7. To prepare, execute and file, by way of illustration and not by limitation, reports, returns, declarations, forms and statements of all and any kinds for tax purposes including, but not limited to, federal, state, local, income, gift, real estate, personal property, business, and intangibles taxes and any other kind of tax whatsoever; to receive any and all information whatsoever bearing upon my obligations to pay taxes; to adjust, settle, pay and compromise any and all claims regarding my tax liabilities; to appear for me and represent me in connection with any tax matter; and to receive any tax refunds due me;

Article II—Scope of Authority

Section 1. This instrument is to be construed and interpreted as a general power of attorney. The enumeration of specific items, acts, rights or powers herein does not limit or restrict and it is not to be construed or interpreted as limiting or restricting the general powers herein granted to my attorney-in-fact.

Section 2. I give and grant to my attorney-in-fact full power and authority to do and perform all and every act and thing whatsoever required, necessary or appropriate, to be determined solely in the discretion of my attorney-in-fact, to be done as fully to all intents and purposes as I might or could do if personally present, hereby ratifying all that my attorney-in-fact shall do or cause to be done by virtue of this power of attorney. The power and authority hereby conferred upon my attorney-in-fact shall be applicable to all matters relating to my financial and business matters, as well as to other matters, as fully as I may decide such matters myself if competent and present.

Section 3. My attorney-in-fact may retain, compensate, and make such use of agents to assist in acting under this power as my attorney-in-fact may deem advisable, and my attorney-in-fact may designate another person as the joint or successor attorney-in-fact, either temporarily or permanently, under this power of attorney if for any reason my attorney-in-fact is unable or unwilling to act individually pursuant to the other provisions of this power of attorney, but my attorney-in-fact has no duty to appoint a joint or successor attorney-in-fact and it would be contrary to my wishes and intent for any person to require that my attorney-in-fact do so or to require that my attorney-in-fact obtain the consent of any other person for any determination which my attorney-in-fact makes.

Section 4. The powers delegated under this power of attorney are separable, so that the invalidity of one or more powers shall not affect any others.

Article III—Revocation

Section 1. This general power of attorney revokes any previous powers of attorney granted by me. This general power of attorney may be voluntarily revoked only by me at any time, either by my written revocation delivered to my attorney-in-fact or by my written revocation entered of record in the deed records of _____ County, _____ (State).

Article IV—Effective Date and Disability

Section 1. Notwithstanding the other provisions of this general power of attorney, the rights, powers, and authorities of my attorney-in-fact shall commence only upon my disability as hereinafter defined and shall remain in full force thereafter until said disability is terminated.

Section 2. Disability shall be defined as a substantial impairment of my ability to manage my business affairs. The inability to manage my business affairs shall mean the inability to know and appreciate the nature and effect of business transactions, notwithstanding a display of poor judgment.

Section 3. For purposes of the exercise of this general power by my attorney-in-fact, my disability shall be conclusively determined by any one of the following:

(a) The filing of a petition in a court of law personally by me to appoint a guardian of my estate or person;

(b) A written declaration of my disability by me to my attorney-in-fact, which declaration shall be attached to this power; or

(c) A written declaration of my disability by my personal physician, _____ (name of physician), and _____ (name of trusted friend or relative),* to me and my attorney-in-fact, which declaration shall be attached to this power.

Section 4. In executing this general durable power of attorney, it is my intent to avoid the necessity of ever having to seek judicial appointment of a guardian of my person and/or for my estate; however, should I ever be adjudged incapacitated or incompetent by a court, I hereby nominate my attorney-in-fact to be appointed as the guardian of my person and/or my estate.

Article V—Indemnification and Ratification of Acts of Attorney-in-Fact

Section 1. I hereby ratify and confirm all that my attorney-in-fact or any successor attorney-in-fact shall lawfully do or cause to be done by virtue of this general power of attorney and the rights and powers granted herein.

The second individual named should be a trusted individual who will have sufficient contact with the principal to be able to make this determination and who is not himself the attorney-in-fact.

Section 2. I hereby bind myself, my heirs, devisees, and personal representatives to indemnify my attorney-in-fact and any other successor attorney-in-fact who shall so act against any and all claims, demands, losses, damages, actions, and causes of action, including expenses, costs, and reasonable attorneys' fees that my attorney at any time may sustain or incur in connection with carrying out the authority granted in this general power of attorney.

Section 3. My death shall not revoke or terminate this agency as to my attorney-in-fact or any successor attorney-in-fact who, without actual knowledge of my death, acts in good faith under this general power of attorney. Any action so taken unless otherwise invalid or unenforcable, shall be binding upon me and my heirs, devisees, and personal representatives. An affidavit, executed by my attorney-in-fact or any successor attorney-in-fact stating that he does not have, at the time of doing an act pursuant to this general power of attorney, actual knowledge of the revocation of termination of this general power of attorney, is, in the absence of fraud, conclusive proof of the nonrevocation or nontermination of the power at that time.

I have signed and delivered this Durable Power of Attorney consisting of _____ pages this _____ day of _____, 19_____.
(name of principal), the Principal named in the foregoing instrument, signed this instrument, on the _____ day of _____, 19_____. At that time, (s)he declared that the instrument reflects his/her will and intent with respect to his/her financial affairs and all other matters contained herein. At the request of (name of principal), in the presence of (name of principal) and in the presence of each other, each of us believing (name of principal) to be now competent, we have signed our names as witnesses.

Witnesses:

_____

_____

_____

State of _____)
) SS.
County of _____)

On the _____ day of _____, 19_____, before me, the undersigned, a Notary Public in and for (jurisdiction of signing), personally appeared (name of principal), known to me to be the person whose name is subscribed to the within instrument, and acknowledged that (s)he executed the same. Witness my hand and official seal.

(Seal) _____
Notary public in and for
(jurisdiction of signing)

My Commission expires _____.

Drafted by:
(Name of attorney
address
telephone number)

Appendix 10
List of Possible Hospital Services

1. Ambulatory surgery services Scheduled surgical services provided to patients who do not remain in the hospital overnight. The surgery may be performed in operating suites also used for inpatient surgery, specially designated surgical suites for ambulatory surgery, or procedure rooms within an ambulatory care facility.

2. Intensive care unit (cardiac care only) Provides patient care of a more specialized nature than the usual medical and surgical care, on the basis of physician's orders and approved nursing care plans. The unit is staffed with specially trained nursing personnel and contains monitoring and specialized support or treatment equipment for patients who, because of heart seizure, open-heart surgery, or other life-threatening conditions, require intensified, comprehensive observation and care. May include myocardial infarction, pulmonary care, and heart transplant units. Beds must be set up and staffed in a unit(s) specifically designated for this service.

3. Intensive care unit (mixed or other) Provides nursing care to adult and/or pediatric patients of a more intensive nature than the usual medical, surgical, pediatric, and/or psychiatric care on the basis of physicians' orders and approved nursing care plans. Included are medical-surgical, pediatric, and psychiatric (isolation) units. These units are staffed with specially trained nursing personnel and contain monitoring and specialized support equipment for patients who, because of shock, trauma, or life-threatening conditions, require intensified, comprehensive observation and care. These units may also include cardiac care when such services are not provided in a distinct cardiac care unit.

4. Open-heart surgery facilities The equipment and staff necessary to perform open-heart surgery.

5. Trauma center Provides emergency and specialized intensive care to critically injured patients.

6. Ultrasound The use of acoustic

Source: American Hospital Association.

waves above the range of 20,000 cycles per second to visualize internal body structures for diagnostic purposes.

7. X-ray radiation therapy The treatment of disease by roentgen rays or other radiant energy, with the exception of radium, cobalt, or radioisotopes.

8. Megavoltage radiation therapy The use of specialized equipment in the supervoltage and megavoltage (above 1 million volts) ranges for deep therapy treatment of cancer. This would include cobalt units, linear accelerators with or without electron beam therapy capability, betatrons, and Van de Graff machines.

9. Radioactive implants The use of radioactive material (radium, cobalt-60, cesium-137, or iridium-192 implants) for the treatment of malignancies.

10. Diagnostic radioisotope facility The use of radioactive isotopes (radiopharmaceuticals), as tracers or indicators, to detect an abnormal condition or disease.

11. Therapeutic radioisotope facility The use of radioactive isotopes (radiopharmaceuticals) for the treatment of malignancies.

12. Histopathology laboratory A laboratory in which tissue specimens are examined by a qualified pathologist.

13. Organ transplant The necessary staff and equipment to perform the surgical removal of a viable human organ, other than a kidney, from a donor, either alive or just deceased, and the surgical

grafting of the organ to a suitably evaluated and prepared patient.

14. Blood bank A medical facility with the responsibility for each of the following: blood procurement, drawing, processing, and distribution.

15. Health promotion services Education and/or other supportive services that are planned and coordinated by the hospital and that will assist individuals or groups to adopt healthy behaviors and/or reduce health risks, increase self-care skills, improve management of common minor ailments, use health care services effectively, and/or improve understanding of medical procedures and therapeutic regimens. Includes the following specific activities:

Educational activities. Written goals and objectives for the patient and/or family related to therapeutic regimens, medical procedures, and self-care; takes place at the hospital.

Community health promotion. Similar to educational activities, but for individuals in the community not within a place of employment or as a patient.

Worksite health promotion. Similar to educational activities, but for employees of a company implemented by the hospital and sponsored by their employer.

16. Respiratory therapy services The equipment and staff necessary for the administration of oxygen and certain potent drugs through inhalation or positive pressure.

17. Magnetic resonance imaging (nuclear magnetic resonance) The use of a uniform magnetic field and radio frequencies to study tissue and structure of the body. This procedure enables the visualization of biochemical activity of the cell *in vivo* without the use of ionizing radiation, radioisotopic substances, or high-frequency sound.

18. Self-care unit Provides minimal nursing care to ambulatory patients who must remain hospitalized. Beds must be set up and staffed in a unit specifically designated for this service.

19. Skilled nursing or other long-term care unit Provides physician services and continuous professional nursing supervision to patients who are not in the acute phase of illness and who currently require primarily convalescent rehabilitative and/or restorative services. May include extended care units. Can include, but not restricted to, Medicare/Medicaid certified skilled nursing care. May also include intermediate, residential, or other long-term care units. Beds must be set up and staffed in a unit(s) specifically designated for this service.

20. Hemodialysis Provision of equipment and personnel for the treatment of renal insufficiency, on an inpatient or outpatient basis.

21. Hospice A program providing palliative care, chiefly medical relief of pain and supportive services, to terminally ill patients and assistance to their families in adjusting to the patient's illness and death.

22. Burn care unit Provides more intensive care to severely burned patients than the usual acute nursing care provided in medical and surgical units. Beds must be set up and staffed in a unit specifically designated for this service.

23. Physical therapy services Facilities for the provision of physical therapy services prescribed by physicians and administered by, or under the direction of, a qualified physical therapist.

24. Occupational therapy services Facilities for the provision of occupational therapy services prescribed by physicians and administered by, or under the direction of, a qualified occupational therapist.

25. Rehabilitation inpatient unit Provides coordinated multidisciplinary physical restorative services to inpatients under the direction of a physician knowledgeable and experienced in rehabilitative medicine. Beds must be set up and staffed in a unit specifically designated for this service.

26. Rehabilitation outpatient services Provision of coordinated multidisciplinary physical restorative services to ambulatory patients under the direction of a physician knowledgeable and experienced in rehabilitation medicine.

27. Psychiatric inpatient unit Provides acute care to emotionally disturbed patients, including patients admitted for diagnosis and those admitted for treatment of psychiatric problems, on the basis of physicians' orders and approved nursing care plans. May also include the provision of medical care, nursing services, and supervision to the chronically mentally ill, mentally disordered, or other mentally incompetent persons. Beds must be set up and staffed in a unit(s) specifically designated for this service.

28. Psychiatric outpatient services Hospital services for the diagnosis and treatment of psychiatric outpatients.

29. Psychiatric partial hospitalization program Organized hospital facilities and services for day care and/or night care of psychiatric patients who do not require inpatient care 24 hours a day.

30. Psychiatric emergency services Hospital facilities for the provision of unscheduled outpatient care to psychiatric patients whose conditions are considered to require immediate care. Staff must be available 24 hours a day.

31. Psychiatric consultation-liaison services Provides organized psychiatric consultation/liaison services to non-psychiatric hospital staff and/or departments on psychological aspects of medical care that may be generic or specific to individual patients.

32. Psychiatric education services Provides psychiatric educational services to community agencies and workers such as schools, police, courts, public health nurses, welfare agencies, clergy, and so forth. The purpose is to expand the mental health knowledge and competence of personnel not working in the mental

health field and to promote good mental health through improved understanding, attitudes, and behavioral patterns.

33. Women's Center An area set aside for coordinated education and treatment services specifically for and promoted to women as provided by this special unit. Services may or may not include obstetrics but include a range of services other than OB.

34. Organized outpatient department Organized hospital services (or clinics) for the provision of nonemergency medical and/or dental services for ambulatory patients.

35. Emergency department Organized hospital facilities for the provision of unscheduled outpatient services to patients whose conditions are considered to require immediate care. Must be staffed 24 hours a day.

36. Birthing room A hospital-managed combination labor and delivery unit with a homelike setting for mothers and fathers who have completed a specified childbirth course.

37. Family planning services Includes any or all of the following:

Contraceptive care.
A family planning service with full range of fertility control methods including education and counseling on all options of contraception.

Fertility services.
A unit which counsels and educates on infertility problems. Includes laboratory and surgical workup and management on infertility to individuals having problems conceiving children.

Sterilization.
A service with capacity to perform total occlusion or ligation, as appropriate, for women and vasectomy for men.

38. Genetic counseling service A service, directed by a qualified physician, equipped with adequate laboratory facilities, to advise parents and prospective parents on potential problems in cases of genetic defects.

39. Extracorporeal shock wave lithotripter (ESWL) A medical device used for treating stones in the kidney or ureter. The device disintegrates kidney stones, noninvasively, through the transmission of acoustic shock waves directed at the stones.

40. Obstetrics unit Provides care to mothers following delivery, on the basis of physicians' orders and approved nursing care plans. Beds must be set up and staffed in a unit specifically designated for this service.

41. Home care program An organized program, administered by the hospital, that provides medical, nursing, other treatment, and social services to patients in their places of residence.

42. Recreational therapy Facilities for the provision of recreational therapy services prescribed by physicians and administered by or under the direction of a qualified recreational therapist.

43. Day hospital Provides diagnostic, treatment, and rehabilitative services to patients who spend the major portion of the day at the hospital but who do not require care for 24 hours a day. More intensive care than provided in an outpatient clinic and of a limited duration.

44. Speech pathology services Personnel available on a routine basis to provide speech therapy for inpatients or outpatients.

45. Hospital auxiliary A volunteer community organization formed to assist the institution in carrying out its purpose and to serve as a link between the institution and the community.

46. Volunteer services department An organized hospital department responsible for coordinating the services of volunteers working within the institution.

47. Patient representative services Organized hospital services providing personnel through whom patients and staff can seek solutions to institutional problems affecting the delivery of high-quality care and services.

48. Alcoholism/chemical dependency inpatient unit Provides medical care and/or rehabilitative services to patients for whom the primary diagnosis is alcoholism or other chemical dependency. Beds must be set up and staffed in a unit specifically designated for this service.

49. Alcoholism/chemical dependency outpatient services Hospital services for the medical care and/or rehabilitative treatment of outpatients for whom the primary diagnosis is alcoholism or other chemical dependency.

50. Geriatric services Includes any or all of the following:

Comprehensive geriatric assessment services.

Services that determine geriatric patients' long-term care service needs. Includes the assessment of medical conditions, functional activities, mental and emotional conditions, individual and family preferences, and financial status.

Geriatric acute care unit.

Provides acute care to elderly patients in specially designed medical and surgical units. These services may have trained staff in geriatrics, architectural adaptations designed to accommodate the decreased sensory perception of older adults, or age 65 + eligibility requirements.

Satellite geriatric clinics.

Clinics or centers which are geographically located at some distance from the hospital and provide health and related services to older adults. Common locations are in senior citizens' centers or senior housing complexes.

51. Neonatal intensive care unit Provides newborn infants with more intensive care than the usual nursing care provided in newborn acute care units, on the basis of physicians' orders and approved nursing care plans. Beds must be set up and staffed in a unit specifically designated for this service.

52. Pediatric inpatient unit Provides acute care to pediatric patients on the basis of physicians' orders and approved nursing care plans. Beds must be set up and staffed in a unit specifically designated for this service.

53. CT scanner Computed tomographic scanners for head and/or whole body scans.

54. Cardiac catheterization laboratory Provides special diagnostic procedures necessary for the care of patients with cardiac conditions. Available procedures include introduction of a catheter into the interior of the heart through a vein or artery or by direct needle puncture.

Appendix 11
The American Hospital Association's Patient's Bill of Rights

1. The patient has the right to considerate and respectful care.

2. The patient has the right to obtain from his physician complete current information concerning his diagnosis, treatment, and prognosis in terms the patient can be reasonably expected to understand. When it is not medically advisable to give such information to the patient, the information should be made available to an appropriate person in his behalf. He has the right to know, by name, the physician responsible for coordinating his care.

3. The patient has the right to receive from his physician information necessary to give informed consent prior to the start of any procedure and/or treatment. Except in emergencies, such information for informed consent should include but not necessarily be limited to the specific procedure and/or treatment, the medically significant risks involved, and the probable duration of incapacitation. Where medically significant alternatives for care or treatment exist, or when the patient requests information concerning medical alternatives, the patient has the right to such information. The patient also has the right to know the name of the person responsible for procedures and/or treatment.

4. The patient has the right to refuse treatment to the extent permitted by law and to be informed of medical consequences of his action.

5. The patient has the right to every consideration of privacy concerning his own medical care program. Case discussion, consultation, examination and treatment are confidential and should be conducted discreetly. Those not directly involved in his care must have the permission of the patient to be present.

6. The patient has the right to expect that all communications and records pertaining to his care should be treated as confidential.

7. The patient has the right to expect that within its capacity a hospital must make reasonable response to the request of a patient for services. The hospital must provide evaluation, service and/or referral as indicated by the urgency of the case. When medically permissible, a patient may be transferred to another facility only after he has received complete information and explanation concerning the needs for and alternatives to such a transfer. The institution to which the patient is to be transferred must first have accepted the patient for transfer.

8. The patient has the right to obtain information as to any relationship of his hospital to other health care and education institutions insofar as his care is concerned. The patient has the right to obtain information as to the existence of any professional relationships among individuals, by name, who are treating him.

9. The patient has the right to be advised if the hospital proposes to engage in or perform human experimentation affecting his care or treatment. The patient has the right to refuse to participate in such research projects.

10. The patient has the right to expect reasonable continuity of care. He has the right to know in advance what appointment times and physicians are available and where. The patient has the right to expect that the hospital will provide a mechanism whereby he is informed by his physician or a delegate of the physician of the patient's continuing health care requirements following discharge.

11. The patient has the right to examine and receive an explanation of his bill regardless of source of payment.

12. The patient has a right to know what hospital rules and regulations apply to his conduct as a patient.

Appendix 12
Sample State Bill of Rights
for Patients

California Code, Section 70707, Patients' Rights

A. Hospitals and medical staffs shall adopt a written policy on patients' rights.

B. A list of these patients' rights shall be posted in both Spanish and English in appropriate places within the hospital so that such rights may be read by patient. This list shall include but not be limited to the patients' rights to:

1. exercise these rights without regard to sex or cultural, economic, educational, or religious background or the source of payment for care.

2. considerate and respectful care.

3. knowledge of the name of the physician who has primary responsibility for coordinating the care and the names and professional relationships of other physicians and nonphysicians who will see the patient.

4. receive information about the illness, the course of treatment and prospects for recovery in terms that the patient can understand.

5. receive as much information about any proposed treatment or procedure as the patient may need in order to give informed consent or to refuse this course of treatment. Except in emergencies, this information shall include a description of the procedure or treatment, the medically significant risks involved in this treatment, alternative courses of treatment or nontreatment and the risks involved in each and to know the name of the person who will carry out the procedure or treatment.

6. participate actively in decisions regarding medical care. To the extent permitted by law, this includes the right to refuse treatment.

7. full consideration of privacy concerning the medical care program. Case discussion, consultation, examination and treatment are confidential and should be conducted

discreetly. The patient has the right to be advised as to the reason for the presence of any individual.

8. confidential treatment of all communications and records pertaining to the care and the stay in the hospital. Written permission shall be obtained before the medical records can be made available to anyone not directly concerned with the care.

9. reasonable responses to any reasonable requests made for service.

10. leave the hospital even against the advice of physicians.

11. reasonable continuity of care and to know in advance the time and location of appointment as well as the identity of persons providing the care.

12. be advised if hospital/personal physician proposes to engage in or perform human experimentation affecting care or treatment. The patient has the right to refuse to participate in such research projects.

13. be informed of continuing health care requirements following discharge from the hospital.

14. examine and receive an explanation of the bill regardless of source of payment.

15. know which hospital rules and policies apply to the patient's conduct while a patient.

16. have all patients' rights apply to the person who may have legal responsibility to make decisions regarding medical care on behalf of the patient.

C. A procedure shall be established whereby patient complaints are forwarded to the hospital administration for appropriate response.

D. All hospital personnel shall observe these patients' rights.

Appendix 13
Sample Federal Bill of Rights for Patients

Patients' Rights in Veterans Administration Facilities

1. Informed consent: Practitioner performing procedure must inform patient of (a) nature of proposed procedure or treatment; (b) expected benefits; (c) reasonable foreseeable risks, complications, or side effects; (d) reasonable and available alternatives; and (e) anticipated results if nothing done.

2. Treatment with dignity in a humane, safe environment.

3. Privacy with regard to personal needs.

4. Prompt and appropriate treatment for physical or emotional disability.

5. Least restrictive conditions necessary to achieve treatment purposes.

6. Exercise such rights as managing property, entering contractual relationships, executing legal instruments, registering to vote, marrying and divorcing, and holding professional occupational or vehicle operator's licenses.

7. Opportunity to communicate freely with persons outside the facility and to receive visitors.

8. Right to wear own clothing and keep and use personal possessions to extent consistent with safety regulations and rights of other patients.

9. Regular physical exercise, indoors and outdoors.

10. Keep and use own personal possessions and money.

11. Opportunity for religious worship.

12. Interact with others.

Source: Adapted from 38 C.F.R., Sections 17.34 and 17.34a (1985).

13. Freedom from physical restraint or seclusion except where there is substantial risk of imminent harm by the patient to self or others.

14. Freedom from unnecessary or excessive medication.

15. Confidentiality of all information obtained from the patient in the course of treatment.

16. Right to present grievances with respect to infringement of rights.

Appendix 14
An Important Message
from Medicare

Your Rights While You Are a Medicare
Hospital Patient

- You have the right to receive all the hospital care that is necessary for the proper diagnosis and treatment of your illness or injury. According to Federal law, *your discharge date must be determined solely by your medical needs*, not by "DRGs" or Medicare payments.

- You have the right to be fully informed about decisions affecting your Medicare coverage and payment for your hospital stay and for any post-hospital services.

- You have the right to request a review by a Peer Review Organization of any written Notice of Noncoverage that you receive from the hospital stating that Medicare will no longer pay for your hospital care. Peer Review Organizations (PROs) are groups of doctors who are paid by the Federal Government to review medical necessity, appropriateness and quality of hospital treatment furnished to Medicare patients. The phone number and address of the PRO for your area are:

_____

_____

_____

Talk to Your Doctor about Your Stay in the Hospital

You and your doctor know more about your condition and your health needs than anyone else. Decisions about your medical treatment should be made between you and

Source: Medicare.

your doctor. *If you have any questions about your medical treatment, your need for continued hospital care, your discharge, or your need for possible post-hospital care, don't hesitate to ask your doctor.* The hospital's patient representative or social worker will also help you with your questions and concerns about hospital services.

If You Think You Are Being Asked to Leave the Hospital Too Soon

- Ask a hospital representative for a written notice of explanation immediately, if you have not already received one. This notice is called a "Notice of Noncoverage." You must have this Notice of Noncoverage if you wish to exercise your right to request a review by the PRO.

- The Notice of Noncoverage will state either that your doctor or the PRO agrees with the hospital's decision that Medicare will no longer pay for your hospital care.

    + If the hospital and your doctor agree, the PRO does not review your case before a Notice of Noncoverage is issued. But the PRO will respond to your request for a review of your Notice of Noncoverage and seek your opinion. You cannot be made to pay for your hospital care until the PRO makes its decision, if you request the review by noon of the first work day after you receive the Notice of Noncoverage.

    + If the hospital and your doctor disagree, the hospital may request the PRO to review your case. If it does make such a request, the hospital is required to send you a notice to that effect. In this situation the PRO must agree with the hospital or the hospital cannot issue a Notice of Noncoverage. You may request that the PRO reconsider your case after you receive a Notice of Noncoverage but since the PRO has already reviewed your case once, you may have to pay for *at least one day of hospital care* before the PRO completes this reconsideration.

If you *do not* request a review, *the hospital may bill you* for all the costs of your stay beginning with the third day after you receive the notice of noncoverage. The hospital, however, cannot charge you for care unless it provides you with a notice of noncoverage.

How to Request a Review of the Notice of Noncoverage

- If the Notice of Noncoverage states that your *physician agrees* with the hospital's decision:

How to Request a Review of the Notice of Noncoverage (continued)

+ You must make your request for review to the PRO by *noon of the first work day* after you receive the Notice of Noncoverage by contacting the PRO by phone or in writing.

+ The PRO must ask for your views about your case before making its decision. The PRO will inform you by phone and in writing of its decision on the review.

+ If the PRO agrees with the Notice of Noncoverage, you may be billed for all costs of your stay beginning at noon of the day *after* you receive the PRO's decision.

+ Thus, you will *not* be responsible for the cost of hospital care before you receive the PRO's decision.

• If the Notice of Noncoverage states that the *PRO agrees* with the hospital's decision:

+ You should make your request for reconsideration to the PRO *immediately* upon receipt of the Notice of Noncoverage by contacting the PRO by phone or in writing.

+ The PRO can take up to three working days from receipt of your request to complete the review. The PRO will inform you in writing of its decision on the review.

+ Since the PRO has already reviewed your case once, prior to the issuance of the Notice of Noncoverage, the hospital is permitted to begin billing you for the cost of your stay beginning with the third calendar day after you receive your Notice of Noncoverage *even if the PRO has not completed its review.*

+ Thus, if the PRO continues to agree with the Notice of Noncoverage, *you may have to pay for at least one day of hospital care.*

Note: The process described above is called "immediate review." If you miss the deadline for this immediate review while you are in the hospital, you may still request a review of Medicare's decision to no longer pay for your care at any point during your hospital stay or after you have left the hospital. The Notice of Noncoverage will tell you how to request this review

Post-Hospital Care

When your doctor determines that you no longer need all the specialized services provided in a hospital, but you still require medical care, he or she may discharge you to a skilled nursing facility or home care. The discharge planner at the hospital will help arrange for the services you may need after your discharge. Medicare and supplemental insurance policies have limited coverage for skilled nursing facility care and home health care. Therefore, you should find out which services will or will not be covered and how payment will be made. Consult with your doctor, hospital discharge planner, patient representative and your family in making preparations for care after you leave the hospital. *Don't hesitate to ask questions.*

Acknowledgment of Receipt. My signature only acknowledges my receipt of this Message from (name of hospital) on (date) and does not waive any of my rights to request a review or make me liable for any payment.

_____

Signature of beneficiary or
person acting on behalf of beneficiary

Appendix 15
Guidelines for Hospital
Discharge Planning

Introduction

The American Hospital Association believes that coordinated discharge planning functions are essential for hospitals to maintain high-quality patient care. Discharge planning is important because it facilitates appropriate patient and family decision making. In addition, it can also help reduce length of stay and the rate of increase of health care costs.

For most patients, discharge planning is a part of routine patient care. For those patients whose posthospital needs are expected to be complex, special discharge planning services are warranted. These guidelines present general information for organizing services for complex discharge planning.

It is recognized that each hospital has different resources and organizes its services differently to meet specific patient needs. It is further recognized that rapid changes in the hospital environment cause rapid changes in discharge planning. These changes, however, have emphasized the importance of discharge planning, and it is in that context that these guidelines are presented.

Definition

Discharge planning is an interdisciplinary hospitalwide process that should be available to aid patients and their families in developing a feasible posthospital plan of care.

Purposes

The purposes of discharge planning are to ensure the continuity of high-quality patient care, the availability of the hospital's resources for other patients requiring admission, and the appropriate utilization of resources. To ensure the continuity of high-quality care, the hospital will:

- Assign responsibility for the coordination of discharge planning
- Identify as early as possible, sometimes before hospital admission, the expected posthospital care needs of patients utilizing admission and preadmission screening and review programs when available
- Develop with patients and their families appropriate discharge care plans
- Assist patients and their families in planning for the supportive environment necessary to provide the patients' posthospital care
- Develop a plan that considers the medical, social, and financial needs of patients

To ensure the availability of hospital resources for subsequent patients with due regard for prospective pricing, the hospital's procedures should be carried out in such a manner as to accomplish timely discharge.

Principles of Discharge Planning

The discharge planning process incorporates a determination of the patient's posthospital care preferences, needs, the patient's capacity for self-care, an assessment of the patient's living conditions, the identification of health or social care resources needed to assure high-quality posthospital care, and the counseling of the patient or family to prepare them for posthospital care. Discharge planning should be carried out in keeping with varying community resources and hospital utilization activities.

Discharge Planning when Multiple Resources Are Required

In addition to discharge instructions for each routine patient discharge plan, the coordination of multiple resources may be required to achieve continued safe and high-quality posthospital care in situations where the patient's needs are complicated.

Essential Elements

The essential elements in accomplishing the hospital's goals for high-quality, cost-effective patient care are:

- *Early Identification of Patients Likely to Need Complex Posthospital Care.* There are certain factors that may indicate a need for early initiation of discharge planning, either before admission or upon admission. Screens for automatic early patient identification are developed for each specialty service by the physician and relevant health care providers and used as guidelines to carry out discharge planning.

- *Planning and Family Education.*　With greater emphasis on self-care, patient and family education is critical to successful discharge planning. The coordination of discharge planning must integrate teaching about physical care to facilitate appropriate self-care in the home.

- *Patient/Family Assessment and Counseling.*　The psychosocial and physical assessment and counseling of patients and families to determine the full range of needs upon discharge and to prepare them for the posthospital stage of care is a dynamic process. This process includes evaluation of the patient's and the family's strengths and weaknesses; the patient's physical condition; understanding the illness and treatment; the ability to assess the patient's and family's capacities to adapt to changes; and, where necessary, to assist the persons involved to manage in their continued care. Discharge planning and the coordination of posthospital care plans requires an ability to adapt the plans to meet changes in the patient's condition.

- *Plan Development.*　The discharge plan development should include the results of the assessment and the self-care instructions, including information from the patient, the family, and all relevant health care professionals. Service needs and options are identified, and the patient and family are helped to understand the consequences of whatever plan they choose to adopt. A supportive climate is critical to facilitate appropriate decision making.

- *Plan Coordination and Implementation.*　The hospital achieves high-quality and effective discharge planning through the delegation of specific responsibilities to the principal and specialized disciplines providing care. In order to minimize the potential for fragmented care and to fulfill the need for a central hospital linkage to the community, there should be assigned responsibility for discharge planning coordination for complex cases.

- *Postdischarge Follow-Up.*　In complex situations requiring coordinated discharge planning, the plans should ensure follow-up with the patient, the family, and/or community service(s) providing continued care to determine the discharge plan outcome.

Quality Assurance

The quality of the discharge planning system should be monitored through the hospitalwide quality assurance program.

Appendix 16
State Peer Review Organizations

Alabama

Alabama Quality Assurance Foundation
Suite 300
236 Goodwin Crest Drive
Twin Towers East
Birmingham, Alabama 35209
1–800–554–5946
(205) 942–0785

Alaska

Professional Review Organization for
Washington Alaska Division
Suite 204
700 West 41st Street
Anchorage, Alaska 99503
1–800–445–6941
(907) 562–2252

Arizona

Health Services Advisory Group, Inc.
Suite 157–B
301 E. Bethany Home Road
Phoenix, Arizona 85012
1–800–626–1577
(602) 264–6382

Arkansas

Arkansas Foundation for
Medical Care, Inc.
P.O. Box 1508
809 Garrison Avenue
Fort Smith, Arkansas 72902
1–800–824–7586
(501) 785–2471

California

California Medical Review, Inc.
Suite 1100
1388 Sutter Street
San Francisco, California 94109
1–800–841–1602
(415) 923–2000

Colorado

Colorado Foundation for Medical Care
Building 2, Suite 400
6825 East Tennessee Avenue
Denver, Colorado 80217
(303) 321–8642

Adapted from *Knowing Your Rights*, American Association of Retired Persons, Washington, D.C.

Connecticut

Connecticut Peer Review Organization
384 Pratt Street
Meriden, Connecticut 06450
1-800-523-8202
(203) 237-2773

Delaware

West Virginia Medical Institute/
   Delaware PRO
Independence Mall
Suite 54
1601 Concord Pike
Wilmington, Delaware 19803
(302) 655-3077

District of Columbia

Delmarva Foundation for Medical Care
Suite 250
650 Pennsylvania Avenue, S.E.
Washington, D.C. 20006
1-800-492-5811
(202) 675-4612

Florida

Professional Foundation for
   Health Care
Suite 100
2907 Bay to Bay Boulevard
Tampa, Florida 33629
1-800-634-6280
(813) 831-6273

Georgia

Georgia Medical Care Foundation/PRO
Suite 1300
4 Executive Park Drive, N.E.
Atlanta, Georgia 30329
1-800-282-2614
(404) 982-0411

Hawaii

Fiscal Intermediary
Hawaii Medical Services Association
P.O. Box 860
Honolulu, Hawaii 96808
(808) 944-2110

Idaho

Professional Review Organization
   for Washington
Idaho Division
Suite 250
815 Park Boulevard
Boise, Idaho 83712
(208) 343-4617

Illinois

Crescent Counties Foundation for
   Medical Care
Suite 240
350 Shuman Boulevard
Naperville, Illinois 60540
(312) 357-8770

Indiana

PEERVIEW, Inc.
Suite 200
501 Congressional Boulevard
Carmel, Indiana 46032
1-800-421-6558
(317) 573-6888

Iowa

Iowa Foundation for Medical Care
Suite 500
3737 Woodland Avenue
West Des Moines, Iowa 50265
1-800-422-2234
(515) 223-2900

Kansas

Kansas Foundation for Medical Care
2947 S.W. Wanamaker Drive
Topeka, Kansas 66614
1-800-432-0407
(913) 273-2552

Kentucky

PEERVIEW, Inc.
10300 Linn Station Road
Suite 100
Louisville, Kentucky 40223
1-800-423-6512
(502) 429-0995

Louisiana

Louisiana Health Care Review, Inc.
Suite 200
9357 Interline Avenue
Baton Rouge, Louisiana 70809
1-800-433-4958
(504) 926-6353

Maine

Health Care Review, Inc.
51 Broadway
Bangor, Maine 04401
1-800-541-9888
(207) 945-0244

Maryland

Delmarva Foundation for
   Medical Care, Inc.
341-B N. Aurora Street
Easton, Maryland 21601
1-800-247-9770
(301) 822-0697

Massachusetts

Massachusetts Peer Review

Organization, Inc.
300 Bear Hill Road
Waltham, Massachusetts 02250
1-800-228-3297
(617) 890-0011

Michigan

Michigan Peer Review Organization
Suite 200
40500 Ann Arbor Road
Plymouth, Michigan 48170
1-800-482-4045
(313) 459-0900

Minnesota

Foundation for Health Care Evaluation
Suite 700
1 Appletree Square
Minneapolis, Minnesota 55420
1-800-888-3423
(612) 854-3306

Mississippi

Mississippi Foundation for
   Medical Care, Inc.
(1900 No. West Street ZIP 39202)
P.O. Box 4665
Jackson, Mississippi 39216
(601) 948-8894

Missouri

Missouri Patient Care Review
   Foundation
311A Ellis Boulevard
Jefferson City, Missouri 65101
1-800-654-1016
(314) 634-4441

Montana

Montana-Wyoming FMC

Montana *continued*

21 No. Main Placer Center, #201
Helena, Montana 59601
1–800–332–3411
(406) 443–4020

Nebraska

Sunderbruck Corp. of Nebraska
Suite 700 CTU Building
1221 N Street
Lincoln, Nebraska 68508
1–800–422–4812
1–800–624–8617 (after 6:00 P.M.)
(402) 474–7471

Nevada

Nevada Physicians Review
  Organization
Building A, Suite 108
4600 Kietzke Lane
Reno, Nevada 89502
1–800–588–0829
(702) 826–1996

New Hampshire

New Hampshire Foundation for
  Medical Care
P.O. Box 578
110 Locust Street
Dover, New Hampshire 03820
1–800–582–7174
(603) 749–1641

New Jersey

Peer Review Organization of
  New Jersey, Inc., Central Div.
Brier Hill Court, Building J
East Brunswick, New Jersey 08816
(201) 238–5570

New Mexico

New Mexico Medical Review
  Association
Box 9900
707 Broadway, NE
Albuquerque, New Mexico 87119
1–800–432–6824
(505) 842–6236

New York

Empire State Medical, Scientific and
  Educational Foundation
420 Lakeville Road
Lake Success, New York 11042
1–800–331–7767
(516) 437–8134

North Carolina

Medical Review of North Carolina, Inc.
P.O. Box 37309
Suite 200
1011 Schaub Drive
Raleigh, North Carolina 27627
1–800–682–2650
(919) 851–2955

North Dakota

North Dakota Health Care Review, Inc.
301 Mount Vernon Building
900 N. Broadway Avenue
Minot, North Dakota 58701
1–800–472–2902
(701) 852–4231

Ohio

Peer Review Systems, Inc.
Suite 250
3700 Corporate Drive
Columbus, Ohio 43229

1–800–233–7337 (in state)
1–800–237–7337 (out of state)
(614) 895–9900

Oklahoma

Oklahoma Foundation for Peer Review
Suite 400
The Paragon Building
5801 Broadway Extension
Oklahoma City, Oklahoma 73118
(405) 840–2891

Oregon

Oregon Medical Professional Review
   Organization
Suite 300
1220 S.W. Morrison
Portland, Oregon 97205
1–800–452–1250
(503) 243–1151

Pennsylvania

Keystone PRO, Inc.
P.O. Box 618
645 N. 12th Street
Lemoyne, Pennsylvania 17043
1–800–322–1914
(717) 975–9600

Puerto Rico

Puerto Rico Foundation for
   Medical Care, Inc.
Mercantile Plaza Building
Suite 605
Hato Rey, Puerto Rico 00918
(809) 753–6706

Rhode Island

Health Care Review, Inc.

The Weld Building
345 Blackstone Boulevard
Providence, Rhode Island 02906
1–800–662–5028
(401) 331–6661

South Carolina

South Carolina Peer Review
   Organization
1000 Carolina Commerce Center
Fort Mill, South Carolina 29715
1–800–843–0130
(803) 548–8400

South Dakota

South Dakota FMC
1323 South Minnesota Avenue
Sioux Falls, South Dakota 57105
1–800–952–3691
(605) 336–3505

Tennessee

Mid-South Foundation for
   Medical Care, Inc.
Suite 400
6401 Poplar Avenue
Memphis, Tennessee 38119
1–800–873–2273
(901) 682–0381

Texas

Texas Medical Foundation
Suite 200
901 Mopac Expressway, South
Austin, Texas 78746
1–800–252–9216
(512) 329–6610

Utah

Utah PSRO

Utah continued
Suite 200
540 East 5th South
Salt Lake City, Utah 84102
(801) 532–7547

Vermont
New Hampshire FMC
P.O. Box 578
110 Locust Street
Dover, New Hampshire 03820
1–800–582–7174
(603) 749–1641

Virginia
Medical Society of Virginia Review
   Organization
P.O. Box 6569
1904 Byrd Avenue
Room 120
Richmond, Virginia 23230
1–800–533–1745
(804) 289–5320

Washington
Professional Review Organization for
   Washington
Suite 200

2150 N. 107th Street
Seattle, Washington 98133
1–800–233–5439 (residents)
1–800–445–6941 (outside of state)
(206) 364–9700

West Virginia
West Virginia Medical Institute, Inc.
3412 Chesterfield Ave., SE
Charleston, West Virginia 25304
1–800–642–8686
(304) 925–0461

Wisconsin
Wisconsin Peer Review Organization
P.O. Box 1109
2001 West Beltline Highway
Madison, Wisconsin 53713
1–800–362–2320
(608) 274–1940

Wyoming
Montana-Wyoming FMC
Placer Center, #201
21 N. Main Street
Helena, Montana 59601
1–800–826–8978
(406) 443–4020

The Office of Medical Review, Health Standards and Quality Bureau, Meadows East Building, 6325 Security Boulevard, Baltimore, Maryland 21207, (301) 966–6851, can assist individuals who have difficulty reaching any of the offices listed here.

Appendix 17
Model Discharge Notices

Sample Letters Denying Continued Stay

Sample 1: Attending Physician Concurs
(Hospital Letterhead)

Mr. Bert Smith
3 Payne Boulevard
Evanston, Proland 00001

002–59–2300A
(Health Insurance (HI) number)
Dr. Cho
(Attending physician's name)
June 1, 1985
(admission date)

Dear Mr. Smith:

The Nowhere General Hospital has reviewed the medical services you have received for the treatment of the ulcerations of your left leg from June 1, 1985, through June 11, 1985. Your attending physician has been advised and has concurred that beginning June 13, 1985, further treatment of the ulcerations of your left leg could be safely rendered in another setting. You should discuss with your attending physician other arrangements for any further health care you may require.

You will not be responsible for payment of the services which are rendered by this hospital from June 13, 1985, through June 14, 1985, except for payment of deductible, coinsurance, or any convenience services or items normally not covered by Medicare. If you decide to stay in the hospital, you will be responsible for payment of all services

Source: Health Care Financing Administration.

provided to you by this hospital except for those services for which you are eligible under Part B beginning June 15, 1985.

The Foundation for Medical Care, Inc. is the Peer Review Organization (PRO) authorized by the Medicare program to review inpatient hospital services provided to Medicare patients, including those services denied by hospitals in the State of Proland.

If you disagree with our decision and you remain in the hospital beginning June 15, 1985, you may request by telephone or in writing an immediate review by the PRO. You make that request through the Hospital or directly to:

_____

(PRO name)

_____

(address, including zip code)

_____

(telephone number)

The PRO will respond to you within 3 working days of receipt of your request. However, if you do not wish an immediate review and you remain in the hospital beginning June 15, 1985, the PRO will automatically review your case. The PRO will send you a formal determination of the medical necessity and appropriateness of your hospitalization and will inform you of your appeal rights. If the PRO determines that you required further inpatient hospital care beyond the point indicated by the hospital, you will be refunded any amount collected by the hospital except for payment of deductible, coinsurance, or any convenience services or items normally not covered by Medicare. However, if the PRO agrees with the hospital's decision, you are still responsible for payment of all services beginning on June 15, 1985, as explained in this notice.

If you are discharged from this hospital on June 15, 1985, you may still request a review within 30 days from the date of this notice to the address specified above.

Sincerely,

_____

(chairperson of Utilization Review Committee)

cc: attending physician

Acknowledgment of Receipt of Notice

This is to acknowledge I received this notice of noncoverage of services from Nowhere Hospital on June 13, 1985.

_____
(signature of beneficiary or person acting on behalf of beneficiary)

_____
(date of receipt)

Sample 2: Attending Physician Concurs
(Hospital Letterhead)

(date of notice)   (Health Insurance [HI] number)

(name of patient)   (attending physician's name)

(address)   (admission date)

(city, state, zip code)

Dear _____:

The (hospital name) has reviewed the medical services you have received for (specify services or condition) from (date of admission) through (date of last day reviewed). Your attending physician has been advised and has concurred that beginning (specify date of first noncovered day), further (specify services to be rendered or condition to be treated) (specify: is/are medically unnecessary) or (could be safely rendered in another setting). You should discuss with your attending physician other arrangements for any further health care you may require.

You will not be responsible for payment of the services which are rendered by this hospital from (date of receipt of notice) through (second day after receipt of notice) except for payment of deductible, coinsurance, or any convenience services or items normally not covered by Medicare. If you decide to stay in the hospital, you will be responsible for payment of all services provided to you by this hospital except for those services for which you are eligible for under Part B beginning (third day after receipt of notice.).

The (name of PRO) is the Peer Review Organization (PRO) authorized by the

Medicare program to review inpatient hospital services provided to Medicare patients including those services denied by hospitals in the state of _____.

If you disagree with our decision and you remain in the hospital beginning (date of the third day of receipt of notice), you may request by telephone or in writing an immediate review by the PRO. You may make this request through the hospital or directly to the PRO at:

_____
(PRO name)

_____
(address)

_____
(telephone number)

The PRO will respond to you within 3 working days of receipt of your request. However, if you do not wish an immediate review and remain in the hospital beginning (date of third day after receipt of notice), the PRO will automatically review your case. The PRO will send you a formal determination of the medical necessity and appropriateness of your hospitalization and will inform you of your appeal rights. If the PRO determines that you required further inpatient hospital care beyond the point indicated by the hospital, you will be refunded any amount collected by the hospital except for payment of deductible, coinsurance, or any convenience services or items normally not covered by Medicare. However, if the PRO agrees with the hospital's decision, you are still responsible for payment of all services beginning on (date of third day from receipt of notice) as explained in this notice.

If you are discharged from this hospital on (date of third day of receipt of notice), you may still request a review within 30 days from the date of this notice to the address specified above.

Sincerely,

_____
(chairperson of Utilization Review Committee, medical staff, hospital representative, etc.)

cc: attending physician

Acknowledgment of Receipt of Notice

This is to acknowledge I received this notice of denial of services from (name of hospital) on (date).

_____
(signature of beneficiary or person acting on behalf of beneficiary)

_____
(date of receipt)

_____

Sample 3: PRO Concurs
(Hospital Letterhead)

(date of notice)

_____   _____
(name of patient)   (Health Insurance [HI] number)

_____   _____
(address)   (attending physician's name)

_____   _____
(city, state, zip code)   (admission date)

Dear _____.

The (hospital name) has reviewed the medical services you have received for (specify services or condition) from (date of admission) through date of last day reviewed) and has determined that further hospitalization is not necessary.

The (name of PRO) is the Peer Review Organization (PRO) authorized by the Medicare program to review inpatient hospital services provided to Medicare patients including those services denied by the hospitals in the state of _____. The (name of PRO) has concurred with our decision that beginning (specify date of first noncovered day), further (specify services to be rendered or condition to be treated) (specify: is/are medically unnecessary) or (could be safely rendered in another setting).

We have advised your attending physician of the denial of further inpatient hospital care. You should discuss with your attending physician other arrangements for any further health care you may require.

You will not be responsible for payment of the services which are rendered by this hospital from (date of receipt of notice) through (second day after receipt of notice) except for payment of deductible, coinsurance, or any convenience services or items normally not covered by Medicare. If you decide to stay in the hospital, you will be responsible for payment of all services provided to you by this hospital except for those services for which you are eligible for under Part B beginning (third day after receipt of notice).

If you disagree with our decision and you remain in the hospital beginning (date of third day after receipt of notice), you may request by telephone or in writing an expedited reconsideration. You may make this request through the hospital or to the PRO at:

_____

(PRO name)

_____

(address, including zip code)

_____

(telephone number)

The PRO will respond to you within 3 working days of receipt of your request. The PRO will send to you a formal reconsideration determination of the medical necessity and appropriateness of your hospitalization and will inform you of your appeal rights. If the PRO determines that you required further inpatient hospital care beyond the point indicated by the hospital, you will be refunded any amount collected by the hospital except for payment of deductible, coinsurance, or any convenience services, or items normally not covered by Medicare. However, if the PRO reaffirms the hospital's decision, you are still responsible beginning (date of third day from receipt of notice) as explained in this notice.

If you are discharged from this hospital on (date of third day of receipt of notice), you may still request a reconsideration. Instructions on how to request this reconsideration will be given to you in a notice sent by (name of PRO).

Sincerely

_____

(chairperson of Utilization Review Committee, medical staff, etc.)

_____

(date of receipt)

cc: attending physician

Acknowledgment of Receipt of Notice

This is to acknowledge I received this notice of noncoverage of services from (hospital name) on _____.

                             (date)

_____
(signature of beneficiary or person
acting on behalf of beneficiary)

_____
(date of receipt)

Appendix 18
Medicare Quality Screen

Medicare Generic Screening Criteria

These criteria were developed by the Medicare program. The Medicare Peer Review Organization (PRO) is required to apply these screens to each Medicare case selected for review.

1.* Adequacy of discharge planning
   No documented plan for appropriate follow-up care or discharge planning as necessary, with consideration of physical, emotional, and mental status/needs at the time of discharge.

2. Medical stability of the patient at discharge
   a. Blood pressure on day before or day of discharge
      Systolic—less than 85 or greater than 180
      Diastolic—less than 50 or greater than 110
   b. Temperature on day before or day of discharge greater than 101 degrees oral (rectal 102 degrees).
   c. Pulse less than 50 (or 45 if the patient is on a beta blocker), or greater than 120 within 24 hours of discharge.
   d. Abnormal results of diagnostic services which are not addressed and resolved or where the record does not explain why they are unresolved.
   e. IV fluids or drugs on the day of discharge (*excludes* KVOs [to keep vein open], antibiotics, chemotherapy, or total parenteral nutrition).
   f. Purulent or bloody drainage of postoperative wound within 24 hours prior to discharge.

3. Deaths
   a. During or following elective surgery performed during the current admission.

Source: Medicare.

   b. Following return to intensive care unit, coronary care, or special care unit within 24 hours of being transferred out.

   c. Other unexpected death.

4*. Nosocomial infections

   a. Temperature elevation greater than two degrees more than 72 hours from admission.

   b. Indication of an infection following an invasive procedure (e.g., suctioning, catheter insertion, tube feedings, surgery, etc.)

5. Surgery

   a. Unscheduled return to surgery within same admission for same condition as previous surgery or to correct operative problem (exclude "staged" procedures).

6. Trauma suffered in the hospital

   a. Unplanned removal or repair of normal organ (i.e., removal or repair not addressed specifically in operative consent).

   b.* Fall with injury or untoward effect (including, but not limited to fracture, dislocation, concussion, laceration, etc.).

   c. Life-threatening complications of anesthesia.

   d. Life-threatening transfusion error or reaction.

   e. Hospital-acquired decutibus ulcer.

   f. Care resulting in (1) *serious* or (2) *life-threatening complications,* not related to admitting signs and symptoms, including, but not limited to the neurological, endocrine, cardiovascular, renal, or respiratory body systems (e.g., resulting in dialysis, unplanned transfer to special care unit, lengthened hospital stay).

   g. Major adverse drug reaction or medication error (1) *with serious potential for harm* or (2) *resulting in special measures to correct* (e.g., intubation, cardiopulmonary resuscitation, gastric lavage) including but not limited to the following:

      1. Incorrect antibiotic ordered by the physician (e.g., inconsistent with diagnostic studies or the patient's history of drug allergy);

      2. No diagnostic studies to confirm which drug is correct to administer (e.g., C & S);

      3. Serum drug levels not performed as needed;

      4. Diagnostic studies or other measures for side effects not performed as needed (e.g., BUN, creatinine, intake and output).

Source: Medicare.

*PRO reviewer is to record the failure of the screen with "B" (exception) but need not refer to physician reviewer.

Appendix 19
State Long Term Care
Ombudsman Program Offices

Alabama
Commission on Aging
136 Catoma Street, 2nd Floor
Montgomery, Alabama 36130
(205) 261–5743

Alaska
Office of the Older Alaskans
    Ombudsman
3601 C Street, Suite 380
Anchorage, Alaska 99503
(907) 279–2232
(accepts collect calls from older persons)

Arizona
Aging and Adult Administration
P.O. Box 6123–950A
1400 West Washington Street
Phoenix, Arizona 85007
(602) 255–4446

Arkansas
Division of Aging and Adult Services
Arkansas Department of Human Services
1417 Donaghey Plaza South—POB 1437
7th and Main Streets
Little Rock, Arkansas 72201–1437
(501) 682–2441

California
California Department of
    Aging
1600 K Street
Sacramento, California 95814
(916) 323–6681
1–800–231–4024

Colorado
The Legal Center
455 Sherman Street, Suite 130
Denver, Colorado 80203
(303) 722–0300
1–800–332–6356

Connecticut
Connnecticut Department on
    Aging
175 Main Street
Hartford, Connecticut 06106
(203) 566–7770

Delaware
Division on Aging
1113 Church Street
Milford, Delaware 19963
(302) 422–1386
1–800–223–9074

District of Columbia
Legal Counsel for the Elderly
1909 K Street, NW
Washington, D.C. 20049
(202) 662–4933

Florida
State LTC Ombudsman Council
Department of Health and
  Rehabilitation Services
1317 Winewood Boulevard, Building 1,
  #308
Tallahassee, Florida 32301
(904) 488–6190

Georgia
Office of Aging
Department of Human Resources
878 Peachtree Street, NE, Room 632
Atlanta, Georgia 30389
(404) 894–5336

Hawaii
Hawaii Executive Office on Aging
335 Merchant Street, Room 241
Honolulu, Hawaii 96813
(808) 548–2593

Idaho
Idaho Office on Aging
State House, Room 114
Boise, Idaho 83720
(208) 334–3833

Illinois
Department on Aging
421 East Capitol Avenue
Springfield, Illinois 62701
(217) 785–3140

Indiana
Indiana Department on Aging
251 N. Illinois—POB 7083
Indianapolis, Indiana 42607–7083
(317) 232–7020
1–800–622–4484

Iowa
Department of Elder Affairs
Jewett Building
Suite 236
916 Grand Avenue
Des Moines, Iowa 50319
(515) 281–5187

Kansas
Department on Aging
Docking State Office
  Building, 122–S
915 S.W. Harrison
Topeka, Kansas 66612–1500
(913) 296–4986
1–800–432–3535

Kentucky
Division for Aging Services
Cabinet for Human Resources
CHR Building—6th Floor, West
275 East Main Street
Frankfort, Kentucky 40601
(502) 564–6930
1–800–372–2991

Louisiana
Governor's Office of Elderly Affairs
P.O. Box 80374
4528 Bennington Avenue
Baton Rouge, Louisiana 70898–3074
(504) 925–1700

Maine
Maine Committee on Aging
State House, Station 127
Augusta, Maine 04333
(207) 289-3658
1-800-452-1912

Maryland
Maryland Office on Aging
301 W. Preston Street, Rm. 1004
Baltimore, Maryland 21201
(301) 225-1083

Massachusetts
Massachusetts Executive Office of
  Elder Affairs
38 Chauncy Street
Boston, Massachusetts 02111
(617) 727-7273

Michigan
Citizens for Better Care
1627 East Kalamazoo
Lansing, Michigan 48912
(517) 482-1297
1-800-292-7852

Minnesota
Minnesota Board on Aging
Office of Ombudsman for Older
  Minnesotans
444 Lafayette Road
St. Paul, Minnesota 55155-3843
(612) 296-7465
1-800-652-9747

Mississippi
Mississippi Council on Aging
421 West Pascagoula
Jackson, Mississippi 39203
(601) 949-2070

Missouri
Division of Aging
Department of Social Services
P.O. Box 1337
2701 W. Main Street
Jefferson City, Missouri 65102
(314) 751-3082

Montana
Seniors' Office of Legal and
  Ombudsman Services
P.O. Box 232
Capitol Station
Helena, Montana 59620
(406) 444-4676
1-800-332-2272

Nebraska
Department on Aging
P.O. Box 95044
301 Centennial Mall South
Lincoln, Nebraska 68509
(402) 471-2307

Nevada
Division of Aging Services
Department of Human Resources
Kinkead Building
Room 101, 505 E. King Street
Carlson City, Nevada 89710
(702) 885-4210

New Hampshire
Division of Elderly and Adult
  Services
6 Hazen Drive
Concord, New Hampshire 03301-6508
(603) 271-4375
1-800-442-5640

New Jersey
Office of the Ombudsman for the
  Institutionalized Elderly
28 W. State Street, Room 305, CN 808
Trenton, New Jersey 08625–0807
(609) 292–8016
1–800–624–4262

New Mexico
State Agency on Aging
LaVilla Rivera Building, 4th Floor
224 E. Palace Avenue
Santa Fe, New Mexico 87501
(505) 827–7640

New York
Office for the Aging
Agency Building #2
Empire State Plaza
Albany, New York 12223
(518) 474–7329
1–800–342–9871

North Carolina
North Carolina Department of
  Human Resources
Division of Aging
Kirby Building
1985 Umstead Drive
Raleigh, North Carolina 27603
(919) 733–3983

North Dakota
Aging Services Division
Department of Human Services
State Capitol Building
Bismarck, North Dakota 58505
(701) 224–2577
1–800–472–2622

Ohio
Ohio Department on Aging
50 W. Broad Street, 9th Floor
Columbus, Ohio 43266–0501
(614) 466–9927
1–800–282–1206

Oklahoma
Division of Aging Service
Department of Human Services
P.O. Box 25352
Oklahoma City, Oklahoma 73125
(405) 521–2281

Oregon
Office of LTC Ombudsman
2475 Lancaster Drive, Building B, #9
Salem, Oregon 97310
(503) 378–6533
1–800–522–2602

Pennsylvania
Department of Aging
Barto Building, 231 State Street
Harrisburg, Pennsylvania 17101
(717) 783–7247

Puerto Rico
Governor's Office on Elderly Affairs
Call Box 50063
Old San Juan Station
Puerto Rico 00902
(809) 722–2429

Rhode Island
Rhode Island Department of
  Elderly Affairs
79 Washington Street
Providence, Rhode Island 02903
(401) 277–6883

South Carolina
Office of the Governor
Division of Ombudsman and
  Citizens' Services
1205 Pendleton Street
Columbia, South Carolina 29201
(803) 734-0457

South Dakota
Office of Adult Services and
  Aging
Department of Social Services
Richard F. Kneip Building
700 North Illinois Street
Pierre, South Dakota 57501-2291
(605) 773-3656

Tennessee
Commission on Aging
706 Church Street
Suite 201
Nashville, Tennessee 37219-5573
(615) 741-2056

Texas
Department on Aging
P.O. Box 12786, Capitol Station
1949 IH 35 South
Austin, Texas 78741-3702
(512) 444-2727
1-800-252-9240

Utah
Division of Aging and Adult Services
Department of Social Services
120 North—200 West
Box 45500
Salt Lake City, Utah 84145-0500
(801) 538-3910

Vermont
Vermont Office on Aging
103 South Main Street
Waterbury, Vermont 05676
(802) 241-2400
1-800-642-5119

Virginia
Department for the Aging
10th Floor
700 East Franklin Street
Richmond, Virginia 23219-2327
(804) 225-2271
1-800-552-3402

Washington
South King County Multi—Service
  Center
1505 South 356
Federal Way, Washington 98003
(206) 838-6810
1-800-442-1384

West Virginia
Commission on Aging
State Capitol Complex
Charlestown, West Virginia 25305
(304) 348-3317

Wisconsin
Board on Aging and Long-Term Care
819 N. 6th, Room 619
Milwaukee, Wisconsin 53203-1664
(414) 227-4386
1-800-242-1060

Wyoming
Wyoming State Bar Association
900 8th Street
Wheatland, Wyoming 82201
(307) 322-5553

Appendix 20
State Units on Aging

Alabama
Commission on Aging
Second Floor
136 Catoma Street
Montgomery, Alabama 36130
(205) 242-5743

Alaska
Older Alaskans Commission
Department of Administration
Pouch C-Mail Station 0209
Juneau, Alaska 99811-0209
(907) 465-3250

Arizona
Aging and Adult Administration
Department of Economic Security
1400 W. Washington Street
Phoenix, Arizona 85007
(602) 542-4446

Arkansas
Division of Aging and Adult Services
Arkansas Department of Human
  Services
P.O. Box 1417, SLOT 1412
7th and Main Street
Little Rock, Arkansas 72201
(501) 682-2441

California
Department of Aging
1600 K Street
Sacramento, California 95814
(916) 322-5290

Colorado
Aging and Adult Services
Department of Social Services
10th Floor
1575 Sherman Street
Denver, Colorado 80203-1714
(303) 866-3851

Connecticut
Department on Aging
175 Main Street
Hartford, Connecticut 06106
(203) 566-3238

Delaware
Division on Aging
Department of Health and
  Social Services
1901 N. DuPont Highway
New Castle, Delaware 19720
(302) 421-6791

District of Columbia
Office on Aging
1424 K Street, NW, 2nd floor
Washington, DC 20005
(202) 724–5666

Florida
Program Office of Aging and
   Adult Services
Department of Health and
   Rehabilitation Services
1317 Winewood Boulevard
Tallahassee, Florida 32301
(904) 488–8922

Georgia
Office of Aging
Room 632
878 Peachtree Street, NE
Atlanta, Georgia 30309
(404) 894–5333

Hawaii
Executive Office on Aging
Office of the Governor
335 Merchant Street, Room 241
Honolulu, Hawaii 96813
(808) 548–2593

Idaho
Office on Aging
Room 114—Statehouse
Boise, Idaho 83720
(208) 334–3833

Illinois
Department on Aging
421 East Capitol Avenue
Springfield, Illinois 62706
(217) 785–2870

Indiana
Division of Aging Services
Department of Human
   Services
251 N. Illinois Street
P.O. Box 7083
Indianapolis, Indiana 46207–7083
(317) 232–7020

Iowa
Department of Elder Affairs
Suite 236
Jewett Building
914 Grand Avenue
Des Moines, Iowa 50319
(515) 281–5187

Kansas
Department on Aging
Docking State Office
   Building, 122–S
915 S.W. Harrison
Topeka, Kansas 66612–1500
(913) 296–4986

Kentucky
Division for Aging Services
Cabinet of Human Resources
CHR Building—6th West
275 E. Main Street
Frankfort, Kentucky 40621
(502) 564–6930

Louisiana
Office of Elderly Affairs
4550 N. Boulevard
P.O. Box 80374
Baton Rouge, Louisiana 70806
(504) 925–1700

Maine
Bureau of Elder and Adult Services
Department of Human Services
State House—Station #11
Augusta, Maine 04333
(207) 289-2561

Maryland
Office on Aging
State Office Building
301 W. Preston Street, Rm. 1004
Baltimore, Maryland 21201
(301) 225-1100

Massachusetts
Executive Office of Elder Affairs
38 Chauncy Street
Boston, Massachusetts 02111
(617) 727-7750

Michigan
Office of Services to the Aging
P.O. Box 30026
Lansing, Michigan 48909
(517) 373-8230

Minnesota
Board on Aging
4th Floor
Human Services Building
444 Lafayette Road
St. Paul, Minnesota 55155-3843
(612) 296-2770

Mississippi
Council on Aging
Division of Aging and Adult Services
421 W. Pascagoula Street
Jackson, Mississippi 39203
(601) 354-6100

Missouri
Divsion on Aging
Department of Social Services
P.O. Box 1337—2701 W. Main Street
Jefferson City, Missouri 65101
(314) 751-3082

Montana
Department of Family Services
48 N. Last Chance Gulch
P.O. Box 8005
Helena, Montana 59604
(406) 444-5900

Nebraska
Department on Aging
P.O. Box 95044
301 Centennial Mall South
Lincoln, Nebraska 68509
(402) 471-2306

Nevada
Division for Aging Services
Department of Human Resources
340 N. 11th Street
Las Vegas, Nevada 89101
(702) 486-3545

New Hampshire
Division of Elderly and Adult Services
6 Hazen Drive
Concord, New Hampshire 03301-6501
(603) 271-4680

New Jersey
Division on Aging
Department of Community Affairs
CN 807
South Broad and Front Streets
Trenton, New Jersey 08625-0807
(609) 292-4833

New Mexico
State Agency on Aging
224 E. Palace Avenue, 4th Floor
La Villa Rivera Building
Santa Fe, New Mexico 87501
(505) 827–7640

New York
Office for the Aging
New York State Plaza
Agency Building #2
Albany, New York 12223
(518) 474–4425

North Carolina
Division on Aging
1985 Umstead Dr. Kirby Building
Raleigh, North Carolina 27603
(919) 733–3983

North Dakota
Aging Services
Department of Human Services
State Capitol Building
Bismarck, North Dakota 58505
(701) 224–2577

Ohio
Department of Aging
50 W. Broad Street, 9th floor
Columbus, Ohio 43266–0501
(614) 466–5500

Oklahoma
Aging Services Division
Department of Human Services
P.O. Box 25352
Oklahoma City, Oklahoma 73125
(405) 521–2281

Oregon
Senior Services Division
313 Public Service Building
Salem, Oregon 97310
(503) 378–4728

Pennsylvania
Department of Aging
231 State Street
Harrisburg, Pennsylvania 17101–1195
(717) 783–1550

Rhode Island
Department of Elderly Affairs
160 Pine Street
Providence, Rhode Island 02903–3708
(401) 277–2858

South Carolina
Commission on Aging
Suite B–500
400 Arbor Lake Drive
Columbia, South Carolina 29223
(803) 735–0210

South Dakota
Office of Adult Services and Aging
700 N. Illinois Street
Kneip Building
Pierre, South Dakota 57501
(605) 773–3656

Tennessee
Commission on Aging
Suite 201
706 Church Street
Nashville, Tennessee 37219–5573
(615) 741–2056

Texas
Department on Aging
1949 IH 35, South
P.O. Box 12786, Capitol Station
Austin, Texas 78704
(512) 444-2727

Utah
Division of Aging and Adult Services
Department of Social Services
120 North—200 West
Box 45500
Salt Lake City, Utah 84145-0500
(801) 538-3910

Vermont
Department of Rehabilitation and Aging
103 S. Main Street
Waterbury, Vermont 05676
(802) 241-2400

Virginia
Department on Aging
700 Centre, 10th Floor
700 East Franklin Street
Richmond, Virginia 23219-2327
(804) 225-2271

Washington
Aging and Adult Services
    Administration
Department of Social and
    Health Services, OB 44A
Olympia, Washington 98504
(206) 586-3768

West Virginia
Commission on Aging
Holly Grove—State Capitol
Charleston, West Virginia 25305
(304) 348-3317

Wisconsin
Bureau of Aging
Division of Community Services
Suite 300
217 S. Hamilton Street
Madison, Wisconsin 53707
(608) 266-2536

Wyoming
Commission on Aging
Hathaway Building—Room 139
Cheyenne, Wyoming 82002
(307) 777-7986

Appendix 21
State Public Guardianship Programs

Statewide Program	Limited Program	No Program
Alaska	Alabama	Arkansas
Arizona	Florida	Colorado
California	Idaho	District of Columbia
Connecticut	Iowa	Indiana
Delaware	Maryland	Kansas
Georgia	Michigan	Louisiana
Hawaii	Minnesota	Massachusetts
Illinois	Missouri	Mississippi
Kentucky	Nevada	Montana
Maine	New York	Nebraska
New Hampshire	North Carolina	New Mexico
New Jersey	North Dakota	Oklahoma
Tennessee	Ohio	Rhode Island
	Oregon	South Carolina
	Pennsylvania	Utah
	South Dakota	Vermont
	Texas	Washington
	Virginia	Wisconsin
	West Virginia	Wyoming

(As of 1988)

Appendix 22
State Requirements for Personal Status Reports on Wards

Reports Required	Reports Not Required
Alaska	Alabama
California	Arizona
Connecticut	Arkansas
District of Columbia	Colorado
Florida	Delaware
Georgia	Idaho
Hawaii	Illinois
Iowa	Indiana
Kansas	Maine
Kentucky	Massachusetts
Louisiana	Mississippi
Maryland	New Jersey
Michigan	New Mexico
Minnesota	North Carolina
Missouri	North Dakota
Montana	Ohio
Nebraska	Oklahoma
Nevada	Pennsylvania
New Hampshire	Rhode Island
New York	South Dakota
Oregon	Tennessee
South Carolina	Utah

(As of 1988)

Reports Required	Reports Not Required
Texas	Virginia
Vermont	Washington
Wisconsin	West Virginia
	Wyoming

Appendix 23
State Requirements for Ward Estate Accounting

Not Required	Required Periodically	Required Annually
Maine	Alabama	Alaska
Mississippi	California	Arizona
New Jersey	Connecticut	Arkansas
North Dakota	Delaware	Colorado
Pennsylvania	Illinois	District of Columbia
Utah	Indiana	Florida
	Kentucky	Georgia
	Ohio	Hawaii
	South Dakota	Idaho
		Iowa
		Kansas
		Louisiana
		Maryland
		Massachusetts
		Michigan
		Minnesota
		Missouri
		Montana
		Nebraska
		Nevada
		New Hamshire
		New Mexico

(As of 1988)

Not Required	Required Periodically	Required Annually
		New York
		North Carolina
		Oklahoma
		Oregon
		Rhode Island
		South Carolina
		Tennessee
		Texas
		Vermont
		Virginia
		Washington
		West Virginia
		Wisconsin
		Wyoming

Appendix 24
State Requirements for Legal Representation of Wards

No Requirements	Court Lawyer Required (1)	Guardian Required Ad Litem (2)	Both 1 and 2 Required	Court Determines, See 3
Arkansas	Connecticut	Alabama	Alaska	California
Nevada	Delaware	Idaho	Arizona	Florida
Ohio	Georgia	Illinois	Colorado	Hawaii
Oklahoma	Iowa	Michigan	District of Columbia	Indiana
Oregon	Kansas	Montana		Maine
Pennsylvania	Kentucky	New Mexico		Massachusetts
South Dakota	Louisiana	North Carolina		Minnesota
Utah	Maryland	North Dakota		Mississippi
Vermont	Missouri	South Carolina		Nebraska
Wyoming	New Hampshire	Tennessee		New York
	New Jersey	Virginia		Rhode Island
		Washington		Texas
		West Virginia		
		Wisconsin		

1. Court-appointed lawyer to represent client's wishes.
2. Guardian Ad Litem, usually a lawyer, who advises court on what would be best for client.
3. Court decides if it wants to appoint a lawyer or guardian ad litem.

(As of 1988)

Appendix 25
Sample Petition for Appointment of Conservators (Guardians) of the Person and the Property

In re
A.B.C.   Fiduciary No. _____

COMES NOW D.E.C., a resident of Las Cruces, New Mexico ("Petitioner"), and petitions the Court to appoint her as conservator of the person and the property of her natural father, Mr. A.B.C. ("Mr. C.") a resident of _____.

In support thereof, Petitioner states:

1. This court has jurisdiction pursuant to §xxx *et seq.*, of the Code of the _____ ("Code").

2. Mr. C., the proposed ward, resides in _____ at 1434 Maplewood Ct., _____, which residence he owns with the real property thereunder free and clear of encumbrances.

3. Mr. C. was born on _____, in _____ and holds the social security number 123–45–6789. He is now _____ years old.

4. Mr. C. has, within the last 30 days, sustained a major stroke and has been diagnosed as suffering from Alzheimer's Disease. As a result of these debilitating mental and physical conditions, Mr. C. is, in the opinions of his consulting physicians, Dr. _____ and Dr. _____, unable to care for his property, his own personal welfare or health care. (See affidavits attached.) He is, therefore, because of mental weakness not amounting to unsoundness of mind, unable to consent to or participate fully in matters affecting his personal health care or his financial well-being.

5. At present, Mr. C. is being cared for at the _____ Hospital, under the supervision of the physicians above.

6. Petitioner is Mr. C.'s natural daughter and only child. Other known relatives are:
_____ (sister) ADDRESS
_____ (brother) ADDRESS
Said relatives have been contacted by Petitioner and have given their verbal consent to and do not intend to oppose Petitioner's appointment as conservator.

7. The Guardian *ad litem* may also find it useful to contact Delores S. C., former wife of Mr. C. (Office: TELEPHONE NO., home address: _____ for information and documents gathered by Ms. C. and Petitioner to date.

8. Appointment of Petitioner as conservator of the person and the property is clearly in the best interests of her father, Mr. C. She has always demonstrated great love and care for her father, and since his stroke and advancing Alzheimer's Disease, she has taken leave from her husband and employment to travel at her own expense to the jurisdiction. Here she has sat with her father and, with her mother, she has taken what lawful actions she could to assure proper health care for her father and to safeguard his financial well-being while he has been unable to act for himself.

9. If Petitioner's request to be appointed conservator is granted, she intends to file an irrevocable power of attorney for service of process in _____. Moreover, she is aware of the requirements to file inventories and accounts. She is further aware of the need to petition for authorization of expenditures. In addition, Petitioner intends personally to exercise all health care and welfare decisions for Mr. C.

10. If for any reason the Court in its discretion decides not to appoint Petitioner as conservator, Petitioner hereby asks the Court to appoint her mother, Delores S. C., to act as conservator for Mr. C. with all of the duties and responsibilities sought herein. The reason for appointing her include her continuing care for and love of Mr. C., her familiarity with his assets and his needs, her residence in the _____, and the confidence and trust in which she is held by the Petitioner.

11. Petitioner states that, in her opinion, a reasonable estimate of the total assets of Mr. C.'s estate at this time, including his residence, is $_____. The assessed value of his home is approximately $_____. Bank accounts, certificates of deposit, and other personal property comprise the remaining $_____.

Wherefore, the premises considered, the Petitioner prays:

(1)   that she be appointed as conservator of the person and property of her father, Mr. C., or, in the alternative, to appoint her mother, Delores S. C. so to serve, and

(2)   for such other and further relief as the Court may deem just and proper.

Respectfully submitted,

_____

D.E.C.

Verification

)
)SS.
)

I, D.E.C., being first duly sworn, on oath, depose and say that I have read the foregoing petition by me subscribed and that the facts therein stated are true to the best of my knowledge, information and belief.

_____

D.E.C.

Sworn to before me and subscribed in my presence this _____ day of _____, 19_____.

_____

Notary Public

My commission
expires:

_____
_____

Attorneys Name
etc.
Counsel for Petitioner

Appendix 26
Sample Conservatorship (Guardianship) Order for the Person and the Property

Superior Court of _____
Probate Division

In re
A.B.C.   Fiduciary No. _____

Upon consideration of the petition of D.E.C. for the appointment of a conservator of the person and the estate of A.B.C., the Court having heard argument of counsel and the report of the Guardian *ad litem,* and it appearing to the Court that by reason of physical and mental weakness not amounting to unsoundness of mind, A.B.C. needs assistance in caring for himself and his property and that A.B.C.'s best interest would be best served by appointment of a conservator of his estate and of his person, who shall have the charge and management of A.B.C.'s property and person subject to the direction of the Court, it is by the Court this _____ day of _____, 19____.

ORDERED that D.E.C. be and the same hereby is appointed permanent Conservator of the person and of the estate of A.B.C. upon the execution of a non-resident power of attorney and upon entering into an undertaking with surety approved by the Court in the penal sum of $_____, conditioned upon faithful discharge of trust, and provided that prior to the receipt of any assets in excess of $_____ said conservator shall first petition the Court for additional undertaking as may be required.

Judge

_____

Judge

Copies to:
Attorney for Petitioner: _____
Guardian *ad litem:* _____
Conservator: D.E.C.

Appendix 27
Social Security Payee
Application Form

DEPARTMENT OF HEALTH AND HUMAN SERVICES
Social Security Administration

TOE 250

Form Approved
OMB No. 0960-0014

REQUEST TO BE SELECTED AS PAYEE

FOR SSA USE ONLY

Name or Ben. Sym.	Program	Date of Birth	Type	Gdn.	Cus.	Inst.	Nam.

FOR SSA USE ONLY

DISTRICT OFFICE DESIGNATION:

STATE AND COUNTY CODE:

PRINT name of wage earner, self-employed person, eligible SSI beneficiary, Black Lung beneficiary

ENTER SOCIAL SECURITY NUMBER

— — — | — — | — — — —

PRINT name of person or persons for whom you are applying to be payee

ENTER SOCIAL SECURITY NUMBER(S)

— — — | — — | — — — —

PRINT your name *(If different from either of the above)*

ENTER YOUR SOCIAL SECURITY NUMBER

— — — | — — | — — — —

Answer item 1 ONLY if you are the beneficiary and wish benefits paid directly to you.

1. I request that I be paid directly.

CHECK HERE ☐ and answer only item 5 before completing the signature block on page 4.

I REQUEST THAT THE SOCIAL SECURITY BENEFITS, SPECIAL AGE 72 BENEFITS, SUPPLEMENTAL SECURITY INCOME BENEFITS, OR BLACK LUNG BENEFITS FOR THE PERSON OR PERSONS NAMED ABOVE BE PAID TO ME AS REPRESENTATIVE PAYEE.

2. (a) Are you related by blood or marriage to the person(s) for whom you are filing? ➤

☐ Yes *(If "Yes," answer (b) and go on to item 5.)*   ☐ No *(If "No," go on to item 3.)*

(b) How are you related? ➤ *(For example: spouse, child, etc.)*

3. (a) Do you represent a bank, social agency, government office or institution? ➤

☐ Yes *(If "Yes," answer (b) and go on to item 5.)*   ☐ No *(If "No," go on to item 4.)*

(b) Check (✓) below which you represent

☐ BANK (or other financial organization)   ☐ SOCIAL AGENCY   ☐ PUBLIC OFFICIAL *(Representing government office other than social agency or institution)*   ☐ INSTITUTION *(Check one below)*

☐ FEDERAL   ☐ STATE OR LOCAL   ☐ PRIVATE NON-PROFIT   ☐ PRIVATE PROPRIETARY If so, is it licensed under State or local law? ☐ Yes ☐ No

4. If you answered "No" to items 2 and 3, what is your relationship to the person(s) for whom you are filing? ➤

5. (a) Is there a legal representative *(guardian, conservator, curator, etc.)* for the person(s) for whom you are filing? ➤

☐ Yes *(If "Yes," answer (b) and (c) below.)*   ☐ No *(If "No," go on to item 6.)*

(b) Write the following information about the legal representative(s)

NAME *(First name, middle initial, last name)*	ADDRESS *(include ZIP code)*	TELEPHONE NUMBER *(include area code)*

(c) Briefly explain the circumstances which led the court to appoint a legal representative.

Source: Social Security Administration.

6. **(a)** Is the person(s) for whom you are filing living with you or in the institution you represent? ⟶ ☐ Yes *(If "Yes," answer (b) through (f).)* ☐ No *(If "No," go on to item 7.)*

NOTE: If you are the natural or adoptive parent with custody of a minor child or childhood disability beneficiary, or the spouse with custody, or if you are already serving as the beneficiary's payee for SSA, SSI or Black Lung benefits, or if you are the conservator appointed under a voluntary conservatorship, omit the remaining items and go on to page 4.

(b) Why is he/she living with you? ⟶

(c) Who placed him/her with you? ⟶

(d) When was he/she placed with you? ⟶

(e) How long will he/she be with you? ⟶

(f) If you are not the representative of a financial organization, social agency, government office or institution, does work or other activity take you away from home? ⟶ ☐ Yes ☐ No

If "Yes," who takes care of the person for whom you are filing when you are away? ⟶ | Name *(First name, middle initial, last name)*

7. **(a)** If the person(s) for whom you are filing is not living with you, give the following information:

NAME OF PERSON(S) NOT LIVING WITH YOU	NAME, ADDRESS AND TELEPHONE NUMBER OF PERSON OR INSTITUTION WITH WHOM HE/SHE IS NOW LIVING. *(Hereafter this person is called the custodian)*	CUSTODIAN'S RELATIONSHIP TO HIM/HER	DATE HE/SHE BEGAN LIVING WITH CUSTODIAN	
			Month	Year

(If you are an official or the representative of a financial organization or social agency, or otherwise applying in your professional capacity such as an attorney or accountant, answer (d) and go on to question 8. Otherwise, continue with (b).)

(b) Why isn't he/she living with you or in the institution you represent? ⟶

(c) Do you visit the child(ren) or adult not living with you, send him/her clothing or other gifts, write letters, etc.? ⟶ ☐ Yes *(If "Yes," show below how often you do any of those things.)* ☐ No *(If "No," please explain under "Remarks" on page 3 how you will find out about his/her needs.)*

NAME OF PERSON	VISIT	SEND CLOTHING	MAKE OTHER GIFTS	WRITE LETTERS	OTHER *(Describe)*

(d) Do you or any other person or agency give money for his/her support? ⟶ ☐ Yes *(If "Yes," give the following information.)* ☐ No *(If "No," go on to item 8.)*

NAME OF PERSON(S)	PERSON OR AGENCY CONTRIBUTING, ADDRESS AND TELEPHONE NUMBER. SHOW "SELF" IF YOU ARE CONTRIBUTING.	HOW OFTEN CONTRIBUTIONS ARE MADE	AMOUNTS OF EACH CON- TRIBUTION	DATE CON- TRIBUTION BEGAN

Answer item 8 if you are filing on behalf of a child(ren) who is under age 18 and you are not the natural or adoptive parent.

8.

(a) Does the child(ren) for whom you are filing have a living natural or adoptive parent? ➤ ☐ Yes *(If "Yes," answer (b), (c), and (d).)* ☐ No *(If "No," go on to item 9.)*

(b) Give this parent's name, address and telephone number:

NAME OF PARENT ➤ *(First name, middle initial, last name)*

ADDRESS OF PARENT ➤ *(Number and street, city, State, and ZIP code)*

TELEPHONE NUMBER *(include area code)* ➤ (   )

(c) Does this parent show interest in the child(ren)? ➤ ☐ Yes ☐ No

EXPLAIN YOUR ANSWER ➤

(d) Why do you wish to have benefits paid to you instead of to the parent named above? ➤

Answer item 9 if you are not a relative of the person(s) for whom you are filing.

9.

(a) Does the person for whom you are filing have a relative *(other than a parent named above)?* ➤ ☐ Yes *(If "Yes," answer (b) and (c).)* ☐ No *(If "No," go to item 10.)*

(b) Give the name, address, and telephone number of this relative, and his/her relationship to the person(s) for whom you are filing.

Name of Relative ➤ *(First name, middle initial, last name)*

Address of Relative ➤ *(Number and street, city, State, and ZIP code)*

Telephone Number of Relative *(include area code)* ➤ (   )

Relative's relationship to person(s) for whom you are filing. ➤

(c) Why do you wish to have benefits paid to you instead of to the relative named above? ➤

Answer item 10 ONLY if you are not applying in your professional capacity.

10.

(a) Are you under age 18? ➤ ☐ Yes *(If "Yes," show your age.)* _____ ☐ No

(b) Are you employed? ➤ ☐ Yes ☐ No *(If "No," enter below your main source of income.)*

Main source of income ➤

Answer item 11 ONLY if you are a creditor (e.g., a nursing home, landlord).

11.

(a) Is the person for whom you are filing indebted to you or your facility for past care or services? ➤ ☐ Yes ☐ No *(If "Yes," answer (b) and (c).)*

(b) Amount of debt   Date(s) debt incurred   (c) Description of care or services provided in connection with this debt

REMARKS: *(This space may be used for explaining any answers to the questions. If you need more space, attach a separate sheet.)*

_____

_____

PLEASE READ THE FOLLOWING INFORMATION CAREFULLY BEFORE SIGNING THIS FORM

I UNDERSTAND THAT ALL PAYMENTS MADE TO ME AS REPRESENTATIVE PAYEE MUST BE SPENT FOR THE BENEFICIARY'S PRESENT NEEDS OR (IF NOT PRESENTLY NEEDED) SAVED FOR THE BENEFICIARY'S FUTURE NEEDS AND I AGREE TO USE THE PAYMENTS THAT WAY. I ALSO UNDERSTAND THAT I MAY BE HELD PERSONALLY LIABLE FOR REPAYMENT IF I MISUSE THE PAYMENTS OR IF I AM FOUND AT FAULT WITH RESPECT TO ANY OVERPAYMENT OF BENEFITS. I AGREE TO FILE AN ACCOUNTING REPORT OF THE USE MADE OF THE PAYMENTS WHEN REQUESTED BY THE SOCIAL SECURITY ADMINISTRATION.

I AGREE TO NOTIFY THE SOCIAL SECURITY ADMINISTRATION PROMPTLY WHEN ANY PERSON FOR WHOM I RECEIVE PAYMENTS DIES, LEAVES MY CUSTODY, IS LIVING ALONE OR WITH SOMEONE ELSE AND MOVES ELSEWHERE, OR WHEN I NO LONGER HAVE RESPONSIBILITY FOR SUCH PERSON'S WELFARE AND CARE. I ALSO AGREE TO COMPLY WITH THE CONDITIONS FOR REPORTING CERTAIN EVENTS (AS LISTED ON THE ATTACHED SHEET(S) WHICH I WILL MAINTAIN FOR MY RECORDS) AND FOR RETURNING CHECKS TO WHICH THERE IS NO ENTITLEMENT. WHEN AN ANNUAL REPORT OF EARNINGS IS REQUIRED, I AGREE TO FILE SUCH ANNUAL REPORT.

I ALSO AGREE TO NOTIFY THE SOCIAL SECURITY ADMINISTRATION AS SOON AS I BELIEVE I WILL NO LONGER BE ABLE TO OR WISH TO ACT AS A REPRESENTATIVE PAYEE. (SUCH ADVANCE NOTIFICATION WILL ASSIST IN THE DEVELOPMENT OF AN ALTERNATE PAYEE AND WILL AVOID UNNECESSARY SUSPENSION OF PAYMENTS.)

I know that anyone who makes or causes to be made a false statement or representation of material fact in an application or for use in determining a right to payment under the Social Security Act commits a crime punishable under Federal law by fine, imprisonment or both. I affirm that all information I have given in this document is true.

SIGNATURE OF APPLICANT	Date *(Month, day, year)*
Signature *(First name, middle initial, last name) (Write in ink)*	Telephone Number(s) at which you may be contacted during the day
SIGN HERE ▶	___ ___ ___ Area Code

Mailing Address *(Number and street, Apt. No., P.O. Box, or Rural Route)*

City and State	ZIP Code	Enter Name of County (if any) in which you now live

Witnesses are required ONLY if this application has been signed by mark (X) above. If signed by mark (X), two witnesses to the signing who know the applicant must sign below, giving their full addresses.

1. Signature of Witness	2. Signature of Witness
Address *(Number and street, City, State, and ZIP Code)*	Address *(Number and street, City, State, and ZIP Code)*

Appendix 28
Social Security Administration's Order of Preference in Selecting Representative Payee

As a guide in selecting a representative payee, categories of preferred payees have been established. These preferences are flexible. Our primary concern is to select the payee who will best serve the beneficiary's interest. The preferences are:

(1) For beneficiaries 18 years or older, our preference is:

  (a) A legal guardian, spouse (or other relative) who has custody of the beneficiary or who demonstrates strong concern for the personal welfare of the beneficiary;

  (b) A friend who has custody of the beneficiary or demonstrates strong concern for the personal welfare of the beneficiary;

  (c) A public or nonprofit agency or institution having custody of the beneficiary;

  (d) A private institution operated for profit and licensed under State law, which has custody of the beneficiary; and

(2) Persons other than above who are qualified to carry out the responsibilities of a payee and who are able and willing to serve as a payee for a beneficiary; e.g., members of community groups or organizations who volunteer to serve as payee for a beneficiary.

Source: Social Security Administration.

Appendix 29
Social Security Payee Report Form

Social Security Administration Representative Payee Report

We are writing to ask you to complete the enclosed **Representative Payee Report** and return it to us. We must ask you to complete this report when you receive Social Security or Supplemental Security (SSI) payments for another person. We use the facts you give us to make sure that this person's needs are being met. If you receive payments for your spouse or child, you may not have completed this report in the past. A court ruling now requires us to ask you to complete this report once a year.

What You Need To Do

First, please read the instructions below. This is important because **not all questions are self-explanatory.** Then, complete your report and send it to us in the enclosed envelope **within 10 days** from the day you receive it. If you do not return it promptly, we may stop sending checks to you.

General Instructions

To help us process your report and avoid having to recontact you, please follow these instructions.

1. Use black ink or a #2 pencil to complete the report.

2. Keep your numbers and "X's" inside the boxes.

3. Try to make your numbers look like these:

    0 1 2 3 4 5 6 7 8 9

4. Do not use dollar signs.

5. Enter money amounts like this: Show $540.00 as

6. Continue to keep records of how you use the Social Security or SSI money, but do not submit receipts, cancelled checks or any other records with this report. If we need to verify the facts you gave us, we will tell you after we look at your report.

Some Definitions

Benefits—The Social Security (Retirement, Survivors, Disability) and SSI money you receive.

Beneficiary—The person for whom you receive Social Security or SSI benefits.

Custodian—The person with whom the beneficiary lives. If the beneficiary lives alone, he or she is the custodian. A nursing home or institution can also be a custodian.

Report Period—The months for which you must account. This period is shown in the top right corner of the report form.

How To Fill Out The Form

The numbers below match the numbered questions on the report.

1 — Custody of the Beneficiary

Place an "X" in the "YES" box if the beneficiary:

• Lived with you for **some but not all months** in the report period, or

• Lived in an institution or nursing home for **some but not all months** in the report period, or

• Lived alone for **some but not all months** in the report period, or

• Moved from one institution or nursing home to another.

Place an "X" in the "NO" box if the beneficiary lived:

• With the same person during the entire report period, or

• In the same institution or nursing home during the entire report period, or

• Alone during the entire report period.

Do not consider short visits (vacations, weekend or holiday visits) with another person when you answer this question.

2 — Turning Over Payments To Another Person

Place an "X" in the "YES" box if you gave the full amount of the payments to:

• Another person and that person decided how to use the money.

• The beneficiary and he or she decided how to use the money.

Place an "X" in the "NO" box if you:

• Decided how to use the money.
• Told an institution or nursing home how to use the money.

3 — How You Used The Benefits

Place an "X" in the "YES" box if you used all the benefits you received to pay for the beneficiary's day-to-day needs.

Place an "X" in the "NO" box if you:

- Saved all or part of the benefits.
- Used all or part of the benefits for someone other than the beneficiary or for something other than the beneficiary's current needs.

4 — Personal Needs

In this item include the amount of money you spent on clothing, medical and dental care, education, and recreational items like toys, movies, cameras, radios, and musical instruments. Also include other personal items like stationery, grooming aids, candy and tobacco. **Do not include the money you spent on food and shelter.**

5 — Amounts Left At The End Of The Report Period

If you had no SSI or Social Security money left at the end of the report period, put an "X" in box **5.A.**

If you had SSI or Social Security money left at the end of the period, show how much in box **5.B.** This includes money that you have held from earlier years.

6 — Unused Benefits

If you had Social Security or SSI money left at the end of the report period, be sure to answer items 6.A. **and** 6.B.

In item **6.A.**, place an "X" in the boxes which show how you are holding the benefits that you have not spent.

In item **6.A.**, place an "X" in the "OTHER" box if:

- The type of account in which you are holding benefits is not shown, or
- You are not holding the money in an account.

In item **6.B.**, place an "X" in the box which describes the title (name) on the account in which you are holding the unused benefits.

If the title of the account in which you are holding the unused benefits is not shown or if you are not holding the money in an account, place an "X" in the "OTHER" box.

Benefits should be held in an account which shows that the money belongs to the beneficiary. If you are not sure whether the account you established does this, you should check with your bank and change the account title if necessary.

7 — Type And Title Of "Other" Account

If you answered "OTHER" in item 6.A., in item **7.A.** describe the type of account or way in which you are holding the unused benefits. For example, U.S. Savings Bonds, Treasury Bills, cash, etc.

If you answered "OTHER" in item 6.B., in item **7.B.** show the title on the account, if there is one. If there is no title on the account, show "NONE."

8 — Signature

You, the payee, must sign your name in this block. If you sign your name by mark ("X"), please have two witnesses sign their names and show the date.

9 — Relationship To The Beneficiary

Show your relationship to the beneficiary. For example, "parent, brother, friend, legal guardian or none." If you represent a bank, institution or agency, show your title.

Your Job As A Representative Payee

As a payee, you must use the Social Security and SSI money you receive for the care and well-being of the beneficiary. You need to be aware of what the beneficiary needs so that you can decide how best to use the money.

You must also tell us about any changes which may affect the checks you receive. You need to tell us if:

- The beneficiary moves, especially if he or she enters or leaves a hospital or institution, marries, goes to work, dies or is adopted.

- You are no longer responsible for the beneficiary.

Your Right To Privacy

We are required by section 205(j) of the Social Security Act to ask you to complete this report. Although the report is voluntary, the law states that as a representative payee, you have a responsibility to complete the report. If you do not return this report to us, we may not be able to continue sending the beneficiary's payments to you.

Sometimes the law requires us to give out the facts on this form without your consent. We must release this information to another person or Government agency if Federal law requires that we do so or to do the research and audits needed to administer or improve our representative payee program. These and other reasons why facts on the Representative Payee Report may be used or given out are explained in the Federal Register. If you would like more information, contact us.

If You Have Any Questions

If you have any questions, you should call, write or visit your local Social Security office. Almost all questions can be answered by phone. If you visit an office, please bring this report with you. This will help us answer your questions.

Social Security Administration Representative Payee Report

FORM APPROVED
OMB NO. 0960-0068

PAYEE'S NAME AND ADDRESS	REPORT PERIOD		SOCIAL SECURITY NO.	
	FROM:	TO:		
	BENEFICIARY		PSY	FP
	ID PIC BIC	D	TP	CC
	GS PC	DOC		TYA
	DOB		MBC	
	CF	FUN		CFL

Please read the enclosed instructions before completing this form. It will help you answer each question.

		YES	NO
1.	Has the beneficiary's custodian changed during the report period? Please refer to the instructions on page 1 before you answer this question. ➤	☐	☐
2.	Did you turn over the full amount of the payments to another person during the report period (for example, to the beneficiary's custodian or to the beneficiary)? If you answer yes, please explain on the reverse of this page. ➤	☐	☐
3.	Did you use **all** the benefits you received during the report period for the beneficiary? ➤	☐	☐

4. Show the amount you spent for the beneficiary during the report period on things such as clothing, medical care, education, recreation and personal items. Do not include money you used for food and shelter. ➤

DOLLARS   CENTS
☐☐,☐☐☐.☐☐

5.

A. If there were NO benefits left at the end of the report period, including money from earlier years, place an "X" here. ➤ ☐

B. If there were benefits left at the end of the report period, including money from earlier years, show the amount you have left here. ➤

DOLLARS   CENTS
☐☐,☐☐☐.☐☐

6. If you showed an amount in 5.B. above, place an "X" in the boxes below to show how you are holding the remaining money. If you have more than one account, you can mark more than one box in each section.

A. TYPE OF ACCOUNT				**B.** TITLE OR OWNERSHIP		
Checking Account	Savings Account	Collective Savings/ Patients' Fund	Other	Beneficiary's Name by Your Name	Your Name for Beneficiary's Name	Other
☐	☐	☐	☐	☐	☐	☐

7. A. If you answered "OTHER" in 6.A. above, show the type of account or investment in which the benefits are held. ➤   TYPE OF ACCOUNT

7. B. If you answered "OTHER" in 6.B. above, show the title of the account in which the benefits are held. ➤   TITLE OF ACCOUNT

I CERTIFY THAT THE INFORMATION I HAVE GIVEN ON THIS FORM IS TRUE.

8. SIGNATURE OF PAYEE *(If signed by mark (X), two witnesses must sign below)*   DATE

9. RELATIONSHIP TO BENEFICIARY OR TITLE

10. TELEPHONE NUMBERS *(Include area code)*
_____ / _____   _____ / _____
AREA CODE   BUSINESS   AREA CODE   HOME

WITNESS SIGNATURES ARE REQUIRED ONLY IF THE PAYEE'S SIGNATURE ABOVE HAS BEEN SIGNED BY MARK (X).
SIGNATURE OF WITNESS   DATE   SIGNATURE OF WITNESS   DATE

FORM **SSA-623-F3** (4-88)   3

Appendix 30
Social Security Payee Evaluation Form

DEPARTMENT OF HEALTH AND HUMAN SERVICES
SOCIAL SECURITY ADMINISTRATION

Form Approved
OMB No. 0960-0069

REPRESENTATIVE PAYEE EVALUATION REPORT

TP	CC	GS	NAM
TYA	MBA	CF	

BENEFICIARY'S NAME	SOCIAL SECURITY NUMBER
	___ ___ ___ / ___ / ___ ___ ___ ___

PAYEE'S NAME	REPORT PERIOD	
	FROM	TO

PAYEE'S ADDRESS

CITY AND STATE	ZIP CODE	PHONE NUMBER (Include area code)

PART I INFORMATION FROM PAYEE

1. GUARDIANSHIP STATUS

Is legal guardianship now in effect? ⟶ ☐ YES ☐ NO

If yes, show guardian's name and address below (if other than payee).

GUARDIAN'S NAME	GUARDIAN'S ADDRESS

2. CUSTODY

(a) Did the beneficiary live alone or with someone other than the payee? ⟶ ☐ YES ☐ NO

If yes, answer 2(b). If no, skip to item 4.

(b) Show below where the beneficiary lived. Show the relationship of the custodian to the beneficiary, the dates of residence and the reason for any change in custody.

NAME	ADDRESS	RELATION-SHIP	DATES OF RESIDENCE	REASON FOR CHANGE

3. DEMONSTRATION OF CONCERN

(a) How did the payee learn of the beneficiary's needs?

(b) Did the payee maintain contact with the beneficiary? If yes, show type of contact (visits, phone, letters) and frequency. If no, explain. ⟶ ☐ YES ☐ NO

(c) Did the payee provide the beneficiary with funds for personal spending? If yes, show to whom the funds were given (e.g., directly to the beneficiary, the custodian). If no, show why not. ⟶ ☐ YES ☐ NO

4. USE OF BENEFITS

(a) Did the payee turn over the checks or the full amount of the checks to another party? If yes, show to whom the funds were given (e.g., the beneficiary, the custodian). ⟶ ☐ YES ☐ NO

(b) Amount used for beneficiary's care and maintenance. If paid to another party, show to whom. ⟶

AMOUNT	NAME
$ _____	

Form SSA-624-F4 (9-86)

PART I (continued)

4. (cont)

(c) Amount used for beneficiary's clothing. If less than $20, or more than $300. explain. ➡

Amount

$ _____

(d) Amount used for beneficiary's personal spending. If less than $300, explain. ➡

Amount

$ _____

(e) Amount used for other than items (b) through (d) above. (Exclude savings.) Explain. ➡

Amount

$ _____

(f) Total amount of benefits used. ➡

Total Amount (add (b) through (e) above)

$ _____

(g) Did the payee record expenditures (receipts, cancelled checks, etc.)? ➡

☐ YES   ☐ NO

5. CONSERVED FUNDS

(a) Total amount of conserved funds. Subtract item 4(f) from TYA and add conserved funds from prior years. ➡

Amount

$ _____

(b) How are conserved funds held?

☐ CASH   ☐ U.S. SAVING BONDS   ☐ OTHER (explain)

☐ CHECKING ACCOUNT   ☐ SAVINGS ACCOUNT

_____

(c) HOW ARE CONSERVED FUNDS TITLED?

TYPE OF HOLDING	TITLE OR OWNERSHIP	NAME AND ADDRESS OF BANK	ACCOUNT NUMBER

(d) Are the funds mingled with funds of another person(s)?

☐ YES   ☐ NO

If yes, answer (e).

(e) Are funds clearly recorded as belonging to the beneficiary?

☐ YES   ☐ NO

6. OTHER INCOME

(a) Did the beneficiary have other income which affects the entitlement to or use of Social Security benefits? ➡

☐ YES   ☐ NO

If yes, answer (b) and (c).

(b) TYPE OF OTHER INCOME

☐ WORKMEN'S COMPENSATION   ☐ VA BENEFITS

☐ OTHER (Explain)   ☐ PUBLIC ASSISTANCE (Explain)

(c) Is there a payee for other income? ➡

☐ YES   ☐ NO

If yes, show name and address of payee below.

NAME OF PAYEE	ADDRESS OF PAYEE

7. REMARKS

I certify that the information I provided in Part I above is true.

SIGNATURE

▶

DATE

Form **SSA-624-F4** (9-86)   2.

PART II INFORMATION FROM BENEFICIARY	

1. ALL CUSTODY SITUATIONS

(a) Is the beneficiary aware of entitlement to Social Security benefits?	(b) Did the beneficiary participate in decisions on expenditures?
☐ YES ☐ NO	☐ YES ☐ NO

(c) Did the beneficiary receive funds for personal spending?	(d) Were any large purchases made for the beneficiary?
☐ YES ☐ NO	☐ YES ☐ NO

(e) Does the beneficiary have any unmet needs?	EXPLANATION
☐ YES ☐ NO If yes, explain ⟶	

(f) Did the beneficiary live with someone other than the payee?	(g) Did the beneficiary live alone?
☐ YES ☐ NO If yes, answer 2. below.	☐ YES ☐ NO If yes, answer 2. and 3. below.

2. BENEFICIARY NOT IN PAYEE'S CUSTODY

(a) Did the payee maintain contact with the beneficiary?

☐ YES ☐ NO

If yes, show type of contact (visit, phone, letters) and frequency. If no, explain.

(b) Did anyone other than the payee demonstrate concern for the beneficiary?

☐ YES ☐ NO

If yes, show who and type and frequency of contacts.

3. BENEFICIARY LIVED ALONE

(a) Was the beneficiary responsible for his/her maintenance expenses? (Rent, utilities)	(b) Did the beneficiary purchase his/her food and clothing?
☐ YES ☐ NO	☐ YES ☐ NO

4. REMARKS

PART III INFORMATION FROM CUSTODIAN

CUSTODIAN'S NAME	ADDRESS	PHONE (Include area code)

1. PAYEE AND CUSTODIAN ARE NOT THE SAME PERSON OR ORGANIZATION

(a) Did the beneficiary live with the custodian during the entire report period? ⟶ ☐ YES ☐ NO
If no, show other custodians if known.

(b) Who would the custodian notify in cases of emergency?

(c) Was a charge made for care and maintenance of the beneficiary? ☐ YES ☐ NO
If yes, show the amount paid by the payee ⟶ Amount $ _____

(d) Did the payee demonstrate personal concern for the beneficiary? ⟶ ☐ YES ☐ NO
If yes, explain below

FREQUENCY OF VISITS	PROVIDES CLOTHING	GIFTS	OTHER (Specify)
	☐ YES ☐ NO	☐ YES ☐ NO	

(e) Did the payee contribute money for the beneficiary's personal use? If yes, show the amount contributed by the payee. ⟶ ☐ YES ☐ NO
Amount $ _____

(f) Does the custodian hold and control the beneficiary's personal use funds? ⟶ ☐ YES ☐ NO
If yes, answer (g).

(g) Are the beneficiary's funds mingled with funds of other persons? ☐ YES ☐ NO ⟶
If yes, are the funds clearly designated as the beneficiary's? ☐ YES ☐ NO

2. ALL CUSTODIANS

Were any group purchases made? ☐ YES ☐ NO ⟶
If yes, were the purchases approved by SSA? ☐ YES ☐ NO

3. REMARKS

PART IV EVALUATION AND ACTION TAKEN

SIGNATURE AND TITLE	OFFICE	DATE

Form **SSA-624-F4** (9-86)   4.   ⁕U.S. Government Printing Office: 1983-241-312/80032

Appendix 31
States with Family Consent Statutes

The family may make health care decisions for
(A) incapacitated adults in:

Arkansas	Excludes patients who are pregnant.
Georgia	
Idaho	
Louisiana	
Maine	
Maryland	
Mississippi	
New Mexico	Patients must be in an irreversible coma.
Utah	

(B) terminally ill and incapacitated adults (including termination of treatment) in:

Arkansas	Excludes patients who are pregnant.
Connecticut	Excludes patients who are pregnant. May not withdraw nutrition or hydration.
Florida	Excludes patients who are pregnant. May not withdraw "sustenance." Doctor can make decisions if no family members are available.
Iowa	May not withdraw "sustenance."
Louisiana	
New Mexico	Patients must be terminally ill and comatose.
North Carolina	Patients must be terminally ill and comatose. Doctor can make decisions if no family members are available.
Oregon	Excludes patients who are pregnant. Patients must be terminally ill and comatose. Doctor decides how much nutrition patients can tolerate. Doctor can make decisions if no family members are available.
Texas	Excludes patients who are pregnant. Doctor can make decisions if no family members are available.
Utah	May not withdraw "sustenance."
Virginia	

Source: B. Mishkin, *A Matter of Choice: Planning Ahead for Health Care Decisions*, Senate Special Committee on Aging, 1986.

Appendix 32
Provisions of Family Consent Laws

State	Patient Must Be — Terminally Ill	Patient Must Be — Comatose	Family Members — Spouse	Family Members — Adult Child	Family Members — Parent	Family Members — Adult Sibling	Family Members — Other	Priority Given	Consent Not Valid for — Abortion	Consent Not Valid for — Sterilization	Consent Not Valid for — Mental Health Care
Arkansas			X	X	X	nearest relative	grandparent				
Connecticut[A]											
Florida	X		X	X[C]	X		nearest relative	X			
Georgia			X		X[B]	X[B]	grandparent	X	X		
Idaho			X		X		any competent relative				
Iowa	X		X	X[C]	X	X					
Louisiana			X		X[B]	X[B]	grandparent[B]		X	X	
Louisiana[1]	X		X	X[C]	X[C]	X[C]	other ascendents or descendents[C]	X			X
Maine			X		X		nearest relative				
Maryland			X	X	X	X	grandparent; adult grandchild	X	X	X	X
Mississippi			X	X	X	X	grandparent				
New Mexico	X or	X	X	X	X	X	family members[E]	X			
North Carolina	X and	X	X	X	X	X		X			
Oregon	X and	X	X	X[C]	X	X					
Texas	X		X	X[C]	X		nearest relative	X[D]			
Utah			X	X	X[B]	X[B]	grandparent[B]				
Virginia	X		X	X	X		nearest relative	X			

Source: Adapted from B. Mishkin, *A Matter of Choice: Planning Ahead for Health Care Decisions*, Senate Special Committee on Aging, 1986.

A—requires consent of "next of kin," if known
B—for minor child
C—majority of this class required (if available)
D—requires consent of at least two family members, if reasonably available.
E—all who can be contacted must agree on what patient would choose
1 Louisiana has two family consent laws.

Appendix 33
American Medical Association Statement on Withholding or Withdrawing Life-Prolonging Medical Treatment

T HE social commitment of the physician is to sustain life and relieve suffering. Where the performance of one duty conflicts with the other, the choice of the patient, or his family or legal representative if the patient is incompetent to act in his own behalf, should prevail. In the absence of the patient's choice or an authorized proxy, the physician must act in the best interest of the patient.

For humane reasons, with informed consent, a physician may do what is medically necessary to alleviate severe pain, or cease or omit treatment to permit a terminally ill patient whose death is imminent to die. However, he should not intentionally cause death. In deciding whether the administration of potentially life-prolonging medical treatment is in the best interest of the patient who is incompetent to act in his own behalf, the physician should determine what the possibility is for extending life under humane and comfortable conditions and what are the prior expressed wishes of the patient and attitudes of the family or those who have responsibility for the custody of the patient.

Even if death is not imminent but a patient's coma is beyond doubt irreversible and there are adequate safeguards to confirm the accuracy of the diagnosis and with the concurrence of those who have responsibility for the care of the patient, it is not unethical to discontinue all means of life-prolonging medical treatment.

Life-prolonging medical treatment includes medication and artificially or technologically supplied respiration, nutrition or hydration. In treating a terminally ill or irreversibly comatose patient, the physician should determine whether the benefits of treatment outweigh its burdens. At all times, the dignity of the patient should be maintained.

Source: *Current Opinions of the Council on Ethical and Judicial Affairs of the American Medical Association*, 1986, with permission.

Appendix 34
Health-Related State Agencies and Organizations (Including Licensure Agencies)

Alabama

Commission on Aging
740 Madison Avenue
Montgomery 36104

Home Health Care Medical Directors Association (1)
P.O. Box 16626
Mobile 36616
(205) 476–0192

Alabama State Hospice Organization (2)
701 Princeton Avenue SW
Birmingham 35211
(205) 592–1738

Alabama Medicaid Agency (3)
2500 Fairlane Drive
Montgomery 36130
(205) 277–2710

---

1. State home care associations
2. State hospice organizations
3. Medicaid assistance offices
4. Self-help clearinghouses
5. Hospital licensure agencies
6. Medical and nursing licensure agencies

State Hospital Licensure Agency (5)
Division of Licensure and Certification
Alabama Department of Public Health
654 State Office Building
Montgomery 36130
(205) 261–5113

Alabama Board of Nursing (6)
One East Building, Suite 203
500 Eastern Boulevard
Montgomery 36117
(205) 261–4060

Alaska

Department of Health and Social Services
Pouch H
Juneau 99811

Office on Aging
Department of Health and Social Services
Pouch H
Juneau 99811

Hospice of Juneau (2)
419 6th Street
Juneau 99802
(907) 586–3414

Division of Medical Assistance (3)
Department of Health and Social Services
PPO Box H–07
Juneau 99811
(907) 586–9496

Health Facilities Licensing and Certification (5)
4041 B Street #101
Anchorage 99503
(907) 561–2171

Alaska Medical Board (6)
Department of Commerce and Economic Development
Division of Occupational Licensing
P.O. Box D-Lic

Juneau 99811
(907) 465–2541

Alaska Medical Board of Nursing (6)
3601 C Street
Suite 722
Anchorage 99503
(907) 561–2878

Arizona

Department of Economic Security
1717 West Jefferson
Phoenix 85007

Bureau on Aging
Department of Economic Security
P.O. Box 6123
Phoenix 85004

Arizona Association for Home Care (1)
3602 East Campbell
Phoenix 85018
(602) 957–0773

Arizona State Hospice Organization (2)
St. Mary's Hospice
1601 West St. Mary's Road
Tucson 85705
(602) 622–5833

Arizona Health Care Cost Containment System (AHCCS) (3)
801 East Jefferson
Phoenix 85034
(602) 234–3655

Office of Health Care Institution Licensure (5)
Arizona Department of Health Services
411 North 24th Street

---

1. State home care associations
2. State hospice organizations
3. Medicaid assistance offices
4. Self-help clearinghouses
5. Hospital licensure agencies
6. Medical and nursing licensure agencies

Phoenix 85008
(602) 220–6407

Arizona Board of Medical Examiners (6)
1990 West Camelback Road
Suite 401
Phoenix 85015
(602) 255–5092

Arizona State Board of Nursing (6)
5050 North 19th Avenue, Suite 103
Phoenix 85015
(602) 255–5092

Arkansas

Department of Human Services
406 National Old Lind Building
Little Rock 72201

Office on Aging and Adult Services
Department of Human Services
7107 West 12th Street
P.O. Box 2179
Little Rock 72203

Arkansas Association for Home Health Agencies (1)
1501 North University, Suite 400
Little Rock 72207
(501) 664–7870

Arkansas State Hospice Organization (2)
P.O. Box 725
Jonesboro 72401
(501) 972–6270

Office of Medical Services (3)
Division of Economic and Medical Services
Arkansas Department of Human Services
P.O. Box 1437
Little Rock 72203
(501) 682–8338

Office of Long-Term Care (3)
Division of Economic and Medical Services

Arkansas Department of Human Services
P.O. Box 1437
Little Rock 72203
(501) 682–8430

Division of Health Facility Services (5)
Arkansas Department of Health—Area 2300
4815 West Markham Street
Little Rock 72205
(501) 681–2201

Arkansas State Board of Nursing (6)
4120 West Markham Street, Suite 308
Little Rock 72205
(501) 371–2751

California

Health and Welfare Agency
926 J Street, Room 917
Sacramento 95814

Department of Aging
Health and Welfare Agency
918 J Street
Sacramento 95814

California Association for Health Services at Home (CAHSAH) (1)
660 J Street, Suite 290
Sacramento 95814
(916) 443–8055

Hospice Organization of Southern California (2)
637 South Lucas
Los Angeles 90017
(818) 788–3295

Northern California Hospice Association (2)
703 Market Street, Suite 550

1. State home care associations
2. State hospice organizations
3. Medicaid assistance offices
4. Self-help clearinghouses
5. Hospital licensure agencies
6. Medical and nursing licensure agencies

San Francisco 94103
(415) 543–9393

Medical Care Services (3)
Department of Health Services
714 P Street, Room 1253
Sacramento 95814
(916) 322–5824

Self-Help and Mutual Aid Association (SHAMA) (4)
c/o Alfred Katz
UCLA School of Public Health
405 Hilgard Avenue
Los Angeles 90024
(213) 825–5418

San Diego Self-Help Clearinghouse (4)
1172 Morena Boulevard, P.O. Box 86246
San Diego 92138
(619) 275–2344

San Francisco Self-Help Clearinghouse (4)
Mental Health Association of San Francisco
2398 Fine Street
San Francisco 94115
(415) 921–4401

Licensing and Certification (5)
Department of Health Services
714 P Street, Room 823
Sacramento 95814
(916) 445–3054

California Board of Medical Quality Assurance (6)
1430 Howe Avenue
Sacramento 95825
(916) 920–6411

Board of Registered Nursing (6)
1030 13th Street, Suite 200
Sacramento 95814
(916) 322–3350

Board of Vocational Nurse and Psychiatric Technician Examiners (6)
1020 N Street, Room 406

Sacramento 95814
(916) 445–0793

Colorado

Department of Social Services
1575 Sherman Street
Denver 80203

Division of Services for the Aging
Department of Social Services
1575 Sherman Street
Denver 80203

Colorado Association of Home Health Agencies (1)
7235 South Newport Way
Englewood 80122
(303) 694–4728

Colorado Hospice Coalition (2)
3534 Kirkwood Place
Boulder 80302
(303) 449–7740

Bureau of Medical Services (3)
Department of Social Services
1575 Sherman, 6th floor
Denver 80203
(303) 866–5901

Division of Health Facilities Regulation (5)
Colorado Department of Health
4210 East 11th Avenue
Denver 80220
(303) 331–4930

Colorado Board of Medical Examiners (6)
1525 Sherman Street #132
Denver 80203
(303) 868–2468

1. State home care associations
2. State hospice organizations
3. Medicaid assistance offices
4. Self-help clearinghouses
5. Hospital licensure agencies
6. Medical and nursing licensure agencies

Connecticut

Department on Aging
90 Washington Street, Room 312
Hartford 06115

Connecticut Association for Home Care (1)
110 Barnes Road
P.O. Box 90
Wallingford 06492
(203) 265–8931

Hospice Council of Connecticut (2)
461 Atlantic Street
Stamford 06901
(203) 324–2592

Medical Care Administration (3)
Department of Income Maintenance
110 Bartholomew Avenue
Hartford 06106
(203) 566–2934

Hamden Mental Health Center (4)
300 Dixwell Avenue
Hamden 06514
(203) 789–7645

Connecticut Self-Help Mutual Support Network (4)
19 Howe Street
New Haven 06511
(800) 842–1501 or (203) 789–7645

Hospital and Medical Care Division (5)
Connecticut State Department of Health Services
150 Washington Street
Hartford 06106
(203) 566–1073

Department of Health Services
Division of Medical Quality Assurance
Physician Licensure
150 Washington Street
Hartford 06106
(203) 566–7398

Connecticut Board of Examiners for Nursing (6)
Department of Health Services
Division of Medical Quality Assurance
150 Washington Street
Hartford 06106
(203) 566–1032

Delaware

Department of Health and Social Services
Delaware State Hospital, 3rd floor
Administration Building
New Castle 19720

Delaware Hospices, Inc. (2)
3509 Silvergate Road, Suite 109, Talley Building
Wilmington 19810
(302) 478–5707

Medical Services (3)
Department of Health and Social Services
Delaware State Hospital
New Castle 19720
(302) 421–6139

Office of Health Facilities Licensing and Certification (5)
Department of Health and Social Services
3000 Newport Gap Pike
Wilmington 19808
(302) 571–3499

Board of Medical Practice of Delaware (6)
Margaret O'Neill Building, 2nd Floor
Dover 19903
(302) 736–4522

Delaware Board of Nursing (6)
Margaret O'Neill Building, 2nd Floor

1. State home care associations
2. State hospice organizations
3. Medicaid assistance offices
4. Self-help clearinghouses
5. Hospital licensure agencies
6. Medical and nursing licensure agencies

Dover 19903
(302) 736–4522

District of Columbia

Office of Aging
Office of the Mayor
1012 14th Street NW, Suite 1106
Washington 20005

Capitol Home Health Association (1)
P.O. Box 70407
Washington 20088
(202) 547–7424

Hospice Care of the District of Columbia (2)
1749 St. Matthews Court NW
Washington 20036
(202) 347–1700

Office of Health Care Financing (3)
D.C. Department of Human Services
1331 H Street NW, Suite 500
Washington 20005
(202) 727–0735

Greater Washington Self-Help Coalition (4)
Mental Health Association of Northern Virginia
100 North Washington Street, Suite 232
Falls Church, VA 22046
(703) 536–4100

Service Facility Regulation Administration (5)
614 H Street NW
Washington 20001
(202) 727–7190

Occupational and Professional Licensing Administration (6)
P.O. Box 37200, Room 904
Washington 20013
(202) 727–7424

Florida

Department of Health and Rehabilitation Services
1323 Winewood Boulevard
Tallahassee 32301

Program Office of Aging and Adult Services
Department of Health and Rehabilitation Services
1323 Winewood Boulevard
Tallahassee 32301

Florida Association of Home Health Agencies (1)
201 South Monroe Street, Suite 201
Tallahassee 32301
(904) 224–4226

Florida Hospices, Inc. (2)
Hospice of Volusia
P.O. Box 1990
Daytona Beach 32724
(904) 254–4237

Department of Health and Rehabilitative Services (3)
1321 Winewood Boulevard
Tallahassee 32301
(904) 488–3560

Office of Licensure and Certification (5)
Department of Health and Rehabilitation Services
27237 Mahan Drive
Tallahassee 32308
(904) 487–2527

Florida Board of Medicine (6)
130 North Monroe Street
Tallahassee 32399
(904) 488–0595

Board of Nursing (6)
111 Coast Line Drive East, Suite 504
Jacksonville 32202
(904) 359–6331

---

1. State home care associations
2. State hospice organizations
3. Medicaid assistance offices
4. Self-help clearinghouses
5. Hospital licensure agencies
6. Medical and nursing licensure agencies

Georgia

Department of Human Resources
618 Ponce de Leon Avenue N.E.
Atlanta 30308

Office of Aging
Department of Human Resources
618 Ponce de Leon Avenue N.E.
Atlanta 30308

Georgia Association of Home Health Agencies (1)
1260 South Omni International
Atlanta 30303
(404) 577-9144

Georgia Hospice Organization (2)
Hospice of the Golden Isles
1326 Union Street
Brunswick 31520
(215) 265-4735

Georgia Department of Medical Assistance (3)
Floyd Veterans Memorial Building
West Tower, 1220C
2 Martin Luther King, Jr., Drive SE
Atlanta 30334
(404) 656-4479

Standards and Licensure Section (5)
Department of Human Resources
878 Peachtree Street NE, Suite 803
Atlanta 30309
(404) 894-5137

Composite State Board of Medical Examiners (6)
166 Pryor Street SW
Atlanta 30303
(404) 656-3913

Georgia Board of Nursing (6)
166 Pryor Street SW
Atlanta 30303
(404) 656-3913

Guam

Department of Public Health and Social Services
Government of Guam
P.O. Box 2816
Agana 96910

Office of Aging
Social Service Administration
Government of Guam
P.O. Box 2816
Agana 96910

Bureau of Health Care Financing (3)
Department of Public Health and Social Services
P.O. Box 96910
Agana 96910

Guam Board of Nurse Examiners (6)
Box 2816
Agana 96910
(671) 734–2783

Hawaii

Executive Office on Aging
Office of the Governor
State of Hawaii
1149 Bethel Street, Room 307
Honolulu 96813

St. Francis Hospital (2)
Maureen Keleher
2230 Liliha Street
Honolulu 96817
(808) 845–1727

1. State home care associations
2. State hospice organizations
3. Medicaid assistance offices
4. Self-help clearinghouses
5. Hospital licensure agencies
6. Medical and nursing licensure agencies

Health Care Administration Division (3)
Department of Social Services and Housing
P.O. Box 339
Honolulu 96809
(808) 548–3855

State Health Planning and Development Agency (5)
Medical Health Services Division
Hospital and Medical Facilities
Licensing Department of Health
P.O. Box 3378
Honolulu 96801
(808) 548–2048

Board of Medical Examiners (6)
Department of Commerce and Consumer Affairs
P.O. Box 3469
Honolulu 96809
(808) 548–4392

Board of Nursing (6)
P.O. Box 3469
Honolulu 96801
(808) 548–3086

Idaho

Idaho Office on Aging
Statehouse
Boise 83720

Council of Idaho Hospice Organizations (2)
Hospice Mercy Medical Center
1512 12th Avenue
Nampa 83651
(208) 467–1171, ext. 174

Bureau of Medical Assistance (3)
Department of Health and Welfare
450 West State Street
Statehouse Mail
Boise 83720
(208) 334–5794

Facility Standards Program (5)
Department of Health and Welfare
420 West Washington Street
Boise 83720
(208) 334-4169

Idaho State Board of Medicine (6)
650 West State Street
Boise 83720
(208) 334-2822

Idaho State Board of Nursing (6)
700 West State Street
Boise 83720
(208) 334-3110

Illinois

Department on Aging
2401 West Jefferson
Springfield 62706

Illinois Council of Home Health Services (1)
1619 Ashland Avenue
Evanston 60201
(312) 328-6654

Illinois State Hospice Organization (2)
Hospice of Proviso-Leyden
330 Eastern Avenue
Bellwood 60104
(312) 547-8282

Division of Medical Programs (3)
Illinois Department of Public Aid
628 East Adams

1. State home care associations
2. State hospice organizations
3. Medicaid assistance offices
4. Self-help clearinghouses
5. Hospital licensure agencies
6. Medical and nursing licensure agencies

Springfield 62761
(217) 782–2570

Self-Help Center (4)
1600 Dodge Center, Suite S–122
Evanston 60201
(312) 328–0470

Hospital Licensing Section (5)
Division of Health Facilities Standards
Department of Public Health
525 West Jefferson
Springfield 62761
(217) 782–4977

Department of Registration and Education (6)
320 West Washington
Springfield 62786
(217) 785–0800

Indiana

Commission on Aging and Aged
Graphic Arts Building
215 North Senate Avenue
Indianapolis 46202

Indiana Association of Home Health Agencies (1)
P.O. Box 1457
Carmel 46032
(317) 848–2942

Indiana Association of Hospices (2)
2200 Randalea Drive
Fort Wayne 46805
(219) 484–6636, ext. 4183

Assistant Administrator (3)
Medicaid Director
Indiana State Department of Public Welfare
State Office Building, Room 702
Indianapolis 46204
(317) 232–4324

Division of Acute Care Services (5)
Indiana State Board of Health
1330 West Michigan Street
Indianapolis 46206
(317) 633–8488

Health Professions Bureau (6)
Medical Licensing Board of Indiana
P.O. Box 82067
One American Square, Suite 1020
Indianapolis 46282–0004
(317) 232–2960

Indiana State Board of Nursing (6)
Health Professions Bureau
P.O. Box 82067
One American Square, Suite 1020
Indianapolis 46282
(317) 232–2960

Iowa

Commission on Aging
415 West 10th Street
Jewett Building
Des Moines 50319

Iowa Assembly of Home Health Agencies (1)
3000 Southwest 40th Street
Des Moines 50321
(515) 282–6498

Iowa Hospice Organization (2)
205 Loma Street
Waterloo 50701
(319) 273–2702 or 273–2814

---

1. State home care associations
2. State hospice organizations
3. Medicaid assistance offices
4. Self-help clearinghouses
5. Hospital licensure agencies
6. Medical and nursing licensure agencies

Bureau of Medical Services (3)
Department of Human Services
Hoover State Office Building, 5th floor
Des Moines 50319
(515) 281–8794

Division of Health Facilities (5)
Iowa State Department of Inspection and Appeals
Lucas State Office Building
Des Moines 50319
(515) 281–4115

Iowa State Board of Medical Examiners (6)
State Capitol Complex
Executive Hills West
Des Moines 50319
(515) 281–5171

Iowa Board of Nursing (6)
State Capitol Complex
1223 East Court Avenue
Des Moines 50319
(515) 281–3255

Kansas

Department of Aging
Biddle Building
2700 West 6th Street
Topeka 66606

Kansas Association of Home Health Agencies (1)
1526 North Market Street
Wichita 67214
(316) 265–5888

Association of Kansas Hospices (2)
7540 Aberdeen
Prairie Village 66208
(913) 341–5476

Department of Social and Rehabilitation Services (3)
State Office Building
Topeka 66612
(913) 296–3981

Hospital Program (5)
Bureau of Adult and Child Care Facilities
Kansas Department of Health and Environment
Forbes Field, Building 740
Topeka 66620
(913) 296–1240

Kansas State Board of Healing Arts (6)
Landon State Office Building
900 Southwest Jackson, Suite 553
Topeka 66612
(913) 296–7413

Kansas State Board of Nursing (6)
Landon State Office Building
900 Southwest Jackson, Suite 551–S
Topeka 66612
(913) 296–4929

Kentucky

Department for Human Resources
Capital Annex, Room 201
Frankfort 40601

Kentucky Home Health Association (1)
1804 Darien Drive
Lexington 40504
(606) 277–7983

Kentucky Association of Hospices (2)
1105 Nicholasville Road
Lexington 40503
(606) 252–2308

Department of Medicaid Services (3)
Cabinet for Human Resources
275 East Main Street

---

1. State home care associations
2. State hospice organizations
3. Medicaid assistance offices
4. Self-help clearinghouses
5. Hospital licensure agencies
6. Medical and nursing licensure agencies

Frankfort 40621
(502) 564–6535

Division of Licensing and Regulation (5)
Cabinet for Human Resources
Human Resources Building
275 East Main Street, 4th Floor East
Frankfort 40621
(502) 564–2800

Kentucky Board of Nursing (6)
4010 Dupont Circle, Suite 430
Louisville 40207
(502) 897–5143

Louisiana

Health and Human Resources Administration
P.O. Box 44215, Capitol Station
Baton Rouge 70804

Bureau of Aging Services
Division of Human Resources
Health and Human Resources Administration
P.O. Box 44282, Capitol Station
Baton Rouge 70804

Richard N. Murphy Hospice (2)
P.O. Box 111
Hammond 70404
(504) 386–6130

Medical Assistance Division (3)
Department of Health and Human Resources
P.O. Box 94065
Baton Rouge 70804
(504) 342–3956

Division of Licensing and Certification (6)
Louisiana Department of Health and Human Resources
Box 3767
Baton Rouge 70821
(504) 342–5774

Louisiana State Board of Medical Examiners (6)
830 Union Street, Suite 100
New Orleans 70112
(504) 524–6763

Louisiana State Board of Nursing (6)
907 Pere Marquette Building
150 Baronne Street
New Orleans 70112
(504) 568–5464

Louisiana State Board of Practical Nurse Examiners (6)
Tidewater Place
1440 Canal Street, Suite 2010
New Orleans 70112
(504) 568–6480

Maine

Department of Human Services
State House
Augusta 04333

Bureau of Maine's Elderly
Community Services Unit
Department of Human Services
State House
Augusta 04333

Maine Community Health Association (1)
71 Sewall Street
Augusta 04330
(207) 622–3276

Coalition of Maine Hospices (2)
32 Thomas Street

---

1. State home care associations
2. State hospice organizations
3. Medicaid assistance offices
4. Self-help clearinghouses
5. Hospital licensure agencies
6. Medical and nursing licensure agencies

Portland 04102
(207) 774–4417

Department of Human Services (3)
State House, Station 11
Augusta 04333
(207) 289–2674

Division of Licensing and Certification (5)
Department of Human Services
State House, Station 11
Augusta 04333
(207) 289–2606

Board of Registration in Medicine (State of Maine) (6)
RFD 3, Box 461
Waterville 04901
(207) 873–2184

Maine State Board of Nursing (6)
285 Water Street
Augusta 04330
(207) 289–5324

Maryland

Office on Aging
State Office Building
301 West Preston Street
Baltimore 21201

Maryland Association of Home Health Agencies (1)
P.O. Box 1307
Columbia 21044
(301) 964–9698

Maryland State Hospice Network (2)
Sinai Hospital Home Care/Hospice
2401 Belvedere Avenue
Baltimore 21215
(301) 587–5600

Department of Health and Mental Hygiene (3)
201 West Preston Street
Baltimore 21201
(301) 225–6525

Department of Health and Mental Hygiene (5)
201 West Preston Street
Baltimore 21201
(301) 383–6197

Board of Medical Examiners of Maryland (6)
201 West Preston Street
Baltimore 21201
(301) 225–5900

Maryland State Board of Examiners of Nurses (6)
201 West Preston Street
Baltimore 21201
(301) 225–5880

Massachusetts

Department of Elder Affairs
110 Tremont Street
Boston 02108

Massachusetts Association of Community Health Agencies (1)
6 Beacon Street, Suite 915
Boston 02108
(617) 893–4792

Hospice of Lynn (2)
VNA of Lynn
196 Ocean Avenue
Lynn, MA 01902
(617) 598–2454

Department of Public Welfare (3)
180 Tremont Street
Boston 02111
(617) 574–0205

Division of Health Care Quality (5)
Massachusetts Department of Public Health

---

1. State home care associations
2. State hospice organizations
3. Medicaid assistance offices
4. Self-help clearinghouses
5. Hospital licensure agencies
6. Medical and nursing licensure agencies

80 Boylston Street, Room 1125
Boston 02116
(617) 727–5860

Board of Registration in Medicine (6)
Commonwealth of Massachusetts
10 West Street
Boston 02111
(617) 727–3086

Board of Registration in Nursing (6)
100 Cambridge Street, Room 1519
Boston 02202
(617) 727–7393

Michigan

Office of Services to the Aging
300 East Michigan
P.O. Box 30026
Lansing 48909

Michigan Home Health Association (1)
4990 Northwind Drive, Suite 220
East Lansing 48823
(517) 332–1195

Michigan Hospice Organization (2)
1825 Watson Road
Hemlock 48626
(517) 642–8121

Department of Social Services (3)
921 West Holmes
P.O. Box 30037
Lansing 48909
(517) 334–7262

Berrien County Self-Help Clearinghouse (4)
Riverwood Community Mental Health Center
2681 Morton Avenue
St. Joseph 49085
(616) 983–7781

Bureau of Health Facilities (5)
Michigan Department of Public Health
3500 North Logan, Box 30035

Lansing 48909
(517) 335–8500

Michigan Board of Medicine (6)
611 West Ottawa Street, Box 30018
Lansing 48909
(517) 373–6873

Michigan Board of Nursing (6)
Department of Licensing and Regulation, Box 30018
Lansing 48909
(517) 373–6873

Minnesota

Governor's Citizens Council on Aging
Suite 204 Metro Square Building
7th and Robert Streets
St. Paul 55101

Minnesota Assembly of Home and Community Health Nursing Agencies (1)
P.O. Box 300110
Minneapolis 55403
(612) 374–5404

Minnesota Hospice Organization (2)
Metro Medical Center
900 South 8th Street
Minneapolis 55404
(612) 347–4377

Department of Human Services (3)
P.O. Box 43170
St. Paul 55164
(612) 296–2766

Community Care Unit (4)
Wilder Center
919 Lafond Avenue

---

1. State home care associations
2. State hospice organizations
3. Medicaid assistance offices
4. Self-help clearinghouses
5. Hospital licensure agencies
6. Medical and nursing licensure agencies

St. Paul 55104
(612) 642–4060

Health Resources Division (5)
Minnesota Department of Health
717 Delaware Street Southeast
Minneapolis 55440
(612) 623–5440

Minnesota Board of Medical Examiners (6)
2700 University Avenue West, Suite 106
St. Paul 55114
(612) 642–0538

Minnesota Board of Nursing (6)
2700 University Avenue West, Suite 108
St. Paul 55114
(612) 642–0567

Mississippi

Council on Aging
P.O. Box 5136
Fondren Station
510 George Street
Jackson 39216

Mississippi Home Health Association (1)
455 North Lamar Street, Suite 410
Jackson 39202
(601) 353–0015

South Mississippi Home Health (2)
P.O. Box 888
Hattiesburg 39401
(601) 268–1842

Office of the Governor (3)
Robert E. Lee Building, Room 801
239 North Lamar Street
Jackson 39202–1311
(601) 359–6050

Division of Health Facilities Licensure and Certification (5)
Mississippi State Department of Health
2686 Insurance Center Drive

Jackson 39216
(601) 981–6880

Mississippi Board of Nursing (6)
135 Bounds Street
Jackson 39206
(601) 354–7349

Missouri

Department of Social Services
Broadway State Office Building
P.O. Box 570
Jefferson City 65101

Office of Aging
Division of Special Services
Department of Social Services
Broadway State Office Building
P.O. Box 570
Jefferson City 65101

Missouri Association of Home Health Agencies (1)
101 Madison Street
Jefferson City 65101
(314) 634–7772

Missouri Hospice Organization (2)
527 West 39th Street
Kansas City 64111
(816) 531–1200

Department of Social Services (3)
P.O. Box 6500
Jefferson City 65102
(314) 751–6922

Bureau of Hospital Licensing and Certification (5)
Missouri Department of Health

---

1. State home care associations
2. State hospice organizations
3. Medicaid assistance offices
4. Self-help clearinghouses
5. Hospital licensure agencies
6. Medical and nursing licensure agencies

Box 570
Jefferson City 65102
(314) 751-6302

Missouri State Board of Registration for the Healing Arts (6)
Box 4
Jefferson City 65102
(314) 751-2334

Montana

Department of Social and Rehabilitation Services
P.O. Box 1723
Helena 58601

Aging Services Bureau
Department of Social and Rehabilitation Services
P.O. Box 1723
Helena 58601

Montana Hospice Exchange Council (2)
St. Joseph's Mission Mountain Hospice
P.O. Box 1010
Poison 59860
(406) 883-5377

Department of Social and Rehabilitation Services (3)
P.O. Box 4210
Helena 59604
(406) 444-4540

Health Services Division (5)
State Department of Health and Environmental Sciences
Cogswell Building
Helena 59620
(406) 444-2037

Montana State Board of Nursing (6)
1424 9th Avenue
Helena 59620
(406) 444-4279

Nebraska

Commission on Aging
State House Station 94784

P.O. Box 95044
Lincoln 68509

Nebraska Hospice Association, Inc. (2)
1010 East 35 Street
Scotts Bluff 69361
(308) 635–3171 or 632–5549

Department of Social Services (3)
301 Centennial Mall South, 5th Floor
Lincoln 68509
(402) 471–9330

Self-Help Information Services (4)
1601 Euclid Avenue
Lincoln 68502
(402) 476–9668

Division of Licensure and Standards (5)
State Department of Health
301 Centennial Mall South
Lincoln 68509
(402) 471–2946

Bureau of Examining Boards (6)
301 Centennial Mall South
Box 95007
Lincoln 68509
(402) 471–2115

Nevada

Department of Human Resources
505 East King Street, Room 600
Carson City 89710

Division for Aging Services
Department of Human Resources

---

1. State home care associations
2. State hospice organizations
3. Medicaid assistance offices
4. Self-help clearinghouses
5. Hospital licensure agencies
6. Medical and nursing licensure agencies

505 East King Street, Room 600
Carson City 89710

Nathan Adelson Hospice (2)
4141 South Swenson
Las Vegas 89109
(702) 733–0320

Welfare Division, Department of Human Resources (3)
Capitol Complex
2527 North Carson Street
Carson City 89710
(702) 885–4698

Bureau of Regulatory Health Services (5)
Nevada State Division of Health
505 East King Street
Carson City 89710
(702) 885–4475

Nevada State Board of Medical Examiners (6)
P.O. Box 7238
Reno 89510
(702) 329–2559

Nevada State Board of Nursing (6)
1281 Terminal Way, Room 116
Reno 89502
(702) 786–2778

New Hampshire

Council on Aging
P.O. Box 786
14 Depot Street
Concord 03301

Community Health Care Association of New Hampshire (1)
117 Manchester Street
Concord 03301
(603) 225–5597

Hospice Affiliates of New Hampshire (2)
Concord Regional VNA
8 Loudoun Road

Concord 03301
(603) 224–4093

New Hampshire Division of Human Services (3)
Department of Health and Human Services
6 Hazen Drive
Concord 03301–6521
(603) 271–4353

Bureau of Health Facilities Administration (5)
Division of Public Health Services
Health and Human Services Building
6 Hazen Drive
Concord 03301
(603) 271–4592

New Hampshire Board of Registration in Medicine (6)
Health and Welfare Building
6 Hazen Drive
Concord 03301
(603) 271–4502

New Hampshire Board of Nursing Education and Nurse Registration (6)
State Office Park South
101 Pleasant Street
Concord 03301
(603) 271–2323

New Jersey

Division on Aging
Department of Community Affairs
P.O. Box 2768
363 West State Street
Trenton 08625

Home Health Agency Assembly of New Jersey (1)
760 Alexander Road, CN–1

1. State home care associations
2. State hospice organizations
3. Medicaid assistance offices
4. Self-help clearinghouses
5. Hospital licensure agencies
6. Medical and nursing licensure agencies

Princeton 08540
(609) 452–9280

New Jersey Hospice Organization (2)
760 Alexander Road
Princeton 08540
(609) 452–9280

Department of Human Services (3)
CN–712 Quakerbridge Plaza
Trenton 08625
(609) 588–2602

Self-Help Clearinghouse of New Jersey (4)
St. Clare's Hospital
Pocono Road
Denville 07834
(800) 452–9790 or (201) 625–6395

Licensing, Certification, and Standards (5)
New Jersey State Department of Health
Division of Health Facilities Evaluation, CN 367
Trenton 08625
(609) 292–5764

State Board of Medical Examiners of New Jersey (6)
28 West State Street
Trenton 08608
(609) 292–4843

New Jersey Board of Nursing (6)
1100 Raymond Boulevard
Newark 07102
(201) 648–2490

New Mexico

Commission on Aging
408 Galisteo-Villagra Building
Santa Fe 87503

Visiting Nurse Services Hospice (2)
P.O. Box 1951
Santa Fe 87501
(505) 471–9201

Department of Human Services (3)
P.O. Box 2348
Santa Fe 87503–2348
(505) 827–4315

Health Services Division, Federal Program Certification Section (5)
Health and Environment Department
1190 St. Francis Drive, Box 968
Santa Fe 87504
(505) 827–2416

New Mexico Board of Medical Examiners (6)
P.O. Box 1388
Santa Fe 87504
(505) 827–9933

State of New Mexico Board of Nursing (6)
4125 Carlisle Northeast
Albuquerque 87107
(505) 841–6524

New York

Office for the Aging
Agency Building
2 Empire State Plaza
Albany 12223

New York City Field Office
Office for the Aging
2 World Trade Center, Room 5036
New York 10047

Home Care Association of New York State (1)
840 James Street
Syracuse 13203
(315) 475–7229

---

1. State home care associations
2. State hospice organizations
3. Medicaid assistance offices
4. Self-help clearinghouses
5. Hospital licensure agencies
6. Medical and nursing licensure agencies

New York State Hospice Association, Inc. (2)
468 Rosedale Avenue
White Plains 10605
(914) 946–7699

Division of Medical Assistance (3)
State Department of Social Services
Ten Eyck Office Building
40 North Pearl Street
Albany 12243
(518) 474–9132

New York City Self-Help Clearinghouse, Inc. (4)
186 Joralemon Street
Brooklyn 11201
(718) 852–4291

Long Island Self-Help Clearinghouse (4)
New York Institute of Technology
6350 Jericho Turnpike
Commack 11725
(516) 499–8800 or 686–7505

Orange County Department of Mental Health (4)
Consultation and Education Department
Harriman Drive, Drawer 471
Goshen 10925
(914) 294–6185

New York City Self-Help Clearinghouse (4)
Graduate School and University Center/CUNY
33 West 42nd Street
New York 10036
(212) 840–7606

Rockland County CMHC (4)
Sanitorium Road
Pomona 10970
(914) 354–0200, ext. 2237

Westchester Self-Help Clearinghouse (4)
Westchester Community College
Academic Arts Building

75 Grasslands Road
Valhalla 10595
(914) 347–3620

Bureau of Project Management (5)
Office of Health Systems Management
Department of Health
Empire State Plaza
Albany 12237
(518) 473–7915

New York State Board for Medicine (6)
Cultural Education Center
Albany 12230
(518) 474–3841

State Board of Nursing (6)
State Education Department
Cultural Education Center, Room 3013
Albany 12230
(518) 474–3843

North Carolina

Department of Human Resources
Albemarle Building
Raleigh 27603

North Carolina Association for Home Care (1)
714 West Johnson Street
Raleigh 27603
(919) 821–3575

Hospice of North Carolina, Inc. (2)
800 St. Mary's Street, Suite 401
Raleigh 27605
(919) 829–9588

---

1. State home care associations
2. State hospice organizations
3. Medicaid assistance offices
4. Self-help clearinghouses
5. Hospital licensure agencies
6. Medical and nursing licensure agencies

Department of Human Resources (3)
1985 Umstead Drive
Raleigh 27603
(919) 733–2060

Division of Facility Services (5)
Department of Human Resources
701 Barbour Drive
Raleigh 27603
(919) 733–2342

North Carolina Board of Medical Examiners (6)
222 North Person Street, Suite 214
Raleigh 27601
(919) 833–5321

North Carolina Board of Nursing (6)
Box 2129
Raleigh 27602
(919) 828–0740

North Dakota

Social Services Board of North Dakota
State Capitol Building
Bismarck 58505

Aging Services
Social Services Board of North Dakota
State Capitol Building
Bismarck 58505

North Dakota Nurse Corps, P.C. (1)
212 North 5th, Greentree Square
Bismarck 58501
(701) 223–1385

St. Joseph's Hospice (2)
7th Avenue West
Dickinson 58601
(701) 225–7200

North Dakota Department of Human Services (3)
State Capitol Building
Bismarck 58505
(701) 224–2321

Health Resources Section (5)
State Department of Health
State Capitol
Bismarck 58505
(701) 224–2352

North Dakota State Board of Medical Examiners (6)
418 East Broadway Avenue, Suite C–10
Bismarck 58501
(701) 223–9485

North Dakota Board of Nursing (6)
Kirkwood Office Tower, Suite 504
Bismarck 58501
(701) 224–2974

Ohio

Commission on Aging
50 West Broad Street
Columbus 43216

Ohio Council of Home Health Agencies (1)
175 South Third Street, Suite 925
Columbus 43215
(614) 461–1960

Ohio Hospice Organization, Inc. (2)
2181 Embury Park Road
Dayton 45414
(513) 278–0060

Medicaid Administration (3)
Department of Human Services
30 East Broad Street, 31st Floor
Columbus 43266–0423
(614) 466–3196

---

1. State home care associations
2. State hospice organizations
3. Medicaid assistance offices
4. Self-help clearinghouses
5. Hospital licensure agencies
6. Medical and nursing licensure agencies

State Medical Board of Ohio (6)
Suite 510, C–10
85 South Front Street
Columbus 43266
(614) 466–3934

State of Ohio Board of Nursing Education and Nurse Registration (6)
65 South Front Street, Room 509
Columbus 43266
(614) 466–3947

Oklahoma

Department of Institutions, Social and Rehabilitative Services
P.O. Box 25352
Oklahoma City 73125

Special Unit on Aging
Department of Institutions, Social and Rehabilitative Services
P.O. Box 25352
Oklahoma City 73125

Oklahoma Hospice Organization (2)
Hospice of Central Oklahoma
4500 North Lincoln
Oklahoma City 73105
(405) 424–7263

Department of Human Services (3)
P.O. Box 25352
Oklahoma City 73125
(405) 557–2540

State Department of Health (5)
1000 Northeast 10th
Oklahoma City 73152
(405) 271–4200

Oklahoma State Board of Medical Examiners (6)
5104 North Francis, Suite C
Oklahoma City 73118
(405) 848–6841

Oklahoma Board of Nurse Registration and Nursing Education (6)
2915 North Classen Boulevard, Suite 624

Oklahoma City 73106
(405) 525–2076

Oregon

Human Resources Department
315 Public Service Building
Salem 97310

Office of Elderly Affairs
Human Resources Department
772 Commercial Street Southeast
Salem 97310

Oregon Association for Home Care (1)
Box 510
Salem 97308
(503) 399–9395

Oregon Council of Hospices (2)
Maryanne Memorial Hospice
P.O. Box 191
Forest Grove 97116
(503) 640–2737

Adult and Family Services Division (3)
Department of Human Resources
203 Public Service Building
Salem 97310
(503) 378–2263

Senior Services Division (3)
Department of Human Resources
313 Public Service Building
Salem 97310
(503) 378–4728

Portland Self-Help Information Service (4)
Regional Research Institute

1. State home care associations
2. State hospice organizations
3. Medicaid assistance offices
4. Self-help clearinghouses
5. Hospital licensure agencies
6. Medical and nursing licensure agencies

Portland State University
1912 Southwest 6th
Portland 97207
(503) 222–5555 or 229–4040

Health Facilities Section (5)
Office of Environment and Health Systems
Box 231
Portland 97207
(503) 229–5686

Oregon Board of Medical Examiners (6)
1002 Loyalty Building
317 Southwest Alder Street
Portland 97204
(503) 229–5770

Oregon State Board of Nursing (6)
1400 Southwest 5th, Room 904
Portland 97201
(503) 229–5653

Pennsylvania

Department of Public Welfare
Health and Welfare Building
Harrisburg 17120

Office for the Aging
Department of Public Welfare
Health and Welfare Building, Room 540
P.O. Box 2675
7th and Forster Street
Harrisburg 17120

National Association of Meal Programs (1)
Box 6344
604 West North Avenue
Pittsburgh 15212

Pennsylvania Association of Home Health Agencies (1)
1200 Camp Hill Bypass
P.O. Box 608

Camp Hill 17011
(717) 763–7053

Pennsylvania Hospice Network (2)
South Hills Family Hospice
1000 Bower Hill Road
Pittsburgh 15243
(412) 561–4900

Department of Public Welfare (3)
Room 515
Health and Welfare Building
Harrisburg 17120
(717) 787–1870

Philadelphia Self-Help Clearinghouse (4)
John F. Kennedy, CMHC/MR
112 North Ercad Street, 5th Floor
Philadelphia 19102
(215) 568–0860, ext. 276

Division of Hospitals (5)
Bureau of Quality Assurance
Health and Welfare Building
Harrisburg 17120
(717) 783–8980

Pennsylvania State Board of Medicine (6)
P.O. Box 2649
Harrisburg 17105
(717) 787–2381

State Board of Nursing (6)
Department of State
P.O. Box 2649
Harrisburg 17105
(717) 783–7142

1. State home care associations
2. State hospice organizations
3. Medicaid assistance offices
4. Self-help clearinghouses
5. Hospital licensure agencies
6. Medical and nursing licensure agencies

Puerto Rico

Department of Social Services
P.O. Box 11398
Santurce 00910

Gericulture Commission
Department of Social Services
P.O. Box 11398
Santurce 00910

Health Economy Office (3)
Department of Health
P.O. Box 9342
San Juan 00936
(809) 765–9941

Office of Registration and Certification of Professional Health (6)
Call Box 10200
Santurce 00908
(809) 725–7506

Rhode Island

Department of Community Affairs
150 Washington Court
Providence 02903

Division on Aging
Department of Community Affairs
150 Washington Court
Providence 02903

Association of Home Health Agencies of Rhode Island (1)
2845 Post Road
Warwick 02886
(401) 738–8280

Hospice Care of Rhode Island (2)
1400 Pawtucket Avenue
Rumford 02916
(401) 434–4740

Division of Medical Services (3)
Department of Human Services
Aime J. Forand Building

600 New London Avenue
Cranston 02920
(401) 464–3575

Department of Health (5)
75 Davis Street
Providence 02908
(401) 277–2231

Division of Professional Regulation (6)
Rhode Island Department of Health
104 Cannon Building
75 Davis Street
Providence 02908
(401) 277–2827

Samoa

Territorial Administration on Aging
Government of American Samoa
Pago Pago
American Samoa 96799

South Carolina

Commission on Aging
915 Main Street
Columbia 29201

Hospice of Charleston, Inc. (2)
P.O. Box 1125
Charleston 29402
(803) 577–0186

Health and Human Services Finance Commission (3)
P.O. Box 8206
Columbia 29202
(803) 253–6100

---

1. State home care associations
2. State hospice organizations
3. Medicaid assistance offices
4. Self-help clearinghouses
5. Hospital licensure agencies
6. Medical and nursing licensure agencies

Office of Health Licensing (5)
Division of Health Licensing and Certification
South Carolina Department of Health and Environmental Control
2600 Bull Street
Columbia 29201
(803) 734-4680

State Board of Medical Examiners of South Carolina (6)
1315 Blanding Street
Columbia 29201
(803) 734-8901

State Board of Nursing for South Carolina (6)
1777 St. Julian Place, Suite 102
Columbia 29204
(803) 737-6594

South Dakota

Department of Social Services
State Office Building
Illinois Street
Pierre 57501

Office on Aging
Department of Social Services
State Office Building, Illinois Street
Pierre 57501

Department of Social Services (3)
Kneip Building
701 North Illinois Street
Pierre 57501
(605) 773-3495

Licensure and Certification Program (5)
State Department of Health
Joe Foss Building
523 East Capitol
Pierre 57501
(605) 773-3364

South Dakota State Board of Medical and Osteopathic Examiners (5)
1323 Minnesota Avenue

Sioux Falls 57105
(605) 336–1965

Tennessee

Commission on Aging
Room 102 S and P Building
306 Gay Street
Nashville 37201

Tennessee Association for Home Health (1)
4711 Trousdale Drive
Nashville 37220
(615) 331–0463

Tennessee Council for Home Care Services (1)
394 West Main Street
Hendersonville 37075
(615) 822–3094

Hospice of Tennessee (2)
Alive—Hospice of Nashville
1908 21st Avenue South
Nashville 37212
(615) 298–3351

Bureau of Medicaid (3)
Department of Health and Environment
729 Church Street
Nashville 37219
(615) 741–0213

Overlook Mental Health Center (4)
6906 Kingston Pike
Knoxville 36919
(615) 588–9747

Division of Health Care Facilities (5)
Tennessee Department of Health and Environment

---

1. State home care associations
2. State hospice organizations
3. Medicaid assistance offices
4. Self-help clearinghouses
5. Hospital licensure agencies
6. Medical and nursing licensure agencies

283 Plus Park Boulevard
Nashville 37219
(615) 387-6303

Tennessee Board of Medical Examiners (6)
283 Plus Park Boulevard
Nashville 37219
(615) 367-6231

Tennessee Board of Nursing (6)
283 Plus Park Boulevard
Nashville 37219
(615) 367-6232

Texas

Governor's Committee on Aging
Executive Office Building
411 West 13th Street, Floors 4 and 5
Austin 78703

Texas Association of Home Health Agencies (1)
One La Costa Office Building
1016 La Posada Drive, Suite 296
Austin 78752
(512) 459-4303

Texas Hospice Organization, Inc. (2)
2525 Wallingwood #104
Austin 78746
(512) 327-9149

Texas Department of Human Services (3)
P.O. Box 2960, Mail Code 600-W
Austin 78769
(512) 450-3050

Deputy Commissioner for Services to the Aged and Disabled (3)
Department of Human Services
P.O. Box 2960
Austin 78769
(512) 450-3020

Dallas County Self-Help Clearinghouse (4)
Dallas County Mental Health Association
2500 Maple Avenue

Dallas 75206
(214) 748–7825

Tarrant County Self-Help Clearing House (4)
Tarrant County Mental Health Association
904 West 7th Street
Fort Worth 76102
(817) 335–5405

Hospital and Professional Licensure Division (5)
Texas Department of Health
1100 West 49th Street
Austin 78756
(512) 458–7512

Board of Nurse Examiners for the State of Texas (6)
1300 East Anderson Lane
Building C, Suite 225
Austin 78752
(512) 835–4880

Texas Board of Vocational Nurse Examiners (6)
1300 East Anderson Lane
Building C, Suite 285
Austin 78752
(512) 835–2071

Trust Territory of the Pacific

Office of Aging
Community Development Division
Government of the Trust Territory of the Pacific Islands
Saipan, Mariana Islands 96950

Department of Public Health and Environmental Services (3)
Commonwealth of the Northern Mariana Islands
Saipan, CM 96950
(670) 234–8950, ext. 2905

---

1. State home care associations
2. State hospice organizations
3. Medicaid assistance offices
4. Self-help clearinghouses
5. Hospital licensure agencies
6. Medical and nursing licensure agencies

Utah

Department of Social Services
State Capitol Building, Room 221
Salt Lake City 84102

Division of Aging
Department of Social Services
150 West North Temple
Salt Lake City 84102

Utah Hospice Organization, Inc. (2)
1370 South West Temple
Salt Lake City 84115
(801) 627-2504

Division of Health Care Financing (3)
Utah Department of Health
P.O. Box 16580
Salt Lake City 84116-0580
(801) 538-6151

Utah State Department of Health (5)
Bureau of Health Facility Licensure
P.O. Box 16660
Salt Lake City 84116
(801) 538-6152

Division of Occupational and Professional Licensing (6)
P.O. Box 45802
160 East 300 South
Salt Lake City 84145
(801) 530-6628

Vermont

Agency of Human Services
79 River Street
Montpelier 05602

Office on Aging
Agency of Human Services
81 River Street (Heritage 1)
Montpelier 05602

Vermont Assembly of Home Health Agencies (1)
148 Main Street
Montpelier 05602
(802) 229–0579

Vermont Ecumenical Council (2)
Visiting Nurse Association, Inc.
260 College Street
Burlington 15401
(802) 658–1900

Department of Social Welfare (3)
Vermont Agency of Human Services
103 South Main Street
Waterbury 05676
(802) 241–2880

Medical Care Regulation Division (5)
Vermont Department of Health
60 Main Street, P.O. Box 70
Burlington 05402
(802) 863–7272

Vermont State Board of Nursing (6)
26 Terrace Street
Montpelier 05602
(802) 828–2396

Virginia

Office on Aging
830 East Main Street, Suite 950
Richmond 23219

Virginia Association of Hospices (2)
Hospice of North Virginia
4715 North 15th Street

---

1. State home care associations
2. State hospice organizations
3. Medicaid assistance offices
4. Self-help clearinghouses
5. Hospital licensure agencies
6. Medical and nursing licensure agencies

Arlington 22205
(703) 525–7070

Virginia Department of Medical Assistance Services (3)
600 East Broad Street, Suite 1300
Richmond 23219
(804) 786–7933

Division of Licensure and Certification (5)
Virginia Department of Health
109 Governor Street
Richmond 23219
(804) 786–2081

Virginia State Board of Medicine (6)
1601 Rolling Hills Drive
Surry Building, 2nd Floor
Richmond 23229
(804) 662–9908

Virgin Islands

Commission on Aging
P.O. Box 539
Charlotte Amalie Street
Saint Thomas 00801

Bureau of Health Insurance and Medical Assistance (3)
Department of Health
P.O. Box 7309
Government of the Virgin Islands
Charlotte Amalie, St. Thomas 00801
(809) 774–4624 or 773–2150

Virgin Islands Department of Health (6)
Box 7309
St. Thomas 00801
(809) 774–0117

Virgin Islands Board of Nurse Licensure (6)
Knud-Hansen Complex Hospital Ground
St. Thomas 00801
(809) 774–9000 ext. 132

Washington

Department of Social and Health Services
P.O. Box 1788, M.S. 45–2
Olympia 98504

Office on Aging
Department of Social and Health Services
P.O. Box 1788, M.S. 45–2
Olympia 98504

Home Care Association of Washington (1)
P.O. Box 55967
Seattle 98155
(206) 363–3801

Washington Hospice Organization (2)
7814 Greenwood Avenue North
Seattle 98103
(206) 784–9221

Division of Medical Assistance (3)
Department of Social and Health Services
Mail Stop HB–41
Olympia 98504
(206) 753–1777

Health Facilities Survey Section (5)
DSHS Division of Health, ET–31
Olympia 98504
(206) 753–5851

Licensing Division (6)
Box 9649
Olympia 98504
(206) 586–4561

---

1. State home care associations
2. State hospice organizations
3. Medicaid assistance offices
4. Self-help clearinghouses
5. Hospital licensure agencies
6. Medical and nursing licensure agencies

Washington State Board of Nursing (6)
Licensing Division
Box 9649
Olympia 98504
(206) 753–2686

Washington State Board of Practical Nursing (6)
Department of Licensing
Division of Professional Licensing
Box 9649
Olympia 98504
(206) 753–3728

West Virginia

Commission on Aging
State Capitol
Charleston 25305

West Virginia Council of Home Health Agencies (1)
P.O. Box 4227
Star City 26504–4227
(304) 599–9583

Hospice Council of West Virginia (2)
Morgantown Hospice, Inc.
P.O. Box 4222
Morgantown 26505
(304) 598–3424

Bureau Administrator (3)
Bureau of Medical Care
West Virginia Department of Human Services
1900 Washington Street East
Charleston 25305
(304) 348–8990

Health Facilities Licensure and Certification Section (5)
West Virginia Department of Health
1800 Washington Street East
Charleston 25305
(304) 348–0050

West Virginia Board of Medicine
100 Dee Drive, Suite 104

Charleston 25311
(304) 348–2921

West Virginia Board of Examiners for Registered Professional Nurses (6)
Embleton Building
922 Quarrier Street, Suite 309
Charleston 25301
(304) 348–3728

West Virginia Board of Examiners for Licensed Practical Nurses (6)
Embleton Building
922 Quarrier Street, Suite 506
Charleston 25301
(304) 348–3572

Wisconsin

Department of Health and Social Services
State Office Building, Room 700
1 West Wilson Street
Madison 53702

Division on Aging
Department of Health and Social Services
1 West Wilson Street, Room 686
Madison 53702

Wisconsin Homecare Organization (1)
330 East Lakeside Street
Madison 53715
(608) 257–6781

Milwaukee Hospice Home Care (2)
1022 North 9th Street
Milwaukee 53233
(414) 271–3686

Bureau of Health Care Financing (3)
Division of Health

---

1. State home care associations
2. State hospice organizations
3. Medicaid assistance offices
4. Self-help clearinghouses
5. Hospital licensure agencies
6. Medical and nursing licensure agencies

Wisconsin Department of Health and Social Services
One West Wilson Street, Room 244
P.O. Box 309
Madison 53701
(608) 266–2522

Continuing Education in Mental Health (4)
University of Wisconsin Extension
414 Lowell Hall
610 Langden Street
Madison 53706
(608) 263–4432

Mutual Aid Self-Help Association (MASHA) (4)
P.O. Box 09304
Milwaukee 53209
(414) 461–1466

Bureau of Quality Compliance (5)
Division of Health
Department of Health and Social Services
One West Wilson Street, Box 309
Madison 53701
(608) 267–7185

Wisconsin Medical Examining Board (6)
1400 East Washington Avenue
Madison 53702
(608) 266–2811

Bureau of Health Services Professions (6)
Department of Regulation and Licensing
P.O. Box 8935
1400 East Washington Avenue, Room 174
Madison 53708
(608) 266–3735

Wyoming

Department of Health and Social Services
Division of Public Assistance
New State Office Building West, Room 380
Cheyenne 82002

Aging Services
Department of Health and Social Services
Division of Public Assistance and Social Services
New State Office Building West, Room 288
Cheyenne 82002

Sheridan County Hospice, Inc. (2)
2000 Suite 515
Sheridan 82801
(307) 672-3473

Medical Assistance State Program Manager (3)
Department of Health and Social Services
448 Hathaway Building
Cheyenne 82002
(307) 777-7531

Department of Health and Social Services (5)
Division of Health and Medical Facilities
Hathaway Building
Cheyenne 82002
(307) 777-7121

Wyoming Board of Medical Examiners (6)
Hathway Building, 4th Floor
Cheyenne 82002
(307) 777-6463

Wyoming State Board of Nursing (6)
Barrett Building, 4th Floor
2301 Central Avenue
Cheyenne 82002
(307) 777-7601

---

1. State home care associations
2. State hospice organizations
3. Medicaid assistance offices
4. Self-help clearinghouses
5. Hospital licensure agencies
6. Medical and nursing licensure agencies

Appendix 35
National Health Care and
Self-Help Groups

T HERE are numerous places people can turn to for information on how to get help for the elderly. Many such resources have local offices in towns across the country. The Yellow Pages will list some groups under "Associations" or "Social Service Organizations," or the local public library will have an encyclopedia of associations that lists groups as well. For further information on self-help groups, contact the following.

Federal
U.S. Department of Health and
  Human Services
Administration on Aging
330 Independence Avenue SW
Washington, DC 20201
(202) 245-0724

U.S. Department of Health and
  Human Services
Health Care Financing Administration
310G Humphrey Building
200 Independence Avenue SW
Washington, DC 20201
(202) 245-6726

National
National Self-Help Clearinghouse
33 West 42nd Street
New York, NY 10003
(212) 840-7606

National Association of Area Agencies
  on Aging
600 Maryland Avenue, SW
Washington, DC 20024
(202) 484-7520

U.S. Department of Health and Human Services
Public Health Service
716G Humphrey Building
200 Independence Avenue SW
Washington, DC 20201
(202) 245-7694

U.S. Federal Trade Commission
Correspondence Branch
Pennsylvania Avenue at 6th Street NW
Washington, DC 20580
(202) 523-3567

U.S. Veterans Administration
Department of Medicine and Surgery
810 Vermont Avenue NW
Washington, DC 20420
(202) 389-2596

Professional

Alexander Graham Bell Association for the Deaf
2317 Volta Place
Washington, DC 20007

The Alzheimer's Association
360 North Michigan Avenue
Chicago, IL 60601
(national office; local chapter addresses available on request)

American Affiliation of Visiting Nurse Associations and Services
21 Maryland Plaza, Suite 300
St. Louis, MO 63108
(314) 367-7744

American Association for Continuity of Care
1101 Connecticut Avenue NW, Suite 700
Washington, DC 20024
(202) 857-1194

American Association of Homes for the Aging
1050 17th Street NW
Washington, DC 20036

American Association of Retired Persons
1909 K Street NW
Washington, DC 20049

American Cancer Society
219 East 42nd Street
New York, NY 10021

American Diabetes Association
18 East 48th Street
New York, NY 10017

American Federation of Home Health Agencies
429 N Street SW, Suite S–605
Washington, DC 20024
(202) 554–0526

American Foundation for the Blind
15 West 16th Street
New York, NY 10011

American Geriatrics Society
10 Columbus Circle
New York, NY 10019

American Heart Association
44 East 23rd Street
New York, NY 10010

American Hospital Association
Division of Ambulatory Care
840 North Lake Shore Drive
Chicago, IL 60611
(312) 280–6216

American Lung Association
1740 Broadway
New York, NY 10019

American Nurses Association, Inc.
10 Columbus Circle
New York, NY 10019

American Nursing Home Association
(American Health Care Association)
1025 Connecticut Avenue NW
Washington, DC 20036

American Occupational Therapy Association
251 Park Avenue South
New York, NY 10010

American Parkinson's Disease Association
Room 602, 47 East 50th Street
New York, NY 10022

American Physical Therapy Association
1740 Broadway
New York, NY 10019

American Psychological Association
Division of Adult Development and Aging
1200 17th Street NW
Washington, DC 20036

American Society for Parenteral and Enteral Nutrition
1025 Vermont Avenue NW, Suite 810
Washington, DC 20005
(202) 638-5881

Arthritis Foundation
1212 Avenue of the Americas
New York, NY 10036

Association of Rehabilitation Facilities
5530 Wisconsin Avenue NW
Washington, DC 20015
(information about rehabilitation centers nationwide serving older people)

Cancer Care
One Park Avenue
New York, NY 10016

Council on Accreditation of Services for Families and Children
67 Irving Place
New York, NY 10003
(212) 254-9330

Family Service Association of America
44 East 23rd Street
New York, NY 10010
(212) 674-6100

Gerontological Society
One Dupont Circle NW
Washington, DC 20036

Gray Panthers
3700 Chestnut Street
Philadelphia, PA 19104

Health Insurance Association of America
1850 K Street NW
Washington, DC 20006–2284
(202) 331–1336

Home Health Care Medical Directors Association
P.O. Box 16626
Mobile, AL 36616
(205) 476–0192

Home Health Services and Staffing Association
2101 L Street NW, Suite 800
Washington, DC 20037
(202) 775–4707

Joint Commission on Accreditation of Hospitals
875 North Michigan Avenue
Chicago, IL 60611
(312) 642–6061

National Association for Home Care
519 C Street NE
Washington, DC 20002
(202) 547–7424

National Association for Mental Health
1800 North Kent Street
Arlington, VA 22209

National Association for the Deaf
814 Thayer Avenue
Silver Spring, MD 20910

National Association for the Visually Handicapped
305 East 24th Street
New York, NY 10010

National Association of Hearing and Speech Agencies
814 Thayer Avenue
Silver Spring, MD 20910

National Association of Meal Programs
Box 6344
604 West North Avenue
Pittsburgh, Pa 15212

National Association of Social Workers
1425 H Street NW, Suite 600
Washington, DC 20005

National Citizens' Coalition for Nursing Home Reform
1825 Connecticut Avenue NW, Suite 417
Washington, DC 20009
(202) 797-0657

National Council for Homemakers, Home Health Aide Services
1790 Broadway
New York, NY 10019

National Council of Health Care Services
407 N Street SW
Washington, DC 20024

National Council of Senior Citizens
1511 K Street NW
Washington, DC 20005

National Council on the Aging
600 Maryland Avenue SW
Washington, DC 20024
(information, services, and research on aging; publications on day care and senior centers, retirement housing)

National Federation of Licensed Practical Nurses
250 West 57th Street
New York, NY 10001

National Foundation of Dentistry for the Handicapped
1250 14th Street, Suite 610
Denver, CO 80202
(303) 573-0264

National HomeCaring Council
235 Park Avenue South, 11th Floor
New York, NY 10003
(212) 674–4990

National Hospice Organization
1901 North Fort Myer Drive
Arlington, VA 22209
(703) 243–5900

National Institute of Adult Daycare
600 Maryland Avenue SW, West Wing 100
Washington, DC 20024
(202) 479–1200

National Institute of Neurological and Communicative Disorders and Stroke
Office of Scientific and Health Reports
Building 31, Room 8A–06
National Institutes of Health
Bethesda, MD 20205

National Institute on Aging
Information Office
Building 31, Room 5C–36
National Institutes of Health
Bethesda, MD 20205

National League for Nursing
10 Columbus Circle
New York, NY 10010
(212) 582–1022

National Society for the Prevention of Blindness, Inc.
79 Madison Avenue
New York, NY 10016

Society for the Right to Die
250 West 57th Street
New York, NY 10107

Glossary

ACTIVITIES DIRECTOR.   The person in charge of a nursing facility's schedule of activities.

ADMISSION FORMS.   Forms to be signed agreeing to enter a hospital and receive the general care provided.

ADULT DAY CARE.   Care given during the day to elderly individuals by churches, community centers, and so on; may be part- or full-time.

ADVOCATES.   Family members, friends, or professionals employed by hospitals and some state agencies concerned with the patient's condition and willing to ask questions, intercede, or argue on the patient's behalf.

AGENT.   The person appointed in a power of attorney to make decisions and handle the affairs of a principal.

AID TO FAMILIES WITH DEPENDENT CHILDREN (AFDC).   A social welfare program that gives financial assistance to needy families with children.

ALLOWABLE RESOURCES.   The amount of money a state allows individuals to keep and still be eligible for Medicaid (the amount varies from state to state).

ANESTHESIOLOGIST.   A doctor trained to give anesthesia.

ATTENDING DOCTOR.   The doctor who has primary responsibility for a patient; he or she may also supervise interns and residents working with the patient.

AUTOMATIC BANKING.   A service provided by some banks to pay regular bills, such as mortgages or utilities, for persons who can no longer do so themselves.

BENEFICIARY OR RECIPIENT.   The person paid money by any entitlement program.

BENEFITS.   Money paid to reimburse patients and pay doctors, hospitals, and other health care providers.

BEQUEST.   A gift bequeathed after death, in accordance with the will of the deceased person.

BEST-INTERESTS STANDARD.   A standard used by a guardian to make decisions based on the best interests of an incompetent or ill individual.

BOARD AND CARE HOMES.   A home providing "residential care," "domiciliary care," or "assisted living care." Such a home does not provide medical care, but it does house chronically ill or frail elderly people who require supervision and assistance with things like bathing, grooming, and eating.

BOARD CERTIFICATION IN SURGERY. Certification granted by the American College of Surgeons giving formal recognition that a doctor is capable of performing surgery.

CARDIAC CARE. Care for patients with heart conditions.

CARDIOPULMONARY RESUSCITATION (CPR). A procedure reviving a patient after a heart attack.

CASE MANAGER. The individual whose job it is to manage, plan for, and arrange continuing health care services for ill individuals.

CATEGORICALLY NEEDY. A classification of individuals who qualify for Medicaid based on income and financial resource levels.

CHARGE NURSES, NURSING SUPERVISORS, AND NURSING ADMINISTRATORS. Those who supervise nursing staff.

CLAIM. A bill for medical care or services that a beneficiary wants reimbursed under a entitlement program or an insurance policy.

COINSURANCE. The amount or percentage that patients are required to pay toward Medicare-reimbursed bills.

COMATOSE. Unconscious for a long period; possibly a permanent condition.

COMMUNITY ADVISORY COMMITTEE. A committee, usually made up of concerned and knowledgeable citizens, that works to improve nursing home conditions and hear grievances from patients and their families.

COMPETENCE OR CAPACITY. An individual's ability to think clearly, make rational decisions, and appreciate their consequences.

CONSENT TO TREATMENT FORMS. Forms to be signed consenting to specific surgical or medical treatments.

CONSERVATOR. A person appointed by the court to handle the financial affairs of individuals incapable of doing so for themselves. Also known as the *conservator* (or *guardian*) *of the estate.*

CONTINGENCY FEE. A fee charged by a lawyer only if the case is won; usually the amount is a predetermined percentage of the settlement.

COPAYMENT. Money still owed on a medical bill after Medicare has paid its approved amount.

CUSTODIAL CARE. Nonmedical care for elderly individuals; may include grooming, bathing, and so on.

DEDUCTIBLE. The amount of money an individual pays for medical bills before his or her insurance company begins to pay.

DE FACTO DECISION MAKER. An individual who makes decisions for an incompetent person without any legal authority to do so; also called a *de facto surrogate.*

DE FACTO INCOMPETENT. A description of an individual who is considered incompetent by doctors and family members but who has not been found incompetent by a court.

DIAGNOSTIC RELATED GROUPS (DRGs).   Groups of Medicare-categorized diseases, each group assigned a specific amount of money to cover the hospital care of patients whose diseases fall into that group.

DIRECT-DEPOSIT BANKING.   An arrangement whereby paychecks and Social Security or pension payments are sent directly to a bank.

DISCHARGE PLANNERS OR SOCIAL WORKERS.   Persons employed by a hospital to place patients in nursing homes, if necessary, or to arrange for other special services required after patients are discharged from the hospital.

DOCTOR'S PRIVILEGES.   A phrase referring to those hospitals in which a doctor is allowed to admit, see, and care for patients.

DONEE.   The person who receives gifts or bequests in a will.

DONOR.   The person who makes gifts or bequests in a will.

DREAD DISEASE POLICIES.   Insurance policies covering only one disease.

DURABLE POWER OF ATTORNEY.   A legal document designed to let a principal appoint an agent to make decisions for him or her in the event the principal becomes incompetent.

DURABLE POWER OF ATTORNEY FOR HEALTH CARE.   A legal document designed to let a principal appoint an agent to make health care decisions for him or her in the event the principal becomes incompetent.

EARNINGS RECORD.   A statement submitted annually by an institutional payee to the Social Security Administration to show how a patient's Social Security benefits are being spent.

EMPLOYEE GROUP HEALTH INSURANCE.   A group insurance policy purchased at an individual's place of work that may continue to cover him or her after retirement but that may change in character when the individual reaches age sixty-five.

ENTITLEMENT PROGRAM.   Any program that provides financial or other types of assistance to people meeting specific criteria.

EXECUTOR OR EXECUTRIX.   The male or female named in a will or otherwise appointed to see that the wishes in a will are carried out.

FAMILY CONSENT STATUTES.   Laws in some states that automatically authorize family members to make certain necessary decisions for incompetent individuals; in these states, court appointment of a guardian may be unnecessary.

FAMILY SERVICE AGENCIES.   Social service agencies that help families or individuals arrange for and receive care.

FELLOWS.   Doctors in the process of being trained in a particular specialty.

FULL GUARDIANSHIP OR PLENARY GUARDIANSHIP.   Guardianship arrangements whereby the guardian has the right to make almost all decisions over a ward.

GENERAL PUBLIC ASSISTANCE (GPA).   A social welfare program, funded by only some states or communities, that gives financial help to the very needy.

GENERIC SUBSTITUTES.   Pharmaceuticals containing the same ingredients as more expensive name brands.

GERIATRIC MENTAL STATE EXAMINATION.   An evaluation of a patient's state of mind and/or competency.

GRAY PANTHERS.   An activist group of elderly individuals who fight for elder rights.

GUARDIAN.   The person appointed by a court to handle the personal (and sometimes financial) affairs of individuals incapable of doing so for themselves. Also known as the *guardian* (or *conservator*) *of the person.*

GUARDIAN *ad litem.*   The court-appointed individual authorized to represent a ward in specific matters being heard before the court; this is not to be confused with a lawyer's representation of a client.

GUARDIANSHIP HEARING.   A proceeding in which a judge rules on the competency of an individual and may assign him or her a guardian and/or conservator.

HEALTH CARE PROVIDER.   Any person or organization providing health care (including doctors, hospitals, home care services, "meals on wheels," and so on).

HEALTH MAINTENANCE ORGANIZATION (HMO).   An organization offering a prepaid health insurance plan that provides all acute medical services the policyholder may need.

HEARING.   A legal proceeding before a judge.

HOSPICE.   A special facility that cares for dying patients or assists them to be cared for in their homes.

HOSPITAL DISCHARGE PLANNER.   The hospital employee, usually a social worker or a nurse, who plans for the discharge of patients, notifies patients or family members of the discharge, and prepares a formal discharge plan on request.

IATROGENIC DISEASES OR DISORDERS.   Conditions, such as viruses, resulting from medical personnel, treatment, diagnostic procedures, and so on.

INCOMPETENCE OR INCAPACITY.   An individual's inability to think clearly, or make rational decisions, and appreciate their consequences.

INDEMNITY.   Insurance benefits that pay on specific dollar amounts or a percentage of the costs of care.

INFORMED CONSENT.   The state whereby a patient has the necessary information and understanding to agree to or refuse treatment. A patient usually has to sign a form to this effect before treatment is started.

INSTITUTIONAL ETHICS COMMITTEE.   A hospital or nursing home committee made up of health care professionals, religious representatives, philosophers, and ethicists; such a committee may be helpful in resolving disputes between family members over treatment decisions.

INSURANCE COVERAGE FORMS.   Forms that give a hospital permission to share information on a patient with his or her insurance company.

INTERMEDIATE CARE FACILITY (ICF). A facility providing general and limited medical care for patients who will eventually be able to return home or for those who can no longer care for themselves without supervision.

INTERN. A medical school graduate with one or two years of experience.

INTER VIVOS TRUST. A trust that goes into effect while the grantor is still alive.

INTESTACY LAWS. State laws determining the disposition of assets left by individuals who did not make a will.

INTESTATE. Describes an individual who has died without leaving a will (he or she is said to have died *intestate*).

INVOLUNTARY COMMITMENT. The holding of a person in a hospital or other facility against his or her will for seventy-two hours for psychiatric reasons.

IRREVOCABLE LIVING TRUST. An *inter vivos* trust that cannot be revoked or canceled.

JOINT BANK ACCOUNT. A type of bank account that allows either owner to transact business and sign checks (joint accounts are not available at all banks).

JOINT BANK ACCOUNT WITH RIGHT OF SURVIVORSHIP. A type of joint bank account that guarantees that one owner will receive funds in the event the other owner dies.

JOINT PROPERTY ARRANGEMENTS. Arrangements that permit joint ownership of a house or other assets.

LAETRILE. A controversial anticancer drug, not approved in some states.

LEGAL AID LAWYER. A lawyer who works in a clinic offering low-cost legal services to those in need.

LEGALLY INCOMPETENT. The declaration a court makes about people who are incapable of understanding the consequences of their decisions and who, as a result of this inability, are incapable of handling their affairs.

LICENSED PRACTICAL NURSE (LPN). A nurse who monitors and observes hospital patients and gives care, medication, and treatment on doctors' orders.

LICENSED VOCATIONAL NURSE (LVN). A nurse who monitors and observes hospital patients and gives care, medication, and treatment on doctors' orders.

LIMITED OR PARTIAL GUARDIANSHIP. A guardianship arrangement in which the powers of a guardian are expressly limited by the court and the ward retains some rights.

LIVING WILL. A document that allows individuals to state their medical treatment preferences in advance of their becoming incompetent and unable to speak for themselves.

LONG-TERM CARE. Ongoing care provided by a nursing home or by other residential facilities.

LONG-TERM CARE INSURANCE POLICIES. Health insurance policies to cover the cost of long-term or nursing home care.

LONG TERM CARE OMBUDSMAN PROGRAM (LTCOP). A program, established by the federal Older Americans Act, that helps resolve complaints and protects and defends those elderly whose rights are abused; usually used by the residents of nursing homes. By law, each state is required to have an ombudsman program.

Loss ratio.　The minimum level of benefits an insurance company expects to pay out in comparison with money gathered through premiums.

Medically needy.　A classification of persons eligible for optional state medically needy Medicaid programs because their medical bills offset their income.

Medicaid.　A public assistance program that in certain low-income cases pays for nursing home care.

Medicare.　A government insurance program that covers only the costs of medical services (that is, hospital care and doctors' services) for patients over age sixty-five who are suffering from acute illnesses.

"Medigap" or Medicare supplemental insurance policies.　Policies sold by private companies to cover the cost of services not covered by Medicare.

Non-routine-treatment decisions.　Medical care decisions involving definite changes in treatment for which consent of a guardian or a family member is necessary.

Nosocomial infections.　Infections that develop as a result of a patient's hospital stay and are caused by bacteria or viruses.

Nurse anesthetist.　A nurse trained in advanced courses to give anesthesia.

Nursing administrators, nursing supervisors, and charge nurses.　Individuals who supervise nursing staff.

Nursing assistants, orderlies, and aides.　Persons who assist nurses in providing for patients' nonmedical needs.

Nursing home.　A health care facility providing residential or long-term care. There are two types: Skilled Nursing Facilities (SNF) and Intermediate Care Facilities (ICF).

Office of the Inspector General.　Part of the U.S. Department of Health and Human Services (HHS), an office that reviews cases of misuse of Social Security benefits, among other things.

Ombudsman.　The individual working in the state-level office of the Long Term Care Ombudsman Program to investigate and resolve complaints made by or on behalf of older residents of long-term care facilities.

On-site review program.　A program in which the Social Security Administration audits state institutions that receive Social Security benefits on behalf of their occupants.

Patient representative or advocate.　The individual employed by a hospital or other group to act on behalf of a patient when no family member or friend is available.

Payee or Representative payee.　The individual or institution appointed to receive Social Security checks on behalf of an elderly person incapable of handling his or her own finances.

Peer Review Organization (PRO).　A group of doctors and nurses who review a patient's case and help determine the patient's length of stay in the hospital.

PETITION. A request that a court begin a hearing or proceeding.

PETITIONER. The individual who files a petition requesting a hearing by a court.

POWER OF ATTORNEY. A written agreement between a principal and an agent, in which the principal authorizes the agent to sign documents and conduct business for him or her. The agreement is valid only if the principal is competent.

PRINCIPAL. The person who appoints someone else to take care of his or her affairs and to make decisions in his or her behalf.

PRIVATE-DUTY NURSING SERVICES. Services in which nurses are hired by a patient to give additional care.

PROBATE COURT. Usually a county or local court that, among other things, handles guardianship petitions.

PROGNOSIS. The probable course of a disease.

PUBLIC GUARDIANSHIP PROGRAM. A state, county, or private organization that acts as a guardian for those incompetent individuals who have no family or friends able to fill that role.

QUALITY SCREEN. A series of questions about a patient's condition that can help determine a patient's physical readiness to leave the hospital. Quality screens are tools that can help identify possible cases of premature hospital discharge.

REGISTERED NURSE (RN). A nurse who coordinates the nursing care of hospital patients.

REPRESENTATIVE PAYEE EVALUATION REPORT. A detailed report requested by the Social Security Administration to help determine whether a payee is handling a beneficiary's checks correctly.

REPRESENTATIVE PAYEE OR PAYEE. An individual or institution appointed to receive Social Security checks on behalf of an elderly person incapable of handling his or her own finances.

REPRESENTATIVE PAYEE REPORT. A short accounting statement completed by a payee or representative payee about once a year, detailing how benefits were spent on behalf of a beneficiary.

RESIDENTS' COUNCIL. A committee usually made up of nursing home facility residents to examine and help resolve residents' problems.

RESPITE CARE. Part-time care offered for elderly individuals or victims of Alzheimer's disease who are living at home; it gives a break, or respite, to family caretakers.

RESPONDENT. The term used for a person during the court process that determines the need for his or her guardianship.

ROUTINE TREATMENT DECISIONS. Relatively minor medical care decisions involving a change of diet or medication, physical exercise, and so on.

SKILLED NURSING FACILITY (SNF). A facility that provides specialized medical care for seriously ill or disabled patients who do not need to be hospitalized.

SOCIAL SECURITY INCOME.   A federal supplemental monthly income based on a person's work performance before retirement at age sixty-two.

SOCIAL SECURITY DISABILITY INCOME (SSDI).   A government-funded social insurance program that provides assistance to people who, because of their physical or mental disability, are no longer capable of working.

SPECIALISTS OR CONSULTANTS.   Doctors who have been trained in a particular specialty.

SPEND DOWN.   The process of contrasting individual income and resources against personal medical expenses to qualify for Medicaid.

SPRINGING DURABLE POWER OF ATTORNEY.   A type of durable power of attorney that takes effect only if the principal becomes incompetent.

STATUTORY SHORT FORM POWER OF ATTORNEY.   A form used by some states to execute a power of attorney.

SUBSTATE OMBUDSMAN PROGRAM.   The local office of the state ombudsman, active in investigating and solving the complaints of long-term care facility residents or their spokespersons.

SUPPLEMENTAL MEDICAL INSURANCE (SMI).   Insurance provided under Part B of Medicare, requiring a monthly premium to be paid by the consumer for doctor's visits, medical supplies, and equipment.

SUPPLEMENTAL SECURITY INCOME (SSI).   A government-funded social welfare program that provides financial aid to poor people over age sixty-five, the blind, and the permanently disabled.

SURROGATE DECISION MAKER.   Someone who makes decisions on behalf of people who are unable to do so themselves.

TERMINAL ILLNESS.   An illness that cannot be cured and leads to death.

TESTAMENTARY TRUST.   A trust that is created within a will and takes effect upon the grantor's death.

THERAPEUTIC PRIVILEGE.   A doctor's right to keep the particulars of a patient's record from him or her in the event that the doctor believes such information will harm the patient.

TRUST.   An arrangement whereby property is transferred by one person (*grantor* or *settlor*) to benefit himself or herself or someone else. A trust is managed by a *trustee*.

TRUSTEE.   The person who manages a trust.

VETERANS' BENEFITS.   Benefits available to eligible veterans of foreign wars.

WARD.   An individual who is incapable of handling his or her personal and financial affairs and for whom a court has appointed a guardian or conservator.

WILL.   A document written by an individual to specify the disposition of his or her money and property after death.

WILL IN PROBATE.   The period during which instructions in a will are carried out and bequests are administered.

Additional Reading

1. Wills, Trusts, and Joint Accounts: Using Them Now

There are excellent books and computer software that provide more information on the writing of wills, the establishment of joint tenancies and trusts, and the giving of assets.

Books

Theodore Hughes and David Klein, *A Family Guide to Estate Planning, Funeral Arrangements, and Settling an Estate after Death,* Scribner, New York, 1983.

Alex Soled, *The Essential Guide to Wills, Estates, Trusts, and Death Taxes,* American Association of Retired Persons Books, Chicago, 1988. To order, write AARP Books, Department L078, Scott, Foresman and Company, 1865 Miner Street, Des Plaines, Illinois 60016, or call 1-800-238-2300 to order by credit card.

Software

Willmaker, Nolo Legisoft, Nolo Press, Berkeley, California, 1985.

2. "Medigap" Long-Term Care Insurance Policies

For more information on purchasing Medigap or Medicare supplemental insurance, the following publications might be of interest:

National Association of Insurance Commissioners and Health Care Financing Administration, *Guide to Health Insurance for People with Medicare.* This is available in English and Spanish from state Social Security offices.

Consumer Reports, "Medicare Supplement Insurance," June 1984, p. 347. This includes a policy comparison worksheet and ratings of many policies; it should be available through a public library.

Health Insurance Association of America (HIAA), *How to Use Private Health Insurance with Medicare.* This free book, publication #702, is available from HIAA, 1025 Connecticut Avenue NW, Suite 1200, Washington, D.C. 20036, telephone 1–202–223–7780.

Your Medicare Handbook, U.S. government. This is published annually by the federal government to explain Medicare coverage. It is available from local Social Security offices.

Also see appendix 1 for a reprint of *Medicare,* a pamphlet published by the Social Security Administration.

For more information on purchasing long-term care insurance, the following publications might be of interest:

"Who Can Afford a Nursing Home?" *Consumer Reports,* May 1988, p. 300. This publication should be available through a public library or can be purchased by sending $3.00 for publication #RO77, *Who Can Afford a Nursing Home,* to Reprints, *Consumer Reports,* P.O. Box 53016, Boulder, Colorado 80322. This is highly recommended, as it is an excellent article and includes a checklist for evaluating long-term care policies.

Schaeffer, C., "Insurance for Long Term Care," *Changing Times,* January 1987, pp. 113–118. This publication should be available through a public library.

Health Insurance Association of America (HIAA), *The Consumer's Guide to Long Term Care Insurance.* This free book, publication #1262, is available from HIAA, 1025 Connecticut Avenue NW, Suite 1200, Washington, D.C. 20036, telephone 1–202–223–7780.

Health Insurance Association of America (HIAA), *How to Use Private Insurance with Medicare.* This free book, publication #702, is available from HIAA at the address and phone number listed above.

American Association of Retired Persons (AARP), *Before You Buy: A Guide to Long Term Care Insurance.* This book, stock #D12893, is available free from AARP, Fulfillment Section, 1909 K Street NW, Washington, D.C. 20049. AARP has several publications on long-term care services; for more information, write them at the address listed.

Nancy Chasen, *Policy Wise: The Practical Guide to Insurance Decisions for Older Customers,* American Association for Retired Persons, Chicago, 1988. To order, write AARP Books, Department L078, Scott, Foresman and Company, 1865 Miner Street, Des Plaines, Illinois 60016, or call 1–800–238–2300 to order by credit card.

4. Is a Living Will a Good Idea for You?

Publications

American Association of Retired Persons (AARP), *A Matter of Choice: Planning Ahead for Health Care Decisions.* This very useful publication is available through the AARP by calling (202) 872–4700 or writing American Association of Retired Persons, Special Projects Section, Program Department, 1909 K Street NW, Washington, D.C. 20049.

Taking Charge of the End of Your Life: Proceedings of a Forum on Living Wills and Other Advance Directives, Older Women's League, Washington, D.C., 1985. This publication can be ordered by sending $4.50 to Older Women's League, 1325 G Street NW, Lower Level, Washington, D.C. 20005.

Videos

American Bar Association, Commission on Legal Problems of the Elderly, *In Your Hands: The Tools for Preserving Personal Autonomy,* Modern Talking Picture Service. This 16-minute video, narrated by Helen Hayes, comes with a 31-page program guide and fifty copies of a 12-page viewer's pamphlet. It can be rented for $18 or purchased for $48 from Modern Talking Picture Service, Inc., 5000 Park Street North, St. Petersburg, Florida 33709.

American Bar Association, Commission on Legal Problems of the Elderly, *You're in Control: Older Americans and the Law,* Modern Talking Picture Service. This 19-minute video can be rented for $20 from Modern Talking Picture Service, Inc., 5000 Park Street North, St. Petersburg, Florida 33709.

5. Powers of Attorney and Other Ways to Plan Ahead

Publications

Collin, F., et al., *Drafting the Durable Power of Attorney: A Systems Approach,* RPW Publishing Corporation, Lexington, South Carolina, 1984. Lawyers and local university law libraries should have this book, which is very useful in explaining various kinds of durable power-of-attorney documents.

American Association of Retired Persons (AARP), *A Matter of Choice: Planning Ahead for Health Care Decisions.* This very useful publication is available through the AARP by calling (202) 872–4700 or writing American Association of Retired Persons, Special Projects Section, Program Department, 1909 K Street NW, Washington, D.C. 20049.

Taking Charge of the End of Your Life: Proceedings of a Forum on Living Wills and Other Advance Directives, Older Women's League, Washington, D.C., 1985. This publication can be ordered by sending $4.50 to Older Women's League, 1325 G Street NW, Lower Level, Washington, D.C. 20005.

Videos

American Bar Association, Commission on Legal Problems of the Elderly, *In Your Hands: The Tools for Preserving Personal Autonomy,* Modern Talking Picture Service. This 16½-minute video, narrated by Helen Hayes, comes with a 31-page program guide and fifty copies of a 12-page viewer's pamphlet. It can be rented for $18 or purchased for $48 from Modern Talking Picture Service, Inc., 5000 Park Street North, St. Petersburg, Florida 33709.

American Bar Association, Commission on Legal Problems of the Elderly, *You're in Control: Older Americans and the Law,* Modern Talking Picture Service. This 19-minute video can be rented for $20 from Modern Talking Picture Service, Inc., 5000 Park Street North, St. Petersburg, Florida 33709.

6. Saying Yes to Medical Care: What You Should Know First

American Medical Association's Family Medical Guide, Reader's Digest Association, New York, 1982 (or current edition).

Belsky, M., and Gross, L., *How to Choose and Use Your Doctor,* Arbor House, New York, 1975.

Berman, H., et al., *The Complete Health Care Advisor,* St. Martins/Marek, New York, 1986.

Inlander, C., and Weiner, E., *Take This Book to the Hospital with You: A Consumer Guide to Surviving Your Hospital Stay,* Warner Books, New York, 1987.

Williams, S., *A Consumer's Guide to Health Care Services,* Prentice Hall, New Jersey, 1985.

7. Patients Have Rights, Too

Annas, G., *The Rights of Hospital Patients: The Basic ACLU Guide to a Hospital Patient's Rights,* Avon Books, New York, 1975.

Belsky, M., and Gross, L., *How to Choose and Use Your Doctor,* Arbor House, New York, 1975.

Huttman, B., R.N., *The Patient's Advocate: The Complete Handbook of Patient's Rights,* Viking Press, Penguin, New York, 1981.

Inlander, C., and Weiner, E., *Take This Book to the Hospital with You: A Consumer Guide to Surviving Your Hospital Stay,* Warner Books, New York, 1987.

Maurer, J., M.D., *How to Talk to Your Doctor: Getting Beyond the Medical Mystique,* Simon and Schuster, New York, 1986.

Pinckney, C., and Pinckney, E., *The Patient's Guide to Medical Tests,* 3rd ed., Facts on File Publications, New York, 1986.

Robertson, J., *The Rights of the Critically Ill,* Bantam Books, New York, 1983.

Eugene, Robin, *Medical Care Can Be Dangerous to Your Health,* Harper and Row, New York, 1986.

10. The Medicare/Medicaid Maze

More information on entitlement programs can be found in chapters 2 and 3 and appendix 1 of this book. Other publications that make worthwhile reading are the following:

Office of Technology Assessment, *Losing a Million Minds: Confronting the Tragedy of Alzheimer's Disease and Other Dementias,* Government Printing Office, Washington, D.C., 1987.

Miriam K. Aronson, *Understanding Alzheimer's Disease: What It Is, How to Cope with It, Future Directions,* Alzheimer Disease and Related Disorders Association, Chicago, 1988.

11. Competence and Incompetence: What They Mean

*Annas, G., and Densberger, J., *Competence to Refuse Medical Treatment: Autonomy vs. Paternalism,* Toledo Law Review, vol. 15, 1984.

Brown, R., *Legal Rights of Older Persons,* Avon Press, New York, 1979 (or current edition).

*Kapp, M., *Preventing Malpractice in Long Term Care: Strategies for Risk Management,* Springer, New York, 1987.

14. Limits on Decisions Made for Someone Else

A Matter of Choice: Planning Ahead for Health Care Decisions, American Association of Retired Persons. To purchase a copy, write to AARP, Special Projects Section, Program Department, 1909 K Street NW, Washington, D.C. 20049.

Office of Technology Assessment, *Losing a Million Minds: Confronting the Tragedy of Alzheimer's Disease and Other Dementias,* U.S. Congress, Government Printing Office, Washington, D.C., 1986.

---

*These books may not be of great use to those other than lawyers, health care professionals, or ethicists.

Index

About the Advisory Board

WILLIAM BENSON, the consultant and reviewer for chapter 9 ("What to Do if You Have a Problem or Complaint") and the adviser for chapter 15 ("People Will Listen—If You Talk"), is the Staff Director of the Subcommittee on Housing and Consumer Interests, Select Committee on Aging, U.S. House of Representatives. He has also served on the staff of the Senate Special Committee on Aging, was California's state long-term care ombudsman, and managed that state's Advocacy and Civil Rights Office in the Department of Aging. He has also worked on the staff of a federally funded national model project to train and assist advocates to aid the elderly with public entitlement and other legal problems, directed a senior citizens' center, and established and directed a retired senior volunteer program. He has had extensive experience in preparing and providing testimony before legislative and administrative bodies, in drafting and lobbying major legislative initiatives, and in speaking on issues affecting the elderly.

DAVID F. CHAVKIN, the consultant and reviewer for chapter 10 ("The Medicare/Medicaid Maze"), is the Director of Legal Advocacy for the Epilepsy Foundation of America and specializes in representing persons with disabilities. He is a member of the U.S. Advisory Panel on Alzheimer's Disease and has served as directing attorney of the Maryland Disability Law Center, member of the Maryland Governor's Task Force on Alzheimer's Disease, and consultant to the Congressional Office of Technology Assessment for its report on dementia.

JOHN G. FEARS, ESQ., the consultant and reviewer for chapter 13 ("When Social Security Payments Go to Someone Else"), is the Managing Attorney of the Norman Law Center of Legal Aid in Western Oklahoma, which provides civil legal services to low-income individuals. He was the attorney for a landmark beneficiary's case that eventually resulted in the court's requiring all payees to provide annual accountings, to be reviewed by the Social Security Administration. He was also instrumental in working on federal legislation that provided for timely investigation into the backgrounds of prospective payees, as well as increased penalties and fines for the misuse of funds. He has specialized in issues of elder law for more than ten years.

PENELOPE HOMMEL, the consultant and reviewer for chapter 12 ("Guardians and Conservators: When, If, and How"), is the Executive Director of The Center for Social Gerontology (TCSG), a nationally recognized support center in law and aging, in Ann Arbor, Michigan. She developed, with the University of Michigan Law School, a law and aging program for the Institute of Gerontology. She directed a guardianship standards project and is well versed in guardianship issues throughout the country. She was the editor of TCSG's 1986 publication *Guardianship and Its Legal Alternatives* and has conducted countless training programs on protective services issues.

TOM JAZWIECKI, the consultant and reviewer for chapter 3 ("Paying for Nursing Home Care"), is the National Advisor for Long Term Health Care for Ernst and Whinney, the world's leading health care accounting and consulting firm. He is also president of Evergreen Health Care, Inc., a nursing home management corporation, and a member of the Congressional Advisory Panel on Alzheimer's Disease. A former director of the Office of Reimbursement and Financing for the American Health Care Association in Washington, D.C., he was an independent consultant to the California Department on Aging and the California Alzheimer's Task Force. He has written several articles dealing with the financing of long-term care services and recently coauthored a book on long-term care reimbursement.

MARSHALL B. KAPP, ESQ., the consultant and reviewer for chapters 5 ("Powers of Attorney and Other Ways to Plan Ahead"), 11 ("Competence and Incompetence: What They Mean"), and 14 ("Limits on Decisions Made for Someone Else"), is a professor at Wright State University's School of Medicine and at the University of Dayton's School of Law in Ohio. He is the author of numerous articles, reviews, and books on the law and ethics surrounding health care. He has served as a consultant to the Congressional Office of Technology Assessment, the Federal Administration on Aging, the American Hospital Association, and the Retirement Research Foundation. He was a Robert Wood Johnson Faculty Fellow in Health Care Finance and is a Fellow of the Gerontological Society of America.

JOHN LASTER, ESQ., the consultant and reviewer for chapter 1 ("Wills, Trusts, and Joint Accounts: Using Them Now") and the reviewer for chapter 4 ("Is a Living Will a Good Idea for You?"), is a partner at Landsman, Eakes and Laster, a general civil practice firm specializing in estate planning for older people and families in which a member faces long-term illness. A founding member of the National Academy of Elderlaw Attorneys, he has served as chairman of the legal issues section of the Foundation of Thanatology and continues to serve as counsel to the Hospice Council of Metropolitan Washington, Inc. He has taught university courses in estate planning and probate and served as a guest lecturer on legal issues of the elderly for many institutions. He created a popular will-writing workshop in the District of Columbia area and works frequently with the American Bar Association's Commission on Legal Problems of the Elderly.

BARBARA MISHKIN, ESQ., the consultant for chapter 4 ("Is a Living Will a Good Idea for You?"), is an attorney at Hogan and Hartson in Washington, D.C. She is extremely active in many aspects of elder law and is a board member of the Foundation for Critical Care Medicine; Bon Secours Health System, Inc., and the Hebrew Home of Greater Washington. In addition, she is a member of the executive committee on the Legal Counsel for the Elderly; a member of the Committee on Scientific Freedom and Responsibility of the American Association for the Advancement of Science; and a trustee of Mt. Holyoke College. She has published frequently, prepared numerous reports for federal advisory committees, and made many presentations to professional groups involved in elder law and issues.

CYNTHIA E. NORTHROP, ESQ., the consultant and reviewer for chapters 6 ("Saying Yes to Medical Care: What You Should Know First") and 7 ("Patients Have Rights, Too"), was a nurse attorney who specialized in nursing issues in her private law practice in New York City. She also served as adjunct associate professor on nursing law at Columbia University's Teachers College, Department of Nursing Education. She taught community health nursing, law, and ethics at various schools of nursing for more than ten years. She was the founder of the American Association of Nurse Attorneys and president of the American Association of Nurse Attorneys Foundation. Ms. Northrop lectured extensively and published numerous articles on nursing law, as well as an award-winning book on the subject. She died of cancer in November, 1989.

SUSAN M. PETTEY, ESQ., M.P.A., the consultant and reviewer for chapter 2 (" 'Medigap' and Long-Term Care Insurance Policies"), Director of Health Policy for the American Association of Homes for the Aging. Previously she was the Deputy Counsel and Associate Director of Government Affairs for the National Association for Home Care. She has also been director of government affairs for the Home Health Services and Staffing Association and a presidential management intern and legislative analyst for the Health Care Financing Administration in the U.S. Department of Health and Human Services. Ms. Pettey has taught graduate courses in health care law and health care financing, as well as many workshops on the legislative and regulatory processes.

DAVID SCHULKE, the consultant and reviewer for chapter 8 ("If the Hospital Tells You to Go Home Too Early"), is a staff member of the Special Senate Committee on Aging. In that capacity, he researched and prepared numerous hearings on problems of quality, access, and cost in Medicare, Medicaid, and Food and Drug Administration programs. Several of these hearings—based on an unprecedented two-year investigation—focused on problems in the quality of care provided under the Medicare prospective payment system for hospitals. As a result of these hearings, the Heinz/Stark Medicare Quality Protection Act of 1986 was enacted by Congress, creating broad new protections for beneficiaries needing acute hospital services. Mr. Schulke has worked for more than ten years in positions overseeing public health policy and focusing on long-term care services and financing.

About the Author

TERESA SCHWAB MYERS is a freelance writer who specializes in issues facing the elderly and in the interaction between medicine and society. She has written extensively on the legal, medical, and ethical issues that confront the elderly and their families; the impact of genetic testing; and medical safety issues. She cowrote *Losing a Million Minds: Confronting the Tragedy of Alzheimer's Disease and Other Dementias* for Congress, and *Caring for an Aging World,* an examination of how different countries approach the universal problem of caring for their sick and elderly individuals. She has lived around the world, and was educated in Africa, Asia, Europe, and the United States.